Method and Theory
in Paleoethnobotany

Method and Theory in Paleoethnobotany

EDITED BY

JOHN M. MARSTON,
JADE D'ALPOIM GUEDES,
AND CHRISTINA WARINNER

UNIVERSITY PRESS OF COLORADO
Boulder

© 2014 by University Press of Colorado

Published by University Press of Colorado
5589 Arapahoe Avenue, Suite 206C
Boulder, Colorado 80303

The University Press of Colorado is a proud member of
The Association of American University Presses.

The University Press of Colorado is a cooperative publishing enterprise supported, in part,
by Adams State University, Colorado State University, Fort Lewis College, Metropolitan
State University of Denver, Regis University, University of Colorado, University of Northern
Colorado, Utah State University, and Western State Colorado University.

ISBN: 978-1-60732-315-0 (pbk.)
ISBN: 978-1-60732-316-7 (ebook)

Library of Congress Cataloging-in-Publication Data

Method and theory in paleoethnobotany / edited by John M. Marston, Jade D'alpoim Guedes,
and Christina Warinner.
      pages cm
   Includes bibliographical references.
   ISBN 978-1-60732-315-0 (pbk.) — ISBN 978-1-60732-316-7 (ebook)
   1. Paleoethnobotany. 2. Plant remains (Archaeology) 3. Paleoethnobotany—Methodology.
4. Archaeology—Methodology. I. Marston, John M.
   CC79.5.P5M48 2014
   930.1'2—dc23
                              2014010694

Cover illustration © Hein Nouwens / Shutterstock

Contents

As its title suggests, this book presents the current state of method and theory in paleoethnobotany, synonymously termed archaeobotany, the study of archaeological plant remains and human-plant interactions in the past. We conceive of this volume as an homage to, and descendent of, two defining works in the field: the edited volume, *Current Paleoethnobotany: Analytical Methods and Cultural Interpretations of Archaeological Plant Remains* (Hastorf and Popper 1988) and the two editions of *Paleoethnobotany: A Handbook of Procedures* (Pearsall 1989, 2000). Both are staples of any paleoethnobotanist's office or laboratory reference shelf and both engage with the challenge of interpreting plant data from archaeological sites. It speaks to the continuing relevance of *Current Paleoethnobotany* in particular that even after twenty-five years many of its chapters continue to be relevant and regularly cited. Here we attempt to build upon the success of these two seminal volumes by covering subjects that reflect recent technical, methodological, and theoretical advances in the field and by inviting a wide variety of scholars to write on the subjects in which they are expert. We have also taken advantage of this opportunity to update bibliographies to reflect the expansion of botanical studies in archaeology over the past two and a half decades and to incorporate the increasing diversity of scientific studies of human-plant interactions in the past.

This volume builds upon the tradition of edited volumes in the field of paleoethnobotany. Such volumes have often come about as published versions of conference sessions, typically at meetings of the Society for American Archaeology (SAA; e.g., Gremillion 1997; Hastorf and Popper 1988; Scarry 1993b) or the International Work Group for Palaeoethnobotany (IWGP; e.g., van Zeist and Casparie 1984; van Zeist et al. 1991), but also resulting from ad hoc symposia (e.g., Hart 1999, 2008). This book has a similar origin: it was conceived during a session at the 2010 Annual Meeting of the SAA in St. Louis organized by two of us (d'Alpoim Guedes and Warinner), in which Marston and several of the contributing authors were participants. We three editors then planned and organized an electronic symposium at the 2011 Annual Meeting of the SAA in Sacramento and invited authors to write on specific topics that would form the basis for this volume. We are thankful that additional authors who were not able to attend the session were able to submit chapters in the following months to expand and strengthen this volume.

The structure of this book roughly follows the process of paleoethnobotanical analysis. Part I deals with formation processes of macro- and microbotanical remains, whereas part II discusses their recovery and identification, as well as strategies for data management. Part III focuses on quantitative analysis of plant macroremains and methods for interpreting intra- and intersite variation. Part IV describes the integration of botanical macroremains with other allied data types, focusing especially on nascent molecular technologies and remote sensing. Finally, the three chapters of part V take three distinct theoretical approaches to the interpretation of archaeological plant remains and illustrate potential avenues for future investigation. We leave out the integration of plant and animal remains deliberately, as it has been treated fully in a recent edited volume (VanDerwarker and Peres 2010) and multiple articles (especially see Smith and Miller 2009 and associated articles).

Our hope is that this volume will serve the field for the next three decades as well as *Current Paleoethnobotany* has for the past twenty-five years. As we describe in chapter 1 of this volume, many of the technologies and analyses described at length here were not possible in the 1980s, nor even imagined to affect archaeology as much as they have. Certainly, as Ford recently predicted (2003:xvi; 2004:xiv), the successor to this volume will focus increasingly on recent and future advances made in molecular and computational archaeology and on the expansion of a truly global archaeology, including work beyond the traditional European and North American sites so well studied to date. The inclusion of the diverse voices of paleoethnobotanists from developing countries will be a welcome addition to the already rich and productive dialogues in our field.

JOHN M. MARSTON
Boston, MA

JADE D'ALPOIM GUEDES
Pullman, WA

CHRISTINA WARINNER
Norman, OK, and Zürich, Switzerland

Method and Theory
in Paleoethnobotany

1

Paleoethnobotanical Method and Theory in the Twenty-First Century

JOHN M. MARSTON,
CHRISTINA WARINNER, AND
JADE D'ALPOIM GUEDES

The origins of the study of relationships between people and plants in the past began as early as the nineteenth century with the identification of desiccated plant remains recovered from rockshelters in the American Southwest (Ford 2003:xii; 2004:x; Pearsall 2000:1) and waterlogged remains from Swiss lake-dwelling sites (Hastorf 1999:55). This field of study, first termed *ethno-botany*, today is termed either *paleoethnobotany* or *archaeobotany*, with the two synonymous terms generally preferred in North America and Europe, respectively (figure 1.1). Paleoethnobotany expanded tremendously as a field in the second half of the twentieth century, as reflected in the growing number of publications since the 1970s (see the extensive bibliographies in Hastorf 1999 and Pearsall 2000), and continues to make substantial contributions to archaeology today.

This volume is conceived as a reflection on the state of the field after the first decade of the twenty-first century. Paleoethnobotany has changed dramatically since its earliest days and since the publication of the first seminal volumes in the 1970s and 1980s (Hastorf and Popper 1988; Pearsall 1989; Renfrew 1973; van Zeist and Casparie 1984; van Zeist et al. 1991). It is time for a new and updated overview of the methods and theory of paleoethnobotany that addresses what we do and why we do it. This volume assembles a diverse group of authors to write about their areas of expertise in the practice and theory of paleoethnobotany. We cover topics from the formation processes of plant remains

DOI: 10.5876/9781607323167.c001

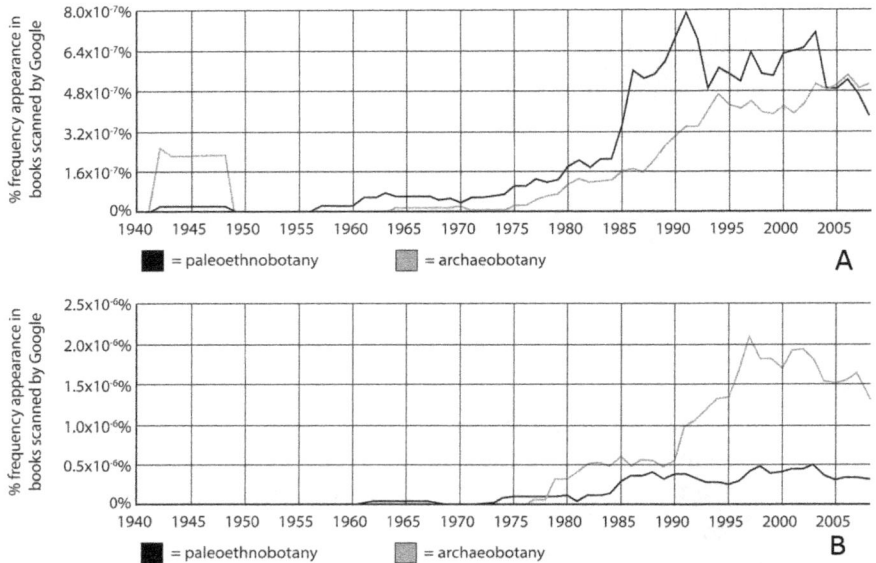

FIGURE I.I. *Relative trends in the use of the terms* paleoethnobotany *and* archaeobotany *in American (a) and British (b) books published between 1940 and 2008, as three-year running averages, originally created using Google Ngram Viewer (https://books.google. com/ngrams, searched May 30, 2013). These data come from the Google Books project and include over 5.8 million texts, more than 4% of books ever published (Michel et al. 2011).*

in the archaeological record to methods for their recovery and analysis to diverse modes of interpretation, both alone and in concert with other types of archaeological analyses.

This book differs from prior contributions to the field in three ways. First, this is the only comprehensive edited volume focusing on method and theory to appear since the 1988 publication of *Current Paleoethnobotany* (Hastorf and Popper 1988), still an influential and frequently cited volume but now dated in bibliography and without the benefit of technical advances in the field since the 1980s. Due to the high quality of the chapters in that volume, we aim to supplement (rather than replicate) the topics covered in 1988 with new areas of inquiry (e.g., starch grain analysis, stable isotope analysis, ancient DNA, digital data management, and ecological and postprocessual theory) that have become central to contemporary archaeological debates. Second, we aim for worldwide coverage in the literature referenced, in contrast to many excellent recent volumes that synthesize regional bodies of data and literatures in the Northeastern United States (Hart 1999, 2008), the Eastern United States (Gremillion 1997; Minnis 2003; Scarry 1993b), the Western United States (Minnis 2004), China (Zhao 2010), Africa (van der Veen 1999b), the tropics (Hather 1994), and Europe and the Near East (van Zeist and Casparie 1984; van Zeist et al. 1991). Finally, although Pearsall's (2000) *Paleoethnobotany: A Handbook of Procedures*, currently in its second edition, is a critical reference for all paleoethnobotanists (as well as archaeologists of other specialties), its focus lies on providing a broad overview of methods in the discipline, rather than a critical examination of particular areas of study. This volume, in contrast, includes chapters that focus narrowly on individual topics and assesses the current state of theoretical, methodological, and empirical work in each area. We intend for this book to be used alongside the seminal works listed above, as well as myriad monographs and articles, and to serve as the next milestone along the path of paleoethnobotanical knowledge.

This chapter serves two purposes: it reviews briefly the state of the field to date and it suggests future directions in paleoethnobotany. Rather than list or summarize the other chapters in this volume, we reference them within this discussion to show how the questions addressed in subsequent chapters fit into the overall trajectory of both recent advances and predicted future trends in the field. Paleoethnobotany is poised at the intersection between study of the past and concerns of the present, including food security, biodiversity, and global environmental change, and has much to offer to archaeology, anthropology, and interdisciplinary studies of human relationships with the natural world. This volume, as a whole, illustrates many of these connections and highlights the increasing relevance of the study of past human-plant interactions for understanding the present and future (cf. van der Leeuw and Redman 2002).

THE DEVELOPMENT OF PALEOETHNOBOTANY

THE STATE OF THE FIELD IN THE 1980S

The state of the field of paleoethnobotany through the 1980s is well summarized by books published late in that decade (Hastorf and Popper 1988; Pearsall 1989; van Zeist et al. 1991) and need not be repeated here (see Ford 2003, 2004; Hastorf 1999:55–57; Pearsall 2000:1–10; Popper and Hastorf 1988; Renfrew 1973:1–6 for excellent summaries of this period). Early work in the field stemmed from chance finds of desiccated or waterlogged plant remains in archaeological contexts, the analysis of which first began in the late nineteenth century and continued through the 1960s (Pearsall 2000:4–6). The major tipping point for the study of paleoethnobotanical remains was the application of flotation to recover carbonized plant remains from archaeological sediments, a technique suitable for a wide variety of archaeological contexts. First publicized to the American archaeological community in 1968 (Struever 1968), flotation rapidly became adopted for use at an increasing number of sites across the Americas, Europe, and the Near East (Pearsall 2000:4–6). Coupled with the expansion of large salvage archaeology projects in the United States in the 1970s and 1980s (henceforth termed *Cultural Resource Management*, or *CRM*, projects), massive botanical data sets were recovered using flotation, studied, and published, driving the need for comprehensive methodological treatments of paleoethnobotany (i.e., Hastorf and Popper 1988; Pearsall 1989) that went beyond prior works that were more narrowly concerned with identification and interpretation of cultigens (e.g., Renfrew 1973; van Zeist and Casparie 1984).

Pearsall's (1989) and Hastorf and Popper's (1988) volumes had two far-reaching implications for paleoethnobotanical research in the 1990s and beyond. First, they popularized the study of plant remains as a theoretically grounded discipline that had the potential to address a variety of research questions. Chapters dealing with formation processes (Asch and Sidell 1988; Pearsall 1988), agricultural activities (Hastorf 1988), paleoenvironmental reconstruction (Smart and Hoffman 1988), and culture change (Johannessen 1988) highlight some of the applications of paleoethnobotanical data sets. Second, these books explained the recovery of plant remains in a way accessible to the general population of archaeologists (Toll 1988; Wagner 1988; and especially Pearsall 1989:chapter 2) and dealt with the basic quantitative methods employed in paleoethnobotanical analysis (Miller 1988; Pearsall 2000:chapter 3; Popper 1988). These references, and in particular the second edition of Pearsall's book, continue to be consulted by archaeologists during excavation as a "how-to" guide for the recovery of plant remains, especially when a paleoethnobotanist is not available to oversee sample collection and processing in the field. Undoubtedly these texts have contributed to the expansion of flotation and paleoethnobotanical analysis since the late 1980s.

Trends in Paleoethnobotanical Analysis since 1989

We identify seven trends that have occurred in paleoethnobotany since the late 1980s, leading to significant changes in the field today. We briefly outline these trends, and their implications, in this section. These trends include (1) improved understanding of the formation and depositional processes that affect botanical macro- and microremains; (2) improved methods for and frequency of paleoethnobotanical sampling, of both macro- and microremains; (3) new methods for quantification; (4) advances in computing and digital technologies, which have enabled new methods of interpretation; (5) the application of new theoretical approaches to the analysis of paleoethnobotanical remains; (6) the integration of paleoethnobotany with other methods of environmental archaeology; and (7) the increasingly mainstream role of paleoethnobotanical analyses and specialists within archaeological discourse. These trends are the result of a steady accumulation of knowledge within the field of paleoethnobotany, the increased number of trained paleoethnobotanists, and broader changes in the field of archaeology that have benefited paleoethnobotanical analysis.

Improved Understanding of Formation and Depositional Processes
Basic research continues on the processes that affect the deposition, decay, and preservation of botanical remains in a variety of archaeological contexts. These processes have not been a primary focus of earlier texts in the field (but see Pearsall 2000; Piperno 2006b; Torrence and Barton 2006). Five chapters in this book summarize recent advances in our understanding of the chemical, physical, and biological processes that affect botanical preservation at the macroscopic, microscopic, and biomolecular levels. Gallagher (chapter 2, this volume) describes both cultural and natural processes that affect the patterning of macrobotanical remains. Henry (chapter 3, this volume) and Pearsall (chapter 4, this volume), in contrast, focus on the physical and chemical structure of botanical microremains (starch grains, and pollen and phytoliths, respectively) and recent experimental work that gives insight into how and why certain microremains may be preserved (or not) in specific archaeological contexts. Finally, Warinner (chapter 14, this volume) and Wales et al. (chapter 15, this volume) discuss the factors that influence biochemical and biomolecular (DNA, RNA, and protein) preservation in archaeobotanical remains. This basic knowledge has improved the ability of paleoethnobotanists to make claims about the presence and absence of certain taxa at the time of deposition, rather than at the time of analysis.

Improved Paleoethnobotanical Sampling Methods
and Increased Sampling Frequency
The "flotation revolution" of the 1970s was responsible for making the collection of plant remains a part of mainstream archaeological fieldwork in many parts of the world, as described above, and sampling has continued to

increase ever since. This is mainly the result of the penetration of flotation, and other appropriate methods for recovering botanical remains, into parts of the world where such work was not previously practiced. Archaeologists in South and East Asia and Africa, in particular, have only recently begun to adopt flotation on a large scale (e.g., Crawford 2006, 2009; D'Andrea et al. 2001; D'Andrea 2008; Di Piazza 1998; Fairbairn 2007; Fuller 2006; Fuller and Weber 2005; Gallagher 2010; Kajale 1991; Lee et al. 2007; Logan 2012; McConnell and O'Connor 1997; Neumann et al. 2003; van der Veen 1999b; Zhao 2010). Improvements in the identification and interpretation of microremains (here phytoliths and starch grains) from archaeological contexts, especially in tropical soils where macroremains are poorly preserved, have further expanded our understanding of plant use on a global scale (Denham et al. 2003; Fahmy 2008; Fahmy and Magnavita 2006; Pearsall 2000:chapter 5; Piperno 2006a, 2009; Piperno and Holst 1998; Torrence and Barton 2006). The availability of methods guides for sampling both macro- and microremains (Fritz 2005; Pearsall 2000; Piperno 2006b; Torrence and Barton 2006) has further increased the ubiquity of such sampling. D'Alpoim Guedes and Spengler (chapter 5, this volume) and White and Shelton (chapter 6, this volume) address recent trends in methods for sampling and recovering paleoethnobotanical remains, including recent improvements in flotation device efficiency and portability, such as the hand-pump flotation device (Shelton and White 2010).

New Methods in Quantification

An increase in computing technology and the development of statistical software programs have allowed major contributions to the quantification and interpretation of archaeological plant remains through multivariate statistics, especially correspondence analysis and various derivative methods (see discussion in A. Smith, chapter 10, this volume). These methods extract significant axes of variation from large and complex data sets and can be used for the direct integration of plant and animal remains from an archaeological site (VanDerwarker 2010a). The interpretation of multivariate statistics remains subjective and such statistical methods are not appropriate for every data set (Jones 1991). Multivariate approaches, however, have been essential to new advances in understanding large-scale patterning of archaeological plant remains at both the sitewide and regional scales (e.g., Colledge et al. 2004; Jones et al. 2010; Peres et al. 2010; Smith and Munro 2009; Torrence et al. 2004; van der Veen 1992a, 2007b; VanDerwarker 2006).

Improvements have also been made in the use of simple (i.e., non-multivariate) statistics and their applications to interpretation of paleoethnobotanical assemblages, especially related to hypothesis testing (see Marston, chapter 9, this volume). Such applications extend to the interpretation of both intrasite (VanDerwarker et al., chapter 11, this volume) and intersite (Stevens, chapter 12, this volume) variation in the deposition of plant remains.

Advances in Computing and Digital Technologies

Perhaps no change over the past thirty years has affected archaeology as much as the exponential increase in computing power and the increased availability and usability of digital imaging on devices ranging from microscopes to multispectral satellites. As Warinner and d'Alpoim Guedes (chapter 8, this volume) discuss, these advances have had profound implications for the field of paleoethnobotany by enhancing our ability to record, store, sort, analyze, publish, and share the results of our analyses. Powerful desktop and portable computers make possible the widespread use of multivariate statistics, as described above, and spatial analysis, including the analysis of remotely sensed data (Casana, chapter 16, this volume). Online archives have enabled unprecedented sharing of data and publications (Warinner and d'Alpoim Guedes, chapter 8, this volume) and enhance the utility of reference collections (e.g., botanical collections imaged and available online in high resolution; Fritz and Nesbitt, chapter 7, this volume). Computing advances have also greatly enhanced other areas of science, such as genomics, that have had tremendous implications for paleoethnobotany (Londo et al. 2006; Olsen and Schaal 1999; Smith 2001a, 2014; Smith and Zeder 2013; Zeder, Bradley, et al. 2006; Zeder, Emshwiller, et al. 2006; see also Wales et al., chapter 15, this volume).

New Theoretical Approaches

The major theoretical shift in archaeology during the 1980s and 1990s that culminated in the division of theoretical approaches between so-called processual and postprocessual theoretical stances is one of the defining trends of archaeology as a whole over the past three decades, as have been attempts to find common cause between these approaches (Fogelin 2007; Trigger 2006). Paleoethnobotany has traditionally fallen into the "processual" camp, as the rise in scientific analysis during the 1970s that included the flotation revolution was tied to the rise of the "New Archaeology" that formed the basis for processual approaches to archaeology (Trigger 2006; Watson et al. 1971). Paleoethnobotanical data, however, have always been amenable to a variety of interpretive approaches, and publications since the 1980s highlight that variation. The application of "postprocessual" gender theory (Hastorf 1991) and

Bourdieu's concept of *habitus* (Atalay and Hastorf 2006; Bourdieu 1977) to the interpretation of food remains has led to important insights into practices of food preparation and consumption, as well as the origins of agriculture (Asouti and Fuller 2013). Similarly, practice theory offers another approach to understanding the social setting for food preparation in the past (Morell-Hart, chapter 19, this volume).

Other theoretical approaches derived from biology, and especially ecology, have been important avenues for understanding plant gathering, domestication, and crop selection. Human behavioral ecology, the study of how people make foraging decisions under particular environmental conditions, has offered new perspectives on hunting and gathering, transitions to agriculture, agricultural risk management, and settlement location (Gremillion, chapter 17, this volume; see also Bird and O'Connell 2006; Gremillion 2002a, 2002b; Gremillion and Piperno 2009a; Gremillion et al. 2008; Kennett and Winterhalder 2006; Marston 2009, 2011; Zeanah 2004). Niche construction theory, which addresses the ways in which people shape their environments and the ecological and social implications of such practices, informs our understanding of pre-agricultural practices, including incipient stages of domestication (B. Smith, chapter 18, this volume; see also Odling-Smee et al. 2003; Smith 2007a, 2007b, 2009a, 2009b, 2011a, 2011b). Combined with more traditional evolutionary approaches to understanding domestication (e.g., Rindos 1984), biological theory offers a counterpoint to social theory as a meaningful framework for interpreting paleoethnobotanical assemblages.

Integrated Environmental Archaeology

The term *environmental archaeology*, which describes the broad suite of methods used to understand human-environmental interaction in the past and includes paleoethnobotany, has been used increasingly to describe integrated paleoenvironmental and archaeological analyses over the past twenty-five years as these integrated approaches have become more common, generally outpacing the growth of both paleoethnobotany and zooarchaeology as a key term (figure 1.2; Dincauze 2000; Reitz et al. 1996; Reitz et al. 2008). An integrated approach to environmental archaeology beginning at the stage of project design is highly recommended, as it allows for comprehensive sampling strategies and sharing of data between specialists, leading to a more nuanced understanding of human-environmental interactions in the past.

Recent publications have focused on the integration of animal and plant remains (Smith and Miller 2009; VanDerwarker and Peres 2010), a topic not addressed in this volume, but the integration of other environmental

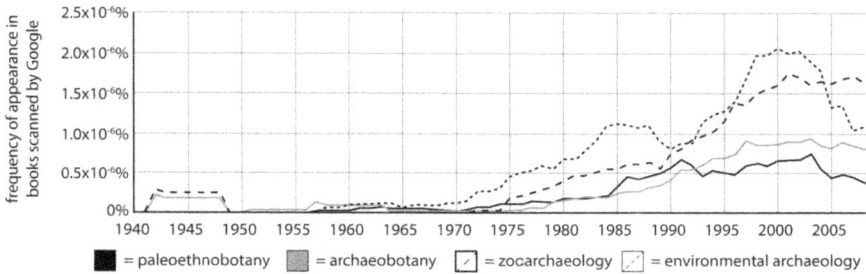

FIGURE 1.2. *Relative trends in the use of the terms* paleoethnobotany, archaeobotany, zooarchaeology, *and* environmental archaeology *in English-language books published between 1940 and 2008, using Google Ngram Viewer (https://books.google.com/ngrams, searched May 30, 2013). These data come from the Google Books project and include over 5.8 million texts, more than 4% of books ever published (Michel et al. 2011).*

archaeology techniques with paleoethnobotanical analysis has been pursued less often. Several chapters of this volume address how botanical remains can be used in concert with other data sets, including soil chemistry and geomorphology (Messner and Stinchcomb, chapter 13, this volume), human and plant stable isotope data (Warinner, chapter 14, this volume), and remote sensing satellite imagery (Casana, chapter 16, this volume). New methods and applications in the fields of genetics and proteomics are also presented, with an emphasis on the use of botanical remains in ancient DNA and paleoproteomic studies (Wales et al., chapter 15, this volume).

Paleoethnobotany Becomes Mainstream

Although paleoethnobotanists, much like other environmental archaeologists and archaeological scientists, were once considered specialists restricted to the analysis of specific bodies of data, now many paleoethnobotanists direct or codirect archaeological projects, putting paleoethnobotanical research questions at the forefront of excavation goals. A review of articles published since 1990 in *American Antiquity*, the flagship journal of the Society for American Archaeology and a methods-agnostic forum for publication of North American archaeology, shows an increase in publications that incorporate paleoethnobotanical methodologies in the mid-late 1990s (figure 1.3).

This period, the five to ten years following the publication of both *Current Paleoethnobotany* (Hastorf and Popper 1988) and *Paleoethnobotany: A Handbook*

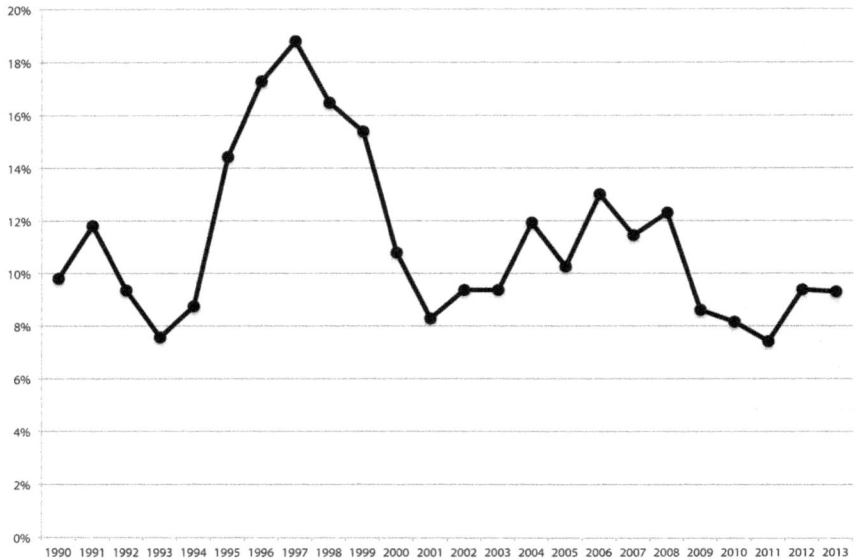

FIGURE I.3. *Trends in the frequency of paleoethnobotany as a major research component of research articles published in* American Antiquity *between 1990 and 2013 (through April issue), represented as the three-year trailing average of the percentage of total research articles published (e.g., the 1990 data point is the average of the years 1988, 1989, and 1990).*

of Procedures (Pearsall 1989), also saw the publication of several major edited volumes in the field (e.g., Gremillion 1997; Hart 1999; Scarry 1993a). Since 2000, the number of articles focused on paleoethnobotany in *American Antiquity* has remained relatively constant at around 10 percent of the total. US National Science Foundation (NSF) funding for paleoethnobotanical research peaked during the early 1990s, after which funding rates for projects incorporating paleoethnobotany stabilized to approximately 5–20 percent of the total (figure 1.4).

Since 1988, the NSF has supported more than 200 projects involving paleo-ethnobotanical research, representing approximately 14 percent of all funded archaeological projects.[1] For more than half of these projects, paleoethnobo-tanical analysis is a major component of the project and is fundamental to the project goals. We suggest that the evident "bump" in NSF-funded paleo-ethnobotany projects between 1990 and 1993 may have further contributed to the increase in paleoethnobotanical articles published in *American Antiquity* between 1995 and 1999 (figures 1.3 and 1.4). The PhD students who have been

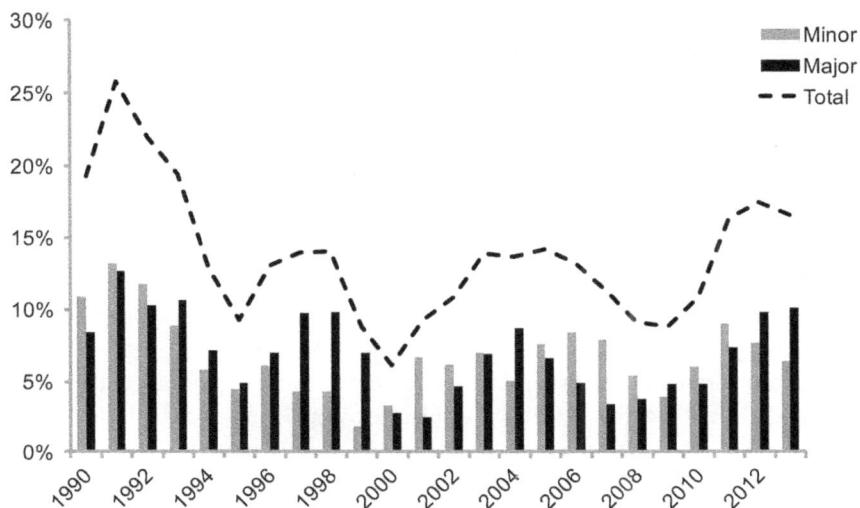

FIGURE 1.4. *Trends in the frequency of NSF-funded projects involving paleoethnobotanical research, 1988–2013, represented as the three-year trailing average of the percentage of total NSF-funded archaeology projects (e.g., the 1990 data point is the average of years 1988, 1989, and 1990). The contribution of paleoethnobotanical inquiry to the project as a whole was scored as major or minor.*

trained on these projects have gone on to start their own integrative, multi-disciplinary projects, leading to an expansion of the use of botanical data in mainstream archaeological publications and a broadening of questions that paleoethnobotanical methods and data are used to address.

FUTURE DIRECTIONS IN PALEOETHNOBOTANY

According to an often-quoted line, it is always difficult to make predictions, especially about the future. Nonetheless, we see many of the trends listed above continuing into the future, in particular those related to increased collection and study of botanical remains, and further integration of paleoethnobotany with other environmental archaeology methods, especially those operating at the molecular level. In addition, we suggest three new ways in which we see the field of paleoethnobotany changing over the next twenty to thirty years: (1) increased accessibility of published data sets online, leading to broader-scale (and more powerful) analyses; (2) increased training of paleoethnobotanists in developing countries and more publications from those countries; and (3) increased relevance of paleoethnobotany beyond archaeology, particularly in environmental and climate-change science. We outline briefly why we see these as likely future directions for the field and how we see these developments affecting the practice of paleoethnobotany and its role within archaeology.

INCREASED ACCESSIBILITY OF PALEOETHNOBOTANICAL DATA SETS

The Internet has proven to be a remarkable tool for sharing primary data sets. Well-managed public scientific data repositories, such as GenBank, have transformed research in other fields (e.g., evolutionary genetics and genomics), and similar databases show promise for improving archaeological practice as well (see Warinner and d'Alpoim Guedes, chapter 8, this volume). Existing paleoethnobotanical database websites host images (e.g., Paleobot. org) and distributional maps (e.g., the Archaeobotanical Database of Eastern Mediterranean and Near Eastern sites, http://www.cuminum.de/archaeobotany), as well as bibliographic references (e.g., Literature on Archaeological Remains of Cultivated Plants 1981–2004, http://www.archaeobotany.de/). The Archaeobotany Listserv (https://www.jiscmail.ac.uk/cgi-bin/webadmin?A1 =ind1407&L=ARCHAEOBOTANY) accomplishes similar goals through email communication. In addition, the deposition of entire primary data sets into online data repositories such as PANGAEA, tDAR, OpenContext, and DRYAD is increasingly being encouraged by scientific journals and government funding bodies (see Warinner and d'Alpoim Guedes, chapter 8, this volume).

The possibility offered by centralized data repositories of primary archaeobotanical data is reuse of published data sets, which remains uncommon in the field, and integration of data sets to produce regional syntheses (e.g., Miller and Marston 2012). This has the potential to reduce Balkanization of the field and contribute to larger-scale and more powerful statistical analyses, leading to more significant and meaningful results. We see ongoing trends in computing and digital visualization contributing to this goal, allowing better sharing and more rapid analysis of large data sets. Perhaps most important, should governmental regulations for CRM institute mandatory digital archiving in a limited number of permanent online data repositories, such as those listed above, large numbers of botanical data sets that have been buried in gray literature will become accessible and contribute to future paleoethnobotanical research.

INCREASED TRAINING IN AND ADOPTION OF
PALEOETHNOBOTANY IN DEVELOPING COUNTRIES

Paleoethnobotany has historically been practiced by North American–
or European-based scholars working in traditional areas of archaeological
focus: the Americas, Europe, and the Mediterranean and Near East. Naomi
F. Miller's 2010 survey of archaeobotanists identified 86 percent of respondents (total number of respondents was 118) as being based in North America
(United States or Canada), the British Isles, or mainland Europe. Similarly,
only 10 percent of respondents described their primary geographic area of spe-
cialty as something other than the Americas, Europe, or the Mediterranean
and Near East (Miller 2010a:22; 2011a:10). Until the last two decades, nontra-
ditional areas such as East and South Asia, Sub-Saharan Africa, Oceania, and
the tropics of both the New and Old Worlds were studied infrequently and
only by a few scholars. This is changing today and will continue to change as
more paleoethnobotanists are trained in those countries and go on to careers
in archaeology. Even a small number of well-trained specialists can have a
dramatic impact on the amount of data analyzed in a developing country, and
continued partnerships with well-established scholars in North America and
Europe will facilitate publication and dissemination of the results of those
analyses. Furthermore, training new generations of scholars with distinct edu-
cational and cultural backgrounds will broaden the diversity of the field and
allow the practice of paleoethnobotany to move in new directions not previously pursued. More than any other trend, the growth of scientific archaeology
worldwide will have tremendous implications for the future of paleoethnobotany and our collective understanding of the human past.

RELEVANCE OF PALEOETHNOBOTANY BEYOND ARCHAEOLOGY

Research attention (and funding) in many fields has moved toward
understanding the human role in global environmental change, including
climate change, and the future implications of ongoing present-day interactions between people and their natural environments. One thread in this
research has focused on the past, partly to establish an accurate baseline for
natural processes of climate change and extinction events in the pre-human
past, and partly to establish how humans affected environmental systems
in the pre-industrial period (Foley et al. 2005; Jackson et al. 2001; Lotze
2010; Pauly 1995). Archaeology as a whole has much to offer this effort, as
it is the one discipline that directly investigates the holistic past across the
entire span of human existence (Redman et al. 2004; van der Leeuw and

Redman 2002). Paleoethnobotany has a major role to play in this endeavor by providing robust data sets that reflect interactions between human and botanical communities over long spans of time and across economic, social, geographic, and climatic transitions. Recent work in the field highlights the value of such data: for example, synthetic analyses of long-term coupled changes in both human societies and vegetation communities in the Near East, as reconstructed through both macrobotanical (Riehl 2009) and pollen analysis (Rosen 2007), have clarified how climate and environmental change influenced agricultural practices on a regional scale over time. In some cases, however, paleoethnobotanical data are still largely neglected in the study of environmental change associated with agricultural systems (e.g., the case studies in Fisher et al. 2009), offering an opportunity for increased future contributions for paleoethnobotany.

CONCLUSIONS

Paleoethnobotanical inquiry is a rich and varied field, providing everything from basic science on depositional processes to interpretation about human adaptation to local environments on a global scale. The field has expanded in the number of practitioners, frequency of sampling and analysis, areas of the world in which such work is routinely conducted, and breadth of research questions addressed. The flotation revolution of the 1970s is still expanding in Africa and Asia, and the theoretical debates of the 1980s have brought a multivocal perspective to the interpretation of plant remains. In addition, the technological improvements of the 1990s and 2000s have led to unprecedented opportunities for data analysis, publication, and sharing. This volume highlights the implications of these developments and complements earlier volumes in the field that have driven research inquiry over the past quarter century.

Furthermore, we argue that the field is poised for further contributions to study of not only the human past but also the human present and future. We believe that paleoethnobotanical data sets are rich and robust sources of information on human adaptation to climate change and offer case studies of successful and unsuccessful agricultural and land-use systems in the past that are directly relevant to assessing the sustainability of such systems in the present. Despite persistent challenges in funding, employment, and integration with other areas of archaeology and the social and natural sciences (Miller 2011a:9), paleoethnobotany is poised for a new set of revolutions. We hope this volume contributes to that bright future.

NOTE

1. Survey conducted on all active and expired records with start dates from 1988 to 2013 with the Field of Application = anthropology and/or Search Award For = archaeology. The first complete year for which the public NSF project records include abstracts, allowing project content statistics to be calculated, is 1988. Abstracts for records related to archaeology and including the terms *botan**, *plant*, or *flora* were then read and scored for content. The paleoethnobotanical content of each abstract was scored as: 0 = none, 1 = minor, and 2 = major. Projects were deemed as having paleoethnobotanical content if they involved the direct investigation of ancient plant remains (macroscopic, microscopic, biomolecular, or biochemical) or involved targeted work towards producing modern reference collections or data sets for the interpretation or modeling of ancient plant remains. Surveys of modern vegetation without the purpose of being used for paleoethnobotanical interpretation were excluded.

PART I

*Formation
Processes*

2

Formation Processes of the Macrobotanical Record

DAPHNE E. GALLAGHER

THE MACROBOTANICAL RECORD

The macrobotanical record consists of all plant remains that are large enough to be seen with the naked eye and that can usually be identified with a low-power microscope (Ford 1979:301; Pearsall 2000:11). Macroremains can range in size from tobacco seeds (< 1 mm diameter) to a preserved dugout canoe several meters long. They can encompass every part of the plant including roots, stems, wood, fibers, sap, leaves, spines, flowers, fruits, nuts, seeds, and more. Consequently, the macrobotanical record has the potential to illuminate a wide range of human-plant interactions from management and environmental impact to cultural modification of plant products and the plants themselves. Given the scope of plant materials included and the comparatively minimal laboratory requirements for their recovery and study (see White and Shelton, chapter 6, and Fritz and Nesbitt, chapter 7, this volume), it is unsurprising that the majority of archaeological studies of plants focus on various classes of macroremains, although with improved techniques and awareness, studies of microremains from archaeological sites (i.e., pollen, phytoliths, and starch) are becoming more common (see Henry, chapter 3, and Pearsall, chapter 4, this volume).

Despite the potential diversity of plant parts in the macrobotanical record, analysis of macrobotanical samples and, consequently, research on how these plants enter the archaeological record, has tended to

DOI: 10.5876/9781607323167.c002

focus on two primary categories of macrobotanical remains: wood and seeds (the latter conceptualized broadly to include seedlike structures such as caryopses and achenes). This emphasis is for the most part practical. First, wood and seeds tend to be dense and highly durable, and consequently are good candidates for preservation, particular in conditions where macrobotanical remains are carbonized (see below). Second, both may be comparatively easy to identify. Many species of seeds have unique anatomy and, given their small size, are more likely to be preserved as complete specimens, whereas the nature of wood anatomy is such that identifications can be made from very small fragments (see Fritz and Nesbitt, chapter 7, this volume).

PRESERVATION OF MACROBOTANICAL REMAINS

Macrobotanical specimens in most exposed and subsurface settings decompose as a result of biological, chemical, and geochemical weathering processes (Beck 1989; Ford 1979). Soil-based bacteria, saprophytic fungi, and other microorganisms, as well as earthworms, insects, and other invertebrates, are the primary agents that break down the anatomical structures of deposited plants into their constituent elements (Swift et al. 1979). In general, environments that are warmer, wetter, more alkaline, and that have higher soil carbon and nutrient content will result in faster decomposition. However, these relationships are complex and linked to the nature and biodiversity of both the local decomposing organisms and the plant community (Beck 1989; Berg and McClaugherty 2008; Hättenschwiler et al. 2005; Swift et al. 1979). These biochemical processes can be aided by a variety of natural processes, including exposure to the elements (wind, rain, etc.), in addition to freeze-thaw and wet-dry expansions and contractions of the surrounding matrix that can cause mechanical damage (Beck 1989). Anthropogenic processes also contribute to decomposition of plant remains in archaeological sites. Humans not only grind, cut, pound, trample, and otherwise mechanically damage plants, but also frequently enrich local soil chemistry through the deposition of waste (Beck 1989; Holliday 2004).

Despite these combined effects, which typically destroy the majority of plant material initially deposited, macrobotanical remains are regularly preserved in archaeological contexts. All factors being equal, different plants and plant parts will decompose at different rates. For example, "woody" parts (those high in lignin) will take longer to break down than leaves (Beck 1989; Berg and McClaugherty 2008), and some species and plant parts may be differentially targeted by rodents and insects (Gasser and Adams 1981). Some plant parts are particularly durable. Certain fruit pericarps, such as hackberry (*Celtis* spp.), undergo a process of biomineralization in which they naturally produce carbonates during their lifespan. These deposited carbonates render the pericarp resistant to decomposition, such that they frequently preserve in contexts where other plant parts do not (Fairbairn et al. 2002; Shillito and Almond 2010). Similarly, the hard involucres of Job's tears (*Coix lacryma-jobi*), which are often used as beads, are also resistant to decomposition (Ford and Jones 1974). However, in most cases, preservation in archaeological contexts depends less on the durability of the plant itself and more on environmental conditions and/or processes, such as carbonization, that improve the chances of preservation.

In general, plant material will preserve best in settings that inhibit decomposers. These include environments that are lacking moisture or oxygen, have consistently high or freezing temperatures, and/or have acidic or nutrient-poor substrates. Plants can also preserve in settings where they have undergone transformations pre- or post-deposition (e.g., carbonization, mineralization) that make them resistant to decomposition. Finally, plants may also leave impressions in durable substances that can then be identified after the plant has decomposed. In this section, we examine four frequent contexts of preservation, and the effects of each on archaeological specimens. Note that many archaeological sites include multiple types of preservation.

DRY PRESERVATION

Dry preservation (desiccation) occurs in environments where the sustained absence of moisture inhibits the microrganisms that drive decomposition. Since almost all botanical specimens will preserve (often for thousands of years) in these settings, desiccated assemblages are frequently dense and species rich, sometimes to the point where the sheer quantity of material poses problems for sampling (Bryant 1989; Rowley-Conwy 1994; van der Veen 2007a). For example, at the site of Zinchecra, Libya, almost 800 desiccated plant remains were recovered from each liter of sediment (van der Veen 1992b).

Dry preservation is typically associated with desert environments, where rainfall and humidity are low, but even in these regions, caves frequently yield the best-preserved botanical specimens, as they have been more consistently protected from the elements (e.g., di Lernia et al. 2012; Emslie et al. 1995; Knörzer 2000; Smith 1967). For example, in the Great Basin of the Western United States, caves with dry preservation have yielded foodstuffs, bedding, textiles, baskets, sandals, wooden tools, and other macrobotanical remains dating from over 10,000 BP through the historic period (figure 2.1; Fowler and Fowler 2008). In ancient Egypt and the Xinjiang region of China, man-made subterranean tombs provide similar protection (e.g., Chen et al. 2012; Jiang et al. 2007; Kunth 1826); in Egypt even delicate floral garlands have been recovered intact (Hamdy 2007). Dry preservation can also occur at open-air sites in particularly arid locations, such as coastal Peru, where rich botanical assemblages including well-preserved woven textiles are common (e.g., Beresford-Jones et al. 2011; Doyon-Bernard 1990).

Despite its common association with arid environments, dry preservation can also occur in regions with high rainfall, provided the archaeological site is sufficiently protected. Some of the most famous examples of dry preservation in temperate environments are from a series of caves in Kentucky, among them Newt Kash Hollow, where a wide variety of tools, baskets, and foodstuffs, including early examples of domesticated chenopod (*Chenopodium berlandieri*) and sumpweed (*Iva annua* var. *macrocarpa*), were recovered (Gremillion 1996b; Jones 1936; Smith and Cowan 1987; Yarnell 1972). Excavations in Europe have demonstrated that even in sites that are predominantly subject to decomposition, dry preservation can occur in specific contexts such as protected gaps and holes within medieval buildings (e.g., Ernst and Jacomet 2006).

In cases of dry preservation, much of the water evaporates from the plant specimen. Although this process can cause shrinking and twisting, particularly of softer, moisture-rich plant parts such as leaves, flowers, and fruits, more rigid anatomical structures such as wood and seeds can appear virtually identical to their modern counterparts (Cappers 2006; Neef et al. 2012; Van Bergen et al. 1997). Depending on the speed of desiccation, colors will frequently fade, although van der Veen (2007a:969) notes that in some cases desiccated grains and chaff acquire a darker reddish-brown hue. In all cases, anatomical features, including delicate ones such as hairs, are often intact, improving the possibility of identification to the species level (van der Veen 2007a). The quality of preservation frequently extends to the biomolecular level, where dry specimens are generally good candidates for analysis, although certain lipids may chemically degrade (Brown and Brown 2011; Van Bergen et al. 1997; see Wales et al., chapter 15, this volume, for further discussion). Desiccated specimens have also been used for isotopic analysis (e.g., Reynolds et al. 2005).

WET PRESERVATION

Plant material can also be prevented from decomposing within an anaerobic environment, a situation that most frequently occurs in waterlogged

FIGURE 2.1. *Examples of desiccated and waterlogged botanical preservation. Top: Fort Rock–style sandal from Catlow Cave, Oregon (MNCH cat #1-3563) dated to ca. 9350 cal BP (Connelly and Cannon 1999); photo courtesy University of Oregon Museum of Natural and Cultural History. Bottom: Wood stake from intertidal fish weir dated to earlier than 3000 cal BP, Favorite Bay, Admiralty Island, Alaska; photo courtesy Madonna Moss.*

conditions. Although water saturation will inhibit many microorganisms and slow decomposition in a variety of settings, in practice the degree of preservation also depends on the exposure of the specimen (seasonal fluctuations, burial in sediment, etc.) and the chemical composition of the water (particularly pH and reduction potential) (Caple and Dungworth 1997; Florian 1987; Menotti 2012). For this reason, the density of plant remains in wet sites will vary, but waterlogged assemblages are generally large and species rich (Jacomet 2013).

Some of the best anaerobic preservation occurs in peat bogs, highly acidic wetlands with low reduction potential in which almost all organic matter preserves, although these areas rarely include habitation sites (e.g., Brunning and McDermott 2013; Burov 2001; Coles and Coles 1989 Hillman 1986; Holden 1986; Kaplan et al. 1990; Sands 2013). Other types of inland waterlogged sites, particularly those in colder climates with minimal circulation and inflow (which oxygenate the environment), also have excellent preservation. A well-studied example is the now submerged Late Neolithic lakeside sites of alpine Switzerland, France, and Italy, where wooden house foundations, tools, foodstuffs, and other botanical culture of entire villages have been preserved (e.g., Brombacher 1997; Ebersbach 2013; Jacomet 2009, 2013; Jacomet and Brombacher 2005). These conditions can also occur in warmer climates, such as central Florida, where precontact wood canoes are frequently recovered from lakes lowered by drought (Newsom and Purdy 1990; Wheeler et al. 2003).

In maritime and coastal contexts, the degree of preservation depends not only on the temperature and chemistry of the marine environment but also on the exposure of the artifacts to wave action and other erosional forces (Florian 1987). Most organic material will eventually decay in a marine context (Søreide 2011), but decay can be slowed by cool temperatures, calm, deep water, and, most important, burial in sediment (particularly > 50 cm) (Florian 1987). For example, plant foods, basketry, and wooden objects survived buried 250 m offshore at the Mesolithic site of Tybrind Vig, Denmark (Anderson 1986; Kubiak-Martens 1999). In an area with more wave action, the bases of buried wood stakes forming intertidal fish weirs on the Northwest Coast of North America have been protected by sediment and can be mapped at low tide (figure 2.1; Moss 2013; Moss et al. 1990).

Burial in wet sediment is not confined to underwater contexts. Its significance in producing anaerobic conditions is perhaps best illustrated by the coastal site of Ozette, Washington. Sometimes referred to as the "North American Pompeii," a late prehistoric mudslide at the site covered and preserved the material culture of several plank houses, including boats, hunting and fishing tools, weaving tools, gaming pieces, baskets, boxes, bowls, carvings, nets, foodstuffs, and the houses themselves, providing a precontact perspective on the rich botanical culture of the Makah (Samuels 1991; Whelchel 2005).

Finally, plant material can also be preserved in frozen contexts. Though often technically "wet," in these cases the freezing temperatures are also a major contributor to the preservation. The most famous cases of frozen macrobotanical remains are those associated with individuals preserved in the ice, notable Ötzi in the Austrian Alps and Kwäday Dän Ts'ìnchí in British Columbia. In both cases, analysis of gut contents has provided direct evidence of plant foods, while associated possessions have included plant-based tools, medicines, and foods (Acs et al. 2005; Beattie et al. 2000; Bortenschlager and Oeggl 2000; Dickson et al. 2003; Dickson et al. 2004; Heiss and Oeggl 2009; Oeggl 2009).

In ideal conditions, wet preservation will maintain plant specimens in a condition similar to that of modern specimens, with both anatomical structures and cellular characteristics intact (Jones et al. 2007). However, in many cases specimens may be preserved less well than their appearance suggests. The majority of research on what precise changes occur in waterlogged specimens has focused on wood: despite seeming intact, cell walls are frequently weakened so that a specimen can collapse if it is allowed to dry (Gratten 1987). Waterlogging can cause degradation of biomolecules, although DNA has been recovered from waterlogged plant material in some cases. The exception is frozen sites, which have excellent preservation of biomolecules (Schlumbaum and Edwards 2013; see also Wales et al., chapter 15, this volume).

CARBONIZATION AND MINERALIZATION

Although the wet and dry contexts discussed above produce the most diverse and best-preserved plant assemblages, these conditions only occur in a small percentage of archaeological sites. In the majority of cases, the decomposition processes discussed in the introduction to this section will break down organic material unless the specimen has undergone a transformative process to convert organic compounds to inorganic structures (figure 2.2).

In rare cases, this occurs through mineralization in which organic material within plant structures is gradually replaced by precipitated minerals from the surrounding substrate, preserving the anatomical structure. This process occurs frequently in phosphate-rich contexts (often latrines or coprolites) (Green 1979; McCobb et al. 2003) but is also documented in cases where deposited plants are in direct association with a corroding metal such as bronze, copper, or iron (Chen et al. 1998; Keepax 1975; Miksicek 1987; Moulherat et al. 2002). Mineralized specimens will frequently be unevenly preserved, as the process

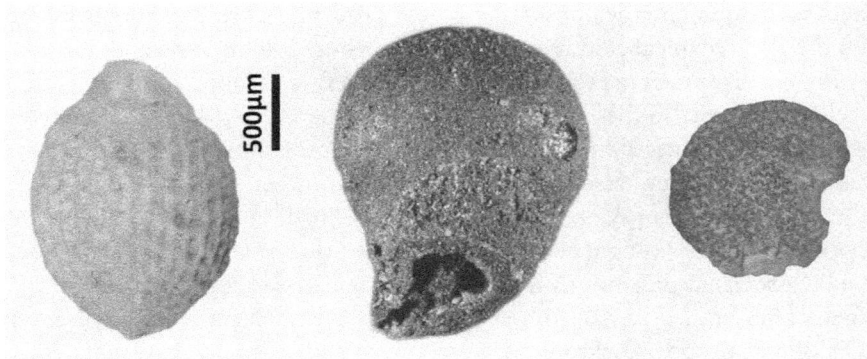

Figure 2.2. *Examples of biomineralized and carbonized seeds from Iron Age archaeological sites in West Africa. Left to Right: biomineralized* Scleria *sp., carbonized* Pennisetum glaucum, *carbonized Solanaceae.*

may proceed at different speeds for different anatomical parts (Green 1979). In contrast to mineralization, which is confined to very specific contexts, carbonization is a common phenomenon accounting for the bulk of macrobotanical remains recovered from archaeological sites.

Carbonization or charring is a process through which exposure to heat, usually in a low-oxygen environment, converts organic material to an inorganic structure consisting primarily of carbon (Bryant 1989; Märkle and Rosch 2008). The advantage of carbonized remains is that, once burned, they preserve in a wide variety of environments, although they can still break down in alkaline contexts and are vulnerable to mechanical damage (Bryant 1989). Consequently, carbonized assemblages are found in sites around the world and account for a significant portion of the macrobotanical record (e.g., Gremillion 1997; Hastorf 1999; Hastorf and Popper 1988; Minnis 2003, 2004; VanDerwarker and Peres 2010). However, carbonization usually only affects a small portion of the original assemblage of deposited macrobotanical remains; even in cases of catastrophic burning, it is rare for every element of the original assemblage to carbonize in identifiable form. For example, at the West African site of Kirikongo, only wood, likely from posts or roof beams, and seeds have been identified in a burned ritual structure that likely included a wider range of botanical culture (Dueppen 2012). Consequently, researchers have invested significant effort in modeling both the relationship between the carbonized sample and the original plant assemblage in use at the site, as described later in this chapter, and the actual carbonization process.

Under ideal conditions, carbonization produces a perfectly preserved specimen. However, specimens also pop, twist, or reduce completely to ash. In addition, the carbonization process frequently shrinks specimens, a phenomenon that has substantial implications for the identification of domestication based on seed size (e.g., Braadbaart and Wright 2007; Smith 2014; Wright 2003, 2008). Extensive experimental research designed to determine the conditions under which various species and plant parts carbonize and the effects of carbonization on morphology has demonstrated that the process is complex and situational (e.g., Boardman and Jones 1990; Braadbaart and Bergen 2005; Braadbaart et al. 2004; Braadbaart and Poole 2008; Braadbaart et al. 2007; D'Andrea 2008; Dezendorf 2013; Guarino and Sciarrillo 2004; Gustafsson 2000; Hather 1993; Hubbard and Azm 1990; Lopinot 1984; Margaritis and Jones 2006; Märkle and Rosch 2008; McParland et al. 2010; Prior and Alvin 1983; Rossen and Olson 1985; Sievers and Wadley 2008; Smith and Jones 1990; Terral and Durand 2006; Théry-Parisot 2001; Théry-Parisot et al. 2010; Théry-Parisot and Henry 2012; Wilson 1984; Wright 2003, 2008). As Wright (2003:577) summarizes, whether and how a specimen carbonizes depends on the species and plant part, the condition of the specimen (e.g., moisture content), and the conditions under which it is exposed to heat (e.g., temperature, oxygen, time, etc.). However, creation of intact carbonized specimens is most likely to occur in reducing (low oxygen) conditions and when fires burn at lower temperatures (e.g., ca. 200–600°F) for shorter amounts of time (Boardman and Jones 1990; Wright 2003). In addition, as specimens with different characteristics (e.g., seeds of different sizes and starch/oil contents) favor different carbonization conditions, systematic preservation biases may occur in particular archaeological sites or contexts.

Although any part of the plant can be preserved through carbonization, the majority of the above studies have focused on seeds and seedlike plant parts (achenes, caryopses), nutshell, and wood charcoal, because, as described above, they preserve well, forming the bulk of most carbonized macrobotanical assemblages. However, studies have demonstrated that other carbonized material can be identified, including roots, tubers, leaves, and fibers, although in many cases these identifications require observation of anatomical features under high-power microscopy (e.g., Cortella et al. 2001; Good 2001; Hather 1993). At a molecular level, DNA, lipids, and other molecules are usually damaged or destroyed by the carbonization process, although there is a growing number of case studies of successful extraction from charred archaeological specimens (e.g., Brown and Brown 2011; Schlumbaum et al. 2008; Wales et al., chapter 15, this volume).

PLANT IMPRESSIONS AND REPRESENTATIONS

Thus far, this discussion has focused on preserved plants in the archaeological record. However, there are two significant categories of macrobotanical data in which the plant itself is not preserved at all. Plants can leave impressions on pliable substances that have since hardened. Impressions may result from the intentional use of plants in decoration, such as the use of *Blepharis* sp. roulettes in West Africa (Haour et al. 2010) or cord decoration on Neolithic beakers in Europe (Grömer and Kern 2010). Plants can also leave impressions when incorporated as a temper for pottery vessels or mud brick or as the underlying structure of wattle-and-daub architecture (e.g., Hovsepyan and Willcox 2008; Peacock 1993; Sherard 2009). Finally, many impressions are the result of fortuitous accidents, such as a jute textile draped over a clay pot prior to firing at Harappa circa 2000 BCE (Wright et al. 2012).

Impressions are often imperfect and lacking in detail. However, when identifications can be made, they may provide a data source in sites with otherwise poor preservation. Perhaps most significant, impressions have been used to document particularly early examples of plant use. Some of the early identifications of cordage from the Upper Paleolithic were based on impressions (Soffer et al. 2000). Likewise, the oldest examples of domestic pearl millet seeds are known from impressions in pottery at Karkarichinkat, Mali (Manning et al. 2011). In other cases, impressions can provide a perspective distinct from other elements of the macrobotanical record. For example, the use of nonlocal plants as temper has been used to identify trade ceramics (Mariotti Lippi et al. 2011; Nixon et al. 2011).

Finally, a brief mention should be made of the importance of artistic representations of plants. Plants in paintings, carvings, and other artistic media can be richly interpreted within an art historical framework as decorative elements; they may also be identified by paleoethnobotanists, who draw on these representations not only to understand the cultural significances of the plants, but also to discover evidence of the use of plants not otherwise present in the archaeological record (e.g., Akers et al. 2011; Eubanks 1999; Ford 1994; Hays-Gilpin and Hegmon 2005; McMeekin 1992; Miller 2000, 2013).

FORMATION OF MACROBOTANICAL ASSEMBLAGES IN ARCHAEOLOGICAL CONTEXTS

As is clear from the descriptions above, preservation conditions will significantly affect the range of macrobotanical specimens recovered from a site. However, to interpret the archaeological assemblage fully, it is equally necessary to understand how these assemblages are initially created and how they are affected by post-depositional processes.

In order to interpret paleoethnobotanical assemblages, as a first step archaeologists model the relationships between living and dead assemblages. Although these models are often most effective when developed for specific environmental and cultural contexts (see below), generalized models provide a basic framework. A recent example is that developed by Lee (2012:651–53), who distinguishes between a life assemblage (living plant population), death assemblage (plants brought into sites), deposited assemblage (discarded and buried plants), and fossil assemblage (preserved plants). At each stage, some elements of the assemblage are lost, consumed, or otherwise removed, a process that, as Ford (1979) reminds us, is shaped by cultural patterns of use and disposal. Ultimately, Lee's and other models formalize the basic concept that plants enter archaeological sites through a variety of routes or paths and once at an archaeological site, they are affected by cultural and noncultural processes that in turn affect their preservation (the sample is then further narrowed by recovery and analysis; see White and Shelton, chapter 6, this volume; Fritz and Nesbitt, chapter 7, this volume). In this section, we look first at three major pathways by which plant species enter sites: direct anthropogenic (plant species intentionally brought to sites by humans), indirect anthropogenic (plant species unintentionally brought to sites, or brought to sites as a secondary effect of another activity), and non-anthropogenic (all other routes by which plants enter sites). We then briefly examine some of the most common post-depositional processes that affect the interpretation of macrobotanical remains.

DIRECT ANTHROPOGENIC

Human societies gather and cultivate a wide range of plants for a large variety of purposes. Plants may be used for food, fuel, fodder, construction material, bedding, basketry, medicine, ritual objects, dyes, fiber and cordage, tools, toys, and more: for example, Burkill (2004) indexes 7 primary and 116 secondary categories of plant use in West Africa. In each case, a plant is intentionally selected for its properties and frequently brought to a cultural space where it may eventually be preserved in an archaeological deposit. The choices made in bringing these plants into archaeological sites can provide insight into the cultural and environmental contexts in which these choices were made (e.g., Lentz and Hockaday 2009; Lepofsky and Lyons 2003; Marston 2009).

Once the choice has been made to bring a plant into the cultural sphere, the mode in which it is collected, transported, processed, used, and discarded will affect its entry into the archaeological record in different ways in different preservation contexts (Dennell 1976; Ford 1979; Miksicek 1987; Minnis 1981). These activities are frequently routinized and reflect local social and cultural practices (Atalay and Hastorf 2006; van der Veen 2007b). Therefore, modeling the processes that ultimately create the archaeological record not only aids in identifying what activities took place at a site, but also allows researchers to utilize the macrobotanical assemblage to address issues such as identity and cultural change.

Given the dominance of carbonized assemblages in the global paleoethnobotanical record, many studies pay particular attention to when plants are exposed to heat, either intentionally or accidentally. As an example, consider the typical representation of three economically valuable West African trees in wood charcoal assemblages. Although the leaves and fruits of the baobab (*Adansonia digitata*) are edible, the tree produces a very poor fuel and construction wood and is therefore virtually never present in archaeological wood charcoal assemblages. In contrast, the wood of the shea tree (*Vitellaria paradoxa*) burns well and at a high temperature, but the tree is more valued for its oil-rich nuts and therefore is frequently protected. Finally, the woods of *Combretum* spp. burn very well and the trees have few other economic uses, making them common in wood charcoal assemblages (Neumann 1999).

Many of the most interesting and comprehensive studies on the entry of plants into the archaeological record have focused on food processing (e.g., Abbo et al. 2008; Atchison et al. 2005; Chernoff and Paley 1998; D'Andrea 2008; Dennell 1974; Fuller and Harvey 2006; Fuller and Stevens 2009; Hastorf 1988; Jones 1987; Jones and Halstead 1995; Munson 1984; van der Veen 1989). A recent example is Margaritis and Jones's (2006) exploration of grape processing in Hellenistic Greece. Through a combination of historical research, ethnographic observation, and experimental charring, they were able to link specific combinations of whole fruits, pips, pressed skins, and other parts of the grape cluster (pedicels, peduncles, and rachises) to various stages in red, white, and rosé wine production as well as fresh and dried grape production. Margaritis and Jones's research is fairly unusual in its focus on fruit, as the majority of crop processing research has been on grains, due not only to the significance of cereal crops, but also to their complex processing, as best demonstrated by Hillman (1981, 1984a, 1984b, 1985). His particularly detailed studies covered plant part distribution, waste production, and opportunities for carbonization for approximately thirty stages from harvest to processing to cooking of Near Eastern grain crops (wheat, barley, rye, and oats).

Indirect Anthropogenic

Though the direct anthropogenic assemblage is a significant component of the plants found at an archaeological site, many plants are brought to sites by humans unintentionally. These plants are frequently accidentally collected with other, desired species or acquired incidentally (e.g., while collecting dung, as described below) and, although not expressly targeted, can still yield a great deal of information. Particularly fruitful has been the study of weeds, which are frequently collected with crops during harvest. Weed assemblages are often particular to certain crops, soil types, and cultivation practices, and can consequently be used to address such questions as the range of crops grown, the farming practices in use, and the health of the field system (Bogaard et al. 2005; Charles et al. 2003; Jones 2002; Jones, Bogaard, Charles, and Hodgson 2000; Jones et al. 2010; Jones et al. 2005).

Determining whether a useful plant was intentionally or unintentionally transported to an archaeological site can be challenging. For example, many "weeds" with edible plant parts may be intentionally encouraged in fields and Behre (2008) notes that cleaning these edible "weeds" from harvested crops can provide an opportunity to collect them in large quantities, encouraging their consumption. In contrast, simply because a plant is edible does not mean it was necessarily brought to a site for that purpose. For example, kram-kram (*Cenchrus biflorus*), a wild small-seeded grass, is documented ethnographically in West Africa as a food plant, but is also a burr that clings to clothing and animal fur, making it easy to transport accidentally to a site.

Particularly well studied by archaeologists working in areas where livestock are common is distinguishing the use of dung as fuel from the direct collection of wild plants (Anderson and Ertuğ-Yaras 1996; Bottema 1984; Charles 1998; Hastord and Wright 1998; Miller 1984; Miller and Smart 1984; Murray 2005; Reddy 1998; Shahack-Gross 2011). Dried dung may be burned directly or mixed with dry plant matter prior to being formed into cakes, although in either case, the included seeds, chaff, and other plant parts can carbonize when the dung is burned. Miller and Smart (1984) have noted that dung burning must be considered as a possibility in sites where burned dung and macrobotanical assemblages with high numbers of fodder seeds are recovered in regions with little wood fuel, particularly if the recovery contexts suggest fuel use rather than food waste. If not recognized, dung-derived samples can be misinterpreted to suggest higher reliance on wild plants in human diets. However, once identified, their analysis can contribute significantly to understanding the local agropastoral system (e.g., Delhon et al. 2008; Miller 1996).

Non-Anthropogenic

Finally, it is important to consider that many of the plants recovered from archaeological contexts may have entered the site through non-anthropogenic means. Seeds are widely dispersed independently of human activity by wind, water, and other vectors (including insects and seed-consuming animals), a process often referred to as "seed rain" (Cappers 1993, 1995; Minnis 1981). Many plants produce hundreds to thousands of seeds, which can be spread over significant distances (particularly by water) although most seed rain assemblages will be fairly localized (Cappers 1993; Minnis 1981). Rodents, ants, termites, and other taxa can also transport seeds both into and within sites (see below). Overall, as Minnis (1981) describes, seed rain can easily contribute thousands of specimens to an archaeological site before, during, and after an occupation.

Many of these incidentally introduced seeds will be uncarbonized and therefore unlikely to preserve in most settings. As Miller (1989) notes, animals and insects will tend to transport uncarbonized and therefore edible seeds. However, non-anthropogenic seeds can become charred through a variety of processes. Seeds that have entered the soil prior to occupation through seed rain can be carbonized when a fire is built over them, seeds can blow into anthropogenic fires during occupation, and wind can easily disperse seeds carbonized in a naturally occurring wildfire. Although much of the research on non-anthropogenic contributions has focused on seeds due to their dispersal mechanisms, many of these same processes apply to other plant parts (e.g., Smart and Hoffman 1988).

Despite their nonhuman-centered pathways to entering the site, these elements of the plant assemblage have interpretive value. Humans have impacts on their surrounding vegetation, even in cases of fairly low-density population (e.g., Smith 2011b; see also B. Smith, chapter 18, this volume). For example, the background flora may include species that colonize recently cleared areas, wind-dispersed weeds from nearby fields, or disproportionate numbers of seeds from useful wild plants, the growth of which may have been encouraged by local populations.

Post-Depositional Processes

Finally, it is worth considering the post-depositional effects that can alter the botanical assemblage once an archaeological site has been abandoned. As already discussed above, plants deposited in archaeological sites will preserve differently depending on the local environment and the condition (e.g., carbonized or not) of the plant when it was deposited. However, all archaeological sites are subject to a range of post-depositional processes, including sediment shifting, cracking, trampling, flooding, bioturbation, and erosion (e.g., Miksicek 1987; Rolfsen 1980; Schiffer 1987; Théry-Parisot et al. 2010; Wood and Johnson 1978).

Burrowing animals and invertebrates, notably rodents, earthworms, ants, and termites, can move both seeds and sediment within a cultural deposit (sometimes over several meters in depth), mixing specimens from different contexts (Bocek 1986; Borojevic 2011; Canti 2003; Johnson 1989; McBrearty 1990; Miksicek 1987; Stein 1983; Tryon 2006; Wood and Johnson 1978). Some of these animals stockpile seeds, creating diverse caches that can give the impression of human harvesting (Borojevic 2011; Gasser and Adams 1981; Miller 1989; Minnis 1981). Roots can also cause compression, soil movement, and damage to macrobotanical specimens (Lopinot and Brussell 1982; Miksicek 1987). Sediment in archaeological sites can shift and move slightly for other reasons, and in some cases may crack, for example due to drying (Erlandson and Rockwell 1987; Wood and Johnson 1978). This can cause seeds to move up and down within the deposit. Although these effects are minimal in most cases, particularly in instances of old, rare, or unexpected finds, it is essential to ensure that the site stratigraphy is intact at both the macro and the micro level. Many post-depositional effects are clearly visible in excavation stratigraphies, but macrobotanical remains are often quite small, and as such may be significantly affected by processes that are not always immediately apparent (Borojevic 2011; Fowler et al. 2004; Miksicek 1987).

CONCLUSION

Macrobotanical assemblages from archaeological sites are cultural but are significantly shaped by the local environment both at the time of site occupation and in post-depositional contexts. As demonstrated above, successfully modeling how plants enter and become preserved in archaeological sites is a complex process that must take into account the intrinsic properties and ecology of those plants being studied; how the plants may be culturally managed/cultivated, processed/modified, and used/consumed; and the effects of differential preservation on the diverse elements of the botanical assemblage.

ACKNOWLEDGMENTS

Thank you to Jade d'Alpoim-Guedes, Christina Warinner, and particularly John M. Marston for inviting me to participate in this volume and for their support during the writing process; to Patti Wright for generously sharing her research on this topic; to Ada Ball for her assistance in formatting the bibliography; and to Richard I. Ford.

3

Formation and Taphonomic
Processes Affecting
Starch Granules

AMANDA G. HENRY

Like pollen and phytoliths, starch granules have proven to be a valuable source of information about ancient plant use. Their semi-crystalline structure and insolubility in water, as well as the sheer numbers in which they are produced in plants (Pérez et al. 2009; Swinkles 1985), all help preserve them in the archaeological record. Their taxon-specific morphology and the manner in which they preserve signs of intentional processing are powerful markers of human dietary behavior. However, because of starch granules' unique biological origins, they can be damaged or destroyed by certain biological, chemical, and human-induced factors. In order to fully interpret and properly analyze the appearance of starch granules in the archaeological context, we must first have a good grasp of the processes leading to the formation and destruction of these granules. Paleoethnobotanists have been using starch granules as a means of identifying ancient use of plants since at least the early 1980s, but our understanding of starch granule formation, damage, and destruction comes primarily from the food science industry, where the properties of starches have been studied for several hundred years (Schwartz and Whistler 2009). The information presented here is more extensively reviewed in the food science literature, and those interested in a more detailed description, particularly of starch formation and gelatinization processes, are encouraged to read Galliard (1987), Tester and colleagues (2004), and BeMiller and Whistler (2009). Finally, a brief note on

DOI: 10.5876/9781607323167.c003

terminology: *starch grain* and *starch granule* are used interchangeably in the literature, but I use *starch granule* or *starches* here to avoid potential confusion over the term *grain*, which can also be used to refer to whole cereal plants or fruit caryopses. The term *native starch* refers to starch granules that have not been heated, ground, or otherwise processed.

WHAT IS STARCH?

Starch is a complex carbohydrate, consisting primarily of two kinds of long-chain polysaccharides, called *amylose* and *amylopectin*. These two compounds make up 98 to 99 percent of the dry weight of starch (Tester et al. 2004) and are chains of greater than ten monosaccharides (carbon chains, usually $C_6H_{12}O_6$) that do not taste sweet and are essentially inert (Belitz et al. 2009). Amylose is a linear molecule and usually accounts for about 20 to 35 percent of the starch granule, though this varies among plant species. So-called waxy plant varieties have less than 15 percent amylose, but high-amylose species have more than 40 percent. Amylopectin is a much larger molecule that has many branches and it forms the backbone of the starch (Biliaderis 2009; Blanshard 1987; Galliard and Bowler 1987). Researchers have noted that some plants have carbohydrate forms that are neither as highly branched as amylopectin nor strictly linear like amylose. Between 5 and 7 percent of normal maize starch has been reported to be of this intermediate form (Lansky et al. 1949), but others have argued that this may be actually the result of imperfect isolation techniques (Tester 1997b). Within commercially prepared starch suspensions, several other minor components have been found, including proteins, lipids, "ash" (metal oxides), phosphorous, and pentosan (monosaccharides with five carbons). Each of these makes up between 0.1 and 1.2 percent dry weight, except phosphorous, which is a much smaller component, between 0.02 and 0.13 percent (Galliard and Bowler 1987). Some of these components are internal constituents of the starch granules, like lipids, which actually form part of the structure of the carbohydrate chains (Blanshard 1987). Others come from broken plant cells or the remains of the amyloplast and simply adhere to the surface of the granules (Galliard and Bowler 1987).

Starch is created by plants as a means of energy storage and transport. It is also found in mosses and ferns, protozoa, algae, and bacteria (Shannon et al. 2009; Stacey and Barker 1960). In algae and bacteria, starch forms only in the cytosol (Shannon et al. 2009) and it is unclear what form this starch takes. In plants, the starch granules form within plastids; mosses, ferns, green algae, and higher plants produce starch within their chloroplasts, but higher plants also have specific plastids dedicated to starch formation, called *amylo-plasts* (Badenhuizen 1965). There are two types of starch granules produced by higher plants, known as transitory and reserve starch (Badenhuizen 1969). Transitory starch granules accumulate briefly before being degraded. They primarily form within chloroplasts during the day as a result of photosynthesis, but are reverted to simple sugars and transported to other areas of the plant at night (Preiss 2009). Transitory starch granules are also known to form in pollen (Dickinson 1968) and in plant cell cultures. Reserve starch granules accumulate and are used for energy storage over long periods. They form in amyloplasts, primarily within the storage tissues of plants, such as roots, seeds, and tubers, and occasionally within unripe fruit. Reserve starches are only degraded back into sugars when the energy stored in these areas is needed, for example during sprouting of a tuber, germination of a seed, or ripening of the fruit (Preiss 2009). It has long been recognized that reserve starches take on genera- or species-specific shapes (figure 3.1; Reichert 1913; Seidemann 1966), but transitory starches are much smaller and do not take on these diagnostic forms (Shannon et al. 2009).

STARCH FORMATION AND ITS RELEVANCE
TO PALEOETHNOBOTANICAL STUDY

The species-specific shapes and physical properties of starch granules make them desirable markers of ancient behavior, but they also make starches vulnerable to certain taphonomic effects. The formation of starch granules is similar in all plants but details vary from species to species. This section describes the formation processes and how they affect what we see under light microscopy and scanning electron microscopy (SEM) and by the use of chemical stains.

The formation of reserve starch granules occurs primarily within the amyloplasts of a plant storage organ. Amyloplasts are membranes made up of lipids and proteins that contain enzymes to catalyze the synthesis of amylopectin and amylose. Sucrose created by photosynthesis enters the amyloplast and is incorporated into long-chain polysaccharides on the lipoprotein matrix on the inside of the amyloplast (Duffus 1979). The formation of these molecules begins at a single point, which is known as the *hilum* (plural *hila*), and proceeds radially. The hilum is often visible on mature starches (figure 3.1). Usually one starch granule is formed within each amyloplast, giving rise to so-called simple starches. Sometimes several individual granules form within one amyloplast, which results in compound starches like those seen in the seeds of rice (*Oryza sativa*) and some species of amaranth (*Amaranthus* spp.). Rarely,

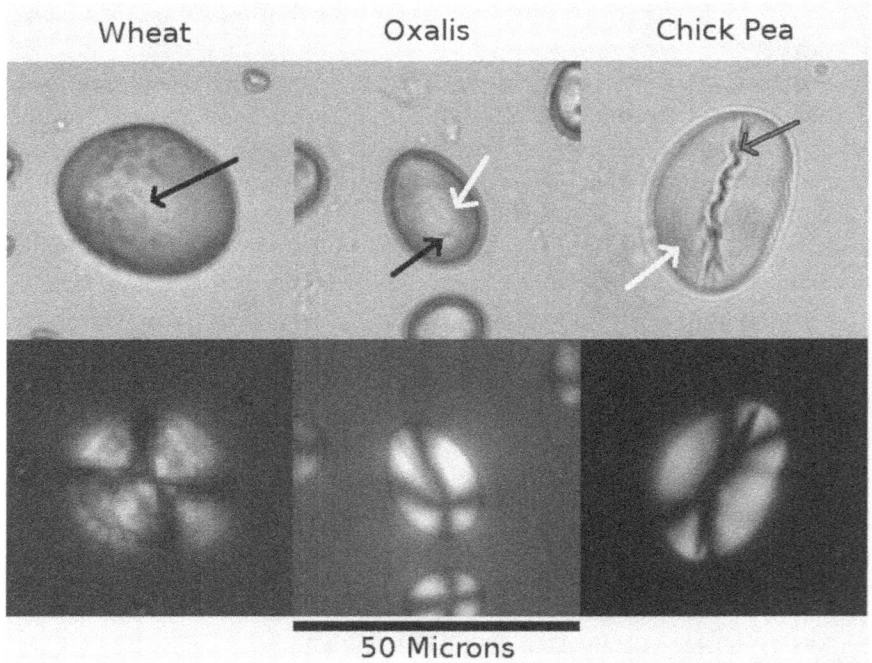

| Wheat | Oxalis | Chick Pea |

50 Microns

FIGURE 3.1. *Starch granules from a wheat (*Triticum aestivum*) seed, an oxalis (*Oxalis pescaprae*) tuber, and a chick pea (*Cicer arietinum*) seed. Note the variation in size, shape and features. Black arrows point to the hila of the starches. White arrows indicate lamellae. The gray arrow points to the large fissure common to many legume starches.*

compound starches are cemented together with a secondary deposit of starch, and such starches are called semi-compound or half compound (Badenhuizen 1965). Starches of this type have been found in the bulb of squill (*Scilla ovati-folia*) and seeds of common amaranth (*Amaranthus retroflexus*) (Badenhuizen 1965; Shannon et al. 2009).

As growth of the starch granule proceeds, the amylose and amylopectin are deposited in lengthening chains that radiate from the hilum toward the margin. Transmission electron microscopy (TEM), X-ray crystallography, and other methods have shown that as these chains lengthen there is a repeating pattern of growth on both the gross and fine scale. On the gross scale, the granule has alternating amorphous and crystalline shells that are between 100 and 400 nm thick (Pérez et al. 2009). These shells are commonly known in the paleoethnobotanical literature as *lamellae*, though in food science literature they are called growth rings, shells, or annular rings (Blanshard 1987; Pérez et al. 2009). The processes that determine the formation of lamellae are unclear. In wheat and barley the number of rings corresponds to the number of days of growth (Buttrose 1962), and the lamellae disappear when the plants are grown under constant light and temperature. In contrast, potato granules form lamellae even under constant conditions, which suggests that these lamellae may be controlled by a different formation process (Evers 1979). Although chains of amylose and amylopectin run through both crystalline and amorphous lamellae, it is generally thought that a more organized branching pattern of amylopectin is responsible for the crystalline shells and that amylose is concentrated in the amorphous ones (Blanshard 1987). The radial orientation of the amylopectin chains within the growth rings is thought to cause the birefringence patterns that appear when the starch granules are viewed under cross-polarized light (figure 3.1; Blanshard 1987; Sterling 1987). These growth rings, or lamellae, are fundamental features of the starch granules and can be diagnostic of particular taxa (figure 3.1). The crystalline and amorphous shells differ in density, resistance to attack by enzymes and chemicals, and, importantly for visualization by light microscopy, in their refractive index. Although starch granules have a mean refractive index of about 1.5 (Frey-Wyssling 1940; Speich 1942), the lamellae have higher and lower values (Blanshard 1987) and may become less visible if the granule is dehydrated (Hanssen et al. 1953). Because of this internal variation in refractive indices, it is vital that an appropriate mounting medium be chosen when attempting to view starch granules; a medium with a refractive index too close to that of the starch may cause the lamellae to be obscured.[1]

On the fine scale, the amorphous growth rings are relatively poorly understood, but the crystalline shells have been well-studied in certain taxa. Within the crystalline shells of all species examined thus far, there is a pattern of radial amylose, amorphous amylose, and tangential bands of amylopectin, which repeats every 5 to 10 nm. Although these repeating features are too small to see with light microscopy or SEM, I mention them because they appear to be a universal feature of starch formation and because in the food science literature the tangential amylopectin bands are sometimes called lamellae, but they should not be confused with the growth rings that paleoethnobotanists call lamellae. The even finer structure of starch granules is still under some debate (e.g., Pérez and Bertoft 2010), but is not discussed further here, as it does not directly affect the appearance and identification of starches under light microscopy or SEM.

Several other features of granules that are visible under light microscopy and SEM are pores, vacuoles, and cracks (figure 3.1). Some species produce starch granules with pores in the surface, which are thought to be channels of amorphous starch that run through the crystalline shells (Pérez et al. 2009). The pores are sites where the crystalline shell is weaker, making it more vulnerable to enzyme digestion in these areas (Jane 2009). Species that produce pores include sorghum (*Sorghum* cf. *bicolor*), millet (either *Setaria italica* or *Panicum miliaceum*, this is not specified in the article), maize (*Zea mays*), tapioca (*Manihot esculenta*), and rice (*Oryza sativa*) (Fannon et al. 1992). The large granules of wheat (*Triticum aestivum*), rye (*Secale cereale*), and barley (*Hordeum vulgare*) have pores in the equatorial groove, but the small granules from these species do not have them. Potato (*Solanum tuberosum*), arrowroot (*Maranta arundinacea*), and canna (*Canna discolor*) do not have pores (Fannon et al. 1992). The hilum of starch granules is usually a disorganized area that sometimes contains proteins or other material from the amyloplast, and in some species this organization is so poor that a vacuole, or "open hilum," appears (French 1984). In some species, cracks or fissures appear within the granule, and among legumes (Fabaceae) in particular they can be a diagnostic feature (Reichert 1913), though care must be taken to differentiate the cracks from those caused by milling (see below).

Finally, other aspects of starch formation can cause variation in its appearance. As mentioned above, the relative amounts of amylose and amylopectin can vary from species to species and even among varieties of the same domesticate. This affects how starch granules appear when stained with various chemical stains (Reichert 1913). For example, iodine solution (iodine dissolved in an aqueous solution of potassium iodide) stains amylose a deep blue, but turns amylopectin red, so different species show different values of purple (Bailey and Whelan 1961). Furthermore, starch granules can vary within individual storage organs. The size of the starch depends on how long it has been maturing. In certain species, the shape also varies with maturity. For example, Evers (1971) demonstrated that in wheat and barley, the granules begin as small spherical bodies, or nuclei, which are subsequently surrounded by deposits that form on the equatorial plane. These secondary deposits form on one side of the nucleus and proceed around the circumference, so that less-developed granules appear somewhat reniform in plane view, and only fully developed starches are fully circular in plane view. It has also been shown in several species that different parts of an individual storage organ mature at different times, so that starch granules may be at different stages of development within the same organ (Shannon et al. 2009 and citations therein). Finally, starches from different organs within a plant have different shapes and sizes (e.g., Messner 2008).

PROCESSES THAT MODIFY STARCH
GRANULE STRUCTURE AND SHAPE

Several physical and chemical processes can affect starch granule structure and shape. The effects of water, heat, and enzymes have been well documented and represent the three main ways in which starches are modified.

Water has a very strong effect on granule properties, as it can be absorbed by native granules even at room temperature. The water uptake occurs in the amorphous part of the granules, and in some species the granules can absorb about 0.5 g of water per dry gram of starch (Brown and French 1977). This uptake of water is reversible and though it causes some swelling of the granule and possibly the increased appearance of the growth rings, these features revert upon drying.

Heat also changes the physical properties of starch through the process of gelatinization. Gelatinization is the breaking of the hydrogen bonds between the carbohydrate chains in the crystalline regions of the starch and appears as the loss of order (as seen by the loss of birefringence) and the swelling of the granule. The water content during heating strongly affects how and at what temperatures the changes occur (Blanshard 1987). If the water content is moderate to high, then the amorphous regions of the granule swell first and then the crystalline regions melt as the temperature rises. If the water content is low, then swelling is minimal and few changes in the starch are observed until the temperature reaches the melting point of the crystalline regions. Finally, if the water content is extremely high, then the swelling of the amorphous regions overcomes the structural integrity of the crystalline regions at lower temperatures, before melting can occur, and the starch appears to have "burst."

In addition to water content and temperature, the biological origin of the starch granule also has a strong effect on how it gelatinizes. Furthermore, not all granules from the same species react identically to the same heat and water application, so we usually speak of a temperature at the onset of gelatinization and a temperature of complete gelatinization, which can be separated by several degrees Celsius. These temperatures vary considerably from species to species (e.g., Reichert 1913). In genera like *Triticum* and *Hordeum* that have a bimodal distribution of granule sizes, the different sizes have different gelatinization profiles (Blanshard 1987).

As a good source of energy, starch granules are actively sought out by a wide variety of organisms, from the plants that produce them to the animals, bacteria, and fungi that feed upon them. In order to access the energy stored in the crystalline structure, starch-consuming organisms have developed a variety of enzymes with the specific function of degrading starch granules, which are known collectively as *amylases*. Though they come from a variety of sources and vary significantly in how they break up amylose and amylopectin chains (Robyt 2009), the effect on the microscopic appearance of the starch granule usually falls into one of two categories. The enzymes either erode the surface of the granule, resulting in a very irregular, rough surface, or they penetrate the surface at local points, possibly through the pores mentioned above, and digest the granule via an "inside-to-out" process, leaving very characteristic pits visible on the surface (Galliard and Bowler 1987).

Several other physical and chemical processes are also known to alter starch granules, such as the addition of salts to starch-water solutions, but this research has primarily been done in the food science realm, where the effects are measured on starch pastes and overall properties, rather than on the microscopic appearance of the starch granules. This remains an area of paleo-ethnobotanical starch analysis that needs much more study.

TAPHONOMY OF STARCH GRANULES IN
THE ARCHAEOLOGICAL RECORD

Though we generally understand how starches are formed and the most common ways in which they are altered, the taphonomic processes that alter starch granule morphology and preservation in the archaeological record are only just beginning to be understood. When observing variation among starch granules, it is important to consider all of the times and places in those gran-ules' "life histories" that may have been the source of that variation (figure 3.2). A starch granule's life history begins with its formation in the plant and pro-ceeds through the initial human interaction, which usually involves some sort of removal from the plant source, processing, and then consumption or use. It then enters the archaeological record through discard of the plant or the tool, or death of the individual, where it becomes vulnerable to environmental and microbial alteration. Finally, it enters a second phase of human interaction during excavation and lab analysis of the artifact or fossil. Each of these stages has many possibilities for damage, distortion, or complete disappearance of the granule, which can confound our attempts to describe and compare starch granule assemblages. I describe below the various places where variation and modification of starch granule assemblages may occur and, though this is not an exhaustive list, it should guide a researcher's thinking prior to making con-clusions about differences between samples.

Starch Granule Life History

Factors affecting starch granule appearance and numbers

1. Starch Production within Plant

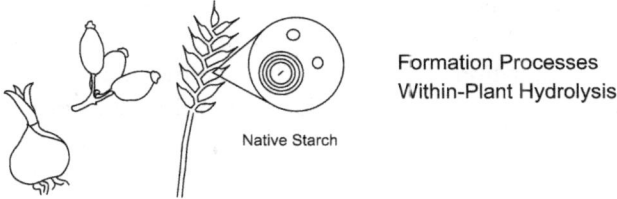

Native Starch

Formation Processes
Within-Plant Hydrolysis

2. First Human Interaction

Partially
Gelatinized
Starch

Processing
Consumption

3. Discard and Burial

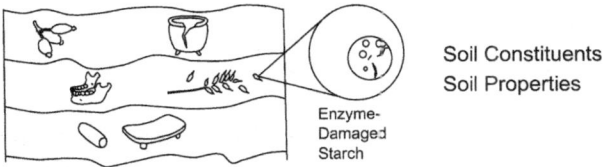

Enzyme-
Damaged
Starch

Soil Constituents
Soil Properties

4. Excavation and Laboratory Processing

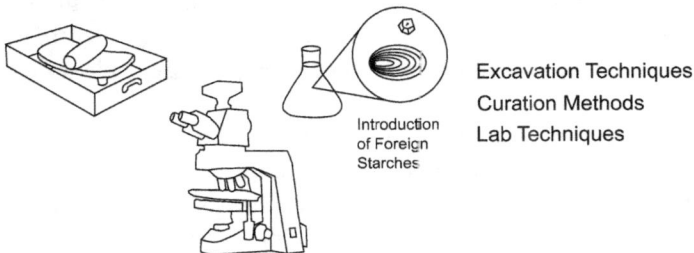

Introduction
of Foreign
Starches

Excavation Techniques
Curation Methods
Lab Techniques

FIGURE 3.2. *Diagram of a starch granule's "life history." Loss, distortion, or damage to the starch granule is possible at any step.*

Production within the Plant

The formation and digestion processes within the plant itself can cause significant variation among starch granules. As mentioned above, granules from different parts of the same organ can be at different stages of development, so granules with different sizes and possibly different shapes can appear within the same sample. When the plant begins to digest its own starch during sprouting or germination, the action of the digestive enzymes can leave characteristic markings on the granules. Sometimes this damage can be successfully identified in the archaeological record. For example, Samuel (1996, 2000) was able to identify the use of sprouted grains in ancient Egyptian bread and beer based on the appearance of partially digested granules.

The First Human Interaction

After being formed in the plant, starch granules then begin their initial interaction with humans. Archaeologists are often interested in the starch-rich plants that have been used as foods, so much of the archaeological literature on starch use is dedicated to studying evidence of cooking and processing. However, it is important to keep in mind that starchy plants can be used for other, non-dietary purposes, like mastics and parts of compound tools. These non-dietary plants may be processed prior to use much in the same way as food plants, so the kinds of damage may be similar, though this area has not been well explored in either the food science or the paleoethnobotanical literature.

The changes to starch granules caused by cooking have been well studied. Native starches are not easily digestible in the human alimentary system, so most starch-rich foods are subjected to some kind of cooking or processing in order to make them more readily attacked by amylolytic digestive enzymes (Galliard 1987). Even after undergoing processing, many starch granules retain some physical and chemical features that allow them to be identified to plant taxon and that may also record how they were processed (Henry et al. 2009; Messner and Schindler 2010).

Many starch-rich foods common in modern diets are ground prior to consumption or prior to further processing. Grinding partially destroys the crystalline structure of the starch granules by breaking some of the hydrogen bonds that hold the macromolecules together, making the granules more amorphous (Lelievre 1974). This in turn leads to increased swelling in cold water, lower gelatinization temperatures, and increased vulnerability to enzymes (Tester 1997a; Tipples 1969). Grinding damage can been seen under light microscopy, either as radial cracks at or near the hilum, or as an increased propensity to swell significantly in room temperature water (Jones 1940). Some researchers have been able to identify ground foods in the archaeological record based on the presence of radial cracks and surface damage to the granules, as well as distortions to the extinction cross (Del Pilar Babot 2003; Del Pilar Babot and Apella 2003).

Cooking experiments conducted by Henry et al. (2009) have shown that the biological origin of the starch granules and the type and intensity of the cooking strongly influence the degree and type of damage to the starch granules. Most cooking processes involve the application of heat with various amounts of water, which results in some degree of gelatinization. Boiling involves starch-water solutions with an excess of water, causing extreme swelling of the granules. Baking can include various amounts of water, resulting in granules that range from moderately to completely swollen. Parching, popping, and other "dry" forms of cooking usually cause melted but less swollen starches. In all of these cooking methods, the time that the food was cooked, the temperature reached, and the particle size of the food determine the extent to which the starch granules are gelatinized. In many cases, some starch granules particles retain all or many of their diagnostic morphological features even after having been cooked (Henry et al. 2009; Messner and Schindler 2010). Cooking can also increase the susceptibility of starch granules to certain dyes, particularly Congo Red, which can be another key way to identify cooked starch granules (Lamb and Loy 2005).

There are several processing methods that do not use heat to make starch granules more digestible, and these can also create distinctive damage patterns. Del Pilar Babot (2003) has shown that freezing can cause bursting and fracturing of the granules and loss of birefringence. Starches gelatinize at low temperatures in solutions of alkali (Galliard and Bowler 1987), so processing with lye or other solutions in the making of hominy or nixtamal should be expected to cause distinctive damage, though thus far this hypothesis has not been tested.

As more researchers recover starch granules from dental calculus (e.g., Henry et al. 2011; Li et al. 2010; Piperno and Dillehay 2008) and from the products of digestion, it is important to recognize that damage can occur both within the mouth during mastication and later in the intestinal tract. When a bolus of food is processed in the mouth, it is ground between the teeth and mixed with salivary amylase, so it could be expected that chewed granules should show both grinding and enzyme damage. However, damage from chewing has not been thoroughly studied, and preliminary data suggest that the physical properties of the food (including particle size and degree and type of cooking) strongly affect the length of chewing and the associated starch damage (Hoebler et al. 1998). Starch granules are occasionally recovered from coprolites and fecal samples (e.g., Horrocks et al. 2004); however, they are rare and the degree of damage on those granules has not been described. Given the large numbers of starch granules consumed on a daily basis in most human diets (particularly agricultural ones), it is not surprising that some granules should survive their passage through the intestinal tract, particularly if they are not damaged by milling or cooking prior to ingestion, therefore retaining their resistance to enzyme attack.

DISCARD AND BURIAL

Once a starch granule leaves the human sphere (e.g., on a discarded tool), it can be subject to a variety of taphonomic processes as it enters the archaeological record. The taphonomy of plant macroremains has been somewhat explored (e.g., Beck 1989), but research on both macro- and microremains is still underdeveloped. A literature review by Haslam (2004) has outlined many of the dangers that starch granules face in sediments. He suggests that two aspects of soils affect starch preservation: soil properties (e.g., moisture, texture, and pH) and soil constituents (e.g., enzymes, bacteria, fungi, and other organisms). The latter category is probably responsible for the degradation of the majority of starch granules in soils (Cheshire et al. 1969). Starch-hydrolyzing enzymes are prevalent in a wide variety of soil types and are particularly common in the top layers of soils (Taylor et al. 2002). However, though carbohydrates are known to be rapidly removed from soils by the action of enzymes (Cheshire et al. 1974; Cheshire et al. 1969), many of these studies have focused on amorphous starch or transitory leaf starches and not on storage starch grains (e.g., Porter and Martin 1952). Transitory starches are known to be much more readily hydrolyzed than storage starches (Bailey and Macrae 1973), so they may not provide a good reference for the behavior of storage starches in soils. Furthermore, the starches from only a few species, notably tobacco (*Nicotiana tabacum*), have been examined. In laboratory studies, the effect of enzymes on starches varies depending on the plant species (Robyt 2009), suggesting that the same would be true of different starches in soils. The effect of soil enzymes on storage starches needs to be better understood.

Outside of the effects of the enzymes themselves, soil properties can create conditions where starch granules are weakened and are therefore more susceptible to the actions of microorganisms. For example, freezing soils can damage starch granules (Del Pilar Babot 2003), making them more easily hydrolyzed. In other cases, however, it is unclear what the effect of certain soil properties might be. For example, drying can increase the susceptibility of a starch granule to enzyme attack (Leach and Schoch 1961), but drier sediments are also known to reduce soil enzyme activities (Speir and Ross 1981), making it unclear if dry soils should have better or worse starch preservation. Extremely high or low pH environments would likely cause considerable damage to starches, since strong acid treatment hydrolyzes starch and breaks it into small pieces (Jane et al. 1992) and strong bases cause gelatinization (Wootton and Ho 1989). Moderately high or low soil pH may have only minor direct effects on the starch granules, but would affect the microorganisms living in the soil, accelerating or inhibiting their consumption of starches (Cheshire 1979; French 1975). A few soil properties are known to reduce soil enzyme action, including the presence of aggregates (Guggenberger et al. 1999), clays (Lynch and Cotnoir 1956), and heavy metals (Joshi et al. 1993), which might provide a better preservation environment for starch granules. In addition to the potential damage caused by soil properties and components, starch granules can also migrate throughout the soil profile, both horizontally and vertically (Horrocks 2005). This would disrupt any associations between the starches and the archaeological layers or areas in which they were deposited.

Despite these potential problems, there is evidence that starches can be preserved in archaeological sediments and reflect ancient behaviors. Balme and Beck (2002) examined the spatial distribution of starches in an Australian rockshelter and found that soil properties, including moisture, pH, and compaction, did not strongly affect the patterning of starches, but that features related to human behavior, like ceiling height and position of barriers, did. In addition, there is mounting evidence that certain contexts, such as within dental calculus, in large particles of plant tissue, or in close association with tools, provide a significant measure of protection to starch granules and other plant microfossils (Barton and Matthews 2006). Wadley et al. (2004) examined the residues remaining on experimental stone tools after one month of burial and found that plant residues were well preserved. Studies of archaeological tools also provide evidence that starch granules are preserved on tool surfaces even when they are not preserved in the surrounding soil (Kelso et al. 1995). Comparisons of archaeological tools to naturally fractured stones have shown that passive transfer from sediments to artifacts is unlikely (Zarrillo and Kooyman 2006). Starches are preserved both in the pits and crevices of coarse-grained materials (e.g., Piperno et al. 2004) and on smoother homogeneous surfaces, like obsidian, pottery, and shell (e.g., Crowther 2005), though some degradation from soil enzymes can occur (Barton 2007). Starches have been recovered from stone tools from a variety of environments, including the humid tropics (e.g., Loy et al. 1992; Pearsall 2004; Piperno and Holst 1998), cold northern plains (Zarrillo and Kooyman 2006), and many other places around the world (e.g., Henry 2010; Yang et al. 2009), suggesting that stone tools protect starches in many different sedimentary contexts.

Dental calculus has also been shown to be a protective context that increases the chances for starch granule survival (Boyadjian et al. 2007; Henry et al. 2011; Henry and Piperno 2008; Li et al. 2010; Piperno and Dillehay 2008; Wesolowski et al. 2010). Dental calculus forms quickly within the mouth and over time becomes heavily mineralized (Friskopp and Isacsson 1984; Lieverse 1999), which probably contributes to its protective effect. Cooked and processed starches have also been recovered from tools and from calculus (Barton 2007; Henry et al. 2011), but their survival depends strongly on the protective nature of these contexts, since these damaged starch granules are at increased risk of enzymatic digestion.

The preservation of starches in different sedimentary contexts is one of the major areas of this field requiring more study. We need to understand the preservation of starch granules in a variety of soil types and to be able to predict, based on soil properties like pH, temperature, and bacterial content, what the preservation of starch granules should be. Currently, when sediments and tools from the same site preserve different starch assemblages, we cannot say with confidence whether this reflects a behavioral difference or a preservation bias (Perry 2007).

Excavation and Laboratory Processing

During and after their removal from an archaeological context, starch granules then enter their second interaction with humans. Aspects of the excavation, curation, and lab processing of sediments and artifacts can expose the remaining starch granules to further damage or destruction, disassociation from their primary contexts, or changes in their relative proportions. A concern in excavation and laboratory environments is the potential for contamination, either from other archaeological sources or from modern ones. In addition to avoiding the more obvious sources of contamination, such as poorly cleaned sampling implements, improper artifact or sediment storage, and use of powdered gloves, the paleoethnobotanist should also consider less obvious potential contaminants. Food residues left on hands or excavation tools can be transferred to artifacts. Tests of experimental artifacts handled immediately after eating revealed several starch granules, from both bread and granola bars (Henry 2010). Simple hand washing after eating and between handling different artifacts would prevent this kind of transfer. Airborne starch is another potential source of contamination. Studies in hospitals have revealed high concentrations of airborne starch granules from powdered gloves, even in rooms where powdered gloves were not worn (Newsom and Shaw 1997a; Newsom and Shaw 1997b). Airborne starches from other sources should also be considered, because things like flour mills can cause starch to become airborne and blown in through windows (see Loy and Barton 2006) and pollen is also known to contain starches (e.g., Baker and Baker 1979). Proper ventilation, clean lab procedures like keeping slides and samples covered, and regular cleaning of surfaces with 5% sodium hydroxide (NaOH) (Crowther et al., 2014) followed by a hot water rinse (> 60°C) should help prevent contamination from these sources.

Common procedures to preserve samples may cause damage to starches, though experimental studies on this topic have not yet been done. Heating or drying of sediments can cause starch granules to gelatinize or dehydrate. The application of preservatives to teeth or to wooden artifacts can damage or destroy starches, or may introduce foreign starch granules. Chemical treatment, particularly by strong acids, bases, and even neutral salts, is known to cause surface gelatinization and damage to the granule (Blanshard 1987; Jane and Shen 1993). Ideally, the paleoethnobotanist would have some control over how samples are collected and curated before they arrive in the laboratory. This is rarely the case, however, so it is necessary that the researcher know as much as possible about these factors and how they might affect a starch granule assemblage.

Finally, though procedures for processing and isolating starch granules from various substrates have been fairly well established (e.g., Torrence and Barton 2006), care must be taken to avoid steps that may cause damage to starches or that may confuse their interpretation. First, whenever adopting a new method, a researcher should first test all the steps on samples of modern starches from plants that they are likely to find on the archaeological specimens. This is particularly important for new chemicals and for any procedure that involves the application of heat, because starches from different biological origins are known to react quite differently, and what works on one plant's starch may in fact damage another's. Second, when seeking to compare several specimens, care should be taken to use the same protocol on all of the samples, particularly keeping in mind those aspects of the methodology, like chemical processing or mounting medium, that may alter the appearance of the granules.

CONCLUSION

In summary, starch granules have a somewhat complex biology that affects their appearance, their response to biological, chemical, and mechanical processes, and ultimately their survival in the archaeological record. Taphonomic processes affecting starch granules can potentially substantially change our interpretation of ancient behavior. Much more research is needed to understand how starches are affected by these processes.

ACKNOWLEDGMENTS

Many thanks to Christina Warinner, Jade d'Alpoim Guedes, and Mac Marston for organizing the symposium and editing this book, and for inviting me to take part. Much of the work leading to this publication was done at The George Washington University and the Smithsonian Institution. Dolores Piperno, Holly Hudson, Linda Perry, Christine Foltz, and Tim Messner provided substantial inspiration for my studies of starch granules. This work was supported by the Max Planck Society.

NOTE

1. Water (refractive index 1.33) is a convenient though impermanent mounting medium. Using a mixture of glycerin (RI 1.44) and water helps slow dehydration, and sealing the edges of the cover glass with nail polish, Permount™, or another permanent medium can prevent dehydration. However, direct mounting in Permount™ (RI 1.52) or Canada Balsam (RI 1.54) is likely to obscure important features in some starch grains.

4

---

*Formation Processes of
Pollen and Phytoliths*

Deborah M. Pearsall

Understanding formation processes of pollen and phytoliths—how these microfossils come to be deposited and preserved in archaeological sediments, artifact residues, and lake and swamp sediments—begins with understanding their biological properties: physical characteristics, production, modes of dispersal, and patterning in the plant kingdom. Although pollen and phytoliths have different natures, they are similar in that they are not transported purposefully into localities that become archaeological sites. Their presence in site sediments follows two pathways. The first is as a by-product of human selection of plants for food, medicine, construction, and other uses: for example, palm fruits are collected and the inedible husks and shells, full of tiny spherical phytoliths, decay in a pit or are burned in a hearth, whereas chamomile flowers, rich in pollen, are ingested as a medicinal tea and eventually deposited in a latrine. The second pathway is through natural dispersal and deposition on the landscape, including into what will become an archaeological site or a locality sampled by coring. Distinguishing these pathways is one of the challenges of pollen and phytolith interpretation in archaeological contexts.

THE BIOLOGICAL PROPERTIES OF POLLEN AND PHYTOLITHS

POLLEN FORMATION

Pollen is formed in the anthers of seed plants. Most, but not all, pollen grains are regular rotation ellipsoids

DOI: 10.5876/9781607323167.c004

(i.e., symmetrical around an axis) that usually have three concentric layers. The outermost, the exine, is preserved in fossil pollen. The exine contains sporopollenin, one of the most resistant natural organic compounds (Faegri et al. 1989). Features of the exine, including the shape and numbers of openings (apertures) in it, surface sculpturing (e.g., shapes of projections), and structure (e.g., whether the outermost surface is continuous, discontinuous, or absent), are important for identifying pollen (Kapp 1969; Kapp et al. 2000). Pollen varies in size from 5 to 200 microns.

POLLEN DISPERSAL

When mature, pollen is released for transfer to the female portion of the flower, effecting fertilization. Four types of pollination have evolved: wind, zoophilous (animal vector), water, and self-pollination (Faegri et al. 1989; Moore et al. 1991). Although all seed plants produce pollen, pollen abundance and morphology are affected by pollination mechanism, as is the likelihood that pollen will become deposited in archaeological sediments, artifacts, or lake and swamp sediments. For example, wind-pollinated plants produce many more pollen grains than do animal-pollinated plants: masses of pollen increase the probability that the right pollen will be blown to the right flower. By contrast, one animal species may pollinate a single plant species, having evolved with it, and little pollen is required. Self-pollinated plants also produce very little pollen. A major pathway by which pollen is deposited on the landscape is through pollen rain: the mix of pollen transported by air currents (Faegri et al. 1989). Pollen of wind-pollinated plants is very aerodynamic, to enhance dispersal (e.g., figure 4.1a), whereas pollen transported by animal vectors has features that insure that grains stick to the pollinator (e.g., figure 4.1b). Another pathway of pollen deposition in marine, river, and lake sediments is fluvial—transport of pollen (and pollen-laden sediments) by streams and rivers (Campbell and Chmura 1994). Understanding pollination ecology—pollen production and dispersal—is an important aspect of interpreting archaeological and environmental pollen records, as it is one factor that leads to over- or underrepresentation of pollen in the record.

POLLEN PRESERVATION AND TAPHONOMY

Sporopollenin is tough, but not indestructible. Another important aspect of understanding over- and underrepresentation of pollen in the record is differential preservation. The forces affecting pollen preservation—mechanical

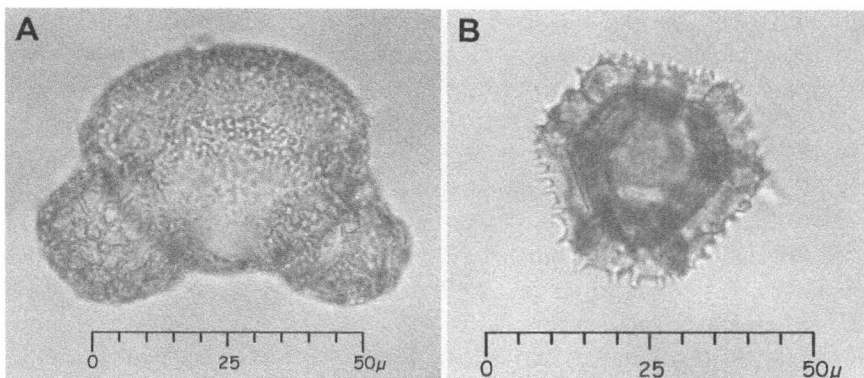

FIGURE 4.1. *Two common pollination mechanisms: (A) wind-pollination; example, buoyant pine pollen (*Pinus contorta*), with flotation bladders (two smaller projections); (B) animal-pollinated; example, dandelion pollen (*Taraxacum officinale*), with spines for adhering to pollinator. Scale: microns. Figure composed by Howard Wilson.*

degradation (e.g., breakage), chemical destruction (e.g., oxidation), and action of biological agents—do not act on all pollen equally (Bryant 1978; Bryant and Holloway 1983; Bryant et al. 1994). For example, comparisons of pollen from modern surface and fossil soil samples taken along a transect in Texas showed that fossil assemblages were reduced in diversity and abundance (total pollen count), and dominated by taxa that could be recognized even when damaged, in comparison to modern samples, which were diverse, with abundant pollen (Bryant et al. 1994). Other "tests" for assessing preservation of pollen in soil include total pollen concentration, percentage severely deteriorated grains, percentage indeterminable grains, percentage "resistant" taxa, and spore:pollen ratio (Bunting et al. 2001).

Experimental studies have contributed valuable insights into pollen preservation. Lebreton et al. (2010) conducted experiments to study how oxidation affected preservation and concentration values of different pollen taxa. Even low oxidation concentrations and duration impacted concentrations of all pollen tested, reducing each by half or more. The extent of the impact on different taxa varied, however, according to the thickness of the pollen exine, and how recognizable damaged grains were (i.e., some pollen taxa are more easily identified, and thus counted, when damaged). Experiments by Twiddle and Bunting (2010) also demonstrated significant differences in oxidation damage to pollen considered resistant and not resistant. In an interesting application of their results, Lebreton et al. (2010) showed how oxidation could lead to a resistant type becoming overrepresented in a model pollen assemblage, leading to an erroneous landscape reconstruction. They also caution, however, against automatically attributing high rates of resistant, easily recognized pollen to differential preservation, without exploring other taphonomic processes or environmental factors. Two aspects of mechanical weathering—freezing-thawing and hydration-dehydration—were the focus of an experimental study by Holloway (1989), which demonstrated that whereas freezing-thawing had little impact on pollen, wetting-drying had marked effects, probably associated with the evaporative process. Differences in the rate of preservation were found for different pollen taxa.

Pollen damage or destruction is reduced in arid or waterlogged soils and in deposits covered by peat formation (acid conditions) because of lower microbial activity (Bryant and Hall 1993; Bryant and Holloway 1983, 1996; Dimbleby 1985). Jones et al. (2007) describe an approach for assessing pollen preservation in waterlogged sites, so that comparisons may be made within and between sites. In their approach, deterioration types present in pollen assemblages were defined (following Delcourt and Delcourt 1980), which, with numbers of indeterminable grains, provided information on the depositional history and watertable fluctuation of sites. Two indices that summarized the state of the grains—index of biochemical deterioration and index of physical deterioration—were also found to be useful. The authors demonstrated a positive and significant correlation between the two indices and number of indeterminable grains, suggesting that the latter was a good proxy for overall state of pollen preservation.

Burial of archaeological deposits (by volcanic ash, sand, under earth mounds, pavements, within burials) and contact of pollen with artifact surfaces (grinding stones, ceramic vessels, metal objects) may enhance preservation. Dissolved salts from copper artifacts may act as a fungicide, for example (King et al. 1975). Pollen deposited on soil surfaces can be moved downward by percolating groundwater, and destroyed by oxygen in the groundwater and aerobic fungi (Kelso et al. 1995). Under these circumstances, preservation of pollen associated with original site matrices and artifacts is possible if pollen is rapidly buried or if percolation is prevented by flat objects, such as artifacts (Kelso et al. 1995) or shells (Kelso et al. 2000). In these studies Kelso and colleagues compared pollen recovered from under artifacts or shells to pollen profiles in the same deposits, and demonstrated that the objects protected the ancient pollen: pollen was found only under artifacts, not in matrix, in a deep refuse pit at Jamestown Island, Virginia; distinctive differences in pollen assemblages were found under shells and in matrix at the shallow Salem Neck shell midden, Salem, Massachusetts. In the latter case, the matrix was dominated by pollen of Eurasian weeds (from the surface), whereas the shells protected pollen of the forest that dominated the area before Euroamerican impact.

Fish (1994) argues that the above model of pollen behavior in soil—that it is dislocated by percolating water and subject to destruction and mixing—should be considered the extreme case, and that the extent of pollen dislocation and degradation in soil needs to be evaluated on a case-by-case basis.

Phytolith Formation

Phytoliths, or plant opal silica bodies, are produced by the deposition of silica from groundwater (as monosilicic acid) into tissues of roots, stems, leaves, and inflorescences of plants. There are two mechanisms: (1) formation within specialized silica-accumulating cells (Esau 1965) (e.g., figure 4.2a), or (2) formation in cellular or intercellular spaces, in which phytoliths take on the shape of the space (Piperno 1991) (e.g., figure 4.2b). There is a strong genetic component to phytolith formation: orders and families show tendencies for deposition or lack of deposition of silica (e.g., Iriarte 2003; Kealhofer and Piperno 1998; Madella and Zurro 2007; Pearsall 2000; Piperno 1988, Piperno 2006b; Piperno and Pearsall 1998a, b; Runge 2000, among others).

This marks a difference between pollen and phytoliths : all seed plants produce pollen, but not all plants produce phytoliths. Within silica-accumulating taxa, water availability and level of evapo-transpiration influence the extent to which cellular or intercellular spaces silicify (Madella et al. 2009). Although silicification patterns are redundant in some groups, distinctively shaped phytoliths are formed in many taxa, providing a means of identifying plants at family, genus, or species level, or even plant tissue (e.g., *Calathea* and *Maranta* root phytoliths; Chandler-Ezell et al. 2006). Most phytoliths are the size of silt soil particles (2–250 microns).

Phytolith Preservation

Another important distinction between phytoliths and other archaeobotanical remains is that phytoliths are inorganic and survive in circumstances under which organic tissues may be lost. For example, in soils of high clay content at sites in the Jama River valley, Ecuador, abundances of charred macroremains declined abruptly with depth, while phytolith counts remained high (Pearsall 2004). Plants not present in the macroremain record, through lack of deposition, charring, or post-depositional destruction, may be represented by phytoliths (table 4.1).

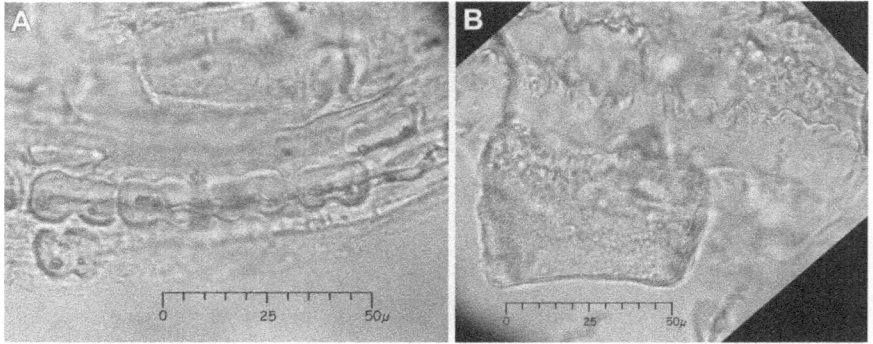

FIGURE 4.2. *The two mechanisms of phytolith formation: (A) formation within specialized silica–accumulating cells; example, bilobates in* Zea mays *leaf tissue; (B) formation in cellular or intercellular spaces; example, silicified bulliform (darker cell above scale) and epidermal cells (with wavy edges) in* Zea mays *leaf tissue. Scale: microns. Figure composed by Howard Wilson.*

Phytoliths are not indestructible, however. Lightly silicified tissues, such as the epidermis illustrated in figure 4.1b, may break up in soil. Silica must be present in the right form to be taken up by plants. If tissues are harvested while immature, silicification may be incomplete. Understanding the geo-chemical nature of sediments is essential for understanding preservation of archaeological materials (Karkanas 2010). In the case of phytoliths, opal silica has a constant solubility up to pH 8.5, and solubility increases rapidly above pH 9, which in soil can lead to phytolith dissolution. Water is required for dissolution, however. Thus, in arid environments, phytoliths may preserve under conditions of very high pH. By contrast, a high rate of water flow through sediments may increase dissolution. Fluctuating wet and dry periods can result in changes in soil pH and phytolith destruction.

Studies reviewed by Karkanas (2010) are contradictory concerning whether dissolution differs based on phytolith morphology. A recent experimental study of wheat by Cabanes et al. (2011) indicated that burnt phytoliths were more soluble than unburnt, and that hairs and ornamentation on long cells were relatively unstable. These authors suggest that preservation of phytoliths depends on solubility of the phytolith mineral, robusticity of morphotypes, nature of the local water regime, and level of plant activity (i.e., whether soil formed over the site, increasing dissolution by roots of living plants, or whether the site was quickly buried). Rapid burial enhances preservation of both macro- and microremains. It would be useful to explore using the ratio

TABLE 4.1. Selected plants documented at sites in the Jama River valley by macroremains and phytoliths*

Category	Identification	Common Name	Macroremains, Phytoliths
Economic			
	Canna	achira	phytoliths
	cf. *Manihot esculenta*	yuca	root
	Phaseolus	bean	seed, phytoliths
	Marantaceae	arrowroot family	phytoliths
	Calathea		phytoliths
	C. allouia	llerén	phytoliths
	Maranta		phytoliths
	M. arundinacea	arrowroot	phytoliths
	Gossypium	cotton	seed
	Zea mays	maize	kernel, cupule, phytoliths
	Cucurbitaceae	squash/gourd family	fruit stalk, phytoliths
	Lagenaria siceraria	gourd	rind, phytoliths
	Cucurbita	squash	phytoliths
Arboreal			
	Annonaceae	soursop family	seed, phytoliths
	Arecaceae	palm family	seed, phytoliths
	Aiphanes	coroso palm	seed
	Phytelephas	cadi palm	seed, fruit
	cf. *Crescentia*	tree gourd	rind
	Bixa orellana	achiote	seed, fruit
	Cordia lutea	mullullu	phytoliths
	Croton		phytoliths
	Cleidion		phytoliths
	Psidium	guava	seed
	cf. *Sideroxylon*	dilly	seed

* Adapted from Pearsall (2004).

between identifiable morphotypes and opaline debris (broken up phytoliths) as an indicator of preservation (Cabanes et al. 2011).

There is also evidence that some kinds of phytoliths can be altered during laboratory processing. Shillito (2011) and Jenkins (2009) investigated the stability of multicellular (conjoined) wheat husk phytoliths. Rosen (Rosen 1987; Rosen and Weiner 1994) observed that multicellular phytoliths formed in contexts in which crops grew under irrigation or high rainfall and pioneered this as an irrigation indicator. An experimental study of wheat and barley by Jenkins et al. (2011) corroborated that numbers of conjoined cells increase with irrigation, although they observed intersite and interyear variability. Multicellular wheat husk phytoliths are fragile, however: fewer and smaller conjoined forms were observed in fully processed samples compared to unprocessed soil smears and thin sections of soil blocks from wheat-rich deposits at Çatalhöyük (Shillito 2011), and acid extraction caused greater breakdown of conjoined phytoliths than dry ashing during a test of alternative methods of organic removal (Jenkins 2009). These results highlight the importance of consistency in methods for sample comparability.

PHYTOLITH DEPOSITION AND TAPHONOMY

Unlike pollen, spores, or seeds, phytoliths are not part of plant reproduction, and so do not have a dispersal mechanism. Phytoliths are released by processes that break down plant tissues: organic decay, burning, and digestion. For example, phytoliths may be released through burning of dung of sheep, goats, and cattle (Shahack-Gross 2011). Burned dung is fragile and in most instances will be found as ash containing spherulites and phytoliths. It may be difficult to identify the contribution of dung to sediments unless deposits are substantial, which can produce thick phytolith-rich sediments (e.g., ethnoarchaeological and experimental results; Shahack-Gross et al. 2005; Shahack-Gross et al. 2004; Shahack-Gross et al. 2003). Burning increases the refractive index of phytoliths and is indicated by 50 percent of phytoliths with an RI greater than 1.440 (Albert et al. 2008; Elbaum et al. 2003).

Because phytoliths are released into soil, not air, a large proportion of phytoliths deposited in sediments or soils represent in situ deposition (Pearsall 2000; Piperno 1985, 2006b). This is referred to as the *decay-in-place model* (Dimbleby 1978; Mulholland 1989; Piperno 1988). Piperno (1988) demonstrated, for example, that phytolith assemblages in soils under tropical forests in Panama corresponded closely to local vegetation. Morris et al. (2010) found that abundances of burnt phytoliths declined rapidly away from the edges of a fire, and also with depth in soil. Research indicates, however, that if soil, especially silt and fine sand fractions, moves, phytoliths move. Phytoliths are part of wind-blown dust (Fredlund and Tieszen 1994; Twiss et al. 1969) and soil washed into lakes and swamps (Piperno 1991, 1995). To reflect this complexity, Fredlund and Tieszen

(1994) proposed the *inheritance-and-dispersal model* of phytolith assemblage formation: inheritance is the long-term incorporation of phytoliths into soil; dispersal is modeled as five processes (decay-in-place, eolian, fire-eolian, herbivory, and fluvial/colluvial). As part of her research into archaeological site formation processes affecting plant remains in an open desert environment, Lawlor (1995) found that phytolith assemblages from experimental plots representing various food preparation activities varied significantly from each other, indicating that decay-in-place characterized some of the phytolith deposition on plots. Dispersal also played a role in assemblage formation. Fredlund and Tieszen (1994) observed that it is possible to predict grassland composition from soil phytolith assemblages despite local, extralocal, and regional sources of phytoliths in grassland soils in the open Great Plains. As studies discussed below illustrate, extralocal or regional phytoliths are in the minority compared to phytoliths released from plants brought into sites and used by people.

Plant tissues break down, resulting in the addition of organic matter to soil, which results in the formation of the A soil horizon. Phytoliths are part of this horizon, and it can be very challenging to break the chemical and electrical bonds between phytoliths and soil constituents (Zhao and Pearsall 1998). Older studies of temperate zone soil profiles, reviewed by Piperno (1985), indicated no significant degree of phytolith illuviation (downward movement through water percolation) out of the A soil horizon and an exponential drop off of phytoliths is expected with depth. Although some illuviation might be expected in sandy sediments, there is no reason to expect it in sediments with finer structure (clays, silts). Piperno argues that if illuviation occurs, it should produce distinctive patterns, for example, presence of phytoliths in sterile deposits located stratigraphically below phytolith-rich deposits, or differences in phytolith assemblages inside and outside the drip line of a cave (i.e., sediments that differed in exposure to water percolation). These patterns were not observed in Panamanian sites: culturally sterile deposits did not contain phytoliths, and patterning in samples inside and outside the cave drip line matched up (Piperno 1985).

A number of recent studies have looked at the potential roles of bioturbation (mixing of soil by fauna) and water percolation in phytolith movement in natural soils. Hart and Humphreys (1997) studied a soil profile with high bioturbation in a loamy A soil horizon, and observed normal phytolith decline with depth, but also recovered phytoliths from faunal channels within the underlying sandy clay B horizon. In a sandier soil profile, phytoliths also declined with depth, but then increased again, with clays, just above a hard pan (a type of B horizon). In the first instance, the interpretation was phytolith movement by fauna; in the second, illuviation of clays and phytoliths and accumulation on the hard pan. Hart (2003), in a study of an A horizon highly bioturbated by ants and termites, also found evidence of phytolith movement by fauna into the B soil horizon, as did Humphreys et al. (2003). The latter study also documented downward movement of phytoliths in a sandy soil, but not in two profiles of finer texture. An experimental study that looked at phytolith displacement over a five-month period in sandy sediments under two irrigation regimes (low, high frequency) demonstrated that 98–99 percent of phytoliths added to the top 1 cm of columns of medium sand remained in the top 1.5 cm (Fishkis et al. 2009). Two modeling approaches were used to simulate long-term effects of this degree of displacement, but returned conflicting results. The authors suggest that in natural sandy soils, organic substances and clays would aggregate with phytoliths and reduce their mobility.

This brief review of studies on phytolith stability in soils and sediments suggests several generalizations. Phytoliths are not "loose" in soil; they are bound up in its organic and inorganic components. Movement of soil results in phytolith movement. When studying phytoliths in soils, it is informative to examine profiles for faunal channels and other evidence of bioturbation, to avoid sampling within such contexts, and to determine soil particle sizes in the profile. Graphing phytolith abundances by depth and soil horizons may provide insights into whether mixing or illuviation has occurred, as may comparisons of phytolith assemblages at various depths in the profile. In other words, does the assemblage in the modern topsoil look like the current vegetation? Does going deeper in the A horizon produce an assemblage that makes sense in terms of past vegetation? In situations of accumulating sediments of finer structure (clays, silts), which characterize many archaeological sites, coring localities, and some soils (e.g., loess, alluvium), minimal downward displacement or mixing of phytoliths occurs. In situations of rapid sedimentation, buried soils may be obvious. Micromorphological analysis of sediments (analysis of plant materials in large-format thin sections) is an approach that shows promise for elucidating formation processes of plant materials, including phytoliths, in complex depositional settings (e.g., Matthews 2010; Shillito 2011).

POLLEN AND PHYTOLITHS IN ARCHAEOLOGICAL SEDIMENTS

In this and the next two sections, I discuss pathways by which pollen and phytoliths become deposited in archaeological sediments (figure 4.3), on artifact residues, and in swamp cores. Issues of representation and preservation are summarized, and basic interpretive approaches presented. I end each section

Models of Formation Processes
in Archaeological Site Sediments

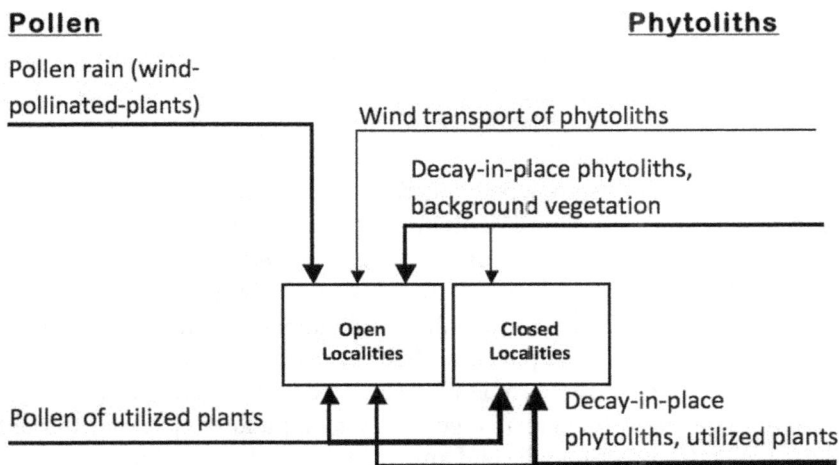

Pollen   **Phytoliths**

Pollen rain (wind-
pollinated-plants)
                    Wind transport of phytoliths

                        Decay-in-place phytoliths,
                        background vegetation

                    ┌──────────┐ ┌──────────┐
                    │ Open   │ │ Closed │
                    │Localities│ │Localities│
                    └──────────┘ └──────────┘

Pollen of utilized plants   Decay-in-place
                                           phytoliths, utilized plants

FIGURE 4.3. *Models of formation processes in archaeological site sediments. Thickness of line (thick, medium, thin) estimates contribution from that source. Figure composed by Cynthia Irsik.*

by discussing issues concerning formation processes for which more research is needed. A basic point to bear in mind: as is also the case for macroremains and starch, there is no direct correspondence between absolute abundances of pollen or phytoliths in the record and representation of those plants at a site, on an artifact, or in the landscape. Most interpretation is based on assessing relative abundances as well as ubiquity (percentage presence), and through the comparative or analogue approach. Concentration values (absolute count per unit analyzed) also provide insight into mode of deposition in some cases.

POLLEN

As discussed earlier, a major pathway of pollen deposition is through pollen rain: the mix of pollen transported by air currents (Faegri et al. 1989). Because this pathway is limited inside closed localities (e.g., structures, pits), inferring cultural uses of wind-pollinated plants may be possible by finding pollen concentrations in contexts less likely to be impacted by pollen rain. A study of experimental floor deposits from a stable and a domestic beaten floor at Butser

Ancient Farm, United Kingdom, provides insight into pollen formation processes within structures (Macphail et al. 2004). Pollen concentrations (predominantly grass pollen) were up to ten times higher in the stable floor "crust" layer (the active use layer) than in the lower layers of the stable floor, or in the domestic floor. In general, stable floor deposits were very homogenous in terms of organic matter, phosphate, and pollen, whereas domestic floors were heterogeneous, indicating that distinctive formation processes were operating in these contexts (but see Canti et al. 2006 for a critique; Macphail et al. 2006 reply). Comparable results were reported by Kelso et al. (2006), who demonstrated that different human activities resulted in distinctive patterning of percentages and concentrations of pollen of meadow hay plants at Bay View stable, and that decades of intermittent human activity after primary uses ceased left concentrations in situ. Pollen from animal-pollinated plants is *not* typically represented in the pollen rain, so the presence of such pollen in site sediments can be used more straightforwardly to infer human behavior.

Incorporation into the human digestive system is another pathway through which pollen from both wind- and animal-pollinated taxa enter the archaeological record. Pollen from an individual's final meals can be recovered from skeletonized burials, because the pelvic girdle (sacrum) acts as a protective "container" for decomposed intestinal contents (Reinhard et al. 1992). By comparing pollen and macroremains recovered from the sacrum to control samples, Reinhard et al. (1992) were able infer the final meals of an Anasazi individual. Coprolites and latrine sediments can be especially productive contexts for pollen sampling, preserving evidence for ingestion of flowers, honey, or other parts of plants to which pollen has adhered, use of medicinal teas, or presence of parasites (e.g., Cahill et al. 1991; Greig 1994; Gremillion and Sobolik 1996; Reinhard et al. 1991), and even the last itinerary of "Ötzi," the Neolithic Iceman (Oeggl et al. 2007).

Dean (2006) investigated whether pollen concentration was a reliable indicator of deliberate ingestion, particularly whether there was a threshold that corresponded to recent ingestion (i.e., Reinhard et al. 1991; Sobolik 1988), by studying a time-series of modern fecal specimens to investigate the rate of elimination of specific pollen grains. Four kinds of pollen, all zoophilous taxa, were ingested. Looking at the data by relative abundance (i.e., the proportion of each taxon in a fixed sum), pollen grains appeared as an initial peak, and then fell evenly as they were eliminated from the system. However, when data were expressed by pollen concentration (i.e., absolute number per unit of analysis), the pattern was bimodal, indicating that pollen was unpredictably divided among the time-series specimens. On the basis of these results, Dean argued that dispersal mode (i.e., zoophilous), rather than an absolute pollen concentration, is a more reliable argument for deliberate ingestion. Kelso and Solomon (2006), in a similar study of modern fecal specimens, found that relative counts were not an accurate reflection of ingestion. However, their study indicated that pollen concentration in fecal matter did increase rapidly a day after ingestion, and remained high for one to three days. They concluded that comparatively high concentration values could be used to indicate deliberate ingestion. They also found variation in pollen content over the time-series of fecal specimens studied. These and other experiments (Bryant and Dean 2006) provide support for the position that inferences on past diet drawn from study of coprolites should be based on multiple specimens from a site or site component.

In many cases, pollen representation in archaeological sediments is a matter of preservation: conditions encountered in many sites are not ideal for pollen preservation (Faegri et al. 1989). If pollen is differentially preserved across a site (e.g., only under flagstones, mounds, in waterlogged areas), or through time (e.g., better preserved in more deeply buried deposits), this is a complicating factor in inferring spatial or temporal patterning in plant use. Assessing the quality of preservation is vital; comparisons may be limited to contexts in which pollen is equally well preserved. In situations of good preservation, understanding the pollination biology of plants potentially targeted by humans is essential. Sampling within closed (e.g., structures) or otherwise protected localities (e.g., under artifacts, within coprolites) maximizes recovery of pollen of used plants and minimizes the contribution from pollen rain. Under these circumstances, spatial patterning of different human activities involving plants may be revealed. Bohrer and Adams (1977) provide a detailed example of sampling strategies for pollen and macroremains for elucidating room functions at Salmon Ruins pueblo, New Mexico.

PHYTOLITHS

Phytolith representation in archaeological site sediments is impacted chiefly by phytolith production patterns: that is, whether or not plants and plant tissues targeted by humans are silica accumulators and produce diagnostic phytoliths. As discussed earlier, once deposited, phytoliths preserve in most archaeological settings.

Phytoliths are not deposited through a process analogous to pollen rain, but phytoliths from background vegetation do occur in archaeological sediments (i.e., decay-in-place deposition before, during, and after site occupation;

deposition through wind transport) (figure 4.3). Closed localities are less subject to background phytolith deposition, and therefore are contexts in which culturally selected plants dominate. For example, house floors at the Real Alto site, Ecuador, contained much higher concentrations of grass phytoliths than did modern soil samples, indicating in situ decay of grasses from roof thatch (Pearsall 1979). In a study of spatial organization of a Neanderthal site, Esquilleu Cave, Spain, Cabanes et al. (2010) interpreted phytolith accumulations in one unit (C unit) as decay from grass bedding and activities related to fire based on phytolith concentrations that were higher than modern control samples and on lack of evidence of plants growing or soil development or animal transport (dung). It is also possible to identify decay-in-place deposition of used plants in open localities. For example, midden deposits at the San Isidro site, Ecuador, showed higher frequencies of palm phytoliths than strata in a contemporaneous off-site river profile: elevated palm concentrations indicated human selection (Pearsall 2004). This interpretive approach is similar to comparing macroremain assemblages from within and outside features, to determine if a distinctive feature pattern is present (Lennstrom and Hastorf 1995).

Phytoliths enter archaeological contexts primarily through the decay or burning of plant tissues brought into the locality by its inhabitants. Plant debris, ash, and other cultural debris may be left in place (like the house floors at Real Alto), or removed from a primary activity context and redeposited, for example, into a trash pit. There is a potential delay between use of plant tissues and phytolith deposition through decay. At the scale of analysis of archaeological sediments (household, community level; long time scale), this has little impact on interpretation in most cases. However, presence of well preserved, uncharred macroremains may indicate reduced in situ decay and release of phytoliths, as argued by Duncan (2010) for the Buena Vista site, Peru. At that site there was some overlap in taxa identified by phytoliths and dried macroremains, but leren (*Calathea allouia*), *Heliconia*, and palms were only represented by phytoliths, leading Duncan to conclude that burning was the likely mode of their deposition.

Traditional agricultural practices lead to the deposition of distinctive assemblages of phytoliths. Harvey and Fuller (2005), for example, outlined traditional crop-processing models for rice and millets (e.g., Reddy 1997, 2003; Thompson 1996) and developed expectations for phytolith deposition. First winnowing of rice, for example, should produce grains with spikelets, rice waste, and weeds, as well as the associated phytoliths. They applied the resulting interpretive framework to archaeological samples from Mahagara, India.

Rice macroremains were present, but only seeds, leaving open the question of whether rice was locally grown or traded. Phytolith analysis indicated that both early and later stages of rice processing were carried out. In a study with a similar research design, Korstanje and Cuenya (2010) integrated microfossil assemblages (phytoliths, pollen, diatoms, spherulites, cellulose rings, starch, calcium oxalates, micro-charcoal) and soil physical and chemical characteristics to develop expectations for identifying agricultural fields, corrals, and domestic structures. Applying the model to two archaeological sites in Argentina, they were able to infer crop rotation and fallowing, as well as areas used as corrals. Household activities in domestic contexts proved to be more challenging to identify, as many more combinations of soil features and microfossils were possible. A number of other recent studies illustrate the interpretive power of the comparative or analogue approach based on ethnographic modeling (e.g., Shahack-Gross et al. 2009; Shahack-Gross et al. 2004; Shahack-Gross et al. 2003; Tsartsidou et al. 2008, 2009; Zurro et al. 2009).

Pollen, phytoliths, and other microscopic plant remains can provide insights into past human behavior even in underwater archaeological sites (Gorham and Bryant 2001). It is critical to understand the formation processes of underwater sites that affect preservation, removal, or redeposition of microremains. For example, alluvial and coastal-marine processes affect shipwrecks and submerged terrestrial sites, both depositing and removing sediments. High-energy environments such as shallow coastal waters can severely damage both pollen and phytoliths. Biological microbes in water or marine sediments feed on fresh and fossil pollen. Potentially valuable contexts for sampling include underwater sediment cores (taken from above, beside, and beneath shipwrecks), bilge mud, contents of amphoras and other containers, rope fragments, basketry and matting, and caulking, resin, and pitch. Control samples (from sediments away from the ship or site, and of water) greatly aid interpretation.

FUTURE RESEARCH DIRECTIONS

Models of formation processes of pollen and phytoliths in archaeological sediments are well understood at a basic level, as illustrated in figure 4.3 and discussed here. Continued experimentation and/or ethnographic/ethnoarchaeological studies on patterns of deposition of microfossils in a broader range of domestic contexts would expand applications of the comparative (analogue) approach, which has considerable interpretive power. Quantitative methods for formalizing such comparisons could be explored further. Proxy measures exist to indicate degraded microfossil assemblages; these are better developed for pollen than for phytoliths. In general, there is more to learn about phytolith dissolution and whether different kinds of phytoliths are affected differentially. Debate continues among coprolite analysts concerning best approaches for interpreting pollen of wind-pollinated taxa, suggesting the need for further experimentation or modeling.

POLLEN AND PHYTOLITHS IN ARTIFACT RESIDUES

POLLEN

There are several pathways through which pollen becomes deposited onto the surfaces of artifacts (figure 4.4).

Artifacts are exposed to pollen rain, both during their use lives and after discard. Depending on the artifact type, a variety of human behaviors result in the deposition of pollen from wind- or animal-pollinated plants, whereas others may lead to loss of pollen (e.g., exposure of artifact to heat). Perhaps the most common inference for ground stone artifacts is deposition of pollen as a by-product of seed grinding or other food processing (e.g., Bryant and Morris 1986).

Geib and Smith (2008) conducted experiments to investigate the relationship between seed grinding and pollen deposition, and to determine whether pollen rain "swamps" pollen deposited by seed grinding. One general trend for all washes of seeds and artifacts conducted in a controlled laboratory setting (i.e., minimizing exposure to pollen rain) was that concentrations of target pollen exceeded the combined concentrations of all other pollen. Pollen concentrations dropped off with each step of processing, suggesting that places where harvests were stockpiled or processed would be good contexts to sample for pollen. Concentrations varied among species, in part due to pollination ecology, but also according to whether it was possible to remove tissues that held pollen (e.g., grass glumes) from seeds prior to grinding: for instance maize pollen was only recovered from washes of the husks but not from other plant parts. They also found that pollen abundance (density) was higher from archaeological grinders with many vesicles and coarse grain size. Experiments in which the same seeds were ground in the laboratory and outdoors (i.e., exposed to pollen rain) produced inconclusive results. While this study illustrates the potential complexity of formation processes of pollen deposited on artifact surfaces, it does provide some support for the inference that pollen recovered from artifacts from protected contacts provides evidence of past plant processing.

Models of Formation Processes on Artifacts

Pollen   ### Phytoliths

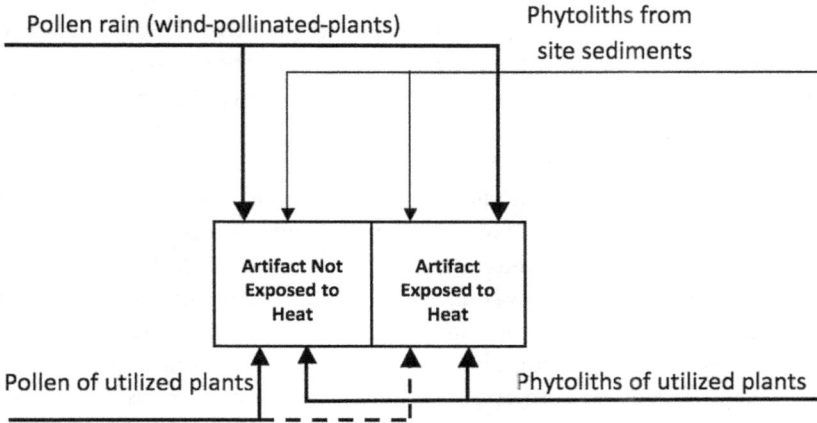

FIGURE 4.4. *Models of formation processes on artifacts. Thickness of line (thick, medium, thin) estimates contribution from that source. Figure composed by Cynthia Irsik.*

As is the case for pollen in archaeological sediments, pollen representation on artifact surfaces or in artifact residues is subject to quality of preservation. I found no experimental studies focused on pollen preservation in residues, and no examples of pollen recovered from cooking vessels, suggesting that exposure to heat may lead to pollen destruction (dashed line in Figure 4.4). However, a study on preservation of pollen in the clay of poorly fired pottery indicates the situation may be more complex (Ghosh et al. 2006). In this study, pots made of clay with known pollen content (six types added) were fired one to six hours in a kiln that rose 170°C per hour. Well-preserved pollen and spores were recovered from pots fired for one hour; two hours yielded grains that were deformed, but still recognizable; after three hours only highly deformed grains of two taxa could be identified. None survived higher firing. The authors successfully recovered pollen from food plants and arboreal taxa from poorly fired pottery from the Pakhanna site, India. Because starch can be recovered from cooking vessel residues (see Henry, chapter 3, this volume), perhaps the issue is rare deposition (i.e., of pollen associated with seeds) rather than rare preservation. Under the right circumstances, pollen can indicate the original content of storage or serving vessels (e.g., Bryant and Murry 1982; Rösch 2005).

PHYTOLITHS

The major pathways through which phytoliths become deposited in or on artifacts are through human behaviors involving plant tissues that contain phytoliths (e.g., cooking, pounding, grinding, cutting, brewing, storage) and exposure of artifacts to sediments containing phytoliths (figure 4.5). As in the case for phytoliths in archaeological sediments, phytolith representation in artifacts is chiefly a matter of phytolith production patterns in used plants and plant tissues.

In some cases, phytoliths may be underrepresented on stone tools used for food processing relative to starch (Pearsall et al. 2004). In a study from Real Alto, Ecuador, maize starch was ubiquitous on the tools (i.e., occurred on all examined), however maize cob phytoliths occurred on few tools, suggesting that repetitive grinding accumulated starch (from maize kernels) more consistently than phytoliths (from chaff adhering to kernels—kernels do not accumulate silica).

Experiments conducted by Raviele (2010, 2011) on the incorporation of phytoliths into charred food residues provide additional insight into phytolith representation on/in artifacts. Charred residues of different forms of maize (flour, dried mature kernels, green kernels, whole green ears [i.e., corn-on-the-cob]) and different concentrations of maize (10–100% by weight, mixed with venison) were produced. Maize starch survived charring and the phytolith extraction procedure. Only residues made with green ears contained abundant phytoliths; 0–1 phytoliths were recovered from all other forms and concentrations. Starch was most abundant in residues from mature maize, and reduced in green maize residues. Raviele argued that cooking of green corn-on-the-cob, rather than incidental inclusion of glumes with mature kernels, created archaeological cooking residues high in phytoliths. Finding only starch would be an indication of use of mature grain.

Because artifacts are exposed to site sediments both during their use lives and after disposal, interpreting artifact phytolith assemblages involves distinguishing between phytoliths deposited from used plants and those from site sediments. One approach is to compare phytolith assemblages from sediments adhering to the artifact (or sampled near it) to phytoliths recovered from artifact surfaces. In a study of grinding and pounding stones from Real Alto, Ecuador, Pearsall et al. (2004) recovered distinctive phytolith assemblages from soil brushed from artifact surfaces (Sediment 1), washed from

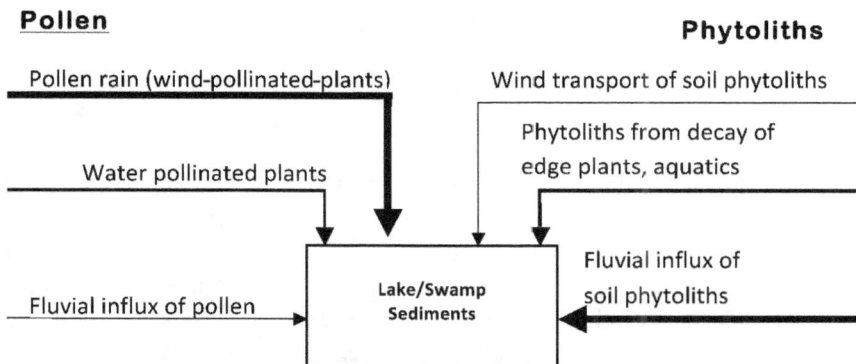

Pollen

Phytoliths

Pollen rain (wind-pollinated-plants)

Wind transport of soil phytoliths

Phytoliths from decay of
edge plants, aquatics

Water pollinated plants

Lake/Swamp
Sediments

Fluvial influx of
soil phytoliths

Fluvial influx of pollen

FIGURE 4.5. *Models of formation processes in lake and swamp sediments. Thickness of line (thick, medium, thin) estimates contribution from that source. Figure composed by Cynthia Irsik.*

surfaces (Sediment 2), and sonicated from artifacts (Sediment 3). Sediment 1 assemblages resembled those from house floor deposits.

FUTURE RESEARCH DIRECTIONS

Experimental and ethnographic/ethnoarchaeological studies of different kinds of tools, foods, and preparation and cooking techniques would provide further insights into over- and underrepresentation of pollen and phytoliths in residues, important for a nuanced understanding of plant use. Recent articles also suggest there is potential for investigating food preparation methods using isotope analysis (Hart, Lovis, Schulenberg, and Urquhart 2007; Hart and Matson 2009; Warinner, chapter 14, this volume).

LAKE AND SWAMP SEDIMENTS

POLLEN

Permanently waterlogged swamp and lake sediments are environments in which biological decomposition, including of pollen grains, is inhibited (Faegri et al. 1989; Moore et al. 1991). Such contexts are thus prime sampling localities for paleoenvironmental research. A major source of pollen in lakes and swamps is pollen rain (figure 4.5). Pollen of wind-pollinated plants from the surrounding region falls on water surfaces, which serve as pollen sinks, and becomes incorporated into bottom sediments. Importantly for archaeology, the record of past vegetation captured in the deposition of pollen from wind-pollinated plants often reflects human interactions with the environment, such as cutting trees or planting crops.

As long as lakes or swamps do not dry up, preservation has relatively little impact on pollen representation in lake and swamp sediments (Faegri et al. 1989). Changes in pollen condition can in fact yield insights into changing conditions of preservation or transport. For example, if conditions on a slope above a lake changed, affecting degree of run-off, changes in abundance and type of reworked pollen may occur (Campbell 1999). Pollen from animal-pollinated plants is rarely deposited in lakes, and in some cases this can have a significant impact on reconstructing past vegetation and detecting human impacts on past environments. Different wind-pollinated plants also contribute differentially to the pollen rain (Faegri et al. 1989). For example, in a forested setting, the upper canopy contributes more pollen than do understory plants (Newsome 1988). Larger, heavier pollen grains, such as maize, travel shorter distances than smaller grains, which influences the likelihood of deposition. For example, maize phytoliths, deposited through fluvial transport of sediments (see below) were found in earlier strata than maize pollen in mangrove swamp cores from Pacific coastal Guatemala (Neff et al. 2006), perhaps because early maize fields were not located very near the coring locality.

Paleoenvironmental studies sometimes rely on a single pollen core from a lake basin, based on the assumption that differences in pollen deposition do not significantly affect the record. But is this a valid assumption, given that different kinds of pollen grains differ in mass, and might be selectively accumulated in sediments in different parts of a lake basin (Beaudoin and Reasoner 1992)? In a study of a lakewide series of nineteen cores from Lake O'Hara, British Columbia, Beaudoin and Reasoner (1992) demonstrated that percentages of major pollen taxa showed basinwide consistency. There was no evidence for preferential sorting and deposition of any individual taxon, and a single record represented the whole. However, minor components (< 1% of sum) were much more variable; a single core did not give a representative record. Pollen influx was also highly variable across the basin. With careful coring site selection, most of the factors that influence pollen deposition in lakes (lake size, fluvial transport of pollen, sediment redeposition and focusing) can be rendered unimportant or held constant (Giesecke and Fontana 2008). These authors agree with earlier research showing that a coring locality with even, undisturbed sedimentation is best, and that sites with incoming streams or high bank erosion should be avoided (as these increase the likelihood of fluvial transport).

Formation processes of lake sediments are relatively simple in cases where there is no significant stream inflow. But sometimes marine, river, or delta deposits cannot be avoided (e.g., Neff et al. 2006, coring in coastal mangrove swamps). Campbell and Chmura (1994) concluded that pollen deposited in coastal and marine sediments influenced by major river systems can include a significant input from fluvial sources.

Stratigraphic pollen (and phytolith) data are presented in a pollen diagram, a standardized graph that depicts the proportion or absolute count of each type in each sampled stratum. The conventional order for listing identifications is arboreal taxa, shrubs, herbs, and spores, but taxa may be ordered by ecological groups or include categories such as disturbance or cultivated plants as an aid to interpretation (Faegri et al. 1989; Moore et al. 1991). Because it is difficult to interpret a long stratigraphic record with many types, sequences are divided into smaller units, or pollen biozones, places in the sequence in which the analyst sees several concurrent changes in frequencies or absolute counts of types (e.g., a decrease in primary forest taxa and an increase in taxa favoring open habitats). Numerical approaches are often used to delineate pollen zones (Birks and Gordon 1985). Pollen and spore assemblages—the taxa present and their abundances—along with absolute pollen concentration and patterning in microscopic charcoal concentration are key to establishing pollen biozones and interpreting changes in terms of past regional vegetation and human impact.

Human interactions with their environments are often "captured" in stratigraphic pollen and phytolith records, which provide landscape-level views to complement archaeological site-level data. Piperno and Jones (2003), for example, identified significant burning around Lake Monte Oscuro in Pacific coastal Panama, which in association with increases of weedy plants, indicated that slash-and-burn cultivation was being practiced, whereas Atahan et al. (2008) identified localized environmental impacts (deforestation) of early agriculture in the lower Yangtze delta, China. Understanding the nature of human interactions with the environment is facilitated by multiple lines of evidence at different scales of analysis. In the case of paleoenvironmental studies, incorporating pollen, phytolith, and particulate charcoal data give a more nuanced view of vegetation than relying on single indicators. For example, palynologically underrepresented plants may be phytolith producers; patterning within the particulate charcoal signal may serve as a proxy for intensity/frequency of burning. Further, regional-scale data provided by environmental cores may provide the earliest glimmers of human impacts on landscapes. Neff et al. (2006), for example, were able to examine the impact of archaeologically "invisible" Archaic period populations on the landscape of Pacific coastal Guatemala through a regional coring program.

PHYTOLITHS

Phytoliths move with soil washed into lakes and swamps, as the major mode of deposition is fluvial (figure 4.5). As discussed earlier for archaeological sediments and artifacts, phytolith production patterns are important factors influencing phytolith representation in lake and swamp sediments.

Logically, core location relative to the source of phytolith-laden sediments may be a factor in phytolith influx and deposition, but to my knowledge this relationship has not been systematically studied. In coastal mangrove swamps, for example, influx comes from the landward side. Changes in coastline and sea level may alter the sedimentary environment in a locality over the time frame sampled by a core. Phytolith concentrations in mangrove swamp cores can be highly variable; it may be possible to model the relationships among environmental variables (e.g., watershed size, river flow, core location, rainfall, pH, density of vegetation) and phytolith deposition in such settings. Anaerobic sediments, such as peats encountered in lake and swamp cores, may slow release of phytoliths from deposited plant tissues and reduce phytolith accumulations; this is another potentially testable relationship.

There is a large literature of case studies that illustrate how environmental phytolith and pollen records inform issues of interest in archaeology by "capturing" human-landscape interactions. In forested environments, for example, stratigraphic pollen and phytolith sequences may record reductions in forest cover and increases in open habitat taxa, which, in combination with particulate charcoal increases and the appearance of domesticated plants, mark the beginning of agriculture. Shifting abundances of open and secondary forest taxa or marked increases in grasses provide insight into cropping practices, as does the frequency of burning and changes in sediments accumulating in lakes or swamps. Human migration and population growth and decline all leave their mark on vegetation. Environmental phytolith and pollen records have stories to tell any student of paleoethnobotany.

FUTURE RESEARCH DIRECTIONS

Formation processes of pollen in lake and swamp settings are better studied than those of phytoliths. Modeling phytolith influx under different environmental conditions would aid interpretation of swamp core sequences. Pollen diagrams do not always give an unambiguous picture of human presence and disturbance of the environment. Recent research on the ancient DNA (aDNA) of bacteria known to be markers of human fecal contamination could help determine local human presence (Madeja et al. 2009). A study in Poland correlated levels of bacterial aDNA with charcoal concentrations and pollen assemblages, suggesting an increasing human presence in the local environment (Madeja et al. 2009). Further study into formation processes of aDNA in sediments are needed, but the method appears promising. Lane et al. (2009) illustrate the potential of stable carbon isotope analysis of core sediments for improving estimates of the scale of human impacts on environments, namely, for inferring the extent of vegetation change under agriculture from increasingly positive (more C_4) isotope signatures. See also the discussions by Messner and Stinchcomb (chapter 13, this volume) and Warinner (chapter 14, this volume).

CONCLUSIONS

Pollen and phytoliths are very different microfossils in terms of production patterns, dispersal, and preservation. This contributes to some fundamental differences in formation processes, as reviewed in this chapter. Although different formation processes contribute to complexity in interpretation, these differences may also enhance our understanding of human behaviors. For example, finding starch but no phytoliths in a cooking pot residue may indicate the degree of maturity of the food being used; whether or not pollen is present with seeds in a coprolite may indicate seasonality or storage; recovering phytoliths but no dried macroremains may indicate mode of food processing; phytoliths and pollen in combination may double the number of plant taxa identified in an environmental core.

Phytoliths and pollen are alike in that they become deposited in archaeological sites both through human action (by use of plants producing/containing them) and through different natural processes. Insights from experimental and ethnographic/ethnoarchaeological research help us disentangle these pathways, and infer past plant-people interrelationships.

ACKNOWLEDGMENTS

I thank Vaughn Bryant Jr. for providing a number of important references for pollen analysis. Errors in interpretation are mine.

Part II

Recovery,
Identification, and
Data Management

5

Sampling Strategies
in Paleoethnobotanical
Analysis

JADE D'ALPOIM GUEDES AND
ROBERT SPENGLER

The archaeological record is by nature fragmentary. In addition, because of finite resources it is impossible for archaeologists to have access to the entirety of the archaeological record. Choosing when, how, and where to sample is thus a crucial aspect of any archaeological investigation, and it is important to consider the effects that different sampling strategies have on the types of questions one wishes to answer. These issues are present in every approach to archaeological data, and archaeobotany is no exception. As paleoethnobotanists, our target populations are the plant remains brought into archaeological sites and deposited in areas surrounding them; however, we are only able to examine a limited portion of these remains.

When sampling for macro- and microbotanical remains, either in an archaeological context or non-anthropogenic sediments, careful consideration must go into choosing sampling methods. When deciding where to sample and how many samples to take one should keep in mind a list of variables, including (1) what research questions are being asked and how sampling will impact their answers, (2) how many samples can feasibly be analyzed by the project, (3) how many samples should be stored for future analysis, (4) which contexts have archaeological significance to the project, and (5) how best to provide a standard for comparison both regionally and within a site.

Research questions can dictate where and how to collect samples. For example, questions relating to

DOI: 10.5876/9781607323167.c005

the introduction of domesticates or simple presence/absence of plants in the economy may require fewer samples than questions relating to spatial or temporal variation. Likewise, documenting regional intersite variation in plant remains requires fewer samples from one site but more samples from a wider range of sites. Documenting intrasite variation, on the other hand, requires more intensive sampling from features within a given site. Since excavation is a destructive process, taking more samples is always preferable, especially when samples can be stored for future research.

When possible, a specialist should be on site to observe the soil and contexts from which the samples come. As interpretations rely on understanding site formation processes, it is important that archaeobotanists at least visit the site (Fritz 2005; Maloney 1994). When a specialist cannot spend at least part of the season working at the site, careful handling of samples and detailed notes are necessary. The specialist should meet with the excavators before the field season and discuss the procedures that he/she wants followed. This is especially important if undergraduates or inexperienced excavators will be doing the sampling and flotation. A short lecture or training session given to the excavators can help ensure that everyone understands the process and final goals.

SAMPLING FOR MACROBOTANICAL REMAINS
SAMPLING FOR INTRASITE VARIATION

Several different kinds of sampling strategies are widely employed in paleoethnobotanical analysis. Sampling strategies can be divided into those concerning (1) approaches to the whole site and (2) sampling within features or units. A sampling strategy at the site level lies at the core of any archaeological project and researchers should consider the use of one or a combination of the following strategies:

1. *Full coverage* (Renfrew and Bahn 2008), *blanket* (Pearsall 2000), or *total* (Jones 1991) *sampling*: samples are taken from each unit and from all features.
2. *Probabilistic sampling* (Renfrew and Bahn 2008) or *judgmental sampling*: samples are taken intensively from features or areas thought to be of interest.
3. *Random sampling*: can be carried out on either a *simple random basis*, in which samples are selected on a completely random basis, or on a *stratified random sampling basis*, in which the site is first divided into categories (i.e., different types of features or strata) that are then randomly subsampled; the latter method ensures that each category is accurately represented.
4. *Systematic sampling*: samples are taken at regular intervals across the site.

Pearsall (2000) recommends that excavators employ blanket sampling where possible. She argues that it is difficult to tell which contexts will yield carbonized plant remains and that it is easier to subsample from those already taken. Furthermore, knowing where plant remains do not occur in the site is important for understanding the mechanisms underlying the preservation of remains and is essential for functional interpretation of features (Lennstrom and Hastorf 1995). In an ideal world, a full coverage sampling strategy would aim to take samples from all features and their surrounding matrices and strata.

All too often, probabilistic or judgmental sampling is employed and selection of loci for sampling is based on the quantity of charcoal visible to the excavators. Although, clearly, one should make sure areas dense in carbonized remains are sampled, care should be taken to avoid "feature bias" (Lennstrom and Hastorf 1995:702). It is important to select samples not only from features or units but also from contexts that can provide a baseline reading of botanical material (unless time and resources are particularly limited; Lennstrom and Hastorf 1995).

Using a random sampling strategy can prove difficult to carry out during excavation, as it is impossible to predict how many features will be uncovered and what percentage of these should be sampled. A completely random sampling strategy means that areas crucial to the interpretation of the site might be ignored. Similar problems arise from systematic sampling. To avoid these problems, we recommend that a large number of samples be collected in the field and that a blanket strategy be used. If a large number of samples are collected from a site, a stratified random sampling can later be used to reselect a smaller number of samples for analysis. When approaching the entire site, one should be sure to take samples both horizontally (i.e., across features) and vertically (to document time depth).

A variety of these sampling methods can be combined. For instance, in waterlogged sites, Jacomet and Brombacher (2005) recommend using a grid to take systematic samples every meter to record baseline archaeobotanical data and to document the spatial distribution of archaeobotanical remains across features, such as floors. In addition to these systematic samples, they recommend taking column samples to record change through time, as well as judgment samples from visible features (Jacomet and Kreuz 1999).

The researcher should also take into account factors that will aid in feature interpretation. For example, taking "companion samples" from the matrix above and below features can later help with functional interpretation and allow analysts to certify that finds in a feature are independent and not the result of mixing or bioturbation (Adams and Gasser 1980; Lennstrom and

Hastorf 1995; Pearsall 2000). At the site of Pancan in Peru, Lennstrom and Hastorf (1995) took companion samples above and below visible and well-defined hearth features. They then used pie charts to define the relative quantities of different taxa in the hearths (see figure 9.1, for example) and in sample companions and found that for most of the contexts, the content of hearths was distinct from that of the surrounding matrix, suggesting that the remains of food were still in situ (Lennstrom and Hastorf 1995:706). In two hearths, remains were sparse and their content was also similar to that of the surrounding matrix, suggesting that their original content had been removed and replaced by this sediment (Lennstrom and Hastorf 1995:707).

Where possible, samples for micromorphological work should be taken alongside flotation samples to aid in the interpretation of site formation processes. Matthews (2010) and Goldberg and Macphail (2003) provide guidelines for taking samples for micromorphological analysis also discussed later in this chapter.

When sampling within features or strata it is often not possible to collect all soil in a context, and a subsample, therefore, needs to be taken. The following strategies can be used for sub-sampling:

1. *Point* (Pearsall 2000), *bulk* (Lennstrom and Hastorf 1992), or *spot* (Dimbleby 1985): soil is collected from a contiguous matrix within a single context. This strategy is often used for sampling inside small features like ashpits, sediment inside vessels, or graves.

2. *Pinch/composite* (Pearsall 2000) or *scatter* (Lennstrom and Hastorf 1992): small amounts of sediment are collected from the whole context and combined in a bag so that the sample is representative of the context as a whole. This strategy can be used for cultural layers, sublevels in large features, and fill levels.

3. *Column* (Jacomet and Kreuz 1999; Pearsall 2000): samples are taken from a column of soil bisecting contiguous stratigraphic layers in the archaeological site (usually in a completed excavation unit and often from a baulk wall) and collected from discrete stratigraphic layers down the column. In order to document time depth, we suggest that at least one column sample be taken from a site. An illustration of these different sampling strategies is provided in figure 5.1.

Pinch and point sampling produce roughly similar results. However, Lennstrom and Hastorf (1992) found that pinch samples produced a higher diversity of taxa and less variability in density. Point sampling produced a more detailed view of the spatial patterning than pinch sampling. Pearsall

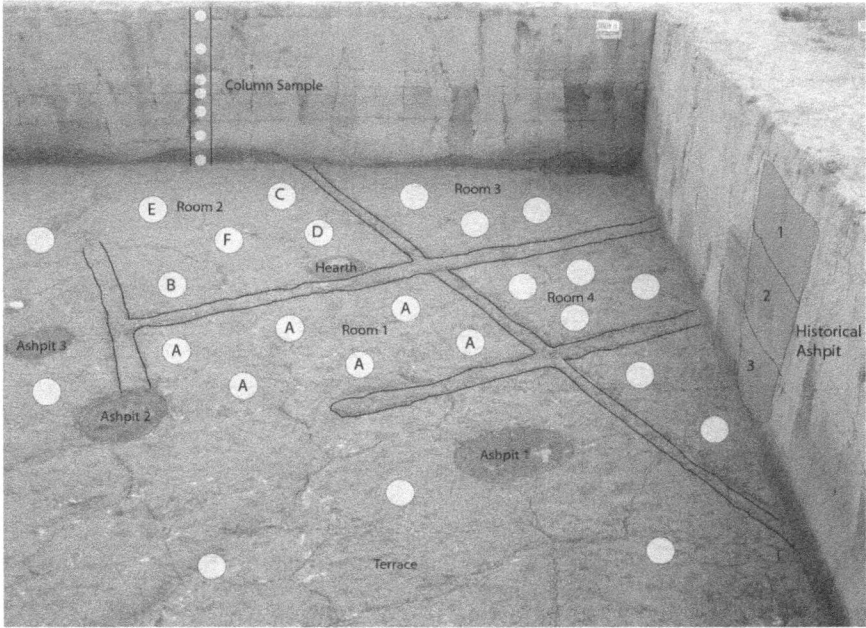

FIGURE 5.1. *An example of how different areas of an excavation unit can be sampled for archaeobotanical remains. The remains of a habitation structure, as well as ashpits, are visible. Two different sampling strategies can be used to understand feature function. To gain an accurate representation of the taxa spread across the floor of room 1 a "pinch" sampling strategy is used. Small quantities of earth (labeled A) are taken across the surface of the floor and then combined for analysis. In a scenario, where spatial distribution of plant remains within a given room is of interest, "point" samples can be taken. Point samples (labeled B, C, D, E and F) are taken in room 2 and are analyzed separately to provide a picture of different use areas within the room. Either pinch or point samples could be used in the terrace space outside the structure, depending on the research question(s) being asked. Although these two different strategies are pictured together here for illustrative purposes, it is advisable to use only one of these strategies within a feature category at one site for comparability of results. For the ashpits, a bulk sample of soil is taken. As these ashpits are small, the entire context of the pit was recovered. Clear stratigraphy was visible in the context of a later historical period pit, and bulk samples were taken according to strata. In order to provide time depth to the site a column sample was taken from one of the baulk walls.*

(2000) thus recommends using point sampling when dealing with excavation units larger than 1 × 1 m. An example is given in figure 5.1, which uses different strategies to understand how taxa are distributed across the floor of a domestic structure. In room 1, pinch samples from within the room are combined to give us an overall understanding of its function. In room 2, point sampling is used to examine the spatial distribution of taxa across the different areas within this space. Point sampling is used outside the structure to understand activities outside the house. Point sampling should be used for small features, particularly when the entire context can be retrieved for flotation, such as small ashpits or hearths in the figure. However, for large, stratified features like the historical ashpit, bulk samples were collected from each layer to examine temporal change. Although it is often useful to employ a combination of sampling strategies in an excavation, we recommend that only one strategy be employed within a given category of features to maximize comparability of results (Lennstrom and Hastorf 1992; Pearsall 2000).

Sampling for Intersite Variation

Several authors (Fuller and Stevens 2009; Hillman 1981; Jones 1985) have argued that the content of samples can be similar across a site regardless of the feature. According to these scholars, the majority of archaeobotanical material deposited in a site is the result of routine activities carried out on a daily basis that have been mixed and redeposited. Assemblages within a site should be relatively homogeneous across contexts because deposits reflecting discrete events are rare. When true, this homogeneity allows samples from different sites to be compared. However, it is necessary first to demonstrate this degree of homogeneity using a proper archaeobotanical sampling strategy. Many sites contain deposits related to one single event, such as feasting or goods placed in a grave (e.g., Pauketat et al. 2002).

The comparison of data from several sites to examine intersite variation usually occurs after excavations have been completed, often using data from published archaeobotanical reports. It is thus critical to consider the sampling strategies used at different sites. It is important first to demonstrate statistically that the samples are indeed comparable: for example, that samples to be compared result from routine activities such as crop processing or waste disposal. Any anomalous samples resulting from either discrete events or noncomparable sampling strategies should be dropped from analysis. Lee (2012) presents a useful formula for calculating the representativeness and comparability of samples.

Survey Archaeobotany

Growing interest in documenting regional variation has led to increasing attempts to extract archaeobotanical remains from archaeological surveys. The earliest examples of a survey that explicitly incorporated the collection of archaeobotanical remains is that of the Deh Luran Plain survey in Iran (Helbaek 1969). More recently, survey archaeobotany has been employed as a means of retrieving data from sites that are either unexcavated or that were not sampled for archaeobotanical remains in previous seasons of excavation. This approach has become increasingly popular in East and Southeast Asia, where it has been instrumental in documenting the introduction of domesticates and changes in agricultural regimes. Examples include Fuller's work in the Kunderu River basin (Fuller et al. 2001) and central China (Fuller and Zhang 2007; Zhang et al. 2010), the work of Lee et al. (2007) in the Yiluo River basin, Barton's (2003) work in northwest China, and the Chengdu Plain Archaeological Survey's work in Sichuan (Flad et al. n.d.).

Previously excavated sites can be sampled by returning to visible trenches of old excavations (Barton 2003; Fuller 2000). Unexcavated sites are more problematic. Known sites can be sampled opportunistically using construction or agricultural terrace cuts, an approach that has proven particularly useful on the loess plains of northern China, where archaeological features are often visible in terrace cuts in the loess plateaus (Barton 2003; Flad et al. 2010; Lee et al. 2007). Digging small-scale test pits is another solution for extracting archaeobotanical data from unexcavated sites (Barton 2003; Harvey et al. 2006; Helbaek 1969). Deciding where to place a test pit can be challenging in environments where stratigraphic cuts through sites are rare or site features are otherwise invisible on the surface. Recent archaeobotanical work in the context of the Chengdu Plain Archaeological Survey in Sichuan, China, used magnetometry to determine the location of ashpits and other subsurface features likely to yield archaeobotanical remains. These were targeted for archaeobotanical sampling using small-scale test pits (Flad et al. n.d.).

Regional surveys also offer good opportunities for obtaining complementary offsite information that can be used for environmental reconstruction. Waterlogged macrobotanical remains from contexts such as lakes and buried A horizons have been used extensively for the purposes of environmental reconstruction and paleoecology. Such sampling is often carried out in conjunction with pollen analysis. Procedures for sampling such remains are well established and we refer readers to Birks (1980, 2001) and Watts (1978) for detailed sampling instructions.

SAMPLE COLLECTION

Recommendations for sampling macrobotanical remains are summarized in table 5.1. Table 5.2 provides a list of information to be recorded when sampling. Once samples have been collected it is important to prevent them from "sweating" in a plastic bag by using cloth bags that allow the sample to breathe, or keeping bagged samples in cool, shaded areas. Since prolonged humidity combined with drastic changes in temperature and freeze-thaw cycles can damage carbonized material, it is better if they are stored in a dry state if flotation cannot be carried out immediately. If plastic bags will be used for storage, we recommend first drying the sample in a large sieve or basket on a plastic tarp (covered to avoid contamination) or drying it in a fine mesh muslin pouch before placing it in the bag.

Although consistency in sample size is good, it is not necessary, as density ratios account for differences soil volume (Marston, chapter 9, this volume). It is thus essential that soil volume be recorded accurately. Pearsall (2000) recommends starting with 10 L samples[1] and evaluating the quantity of material recovered; quantities might be adjusted according to the kind of feature sampled: for example, for features containing large quantities of nonorganic material, such as burnt clay from mudbrick houses, sample size should be increased. The nature of the soil matrix should also be taken into consideration. In particular, soils with high clay content are deleterious to the preservation of charred remains (Gallagher, chapter 2, this volume). In these contexts, larger samples should be taken to ensure that a satisfactory number of plant remains are recovered. When working in soils with high clay content on the Chengdu Plain in China, d'Alpoim Guedes and Ming (2011) recommended taking a minimum 25 L sample. If no paleoethnobotanist is present at the site to carry out flotation or experiment with the number of liters required, take larger samples rather than smaller samples. Larger samples can always be subsampled later.[2] At waterlogged sites, smaller samples sizes are acceptable because of the large quantities of uncarbonized organic remains preserved in these contexts. In general, roughly 1–5 L should yield enough material at such sites, however a test should be carried out in order to evaluate the quantity of material recovered before the final sampling strategy is established (Jacomet and Brombacher 2005; Jacomet and Kreuz 1999). Similar guidelines can be used at sites where plant remains are preserved through desiccation. In these sites, high densities of uncarbonized remains make it unnecessary to extract large samples.[3]

TABLE 5.1. Sampling checklist for micro- and macrobotanical sampling

	Macrobotanical Remains	Pollen	Phytoliths	Starch
Volume of soil needed	Between 10 and 30 L	60 ml	60 ml	60 ml
Use permanent marker to label samples both inside and outside of bag	YES	YES	YES	YES
Treat sample bags gently; do not crush	YES	N/A	N/A	N/A
Clean trowel and tools	Recommended	YES	YES	YES
Sample from a freshly exposed soil surface	YES	YES	YES	YES
Powder free gloves and bags or sterile test tubes	Not necessary	YES	Recommended	YES: Test tubes should be boiled for 2 hours prior to use*
Dry samples before storing	Recommended	YES	Recommended	YES
Refrigerate samples if cannot be dried	NO	Recommended if sample cannot be dried	NO	Will damage sample
Fungicide or 100% EtOH to sterilize samples	NO	Recommended if sample cannot be dried	NO	Will damage sample

* Experiment carried out by Jade d'Alpoim Guedes on starch contamination in test tubes. Unpublished data.

TABLE 5.2. List of information to record when sampling

- Site name
- GPS coordinates (if available)
- Depth and provenience
- Stratigraphic position
- Feature number
- Sample type (Macro, Pollen, Phytolith, Starch, or Combined)
- Evidence for bioturbation
- Soil color (use Munsell) and texture (i.e., sandy loam, clay, etc.)
- Assessment of amounts of carbonized material present*
- Soil volume sampled
- Name and contact information of person who took the sample
- Sample date

*A visual assessment of the amount of organic material in the soil of a specific context can be useful when selecting subsamples for analysis due to insufficient time available to analyze everything collected.

SAMPLING FOR MICROBOTANICAL REMAINS

This section is intended to provide an overview of sampling strategies for microbotanical remains (pollen and diatoms, phytolith, and starch grains). Interested readers are directed to a number of more detailed sources for follow-up reading: Brooks and Johannes (1990), Bryant and Holloway (1983), Dimbleby (1985), Pearsall (2000), Pearsall and Piperno (1993), Piperno (2006b), Rovner (1983), and Torrence and Barton (2006).

Pollen, diatoms, phytoliths, and starch grains are physiologically very different, but approaches to sampling them in archaeological sediments overlap and are similar to macrobotanical sampling strategies, although burnt areas and ash, which provide good results for macrobotanical remains and phytoliths, tend not to be productive sampling areas for pollen (Bryant and Holloway 1983). Overlaps among microbotanical sampling strategies are, in part, a reflection of the fact that many approaches to phytolith studies have been adopted from palynology. Consequently, we discuss pollen and phytoliths together in this chapter. Diatoms, the remains of single-celled algae, can be used as proxies of environmental change and are typically collected using the same methods needed for pollen (Juggins and Cameron 2010). We treat them together below. Starch grains are the most fragile of the microremains and require more careful sampling; we describe them separately.

Pollen, phytolith, and starch grain analyses are complementary methods for building a model of economy. Pollen provides a broad-spectrum picture of local vegetation and, in some cases, can identify plants associated with specific anthropogenic features (see Pearsall, chapter 4, this volume). Phytoliths represent parts of plants and are often more closely associated with anthropogenic activities (see Pearsall, chapter 4, this volume). Starch grains can represent perishable and rarely preserved parts of economic plants (see Henry, chapter 3, this volume). By combining these microremains, a more comprehensive picture of ancient plant use can be formed.

POLLEN

Most open-air sites do not provide ideal settings for pollen preservation (Bryant and Holloway 1983; King et al. 1975; Pearsall 2000; Pearsall, chapter 4, this volume). Despite this, palynology can be a useful tool for answering questions related to both economy and environment. Archaeological soils contain a mixture of pollen from naturally occurring processes as well as pollen brought into the site by anthropogenic processes. Therefore, if pollen from an archaeological site is being used to reconstruct paleoenvironments, it is necessary to contrast it with non-anthropogenic sediment columns.

The original foundations of palynology in Europe were focused on paleoenvironmental studies (Erdtman 1969), and these applications are still the main use of palynology today; such work is primarily conducted using lake or bog cores.[4] For sampling outside of anthropogenic contexts we refer the reader to other sources: Faegri and Iversen (1975), Nilsson and Praglowski (1992), Moore and Webb (1978), and Stewart and Rothwell (2010).

Poor pollen preservation has led many researchers to abandon on-site pollen sampling. King et al. (1975) notes that most open-air sites in the Northeastern United States do not have good preservation, but if taphonomy is taken into account, valuable on-site pollen data can be produced. King et al. (1975) presents a case study for the Rhoads site, in central Illinois, where economically relevant pollen grains preserved through oxidation were found in a pit associated with large metal pots.

PHYTOLITHS

Phytoliths are silica and therefore are extremely resistant to biodegradation. In addition, they are generally preserved in situ where a plant decomposed (Piperno 2006b). These two characteristics (durability and localization) make phytoliths a good tool for studying paleoeconomies and paleoenvironments. However, bioturbation is always an issue in anthropogenic contexts, especially with microscopic material. Phytoliths may provide either a complement to macrobotanical analysis or a replacement for it in cases where macrobotanical remains do not preserve well (e.g., tropical soils) (Piperno 2006b; Pearsall, chapter 4, this volume).

Sampling for Pollen and Phytoliths

As with all paleoethnobotanical sampling, two general categories of approaches exist: vertical sampling (column sampling) and horizontal sampling (blanket sampling). Each approach to sampling has advantages and disadvantages, and if feasible a combination of the two approaches is recommended. Vertical sampling is not possible if the site does not have stratigraphic depth. However, Piperno (2006b) claims that a column sample can be taken from sites with as little as 30 cm in profile depth.

Column Sampling

With a column sample, pollen curves can be calculated that portray trends through time, including changes in the microenvironment around a site.[5] Many researchers take column samples from baulk walls left in situ, but trench walls can be used after mapping is complete. Cleaning the profile with a trowel or brush allows for final confirmation of stratigraphy before sampling and ensures the stratigraphic association of each sample is accurately reported.[6] Column samples can be taken either stratigraphically (sampling horizons) (Dimbleby 1985) or at standard increments down the column (incremental sampling). It is more common to use standard increments, although in such cases stratigraphy should be recorded.

Incremental samples in more compact stratigraphic contexts may be taken as close as 0.5 cm apart. The closer the samples are taken to each other the more detailed short-term environmental changes can be identified, provided that a detailed, datable stratigraphic sequence exists and it is possible to process numerous samples. Dimbleby (1985) argues that samples should be *contiguous*, meaning one sample in a column should touch the next with no space between. A contiguous serial column sample provides the most comprehensive chronological view of the site, and is recommended when time and labor permit. A column sample should span the entire occupation sequence from the modern surface layer to the subsoil below the basal occupation layer. These two samples will help the researcher determine if there has been vertical turbation in the soil column, which may have moved surface sediments down or subsoil up. When determining how many columns to sample, we refer to Piperno's (2006b:82) rule of thumb, "the more the better," keeping in mind financial and labor constraints. More than one column sample from a site allows for intrasite comparison.

Horizontal sampling

Horizontal sampling is often used to complement column sampling. Horizontal blanket sampling allows for a comparison between contemporaneous features and can help researchers interpret use areas and provide comparative data for column samples. Pearsall (1982:863) notes that "sampling in well-defined, tightly controlled contexts (e.g., hearths, burial pits, closely spaced intervals on a house floor, stratified middens) is preferable."

Pinch sampling can be useful when sampling for multiproxy analysis. Piperno (2006b) recommends pinch sampling across an entire feature (house floor or hearth) and combining the various pinch samples into a composite sample of about 200 g. Point sampling also has applications in microbotanical research. It is often difficult to determine the vector of pollen introduction into archaeological sediments, and point sampling may help achieve this goal. Point sampling distinguishes concentrations of pollen or phytoliths in certain parts of a site. This may lead to the identification of processing areas for crops or storage locations. Shishlina et al. (2008) used point sampling of pollen to compare burials in the Caspian steppe region, and found that different burials had different species placed in them. Anthony et al. (2005) used point sampling to identify concentrations of *Allium* pollen at Krasnosamarskoe on the Russian steppe. The presence of pollen from this insect-pollinated plant in houses indicated that individuals brought this plant into the settlement to be used for economic purposes.

Sample collection

There are no established standards for sample collection size for microremain analysis. Bryant and Holloway (1983) suggest samples be between 0.5 and 1 L; Dimbleby (1985) claims 30 g is enough; Bohrer and Adams (1977) suggest about 60 ml; Pearsall (2000) suggests 50 g, or 200 g of sediment, for a multiproxy sample. The amount of pollen or phytoliths in a sediment sample can be highly variable and less soil is required in organic-rich, rather than sandy or clay sediment.[7] A 200 g sample usually includes enough sediment for pollen, phytolith, and starch grain analyses, while leaving significant quantities in case of laboratory errors and for future research. If samples are collected for only one form of analysis, 60 g is sufficient. Samples for multiple analyses can be divided into separate bags in the field or in the lab. The fewer steps done in the field the better, as there are more sources of contamination in the field. Table 5.1 provides sampling recommendations. For the collection of both pollen and phytolith it is essential that sampled surfaces are fresh and that tools are cleaned between samples. For a more detailed description of sample collection, refer to Pearsall's (2000:279–89) discussion of the three procedures for taking soil samples based on Bryant and Holloway (1983), Bohrer and Adams (1977), and Dimbleby (1985).

As with macrobotanical remains, it is essential to employ a sampling strategy that can demonstrate that the patterns seen are a result of human activity and not post-depositional processes. Control samples are necessary because they provide a background botanical signature to help researchers distinguish pollen and phytoliths from plants associated with human activity from native vegetation and to assess differential preservation. Although macrobotanical remains are capable of moving considerable distances through archaeological sediments (Brantingham et al. 2007), microbotanical remains are even more susceptible to movement in sediment (Blake 2006; Haslam 2004; cf. Piperno 2006b) and any sampling strategy must take this into account. Rodent activity or other turbation can be identified during excavation and should be noted.

Control samples should be taken off-site at varying depths. If possible, it is best to take a series of control column samples at regular or exponential distances (i.e., 50 m, 100 m, 200 m) away from the site. Column samples can be obtained by digging a 1 × 1 m test unit at each of these locations or by using split-spoon samplers or percussion augers. The cleaned surface of naturally or anthropogenically exposed stratigraphy can also be used. Pearsall (2000) has discussed contamination issues with the use of an open-face corer (split spoon). A variety of closed-face corers also exist (auger or split-barrel corer).

Pollen and phytolith analyses are also important tools for studying garden archaeology (Currie 2005) and ancient field systems (Miller and Gleason 1994; Pearsall and Trimble 1984; Zheng et al. 2009), which require different sampling strategies. Phytoliths can also be useful in detecting concentrations of dung and organic refuse, which are rich in phytoliths, as they are essentially condensed decomposed plant material (Shahack-Gross et al. 2003).

STARCH GRAINS AND RESIDUES

As with other microremains, sampling for starch requires continual awareness of potential contamination in the field. Because large quantities of starch are present in most foods, field workers should not snack on site. In addition, workers should thoroughly wash their hands before analysis and avoid the use of lotions and creams, many of which contain starch. Powdered gloves also contain substantial amounts of starch, and thus only powder-free gloves should be used (Newsom and M. Shaw 1997b).

Many concerns have been voiced about the reliability of starch grain studies from soil samples. In particular, critiques have centered on our poor understanding of the mechanisms underlying starch preservation (Haslam 2004), as well as movement in sediment (Therin 1998, 2006). Lentfer et al. (2002) carried out an experimental study on starch associated with modern sediments to examine the potential for environmental reconstruction in Papua New Guinea. Pinch samples were collected randomly within a 10×10-m quadrant from modern sediment layers and both starch grains and phytoliths correlated well with known land use. Bulk samples were also taken in similar studies conducted by Therin et al. (1999) and Torrence (2006). Other studies have sampled for starch grains in archaeological sediments and have extracted ancient starch from column samples in caves both in arid (Atchison and Fullagar 1998; Balme and Beck 2002) and tropical environments (Barton 2005; Horrocks et al. 2004).

In their study, Balme and Beck (2002) evaluated the presence/absence of starch across a rockshelter site to explore mechanisms related to preservation. Samples were taken across the surface of the cave at 25-cm intervals, and after an evaluation of different physical characteristics of the surrounding matrix, the authors concluded that the distribution of starch and charcoal in the cave was related to human use patterns and not to post-depositional processes. If researchers intend to use starch grains to demonstrate feature function, we recommend using blanket sampling and taking control samples from every stratigraphic layer to demonstrate that the starch grains examined in a given deposit are indeed independent from those in the surrounding matrices above and below.

Sampling from Artifacts

Pollen, phytoliths, and starch grains can also be recovered from artifacts to document tool use. Usually extraction of starch or phytoliths is performed on stone tools (Barton 2007; Barton et al. 1998; Del Pilar Babot and Apella 2003; Dickau et al. 2007; Fullagar et al. 2006; Loy 1994; Loy et al. 1992; Perry 2004; Piperno and Holst 1998; Piperno et al. 2000; Piperno et al. 2004; Zarrillo and Kooyman 2006) or similar artifacts such as carbonized ceramic residues (Zarrillo et al. 2008). Both phytoliths and starch have been extracted from dental calculus (Boyadjian et al. 2007; Cummings and Magennis 1997; Henry and Piperno 2008; Juan-Tresserras et al. 1997; Lalueza Fox et al. 1996; Lalueza Fox et al. 1994; Piperno and Dillehay 2008). Starch has also been extracted from desiccated plants, uncarbonized macroscopic plant remains, and coprolites (Horrocks et al. 2004).

Special treatment should be given to artifacts or ecofacts that will be analyzed. Artifacts should be dried in a box or otherwise sealed environment and should then be sealed in airtight bags to reduce airborne contamination and not washed in the field. There are multiple protocols for a pollen or phytolith wash to remove microremains from an artifact. Bohrer and Adams (1977) and Pearsall (2000) describe a pollen wash method using a dilute HCl solution. Double-distilled water can also be used. The wash solution can then be centrifuged and processed to extract microremains. Adhered sediment matrix should be removed from the artifact prior to washing and test samples should be taken from the surrounding matrix using mechanical scraping to ensure that sampled microremains are not simply part of the surrounding sediment (Barton 2006). Piperno suggests that the control samples should be taken from beneath and around the artifact at a distance of 5 to 10 cm. Starch is primarily extracted from the surface of artifacts by either scraping or using an ultrasonicating tool. A sonicator (sonic water bath) can be used either in the field or in the lab (Perry et al. 2007). Loy (1994) describes how to scan an artifact to determine if starch grains are present and if extraction would be fruitful, and how to extract starch grains from artifacts. We refer readers to the edited volume by Torrence and Barton (2006) for a number of case studies on how to extract starch from different kinds of artifact surfaces.

INTEGRATING MACROBOTANICAL AND
MICROBOTANICAL SAMPLING

We suggest that excavators should keep a portion of all flotation samples (especially if taken using blanket sampling) for microbotanical analyses. Keeping a bag of soil (200 g) from flotation samples should be standard protocol even if a microbotanical specialist is not on hand to analyze them. Micro- and macrobotanical data sets are complementary and multiple lines of evidence should be used under optimal funding and labor conditions. Pairing macrobotanical with microbotanical analyses can provide particularly insightful results because phytoliths and starch provide evidence for plant parts that often do not preserve macroscopically, whereas macrobotanical analyses may provide more detailed taxonomic identification.

CONCLUSION

In paleoethnobotany, we are left with only a fragmentary portion of the plant communities around a site and the plant resources brought into it. Based on this fragmentary assemblage, we must develop an understanding not only of the surrounding environment and human economy, but also of social aspects such as technology, craft, and ritual. Therefore, it is important to know where to take samples, how many to take, and how to take them. These variables depend on the research questions being asked and on the local conditions of the site and lab. Sampling strategies are site specific and will vary depending upon researcher preference.

One unfortunate trend in paleoethnobotany has been the use of microbotanical studies solely as a supplement for macrobotanical analysis. Although microbotanical data provide unique information and are important for understanding any archaeological site, the nature of information derived from each type of remain is different and sampling for one class of remains is not a substitute for sampling for another. Micro- and macrobotanical data sets are complementary; therefore, wherever possible, excavators and researchers should design sampling strategies with multiproxy analysis in mind. Micromorphological studies can further complement a multiproxy data set. When flotation samples are taken from a site, it is good practice to keep 200 g of soil for future pollen, phytolith, and starch studies. Keep in mind that the archaeobotanical significance of a site is rarely known during excavation and that it is difficult or even impossible to resample after an excavation. When integrated, multiproxy analyses allow us to understand not only which plants were present at the site but also which plant parts were present and where concentrations of plant materials were located. In addition, a combination of vertical and horizontal sampling methods allows us to understand both patterning through time and contemporaneous feature use. Once these strategies have been applied at multiple sites, we can start to answer economic questions on a regional scale. Without a regional baseline, it is not possible to understand the significance of patterns at a single site. Once intersite analyses are implemented, taphonomic processes can be understood and topics such as exchange, value of resources, labor patterns, exotic goods, resource use and origin, decision-making processes, and even cultural preferences can be explored.

NOTES

1. In the Americas, 10 L samples have tended to be the standard, whereas in Eurasia sample size has been more variable.

2. Subsampling can be done simply by splitting by weight or volume or by using a riffle box (Toll 1988; van der Veen and Fieller 1982).

3. Flotation is usually not used for desiccated or waterlogged material; see Pearsall 2000 for appropriate protocols.

4. Waterlogged contexts have much better preservation than terrestrial contexts and, although turbation occurs, they often do not have as many problematic variables as anthropogenic contexts.

5. Pollen curves produced from soil in an archaeological site reflect the localized anthropogenic microenvironment. However, R-values are required to calibrate for pollen that may be overrepresented locally due to extended transportability (such as with saccate pollen of many conifers) or extreme pollen productivity (as in most wind-transported pollen); a good understanding of pollination syndromes is necessary (for a discussion of R-values see Broström et al. 2005; Ford 2008; Sugita 1994).

6. It is especially important with microbotanical sampling to take samples only from freshly exposed surfaces to reduce contamination by airborne pollen or plant material.

7. A full liter of sediment is more than necessary and such a large sample may cover more than one pollen stratum in a column.

6

Recovering Macrobotanical Remains

Current Methods and Techniques

Chantel E. White and China P. Shelton

A wide variety of techniques are currently used by paleo-ethnobotanists to recover macrobotanical remains. The methods chosen by paleoethnobotanists are influenced by a multitude of factors, but one of the most important issues is the type(s) of botanical preservation found at an archaeological site. In the case of macrobotanical remains (i.e., seeds, wood, and other plant parts identifiable at low magnifications typically ranging from 5× to 30×), the most frequently preserved forms are charred, desiccated, and waterlogged remains (Pearsall 2000; Tolar et al. 2010; van der Veen 2007a). The goal of all recovery methods is to successfully isolate plant remains from their surrounding sediment matrix without loss or damage. A frequent additional goal is the simultaneous collection of other types of archaeological material including lithics, ceramics, and bone. Deciding which method to employ can be a complex process that often involves extensive modifications to fit a particular site and situation. Each technique has specific benefits and drawbacks that must be considered along with the parameters of the project and the goals of the paleoethnobotanist.

The history and development of macrobotanical recovery methods over the past seventy years have been thoroughly summarized by scholars such as Pearsall (2000), Wagner (1988), and Watson (1997). Here we provide an overview of various methods currently used by paleoethnobotanists and detail recent advancements in techniques and equipment. We then discuss important factors to consider in choosing a method, the individual

DOI: 10.5876/9781607323167.c006

95

strengths and limitations of certain techniques, and under what circumstances they can be best employed. Case studies and examples from multiple contexts and regions are provided, drawing on personal experiences from both academic and contract paleoethnobotany, to illustrate the level of innovation and flexibility required in implementing a macrobotanical recovery program.

DISCUSSION OF RECOVERY METHODS

In the field, archaeologists often recognize the presence of small, visible plant remains during excavation. These remains may take the form of dark flecks of wood charcoal embedded in sediment or desiccated seeds preserved within a pottery vessel. The identification of in situ botanical remains can provide essential information about the function of a feature and help to establish an association between the remains and other nearby artifacts (Pearsall 2000). However, small seeds are often difficult to detect with the naked eye, especially if they are waterlogged in dark organic sediment. Because these small remains may be easily overlooked by excavators, the use of "hand-picked" samples as the only means of macrobotanical recovery may result in an uneven and biased assemblage.

DRY SCREENING

One method of addressing this issue is through the technique of dry screening. Commercial and academic excavations have made dry screening a standard practice and are able to systematically recover small artifacts such as lithics, pottery sherds, bone, and shell (Wagner 1988). However, given the minute size of most seeds and plant parts (< 2 mm), botanical material may be lost if the screen aperture size is too large. Plant remains may also be crushed or have their distinguishing features destroyed when processed alongside stones and other dense material. Nevertheless, in some cases dry screening offers the most practical means for recovering macroremains. Dried/desiccated plant remains are preserved on archaeological sites when bacterial activity is reduced in extremely arid conditions (e.g., a desert environment). The addition of water, often used in other methods of macrobotanical recovery, weakens the dried remains. Although the plant material may appear to be very well preserved, tissue breakdown and decomposition rates are greatly accelerated through wetting. Even carbonized plant remains from arid sites may "explode" upon contact with water (Pearsall 2000:81, 83).

At archaeological sites across North Africa, paleoethnobotanists frequently use a form of dry screening to collect plant remains (Cappers 2006; Hillman

1989; Hillman et al. 1989; van der Veen 1992b, 1996, 1998, 2004; Wasylikowa et al. 1997). Large-scale recovery efforts at sites in Egypt, Libya, and other locations have revealed rich assemblages of grains, legume seeds, and fruit pits, as well as more fragile plant tissues such as cloves of garlic and delicate flower parts (van der Veen 2007a:969). One exciting site is Berenike, a Roman harbor site located along Egypt's Red Sea coast (ca. 275 BC–seventh century AD). Nearly 800 samples from the site were dry screened using a series of nested fine-mesh sieves (5.0–0.5 mm). In addition to dietary staples, plants used for condiments and spices, oils and resins, and components of the dying and tanning process were found (Cappers 2006:159). At the Middle Kingdom port site of Mersa/Wadi Gawasis in Egypt, occupied approximately 1,200 years before Berenike, a dry screening system was also used to collect fragments of ancient ship timbers (Borojevic et al. 2010). The careful use of this technique recovered not only fragile food remains of ancient grains, but also the preserved carapaces of insects that once infested the stored cereals.

A similar dry screening system was designed for an excavation of Maya farmsteads in northwestern Belize in Mesoamerica (Hageman and Goldstein 2009). Dry sediment samples averaging 4 L were processed through a set of nested geological sieves (4.0, 2.0, 1.0, and 0.425 mm). The varying sieve sizes made identification of seeds easier and faster because plant parts were of a similar size. It was not necessary to continuously change magnification during microscopic analysis of each sieve fraction and refocus to account for varying object heights. During this excavation, the dry screening method was also carried out in conjunction with flotation, a technique discussed below. This resulted in a much richer and varied assemblage of plant remains than either method could have provided on its own. The dry screening method recovered 5 percent more charcoal than flotation, as well as eleven unique plant taxa (Hageman and Goldstein 2009:2848). However, flotation recovered twice as many seeds overall. Such a complex situation indicates that conditions of plant preservation need to be evaluated on a site-by-site basis. Analysys of archaeological samples from the Early Bronze Age site of Numayra in Jordan, for example, has also been facilitated by a joint dry screening and flotation processing program (Figure 6.1). The paleoethnobotanist should feel comfortable trying various techniques and may end up employing more than one recovery method.

Wet Screening

Wet screening is an alternative technique that is often used by paleoethnobotanists in waterlogged contexts. In recent literature, wet screening has

FIGURE 6.1. *A set of nested sieves is used to dry screen archaeological sediments from the site of Numayra, Jordan. Photo by Chantel White.*

become synonymous with wet sieving, but Wagner (1988:19) notes that the latter involves submerging the sample in water (often in a basket) and removing small particles through gentle agitation. In wet screening, however, sediment is simply poured through a nested set of geological screens and lightly sprayed with a water hose to ease remains through the mesh (Hosch and

Zibulski 2003). At sites with clay sediments and waterlogged plant remains, the plant material will likely be weighed down with adhering clay and other heavy minerals. Methods of recovery that rely on buoyancy (such as flotation) may thus be out of the question. Wet screening offers a viable solution but is not without its own problems. At times it can be very physically demanding, requiring soils to be hand-kneaded through the screens if clay is abundant. This rough action can also destroy the botanical materials one is trying to recover (Tolar et al. 2010).

At the Neolithic site of Arbon-Bleiche 3 in Switzerland, a method of wet screening was used to recover waterlogged plant remains from a lakeshore context (Hosch and Zibulski 2003). Using a set of nested screens (2.0 and 0.5 mm), approximately 3 L of sediment was spread over the top screen and sprayed with a mist of water. Plant remains were caught in either the larger mesh or washed down into the smaller mesh size, which was also then lightly misted to remove additional sediment (Hosch and Zibulski 2003:850). Processing took a very long time (~2.5 hrs per 3 L sample), and rates of recovery were highly dependent on the technique of the operator. Some samples retained so much sediment that they were considered to be incompletely processed (even after two hours), whereas others had been agitated to the point of seed fragmentation and loss. In light of these experiments, Hosch and Zibulski (2003:856) instead recommend the wash-over technique, a combination bucket and wet screening method described below.

Wash-Over

Commercial archaeologists operating in Britain often excavate sites containing waterlogged plant remains, and they have standardized an improved method of recovery known as the wash-over technique (Jones 2002; Kenward et al. 1980; Monk 2007). A sample of a few liters (1–5 L) is placed in a bucket and water is added. The sample is agitated by hand until the sediment begins to break up. At this point, the operator gently pours out the liquid contents of the bucket, including the waterlogged remains (which are still suspended), into a sieve of 300-micron mesh and carefully leaves the heavy inorganic material at the bottom of the bucket. The bucket is then emptied, refilled with water, and the plant remains are returned to it. The bucket is slowly poured out again, this time into a set of nested sieves of decreasing mesh size (Hosch and Zibulski 2003). This decanting procedure protects the remains from the abrasion of direct screening and size-sorts them for later analysis. Because drying may cause damage or distortion of the remains, samples are kept wet after processing.

Depending on the site and level of waterlogged preservation, recovery rates can be improved through various modifications to the wash-over technique. Specialists may take unprocessed samples back to the laboratory and subject them to pretreatment techniques such as freezing, soaking, and the addition of chemicals including potassium hydroxide. Samples should be carefully double-bagged in the field to retain their moisture content and then stored in a laboratory refrigerator, freezer, or other dark cool place (Pearsall 2000:85). Experiments by Vandorpe and Jacomet (2007) at a Roman site in France revealed that better-preserved, less-fragmented plant remains were collected following two days of freezing samples at −18°C. These experiments suggest that waterlogged remains recovered from clay-rich sediments may benefit from a multistep process in which they are first frozen and then thawed before use of the wash-over technique. If botanical specimens will be subjected to accelerator mass spectrometry (AMS) radiocarbon dating, adhering sediment should be removed and the remains should be kept in their waterlogged or frozen state. Any chemicals used in the recovery process must be reported to the radiocarbon laboratory and may require additional treatments (Brock et al. 2010:107).

In addition to recovering waterlogged material, the wash-over technique may prove useful for recovering carbonized plant remains (figure 6.2). At the site of Mezber in northern Ethiopia, the wash-over technique was used with much success to recover Pre-Aksumite charred plant remains (D'Andrea 2010). A 12-L bucket was filled with water and then 1–2 L of sediment was sprinkled in. The sample was agitated by hand and any clumps of sediment were carefully broken up before the bucket was gently tipped over a set of nested screens (1 mm and 0.25 mm). The skill of bucket pouring at a controlled slow rate was critical to the recovery of the remains; a quick pour resulted in sediment clogging the sieves or water spillage in which remains were lost. A second person assisted by carefully spraying the insides of the flotation bucket with a handheld spray bottle to wash any adhering charcoal into the water. Samples of 10 L typically required multiple pourings and sometimes took over an hour to fully process (Pamela Wadge, personal communication 2009). A video created by Dorian Fuller demonstrating this wash-over technique is available online (Fuller 2007c).

MANUAL FLOTATION

The most common means of recovery for carbonized plant remains is through *flotation*, although this term encompasses a multitude of techniques

FIGURE 6.2. *Carbonized plant remains from the site of Mezber, Ethiopia, are recovered with the wash-over technique. Photo by Chantel White.*

and varying strategies. Flotation systems are based on the principle that charred plant material is less dense than water (1 g/mL). When a sediment sample is submerged in water and agitated, charred plant remains will float to the water's surface where they can be collected with a mesh skimmer or poured off into a sieve or mesh bag (Pearsall 2000). These plant remains, referred to as the *light fraction*, are typically collected using a 0.5-mm mesh or smaller to catch even the smallest plant parts. Stone tools, ceramics, bone, and other items that are denser than water (and thus sink) are retrieved separately as the *heavy fraction*, usually through a 1-mm mesh sieve. Particles of silt, clay, and sand are filtered through the system and are discarded. Many examples of flotation systems can be found online through the websites of paleoethno-botanists, often with plans, photos, and variations (e.g., Crawford 2011; Fuller 2011; White 2011).

Since its first implementation in the 1950s, flotation systems have been modified and improved by both commercial and academic paleoethnobot-anists. The easiest and most basic system to assemble is known as bucket flotation (Struever 1968). In this technique, the bottom of a steel or heavy-duty plastic bucket is removed and a mesh screen is attached with wires and caulk to collect the heavy fraction. The bottom of the bucket is submerged in a water-filled tub and the sediment sample is slowly poured into the modified bucket. The light fraction is then scooped up from the water's surface using a hand-sieve created from fine mesh. A popular variation of this method was created by Gail Wagner for the Illinois Department of Transportation (IDOT) and involves a specially made type of wooden box with three sides of screen mesh (Pearsall 2000; Wagner 1976). The heavy fraction is collected inside the IDOT box and the light fraction can be collected from the water's surface with a hand-sieve.

Hand-Pump Flotation

The recently developed technique of hand-pump flotation is a type of manual flotation. These systems use the same large tanks as machine-assisted flotation but do not require a power source (such as a gas-powered pump). Instead, a manual bilge pump is used to drive water through the system (Shelton and White 2010). Water pressure is applied from below the sample, although an alternative model uses a handheld hose to direct water where needed (figure 6.3). The hand-pump system is well suited for processing small samples (10 L or less) and operates at a slower pace than machine-assisted techniques. It does, however, offer greater flexibility in water flow, which can be essential if carbonized plant remains are very fragile and prone to fragmentation. Instead of nested sieves, one of the authors (C. White) uses a 250-micron mesh bag attached to the spout of the tank, modified from the bags designed by Sue Colledge for a Shell Mound Archaeological Project (SMAP)-style tank in Jordan. The fine-mesh bag allows plant remains to be captured without the impact of water overflow directly hitting a screen, as may occur with nested sieves. This technique has been used with success at the site of el-Hemmeh, where fragile plant remains from the early Neolithic have been recovered with little additional fragmentation (Shelton and White 2010).

Machine-Assisted Flotation

Unlike manual techniques that rely on hand-agitation or bilge pumps, machine-assisted systems typically use a form of water pressure provided by a gas-powered pump. One of the first systems designed was the water separator, or Ankara machine, which used water pressure created from an elevated

FIGURE 6.3. *The hand-pump flotation system from Molyvoti, Greece, using (A) a hand-held hose to direct water into the main flotation tank, (B) a mesh insert to support the heavy fraction screen, (C) a second tank to conserve and recycle water, and (D) the hand-operated bilge pump and the light fraction spout (with attached 250-micron mesh bag). Photos by Chantel White.*

reservoir to clean nonfloating artifacts, break up sediment, and wash charred plant remains into a separate flot box lined with fine mesh (Diamant 1979; French 1971; Limp 1974; Watson 1976). Later modifications used a 55-gallon steel drum as the main tank and modified the flot box into a series of graded sieves attached beneath the trough or spout (Davis and Wesolowsky 1975; Watson 1976; Williams 1973). The SMAP machine pumped water directly into the main tank without the use of an elevated reservoir and had the added benefit of being transportable (Peterson 2009). Because of its versatility and ability to process even difficult clay sediments, many versions of the SMAP tank are currently in use around the world (figure 6.4).

Machine-assisted flotation tanks can also be modified to include settling tanks. Settling tanks capture the outflow from the flotation tank and allow time for fine sediment to settle out of this water, after which clean water can be recycled back into the main tank and reused. This arrangement is useful in situations where water availability is limited and conservation necessary or desirable (Pearsall 2000:48–50).

However, water pressure is not the only means of agitating samples. Froth flotation machines use air pressure, in the form of bubbles created through compressed air and/or a frothing agent, to break up sediment and separate light and heavy fractions (Crawford 1983; Jarman, Legge, and Charles 1972; Ramsay 2010). This may be aided by the addition of kerosene to the water, which helps plant remains to affix to air bubbles and rise to the water's surface for collection (Pearsall 2000). In the late 1980s, Crawford created a hybrid froth flotation/SMAP tank that was transportable and that accommodated large samples (Crawford 2011). In recent years he and his team have developed a hybrid SMAP tank that is smaller in size and now widely used throughout Japan and China (Lee et al. 2007; Zhao 2007).

Another system using both water pressure and aeration to separate sediment is the commercially manufactured Flote-Tech flotation system developed by R. J. Dausman Technical Services, Inc. This self-contained system possesses two 50-gallon tanks, one that serves as the main flotation tank and one as a water reservoir. A ¾-horsepower water pump circulates water through the system and the operator controls both water flow and the level of aeration (Hunter and Gassner 1998). The light fraction is collected in a large tray onto which a fine mesh (typically 300-micron) is placed. Critics of the Flote-Tech machine cite difficulties with cleaning the tank and insert used to collect the heavy fraction (Rossen 1999). The system is generally best used in situations in which a high volume of sediment needs to be processed and where ample electrical power is available to run the system all day.

FIGURE 6.4. *A SMAP-style flotation system from Tell Sakhariya, Iraq, featuring (A) a high-flow water spout and funnel for collecting the light fraction (using a fine mesh, not shown), (B) a removable tank insert for collecting the heavy fraction, (C) a showerhead used to agitate the samples from below, (D) a sludge valve and hand-held showerhead for cleaning the tank, and (E) a gasoline-powered pump. Photos by Demetrios Brellas.*

CHOOSING A METHOD

Practical and logistical factors play important roles in the type of recovery technique chosen and the equipment constructed or purchased. Determining which macrobotanical collection method is appropriate for a given project depends on several factors, including the research questions guiding excavation and macrobotanical collection, funding, field conditions, and local resources such as water and electricity, the length of the field season, and the condition of plant remains. The varying interests of specialists should also be taken under consideration (e.g., the simultaneous sampling of microbotanical remains and microvertebrates), as well as the composition and training level of the excavation team (Bezic 2009; Miller et al. 2010).

PRACTICAL CONSIDERATIONS

With regard to financial cost, recovery systems run the gamut from minimal investment (bucket and screen) to expensive set-ups including power generators. The project budget is necessarily a primary consideration and some equipment such as geological sieves and gasoline-powered pumps can be quite costly. An effective, small-scale macrobotanical processing program can usually be implemented for under two hundred dollars. It is therefore unlikely that cost will be a significant barrier to undertaking macrobotanical recovery at a basic level, even during test seasons or salvage operations. Funding for laboratory work, analysis, and storage of samples should also be planned at the outset of research. Depending on the characteristics of a site—in particular, the preservation of plant remains—channeling more funds toward equipment can improve final results by permitting processing on an increased scale. At the site of Acquachiara in Italy, this has been achieved by operating two flotation tanks simultaneously, doubling the number of samples that can be processed during the workday (Shelton 2009).

Time is another pertinent concern, both in terms of the length of a single field season and with regard to long-term research plans. A multiyear project with good field research and storage facilities should invest in a durable multiyear recovery system, with features that permit flexibility (in terms of water flow, transportability, or technique) in the event that field conditions change or new sites or phases are incorporated into the research program. Projects of shorter duration or exploratory ventures may set up a small-scale system, employing bucket-flotation or a hand-pump tank, until they have a better understanding of preservation and soil conditions.

Other practical considerations stem from the location of the archaeological site and proximity to available resources (e.g., water, electricity, repair facilities, and equipment security). In order to facilitate a dialogue between the project members and the paleoethnobotanical team, it is most beneficial to locate recovery operations near the excavation (Peterson 2009). The more remote

the site, the less likely that convenient transportation of a large, heavy flotation tank will be possible. However, bringing sediment samples back to a
field lab for processing is unlikely to be an appealing option either. In such
a situation, the project should opt for a lightweight system that can be easily transported to the site on a regular basis. The added benefit of this decision is that lighter, simpler systems have less need of specialized maintenance,
including the repair of an electric pump or generator repair, or blacksmith
labor. If resources and location are not an issue, the added processing capacity of heavier-weight systems such as a SMAP-style tank or the Flote-Tech
machine may be a wise choice.

From an archaeological perspective, the nature of the soil matrix and botanical preservation conditions are paramount. These factors may not be known
during initial planning phases and paleoethnobotanists may have to modify
their recovery methods over time. Soils with high clay content present a common problem in sample processing and a high-flow system may be desirable if
plant remains are deemed durable enough to withstand processing. However,
the presence of clay may necessitate a wider-aperture mesh size and subsequently lead to the loss of small remains (Pearsall 2000). Siltier soils break
down more easily and a comparable number of samples can be processed in
less time (Beresford-Jones et al. 2010). Designing a time-effective program is
critical to avoiding a backlog of unprocessed samples, which may have to be
stored until the next field season. Long-term storage may result in damage to
specimens, since off-season facilities often have poor environmental control
and samples or paper tags may become moldy. In some unfortunate scenarios,
samples may be discarded if their provenience is unclear. High-quality storage
space tends to be at a premium and is frequently reserved for artifacts that
appear more fragile than soil.

The fragility of macrobotanical remains is another quality that may not be
known in advance of excavation, though an initial assessment may be possible (e.g., potential methods of preservation, including waterlogging or desiccation). On many sites, remains are preserved in multiple ways depending
on how and where plant materials were incorporated into the archaeological
record. If such is the case, a capacity for multiple processing techniques is
advisable (Hageman and Goldstein 2009). For example, a project that encounters both waterlogged and dry levels might consider a system that can perform
both standard flotation as well as careful wet screening. Every attempt should
be made to avoid altering the state in which plant materials were initially
recovered: ideally, dry remains should stay dry (Jarman, Legge, and Charles
1972; Lopinot 1984; Wagner 1988). Plant remains that are unusually delicate or

fragmentary, whatever their mode of preservation, should be processed with corresponding care despite the fact that this will decrease the total volume of soil investigated. Such remains survive best in systems where the operator has the greatest control and can slow, stop, or start the procedure according to the nature of observed materials, as in the case of the hand-pump flotation tank.

Many of these decisions should be considered in advance to facilitate the timely acquisition of equipment. In some settings, flotation systems can be reserved for use from a research institution (e.g., the Flote-Tech machine at the American Center for Oriental Research in Amman, Jordan). Borrowed tanks can save time and expense and do not need to be stored by the project in the off-season. However, these systems may not be available when needed, may be in need of service, and may not be ideally suited to specific site conditions. Assuming that an archaeological project has available storage facilities, construction of a new system is preferable because it eliminates issues that may slow or halt recovery operations. If a new system is constructed, it may be built beforehand and transported in pieces (both authors frequently transport flotation equipment to international destinations), built by a local blacksmith, or assembled on-site by the specialist. We have found it is best to bring smaller critical items (i.e., high-quality bags, Tyvek® or similar tags, and durable fine mesh) from one's home institution. If essential items are locally unavailable, recovery efforts may quickly become compromised.

TRAINING OF PERSONNEL

The accuracy and reliability of any macrobotanical recovery program is dependent on the project members who collect samples and the individuals who carry out each step of the recovery process. As Fuller (2007a:224) states, "It is essential that all excavators who move, disturb and destroy the sedimentary records of the past have a basic working knowledge of the potential of these datasets." As such, it is the responsibility of both the paleoethnobotanical specialist and the field director to ensure that all personnel are properly trained, aware of appropriate procedures and protocols, and fully invested in recovering and preserving material from the site.

Training ideally begins in the university classroom at the undergraduate level with an overview of archaeological science techniques. Before entering the field, students gain a basic grasp of what paleoethnobotany is and how the analysis of plant remains contributes to a greater understanding of the archaeological record. They become familiar with the basic concepts of macrobotanical recovery (e.g., the principles of flotation), as well as its potential contributions and limitations. At Boston University, an archaeological science course taught to upper-level undergraduates includes a laboratory session focused on paleo-ethnobotanical analysis. Both authors (C. White and C. Shelton) have taught these labs over the years and found that hands-on demonstrations greatly aid in teaching students proper field methods. However, the most important training often occurs outside the classroom setting.

During field school excavations, students ideally learn how and when to sample for plant remains and also spend time learning how to process samples. It is important for specialists to include these students as part of an archaeological education and to help them clarify sampling and recovery methodologies. We have found that an introductory lecture to paleoethnobotany in the field is crucial and that a site-specific written guide/handout is helpful for students to consult. Often there is a positive change in students' record keeping and sampling numbers once they have paid a visit to the project flotation tank. By actually participating in the recovery of carbonized plant remains from their samples, it encourages them to collect more samples in the field and to be vigilant with sample recording.

Paleoethnobotanists must always be careful to supervise students and other project members during recovery efforts. The best results are achieved when the person responsible for analysis and publication is also the person processing the samples, primarily because this individual is the most invested in achieving good results. If this is not feasible, the next-best scenario is a macrobotanical recovery program supervised by someone trained by the specialist (and for whom this is their primary responsibility on the excavation). Careful attention to the many small steps that produce reliable samples is essential. This includes accurate measuring and record keeping, gentle handling of the samples and processed residues, thorough cleaning and maintenance of equipment, and daily interaction with excavation personnel to ensure samples are collected and recorded from all appropriate contexts.

INITIAL SORTING

During excavation, a space designated as the field laboratory is necessary for both sample storage and post-processing activities. Ideally, the field lab will have facilities for the initial examination of light fraction samples (e.g., a microscope or digital microscope attached to a computer) and the space for sorting material recovered in the heavy fraction residue. This sorting is often treated as an activity that can be carried out by untrained individuals, but the careful classification of artifacts and identification of plant material in the heavy fraction requires attention to detail and appropriate training (Bezic 2009). If sorting cannot be completed by the specialist alone, a frequent situation, project members should be carefully taught to identify visible seeds and charcoal. The specialist is therefore expected to have previously sorted several samples from the site and to convey information about types of plant remains and their distinguishing characteristics to project members. As heavy fraction residues may also contain artifacts such as lithics, pottery sherds, and animal bone, individuals sorting through samples should also be able to recognize and collect these remains.

The field lab provides space for many additional activities and excavators and trench supervisors often work there in the evenings. This is a good time to double-check sample information (e.g., tags, logs) and to discuss with project members any inconsistencies or questions. Paleoethnobotanists may also find it useful to set up an area in the lab for a plant press. Local plant species can be collected, photographed, and pressed to create a modern reference collection. When the field laboratory is shut down at the end of the season, modern specimens as well as archaeological material must be carefully packed for transport to the specialist's home institution. Samples in plastic bags should be packed into hard plastic containers for additional protection in shipping. If samples will cross international borders, copies of required permits and documentation should be placed in each individual box. If traveling with samples in one's luggage, paleoethnobotanists should be aware of country-specific customs declaration policies and be ready to explain the archaeological origins of their samples. An official letter from the director of the excavation project is often helpful in these situations.

COMPARABILITY OF RECOVERY METHODS

Many goals of paleoethnobotanical research extend beyond the individual site to include regional paleoenvironmental reconstructions, land-use patterns, and geographic and diachronic variations in human diet. As such, methods of recovery and subsequent analysis should be as comparable as possible between projects. Within a site, data comparability provides the foundation for interpretations of site function, spatial differentiation, and formation processes. Difficulties often arise when incorporating multiple data sets into a single study, particularly those where recording and recovery methods differ (Hunt et al. 2008; Wright 2005).

Fortunately, broad agreement has developed internationally over the past thirty-five years with regard to certain minimum standards, which is encouraging for potential intersite comparisons (Watson 2009). A recent investigation of Iron Age and Roman period plant remains in Italy (Shelton 2009) found that all post-1995 macrobotanical recovery efforts used flotation methods (Arobba et al. 2003; Barker 1995; Bökönyi et al. 1993; Carter 2006; Castiglioni 2005; Ciaraldi 2000; Costantini and Giorgi 2001; Heiss et al. 2005; Monckton 2002; Motta 2002; Sadori and Susanna 2005). Mesh sizes between sites varied minimally and a sub-500-micrometer measure was typical for recovering light fractions. Older studies were characteristically less systematic. Reported recovery methods were based primarily on collecting observed remains during excavation and were not described in detail (Helbaek 1953, 1967; Hjelmqvist 1977). Assuming a level of methodological compatibility in recent reports, comparisons are strongest within similar environments, between local sites, and among deposits with similar forms of botanical preservation. Whenever possible, reports included in a regional analysis should disclose these types of characteristics.

Clarity and specificity in reporting recovery methods are vital to any kind of regional synthesis: the absence of this information makes it impossible to judge the reliability of a data set or the potential absence or overrepresentation of different sets of remains. All archaeobotanical reports should include a detailed description of the recovery system, mesh sizes used, recovery tests performed, and inconsistencies due to varying methods or changes in field personnel (which is not uncommon in multiyear projects; Hosch and Zibulski 2003). All too often reports do not provide even a basic description of the methods and techniques used to recover plant remains.

Clearly, certain recovery methods create biases for the recovery of certain types of materials and against the recovery of others (Wagner 1988:31). A dual-recovery program of Maya sites in Belize highlights this issue (Hageman and Goldstein 2009). Despite using the same minimum sieve size (.425 mm) for both methods, flotation efforts recovered a greater quantity of seeds than dry screening, although dry screening revealed a greater diversity of seeds and larger quantities of wood charcoal (Hageman and Goldstein 2009:2851). Of the thirty-three plant taxa recovered, sixteen were unique to one method or the other, suggesting that a dual-recovery program greatly increased the number of collected and identified remains.

In this case and many others, difficulty with comparability of data sets should not deter paleoethnobotanists from trying new techniques and discovering which methods work best at a given site. Hageman and Goldstein recommend an evolving recovery strategy that takes into account the concerns of both specialists and project directors (Hageman and Goldstein 2009:2849).

At the site of el-Hemmeh in Jordan, one author's (C. White) macrobotanical recovery efforts have included the use of a large SMAP-style tank, a Flote-Tech machine, and a hand-pump flotation system (Makarewicz et al. 2006; Shelton and White 2010). Here a small tank and hand-pump have offered the best option for retrieving fragile carbonized remains. However, without the trial and error of testing various recovery methods, we would not have designed the hand-pump technique and would have lost many fragile plant remains in the process. It is therefore better to try different methods and see what works best than to standardize a recovery system that does not effectively recover plant material at a given site.

In order to mitigate these discrepancies, we suggest three basic standards. The first is the use of a standardized minimum screen size (e.g., 250-micron mesh) in the processing of samples from a site. This was learned, rather embarrassingly, after purchasing locally made mesh and finding that it expanded when submerged in the flotation tank (see warning by Wagner 1988). Standardization can also be difficult to obtain if varying sediment types are present at a site, as silty soils may pass easily through a sieve that clay soils do not (Lopinot and Brussell 1982; Wright 2005). As a general rule, the size of a heavy fraction screen should be large enough to let silt and sand pass through but small enough to capture the smallest seeds possible. This too requires some trial and error.

Our second suggestion is to standardize sample sizes as far as is practicable to increase comparability between individual samples and whole assemblages from different sites. For example, 59.6 percent of surveyed paleoethnobotanists request sediment samples of 10 L or larger from excavations (Miller 2010a). However, sample size standardization is not always feasible: a small feature may not contain a full 10 L of sediment. When absolute counts are included in publications (Jamieson and Sayre 2010; Schmidt 2009:311; Verhoevan 2010), variations in sample size must also be stated. Some of the most useful relative measurements to include are the weights of recovered plant remains per liter of processed soil (g/L) and the number of identified specimens (NISP) per liter of processed soil (see Marston, chapter 9, this volume). These relative measurements provide a very useful means of comparing recovery rates between contexts and illuminate patterns in seed versus charcoal densities, for example.

In order to identify the biases of varying recovery techniques, as well as discrepancies created by different operators, our final suggestion is that all projects test the recovery rates of their system(s) and publish these results. Testing can easily be carried out by adding a known number of exotic seeds to sediment samples (Pearsall 2000; Pendleton 1983; Wagner 1982, 1988). In the case of flotation, batches of 50 or 100 charred foreign seeds can be mixed in with the sediment prior to entering the tank. It is best if the tank operator is unaware which samples contain the test seeds and can therefore avoid preferential treatment (Wagner 1982). Recovery tests carried out by C. White on the hand-pump system at the site of Beisamoun in Israel were very straightforward and quite useful. One hundred quinoa seeds, charred in aluminum foil at 500°F for forty-five minutes, were added to ten samples and then recovered in the sample's light fraction (Shelton and White 2010). Pendleton (1983) has proposed the use of large (> 1 mm) seeds that are known for their lack of natural buoyancy to test the heavy fraction recovery of nonfloating plant remains. If seeds are added *after* samples have been processed, this may prove to be a useful means of testing the efficiency of personnel sorting heavy fraction samples in the field lab.

CONCLUSION

Paleoethnobotanists are specialists, but most are "archaeologists first" (Fuller 2007a:218). These individuals are trained archaeologists but have simultaneously cultivated a specialized knowledge of paleoethnobotanical sampling, recovery, and analysis. Increasingly, paleoethnobotanists are taking on roles as project directors and field supervisors. In addition to developing advanced sampling and recovery programs, field opportunities allow paleoethnobotanists to educate excavators and other project members. This is vital at a time when archaeobotanical research is increasing but the number of paleoethnobotanists is not (Fuller 2007a:218). Since project personnel may be asked to develop and carry out recovery efforts without the expertise of an onsite paleoethnobotanist, their awareness of current methods and protocols is critical.

This chapter discussed a variety of methods for recovering carbonized, desiccated, and waterlogged plant remains. Many factors must be taken into account before implementing a macrobotanical recovery program. Although standardization and comparability between projects is important, each site presents a unique set of conditions and may require time and flexibility to determine which recovery techniques are most successful. Ultimately, paleoethnobotanical publications should provide detailed descriptions of recovery methods and acknowledge potential attendant biases. The recognition of these weaknesses and the motivation to tackle these issues has led to the development of new recovery techniques in paleoethnobotany.

ACKNOWLEDGMENTS

We thank the editors, Mac Marston, Jade d'Alpoim Guedes, and Christina Warinner, for this opportunity. We also thank the many patient project directors who allowed us to test out new recovery techniques and equipment in the field. These include Cheryl Makarewicz, University of Kiel; Fanny Bocquentin, Centre National de la Recherche Scientifique; Hamoudi Khalaily, Israel Antiquities Authority; Susan Kane, Oberlin College; Edward Bispham, Oxford University; Joe Rife, Vanderbilt University; and Nathan Arrington, Princeton University. Photo permission from Cathy D'Andrea, Nathan Arrington, and Elizabeth Stone are much appreciated. Thanks also go to those who gave us our start at the flotation tank, including William Green, Beloit College; Eleni Asouti, University of Liverpool; and Susan Allen, University of Cincinnati. We also greatly appreciate the many students and project members who have helped us with our recovery efforts.

7

*Laboratory Analysis
and Identification of
Plant Macroremains*

Gayle Fritz and
Mark Nesbitt

The laboratory handling and identification of archaeological plant remains is the crucial step between
their recovery in the field (chapters 2–6, this volume)
and their interpretation (chapters 9–19, this volume).
Accurate identification of plant remains is fundamental to the sophisticated interpretation of foraging and
agricultural systems. Inaccurate identification can, at
worst, lead to serious errors in the identification of
early domesticates or plant introductions, as discussed
by Harlan and de Wet (1973) in a classic article that is
still relevant today. Even in less extreme cases, poor-
quality identifications obscure changing patterns of
plant use and present a major challenge to the compilation of regional or supraregional syntheses.

Given the importance of plant identification, and a
history of high-quality archaeobotany that extends as
far back as 150 years in some regions, it might seem
surprising that this essential skill is still highly subjective, based on nuances of shape and texture that are
hard to describe, taught by apprenticeship (with varying degrees of support) in an established archaeobotanical laboratory, and then often practiced in isolation.
The good news is that work in the last 20 years has
addressed these issues, with digital media taking a central role in providing new tools, and enabling easier distribution and exchange of information (Warinner and
d'Alpoim Guedes, chapter 8, this volume).

Our aims in this chapter are threefold. First, we set
out core practice for the handling and identification

DOI: 10.5876/9781607323167.c007

of (mainly) charred plant macroremains in a manner that will be both useful for the beginner and of interest as a baseline for comparison for experienced practitioners. In the available space we can only seek to complement existing handbooks for the New World (Pearsall 2000) and Old World (Jacomet and Kreuz 1999). Second, we highlight examples of good practice in the development and application of identification techniques. Although many of these are drawn from Europe, the Near East, and North America, reflecting the concentration of archaeobotanists working in those regions, there are lessons applicable to other parts of the world. Third, we offer something of a personal perspective on how identification practice has changed and how we would like to see it develop. As becomes clear in the chapter, there is still much to do, and exciting prospects lie ahead for new researchers.

TAPHONOMY AND PRESERVATION

In most cases only a small proportion of plant parts become incorporated into the sediments of an archaeological site and survive until the present day (Gallagher, chapter 2, this volume). Three agents are at work. Humans select which plants and which parts of plants are brought onto archaeological sites. It is often the case that only the edible portion of the plant, typically a propagule such as a seed or fruit, or storage organ such as a root, is harvested and brought back to the site. Other plant parts will only be brought on site if they need processing to separate them from the useful part, or if the other plant parts are also useful. A good example of both is cereals such as rice and wheat, for which the grains are most efficiently stripped from the culms (stems) by bulk processing at or near the settlement, and whose straw is of value as animal feed, fuel, or as a material for craft production or construction (van der Veen 1999a).

The second agent is that of natural and anthropogenic decay. In tropical and temperate climates plant material that is not consumed by humans will be eaten by animals such as rodents or insects or by fungi and other microorganisms. In arid areas such as the Nile valley, American Southwest, and parts of the Andes where these processes are slowed, the quantity of material surviving can be so great as to be overwhelming (van der Veen 2007a). At the same time, the preservation is so good, extending even to color, that conventional techniques of botanical identification can be applied. A recently published example of such sites (with exemplary color illustrations) is the Roman and Islamic ports at Quseir al-Qadim, Egypt, with fresh-looking material such as fragments of sugar cane, ginger rhizome, and banana skin (van der Veen 2011). Comparable preservation can occur with frozen plant remains, as in the case of the Alpine Iceman (Bortenschlager and Oeggl 2000). Dry conditions can also occur in wet countries, for example the medieval sheaves of wheat and accompanying weeds found deep inside thatched roofs in northern Europe (de Moulins 2007). Waterlogged, thus anaerobic, conditions can also lead to the preservation of a remarkably wide range of material. The weaker cells, such as starchy endosperm, however, usually decay, leaving flattened plant remains that look very different from fresh material. Cell patterns in wet preserved material are often much more obvious and useful for identification, but will require comparison to reference material treated with acid to replicate the effects of waterlogging. Waterlogged plant remains are locally abundant in northern Europe and in other areas with waterlogged landscapes such as Florida in the southeast United States, but we do not have space to cover their specialized processing and identification in this chapter (Birks 2007).

The most widespread form of preservation is through charring by fire. Even waterlogged and arid plant assemblages contain significant amounts of charred material. Charring converts plant materials to more or less inert carbon, while preserving its shape. Fire is also destructive: the lighter parts of plants, such as leaves and the bracts surrounding the grain, are likely to burn to ash (Boardman and Jones 1990) and not be recovered (except in the form of phytoliths: see Pearsall, chapter 4, this volume). Both the quantity and quality of plant remains vary enormously by site, in relation to what are still poorly understood factors of burning and site deposition. Because charring often occurs in domestic hearths and ovens in which wood is the main fuel, wood charcoal often forms a significant part of the assemblage.

Archaeological recovery is the third and final destructive agency to act before plant remains reach the laboratory. Although water flotation is proven as the most effective way to retrieve charred plant remains dispersed in archaeological matrix, it is inevitably destructive of fragile material such as light chaff and oil-rich seeds (Märkle and Rosch 2008; White and Shelton, chapter 6, this volume; Gallagher, chapter 2, this volume).

In summary, a series of processes intervenes between a human encounter with plants and the deposition of plant material in archaeological matrix. In most parts of the world, this leads to charred wood and seeds (broadly defined here to include other plant parts such as parenchyma) as being the main form of plant macroremains retrieved and studied by archaeobotanists.

TAXONOMIC GOALS AND LIMITATIONS

In an ideal situation, we could identify all or most archaeological plant remains to the level of species or even subspecies or variety, and we could distinguish clearly between domesticated plants and their wild ancestors or weedy relatives. Generations of archaeobotanists have, in fact, devoted considerable research efforts to recognizing anatomical features and other morphological characteristics that enable key species or subspecies-level identifications to be made, including those that signal domestication. Still, real-world assemblages, whether they consist of charred remains recovered by flotation, or waterlogged or desiccated remains, usually include many specimens that are too fragmentary, too eroded, or too obscured by sediment to be recognized beyond a more inclusive level, whether it be genus, family, or even a broad category such as "nutshell" or "parenchyma." In many cases, too, seeds of different taxa may be so similar in appearance that identification will never be possible beyond genus level, regardless of the quality of preservation.

James Massey, former professor of botany and a plant taxonomy instructor at the University of North Carolina at Chapel Hill, referred to paleoethnobotanists as "wizards" given our apparent ability to recognize a species by examining a barely visible speck of charred matter, whereas botanists usually work with at least a herbarium-sized plant specimen containing leaves, stems, roots, and well-preserved flowers, fruits, or seeds. Of course, we are not wizards, and one of the skills gained by experience is knowing when a specimen is unidentifiable and when it is best to categorize it broadly rather than specifically. Archaeobotanical analysis is guided by research questions and goals, as well as by constraints imposed by preservation. In North America, for example, it may make little difference whether or not one distinguishes between the six or more species of wild grapes (*Vitis* spp.) native to a given region, whereas in Southwest Asia and Europe, the presence of domesticated grapes (*Vitis vinifera*) as opposed to wild grapes has significant cultural and economic consequences. The amount of time and attention spent on species-level identification, therefore, varies according to interpretive yield. More time is usually given to unknown seeds that occur in the greatest quantity or ubiquity.

BASIC SORTING PROCEDURES AND EQUIPMENT

Analysis of plant remains recovered by flotation or a comparable, fine-mesh recovery method entails examining like-sized particles under low-power magnification and recording counts, weights, and often measurements or other attributes of items according to taxonomic grouping. The procedures described here are based on those used in the archaeobotany laboratory at Washington University in St. Louis, but broadly similar procedures are used in most laboratories. Figure 7.1 is an example of an analysis form used at Washington University, and table 7.1 is a list of standard laboratory tools.

SELECTION OF SAMPLES

Where relatively few seeds have been recovered, all samples known to be from secure stratigraphy can be analyzed. However bulk flotation of richer sites, such as those in the Near East, may produce hundreds of samples varying from a few seeds to thousands. Here samples may be chosen on the basis that they are likely to contain at least 500 seeds, as recommended on the basis of statistics (van der Veen and Fieller 1982). Smaller samples might be included because they fill gaps in time periods, or because they come from archaeological contexts of special interest. Any sample might be excluded if its dating is not secure, although AMS radiocarbon dating does allow the dating of individual items of key chronological concern.

Sorting Procedures

If a sample consists of both light and heavy fractions (see White and Shelton, chapter 6, this volume), each is usually analyzed separately, although the numerical data can be combined when reported. Each sample (or each light and heavy fraction) is weighed to the nearest 0.01 g and the contents passed through a series of nested geological sieves, resulting in "splits" of similar-sized objects. It is standard in North America to use a 2.0-mm sieve because this is the cutoff point for complete sorting of larger particles versus removal of selected smaller items that are difficult to identify when smaller than 2.0 mm. When charred items larger than 2.0 mm are very rare, a smaller mesh size can be the cutoff point; however many plant types lose recognizable features with fragmentation below 2.0 mm. All ancient seeds and recognizable seed fragments are pulled from the smaller fractions, regardless of size, along with distinctive plant parts such as gourd rind, maize kernel, and acorn shell fragments, which are too fragile to be well represented in the > 2.0 mm splits. In Europe, where a mesh smaller than 2.0 mm is likely to let through large numbers of cereal grain fragments, the contents of the 1.0 mm sieve may be fully sorted, albeit after subsampling in the case of large samples.

Wood and nutshell might be abundant enough to warrant using as many as four or five splits with mesh sizes larger than 2.0 mm, but samples from sites where charred plant remains are rare or consist mainly of seeds and other

Mound House, IL
Macrobotanical Remains, Center for American Archeology, Paleoethnobotany Workshop

SQ/Fea	Level		Status (Bag#)		Initial Wt. (g)	
					SIEVE SIZE	Wt.(g)
Sample Type (LF or HF)	Analyst	Date		# 4	4.75 mm	_____
				# 5	4.00 mm	_____
				# 6	3.35 mm	_____
Vol. (Soil floated)				# 7	2.80 mm	_____
				#10	2.00 mm	_____
				#12	1.70 mm	_____
LARGER THAN 2.0 mm:	Count	Wt. (g)		#14	1.40 mm	_____
Wood				#18	1.00 mm	_____
Bark	_____	_____			0.50 mm	_____
				#40.	0.425 mm	_____
Stem	_____	_____		#45	0.355 mm	_____
Thick hickory nutshell	_____	_____			Pan	_____
Thin hickory nutshell	_____	_____				
Walnut shell	_____	_____		SMALLER THAN 2.0 mm:		
Juglandaceae nutshell	_____	_____				
Nutmeat	_____	_____			Count	Wt. (g)
Hazelnut	_____	_____		Thin Hickory to 1.4	_____	_____
Acorn shell	_____	_____		Acorn to 1.4	_____	_____
Cucurbita rind	_____	_____		Cucurbita rind	_____	_____
Lagenaria rind	_____	_____		Lagenaria rind	_____	_____
Maize: _____	_____	_____		Maize: _____	_____	_____
	_____	_____			_____	_____
SEEDS, > 2.0 mm: Total Wt.		_____		SEEDS, < 2.0 mm:		Count only
_____	_____	_____		_____	_____	_____
_____	_____	_____		_____	_____	_____
_____	_____	_____		_____	_____	_____
_____	_____	_____		_____	_____	_____
_____	_____	_____		_____	_____	_____
Unknown _____	_____	_____		_____	_____	_____
Other (describe):	_____	_____		_____	_____	_____
_____	_____	_____		_____	_____	_____
Bone	_____	_____		_____	_____	_____
Faunal Globule	_____	_____		_____	_____	_____
Snail	_____	_____		_____	_____	_____
Other Shell	_____	_____		_____	_____	_____
Stone/Soil	_____	_____		_____	_____	_____
Sherd	_____	_____		_____	_____	_____
Uncarbonized (wt. only)		_____				

COMMENTS:

Residue Weight: _____
(0.7 – 2.0 mm)

FIGURE 7.1. *Sample analysis sheet for recording data from a flotation sample.*

relatively small items may require no sieves greater than 2.0 mm. Smaller-sized sieves may include 1.0 and .5 mm (or in Europe, often .3 or .25 mm) only, but intermediate splits might be needed, depending on sample size and composition. Once a sample has been passed through the graduated sieves, the largest items are examined under low-power magnification and grouped

TABLE 7.1. List of basic equipment needed for analysis of macroremains in a paleoethnobotany laboratory

Function	Equipment
Microscopy	Microscope(s); light source for each microscope
Sample sorting	Standard USDA (or other) geological sieves; sorting pans or dishes; pouring spout; riffle-type sample splitter
Sample weighing	Weighing scales; analytic balance (optional)
Sample handling	Dissecting needles; featherlight forceps; spatulas; fine paintbrushes
Sample storage	Gelatin capsules and/or plastic centrifuge tubes; glass vials; 2-mL-density plastic bags; metal tins or glass bottles; acid-free paper for tags
Reference materials	Reference manuals; comparative reference collection

according to taxon or plant type, followed by examining the contents of progressively smaller splits. All items greater than 2.0 mm are normally counted and weighed to the nearest 0.01 g, although we do not always count wood when there is a great deal of it. If a taxon such as walnut shell is found only in a < 2 mm split but is nonetheless clearly identifiable, it can be pulled and given a count of 1 and weight of .01 g in order in include it in ubiquity frequencies (% of samples in which a plant type occurs; Marston, chapter 9, this volume). For items greater than 2.0 mm, quantified categories include charred seeds, sorted as close to species-level as advisable, and fragile but clearly recognizable plant parts such as gourd rind or other distinctive cultigens, as discussed above. In North America, seeds less than 2.0 mm are not weighed, but only counted, but in Europe the 1mm fraction may also be fully counted and weighed.

Uncharred seeds are not pulled from assemblages when they are all modern contaminants, and learning to tell the difference between dark-colored modern seeds and their charred counterparts is one of the challenges of archaeobotanical training. But when samples come from unusual contexts in which ancient seeds and other remains survived without charring, a different strategy is obviously necessary. Samples from Cahokia's sub-Mound 51, for example, consist of 1,000-year-old feasting remains that were purposefully, rapidly, and deeply buried under mound fill after the structures in which feasting activities had taken place were partially burned, leaving both charred and uncharred wood and thousands of seeds in both physical states (Pauketat et al. 2002). In these situations, analysis sheets and published tables should be modified to include separate columns for charred and uncharred materials. Reporting the different frequencies of both uncharred and charred ancient seeds makes it possible to compare results to assemblages in which only the latter are preserved (cf. for ancient Egypt Smith 2003).

Preferences for sorting tools and techniques vary, with choices guided in part by the available microscope base and working area. Plastic dishes or trays are problematic due to static that causes seeds to undergo damage or loss, so glass Petri dishes are used under the microscope. Round metal baking tins, 8–10 cm in diameter, work well for sorting large fractions, but they should not be too dark or so shiny that they blind the analyst with reflected light. Dissecting needles work well for moving items around in the sorting dish, especially if the tip is bent to form an obtuse angle. Some analysts prefer fine paintbrushes for sorting, and these work very well for picking up seeds to transfer them to capsules, tubes, or other containers for curation. Entomologists' forceps serve well to pick up seeds, but must be of the soft ("featherweight") type to avoid breakage. During routine sorting at 10× to 15× magnification, some analysts move fragments across the field of vision, separating them into taxonomic groups. Others recommend dividing the remains according to a grid system and examining them systematically by square (Bohrer and Adams 1977). A small dish filled with clean sand is an essential tool for detailed examination, allowing seeds to be positioned and examined at a variety of angles.

The end result is a set of tins, vials, boxes, tubes, and/or capsules divided into the respective groups of completely sorted (> 2 mm or > 1 mm) plant types, along with all seeds and other "special" remains pulled from the smaller splits, and the resulting residual fragments (< 2 mm or < 1 mm). All containers must be clearly labeled with site name or number and provenience information, and with sample data including plant type, split size, and light versus heavy fraction status. Acid-free paper can be cut into little tags to fit inside capsules or tubes if the containers themselves are too small to label. Careful attention should be given to labeling and storage so that seeds can be restudied. It is also important that the original records of laboratory subsampling and scoring are clear and are retained.

Subsampling

Samples too large to analyze in their entirety can be subsampled by determining the weight of the whole sample and then pouring it through a riffle box sample splitter, using a back-and-forth motion along the length of a riffle box while pouring to divide the sample in half. The procedure is repeated with one-half of the sample in order to acquire a 25 percent subsample. It should not be assumed, however, that all taxa—especially rare ones—will be represented in each split, or that common taxa will be equally divided into the final groups (see Pearsall 2000:112–13, for uneven results of one sorting test).

Major Pieces of Laboratory Equipment

The most expensive laboratory requirement is a good binocular stereomicroscope with continuous zoom magnification beginning at either 7× or 10× at the low end, going up to at least 30× and ideally higher. One eyepiece should be equipped with an optical micrometer, and a microscope model with a phototube for camera mounting is highly recommended. Desirable extras include a camera lucida, for drawing seeds, and a teaching tube with a second pair of eyepieces, so that two people can look at material together. Student-quality or field-quality microscopes are available with built-in, direct, halogen lighting from above (usually combined with florescent or halogen lighting from below in order to view transparent material through a glass stage), but these cause more eye fatigue than dual-armed fiber-optic light sources, which also allow for angle adjustment. Fiber-optic lighting is also cool and will not damage seeds by heat. Higher-power (40× to at least 400×), phase-contrast, compound microscopes are necessary for analysis of microbotanical remains. A metallurgical ("epi-illuminating") microscope with incident and transmitted light is needed for wood analysis.

A small electronic digital balance that weighs to at least the closest 0.01 g is a required piece of equipment, and archaeobotanists who record the weights of individual seeds or low numbers of small seeds need to invest in a more sensitive, enclosed analytic balance. A set of standard, graduated geologic sieves is the last significant expenditure. We recommend buying high quality, heavy-gauge, brass or steel sieves, eight inches (200 mm) in diameter, with stainless steel mesh, and avoiding smaller, cheaper, plastic versions. Laboratory sieves should never be used for fieldwork or be loaned to colleagues working with sediments that might clog up the finer holes.

IDENTIFICATION TOOLS

Charred plant material loses its original color (an important character in many seed guides written for agricultural or botanical use) but retains its shape and sculpturing, with minor changes (Braadbaart and Bergen 2005; Braadbaart and Wright 2007; Märkle and Rosch 2008), and can therefore be identified by comparison to modern reference material. More subtle characters, such as surface cell patterns, are lost in many cases. Charring, however, can sometimes make them more visible by removing the waxy cuticle.

The basis of archaeobotanical identification is the comparison of unknown to known material, whether in a photograph or as a plant specimen. Familiarity with seed reference material is fundamental to both the learning process and to checking identifications in routine work. At the same time, having a mentor to personally tutor students plays a major role in learning seed identification, both in passing on short cuts for identification of common or difficult types, and in developing confidence.

Books and Manuals

The production of a seed atlas is a major undertaking, both in terms of gathering a comprehensive suite of reference material to be illustrated, and in drawing or photographing it. Traditional, film-based, photography of modern and ancient seed is challenging because of the difficulty in avoiding shadows and in maintaining sufficient depth of focus. As an illustration of the work involved, the pioneer archaeobotanist Hans Helbaek took superb photographs of charred seeds in the mid-twentieth century and personally oversaw the production of lithographic printing plates in Copenhagen to ensure the quality of the published result.

The arrival of digital photography (Warinner and d'Alpoim Guedes, chapter 8, this volume) still allows the taking of bad pictures. Nonetheless, digital photography, when combined with skillfully used software, has enabled the production of seed atlases on a larger scale and of higher quality than could have been imagined twenty years ago. So far the Old World has been the beneficiary of the superb photographic seed atlases produced by René Cappers and collaborators in Groningen (Cappers et al. 2006; Cappers et al. 2009; Neef et al. 2012). Drawings (Bojňanský and Fargašová 2007; Nesbitt 2006) and scanning electron microscopy (SEM) (Knapp 2006, 2010; Schoch et al. 1988) continue to be important, with drawings able to show aspects of morphology that would be obscure in photography, and SEM imagery the medium of choice to record complex surface patterning. Fewer seed manuals have been produced recently in North America, where digital photography has tended to be presented on websites (table 7.2).

Most archaeobotanists work closely with several seed atlases in the lab. Much useful information on specific taxa, particularly crops, also exists in the identification sections of published archaeobotanical reports. Some of this work, for example the exemplary publications of Willem van Zeist relating to the Near East (e.g. van Zeist and Bakker-Heeres 1982), is well-known. However, as the volume of publications increases, and existing bibliographies

TABLE 7.2. Standard seed identification references[a]

PRINTED BOOKS AND MANUALS

	Title	Year	Authors
Worldwide	Digital Atlas of Economic Plants, 3 vols.	2009	R. T. Cappers, R. Neef, and R. M. Bekker
	Fruits and Seeds of Genera in the Subfamily Mimosoideae (Fabaceae)	1984	C. R. Gunn
	The Seeds of Dicotyledons, 3 vols.	1976	E. J. H. Corner
New World	Seeds of Amazonian Plants	2010	F. Cornejo and J. Janovec
	Weed Seeds of the Great Plains: A Handbook for Identification	1996	L. W. Davis
	An Illustrated Taxonomy Manual of Weed Seeds	1970	R. J. Delorit
	Seeds of the Continental United States: Legumes (Fabaceae)	1986	R. J. Delroit and C. R. Gunn
	Colorado Weed Seeds	1921	G. E. Eggington
	Identification of Disseminules Listed in the Federal Noxious Weed Act	1988	C. R. Gunn and C. A. Ritchie
	Bobwhite Quail Food Habits in the Southeastern United States with a Seed Key to Important Foods	1976	J. L. Landers and A. S. Johnson
	Seeds of Central America and Southern Mexico: The Economic Species	2005	D. L. Lentz and R. Dickau
	Seed Identification Manual[b]	1961	A. C. Martin and W. D. Barkley
	Seeds and Fruits of Plants of Eastern Canada and Northeastern United States	1977	F. H. Montgomery
	Identification of Crop and Weed Seeds	1963	A. F. Musil
	Arizona Ranch, Farm and Garden Weeds	1958	K. F. Parker

continued on next page

TABLE 7.2—*continued*

PRINTED BOOKS AND MANUALS

	Title	Year	Authors
	Seeds of Woody Plants in the United States	1974	C. S. Shopmeyer
	Woody-plant Seed Manual[c]	1948	US Forest Service
Old World	Atlas of Seeds and Small Fruits of Northwest-European Plant Species, Part 4: Resedaceae–Umbelliferae	1994	A-L. Anderberg
	Atlas of Seeds and Small Fruits of Northwest-European Plant Species, Part 2: Cypreraceae	1969	G. Berggren
	Atlas of Seeds and Small Fruits of Northwest-European Plant Species, Part 3: Salicaceae–Cruciferae	1981	G. Berggren
	Zadenatlas der Nederlandsche Flora (Seed Atlas of Netherlands Flora)	1947	W. Beijerinck
	Atlas of Seeds and Fruits of Central and East-European Flora: The Carpathian Mountains Region	2007	V. Bojňanský and A. Fargašová
	A Manual for the Identification of Plant Seeds and Fruits	2013	R. T. Cappers and R. M. Bekker
	Digitale Zadenatlas van Nederland/Digital Seed Atlas of the Netherlands	2006	R. T. Cappers, R. M. Bekker, and J. E. A. Jans
	Digital Atlas of Economic Plants in Archaeology	2012	R. T. Cappers, R. M. Bekker
	Ackerunkräuter Europas mit ihren Keimlingen und Samen, 4th ed. (Arable Weeds of Europe and their Sprouts and Seeds)	1999	M. Hanf
	Atlas and Keys of Fruits and Seeds Occurring in the Quaternary Deposits of the USSR [In Russian]	1965	N. J. Katz, S. V. Katz, M. G. Kipiani

continued on next page

TABLE 7.2—*continued*

PRINTED BOOKS AND MANUALS

Title	Year	Authors
Samenatlas, Teil 1: Caryophyllaceae; Teil 2: Ranunculaceae (Seed Atlas, Part 1: Caryophyllaceae; Part 2: Ranunculaceae)	2006	H. Knapp
Samenatlas, Teil 3: Fabaceae; Teil 4: Hyperiaceae (Seed Atlas, Part 3: Fabaceae; Part 4: Hyperiaceae)	2010	H. Knapp
Bestimmungsschlüssel für subfossile Juncus-Samen und Gramineen-Früchte (Key to Subfossil Juncus Seeds and Graminae Fruits)	1964	U. Körber-Grohne
Archaeobotany—Research on Seeds and Fruits [in Chinese]	2008	C-J Liu, J-Y Lin, and Z-C Kong
Identification Guide for Near Eastern Grass Seeds	2006	M. Nesbitt
Botanische Makroreste / Botanical Macro-Remains / Macrorestes Botaniques	1988	W. H. Schoch, B. Pawlick, and F. H. Schweingruber

ELECTRONIC RESOURCES

	Title and URL[a]	Authors
Worldwide	USDA Family Guide for Fruits and Seeds, http://nt.ars-grin.gov/seedsFruits/rptSeedsFruitsFam.cfm	J. H. Kirkbride, C. R. Gunn, and M. J. Dallwitz
	Paleobot.org, http://www.paleobot.org	Open Source
New World	Identification Criteria for Plant Remains Recovered from Archaeological Sites in the Central Mesa Verde Region, http://www.crowcanyon.org/ResearchReports/Archaeobotanical/Plant_Identification/plant_identification.asp	K. R. Adams and S. Murray

continued on next page

TABLE 7.2—*continued*

ELECTRONIC RESOURCES

	Title and URL[a]	Authors
	Seed Identification, http://seedbiology.osu.edu/seed_id	Dept. of Horticulture and Crop Sciences, Ohio State University
	Laboratory Guide to Archaeological Plant Remains from Eastern North America, http://pages.wustl.edu/fritz	G. Fritz, ed.
	USDA Woody Plant Seed Manual, http://www.nsl.fs.fed.us/nsl_wpsm.html	US Forest Service
Old World	Archaeobotanical Online Tutorial, http://archaeobotany.dept.shef.ac.uk/wiki/index.php/Main_Page	M. Charles, et al.
	Digital Seed Atlas of the Netherlands website, http://seeds.eldoc.ub.rug.nl/?pLanguage=en	
	A Millet Atlas: Some Identification Guidance (2006),[e] http://www.homepages.ucl.ac.uk/~tcrndfu/archaeobotany.htm	D. Q. Fuller
	HYPPA (HYpermedia for Plant Protection Database of European Weeds), http://www2.dijon.inra.fr/hyppa/hyppa-a/hyppa_a.htm	
	Identification of Cereal Remains from Archaeological Sites (2008), 3rd ed., https://ipna.unibas.ch/archbot/pdf	S. Jacomet, et al.
	Photos of Charred Remains from Early Agricultural Sites in the Near East, http://g.willcox.pagesperso-orange.fr/archaeobotanical%20images/index.htm	G. Willcox

a See bibliography for full bibliographic details.

b A more recent issue of this manual is in print, but the quality of the printed images is not as high.

c A newer print edition is available as USDA FS Agriculture Handbook 727, April 2008, and is also available online (see Electronic Resources section).

d All websites accessed on 09/24/2014.

e Additional helpful resources are also available on the parent website.

become increasingly out-of-date (Delcourt et al. 1979; Jensen 1998; Nesbitt and Greig 1989; Royal Botanic Gardens 1985), there is a risk that existing knowledge embedded in archaeobotanical literature will be forgotten.

DIGITAL RESOURCES

Archaeobotanists have made good use of the Internet as a means to show images (Warinner and d'Alpoim Guedes, chapter 8, this volume) and as a means to distribute laboratory manuals (e.g., from the laboratories of Dorian Fuller, Gayle Fritz, and Stefanie Jacomet; for details see table 7.2). The series of volumes produced by René Cappers is a valuable hybrid, whereby purchasers of the books also have access to a website on which a wider range of images can be searched using selected identification criteria such as seed size.

We consider that printed and digital resources complement each other: books offer easy browsing and a structure that usually stresses plant family affinities—an excellent learning tool, as an understanding of family-level seed characters is the basis of practical identification skills. However, the identification keys in books are usually binary keys that are hard to use on archaeobotanical material that is often fragmentary and missing characters (but see Nesbitt 2006 for an alternative approach to keys). Digital media allow presentation of a far larger number of photographs and are likely to allow more sophisticated searches based on multi-access keys, which are hard to present in printed form.

Automated identification of seeds has been investigated for many years by agronomists, but so far has been largely unsuccessful. Archaeological material is particularly challenging in that seeds all tend to be black, may belong to a wide range of taxa (100–200 species are often found in major archaeobotanical reports), and are often fragmented. Even with restricted data sets and well-orientated and photographed material, as in the case of distinguishing wild and domesticated sunflower seeds, computerized shape analysis has proved unsuccessful (Tarighat et al. 2011). This will undoubtedly change, but probably on the basis of work done in better-funded areas such as face recognition. Careful application of image analysis to cultigens has proved valuable in identifying morphological groups within one taxon that map onto geographical origins, for example in olive, grape, and the date palm (Terral 1997; Terral et al. 2010; Terral et al. 2012), and this technique should be explored further for other crops with subtle variation in seed shape, such as wheat.

Seed Reference Collections

Recently collected seed specimens are the basis of the seed identification aids discussed above, and direct comparison with reference material is always valuable (and often essential) in confirming an identification. Reference material is particularly useful in that it can be cut apart, allowing examination of internal characteristics, which can be particularly helpful if even the plant family cannot be determined using gross morphology (Corner 1976; Martin 1946). Reference material is also useful as seed specimens often bear other plant parts, such as pedicels or bracts, which may also be found in archaeobotanical samples. Finally, a major benefit of regular use of a reference collection is also increased familiarity with seed characteristics by plant family, easing identification of unknown archaeological seeds.

Although we consider the seed reference collection to be an essential resource for seed identification, we also recognize that making a good quality collection is a significant investment (see Nesbitt et al. 2003 for detailed guidance on collection and curation). The seeds may come from different sources: botanic gardens, genebanks, shops, herbaria, and from living plants collected during fieldwork. In general, the ease with which a sample is obtained is in inverse proportion to the reliability of the identification, with seeds from botanic gardens being most likely to be misidentified or mislabeled (Aplin and Heywood 2008). A further advantage of seeds collected directly from the wild or from farmers' fields in the region of interest is that their size will often be more typical of ancient material than that of seeds grown in a garden environment. However, a well-balanced reference collection will draw on all these sources, as some species will be too rare, or even locally extinct, to collect oneself. Building up multiple accessions of the same taxon from different sources has two advantages: first, any incorrect identifications of reference material are more likely to become apparent as specimens will not match each other and, second, the specimens will better represent the diversity of size and shape present in different populations in nature. It is dangerous to build identification criteria on the basis of a single accession of reference material.

The work involved in identifying and housing voucher herbarium specimens (essential for material collected from the field) can be greatly reduced by collaboration with local botanists (for more on voucher specimens and collaboration, see Bye 1986; Nesbitt et al. 2010). At the same time, active participation by the archaeobotanist in collecting seeds and herbarium specimens in the field is an excellent way of increasing understanding of plant ecology and agricultural practices in an area of archaeological interest.

Care must be taken in storing reference collection seeds after field collection. Like all plant material, seeds are vulnerable to pests. They are often stored in clear plastic or glass containers that allow rapid assessment of seed appearance and restrict the movement of insects. The best safeguard for any collection is use: early detection of pests enables rapid treatment, such as freezing to deal with insects or reduction of relative humidity to deal with mold. With the decline of agricultural research, older seed collections in botanical and agricultural institutions are sometimes neglected. Archaeobotanists should seek out these collections; they are often rich in local weeds and crops that are now rare.

BASIC IDENTIFICATION PROCEDURES AND ISSUES
PRINCIPLES

Seed identification (here *seed* is used in the general sense of non-wood plant remains) depends on both the ability to recognize different shapes and a knowledge of the range of candidate species. Identifying candidate species is important because identification criteria must not only enable matching with a species but also *exclusion* of other candidate species. Identification criteria should be based on a study of all likely species. It will be easier to arrive at a narrowly defined identification if there are fewer species in the study area.

Assessment of candidate specimens requires careful consideration of the ecology and abundance of species: for example, at a lowland site it may be possible to exclude mountain species and rare species restricted to specific habitats. However, it is important to be aware that the distribution of species can change and that this is increasingly true the further back in the past one investigates. Sometimes plants become extinct, as in the case of a suite of North American domesticates such as *Iva annua* var. *macrocarpa* and *Chenopodium berlandieri* ssp. *jonesianum* (Smith 1989). In general crop plants are much more likely to see major changes in distribution because of deliberate transfer through cultivation or trade.

Poorly documented wild plant floras can also lead to confusion: for example, it has only recently become clear that two species within the sedge genus *Bolboschoenus* occur today in the Near East. Nutlets of this genus are abundant in pre-agrarian archaeobotanical assemblages and have previously been identified as *B. maritimus*. Reassessment of the genus by taxonomists has shown that *B. glaucus* is the dominant species of inland areas today, and is also the species represented in archaeological samples (Wollstonecroft et al. 2011). There are important ecological (and, potentially, culinary) differences between the two species, but the correct identification was impossible until the current day taxonomy and distribution of these species was understood.

Documenting Identifications

It is good practice to include photographs and, if space allows, written descriptions and measurements of seeds in site reports. In short reports these may be restricted to unusual species or cases in which novel identification criteria have been developed. In full reports, it is also desirable to discuss and illustrate common taxa, both to allow the reader to confirm the analyst's identifications and to show the variability in seed size and shape that is always present for the more abundant taxa. Drawings are still useful for highlighting differences between closely related taxa, although time and cost mean they must be used sparingly.

Seeds and Fruits

Family-level characteristics are as excellent a starting point for seeds as they are for whole plants, enabling the bypass of general identification keys and a focus on a smaller part of the plant kingdom. Many families have highly distinctive seeds: for example, the legumes (Fabaceae), daisy family (Asteraceae), grasses (Poaceae), and cress family (Brassicaceae). Once a family has been identified, identification to genus is the next step. This is usually more manageable than for species. For example, worldwide (these proportions will be reflected in the smaller regional numbers) the Fabaceae has 740 genera but 19,000 species. As seeds often differ substantially in appearance at genus level, initial identification may be a matter of relatively rapid scanning of reference specimens or illustrations.

At species levels, identification criteria may be much more subtle, and it is here that our limited ability to describe differences in shape is most problematic. Although botanists have developed an extensive vocabulary for plant morphology (Beentje 2010), it is probably true to say that communication of differences in shape of seeds and surface cell patterns is best carried out using images. Measurements can be valuable, but we have doubts about the blanket application of absolute figures, whether for distinguishing wild species or wild and domesticated forms. Not only does charring introduce significant and unpredictable changes in shape and size, it is also uncommon for simple measurements of plant parts to clearly distinguish species even on fresh whole plants, where there are often overlaps in size between species. Instead, plotting scattergrams of measurements of archaeological material from one or multiple sites is often an effective way of identifying groups of differently sized seeds that may correspond to different taxa. In other words, absolute differences in size that are visible on fresh material are valuable tools for investigating relative differences in size that are apparent in archaeobotanical material. An example of the problem is the separation of wild and domesticated Old World grape pips (*Vitis vinifera*). Over a century of observations that wild grapes have squatter pips with short beaks have not yet translated into a formula that can distinguish charred material of the two forms across all sites, even though the difference is obvious to the eye, and numerical criteria such as ratios sometimes work within one site (Jacquat and Martinoli 1999; Smith and Jones 1990).

Differentiating between Wild and Domesticated

Crops usually possess a "domestication syndrome" of several characters that make them relatively easy to distinguish from their wild ancestors (Harlan 1975). These characters include larger propagules, loss of ability to disperse seed, and changes in growth habit that, in the case of some plants, such as maize, radically change the appearance of the plant. However, bearing in mind that it tends to be the propagules that end up in archaeological deposits, morphological changes in growth habit, or even in lighter (i.e., more fragile) parts of the fruit such as legume pods, will not be visible. Thus in the case of cereals and legumes, identification of domestication in archaeobotanical macroremains has focused on increase in seed size (in the case of grasses, strictly the grain or caryopsis size), and loss of seed dispersal mechanisms. In the case of amaranths and chenopods, there are clear changes in the thickness of the seed coat, discussed below.

Although a clear size difference is often visible between the seeds or grains of wild and domesticated taxa from recent populations, this difference appears more obscure in early populations of domesticates. In part this is because charred material from early sites is often in poor condition, but it is also likely to reflect the fact that early domesticates are just that: populations that have only been exposed to selection for larger seed size for perhaps a millennium or less, unlike current day landraces of crops that have been exposed to selection over subsequent millennia of agriculture. Further complicating factors include evidence, discussed below, of incomplete domestication processes in early agriculture and the varying effects of charring on seed size (see for example, the case of teff, *Eragrostis tef*, D'Andrea 2008). It is thus rare that seed or grain size can be used as a simple indicator of domestication at early agricultural sites. However, when individual seed sizes are plotted as scattergrams and compared to those of earlier and later levels, both within one site and at other sites, an overall increase in seed size is visible through time, corresponding to domestication. The application of this technique to wheat and barley grain in the Near East has shown gradual increases in grain size during the Pre-Pottery Neolithic period (Willcox 2004); distinct episodes of increased grain size are also seen in ancient pearl millet (*Pennisetum glaucum*) in Africa and India, after domestication (Manning et al. 2011). In the New World, sunflower achenes have presented similar problems; size differences between wild and domesticated taxa that are clear in modern material are obscure in early material, contributing to the controversy over the location and timing of sunflower domestication (Yarnell 1978).

In principle the loss of seed dispersal mechanisms offers more robust criteria for identification of cereal domestication. For example, in wild wheat, barley, rice and many other cereals, the spikelets disarticulate at maturity to allow the grains to disseminate. This natural disarticulation leads to a smooth abscission scar at the spikelet base. In domesticated forms, the spikelets are torn apart during threshing by farmers, leading to torn abscission scars. There are complications: threshing of immature ears of wild grain can lead to torn scars, and the basal spikelets of wild wheat and barley do not disarticulate in the wild, and thus bear torn scars if threshed (Fuller et al. 2009; Kislev 1997; Tanno and Willcox 2012). The use of low numbers of torn spikelet scars to determine domestication status is therefore unwise. Although chaff remains are usually scarcer than grains in archaeological samples, the application of bulk flotation to early sites in the Near East and in China has led to the recovery of a large number of spikelet remains (Fuller et al. 2009; Kislev 1997; Tanno and Willcox 2012). The persistence of large numbers of wild-type scars in farmer's fields in the millennia following the first domestication of cereals suggests that full domestication was a slower and more complex process than thought a decade ago, with implications for the ease of identification of domesticates by morphological criteria (Fuller 2007b; Tanno and Willcox 2006).

Many crops have seeds that are similar in morphology to those of their wild ancestors. Here, changes in the quantity and distribution of archaeobotanical finds can point toward domestication. It is assumed that an increase in the abundance of a seed or its appearance at sites outside the distribution of the wild ancestor are indicators of domestication. These are inevitably subjective criteria, and can be hard to apply when the distances are small and the distribution of the wild ancestor uncertain. Major changes, however, such as the move of olives inland from the coastal strip of wild olives in the eastern Mediterranean can be good evidence for domestication (Liphschitz et al. 1991; Neef 1990).

CROPS

The biggest challenge in identifying crop remains is that human selection has led to the evolution of myriad closely related taxa that vary subtly in morphology, agronomy, and culinary properties. This led to endless taxonomic problems in the past, when overemphasis was given to relatively minor differences with the description of tens or hundreds of species within what is today considered a single biological species. Modern taxonomy handles this by taking a "lumping" approach in which interfertile taxa are considered to belong to a single species and major morphological variants are then recognized at either subspecies or variety level, or as in the case of sorghum, by informal groups (de Wet et al. 1986; Harlan and de Wet 1971). Within these distinct forms are then thousands of landraces characterized by further minor morphological variations. Wheat, maize, rice, and sorghum are examples of highly variable crops that are abundantly represented in archaeobotanical remains.

Similar problems face the archaeobotanist, and beginners faced with highly variable crop seeds have a strong tendency to over-split, creating too many categories. A useful tool to counter this is to arrange seeds in a series by, for example, increasing length, in order to judge whether the "different" types are in fact simply extreme forms of a continuum. Measurement can also be helpful in deciding if more than one taxon is involved, for example when measurements are plotted as a scattergram to show whether more than group can be distinguished.

Once coherent groups of crops have been identified within a site assemblage, the question arises of whether they can be assigned to current-day taxa. This question of candidate species is simpler for wild taxa; as discussed above, the current wild flora of the region (and reference material collected from that region) is likely to match archaeobotanical material, with some provision for species that have since become rare in the locality. The case of crops is more complex, since taxa may have been widespread in the past that are rare or extinct now, as with a highly robust form of emmer wheat once found in the Near East and parts of central Europe (Jones, Valamoti, and Charles 2000), or the once important sumpweed (*Iva annua* var. *macrocarpa*) and goosefoot (*Chenopodium berlandieri* ssp. *jonesianum*) in eastern North America (Smith 1989). In these cases rigorous and multiple identification criteria were established that support the identification of a novel taxon. However, it is more often the case that there are only minor morphological differences between archaeobotanical remains and modern reference material, which in matters such as cereal grain size are partly accounted for by the effects of charring. In this case, it is usually better to document the characteristics of the crop and to explain how they differ from other archaeobotanical or modern material, without assigning it to a novel taxon.

Given the difficulties explained above, archaeobotanists have developed good tools for identification of crops to finer detail than simply that of biological species (e.g., for wheat Jones 1998 and for maize Adams 1994). A major factor in this process is the development of regional identification manuals, and the ease with which material can be shown to colleagues via electronic means and at meetings such as the International Work Group for Palaeoethnobotany. However, we believe there is more room to standardize identification criteria, in discussion formats such as the London workshop on wheat identification (Hillman et al. 1996), and by the blind-testing that has led to greater rigor in the identification of microfossils.

Parenchyma and Vegetative Remains

In charred remains, wood and plant propagules (at most sites, seeds and fruits) will account for the majority of the plant remains found. When other plant parts occur, they are often associated with the plant propagules: for example, fruit pedicels. Charred roots and tubers are often present and have become increasingly recognized by archaeobotanists after the pioneering studies of Jon Hather (1993, 2000). Intact tubers superficially resemble fruits, but often have scars where rootlets or scales were attached. Their interior has more or less spherical cells, rather than the elongated cells of wood fragments. Lumps of different cell types aggregated together are also common, and these are probably fragments of charred food. These have been little studied, but preliminary work suggests that their disaggregation and study by scanning electron microscopy would be worthwhile (Hansson 1994; Valamoti et al. 2008).

In waterlogged and desiccated conditions, it is common to find a far more diverse range of plant materials, including non-woody stems, buds, and leaves. Because waterlogging leads to the decay of the waxy cuticle and of fleshy interiors, including endosperm in grass grains, waterlogged remains are often translucent, allowing their cell patterns to be studied through transmitted light microscopy. Reference material may need to be treated by soaking or heating in dilute acid or a solution of potassium hydroxide in order to arrive at the same translucency. There is an extensive literature on the specialist identification of waterlogged material (Birks 2007; Mauquoy and Van Geel 2007).

WOOD AND STEM MATERIAL

Wood is often abundant in macrobotanical samples, representing fuel and burned architectural features and providing information about the surrounding vegetation and how people of the past used and altered it. Wood anatomy is a specialized field of study and careful analysis of wood requires a higher-powered microscope (at least 400×) than needed for standard sorting of seeds and nutshell. We recommend training with an expert in wood identification of a particular study area, especially in regions of high tree diversity. A start can be made even by nonspecialists by examining transverse (cross) sections of charred wood under a low-power dissecting microscope, with conifers easily distinguished from hardwoods, and ring-porous taxa distinguishable from diffuse-porous ones. Oaks are identifiable by their multiseriate rays (see Pearsall 2000:144–53 and sources cited therein for an excellent overview). Charcoal is usually studied by breaking it so that the structure can be seen in three sectional views, and then examining each section through a high-powered metallurgical microscope.

The structure of charred and waterlogged wood is well preserved. A major difference from seed identification is that work by wood anatomists, under the auspices of the International Association of Wood Anatomists, has led to highly standardized character states that have been recorded for a large number of tree species. Excellent identification manuals exist for many regions and can be used in combination with the comprehensive website *Inside Wood* (2004).

MICROBOTANICAL REMAINS

Palynology has been a fundamental element of archaeobotanical research since the mid-twentieth century (Faegri and Iversen 1975), and it has been joined more recently by the study of phytoliths and starch grains. Combination and integration of macro- and microbotanical remains greatly expand the scope of our understanding of past plant-people relationships, but for one person to acquire the skills and access to laboratory facilities to conduct all of these types of analyses is challenging. Pearsall's (2000) *Paleoethnobotany* handbook contains separate chapters on pollen and phytolith analysis, and

Piperno's (2006b) book on phytoliths is, as the title states, a comprehensive guide. Analysis of starch grains from ancient tools and features is being applied with increasing frequency and exciting results (Messner 2011; Piperno et al. 2004). All of these endeavors utilize potentially caustic chemicals and require scientific laboratory facilities—including fume hoods and centrifuges—for extraction of the remains and preparation of slides, which need to be studied under high-power microscopes (up to 1000×). A cross-polarizing filter is necessary for microscopic analysis of starch grains in order to see the extinction crosses (see Henry, chapter 3, this volume).

NON-PLANT INCLUSIONS

Flotation samples frequently contain insect eggs, fecal pellets from very small animals, and fungal sclerotia that can easily be mistaken for seeds by an untrained observer. When archaeologists presort light fractions before handing them over to an expert, considerable time might be wasted pulling hundreds of round, black sclerotia from the smaller-than-2.0 mm splits (figure 7.2). Therefore, we briefly address the morphological characteristics of these ubiquitous objects. Most assemblages including fungal sclerotia will include enough whole ones to demonstrate the lack of any embryo or hilum scar. Sclerotia may be very round and smooth, but vary morphologically by species. Schoen (1983) gives the general size range as 0.5 to 3.0 mm and illustrates a number of different genera and species. Most that we have observed are smaller than 1.0 mm in diameter. The outer rind or cortex layer appears smooth at low magnification, lacking reticulation or other sculpturing commonly exhibited on seed testas. Sclerotia are easily dissected with one's fingernail or razor blade. The inner filling, called the medulla, when present, is a slightly spongy-looking, solid mass that differs from seed endosperm by its homogeneity, absence of cotyledons, and lack of starchiness. Fungal sclerotia are considered in most cases to be background noise in soil, modern contaminants that usually go unmentioned. However, Matsumoto et al. (2010) recently reported carbonized sclerotia from two sites on the island of Hokkaido, northern Japan, that appear to be from good archaeological contexts, including ash-coated fireplace vestiges. The authors, using scanning electron microscopy, identified the objects to the species *Typhula ishikariensis* and inferred that the fungal bodies entered the archaeological record associated with plant material deposited in the fireplace and elsewhere. European sclerotia are usually identified as *Cenococcum geophilum* and are usually considered modern (Alonso and López 2005).

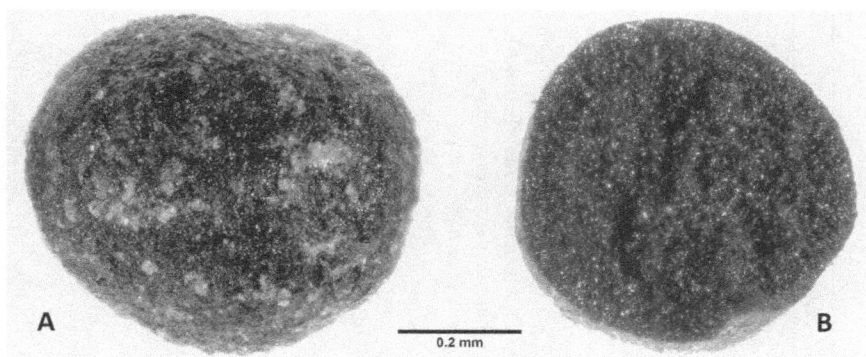

FIGURE 7.2. *Fungal sclerotia, species unknown, recovered during flotation of sediments from the Berry Site, Burke County, North Carolina, United States. A: outer, convex surface. B: cross section of different, slightly smaller specimen.*

SPECIFIC EXAMPLE: IDENTIFYING AMARANTH

Identification of seeds in the genus *Amaranthus* can be tricky for several reasons. First, wild amaranth seeds are black even when uncharred, so it takes close inspection and sometimes physical pressure using one's fingernail or metal tool to determine if an unbroken specimen is modern or ancient. Second, wild or weedy amaranth species produce seeds that look very much alike, and there may be little research incentive to attempt identification below the genus level. The third challenge involves distinguishing between amaranths and their close relatives, especially species in the genus *Chenopodium* (table 7.3), which often occur in the same deposits. Fourth, there are three domesticated species of amaranth—*A. hypochondriacus*, *A. cruentus*, and *A. caudatus*—all native New World cultigens, making it necessary to detect morphological changes that signal agricultural production rather than wild harvesting (Fritz 2007).

Undomesticated amaranth seeds (figure 7.3) have relatively thick, hard seed coats (testas) that cover the interior perisperms (endosperms) and encircling embryos. Analysts should collect and study the seeds of plants native to their research area and observe how they are borne in inflorescences consisting of clusters of chaffy tepals, bracts, and fruits called pyxes (a pyxis is a single-seeded, circumcisally dehiscent utricle.) Unlike chenopods, amaranth seeds are not covered by adhering pericarps.

Native eastern North American amaranth seeds overlap in diameter with local *Chenopodium* species, but whole amaranth seeds are rarely larger than 1.1 mm, whereas most whole chenopod seeds in this region are bigger. In the

TABLE 7.3. Means of distinguishing charred amaranth from chenopod seeds

Trait	Cultigen Amaranth Seeds	Wild/Weedy Amaranth Seeds	Wild/Weedy Chenopod Seeds
Seed coat thickness	Very thin(2–15 μm, usually)	Thicker(17–32 μm)	Thick(20–30 μm for weedy; 40–80 μm for wild)
Diameter	c. 1.0 mm, ± a few mm, usually	c. 1.0 mm, ± a few mm, usually	Can be as large as 2.0 mm, but some species are as small as amaranths
Beak morphology	Liplike meeting of embryo ends	Liplike meeting of embryo ends; some species have one end that projects slightly	Distinctly overlapping beak, but varies by species
Pericarp (presence or absence)	No pericarp adhering to seed	No pericarp adhering to seed	Papery pericarp adheres to seed, but rarely survives charring except as fugitive trace
Seed coat texture	Smooth (but *A. cruentus* seed coats are slightly rugose)	Relatively smooth, with some species exhibiting marginal texture, (e.g., diamondlike pattern)	Can be distinctly pitted (alveolate) or caniculate, but varies by species
Dorsal sulcus (presence or absence)	Absent	Absent	Present, running from center to beak, but varies by species
Cross-section shape	Enlarged, oval embryo creates semi-truncate cross-section; One or more ridges may be present around circumference	Biconvex, lenticular, with circular embryo cross-section	Biconvex, lenticular

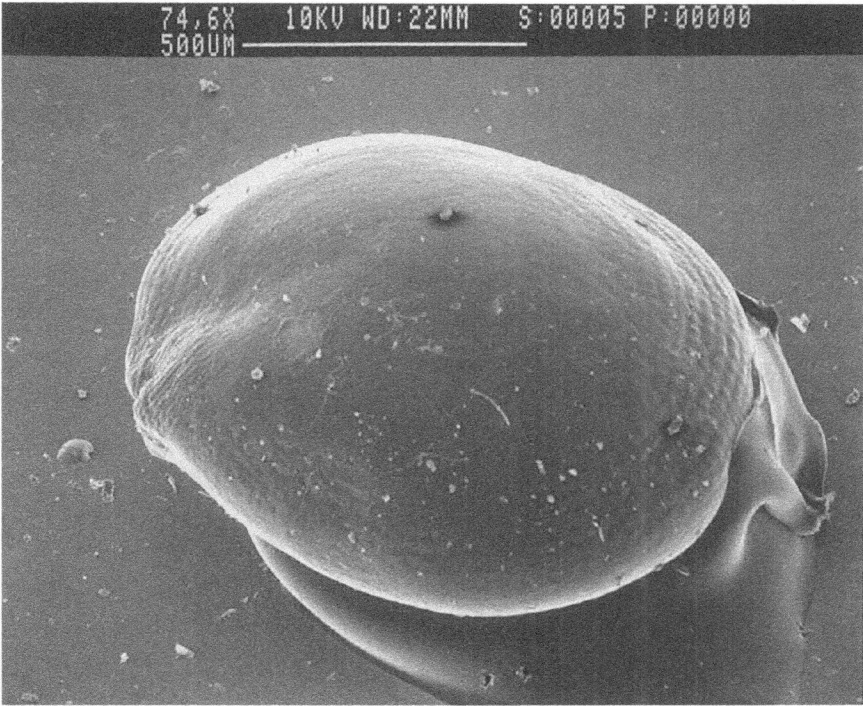

FIGURE 7.3. *Scanning electron micrograph of wild/weedy amaranth seed.*

US Southwest, additional chenopod species exist that have smaller seeds than their eastern relatives, increasing the difficulty of distinguishing between genera. However, the embryos of chenopod seeds wrap around and overlap to form a distinct beak (figure 7.4), whereas amaranth embryos meet to form liplike features, although one lip might protrude beyond the other (figure 7.3). The most common North American wild/weedy archaeological chenopod type, *C. berlandieri*, has a distinctly alveolate (pitted) seed coat, unlike any amaranth, and may retain evidence of its reticulate (netlike) pericarp (fruit coat). Amaranth seed coats tend to be smooth except at the margin, where a subtle diamondlike patterning is visible on some wild specimens, especially under high-power scanning electron microscopy. Amaranth seed coats might be slightly undulating, but they do not exhibit the distinct reticulation of *C. berlandieri* or other chenopods. Finally, amaranths lack the dorsal sulcus extending from the beak to the center of chenopods. If seed coats are entirely missing, or if specimens are otherwise in too poor shape for

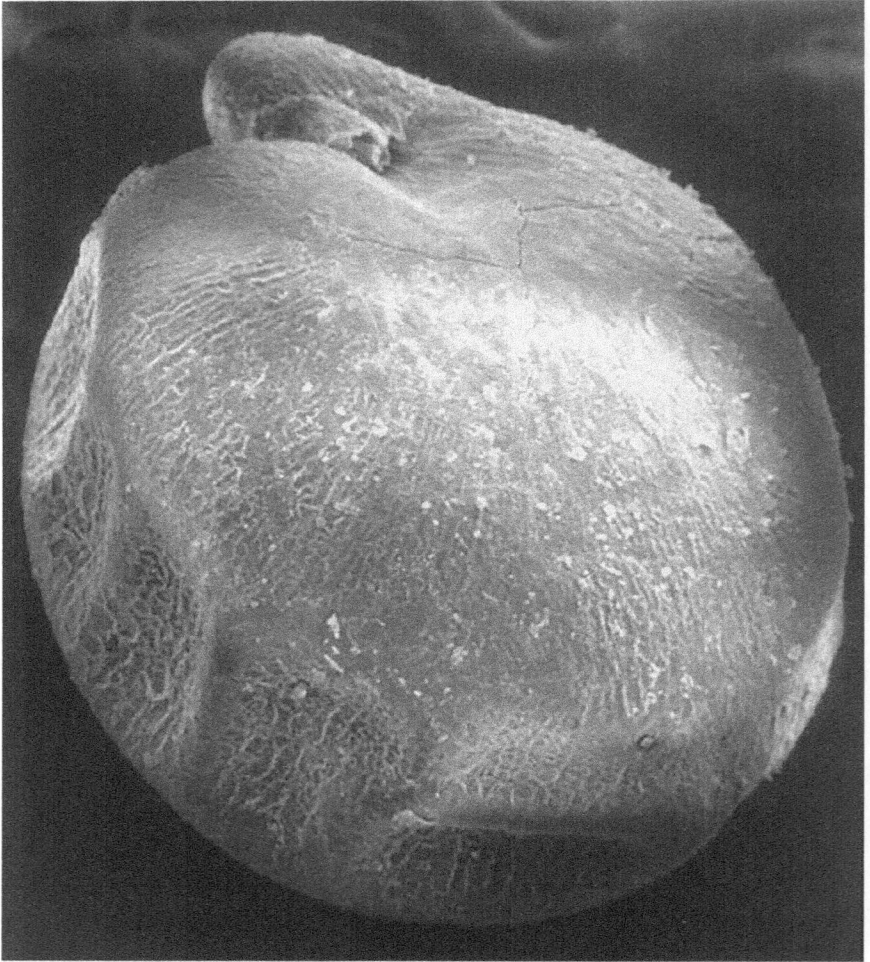

FIGURE 7.4. Chenopodium *seed showing distinct beak and reticulate pericarp (fruit coat). Because this is a domesticated chenopod (*Chenopodium berlandieri *ssp.* jonesianum*) from an archaeological rockshelter in the Arkansas Ozarks, it has a truncate rather than rounded margin and a smooth rather than pitted seed coat (here hidden by pericarp).*

these features to be observed, archaeobotanists relegate them to the category of "cheno-am" (figure 7.5).

Identifying domesticated amaranths can be especially difficult because the primary change that occurred through selection was reduction in seed

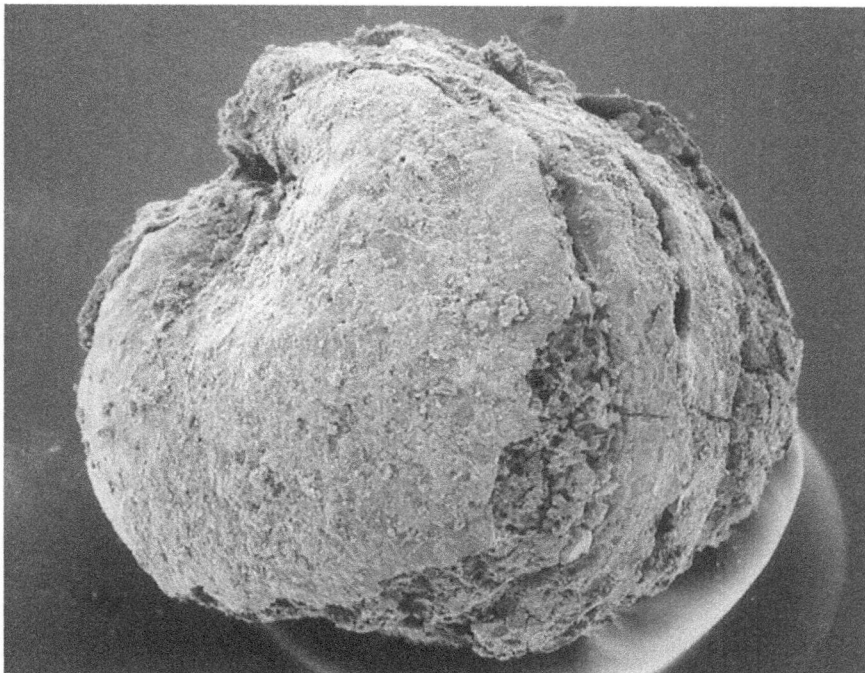

FIGURE 7.5. *"Cheno-am" perisperm with no seed coat that would enable classification to genus.*

coat thickness, resulting in pale rather than black seeds (figure 7.6), the same process that happened during domestication of Andean quinoa (*C. quinoa*) and the eastern North American cultigen, *C. berlandieri* ssp. *jonesianum* (Fritz et al. 2009; Fritz and Smith 1988; McClung de Tapia et al. 1996; Smith 1984, 1985).

The extremely thin seed coats of cultigen amaranths and chenopods are so fragile that they are poorly preserved, if present at all, after charring, and scanning electron microscopy is needed to obtain accurate seed coat measurements. Seed size increase does not seem to have accompanied testa reduction (Sauer 1993), but embryos of cultigen amaranth seeds are enlarged and oval rather than circular, giving the seeds semi-truncate margins with concentric marginal ridges, rather than being biconvex in cross-section.

Making the effort to separate amaranth seeds from chenopods and to recognize the presence of domesticates, although time-consuming, pays off in research dealing with agricultural origins and intensification in North

FIGURE 7.6. *Domesticated amaranth seeds. These specimens came from a 1000-year old storage pit in a dry rockshelter, the Holman Shelter, in the Arkansas Ozarks.*

America, Mesoamerica, and Andean South America (Bruno 2006; Fritz 1984; Fritz et al. 2009).

CONCLUSIONS

Archaeobotanists are continually refining traditional, decades-old practices of laboratory analysis and, at the same time, pioneering new types of research requiring technical skills and equipment not available until recently. Although our field has expanded, a protracted period of one-on-one training in the laboratory is still the ideal method of learning, followed by many years of continuing consultation with colleagues. Communication today, of course, includes options such as the capabilities to attach high-resolution images to email messages and to access websites devoted to archaeobotanical networking (see Warinner and d'Alpoim Guedes, chapter 8, this volume).

Most paleoethnobotanists today are, first and foremost, archaeologists who direct or codirect field projects or, at least, participate fully in research-design planning, excavations, laboratory work, and formulation of results. Ethnographic observations (ethnobotanical, agronomic, culinary, etc.) and experimental activities are increasingly frequent components of our studies. Still, as much as ever, identification of ancient plant remains requires expertise acquired through formal coursework, field biology, and careful scrutiny of reference specimens in comparative collections. The laboratory stage of analysis is a crucial and time-intensive link to interpretive success. This brief chapter covers philosophical and methodological points that we consider fundamental to this step in the pursuit of understanding how human and botanical spheres have intersected and coevolved through the ages.

If we were to choose three conclusions based on the examples and practices discussed in this chapter, they would be:

1. Although useful new techniques are regularly developed—for example, scanning electron microscopy, image analysis, and the extraction of DNA from seeds—none of these have replaced the intensive use of a stereomicroscope and the ability of humans to memorize and compare complex shapes as the main identification tool. The more sophisticated techniques have developed a valuable role, although preservation of DNA in charred material is often poor, limiting its use (Schlumbaum et al. 2008). Image analysis, in particular, merits further application for analyzing variation in ancient crop seeds.

2. Seed reference collections, and the associated knowledge of candidate species based on field experience of the study region, remain central to archaeobotany. Archaeobotanists must not only be archaeologists, but botanists too.

3. Identification cannot be carried out in isolation, and this generation of archaeobotanists is highly fortunate in the ease of travel and the benefits of digital communication available today. There is still scope for further standardization—on a regional basis—of identification criteria, especially for crops, and for blind identification tests. The widespread use in Europe of standardized archaeobotanical recording databases, often based on the ArboDat system developed in Germany (Kreuz and Schäfer 2002), is likely to accelerate the move to more consistent identification.

8

Digitizing the Archaeobotanical Record

CHRISTINA WARINNER AND
JADE D'ALPOIM GUEDES

We now live in a digital age. The rise of digital technology over the last 30 years has provided numerous opportunities for generating, storing, and disseminating paleoethnobotanical data in novel and unexpected ways. The pace of technological innovation is rapidly increasing as computer memory and processing speeds improve, allowing dramatic leaps in software sophistication and global networking. As such, research today proceeds on shifting sands, as technological waves deliver new tools while washing away the detritus of software and hardware *en vogue* just years before. It is difficult to keep pace with this seemingly endless tide of change, especially for the scholars and scientists who are the consumers and not the generators of these new technological advancements.

For those who can learn to navigate these new technological waters the rewards are great. Large-scale archiving, data portability, rapid searching, ease of sharing, interobserver standardization, and automated analysis are just some of the potential benefits of employing a digital research approach. This chapter explores some of the current and emerging online digital resources available to today's generation of paleoethnobotanical researchers and contrasts them with historical practices in the field in order to highlight important changes in paleoethnobotanical practice over the last 30 years.

DOI: 10.5876/9781607323167.c008

TECHNOLOGICAL ADVANCEMENTS, 1988–2013:
FROM DEVELOPED FILM TO PIXELS ONLINE

Until the 1990s, nearly all paleoethnobotanical data were communicated through conventional print media (journals, books) or in person (conferences, meetings, visits, courses). If researchers wished to share unpublished information such as photographs of unidentified seeds or reference collection slides (microscope slides or photographic slides) with colleagues, they would either have to send the materials physically by mail or arrange an in-person visit. The costs of generating and sharing data were high and scaled roughly linearly with the amount of data produced: film and development costs accrued with every photograph taken, and the cost of sharing accumulated in the form of postage and transportation costs. Thus, the more information one acquired and shared, the more money one needed to spend. Such a system posed obvious limitations to the development of the field. By contrast, the rise of digital technology and computing has allowed exponential increases in data acquisition and analysis with relatively few fixed costs. Today, a wide range of online resources and services allow data to be communicated, archived, searched, and shared nearly instantaneously, often with little or no direct monetary cost to the individuals using the service (although website hosting, online advertising, and data tracking impose a different set of costs).

DATA GENERATION

Digital photography offers many advantages over traditional film photography. First, images can be instantly checked for quality and immediately repeated if necessary. There is no delay for film development or processing time. Second, there are few limits on how many images can be taken, and the resolution of each image can be set independently. Finally, the images can be easily downloaded, stored, copied, and rapidly shared. They can be hyperlinked to files, entered into online databases, and even tagged with metadata to allow keyword search functionality. All of these properties allow digital images to be integrated with other forms of data in ways that were never before possible.

The first generation of affordable (less than $1,000) color digital cameras came on the market in the mid-1990s with the Apple QuickTake 100 (1994), the Casio QV (1995), and the Canon PowerShot 600 (1996), among others (Carter 2007). These early digital cameras had many shortcomings with respect to memory, focus, and zoom, and the resulting images could not compete with the resolution and print quality of traditional film. By the mid-2000s, however, optical quality improvements and increased capture resolution resulted in digital cameras superseding film cameras in popularity and sales. In 2005, Kodak announced that digital revenue exceeded that of their traditional formats for the first time (Digital Photography Review 2005), and in 2006 Nikon announced that following seven years of growth in the digital market, digital sales now accounted for 95 percent of their UK business (Nikon Corporation 2006).

Today there are many inexpensive, high-quality digital cameras on the market. Such cameras are good for taking photographs in the field to document excavation and analysis, but automatic lens retraction makes mounting them onto microscopes impractical. Increasingly, however, field archaeologists are forgoing traditional cameras entirely and opting instead for the cameras built into their smartphones and tablet devices. Tablet devices such as the iPad have the added advantage of allowing the archaeologist to edit, annotate, and archive the photos in a project database in real time (DeTore and Bria 2012).

For microscopy, either integrated or independent cameras may be used. Integrated microscope, camera, and software packages have the advantage of being controlled directly through a computer interface in conjunction with other microscopy software, but the costs of such systems are often higher than purchasing a camera separately. Independent cameras offer increased flexibility, including the ability to use the camera on multiple microscopes in the same laboratory. Such cameras can be acquired at a lower cost, although compatibility issues between cameras and software must be considered. Cameras are generally only compatible with the software of their manufacturer, and hence both operating software and camera quality should be taken into consideration before making a purchase. For instance, the software package Cellsens® by Olympus is compatible with a range of recent Olympus cameras and a few third-party cameras such as QImaging, but cannot be used with Nikon cameras. Likewise, Nikon's NIS Elements® package is not compatible with Olympus cameras. Companies such as Hamamatsu or QImaging manufacture hardware that is compatible with a range of different software programs. For individuals wishing to use software that makes use of an automatic stage for multiple image alignment, an integrated microscope, camera, and software package is essential.

In addition to digital cameras, digital scanners also play an important role in paleoethnobotanical research and are frequently used to rapidly digitize large-format botanical voucher specimens. Zooarchaeologists have also found that high-resolution color scanners, such as the ScanMaker 1000XL, are excellent for rapidly imaging relatively flat bones (e.g., ribs, limb bones) at a standardized scale. Digital scanning is currently the preferred method for archiving materials in the Zooarchaeology Laboratory at Harvard University's Peabody Museum of Archaeology and Ethnology, and it is also employed in the Harvard Seed Herbarium Image Project (SHIP).

Data Computing and Storage

Although personal computing emerged in the 1970s and 1980s, it was not until the mid-1990s that computer memory and processing speeds were powerful enough to routinely process high-resolution photographic images. The Apple Macintosh (1984), the first successful personal computer with a graphical interface, had a computer processor speed of just 8MHz and memory of only 128kB. By contrast, a portable 2013 Apple Macbook Pro includes four processors, each with speeds up to 2.8GHz, and 16GB of memory, representing a 1,400-fold increase in processor speed and a 125,000-fold increase in memory.

Another area of major change is data storage. The original Apple Macintosh used a 400kB 3.5-inch floppy disk as its means of computer data storage. The 3.5-inch floppy disk remained the primary data storage and transfer device throughout most of the 1980s and early 1990s, reaching a storage capacity of 1.44MB, which is smaller than most digital photographic image files today. The subsequent availability of CD-ROMs and later DVD-ROMs dramatically expanded external data storage capacity to over 700MB and 4.7GB, respectively, but the limited rewriteability of these devices and their susceptibility to "disk rot" (Svensson 2004) posed serious drawbacks. Today, most computer hard drives can store in excess of 500GB of data, and fully rewriteable USB flash drives (2000), external hard drives, and, most recently, cloud computing are common additional data storage solutions featuring capacities ranging from gigabytes (1,000MB) to terabytes (1,000,000MB). To put this in perspective, a 3-megapixel image (which has sufficient resolution to produce a 5×7-inch print of the same quality as 35mm film) requires 2–10MB of storage space, depending on the file format (JPEG or TIFF). Thus, one TB of storage would be sufficient to store more than 100,000 high-quality digital images.

Alongside advances in hardware, image-related software also underwent rapid development. The first commercial image editing software, PhotoMac (1988) and Adobe Photoshop 1.0 (1990), have given rise to a wide variety of free and affordable image editing software, whereas the 2013 version of Adobe Photoshop, perhaps the most sophisticated photo editing software on the market today, is available for a monthly fee as low as $19. Today, even basic personal computers and off-the-shelf software are powerful enough to manage and manipulate large digital photographic collections, making digital paleoethnobotanical research both possible and practical. In addition, the manufacturers of digital microscopy cameras offer several proprietary computing and photomanipulation software packages that allow users to count and measure specimens, embed accurate scales, manipulate colors, and create uniformly focused images of three dimensional objects, such as seeds, by using multiple image alignment technology.

Data Sharing and Communication

The Internet has proven to be a revolutionary tool for the sharing and communication of paleoethnobotanical data. The first widespread use of the Internet occurred following the creation of the World Wide Web in 1991, and in 1992 the National Center for Supercomputing Applications released Mosaic (later Netscape), the first web browser that allowed users to view photographs on the web (Carter 2007). Nearly 10 years later Google launched Google Images (2001), the first online image search service. Using this service, one can enter a search term, such as "*Zea mays* phytolith," and obtain hundreds of image results in a fraction of a second. In 2008, TinEye launched a reverse image search engine that uses image recognition software to enable users to upload or link to an image and search the web for other similar images without using any text at all, and in 2011 Google also added reverse searching functionality to its image search service (Google 2011).

Scholars now routinely share images and information via email and email listservs such as the Archaeobotany Listserv (archaeobotany@jiscmail.ac.uk). The ability to share data in this way is relatively recent and has largely resulted from the dramatic improvement in Internet download and upload speeds with the transition from dial-up to broadband Internet service, and from the release of web-based email services with free data storage from providers such as Hotmail (1996), Yahoo Mail (1997), and Gmail (2004). Even today, these email providers may allow larger file attachments (in 2013, 25MB for Gmail) and much larger (even unlimited) online storage than university- or company-provided email services. Files of exceptionally large size that exceed even that allowed by these email providers can be sent using free file transfer protocol (FTP) services or other online document delivery services such as Dropbox (2008; https://www.dropbox.com/).

Also linked to improved broadband availability, the emergence of Voice over Internet Protocol (VoIP) has increasingly enabled scholars to coordinate projects and share information by videoconference using free services such as

Skype (2003), Apple's FaceTime (2010), and Google Hangout (2011). In addition, Google Hangout allows users to teleconference and simultaneously view and edit documents in real time—all on the same screen. This service, which is especially popular among scholars working on collaborative grant proposals (Cordell 2011), is supported by Google Docs (2007), a web-based office suite that marks Google's expansion into cloud computing.

In addition to direct communication via email or videoconferencing, scholars are also increasingly communicating, sharing articles, and organizing over social networking sites such as LinkedIn (2003), Facebook (2004), ResearchGate (2008), Academia.edu (2008), and Google+ (2011). Photo-sharing websites such as Google's Picasa (2002) and Ludicorp/Yahoo's Flickr (2004) have also become very popular among scholars wishing to upload, edit, tag, geotag, search, and share large collections of images because they incur little or no direct costs to the researchers and do not require programming skills.

Finally, in addition to using the resources and services described above, scholars also frequently develop their own personal research websites hosted on university servers, use free website development and hosting services such as Google Sites (2008), or build customized websites using open-source software (e.g., Drupal and WordPress), which can be hosted on commercial, subscription-based servers. Research websites tend to be highly heterogeneous and range from minimal descriptive information about research interests and publications to large, fully searchable web-based research databases, such as InsideWood (Wheeler 2011) and Paleobot.org (Warinner et al. 2011).

Publication and Online Access

Digital content from traditional print media sources is also increasingly available online. Today, most academic journals make their articles available online as downloadable Adobe PDF files, although access can vary dramatically between journals. Some journals, such as Elsevier's *Journal of Archaeological Science*, make online articles available weeks or months before the article officially goes to print in physical form, while other journals, such as the Society for American Archaeology's *American Antiquity* and *Latin American Antiquity*, delay the release of their online content for months or years after the physical issue has been mailed to subscribers, a phenomenon known as the "moving wall." Dissertations, once distributed as microfilms by University Microfilms International (UMI), are now available as online PDFs through ProQuest (1995), and scholarly books are increasingly going online through services such as Project Gutenberg (1971, 2004), Google Books (2004),

Project MUSE (1995), Questia (1998), Ebrary (1999), as well as through direct offerings from individual academic presses. Managing the large amount of digital content downloaded from online sources has led many scholars to seek out reference management software to help them organize their PDF libraries, such as Papers (2007) and ReadCube (2011). In addition, although PDFs largely represent static digital versions of print articles, some PDF readers, such as Utopia Documents (2010), are experimenting with making PDFs more interactive with other online resources through dynamic hyperlinking and integration with social media.

Search is another area undergoing rapid change. Gone are the days of library card catalogs; instead, digital citation indexes and bibliographic databases with full text and PDF links to academic articles and books are now available as free (Google Scholar [2004], Google Books [2004], and PubMed [1997]) and subscription-based (JSTOR [1995], Project Muse [1995], Scopus [2004], Web of Knowledge [2004], WorldCat [1971, 2006], and Anthropological Literature [1979, 1992]) services. These online search services allow researchers to rapidly search tens of thousands of journals and books instantly and they have revolutionized the way scientists and scholars conduct research.

DIGITAL ARCHAEOBOTANY: TAKING
STOCK OF THE FIELD IN 2013

The technological advances described above have cultivated a growing assortment of online resources available to archaeobotanists specializing in macro- and microfossil remains (table 7.3). Online resources range from personal research websites of individual analysts to multi-institution searchable photographic collections of particular plant parts or types. Although these websites offer many advantages, there is still a need to overcome a number of practical limitations that affect currently available archaeobotanical online resources.

NEED FOR IMPROVED ONLINE RESOURCES

In 2009, Naomi F. Miller circulated a questionnaire to archaeobotanists working in the field with the goals of determining the state of current archaeobotanical research and identifying areas in need of improvement. The results were presented at the 2010 Annual Meeting of the Society for American Archaeology in a forum entitled, "Quantification and Presentation: Effective Means of Presenting Plant Evidence in Archaeology," organized by Christine

Hastorf (Miller 2010a), and later published in the SAA Archaeological Record (Miller 2011a).

One of the major challenges listed by archaeobotanists in the survey was the lack of identification tools and reference collection images, both for specific regions and globally. When asked what would facilitate or enhance their own archaeobotanical research, respondents listed the development of online identification databases as the single most-desired resource. A strong desire for a website dedicated to the identification of unknown specimens was also expressed (Miller 2010a, 2011a).

At present, archaeobotanists most frequently solicit assistance with difficult identifications by disseminating images over email listservs, but email is poorly suited for such purposes and is ill equipped to handle large image files and complicated discussion threads involving multiple individuals. In addition, listservs make archiving difficult, and in situations in which similar questions arise, it is difficult to access prior conversations and discussions. It has become clear that dedicated online websites capable of dynamically hosting high-quality images, as well as curating associated metadata such as field notes, site information, comments, and discussion threads, would greatly benefit the archaeobotany community.

Mandate for Improved Data Communication

In January 2011, the US National Science Foundation (NSF) mandated that all proposals include a "data management plan" in order to be considered for funding. Previously, this document was required only by some NSF programs, including Archaeology and Archaeometry. The objective of this requirement is to ensure that NSF-generated data are archived and accessible for future use (National Science Foundation 2011a). This new mandate makes the need for online archival of archaeobotanical data in the United States a pressing issue.

One longstanding problem with published archaeobotanical data is that full data sets are often not made publicly available. Journals typically have strict limitations on the number and sizes of figures and tables they allow, and as a result, most archaeobotanists produce only summarized versions of their data tables for publication. As a result, counts of grain fragments and whole grains are often combined, and sometimes even different taxa are grouped together to reduce the size of tables. For sites with many samples, the lack of space allowed in journal articles, book chapters, and monographs means that archaeobotanists forgo presenting real counts and in their place present only summary statistical measures such as ubiquity or frequency.

Although site reports are the conventional repositories of full, or at least expanded, archaeological data sets, a site report is not produced for every excavation. In addition, even in site reports there is often little room for the presentation of photographs of unidentified seeds, a fact that stunts development and reifies conventional ideas and categories. As most publishers require that authors present their work as concisely as possible, there are few venues in which a discussion can be devoted to unidentified seeds. In the majority of publications, unidentified seeds are simply combined and presented as a total sum, thereby closing the door to potential future analysis or reinterpretation.

Too Much of a Good Thing: Journals Awash in Digital Information

Paleoethnobotany is neither the first nor the only field to be seriously hampered by publication restrictions. In recognition of the severe restrictions placed on data presentation, many journals began publishing online article supplemental information in the early 2000s, but even this has turned out to be a limited and controversial solution. A large part of the controversy centers on the purpose of supplemental information: is it to provide access to non-text multimedia files? Is it to provide essential evidence that could not be accommodated in the main body of the article? Is it a venue for primary data publication?

To address both the growing demand for and criticism of supplemental information, many journals have tried to redefine and curtail supplemental information submissions (e.g., Borowski 2011; Maunsell 2010). Some journals restrict the number of files that can be uploaded (in 2013, a maximum of 10 for *Nature* and *Proceedings of the National Academy of Sciences*) or place limits on the cumulative size of supplemental files (e.g., in 2013, 50MB for *Science* and 150MB for *Nature*). Most support only a few static file formats and types. As many science bloggers (e.g., Piwowar 2010) have pointed out, journal supplemental information is a clumsy, inefficient, and heterogeneous way of storing and archiving scientific data, but it has become necessary given the unavailability of established alternative options. As technology improves and data sets become even larger, this problem will only grow.

Public Online Databases for Data Archiving

A few fields, such as genetics, dealt with this issue early and head-on. GenBank, a public, open-access, genetic sequence database was founded in 1982 as an aid to the development of the emerging field of genetics. Since 1992 it has been maintained online by the National Center for Biotechnology Information (NCBI), and as of February 2013 it contained over 162 million sequences contributed by scientists and research institutions around the world (GenBank 2011).

Increasingly, journals encourage authors to submit data to public, online databases for long-term curation and accessibility. *Science*'s database deposition policy, for example, "supports the efforts of databases that aggregate published data for the use of the scientific community" and now requires several classes of data (e.g., DNA and protein sequences, microarray data, climate data, and electron microscopy maps) to be deposited in approved public databases before publication (Science 2011).

However, for many fields, such as paleoethnobotany, there is no established online data repository, although several new resources are emerging. The *Journal of Archaeological Science* and *Vegetation History and Archaeobotany* recommend that authors submit raw data to PANGAEA (www.pangaea.de), an online data archive for earth and life sciences. Another archive popular among biologists and ecologists is DRYAD (http://datadryad.org). In addition, tDAR (the Digital Archaeological Record) repository (http://www.tdar.org) and OpenContext (http://opencontext.org) have also recently emerged as online, open-access data storage and management systems for archaeologists. All four databases meet the NSF's mandate for accessible data storage, and tDAR and OpenContext are specifically noted in the NSF Archaeology Program's guidelines for required data management plans (National Science Foundation 2011b). Submissions to these databases are assigned an enduring, unique identifier that can be used for data retrieval and which also allows submissions to be cited in publications.

NEW DIRECTIONS AND CHALLENGES

Advances in digital technology have revolutionized the field of paleoethnobotany and offer expanded possibilities and new opportunities. Improvements in data generation, computing and storage, and data sharing and communication have increased the pace and scale of paleoethnobotanical research, and the field is evolving to take advantage of the full spectrum of current and emerging technological resources. The rapid rate of change, however, has not been limited only to new advancements in hardware and software technologies. There has also been a major shift in mindset, and the last 20 years have been characterized by a changing relationship between researchers and the information they produce and use. The next generation of paleoethnobotanists will have come of age not only during the Digital Age, but also during the era of social networking and free and immediate access to a level of information that was not even imaginable in the early 2000s.

Growing Pains

This new relationship between researchers and information has at times strained conventional notions of data ownership and fair use. For example, the rise of digital PowerPoint presentations coupled with the easy accessibility of millions of online images has resulted in widespread use of web-downloaded images and graphics in classroom and public presentations, often with little or no source attribution. As a result, some researchers have come to see online data sharing as a liability that merely encourages the theft of their work. The very thing that makes digital information so valuable—its portability, clonability, and rapid transferability—is also what makes it vulnerable. This is just as true in the music and film industry as it is for researchers and scholars.

Perhaps the greatest source of anxiety for scholars wishing to engage more fully with new digital technologies is the fact that the speed of technological innovation has consistently outpaced the standards and rules of data protection, compensation, and attribution over the last two decades. For academics, whose careers are for many years governed by the tenure clock, it may seem risky or even foolhardy to experiment with web design, online database development, or blogging. And yet, blogs, websites, and other online resources are often the first places our students (and many of us) turn when exploring new topics or questions.

The immediacy and ubiquity of the Internet has tremendous appeal, and it is why scientific journals and even popular books are increasingly going online. For example, in 2011 the online bookseller Amazon.com announced that its sales of digital Kindle e-books exceeded that of print titles (Ionescu 2011). Some scientific journals, such as the high-profile Public Library of Science (PLoS) family of journals (http://www.plos.org/), exist entirely online. Among these journals, PLoS Biology has consistently ranked among the top biology journals in the Thompson ISI Journal Citation Report, and its sister journal, PLoS ONE, officially became the world's largest academic journal in 2011, with over 13,000 articles published in that year alone (Taylor 2012). Beyond the merits of the individual articles, the fact that the PLoS family journals are open access, meaning that all articles are free to access and download under a Creative Commons license (http://creativecommons .org/), likely plays a large role in the frequency of citation and overall success of the journals.

And therein lies the crux of the problem. For a scholar to engage in new forms of digital information and media is to expose oneself to risk, but also to opportunity. Attempts to harness the use of digital technology in conventional ways—restrictive licensing, copy protection software, lawsuits, and so on—have largely failed, as evidenced by the protracted and largely ineffective efforts by the music industry to prevent piracy (Boutin 2010). In the end, the music industry regained its market by making it easier to buy music through iTunes or Amazon than to copy it illegally.

Scientific data is not fundamentally different. The challenge for academia is not to hide or restrict data, but rather to share it in more responsible ways. During the development of Paleobot.org (Warinner et al. 2011), we thought for a long time about the problem of online archaeobotanical image "borrowing" without attribution, and we found that people usually do not provide image credits, despite encouragement to do so. For an open-access online database to be successful, we knew it would be essential for contributors to be properly credited for their reference collection images. As a result, we decided to employ software that automatically embeds, or watermarks, copyright information onto all images uploaded to the site, thereby making it easier to include author attribution than to exclude it. Thus, technology can be reframed to provide the solutions to its own problems.

NEW DIRECTIONS

The proliferation of open source software and the increasing popularity of Creative Commons licensing are likely to shape the immediate development of paleoethnobotanical research by facilitating the creation of new online resources and promoting data sharing in responsible and accountable ways. Government-funded data archiving and storage databases such as PANGAEA, tDAR, and DRYAD are making it easier to access and cite large research data sets, and open access archaeobotanical databases, such as Paleobot.org and InsideWood, allow researchers not only to use but also to contribute to a collective resource aimed at improving taxonomic identification.

Digital technology has facilitated collective and collaborative research on a scale that has never before been achieved. GenBank is a testament to the visionary efforts of scientists to create a collaborative online database that is now one of the most influential and widely used resources in biology, connecting laboratories around the world and leading to millions of citations each year.

In a completely different context, Wikipedia (http://www.wikipedia.org/), an open access, multilingual, online encyclopedia, has also demonstrated the power of collaborative effort. Although controversial for its nonconventional approach to editorial control and the anonymity of its contributors (Garfinkel 2008), it nevertheless boasted over 20 million articles in 2011 and was visited by 13 percent of the world's Internet users every day (Alexa 2011). Whether you see it as the bane of a teacher's existence or a helpful research tool, it remains one of the most widely accessed news and information sources in the world and cannot be ignored (Woodson 2007).

The future of learning and research is online, and it is up to scholars and scientists to define how this future will develop. There are now several working models, ranging from GenBank to Wikipedia, and academics need to start taking a more active role in creating and shaping our online research environment, both for our own benefit and for the benefit of the field as a whole. If we ignore new digital media or allow others to define the online content of our work, we risk losing control and even threaten the relevancy of our own research.

FINAL THOUGHTS

Technology is rapidly changing, and it is difficult to predict what the future has in store. Three-dimensional imaging of archaeobotanical remains is likely on the horizon, as is better automated software for macro- and microfossil analysis. However, it is difficult to make predictions beyond a few years. The year 1988, when *Current Paleoethnobotany* (Hastorf and Popper 1988) was published, would be almost unrecognizable to many of today's younger paleoethnobotanists. It was an era with few laptop computers, no World Wide Web or commercial email, no online journals or online search databases, and no mobile phones or digital cameras. Twenty-five years from now may look just as foreign to us, and it is both exciting and amazing to think about all the inventions and innovations that await us.

ACKNOWLEDGMENTS

Many thanks to technology enthusiasts Matthew Collins and Bettina Kreissl-Lonfat for always keeping us informed about the latest in software, gadgets, and other technological marvels. Thank you to software programmer David Goode, who helped us work through many of the technical issues involved in creating an online paleoethnobotanical database. We thank Naomi Miller for allowing us prepublication access to the results of her Archaeobotany Questionnaire presented at the 2010 SAAs, and the staff of the Harvard University Herbaria, who have been so helpful over the years as we have begun to think about the digital future of paleoethnobotanical collections. We would also like to thank our fellow editor, Mac Marston, for his close and constructive reading of this manuscript, and, finally, all of the authors who have contributed their efforts and perspectives to this volume.

Part III

Quantification and Analysis

9

Ratios and Simple Statistics
in Paleoethnobotanical
Analysis

*Data Exploration and
Hypothesis Testing*

JOHN M. MARSTON

From its earliest days as a discipline, paleoethnobotany moved rapidly from simple descriptive lists of macroscopic plant remains from archaeological contexts to quantification of those remains. Quantification is now seen as a critical step between the recovery of archaeological plant macroremains and their interpretation, but a variety of methods for quantification exist, from simple seed counts to multivariate statistics (Pearsall 2000). Matching this diversity of methods for quantification is the diversity in their application, with some scholars using simple quantitative methods for data exploration alone, others using them for data presentation, and still others using them for hypothesis testing. A recent trend toward increasingly complex multivariate methods for data analysis and presentation has led to new insights (see A. Smith, chapter 10, this volume), but such statistics alone are unsuitable for direct integration of paleoethnobotanical reports on a regional scale.

Simple quantitative measures, in contrast, still play an important role in paleoethnobotanical inquiry and offer great potential for intersite comparison and regional interpretation. This chapter reviews simple numerical and statistical methods for quantification of paleoethnobotanical macroremains and emphasizes their utility for both preliminary data exploration and hypothesis testing. Despite the utility and explanatory potential of multivariate statistics, I argue that continued use of non-multivariate methods of analysis is

DOI: 10.5876/9781607323167.c009

needed and that further application of simple statistical measures to answer well-defined research questions offers an avenue for interpretive development in paleoethnobotanical method and theory.

SIMPLE STATISTICS IN PALEOETHNOBOTANY

Within the broad scope of quantitative measures used in paleoethnobotany, I consider those that rely on non-multivariate statistical methods to be *simple*, a term that refers to their degree of interpretability rather than the simplicity of calculations involved (although that is often also the case). These range from absolute taxon counts, surely the simplest quantitative measure, to standardized Z-scores and diversity indices, which require significant calculation. A variety of sources already describe how these measures work and provide primary bibliography on their application (Fritz 2005; Hubbard and Clapham 1992; Jones 1991; Miller 1988; Pearsall 2000; Popper 1988; Wright 2010); the aim of this chapter is not to replicate these earlier works but to review the use of simple statistics in recent paleoethnobotanical literature and to consider future development of such measures for both exploratory data analysis and hypothesis testing.

For the purposes of this discussion, I divide all simple statistics into three categories: descriptive, standardized, and relative. Descriptive methods are methods of quantification based solely on the number of seeds or plant parts observed; this category includes absolute counts, rankings, and food value estimates. Standardized methods are those that peg the absolute count to the category of remains to which a taxon belongs or to some other norming variable, such as the amount of soil floated or number of contexts analyzed, to increase comparability between samples (and sites). Such measures include density, proportions, ubiquity, and Z-scores. Finally, relative methods compare the absolute count value of a taxon to the value of other taxa in the same sample; this category includes a wide variety of comparative ratios as well as diversity indices.

Descriptive Methods

The most straightforward method for quantification of a paleoethnobotanical data set is the absolute count of each taxon identified. This is the raw product of laboratory investigation and has been used to describe archaeobotanical assemblages since the 1960s (Helbaek 1960, 1969; Renfrew 1973). These results may be reported on a sample-by-sample basis, as is often the case in dissertations and comprehensive monographs (e.g., Miller 2010b; Riehl 1999), as well as in some longer articles and book chapters (e.g., Klinge and Fall 2010; Schwartz et al. 2000; van Zeist and Bakker-Heeres 1982, 1984a, 1984b, 1985), or may be summarized by period or area of the site (e.g., Moore et al. 2000; Weiss and Kislev 2004). The strength of this approach, especially for sample-by-sample reporting, is that it presents the complete data set as identified by the paleoethnobotanist without any form of adjustment or data manipulation. These absolute counts can be used freely by other researchers who are interested in intersite comparison or reanalysis of the data set using new statistical techniques. For this reason, absolute counts on a sample-by-sample basis should be required as a standard part of all final site reports and excavation monographs, accompanied by a detailed description of how remains were counted. The downside to absolute counts, however, especially on a sample-by-sample basis, is that they are difficult to present graphically and may take up a massive number of pages. Electronic publication of these data thus may be preferable, despite potential limitations of that medium (Warinner et al. 2011, d'Alpoim Guedes and Warinner, chapter 8, this volume). In addition, absolute counts are dependent on the original sample size and percentage of the sample sorted, so require additional standardization before comparison with other samples or sites (Popper 1988:60).

Ranking systems and conversions to food value estimates are used to regularize the comparison of different botanical elements against one another (Pearsall 2000:206–11; Popper 1988:64–66). These measures attempt to account for differences in productivity or preservation between different plants and to improve comparability of different species across or between sites. In both cases, actual counts are abstracted to a new value, whether a rank order or a food value, based on experimental observation. This new value is still directly dependent on the original count value from each sample, so remains purely descriptive of that sample. Such an approach is useful for mapping intersite variation in plant frequencies (e.g., Jacomet 2007). The limitations of absolute counts listed above still hold for these measures, however, and the additional inferential step taken to produce food value estimates or the range for equivalent ranks introduces an additional source of variation in interpreting these results. As such, studies that make extensive use of rankings and food value estimates (e.g., Diehl and Waters 2006; Flannery 1986) are unlikely to be directly comparable with other analyses done by different researchers, potentially limiting their utility for regional synthesis and reinterpretation.

Box plots represent a powerful and intuitive graphical method for conveying differences between samples, periods, or sites (Scarry 1993a:163–67; Scarry and

Steponaitis 1997; Tukey 1977; VanDerwarker 2006:75–77; Welch and Scarry 1995; see also VanDerwarker et al., this volume, figure 11.1). They are based on simple descriptive statistics calculated from sample counts and represent sample medians, typically indicated by the center of a notch, and the dispersion of values around that median, through box edges and whiskers. Box plots do not assume normal distributions, nor do they require large sample sizes, rendering them useful for representing paleoethnobotanical assemblages. When comparing box plots representing different groups of samples, the notches that do not graphically overlap the samples can be considered significantly different at the 0.05 confidence level. Typically, data will be standardized by density, as described below, and often represented as logarithms or natural logs to enhance discrimination between samples with large and small medians (e.g., Scarry 1993a:166–67; VanDerwarker 2006:99–102); however, such standardization is not required. Box plots are especially useful in spatial or temporal comparison of multiple samples (see examples and further discussion in VanDerwarker et al., chapter 11, this volume).

Standardized Measures

One challenge with quantitative paleoethnobotanical results is that changing the size or number of samples from a given feature or area can produce completely different absolute taxon counts on a sample-by-sample basis: a 10-liter soil sample ought to produce twice as many seeds as a five-liter soil sample from the same context. Standardized measures are used to address this problem and to increase intersample comparability, both over space (within one phase of a site or between synchronic sites) and over time (between different phases of a site or between sites of different periods). The two standardization methods employed most frequently are density measures, in which seed or charcoal counts or weights are normalized by the volume (or, occasionally, weight) of soil sampled, and percentages or proportions, which compare the presence of one taxon to a larger category to which it belongs (e.g., wheat grains to total cereal grains) (Miller 1988:73–75; Pearsall 2000:196–99).

Density measures are one of the most useful measures available to paleoethnobotanists because they control for differences between sample sizes. Although an arbitrary 10- or 20-liter sample may be a target sample size for flotation, real-world conditions often necessitate taking smaller samples from contexts of particular interest (e.g., hearth or vessel contents). Calculating density values for taxa of specific interest (e.g., all wild seeds, maize kernels or cupules, oak charcoal) is a necessary starting place for all intersample analyses. Proportions or percentage measures are another invaluable tool for standardizing the count of one taxon of interest against larger categories of botanical remains; these measures can be used to identify diachronic or contextual differences in the use of a particular plant across a site or between sites (Kreuz et al. 2005; Miller 1988; Miller and Smart 1984; van der Veen 2007a; VanDerwarker and Idol 2008; VanDerwarker and Kruger 2012; VanDerwarker et al. 2013).

Standard scores, also termed *Z-scores*, are values transformed to increments of standard deviations around a population mean (Drennan 2009; Shennan 1997). To be more accurate, these measures are based on computation of a sample mean and sample standard deviation, so are properly Student's *t*-statistics, but I retain the term *Z-score* (or standard score) as it is exclusively used in the paleoethnobotanical literature. The advantage of Z-scores is that they standardize each taxon by its relative abundance in a sample, so that taxa that produce large numbers of seeds per plant (e.g., *Chenopodium quinoa*) can be more meaningfully compared to taxa with low counts in archaeological contexts (e.g., maize cupules) (Pearsall 2000:199, 204).

One final type of standardized measure that has been used widely is ubiquity, which calculates the percentage of samples in which a given taxon appears (Pearsall 2000:212–16; Popper 1988:60–64). This is distinct from the other standardization methods detailed above because it standardizes presence/absence values across all samples, rather than actual count data. The utility of ubiquity has been debated (Kadane 1988:210; Pearsall 2000:214; Popper 1988:63–64; VanDerwarker 2010b:66; Wright 2010:51–52) but it remains in common use because it is easy to calculate and may be more informative than standardized count data when taxon counts in each sample are very low. Ubiquity works best when all samples are taken from similar types of contexts under similar depositional conditions and sampling measures, and can be paired with proportions or density measures to track changes in the use of taxa over time (Hastorf 1990). If samples are variable, however, ubiquity may be more misleading than helpful in identifying meaningful patterns of deposition among plant remains because a simple ubiquity measure will conflate and obscure intrasite variation (Pearsall 2000:214).

The limitations of standardized measures are most evident when counts for each taxon are low, as differences of one or two seeds between samples are magnified into seemingly substantial intersample differences in proportion or percentage. Although ubiquity does not suffer from this limitation, it reduces count data to presence/absence and thus treats samples with large quantities of a taxon the same as those with isolated finds of that taxon (Hubbard 1980:52; Kadane 1988:210). In addition, ubiquity is sensitive to sample number and thus different sampling strategies can produce substantively different results and conclusions (Popper 1988:61).

RELATIVE MEASURES

In contrast with descriptive measures, which are based solely on absolute counts, and standardized measures, which are based on absolute counts as parts of a whole (i.e., taxon, sample, or category of remains), relative measures relate the count of one taxon to that of another. This includes a wide variety of ratios in which the numerator is exclusive of the denominator (termed *comparisons* by Miller [1988:75]) and diversity indices, which indicate the homogeneity or heterogeneity of a sample or group of samples and are calculated based on the relative values of multiple taxa (Pearsall 2000:210–11; Popper 1988; Shannon and Weaver 1949; Simpson 1949). The unique strength of relative values lies in this comparative aspect, which allows straightforward visualization and interpretation of changes in multiple taxa over time or space.

Diversity indices are less commonly used in paleoethnobotany than in other archaeological fields, including zooarchaeology (Peres 2010; Reitz and Wing 2008; VanDerwarker 2010b). This is partially due to inherent issues of equifinality, in that one diversity index value represents both the evenness and species richness of a sample, so samples with few taxa but high evenness may have diversity values similar to those with many taxa and low evenness (Popper 1988). The two most common diversity indices used in archaeology are the Shannon-Weaver index (Shannon and Weaver 1949) and Simpson's diversity index (Simpson 1949), both of which incorporate measures of species evenness and richness to calculate diversity between samples. The Shannon-Weaver index calculates sample diversity on a scale of 0 (only one taxon present, no diversity) to a maximum relative to the number of taxa present (multiple taxa, evenly distributed), whereas the Simpson's diversity index uses the same input variables but produces a value of diversity that ranges from 0 (no diversity) to 1 (infinite diversity). The notable difference between the Shannon-Weaver and Simpson's indices is that the latter is less sensitive to the presence of few rare taxa than the former, so may be more appropriate for the analysis of paleoethnobotanical assemblages that are numerically dominated by a few ubiquitous taxa. In addition, the value of the Simpson's index is bounded between 0 and 1, allowing for a ready comparison with the maximum theoretical diversity measure (i.e., the maximum is independent of the number of taxa present), which aids in comparison of values between sites. A related, though rarely used, measure is niche width, which measures the evenness of resource utilization (Christenson 1980; Wymer 1993).

Comparison ratios, in which the numerator and denominator represent different taxa, are powerful tools for identifying patterns in paleoethnobotanical data, visualizing those patterns, and testing hypotheses. Given appropriate attention to how such ratios can address the specific research question of the analyst (Miller 1988; Wright 2010), it is possible to design ratios that measure specific relationships that might change across time or over space. Such ratios might be indicative of changes in fuel use (Klinge and Fall 2010; Miller 1996, 1997; Miller and Marston 2012; Miller and Smart 1984), crop processing (Scarry 2003; Stevens 2003b; VanDerwarker 2005, 2006; VanDerwarker and Stanyard 2009; Welch and Scarry 1995), agricultural risk management (Marston 2011), or environmental disturbance and degradation (Gremillion et al. 2008; Marston 2012a; Miller and Marston 2012). Comparative ratios are the most versatile simple statistic available to paleoethnobotanical researchers; recent scholarship demonstrates the utility of these ratios and other simple statistics in addressing a broad variety of research questions for both preliminary data exploration and hypothesis testing.

APPLICATIONS FOR DATA EXPLORATION

Simple statistics are well suited to data exploration, as they reduce complex tabular quantitative data into single numerical values that allow comparison between samples over space and time (Tukey 1977). Such "pattern searching" approaches (Jones 1991:70) allow for inductive interpretation of possibly meaningful spatial and temporal trends in the distribution of paleoethnobotanical remains, and are compatible with exploratory uses of multivariate statistics (VanDerwarker 2010a; A. Smith, chapter 10, this volume). Data exploration using simple statistics is thus a recommended first step in the quantitative analysis of paleoethnobotanical samples (Pearsall 2000:246).

In this section, I describe the use of simple statistics for exploring data and identifying patterns across space (within and between sites) and over time, with an emphasis on recent literature in the field. See earlier reviews for additional references from the 1960s through the 1990s (Hastorf 1999; Jones 1991; Miller 1988; Pearsall 2000; Popper 1988), as well as other chapters in this volume for additional approaches to intra- (VanDerwarker et al., chapter 11, this volume) and intersite analysis (Stevens, chapter 12, this volume).

Identifying spatial patterning among paleoethnobotanical macroremains within single sites remains a challenge in reconstruction of the past (VanDerwarker et al., chapter 11, this volume). One limitation when interpreting intrasite variation is sample size, which often precludes applying statistical tests to individual samples and results in samples being grouped by area or (more frequently) by phase, eliminating potential interpretation of spatial variation (Jones 1991).

Simple measures, such as percentage composition of samples, are well suited to this type of intrasite spatial analysis. In one notable study, Hastorf (1991) investigated the spatial distribution of domestic food plants among the pre-Hispanic Sausa of Peru using spatially referenced pie charts that indicate the relative proportion of different domesticates in each sample (figure 9.1). These maps convey patterns of behavior, indicating that certain structures were used for food storage and processing, whereas others were used as dumps or compost areas, and open patios were preferred for maize processing (Hastorf 1991:142–43). This pie chart approach to visualizing relative percentages of taxa within a site or between sites has since been applied to investigate spatial distribution of food plants in other paleoethnobotanical studies in both the Old World (Allen 2005; Alonso et al. 2008; Borojevic 2011; Grabowski 2011; Hald 2010; Hald and Charles 2008) and New World (Lennstrom and Hastorf 1992, 1995). Alternately, density plots overlaid on maps of archaeological sites can illustrate the spatial distribution of botanical remains, perhaps more effectively than pie charts (Bogaard et al. 2009; Hally 1981; Weiss et al. 2008; see especially figures in VanDerwarker et al., chapter 11, this volume).

Intersite variation in paleoethnobotanical remains can show patterns of plant processing that indicate status differences or specialization of labor within a society. Trinary graphs (or triangular scatter plots) are an effective way to depict the relative proportions of three classes of data on one graph and can be used to identify differences in agricultural practices or plant disposal within or between sites (Alonso et al. 2008; Jones and Rowley-Conwy 2007; Stevens 2003b; van der Veen 1992a; figure 9.2). Welch and Scarry (1995) used box plots of logarithmically transformed standardized measures to compare diet and food processing between isolated farmsteads and higher-status residential centers in the Moundville polity. They found significant differences in nutshell and maize processing between farmsteads and population centers, with much higher levels of food processing at farmsteads but similar levels of maize consumption between the two types of sites (Welch and Scarry 1995).

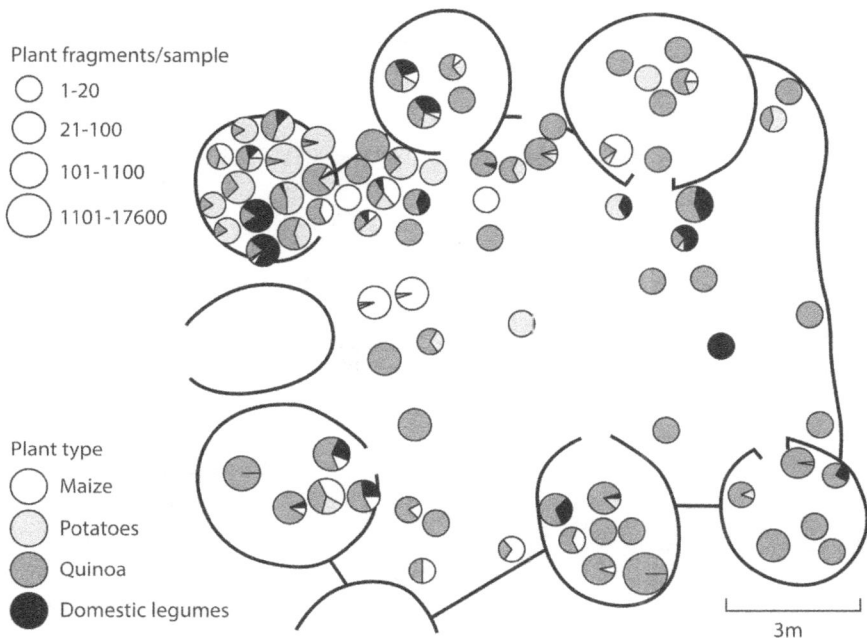

FIGURE 9.1. *Sample pie chart map showing differential use of plants over space within a household compound. Although this image is overly complex, some basic patterning (i.e., maize processed outside, potatoes primarily in upper left structure) can be discerned. After Hastorf 1991:figure 5.1.*

Across Time

The investigation of diachronic change at multiperiod sites is best approached through simple statistics. Any type of standardized or relative measure can be easily tracked over time as a way to identify meaningful patterns of change resulting from environmental or cultural change within a society. Among standardized measures, change in density measures and proportions of certain food or fuel taxa over time is typically grounds for further investigation of why certain plants, or classes of plants, became more or less common during different periods (Crawford 1997; Hastorf 1990; Miller 2010b; Mrozowski et al. 2008; Pearsall 1983). Proportions are especially useful in tracking changes in wood charcoal assemblages between periods, a proxy measure of changes in wood use and forest structure over time. Work in the Mediterranean and Near East has identified declines in slow-growing trees and their replacement by scrub vegetation as an effect of human population expansion throughout

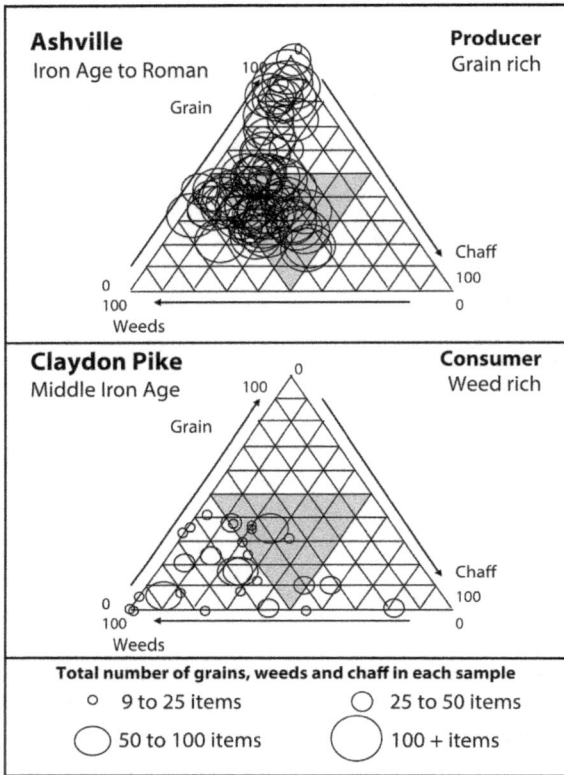

FIGURE 9.2. *Sample trinary graphs distinguishing relative proportions of cereal grain, cereal chaff, and weed seeds in samples from two sites in England, designated as producer and consumer sites. After Stevens 2003:figure 3.*

the region (Eastwood et al. 1998; Marston 2009, 2010; Miller 1999; Rubiales et al. 2011; Willcox 1974); anthropogenic changes in forest succession also have been identified in the area surrounding the Mississippian site of Cahokia in the American Bottom (Lopinot and Woods 1993).

Diversity measures are also well suited to exploratory data analysis. Changes in diversity measures over time at multiphase sites may illustrate chronological trends in the diversity of food remains and human-affected plant communities. Scarry (1993a) found that diversity in maize type declines over time in two different valleys of the Moundville polity, indicating that farmers were increasingly standardized in their production (figure 9.3).

Wymer (1993) found a similar result during the Middle Woodland to Late Woodland transition in the central Ohio River valley, which, combined with declining niche width, indicates agricultural intensification. VanDerwarker and colleagues (VanDerwarker et al. 2013) associated declines in maize production and increases in wild plant food diversity with increasing uncertainty and risk among contact-era Cherokee. I used this statistic to identify diachronic change in steppe grassland health, presumably as a result of different grazing regimens, between periods of occupation at Gordion, in central Anatolia (Marston 2010). Comparison ratios can also be used to identify similar diachronic trends in diet, agriculture, and land use, but are perhaps better suited to hypothesis testing, as detailed below.

APPLICATIONS FOR HYPOTHESIS TESTING

Hypothesis testing has been one primary aim of paleoethnobotanical analysis since the first widespread publication of quantitative data from systematic flotation samples. Although some hypotheses, especially those related to the chronology of certain morphological characteristics related to domestication processes, can be addressed through presence/absence (e.g., Boivin and Fuller 2009; Denham 2005; Diehl 2005; Fuller 2006, 2007b) or categorical data (e.g., Asouti and Fuller 2013), most hypotheses about agricultural production and land use require the use of quantitative data. Simple statistics are well suited to test implications of hypothetical models derived from broader bodies of theory and from previous archaeological exploration in a region.

Several robust bodies of ecological theory give rise to models that can be tested using paleoethnobotanical data and recent efforts in the field have focused on testing models derived from niche construction theory (Smith 2007a, 2009b; B. Smith, chapter 18, this volume) and behavioral ecology (Gremillion 1996a, 1998, 2002b; Gremillion and Piperno 2009a; Kennett and Winterhalder 2006; Marston 2009, 2011; Piperno and Pearsall 1998a; Winterhalder and Goland 1997; Gremillion, chapter 17, this volume). In addition, prior archaeological research in a region may lead to specific hypotheses about diet, land use, and agricultural practices that can be answered through paleoethnobotanical investigation (e.g., Fuller and Stevens 2009; Hillman 1984a; Marston 2012a; Miller 1999; Miller and Marston 2012; Miller et al. 2009; van der Veen 2007a; VanDerwarker 2006). Spatial or diachronic change in standardized measures or relative measures applied to specific taxa provides an especially effective method to test implications of such hypotheses.

In this section, I detail recent approaches to hypothesis testing through the use of simple statistics, with a particular focus on the use of spatial and diachronic change in specially constructed ratios to identify human behavior in the paleoethnobotanical record. Other methods of hypothesis testing using multivariate statistics complement this approach and have additional

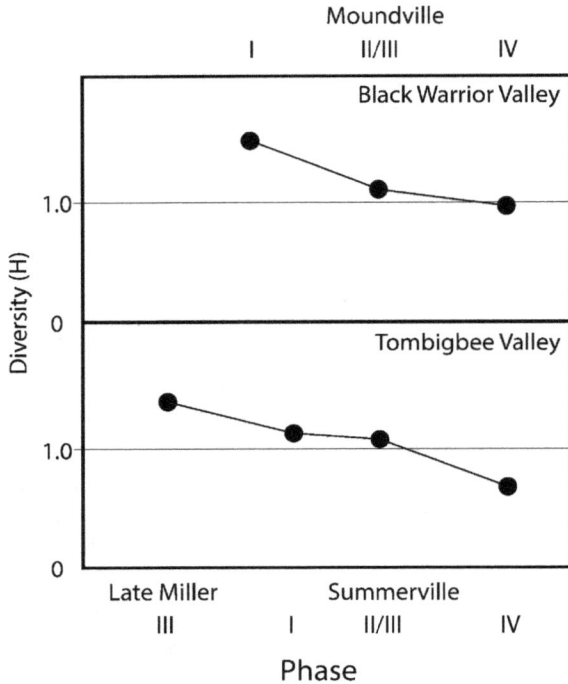

FIGURE 9.3. *Sample Shannon-Weaver diversity graph comparing maize cob row number diversity between two regions over time. After Scarry 1993:figure 11–17.*

benefits for uniting the analysis of animal and plant remains quantitatively (Colledge et al. 2004; Smith and Munro 2009; VanDerwarker 2010a; VanDerwarker and Peres 2010; A. Smith, chapter 10, this volume). Simple statistics, and especially comparative ratios, however, incorporate a smaller set of taxa and can be more specifically tailored to hypothetical test implications, providing greater clarity during analysis and interpretation, and better comparability between sites and regions.

ACROSS SPACE

Both inter- and intrasite variation can be interpreted through the application of comparative ratios that have been designed to test specific hypothetical implications based on the research questions being addressed. One such research question is related to the location of crop processing among sites within a cultural zone. In the New World, a maize kernel-to-cupule ratio (figure 9.4) indicates the relative proportion of cleaned maize kernels to crop processing debris (maize cupules) and can be compared on a regional scale

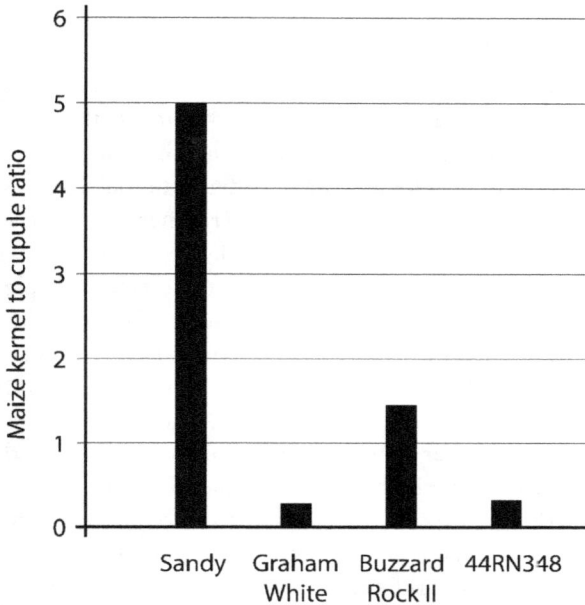

FIGURE 9.4. *Sample comparative ratio: the maize kernel-to-cupule ratio across four Late Woodland sites in the Roanoke valley. After VanDerwarker and Stanyard 2009:figure 3.*

(Peres 2010; Scarry 2003; VanDerwarker 2005, 2006, 2010b; VanDerwarker and Stanyard 2009). Scarry (1993a, 2003; Scarry and Scarry 2005; Scarry and Steponaitis 1997; Welch and Scarry 1995) identified distinct spatial patterns of these remains as evidence for variable locations of crop processing and food preparation in the Southeastern United States.

Similarly, VanDerwarker applied this ratio to Olmec sites on the Gulf Coast of Mexico and Late Woodland sites in Virginia (VanDerwarker 2005, 2006; VanDerwarker and Stanyard 2009). These studies identified differences in the kernel:cupule ratio as evidence for local processing of maize at some settlements (such as the Olmec site of Bezuapan and most Late Woodland sites of the Roanoke valley) but for importation of processed grain to other settlements (the Olmec site of La Joya and the Late Woodland Sandy site). At sites in Europe, regional patterns of labor mobilization can be identified through comparison across several sites of two different measures of crop processing, as measured by the ratio of weeds to cereals combined with the ratio of large to small weed seeds or the ratio of cereal grains to glume bases (Fuller and Stevens 2011; Stevens 2003b).

Alternately, comparative ratios can test the expectations of ecological models relating to the location of cultivation in an ecologically variable environment.

Gremillion and colleagues tested hypothetical upland and lowland cultivation systems in the Cumberland Plateau of eastern Kentucky by comparing the percentages of seeds from lowland, upland, and intermediate plant communities among nine sites in the region; they found that most sites used lowland or intermediate zones for agricultural production (Gremillion et al. 2008). Similar models derived from ecological theory offer potential avenues for quantitative analysis of paleoethnobotanical remains (Kennett et al. 2006; Piperno 2006a; Piperno and Pearsall 1998a; Zeanah 2004).

Naomi F. Miller has applied a seed-to-charcoal ratio (figure 9.5) to multiple prehistoric and early historic sites in the Near East to identify differential patterns of fuel use between sites located in arid steppe environments and wooded areas (Miller 1996, 1997; Miller and Smart 1984). In a recent paper, Miller and I broadened this analysis to six sites on the upper Euphrates, where annual rainfall varies from 500 mm to 200 mm over a few hundred kilometers (Miller and Marston 2012). We tested the hypothesis that reduced rainfall would necessitate increased use of animal dung for fuel across this region through the use of a seed-to-charcoal ratio and identified a general trend in which median seed-to-charcoal ratios are higher at more arid sites, as predicted. We also used a wild-seed-to-cereal ratio as a measure of foddering animals with agricultural products and identified a similar geographic trend, with increased foddering in wetter areas, where crop yields are higher and more consistent (Miller and Marston 2012). This same geographic comparative approach has been applied to Bronze Age sites in Cyprus, Jordan, and Syria, where the authors found similar trends relating forest cover, dung fuel use, and animal foddering across vegetation and rainfall clines (Klinge and Fall 2010).

Across Time

Comparative ratios can be used to identify why different agricultural practices may have been adopted over time at a single site. Research at Gordion, in Central Anatolia, shows substantial variation in agricultural strategies over nearly 3,000 years of occupation (Marston 2010, 2011, 2012a; Miller 2011b; Miller et al. 2009).

I devised a proxy measure of steppe health (figure 9.6) using charred seeds from animal dung burned as fuel; this ratio compares plants that are indicators of healthy, protected steppe to those that resist predation, either through physical (i.e., spines) or chemical defenses, and are often the last plants left in severely overgrazed areas (Marston 2011, 2012a). This ratio is strongly correlated with regional population levels: evidently, high regional population led

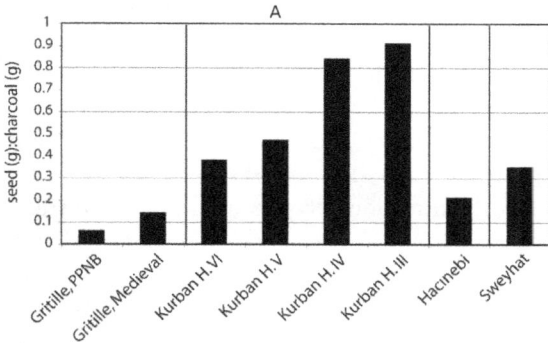

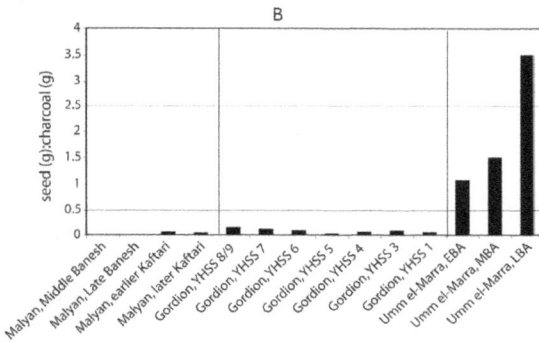

FIGURE 9.5. *Sample comparative ratio: seed to charcoal ratio across time and space among six Near Eastern sites, (a) in the Upper Euphrates valley and (b) outside the valley. From Miller and Marston 2012:figures 3 and 4.*

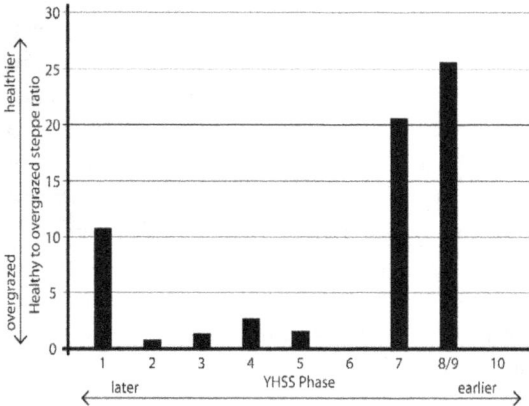

FIGURE 9.6. *Sample comparative ratio: changes in steppe health over time at Gordion, Turkey, measured by a ratio of plants indicative of healthy steppe (mainly perennial grasses) to those present in overgrazed areas (here,* Alhagi *and* Peganum*). YHSS 1 is the latest phase (Medieval) and YHSS 10 the earliest (Middle Bronze Age). From Marston 2012:figure 8.*

to overgrazing. Similar trends are evident in wood use at Gordion and at the site of Malyan in Iran, with increasing regional population leading to forest succession and deforestation (Marston 2010, 2012a; Miller 1985, 1999, 2010b; Miller and Marston 2012).

Wild-seed-to-cereal ratios can be used to identify diachronic change in animal foddering (Marston 2011; Miller 1997; Miller and Marston 2012; Miller et al. 2009) but also changes in cereal cultivation practices resulting from shifts between primary cultivars (Fuller and Stevens 2011). Gremillion and colleagues identified significant increases in the weed-to-canopy-seed and lowland-to-upland-seed ratios over time from a number of sites in the Cumberland Plateau, concluding that human agricultural activities led to increasing disturbance in plant communities over time (Gremillion et al. 2008:400).

CONCLUSIONS AND FUTURE DIRECTIONS

Quantitative reporting of paleoethnobotanical remains, especially on a sample-by-sample basis, permits numerical analysis of trends over space and over time using both simple and multivariate statistics. Simple statistics include descriptive statistics, which are useful for presenting data, and standardized and comparative statistics, which are powerful tools for data exploration and hypothesis testing. Recent scholarship has focused on the use of simple statistics primarily during the data exploration stage of paleoethnobotanical analysis, but comparative ratios in particular offer an avenue for hypothesis testing both within and between sites and regions.

One current trend in paleoethnobotanical analysis is the increased use of multivariate statistics, which have a long history in Europe but have only been widely applied in North America during the last decade (Jones 1991; Pearsall 2000; VanDerwarker 2010a; A. Smith, chapter 10, this volume; VanDerwarker et al., chapter 11, this volume). These methods of analysis are well suited to simplify massive data tables and can produce unique insights into the use of plants in the past (e.g., Colledge et al. 2004; Peres 2010; Smith and Munro 2009; van der Veen 2007a). In contrast, simple statistics rely on selective use of specific taxa from the paleoethnobotanical assemblage, and for this reason can be easily targeted to test hypotheses with clear paleoethnobotanical implications. Simple statistics have the potential to test implications of ecological and behavior models that predict certain dietary or agricultural responses to environmental and cultural change, and should be considered more often for hypothesis testing as well as data exploration.

ACKNOWLEDGMENTS

I thank Naomi Miller, Alexia Smith, and two anonymous reviewers, as well as my fellow editors, for their close and constructive readings of this manuscript. Chris Stevens provided original artwork that was the basis for figure 9.2. Finally, my deepest thanks go out to all the authors in this volume, especially those who participated in our 2011 SAA electronic symposium, for making this book possible.

10

*The Use of Multivariate
Statistics within
Archaeobotany*

Alexia Smith

Over the past decade, the use of multivariate statistics within archaeobotanical analyses has become commonplace, particularly within Europe. This chapter begins with a description of the types of multivariate techniques that have been used by archaeobotanists, followed by a brief history and a survey of studies that have used these techniques to explore plant data, outlining the ways in which the techniques have been applied to consider a broad range of research questions. Emphasis is placed on macrobotanical remains, particularly those from the Old World, but analyses of phytolith, starch grain, and pollen data are also discussed.

MULTIVARIATE TECHNIQUES
USED IN ARCHAEOBOTANY

Multivariate statistics encompass a wide range of statistical techniques that allow for the simultaneous observation and analysis of multiple variables. Baxter (1994:1) notes that within archaeology, the most widely used multivariate techniques are cluster analysis, discriminant analysis (DA), principal components analysis (PCA), and correspondence analysis (CA). The same holds true for archaeobotanical applications with the addition of canonical correspondence analysis (CCA), which has witnessed increased use in recent years. The basic goals and utility of each of these techniques is described below, following by a discussion of how the techniques have been used within archaeobotany. Since

DOI: 10.5876/9781607323167.c010

it is impossible to adequately discuss the mathematical details underlying each of the techniques mentioned here, interested readers are referred to the relevant sources cited within the discussion of each technique.

Multivariate statistics may be used to discover structure or patterning within a data set; highlight relationships between samples and/or species (here *sample* is used to describe the assemblage of plant material recovered from a particular unit of sediment); summarize and succinctly present large data sets; reduce noise within the data and identify outliers; or classify or group samples based on their contents (Gauch 1982). The techniques can be divided into two main approaches: direct and indirect. With direct approaches, such as DA and CCA, it is possible to assess the extent to which *known* variables influence the data. Known variables could include measurements or ecological characteristics of species, or the age of a sample. Indirect approaches, such as cluster analysis, PCA, and CA, allow for more open-ended explorations of the data set and do not presume that the variables affecting the botanical data are known. In these cases, it is the job of the researcher to examine the output of the analysis and determine which variables likely cause the most variation within the data set. Oftentimes, it is advantageous to apply a variety of methods to a single data set (including subsets of the entire data set) since this provides a more detailed understanding of the nature of the variables affecting species composition between samples and also provides a means for assessing the consistency of patterning observed between techniques (Lepš and Šmilauer 2003:38–39).

Prior to conducting any analysis, it is essential to appropriately clean and prepare data sets. Jones (1991:67–69) provides an excellent discussion of data preparation prior to analysis (including data selection, reduction, standardization, and transformation). It is important to stress that for all techniques, in addition to cleaning and preparing data, efforts should be made to ensure that the samples are independent from one another (Jones 1991:67). In practical terms, this means that each sample collected from a site should be archaeologically distinct from all other samples. Species data generated from floated sediment samples that are stratigraphically or contextually indistinguishable must be combined prior to analysis since they are not separate entities. Lee (2012:650) provides a thoughtful discussion of this topic in her consideration of the impacts of taphonomy and sample size on species data.

Cluster Analysis

The term *cluster analysis* describes a variety of classification techniques that can be used to identify groups of sites, samples, or other observations within a data set without presupposing the existence or nature of any particular grouping (Aldenderfer and Blashfield 1984; Baxter 1994:chapters 7 and 8, 2003:chapter 8; Everitt et al. 2001; Shennan 1997:chapter 11; ter Braak 1995). Methods may be hierarchical or nonhierarchical. Hierarchical methods assume that a hierarchical order exists within the data, such that certain groupings of samples or species are more important than others, rendering them higher within the hierarchy (plant classification, for example, employs a hierarchical system with phylum occupying a high level, followed by class, order, family, genus, species, and then subspecies or variety at increasingly lower levels). Nonhierarchical methods, in contrast, do not impose a hierarchy and can be particularly useful for data reduction by helping a researcher identify redundancy, noise, and outliers within the data set that may obscure underlying patterns (van Tongeren 1995:175). The results of nonhierarchical approaches are often presented within a table that summarizes the groups within each cluster (van Tongeren 1995:199).

Hierarchical methods may be divisive or agglomerative. With divisive methods, the entire group of individuals (within archaeobotany, "individuals" are typically represented by samples but can also be represented by individual speciments for classification purposes) is divided into two according to criteria set by the researcher. Each new group is then subdivided further, with the differences between groups progressively getting smaller with each division (van Tongeren 1995). In contrast, agglomerative methods form small groups from the entire set of individuals, which are then grouped into larger groups based on measures of similarity. In each case, the resultant groupings may be depicted visually within a dendogram, or tree diagram (figure 10.1).

Cluster analysis techniques tend to work best when discrete differences between groups exist; the methods are typically less effective when the data form a continuum (van Tongeren 1995). Baxter (2003:92) notes that although "the use of cluster analysis in archaeology is common, there is considerably more skepticism about what it can be expected to achieve" now compared with the 1960s and 1970s, so it is important that the results (as with any technique) are considered carefully and critically: resultant groupings may reflect true divisions within the data set or may be completely arbitrary (Shennan 1997:222). The validity of the groupings can be assessed using a variety of statistical tools (see Baxter 1994:chapter 8; Shennan 1997:chapter 11 for more details on these techniques), but it is the job of researchers to use their expertise and knowledge of taphonomy, preservation, plant processing, ecology, or any other relevant information to interpret the resultant clusterings in meaningful manners.

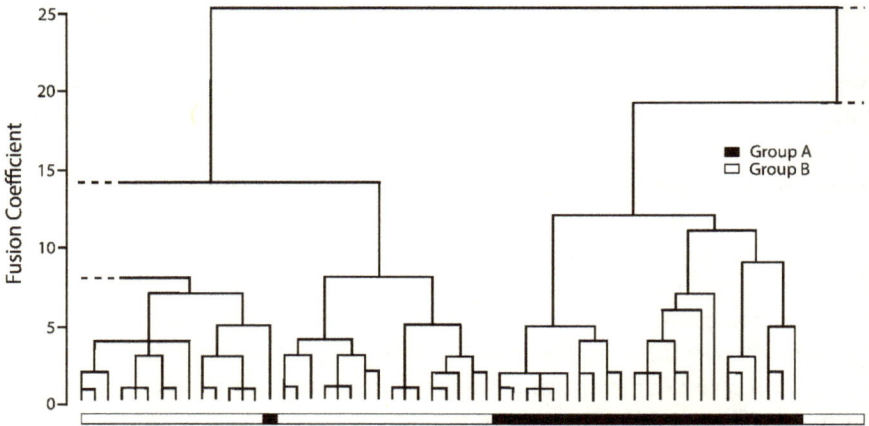

FIGURE 10.1. *Tree diagram illustrating the results of a cluster analysis of prehistoric archaeobotanical assemblages from northern England using Ellenberg's (1979) indicator values of species' position along an ecological gradient to examine differences between samples from two groups. Figure adapted from van der Veen (1992:figure 10.11).*

Within archaeobotany, Jones (1987) and Chernoff (1988) employed cluster analysis to help determine the stages of cereal and legume crop processing present in archaeobotanical samples from Greece and Israel, respectively. Van der Veen (1992a) also used Ward's (1963) method to explore differences in sample composition among samples from sites in northern England (figure 10.1). Ethnographic research has shown that the range of crop parts and the types of weed seeds selectively removed via each crop processing stage such as harvesting, threshing, winnowing, and sieving are fairly predictable (e.g., Hillman 1984a; G. Jones 1984). Building from these studies, Jones (1987) was able to use the density of charred seeds within sediment, the state of seed preservation, the ratio of weed to crop seeds, the degree of seed distortion, and the size, weight, and headedness (i.e., the ability to stay within a seed head) of weed seeds as variables within cluster analysis to help assess the nature and extent of crop processing. She stresses that determining the stage of cereal or crop processing within a sample is not a means unto itself, since archaeobotanical studies consider a wide variety of factors beyond cereals and their processing. By using this approach, however, it is possible to determine whether samples represent cereal storage caches, processing debris associated with a particular state of processing, or mixed assemblages that represent processing debris from crops that cannot be processed together. With this information available, it is possible to more rigorously consider the likely origin of a sample as well as the extent to which crop husbandry practices can be effectively examined since it is challenging to reconstruct crop ecology if most of the weeds have been removed via late stage processing.

Discriminant Analysis

Discriminant analysis (DA) encompasses a range of techniques that use linear combinations of variables to develop a predictive model of how well samples may be discriminated between *known* and defined groups. It is the responsibility of the researcher to define the groupings of samples or objects based on the pertinent research questions and methods of data collection (Baxter 1994:chapters 9 and 10, 2003:chapter 9; Shennan 1997:350–52). Although DA is not considered exploratory, Baxter (1994:185) notes that within archaeology, the approach can take on a "more exploratory nature" when it is used to display results generated through cluster analysis: DA may also be used as a means for assessing or validating the success of cluster analysis results (Baxter 1994:204). The success of DA may be assessed informally by examining the separation of groups on a plot (figure 10.2) or more formally by estimating the extent to which members are misclassified (Baxter 2003:108–10 provides further discussion on estimating the error rate).

Baxter (1994:186) cites a number of uses of DA within archaeology, the most common example being Fisher's linear discriminant function analysis (LDA):

> The aim may be to confirm that the presumed groups are indeed distinct; to characterise groups on the basis of the coefficients associated with the linear combinations of the variables; to identify individuals that do not readily fit into their presumed group; to identify those variables that best discriminate between groups, or to provide a criterion for allocating unclassified individuals to a group.

Within archaeobotany, DA has been used to develop predictive models to help (1) distinguish between a variety of plant taxa based on measurements of modern comparative material (e.g., Ball et al. 2006; Mangafa and Kotsakis 1996; Piperno 1988; Wilson 1985); (2) assess the crop processing stage of an archaeobotanical samples (G. Jones 1984); and (3) infer ancient agricultural practices based on observations of modern weed assemblages collected under differing crop husbandry regimes (Jones et al. 2010). These studies are discussed in greater detail below.

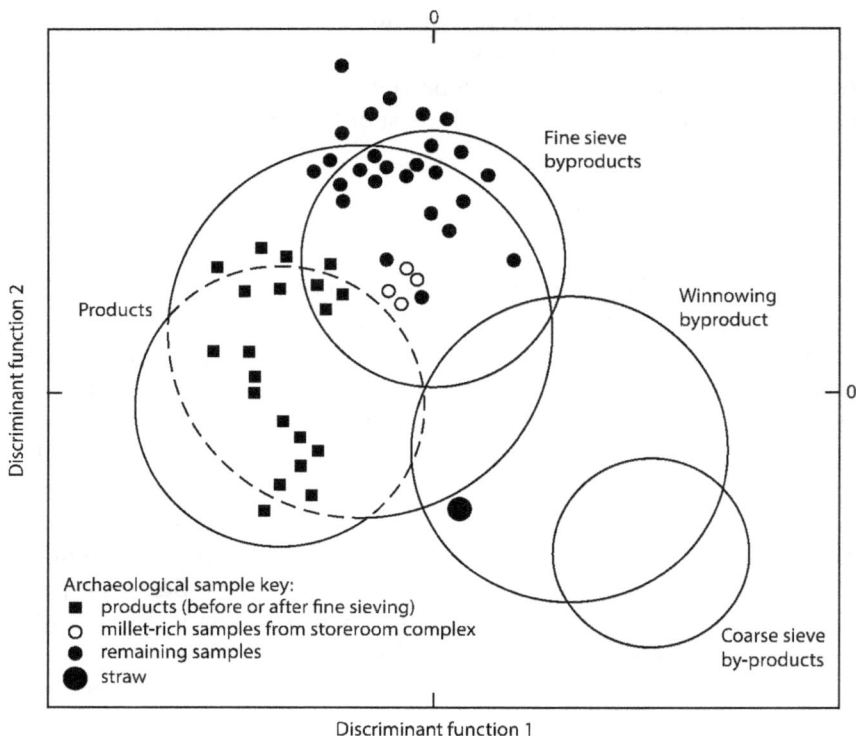

Figure 10.2. *Discriminant analysis plot illustrating the separation of ethnographic crop processing debris from Greece. Figure adapted from Jones (1987:figure 1). Large circles represent ethnographic processing groups and enclose 90% of the samples in each group (Jones 1987:315).*

Principal Components Analysis

Principal components analysis (PCA) and correspondence analysis (CA) are both descriptive, exploratory, unconstrained/open-ended techniques that aim to arrange samples based on their species composition, without assuming any prior knowledge of the variables affecting the species composition (Baxter 1994:chapters 3 and 4, 2003:chapter 7; Gauch 1982:135–44; Jolliffe 2002; Madsen 1988; Shennan 1997:chapter 12; ter Braak 1995:116–32). Both methods may be referred to as indirect gradient ordination analysis, but they differ in that PCA adopts a linear model whereas CA employs weighted averaging (Lepš and Šmilauer 2003:37). Shennan (1997:265) defines ordination as "the representation of relationships between items and between variables in a space of a small number of dimensions which still retains most of the information in the original descriptive variables." As such, the information from a large database can be summarized within biplots that illustrate the sample or site points together with the species data along perpendicular axes. As ter Braak (1995:91) states:

> The aim of ordination is to arrange the points such that points that are close together correspond to sites [or samples] that are similar in species composition, and points that are far apart correspond to sites that are dissimilar in species composition.

Consequently, ordination can reveal patterning within large sample/species data sets and identify similarities or dissimilarities between samples or groups of samples. Although it is possible to observe only two dimensions at any single time within a biplot, by examining multiple biplots, multidimensional space can be considered.

PCA functions by summarizing the variables that affect a data set into a smaller set of variables such that the first principal component explains as much variance within the data as possible (Shennan 1997:chapter 12). It does so by assuming that the more correlated variables are statistically, the more related they are from an interpretive perspective. Gauch (1982:136) notes that the PCA model assumes that the fundamental variables or "components" follow the normal distribution and are uncorrelated, requirements that are rarely met with field/ecological data. He adds that these assumptions need to be adhered to precisely for statistical testing of hypotheses, but strict adherence is not so necessary for descriptive explorations of a data set. PCA has been used by archaeobotanists to some degree (Hillman 1984a; Jones 1983b; VanDerwarker 2010a), but its usage has been surpassed by CA in recent years, given CA's better suitability to the nature of archaeobotanical data (figure 10.3). Examples of PCA studies are provided below.

CORRESPONDENCE ANALYSIS AND DETRENDED
CORRESPONDENCE ANALYSIS

Correspondence analysis (CA; also known as reciprocal averaging), has rapidly become the most widely used multivariate technique within archaeobotany today, and CANOCO (developed by Cajo J. F. ter Braak and Petr Šmilauer) has become the standard software of choice (Baxter 1994:chapters 5 and 6; Greenacre 2007; Lepš and Šmilauer 2003; Shennan 1997:chapter 13; ter Braak 1985, 1995:95–116; ter Braak and Šmilauer 2002). CA is well suited to

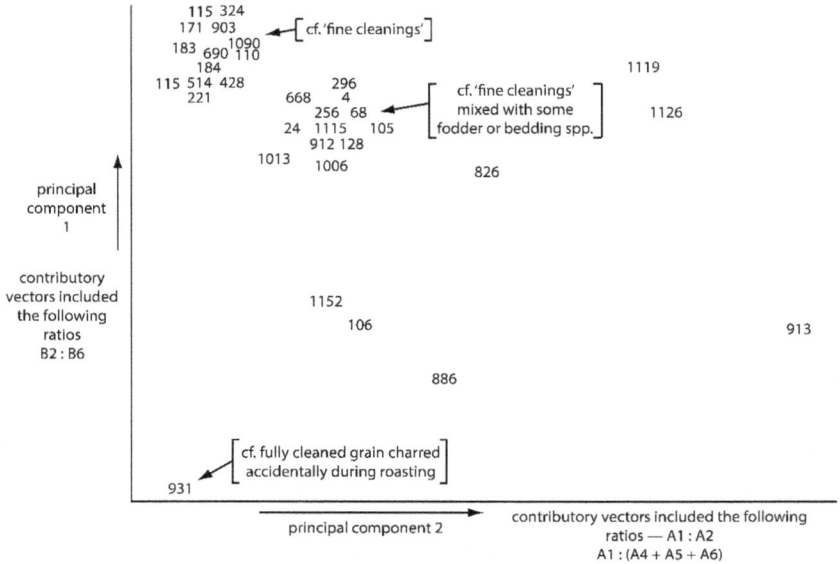

FIGURE 10.3. *Principal components analysis biplot of ratios between major classes of plant remains in some samples from the site of Cefn Graeanog II, Wales. Each three or four digit number represents a separate sample. For some major clusters, tentative identifications are offered in terms of the product or processing debris type represented. These identifications are based on comparisons of the range and ratio values characterizing the samples in each cluster with the equivalent values in present-day plant products. Figure adapted from Hillman (1984:figure 7).*

archaeobotanical data because it can accommodate (1) a large number of species (10–500); (2) presence/absence species data; (3) abundance data sets (i.e., counts of taxa within a sample) that include numerous zero values (given that many species may be present, but not in all samples); and (4) a nonlinear, unimodal relationship between species and quantitative environmental variables whereby a species' abundance peaks within a set range along an environmental gradient (ter Braak 1996:1). PCA, in contrast, adopts a linear model in which species abundance increases or decreases (but does not peak) along an environmental gradient (ter Braak 1995:93–95).

CA simultaneously creates weighted averages of columns and rows of species and sample data matrices, employing eigenanalysis to calculate the "total variance in species data as measured by the chi-square [χ^2] of the sample-by-species table divided by the table's total" (ter Braak and Šmilauer 2002:123).

The results, presented within a biplot, can then be used to assess, for example, the presence of rare or commonly encountered taxa, samples that contain similar assemblages of species, as well as the likelihood of co-occurrence of species within a sample. Detailed rules for interpreting the diagrams are provided by Lepš and Šmilauer (2003:chapter 10), Šmilauer and Lepš (2014: chapter 11), and ter Braak (1988; ter Braak and Šmilauer 2002). In brief, however, the greatest amount of variance within the data is represented along the first (horizontal) axis, with lesser variance represented by the second (vertical) axis (figure 10.4).

Typically, common species tend to cluster around the origin with rarer species falling on the outer edges of the biplot. For short gradient lengths (ca. 2 standard deviation units), the biplot rule can be used, whereby a line is drawn from the species' points through the origin and sample points are then perpendicularly projected onto this line. Samples that join the line closest to the species tend to have a greater relative abundance of the given species than those that connect further away. A hypothetical example of the biplot rule is illustrated in figure 10.4. It is important to stress that in addition to following these rules, thorough interpretation of the plots requires detailed knowledge of the preservation, deposition, and archaeological context of samples as well as plant ecology.

Although CA provides a powerful tool for examining archaeobotanical data, the technique can suffer from the "horseshoe effect" or the "arch effect," whereby the scatter of samples within a biplot resembles an arch. An arch is clearly visible in figure 10.5. This occurs due to the creation of a spurious quadratic arch in the ordination scores of the second axis resulting from distortion of the first axis and can complicate interpretation of the biplots (ter Braak 1995:104–5). In instances in which the arch effect is observed, detrended correspondence analysis (DCA) offers a means for minimizing the problem (Hill and Gauch 1980; Lepš and Šmilauer 2003:52–54; ter Braak 1995:105–9). A variety of methods for detrending the data are outlined by ter Braak and Šmilauer (ter Braak 1995:105–9; ter Braak and Šmilauer 2002). A biplot illustrating the results of a DCA analysis of combined plant and animal data from Southwest Asia where the arch evident in CA analysis (figure 10.5) was effectively removed is illustrated in figure 10.6.

It is important to stress that CA is particularly sensitive to small samples with low seed counts and rare taxa that are represented in only a few samples, both of which create noise that can mask real trends. Data cleaning is necessary prior to conducting CA and many archaeobotanists routinely eliminate samples with a seed count of less than 30 to 50, as well as taxa that occur in

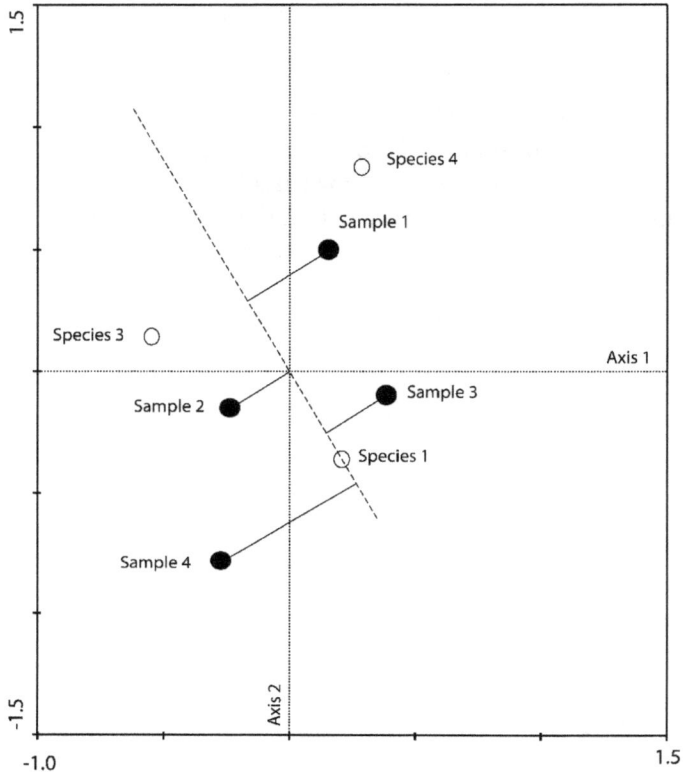

FIGURE 10.4. *Hypothetical unimodal biplot illustrating the biplot rule applied to species and sample points. A line is drawn from the species point through the origin and sample points are projected onto the line perpendicularly. Species 1 is predicted to have the highest relative frequencies in samples 3 and 4 and the lowest relative frequency in sample 1. Sample 2 is predicted to contain species 1 at its average relative frequency. Originally adapted from Lepš and Šmilauer (2003:figure 10–11). Reprinted from Smith and Munro (2009:figure A1). © 2009 by The Wenner–Gren Foundation for Anthropological Research.*

less than 5% to 10% of the samples (e.g., Jones 1991; Lange 1990; Valamoti and Jones 2003; Wasylikowa and Dahlberg 1999). In some instances, rather than delete poorly represented but important categories, researchers have combined functionally similar groups (such as free-threshing cereal chaff)

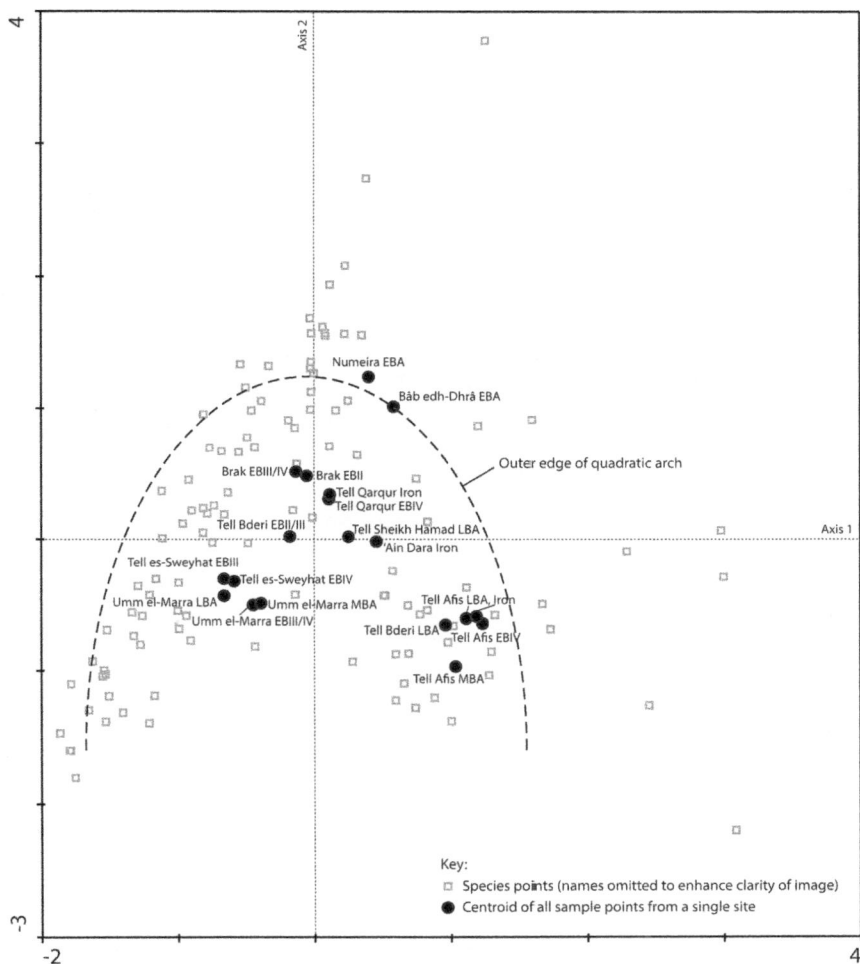

FIGURE 10.5. *Correspondence analysis biplot of integrated plant and animal abundance data from Southwest Asia highlighting the "arch effect." Previously unpublished figure created by Alexia Smith and Natalie Munro.*

in order to minimize loss of data (Jones 1991). In the event that cleaning is insufficient, the biplots produced by CA provide an excellent means for identifying further anomalous taxa or samples that can then be removed prior to repeating the analysis.

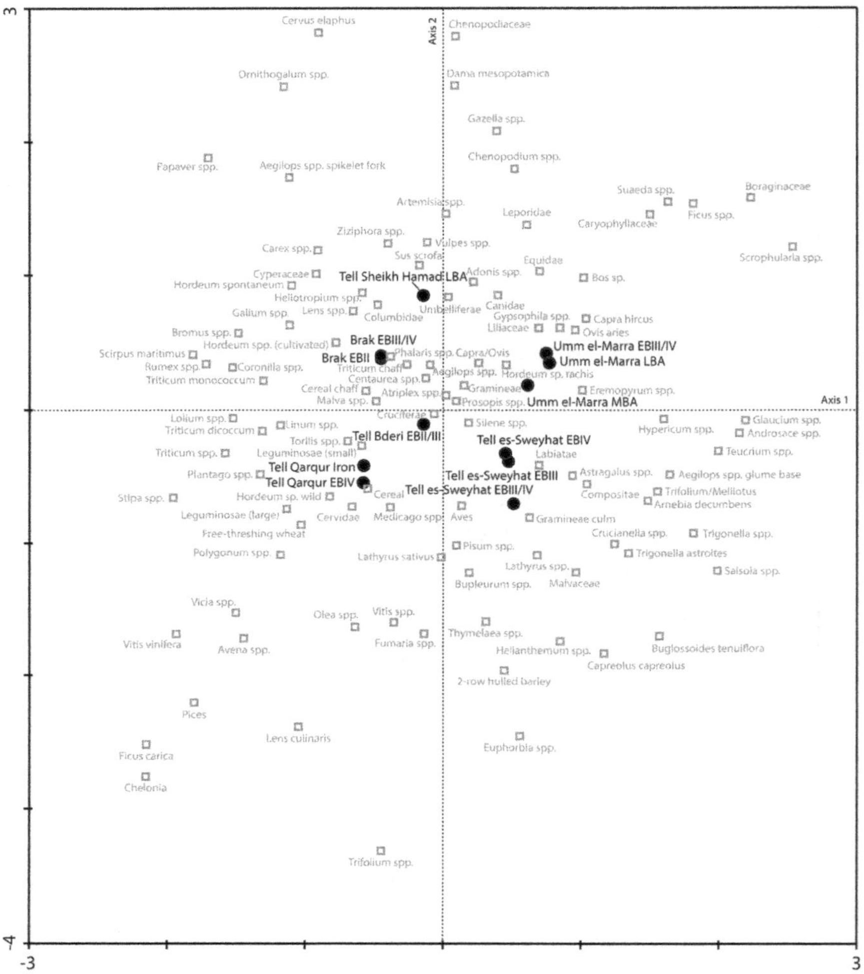

FIGURE 10.6. *Detrended correspondence analysis biplot of integrated plant and animal abundance data illustrating the removal of an "arch" in the species and sample data points. Reprinted from Smith and Munro (2009:figure 4). © 2009 by The Wenner-Gren Foundation for Anthropological Research.*

CANONICAL CORRESPONDENCE ANALYSIS

Canonical correspondence analysis (CCA, a direct gradient analysis technique) differs from open-ended CA in that the ordination is constrained by defined variables (Lepš and Šmilauer 2003:37; ter Braak 1986, 1987, 1994; ter

Braak and Verdonschot 1995). CCA provides a means for assessing the effect that *known* variables have by using these variables to constrain the ordination axes (ter Braak 1994). Variables may be quantitative or nominal (including name of time period or archaeological context type), which is particularly useful within archaeobotany where many ancient environmental variables are difficult, if not impossible, to quantify. In order to measure the impact that a single variable has on species composition, it can be useful to "subtract" the variation caused by other known variables. This can be accomplished by partial canonical correspondence analysis (pCCA) whereby explanatory variables are divided into "variables of interest" and "covariables" and the variance caused by covariables is partialed out (ter Braak 1988). This can be effective, for example, for isolating the variation in data sets caused by the researcher effect, changes in plant use through time, or differences between sites relating to available rainfall (Smith and Munro 2009). Unlike CA, both CCA and pCCA allow for the statistical significance of null hypotheses to be tested via Monte Carlo permutation testing, which provides a further tool for the researcher to consider the validity of the conclusions (Lepš and Šmilauer 2003:64–70; ter Braak and Šmilauer 2002). The use of CCA and pCCA is, at present, fairly limited within archaeobotany, but it has much potential (e.g., Bogaard et al. 1999; A. Smith 2005; Smith and Munro 2009).

CASE STUDIES WITHIN ARCHAEOBOTANY

The use of multivariate statistics to examine macrobotanical data began in the 1980s in Europe following the widespread availability of computers and the increased use of the techniques employed by ecologists (Clark and Stafford 1982; Hillman 1984a; Jones 1983b; G. Jones 1984, 1987; Lange 1990; Paap 1983; van der Veen 1987) and has since been widely popularized by Glynis Jones and her colleagues and students (e.g., Bogaard 2004; Charles et al. 1997; Colledge 1998; Colledge et al. 2004; Jones 1987; Jones et al. 2010; van der Veen 2011). Jones (1983b) was one of the first to use PCA and DA in archaeobotany as part of her doctoral research, the results of which were later published in her widely cited papers on ethnographic models of crop processing in Greece (G. Jones 1984, 1987). Paap (1983) also provides an early use of DA to assess social differentiation in plant use from 10 eighteenth-century samples from Waterlooplein in the Netherlands. Use of CA appeared slightly later. Lange (1990, based on his 1988 thesis at the University of Copenhagen) and van der Veen (1987) present early examples of CA to explore data sets from De Horden in the Netherlands and Thorpe Thewles in northeastern England, respectively.

In general, researchers within the United States have been slower to adopt multivariate statistics in their analyses. Mention of multivariate techniques is not made, for example, in Hastorf and Popper's (1988) important volume, *Current Paleoethnobotany: Analytical Methods and Cultural Interpretations of Archaeological Plant Remains*, a book that otherwise pays significant attention to quantitative methods in archaeobotany. Early studies do exist, however: Pearsall (2000:224), for example, cites Hastorf's (1983) early use of factor analysis in her doctoral dissertation to examine covariation of taxa within archaeobotanical samples from a series of sites in the Jauja region of Peru. Today the use of multivariate techniques is becoming more commonplace among archaeobotanists housed at US institutions working in both the New and Old Worlds (e.g., A. Smith 2005; Smith and Munro 2009; VanDerwarker and Idol 2008; VanDerwarker et al. 2007), but the methods are still not as widely applied as they are in Europe. The reason for the delayed use of multivariate statistics in the United States is not immediately clear. Pearsall (2000:16) attributes the paucity of studies to "lack of familiarity with multivariate approaches, and concern that some may be inappropriate for macroremain data." Because multivariate approaches have repeatedly been proven to be appropriate and highly informative when examining archaeobotanical data, this is likely to change in the future, but the rate of change will depend upon the ease with which students can secure training.

Macrobotanical Remains

Multivariate statistics have been applied within archaeobotany to address a broad range of questions. Numerous examples exist of both open-ended/purely exploratory analyses and problem-oriented studies that seek to address a particular issue or research question. In many respects the shift to more problem-oriented studies reflects a move among archaeobotanists over the past few decades to distance themselves from simple lists of plants recovered and fully embrace the enormous potential of archaeobotanical data to address a broad range of ecological and social questions.

Many of the open-ended analyses employing CA seek to better understand the causes of variation between samples (e.g., Bogaard 2004; Charles and Bogaard 2001; Colledge et al. 2004; Fairbairn et al. 2002; Hollenbach and Walker 2010; Riehl 1999; Riehl and Deckers 2008). In their examination of Final Neolithic and Early Bronze Age archaeobotanical data from Mandalo, Macedonia, for example, Valamoti and Jones (2003) examined spatial and temporal differences in plant remains throughout the site. They used CA to explore the entire data set as well as subsets of the data ("crops/fruits/nuts" and "wild/weedy taxa"). Clear spatial differences in the storage of particular crops across the site emerged. Analyses of the wild/weedy taxa only revealed four different groupings or clusters of wild/weedy taxa within the biplots. By considering the habitats of the species represented, the ratio of weeds to crop debris, and the archaeological context of the samples, Valamoti and Jones (2003) determined that the groupings within the biplot reflect spatial pattern-ing within the weeds that correspond with the distribution of associated crops, habitat preferences of individual taxa, and crop-processing debris. The analysis also demonstrated that many of the samples contained dung, so it was neces-sary to extract these samples before crop husbandry could be examined further.

Crop Processing

In a detailed ethnographic study of cereal crop-processing, Hillman (1984a) observed subsistence farmers in Turkey processing free-threshing wheat by hand. He recorded 26 steps from harvesting, threshing, winnowing, and siev-ing, to hand-picking, and at each stage he detailed the nature and composi-tion of the assemblages produced within the product or by-product fraction (Hillman 1984a). Although some variation in crop processing can exist, most of the recorded steps take place within a predictable order, so it is possible to use knowledge of the plant assemblages produced at each stage to help inter-pret the archaeobotanical record. Hillman (1984a) applied his observations in Turkey to archaeobotanical assemblages from Cefn Graeanog II in Wales, and used PCA to categorize samples by the stage of processing (figure 10.3). Chernoff (1988) critiques Hillman's application of PCA, arguing that cluster analysis is more appropriate, although she reasons that PCA may be useful in reducing the dimensionality of the data prior to conducting cluster analysis.

In a related study, G. Jones (1984) observed traditional plant processing of cereals and legumes by farmers on the Aegean island of Amorgos. She also observed the nature and composition of modern assemblages produced at each stage of processing, but employed DA to examine the data and assess whether they could be distinguished from one another quantitatively. G. Jones (1984:49, 51) concluded that modern winnowing, coarse-sieved, and fine-sieved by-products, and fine-sieved products could be "very successfully discriminated on the basis of weed seeds alone" owing to differences in seed size, the tendency of seeds to remain intact in clusters or heads, and the aero-dynamic qualities of seeds (G. Jones 1984:54). Using DA and cluster analysis to apply this model to Late Bronze Age archaeobotanical samples from Assiros Toumba in Greek Macedonia, Jones (1987) demonstrated that application of the ethnographic models allowed for a more secure interpretation of archaeo-botanical samples, including legumes where chaff is rarely preserved (figure 10.2). Such approaches to examining and interpreting archaeobotanical data hold potential outside of Southwest Asia in regions where detailed ethno-graphic studies of crop processing and the resultant by-products created at each stage have been documented.

Chernoff (1988) partially applied the crop processing model to categorize samples from Tel el-Ifshar in Israel: using cluster analysis she separated sam-ples as hand-sorted by-products, crop products, and fine-sieved by-products. As Jones (1987:321) stresses, by examining data in this way, variation caused by processing can be removed so that a wider range of questions can be addressed. Such an approach was adopted by van der Veen (1992a:chapter 7) in her study of remains from multiple sites in northeastern England. Ratios and DA were used in combination with Jones's crop processing model to assess the most likely crop processing stage evident within each sample. Samples were grouped into either fine-sieved by-products or fine-sieved products, and each grouping was then analyzed separately with PCA and cluster analysis followed by DA. Van der Veen (1992a) observed two main groups of samples that differed in their wheat content and weed assemblages (figure 10.1). Using an autecological approach to interpret the data (which considers the relationship between individual species and environmental variables rather than the co-occurrence of certain taxa within a particular niche), she attributed these groupings to soil preferences and tillage practices (van der Veen 1992a:chapter 10), allowing the investigation to go beyond a simple description of species present and the nature and state of cereal crop processing. In another study examining cultivation practices, Colledge (1998, 2001) employed CA to examine plant remains from five sites in Syria dat-ing to the Natufian and Early Neolithic. Within the biplots she was able to relate clusters to distinct "vegetational fingerprints" (Colledge 1998:127) that corresponded to broad ecological classes among "wild/weed" taxa. Although remains of the "crops" appeared morphologically wild, knowledge of group-ings of "wild/weed" taxa considered alongside chronological and ecological information allowed her to argue for pre- or non-domestication cultivation of wild cereals. The tillage and harvesting techniques employed by the early cultivators were intensive enough to disturb weed flora assemblages, but did not result in the selection of domesticated grain. Consideration of "vegeta-tional fingerprints" has a wide range of applications that may be used else-where to explore regional or temporal differences in plant use (e.g., A. Smith 2005).

Crop Husbandry

Multivariate statistics have also been used to examine modern weed and agricultural field data by a number of scholars in the United Kingdom as part of the Functional Interpretation of Botanical Surveys (FIBS). This work employs autecology to examine how individual taxa respond to changing ecological and agronomic conditions. By amassing data on functional attributes such as length and quality of the growth period, and factors relating to drought tolerance or avoidance, such as maximum canopy height and root diameter, it is possible to apply this information and observe or infer ancient crop husbandry regimes from archaeobotanical assemblages (e.g., Charles et al. 1997; Jones et al. 2010; Jones et al. 2005). Studies have focused on isolating the impacts that changes in soil fertility and crop rotation, sowing times and cultivation intensity, irrigation, fallowing, and level of soil disturbance have on associated weed assemblages (e.g., Bogaard et al. 2005; Bogaard et al. 2001; Bogaard et al. 1999; Charles et al. 2002; Jones, Bogaard, Charles, and Hodgson 2000, 2001; Jones et al. 2010; Jones et al. 2005). Typically both CA and DA have been used to explore the data and assess the best combination of variables that discriminate between the weed assemblages observed under different cropping conditions (Charles et al. 1997). Bogaard et al. (1999) also used CCA to examine weed ecology and crop rotation regimes, constraining the analysis with rotation regime and vegetation zone. Understanding how modern species individually respond to varying environmental and agronomic conditions plays a vital role in interpreting archaeobotanical assemblages.

Spatial Differences in Plant Use

Others have used multivariate statistics to examine spatial differences in plant use across a site. Wasylikowa et al. (1997), for example, employed CA to examine untransformed data from the Early Neolithic site of E-75-6 at Nabta Playa in Egypt to assess variation in plant use both within a single hut and between dwellings. They observed distinct differences in plant remains across the site, particularly in the distribution of wild sorghum, which may have been managed or occasionally cultivated. A similar approach was used by Graham and Smith (2013) to identify distinct use areas at Kenan Tepe, Turkey, that relate to plant processing and use, and the social organization of labor. On a larger geographic scale, Zhang et al. (2010) combined PCA analysis of archaeobotanical data with GIS models of modern environmental data to examine Late Neolithic to Early Bronze Age agriculture from 10 sites in the upper Ying valley of central China. Although the sample size for many of the sites was small, Zhang et al. (2010) cautiously conclude that social and cultural factors explain variation in farming and crop processing between sites, whereas the natural environment was a more important determining factor in shaping wild plant collection strategies. By employing multivariate statistical techniques, therefore, it is possible to address broad questions of social behavior and change.

Identification of Macroremains

To a much lesser extent, multivariate statistics have been used to help develop criteria for quantitatively distinguishing between taxa at the macro level. Mangafa and Kotsakis (1996) employed DA to develop predictive models for separating charred modern wild and cultivated grape from Greece based on a series of size measurements and ratios. They conclude that the predictive power of the resultant formulae is excellent, allowing for secure differentiation of archaeological grape specimens. In an earlier study, Kosina (1984) employed DA and three cluster analysis techniques (single linkage, complete linkage, and Ward's method) to help distinguish between 26 varieties or subspecies of charred and uncharred wheats based on measurements of the grain's cross section and crease morphology. He reports separation of *Triticum monococcum*, *T. spelta*, and ancient *T. aestivum*, but no clear separation between *T. aestivum* and *T. durum*, an observation supported by other morphological studies of grain (summary provided by Zohary and Hopf 2000). Such approaches hold much potential for establishing quantitative guidelines for distinguishing between other taxa frequently encountered on archaeological sites.

Integrating Data

Multivariate statistics have also proven useful for integrating archaeobotanical data from multiple sites although, as several researchers have stressed, the comparability of data needs to be considered very carefully before any intersite study is conducted (Bogaard 2004; Colledge 2001; Colledge et al. 2004; A. Smith 2005; Smith and Munro 2009; Zhang et al. 2010). In a detailed study of Neolithic farming practices in central Europe, Bogaard (2004) combined functional attribute data relating to the time of sowing and intensity of cultivation with CA and DA to help determine which major type of crop husbandry model was used in antiquity. By considering how the data supported prior assertions for shifting cultivation, extensive ard (scratch plough) cultivation, floodplain cultivation, and intensive garden cultivation, she was able to conclude that the latter appeared to be the most probable and widespread.

In another large regional study, Colledge et al. (2004:S47) successfully examined data from 40 Aceramic Neolithic sites spanning Southwest Asia and Southeastern Europe to examine the spread of agriculture via cultural diffusion or population movement. Although issues in integrating large data set do exist, they conclude that:

> From a methodological perspective . . . the quantification and multivariate analysis of properly collated archaeobotanical data, even recorded at the level of taxonomic presence/absence, is of sufficiently high resolution to contribute to our understanding of the earliest phases of the transition to farming.

This observation can also be expanded to different time periods and, most likely, different parts of the world. A. Smith (2005), for example, was able to make a similar conclusion based on her study of Bronze and Iron Age plant data from 19 sites spanning Southwest Asia, where CA and CCA were used to examine spatial and temporal differences in crop production and plant use. The data set proved to be too incomplete to examine temporal trends thoroughly, but distinct regional patterns were evident, and the similarity of assemblages from geographically proximate sites underscored the robustness of archaeobotanical data. The capability of CA to explore very large data sets, therefore, lends itself to questions of large-scale regional and temporal changes in plant uses. Knowledge of these trends may then be considered alongside other archaeological data to assess the extent to which they relate to broad social trends.

In the past few years, multivariate statistics have been used to explore ancient agriculture from a more holistic perspective by integrating archaeobotanical and zooarchaeological data. Smith and Munro (2009) employed CA and pCCA to both independently and simultaneously explore plant and animal data from Bronze and Iron Age sites in Syria. Distinct patterns emerged demonstrating that food production choices in the region were more heavily reliant upon available water than cultural choice. VanDerwarker (2010a) also integrated plant and animal data using CA: she used CA to examine nominal data and PCA to explore ratio/interval data from the Formative site of La Joya in Gulf Coastal Mexico, highlighting that people relied more heavily upon wild resources during times of environmental stress. Both studies report problems related to sampling, differential preservation and quantification of remains, and interpretation, but CA was still deemed to be a powerful tool for considering the two data sets together and was strongly recommended for future studies. By integrating data in this way, it is possible to examine cultural and environmental factors that affect people's choices in food production and acquisition.

PHYTOLITHS

A number of phytolith studies have used DA to help distinguish between closely related taxa based on combined consideration of size and shape attributes. It is possible to use the technique to distinguish between modern comparative material and/or archaeological material, although the most powerful approaches tend to use knowledge of variation among phytoliths extracted from modern specimens to help guide the identification of ancient remains. Wilson (1985), for example, used LDA to help classify *Musa* phytoliths from an early agricultural site in Papua New Guinea based on measurements from modern reference specimens. In a later study of banana phytoliths, Ball et al. (2006:1234) used DA to successfully discriminate between *Musa acuminata* and *M. balbisiana.* Piperno (1988:80–84) employed a similar approach to distinguish maize from a variety of wild grasses, including teosinte, based on cross-bodies and Ball et al. (1996) were able to distinguish between phytoliths from the inflorescence bracts of *Triticum monococcum, T. dicoccon, and T. aestivum.* Zhao et al. (1998) studied the double-peaked glume cells of wild and cultivated rice and were able to develop a fairly accurate predictive model for distinguishing between the two forms archaeologically. With reference to such studies, Piperno (2006b:145) states that "use of multivariate statistics reduces dependence on intuitive inspections of archaeological assemblages in plant identification," although she is quick to add that this "does not mean that other ways of identifying plants become less important, especially because *df* functions are not expected to accurately classify 100% of all species . . . considered." Though such caution is necessary, the use of multivariate tools clearly provide a very useful and powerful augmentary tool to any macro- or microbotanical study that aims to identify or classify sets of remains.

Other researchers have used CA to explore patterning within phytolith data sets that reflect social choices and behavior (Ollendorf 1987; Powers-Jones and Padmore 1993). Powers-Jones and Padmore (1993) examined data from two Late Bronze Age/Early Iron Age sites in the Outer Hebrides, Scotland, and were able to observe differences between samples that they attributed to the organic origin of a phytolith assemblage. They reason that the ability to observe differences in the organic origin of a phytoliths assemblage has important implications for investigating agriculture and site use. Hart and Matson (2009) were also able to successfully apply DA to phytolith data. In their study they examined maize phytoliths from cooking residues on pottery sherds recovered in central New York to explore the question of the dispersal of maize within North America.

STARCH GRAINS

Torrence (2006) cites Loy's (Loy 1994; Loy et al. 1992) study of starch residues on stone tools from the Solomon Islands as the first to use multivariate techniques to distinguish between starch grains morphologically. In a later study of plants from the Pacific, Torrence et al. (2004) employed CA and LDA to help distinguish between starch grains from domesticated and wild species. Torrence (2006) notes that, as with phytoliths, the use of multivariate analyses of granule morphologies can greatly facilitate the construction of identification keys and help identify taxa that are not easily distinguishable from one another.

Others have used multivariate statistics to develop models to help interpret ancient assemblages. Lentfer et al. (2002), for example, combined modern assemblage-based starch grain data with size and shape distributions collected from a variety of different environments in Papua New Guinea, each representing different land use histories. They were able to discriminate garden sites from non-garden sites using PCA. This study highlights the utility of starch grain analysis for investigating palaeoenvironments and ancient land use.

POLLEN

As with the other types of remains, multivariate statistics have been used to differentiate between taxonomic forms, detect chronological changes, and highlight regional or spatial patterning in pollen data. Tweddle et al. (2005), for example, used PCA and DA to help distinguish between pollen from domesticated cereals and wild Poaceae within Holocene profiles in Yorkshire, England. This work enabled them to evaluate the reliability of keys available for distinguishing between the types morphologically. In an earlier study, Birks and John (1974) employed PCA (along with a variety of other statistical techniques) to subdivide Flandrian pollen sequences in England into temporal zones. This, in turn, facilitated comparison of data between pollen cores as well as other archaeological data. PCA also proved useful in integrating pollen spectra from 145 locations across the British Isles dating to 5,000 BP, allowing Birks et al. (1975) to identify major vegetation zones across the region. Cappers et al. (1998) used CA in their attempt to correlate chronologically the Hula, Ghab, and Eski Acıgöl pollen sequences from Southwest Asia. Redundancy analysis, a multivariate analog of regression, has also been used to examine large pollen data sets from the Czech Republic (Kozáková et al. 2009).

GETTING STARTED

For researchers with little experience in statistics wishing to integrate multivariate analyses into their exploration of archaeobotanical data, Pearsall (2000:216) recommends seeking help from an experienced statistician, a sentiment shared by Thomas in his articles outlining uses and abuses of statistics within archaeology. Thomas (1978, 1980) strongly cautions against the use of multivariate statistics where simpler methods suffice, but acknowledges their utility when appropriately applied. Archaeobotanical data are particularly well suited to a multivariate approach. Seeking the assistance of a statistician, and spending the time to make sure that the nature of the data is understood, helps ensure that the methods are applied correctly, but as Jones (1991:63) states, "Whatever the level of expert advice sought from statisticians, archaeobotanists must be able to identify the problems and potential of their data in terms relevant to statistical analysis and to interpret the results in terms relevant to archaeobotany," so some familiarity with the techniques is essential. A number of statistical textbooks directly geared toward archaeologists have been published, providing an accessible entry point to multivariate techniques: Shennan's (1997) *Quantifying Archaeology* provides an excellent introduction. Baxter (1994, 2003: chapters 6–9) provides more detailed and mathematical descriptions, presupposing a familiarity with Shennan's book. Other useful texts that discuss the statistical analysis of ecological data include *Multivariate Analysis of Ecological Data using CANOCO* (Lepš and Šmilauer 2003), *Data Analysis in Community and Landscape Ecology* (Jongman et al. 1987), *Multivariate Analysis in Community Ecology* (Gauch 1982), and *Unimodal Models to Relate Species to Environment* (ter Braak 1996), the last of which is provided with CANOCO software and compiles 15 of ter Braak's most important journal articles. To a beginner, the learning curve may appear prohibitively steep, but with perseverance the techniques can be mastered and, as the examples provided here demonstrate, the range of questions that can be addressed make it well worth the effort.

SUMMARY AND CONCLUSIONS

Over the past several decades, the use of multivariate statistics within archaeobotany has steadily increased, particularly within Europe. The most commonly encountered techniques used today are CA and DA, although cluster analysis and PCA are also popular. Open-ended, indirect techniques such as CA, cluster analysis, and PCA, have proven useful in assessing major differences between samples, identifying variables that affect the species composition of samples, as well as identifying outliers. The direct techniques, such as DA, provide powerful augmentary tools for developing models to distinguish between related taxa based on measurements. Although such use is more popular within studies of phytoliths and starch grains, the approach has much to offer for differentiating between macrobotanical remains. DA has also proven useful for distinguishing between modern weed assemblages recovered from fields subjected to differing crop husbandry practices. As such, models can be developed for interpreting ancient botanical assemblages. Each technique has differing strengths and weaknesses so, oftentimes, the combined application of multiple techniques to a single data set is recommended.

Multivariate techniques are well suited to archaeobotanical data, which are typically represented as either presence/absence or abundance data within a sample/species table with many zero values. CA, in particular, is well suited to the ecological nature of archaeobotanical analysis in that it can accommodate quantitative and nominal environmental variables. By employing CCA or pCCA, it is possible to test the statistical significance of null hypotheses via the Monte Carlo permutations test, providing an independent means for "validating" interpretations of past behavior or plant use. As archaeobotanists become more and more confident in the robustness of their data, and as data sets become larger, the continued use of multivariate statistics will allow a broad range of ecological, social, and anthropological questions to be addressed in a rigorous manner.

ACKNOWLEDGMENTS

I thank Jade d'Alpoim Guedes, John (Mac) Marston, and Christina Warinner for organizing this volume. I am further grateful to them, Philip Graham, Thomas Hart, and Madelynn von Baeyer, as well as several anonymous reviewers for their comments on earlier versions of this chapter. Glynis Jones provided helpful information and bibliographic sources on the early use of multivariate statistics in Europe and kindly allowed me to adapt her discriminant analysis figure. I am also grateful to Marijke van der Veen and Natalie Munro for allowing me to reproduce and adapt previously published diagrams and to Sue Colledge for a very informative discussion on multivariate statistics many years ago.

NOTE

At the time this chapter was in press, Šmilauer and Lepš (2014) published a second edition to their *Multivariate Analysis of Ecological Data*. This volume contains important updates for anyone wishing to use the new Canoco 5 software.

11

Analysis and Interpretation
of Intrasite Variability
in Paleoethnobotanical
Remains

A Consideration and Application
of Methods at the Ravensford
Site, North Carolina

AMBER M. VANDERWARKER,
JENNIFER V. ALVARADO, AND
PAUL WEBB

Within the last decade, spatial analyses of plant remains within sites have become more common in archaeobotany. Despite an increase in the number of studies that focus on spatial variability, this approach nevertheless represents a relatively rare analytical mode in the subdiscipline. There has been no comprehensive treatment of this topic to date, leaving a gap in the literature that we address in this chapter. We begin with a literature review of studies that have attempted intrasite spatial analysis; as the term *analysis* implies some form of quantitative treatment of the data, we do not consider studies that simply describe spatial observations based on tabular data. Our literature review is presented in two parts: the first part summarizes relevant works in terms of (1) how space is defined for the purpose of analysis, and (2) the broader issues addressed (e.g., defining activity spaces, status-based foodways, etc.). The second part of our literature review synthesizes the primary quantitative techniques that archaeobotanists have used to analyze the spatial distribution of plant remains, including multivariate statistics, box plots, density analysis, and the pie chart method. We conclude with a case study from our own research at the Ravensford site, located in southwestern North Carolina. Our analysis focuses on a burnt structure with a floor deposit that appears to represent in situ occupational debris. We demonstrate the use of several quantitative techniques in the analysis of the floor data from this structure as a means to delineate the

DOI: 10.5876/9781607323167.c011

organization of food-related activity areas in the structure's interior. Finally, it is important to note that although our review includes cases from the Old World, it does reflect a bias toward New World archaeobotany.

TRENDS IN INTRASITE SPATIAL ANALYSIS IN ARCHAEOBOTANY

Our review of the literature reveals two general approaches to analyzing space with archaeobotanical data. The first approach assigns spatial contexts prior to conducting quantitative analysis of the plant data (Benz et al. 2006; Fritz, 2003; Gumerman 1994; Hald and Charles 2008; Hastorf 1990; Marston 2010; Peres et al. 2010; VanDerwarker and Detwiler 2002). The most common assignation relates to elite/nonelite contexts and public/domestic architectural areas: sociospatial loci that are defined based on other archaeological data sets. These studies tend to focus on broad anthropological issues related to the intersection of plant-related activities with social status, political economy, gender, ritual, and the public/private division.

A focus on social status as a determinant of plant foodways has been explored in several cases from the New World, especially in Mesoamerica and South America. Benz et al. (2006) compare plant remains from two different sections of a Huitzilapa shaft tomb from Jalisco, Mexico, dating to the Formative/Classic transition (ca. AD 75). Based on the prior analysis of artifactual materials, the northern and southern chambers have been interpreted as representing the interments of elites and non-elites, respectively. Comparison of the macroplant assemblages from the two sections of the tomb revealed little difference in the inventory of plant foods interred with elite versus nonelite individuals; however, there was a clear difference in the quantity of plant food remains recovered from these two different tomb sections, with elite burials yielding a much higher relative abundance of plant foods.

Hastorf's (1990) analysis of plant data from Sausa house floors dating both prior and subsequent to Inka control of the Mantaro River valley of modern-day Peru reveals a shift in plant diet for local elites and nonelites. Prior to Inka domination, during the Wanka II period (AD 1300–1460), elite and nonelite status were clearly marked in plant foodways; the shift to imperial control, however, led to a leveling of local status distinctions. A subsequent study by Gumerman (1994) compares Hastorf's findings to his data from the Chimú occupation of Pacatnamu, along the north coast of Peru. Sociospatial contexts at Pacatnamu were defined based on architecture, beads, copper, and textiles, with categories including nobility, commoners, specialized fishermen, and full-time weavers. Gumerman's analysis indicates that nobles and weavers had very similar diets, dominated by chiles and corn, whereas commoners ate fewer domesticates, relying more heavily on wild greens and fruits. His analysis reveals that the primary food producers (commoners) were engaged in agricultural production to support the leadership and attached specialists.

A similar study was conducted at the epi-Olmec political center of Tres Zapotes, along the Gulf Coast of Mexico by Peres and colleagues. Peres et al. (2010) examine the intersection of space, time, and plant/animal foodways at the site, focusing their comparison on elite, nonelite, and ceremonial contexts. These contexts were defined based on the spatial location of the deposit relative to monumental architecture and the distribution of other artifact categories known to signal elite and/or ceremonial activities. Their findings reveal that more corn processing (shelling) occurred in ceremonial areas, suggesting the importance of food preparation and consumption in public ritual space. Moreover, beans were identified exclusively in elite residential areas, whereas fruit seeds were more numerous in nonelite domestic space. The relationship between food production and social status at Tres Zapotes may be similar to what Gumerman (1994) defined at Pacatnamu, in which nonelites were responsible for the bulk of the farming in order to support the site's leadership; the fact that nonelites (in both cases) heavily supplemented their diets with wild foods suggests that a significant portion of their yields were not meant for their own consumption.

Public and private/domestic spaces have been examined in coordination with plant data from both New World and Old World cases. Fritz and Lopinot (2003) compared a domestic household area (ICT-II) to a ritual feasting deposit (sub-Mound 51) from the Cahokia site in western Illinois. Their findings reveal that corn played a less important role in ceremonialism than it did in daily domestic foodways, challenging the long-held notion regarding the importance of corn in Cahokian ceremonialism. VanDerwarker and Detwiler (2002) analyzed plant remains from a seventeenth-century Cherokee village in southwestern North Carolina, assigning their samples to domestic versus public spaces based on their proximity to domestic structures versus the public-oriented townhouse. Ethnohistoric sources suggest a strict gender dichotomy in which women were tethered to domestic spaces where they carried out their food preparation activities. Analysis of the plant data, however, reveals that virtually all plant food remains were deposited within or around the townhouse, suggesting that women processed plant foods in visible public areas.

In the Old World, at the ancient Anatolian site of Gordion, Marston (2010, 2012b) analyzed wood charcoal from public and domestic contexts defined in architecture. He found that people overwhelmingly chose oak as the primary construction material for everyday domestic architecture; indeed, oak was the most abundant wood source available locally. Public architecture, however, appears to have been constructed primarily of pine, located at a greater distance from the site. Thus, it appears that the construction of public architecture may have mandated community labor to travel significant distances. This interpretation highlights the broader importance of public architecture as seen from the perspective of the local community.

A final example of a study assigning space prior to archaeobotanical analysis was conducted by Hald and Charles (2008) and explores changes in plant storage and disposal from two sequential building complexes at Tell Brak in northeastern Syria. Both building complexes represent special structures that were non-domestic in nature, and room function was determined prior to the analysis of plant remains. Their analysis of plant remains across these building complexes suggests an increase in public storage of crops through time, indicating a greater institutionalization of food production systems.

The second approach to spatial analysis in archaeobotany uses quantitative analysis as the starting point for defining different contexts. In other words, space is not defined according to public/private, elite/nonelite, or other social or functional categories prior to conducting the analysis of the plant data. This type of analysis uses samples, features, or units as baseline data for an exploratory data analysis that either (1) seeks to identify deposits that deviate from the central tendency of the plant assemblage, or (2) plots plant remains on a map in order to determine clusters that may be interpreted in terms of plant-related activities. In this way, social or functional categories that are assigned to space emerge from the data analysis.

The first set of exploratory studies comes from the New World and focuses on native plant foodways in late prehistoric Virginia at the Buzzard Rock site (VanDerwarker and Idol 2008) and contact period North Carolina at the Upper Saratown site (VanDerwarker et al. 2007). Numerous features were excavated and analyzed at both sites, and spatial analysis was employed in order to document variation in plant remains among the various features. At the Buzzard Rock site, plant remains were analyzed from 102 features, most of which represent everyday domestic contexts. VanDerwarker and Idol (2008) used box plots of plant densities to identify statistical outliers, which were apparent for acorn, hickory, and corn remains. Some features appear to have been exclusive dumping zones for these different taxa, suggesting either that they were processed at different times of the year, or that these plants required different processing steps, leading to different processing locales. In addition, two pit features yielded more than 166,000 corn kernels, which appear to have been burned in situ after their deposition in the features; VanDerwarker and Idol (2008) interpret these corn kernels to represent either spoiled stores that were disposed of through burning, or ritual burning of a portion of the new harvest as part of traditional renewal ceremonialism. A similar pattern was documented at Upper Saratown, in which two features yielded significantly more plant foods than the other features, suggesting a ritual nature to the deposits, an interpretation supported by manner of deposition and high quantities of broken figurines (VanDerwarker et al. 2007).

The remainder of the exploratory studies includes those that seek to delineate and interpret activity areas based on the spatial distribution of plant remains. Using a subset of her Sausa data from the 1990 publication discussed above, Hastorf (1991) examines the distribution of plants within two patio groups, dating before and after Inka domination, in order to assess changes in gender roles as reflected by shifts in household activities. Her analysis reveals differences in the use of patio space, suggesting that female activities related to food production became more controlled and circumscribed after the Inka conquered the region. A spatial analysis of flora and fauna from an Archaic site in Michigan by Smith and Egan (1990) revealed a complete separation between food preparation activities of plants and animals, which appear to have occurred in different areas of the site. This pattern may have implications for understanding gendered labor, but has not been interpreted in this way. A similar study from the Early Bronze Age Netherlands plotted the distribution of plant remains at the Swifterbant S3 site in order to reconstruct activity areas related to the processing of wild plants and cultigens (van Zeist and Palfenier-Vegter 1981). This case represents one of the earliest uses of spatial analysis in combination with archaeobotanical remains. Ultimately, the authors interpret their results as representing seasonally consecutive occupations at the site.

Two recent studies from the Old World conduct spatial analyses of plant remains from structure floors of habitations (Bogaard et al. 2009; Weiss et al. 2008). The floor deposits from both cases appear to represent in situ occupational debris, a rarity in archaeology; this type of depositional context (also characteristic of our case presented below) allows for a detailed reconstruction of household activities. Weiss et al. (2008) plot the distribution of more than 60,000 seeds from the sealed floor of an Upper Paleolithic brush hut located in modern-day Israel. GIS maps of plant densities allow them to reconstruct three activity spaces, including an area of food processing at a grinding stone, a flintknapping area, and an area of access between these two work spaces. The authors interpret these two areas to represent a possible gendered-division of labor within the habitation, in which women processed plant foods while men manufactured and repaired their tools (Weiss et al. 2008). Bogaard et al. (2009) compare the floor deposits of two burned buildings from Neolithic Çatalhöyük in order to reconstruct domestic organization, with a particular emphasis on storage location. Based on the distribution of cultigens in various states of processing, the authors conclude that storage facilities were located in side rooms of multiroom buildings.

Ultimately, these spatial analyses permit a greater resolution for understanding archaeobotanical assemblages, allowing us to explore issues that are often difficult to address archaeologically, such as gender, ritual, and household activities occurring prior to abandonment. This literature review presents possible research questions and interpretations that archaeobotanists can pursue if they have the appropriate data sets and the inclination to do so. Below, we discuss the quantitative methods used by these authors as a means to outline a standard set of techniques by which to analyze archaeobotanical data across space.

Quantitative Methods for the Spatial Analysis of Archaeobotanical Data

Our literature review revealed a suite of techniques that archaeobotanists have used in order to conduct intrasite spatial analyses. Four of these techniques were used in multiple publications, demonstrating their utility for this type of analysis: multivariate statistics, box plots, density analysis, and the pie chart method. Given the popularity of these four methods, we explain their application in greater detail below.

Multivariate Statistics

Multivariate techniques like correspondence analysis (CA) or principal components analysis (PCA) are particularly useful when trying to determine spatial clustering of multiple taxa. Unfortunately, an in-depth explanation of multivariate statistics is beyond the scope of this chapter (but see A. Smith, chapter 10, this volume; VanDerwarker 2010a). Although the box plot method can deal with only one taxon at a time, multivariate analysis can determine relationships among multiple taxa, in addition to plotting them against contexts. In order to be appropriate for spatial analysis, the cases must represent spatial contexts (e.g., features, units, houses). For example, VanDerwarker et al. (2007) employ PCA to identify features that stand apart from quotidian food trash. Of the eight features sampled at the site, all but two clustered together at the origin (0, 0 coordinates of the x- and y-axes), which means plants from the majority of the features do not deviate from the average expected value. Thus, this primary cluster of features is interpreted to represent everyday food trash—the two features that plotted outside of this cluster are then interpreted to represent something different, based on the context of the features and the composition of the plant assemblage. Peres et al. (2010) also use PCA, but their analysis employs aggregated spatial categories—elite, domestic, and ceremonial—and combine both plant and animal remains; PCA was chosen as an explicit means to integrate these different data sets. Ultimately, the choice between CA and PCA is one of scale, as CA uses a chi-square statistic and PCA uses a Pearson's r statistic; thus, CA is appropriate for nominal data and PCA for interval/ratio data. We use PCA in our case study below to determine clusters of plant remains along the floor of the final Cherokee structure to be abandoned at the Ravensford site.

Box Plots

Box plots are, not surprisingly, named for their boxlike shape; this type of plot displays distributions of data, in which the actual box (or hinges) represents the middle 50 percent of the data, and the central line portrays the median value of the distribution (figure 11.1; see also Cleveland 1994; McGill et al. 1978; Wilkinson et al. 1992). Lines, or whiskers, extend from the box on either end, representing the remaining top and bottom 25 percent of the distribution. Outliers are depicted as asterisks, and far outliers as open circles. Although box plots are usually employed as a means to compare different distributions (and thus portray more than one box per plot, *sensu* VanDerwarker and Detwiler [2002]), they can also be used to assess variation within a single distribution through the identification of significant outliers. It is this latter use that we consider here.

In order to have spatial meaning, the data for the box plot should be aggregated according to spatial context. For example, Peres et al. (2010) use individual samples that can be associated with specific provenience information. VanDerwarker et al. (2007) and VanDerwarker and Idol (2008) use individual features. Plant data should be standardized per sample or feature or unit (e.g., a density measure), and can then be plotted using the box plot function on any statistical software program. The point is to discover which spatial contexts (if any) depart from the central tendency of the distribution. Any outliers that are plotted (open circles or asterisks) are statistically significantly different from the rest of the distribution. This is not the only technique to determine statistical outliers, but in our opinion, it is the easiest and the most visually pleasing. We use this technique below in our case study of the Late

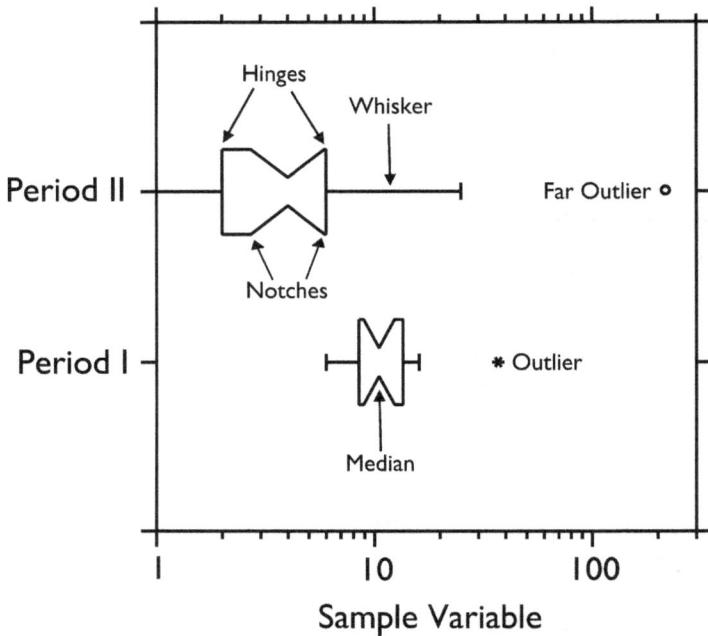

FIGURE 11.1. *Sample box plot.*

Qualla Cherokee structure, presenting each box plot alongside the structure map with the outlier unit(s) shaded.

Density Analysis

Density analysis refers to any visual technique that plots density data (e.g., taxa counts and/or weight divided by soil volume) on a map of a site or part of a site (e.g., house floor). Recently, archaeologists have begun using GIS-based approaches that employ shading techniques to represent different degrees of density (see Bogaard et al. 2009; Weiss et al. 2008; see also below). Before GIS became commonplace in archaeology, however, archaeobotanists plotted their seed counts or densities on a map without all the bells and whistles available now (e.g., Smith and Egan 1990; van Zeist and Palfenier-Vegter 1981; see also Smith 1978 for a density-based spatial analysis that was not plotted on a map). The advantage of GIS-based computer programs is the ability to link data sets directly to a map, which facilitates the creation of the density plots. We use this technique below, employing ArcGIS 9.3 to map the Cherokee structure and to plot plant densities across excavation units.

AMBER M. VANDERWARKER, JENNIFER V. ALVARADO, AND PAUL WEBB

The Pie Chart Method

The pie chart method displays multiple pie charts to show proportions of plant taxa in relation to spatial data. Some uses of this technique plot the pie charts directly onto a map (e.g., Hald and Charles 2008; Hastorf 1991), and others label the pie charts with respect to the type of feature they describe (e.g., hearths, houses) (*sensu* Lennstrom and Hastorf 1995). In the first two examples (Hald and Charles 2008; Hastorf 1991), each pie chart represents a sample that is plotted onto a residential compound, presumably from where the sample was originally taken. Hald and Charles (2008) incorporate six categories of cultigens into their pie charts, whereas Hastorf (1991) uses only four plant categories. When using this technique, it is important to use as few categories as possible (resulting in fewer wedges of pie) in order to retain the visual utility of the pie chart. A reader should be able to visually assess patterning among multiple pie charts with ease; the more categories that are incorporated into the pie charts, the more complicated the visual display.

In addition to these commonly used techniques are other methods that we documented only once in the literature review; these methods were used in the articles that defined spatial contexts prior to conducting quantitative analysis. For example, Hastorf (1990) used bar charts to plot ubiquity values of different taxa against commoner and elite households in order to assess temporal changes; in the same study, she produced a scatterplot of plant ubiquities and size of patio area to demonstrate a positive association between status and household size.

In the section that follows, we present a primary case study in order to demonstrate the use of the first three quantitative techniques for conducting a spatial analysis of archaeobotanical data from a burned house floor. Although the use of three techniques may be statistical overkill, we present them in order to demonstrate the replicability of the different methods, as they all produce similar spatial patterning.

SPATIAL ANALYSIS AT THE RAVENSFORD SITE: STRUCTURE 35

Ravensford is a multicomponent site that was excavated at the behest of the Eastern Band of Cherokee Indians prior to the construction of a local school complex. Located in southwestern North Carolina, the site was excavated by TRC Garrow Associates, Inc., under the direction of Paul Webb and Tasha Benyshek. Occupation at the site encompasses Archaic through Historic periods; the structure of interest (Structure 35) dates to the early part of Late Qualla phase (AD 1700–1830) and marks the final occupation at the site (figure 11.2).

When Structure 35 was first exposed prior to excavation, it was clear that the house had burned in situ. Thus, excavators approached the structure with great care, taking numerous flotation samples directly from the floor. The structure was excavated in a series of contiguous 1×1-m units, totaling 69 units, and is 8×8-m square, not including the east-facing vestibule opening (see figure 11.2). Plant materials from the floor of Structure 35 were identified from both flotation samples and specimens collected by hand. The quantitative analysis presented here deals with flotation samples only.

At the time that Structure 35 was abandoned, all other structures had already been vacated, leaving Structure 35 as the last remaining domestic structure in the community. Prior to its abandonment, large vessels and site furniture (e.g., metates) were removed from the structure, which might lead one to surmise that any materials found in the house represent post-abandonment refuse, unrelated to the activities that occurred in the house prior to its burning. However, as this structure was the final structure occupied at the site, it is highly unlikely that there was anyone living at the site post-abandonment to produce the refuse that was excavated from the structure floor. It seems more likely that the floor debris was produced by the people living in the house, just prior to abandonment. When people know they are leaving and the time of abandonment is imminent, they tend to relax their normal cleaning standards, leading to more refuse on the house floor. After its abandonment, Structure 35 was burned, probably intentionally, leading to the collapse of roof beams and thatching that effectively sealed the floor from the accumulation of post-abandonment refuse. Given the details of timing, burning, and site abandonment, it seems likely that plants recovered from the floor of the structure are related to activities that occurred in the structure toward the end of its uselife. We thus approach our spatial analysis as a means to understand the organization of food storage and processing as reflected in the distribution of plant remains across the house floor.

Flotation samples from the Ravensford site were collected with variable volumes, allowing for the calculation of density measures. Both the light and heavy fractions of the flotation samples were analyzed. Although the materials from the light and heavy fractions were processed and sorted separately, data from the two fractions were combined for analysis. Botanical materials were identified with reference to the paleoethnobotanical comparative collection at the University of California, Santa Barbara (UCSB) Integrative Subsistence Laboratory (ISL), various seed identification manuals (Delorit 1970; Martin and Barkley 1961), the USDA pictorial website (http://www.ars-grin.gov/npgs/images/sbml/), and Minnis (2003), which allowed us to identify the range of

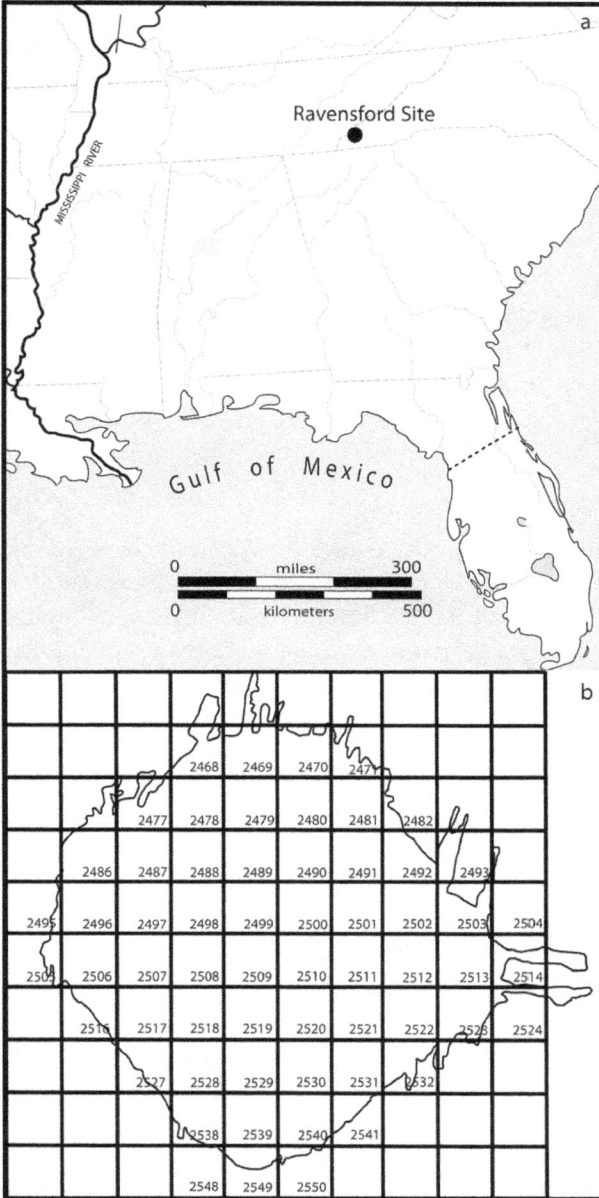

FIGURE 11.2. *(a) Southeastern United States with the location of the Ravensford site. (b) Structure 35 with units labeled.*

taxa native to the region. Given the burned nature of Structure 35, we encountered many species that are infrequently identified in plant assemblages from open-air sites. Sorting and identification of the botanical remains was carried out by Jennifer Alvarado, under the direction of Amber VanDerwarker, who conducted the quantitative analysis of the data. The inventory and frequency of plant remains recovered from Structure 35 are listed in table 11.1.

We employ three methods to explore the spatial arrangement of plant refuse on the structure floor: (1) principal components analysis of units and plant taxa to identify plant groupings and how they correlate with space, (2) box plots to identify excavation units with significant outliers, and (3) plant density analysis using GIS. Ultimately, all three techniques yield similar patterns, and we use this redundancy to demonstrate both the use and appropriateness of these different techniques for use in spatial analysis.

PRINCIPAL COMPONENTS ANALYSIS

The principal components analysis (PCA) uses standardized counts of taxa that occur in a minimum of 5 samples or exceed a count of 10 specimens in at least one sample. Taxa counts were standardized to plant weight (total weight of all carbonized plant material per sample); when more than one flotation sample was taken from a unit, taxa counts and plant weights were summed for all samples from that unit prior to calculating the standardized counts. PCA uses interval/ratio data and calculates multiple correlations using a Pearson's r correlation matrix. The closer the actual computed values are to zero (on both axes), the closer they are to the average expected value. The further away from zero, the more a case (e.g., unit) departs from expected values. The first PCA run identified several units that appear to form two clusters diverging from the average expected value (figure 11.3).

The first cluster (Cluster 1) is represented by a single unit (TU2531) that is located near the southern corner of the structure. Plant taxa that appear to be associated with this unit are tickclover, sumpweed, sunflower, and maypop (figure 11.4b). The second cluster (Cluster 2) includes five units (TU2480, TU2481, TU2490, TU2491, and TU2501) that are all adjacent, located in the northwestern area of the structure. The association of taxa with this cluster is less clear, and thus we draw two taxa clusters, a narrow one in a solid line, and a larger cluster in a dotted line. Taxa that appear to plot midway between unit clusters can be interpreted as being shared by both clusters; the lack of a clear association between taxa with the second cluster indicates such a scenario. Taxa that appear to associate with Cluster 2 include greens (*Polygonum,*

216   AMBER M. VANDERWARKER, JENNIFER V. ALVARADO, AND PAUL WEBB

TABLE 11.1. Counts and weights of plant taxa identified from the floor of Structure 35

N of Samples	65
Total Volume (liters)	1054
Plant Weight (grams)	1214.76
Wood Weight (grams)	1031.43

Common Name	Taxonomic Name	(N)	(g)
CULTIGENS			
Corn cob	*Zea mays*	13	1.46
cf. Corn cob	cf. *Zea mays*	118	0.58
Corn cupule	*Zea mays*	5561	26.1
cf. Corn cupule	cf. *Zea mays*	84	0.05
Corn kernel	*Zea mays*	656	2.95
cf. Corn kernel	cf. *Zea mays*	5	0.03
Common bean	*Phaseolus vulgaris*	30	0.17
cf. Bean	cf. *Phaseolus* sp.	40	0.33
Bean/persimmon	*Phaseolus/Diospyros*	6	0.01
Bottle gourd seed	*Lagenaria siceraria*	62	0.11
cf. Bottle gourd seed	cf. *Lagenaria siceraria*	181	0.3
Bottle gourd rind	*Lagenaria siceraria*	1325	4.34
NUTS			
Acorn cap	*Quercus* sp.	1	0.01
Acorn meat	*Quercus* sp.	2	0.02
cf. Acorn meat	cf. *Quercus* sp.	2	0.01
Acorn nutshell	*Quercus* sp.	196	0.84
cf. Acorn nutshell	cf. *Quercus* sp.	57	0.13
Hickory	*Carya* sp.	8295	99.29
cf. Hickory	cf. *Carya* sp.	13	0.04
Black walnut	*Juglans nigra*	1202	31.53
cf. Walnut family	cf. Juglandaceae	5	0.07
Walnut family meat	cf. Juglandaceae	2	0.05

continued on next page

TABLE 11.1—*continued*

Common Name	Taxonomic Name	(N)	(g)
FLESHY FRUITS			
Blackberry/Raspberry	*Rubus* sp.	43	0
Blueberry	*Vaccinium* sp.	2	0
cf. Blueberry	cf. *Vaccinium* sp.	3	0
Chokeberry	*Aronia* sp.	1	0
Grape	*Vitis* sp.	50	0.12
Groundcherry	*Physalis* sp.	56	0
Gum	*Nyssa* sp.	2	0.03
cf. Hackberry	cf. *Celtis* sp.	1	0
Hawthorn	*Crataegus* sp.	1	0.01
cf. Hawthorn	cf. *Crataegus* sp.	4	0.01
Maypop	*Passiflora incarnata*	146	0.48
cf. Nightshade	cf. *Solanum* sp.	4	0
Peach	*Prunus persica*	1	0.38
cf. Peach	cf. *Prunus persica*	1	0.07
Persimmon	*Diospyros virginiana*	66	1.75
cf. Persimmon	cf. *Diospyros virginiana*	4	0.05
Plum/Cherry	*Prunus* sp.	2	0.01
cf. Plum/Cherry	cf. *Prunus* sp.	4	0.06
Sumac	*Rhus* sp.	178	0.17
GRAINS/OIL SEEDS AND GREENS			
Amaranth	*Amaranthus* sp.	8	0
cf. Amaranth	cf. *Amaranthus* sp.	1	0
Bearsfoot	*Polymnia uvedalia*	1	0
Cheno/am	*Chenopodium/Amaranthus*	24	0
Chenopod	*Chenopodium* sp.	509	0
cf. Chenopod	cf. *Chenopodium* sp.	2	0
Knotweed	*Polygonum* sp.	1	0
cf. Little barley	cf. *Hordeum pusillum*	2	0
Pokeweed	*Phytolacca americana*	6	0

continued on next page

TABLE 11.1—*continued*

Common Name	Taxonomic Name	(N)	(g)
cf. Pokeweed	cf. *Phytolacca americana*	22	0
Purslane	*Portulaca* sp.	19	0
Ragweed	*Ambrosia* sp.	4	0
cf. Sumpweed	cf. *Iva annua*	1	0
Sumpweed/sunflower	*Iva/Helianthus*	1	0
Sunflower	*Helianthus annuus*	9	0.02
Mallow family	Malvaceae	5	0
WILD LEGUMES			
cf. Clover	cf. *Trifolium* sp.	1	0
Tickclover	*Desmodium* sp.	3	0
cf. Tickclover	cf. *Desmodium* sp.	6	0
cf. Wild bean	cf. *Strophostyles* sp.	1	0
Bean Family	Fabaceae	1	0
OTHER SEEDS			
Alder	*Alnus* sp.	19	0
Bedstraw	*Galium* sp.	2	0
Bulrush	*Scirpus* sp.	6	0
cf. Bulrush	cf. *Scirpus* sp.	1	0
Carpetweed	*Mollugo* sp.	34	0
cf. Carpetweed	cf. *Mollugo* sp.	1	0
Copperleaf	*Acalypha virginica*	2	0
cf. Crowngrass	cf. *Paspalum* sp.	5	0
cf. Dogwood	cf. *Cornus* sp.	2	0.04
cf. Falsenettle	*Boehmeria* sp.	3	0
Flatsedge	*Cyperus* sp.	1	0
Goosegrass	*Eleusine indica*	1	0
Grass family	Poaceae	319	0
Holly	*Ilex* sp.	7	0
cf. Holly	cf. *Ilex* sp.	3	0

continued on next page

TABLE II.I—*continued*

Common Name	Taxonomic Name	(N)	(g)
Magnolia	*Magnolia grandiflora*	1	0.03
Mannagrass	*Glyceria* sp.	6	0
cf. Mustard	cf. *Brassica* sp.	1	0
Pine nut	*Pinus* sp.	7	0.02
cf. Pine nut	cf. *Pinus* sp.	5	0
cf. Queensdelight	cf. *Stillingia* sp.	2	0
cf. Sage	cf. *Salvia* sp.	1	0
Sedge	*Carex* sp.	1	0
cf. Sedge	cf. *Carex* sp.	1	0
cf. Selfheal	cf. *Prunella* sp.	1	0
Smartweed	*Polygonum* sp.	5	0
cf. Smartweed	cf. *Polygonum* sp.	2	0
cf. Spikerush	cf. *Eleocharis* sp.	8	0
Spurge	*Euphorbia* sp.	59	0
cf. Spurge	cf. *Euphorbia* sp.	3	0
Verbena	*Verbena* sp.	3	0
cf. Violet	cf. *Viola* sp.	2	0
Violet	*Viola* sp.	6	0
cf. Wax myrtle	cf. *Myrica* sp.	2	0
cf. Wild sunflower	cf. *Helianthus* sp.	4	0
MISCELLANEOUS			
Pine cone flap	*Pinus* sp.	3	0.01
cf. Pine pitch	cf. *Pinus* sp.	15	0.14
UNIDENTIFIED			
Unidentified		108	1.12
Unidentified peduncle		3	0
Unidentified seed		184	0.02
Unidentifiable		2748	11.13
Unidentifiable seed		938	0.27

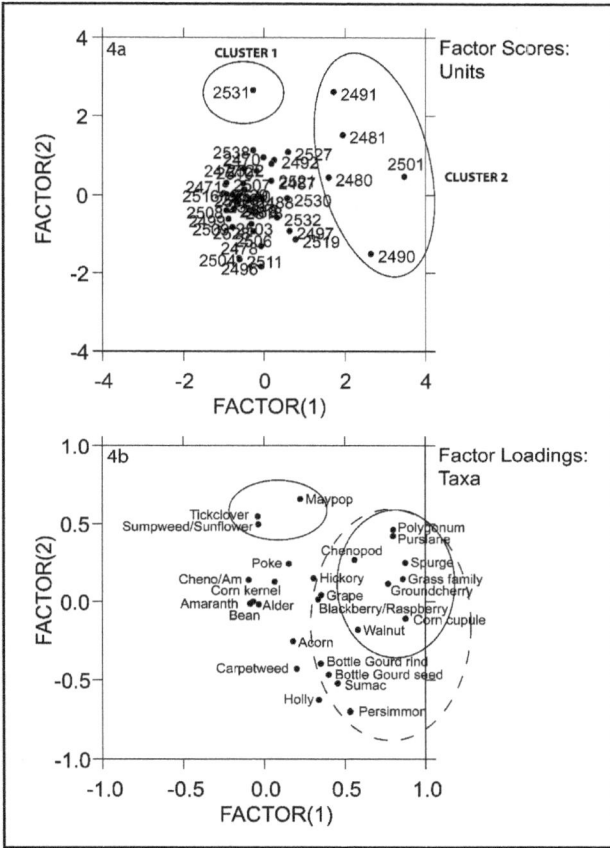

FIGURE 11.3. *Biplot of PCA scores and loadings from first run.*

purslane, spurge, and chenopod), nuts (walnut and hickory), cultigens (corn cupules and bottle gourd seeds and rind), and various fruits (raspberry, grape, sumac, persimmon, and groundcherry).

We conducted a second PCA run, excluding the units from Clusters 1 and 2 in order to determine if any additional patterning could be identified (figure 11.4). The second run resulted in three additional units being pulled away from the origin (TU2530 and TU2470, and TU2497); two of these three units (TU2530 and TU2470) are adjacent to Clusters 1 and 2, respectively. The third unit (TU2497) represents a possible third cluster (Cluster 3).

Figure 11.5 shows the patterning of these clusters on the Structure 35 map. Unfortunately, the PCA did not reveal clear patterning among the

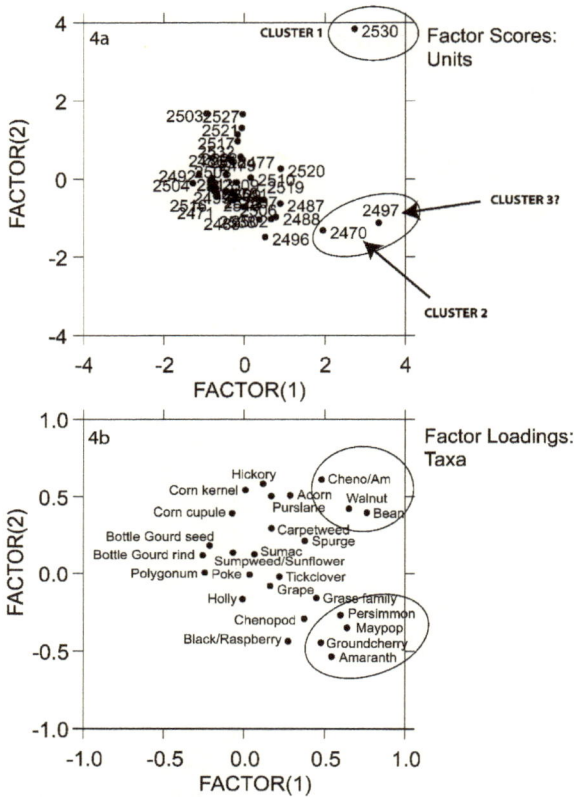

Figure 11.4. *Biplot of PCA scores and loadings from second run.*

taxa (factor loadings) as it did for the units (factor scores). Although we can determine which units form clusters in the structure on the basis of standardized plant counts, it is difficult to identify which plants are responsible for forming these clusters. In order to clarify this patterning, we turn to box plots.

Box Plot Analysis

As discussed above, we use box plots to identify statistical outliers. In this case, we are looking for units that have statistically more of a given taxon than other units. As explained, box plots show a distribution of data by portraying the median value and how the other values vary around the median. Statistical outliers are represented by asterisks, and far outliers by circles. We consider

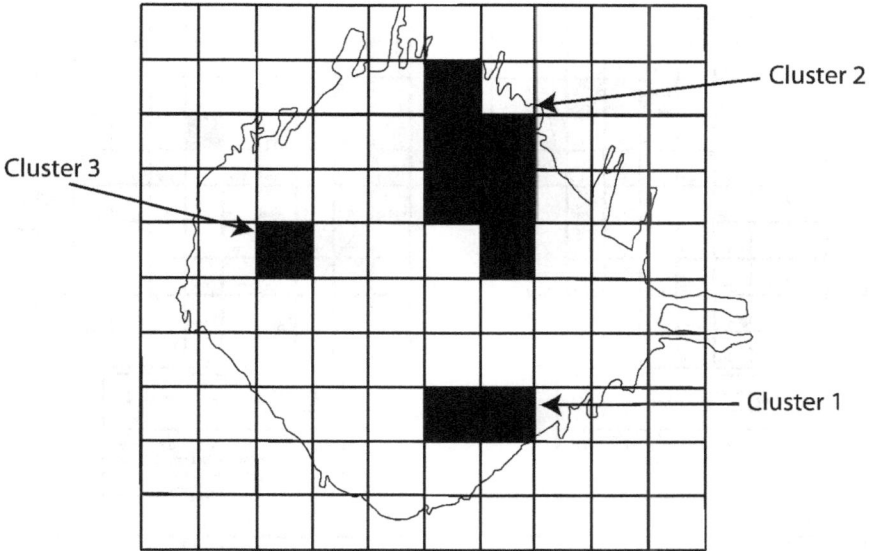

FIGURE 11.5. *Map of Structure 35 showing PCA clusters in black.*

one plant taxon at a time; for each taxon, we present a box plot with outliers labeled (with unit numbers) and a map of Structure 35 showing those units shaded in black.

Only taxa represented in the structure by at least 30 specimens were included, and all counts were converted to density measures prior to inclusion in the analysis. Densities were calculated as seed counts divided by soil volume for each unit. We consider fruits first (figure 11.6), followed by nuts (figure 11.7), and then cultigens and likely cultigens (e.g., chenopod) (figure 11.8).

The PCA identified three clusters of units based on the distribution of plant remains on the floor of Structure 35: Cluster 1 at the southern corner of the house; Cluster 2 along the northeastern wall of the house; and Cluster 3 near the western corner (see figure 11.5). The identification of these clusters is confirmed by the density box plot outlier analysis (figure 11.9).

Moreover, the identification of extreme outliers allows us to better understand what these clusters mean. Cluster 1 is characterized by high outliers of sumac, acorn, hickory, walnut, bean, chenopod, corn, and bottle gourd. Of these taxa in Cluster 1, outliers of acorn, hickory, bean, and corn occur exclusively in this cluster. The remaining taxa also occur in other clusters (sumac and chenopod in Cluster 2, walnut and bottle gourd in Cluster 3). Cluster 2

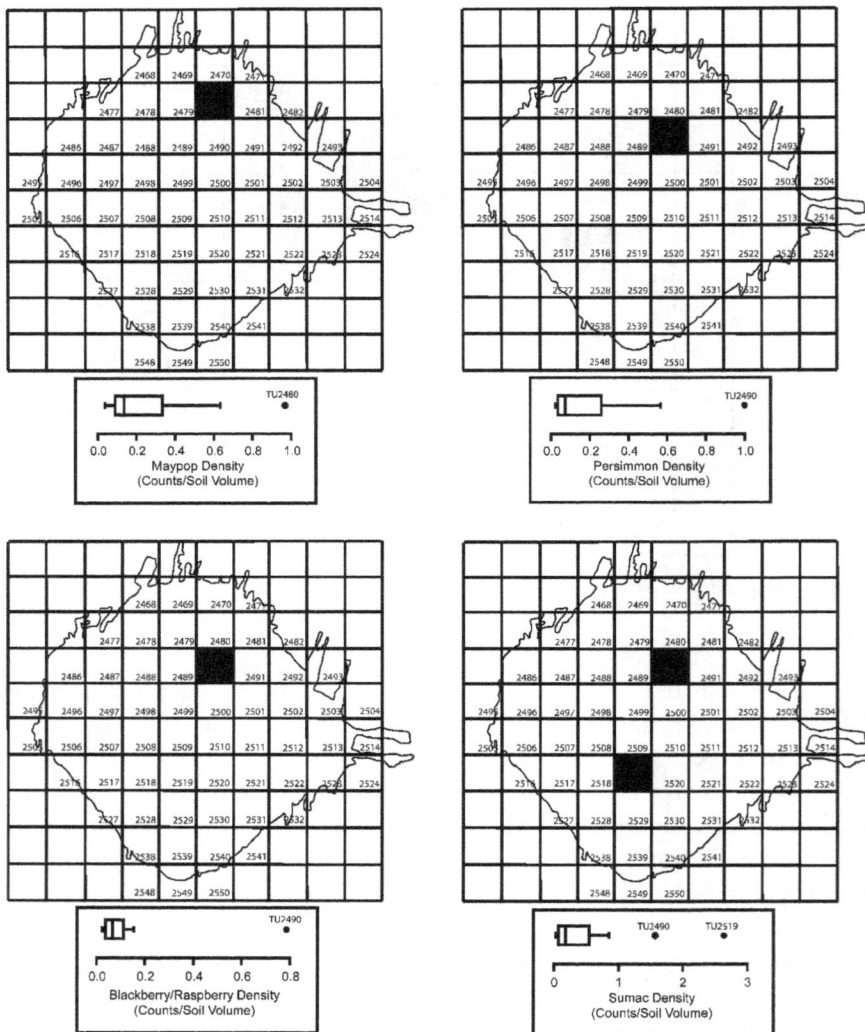

FIGURE 11.6. *Map of Structure 35 showing high outliers of fruits (maypop, blackberry/raspberry, persimmon, and sumac) with corresponding box plots of density values (density calculated as seed counts divided by soil volume per unit).*

is characterized by high outliers of maypop, persimmon, blackberry/raspberry, sumac, and chenopod. With the exception of chenopod, all of these taxa are fruits. Cluster 3 is characterized by high outliers of walnut and bottle gourd. In fact, all but one bottle gourd outlier is found in Cluster 3. It should also be

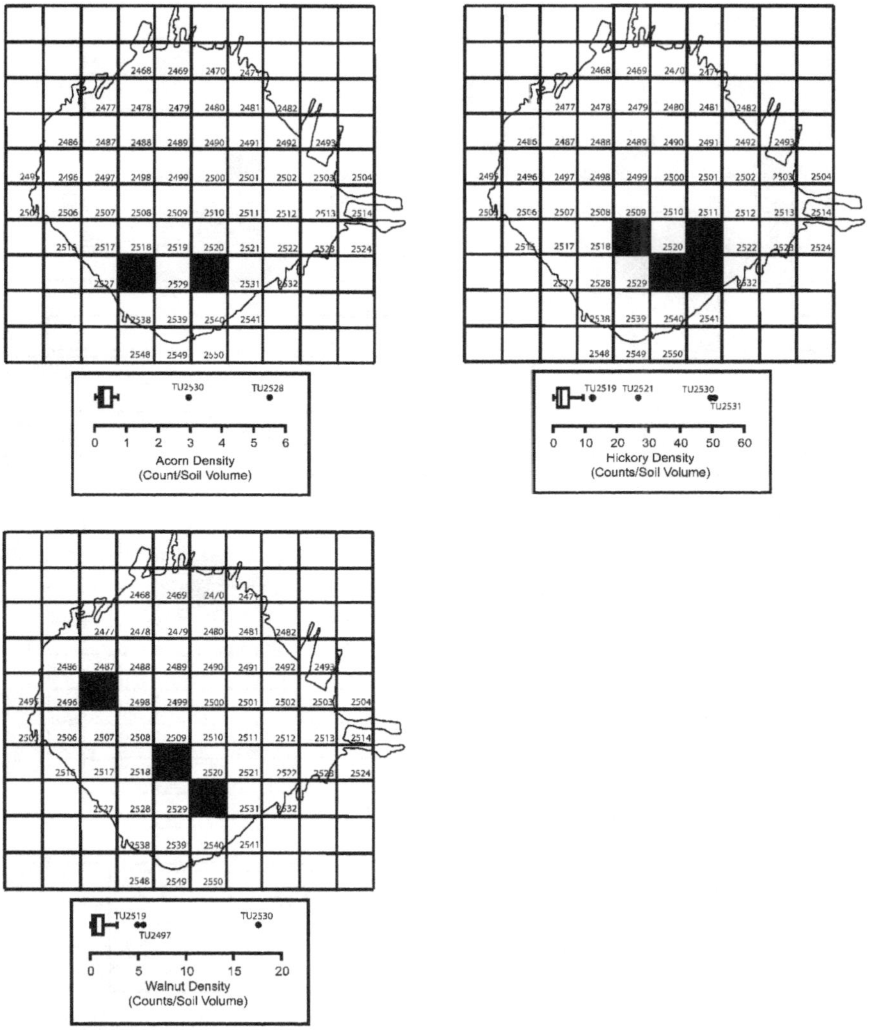

FIGURE 11.7. *Map of Structure 35 showing high outliers of nutshell (acorn, hickory, and walnut) with corresponding box plots of density values (density calculated as nutshell counts divided by soil volume per unit).*

noted that bottle gourd was present in all but five units in Structure 35; thus, it is distributed across most of the structure floor. Cluster 3 then represents an area that is defined by the densest concentration of bottle gourd seeds and rind.

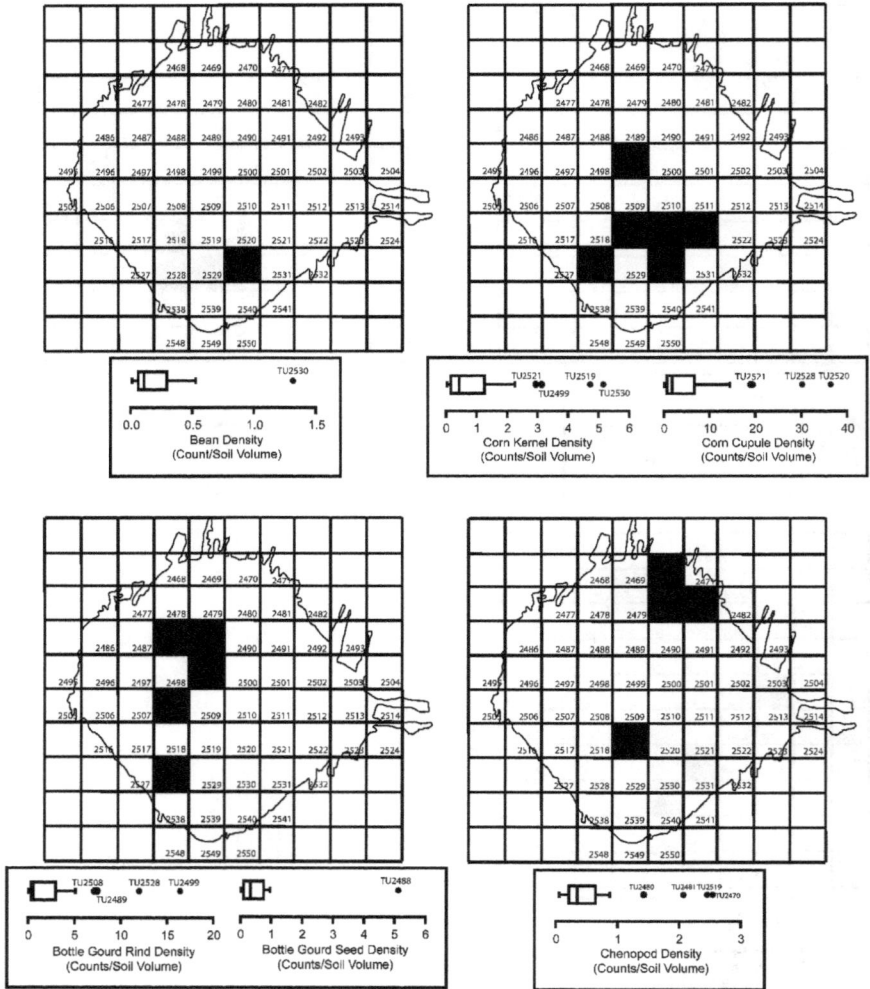

FIGURE 11.8. *Map of Structure 35 showing high outliers of cultigens (bean, corn, bottle gourd, and chenopod) with corresponding box plots of density values (density calculated as seed counts divided by soil volume per unit).*

DENSITY ANALYSIS USING GIS

We employed ArcGIS 9.3 to conduct the density analysis, using the same density values from box plot analysis. The values are linked in the ArcGIS database to the units in which they were identified. The range of density

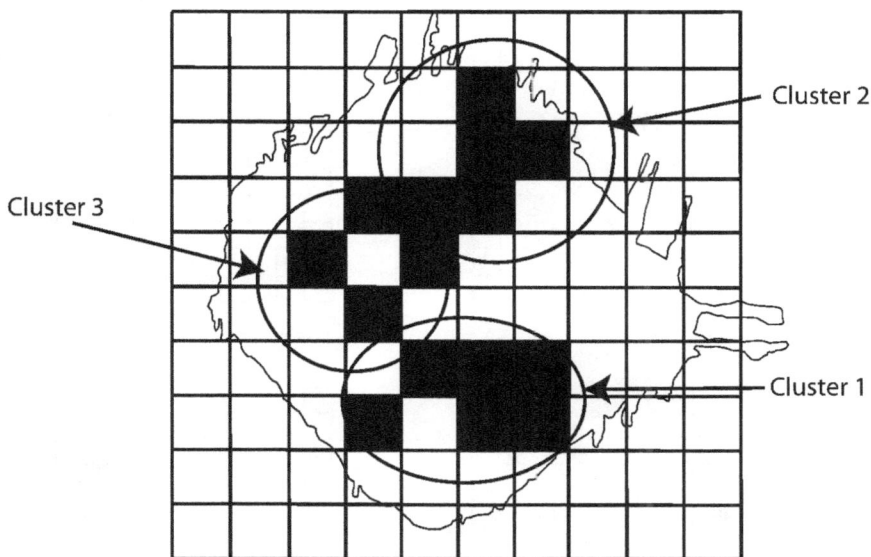

FIGURE 11.9. *Structure 35 showing clusters as revealed by the box plot density/outlier analysis.*

values for each taxon are portrayed along a shaded continuum, in which darker-shaded excavation units represent higher densities and lighter-shaded excavation units represent lower densities. The number of shaded categories was determined for each taxon using a mathematical function in the program that determines natural breaks in the distribution. The results of the density analysis confirm the clusters identified in the PCA and box plot analysis, but also reveal a greater amount of spatial variation in the distribution of more ubiquitous taxa (e.g., hickory, walnut, corn, and bottle gourd). This greater amount of variation is not surprising, given that the density analysis plots the plant data in all the units in which they occur, as opposed to just the outliers. Nevertheless, if we look closely at the densest concentrations of each plant taxon, we find that the high-density concentrations overlap with the clusters defined in the first two analyses.

The fruit density maps displayed in figure 11.10 show that blackberry/raspberry and persimmon are fairly restricted to the northern corner of the structure (Cluster 2); maypop and sumac, however, are distributed more widely along the floor. Indeed, maypop appears to be present in all three defined clusters, although the unit with the greatest density falls within Cluster 2. Sumac

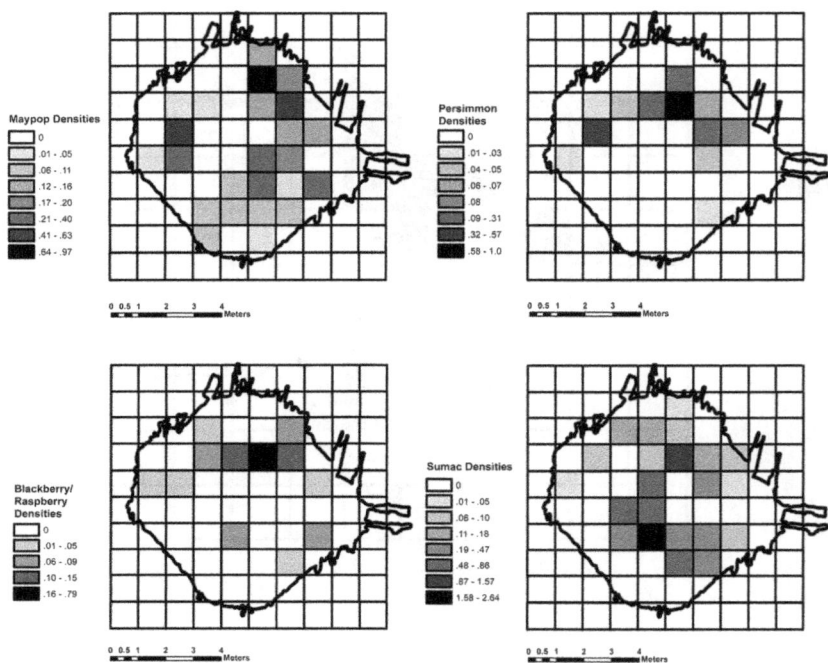

FIGURE 11.10. *GIS map of Structure 35 plotting relative densities of fruits (maypop, blackberry/raspberry, persimmon, and sumac) (density calculated as seed counts divided by soil volume per unit).*

tends to be concentrated throughout the central portion of the structure, with the densest area falling into Cluster 1, the area defined by nut and cultigen processing. Sumac is also present in fairly dense amounts in Cluster 2, which we interpret as an area of dried fruit storage (see below). Perhaps unlike the other fruits, sumac had a different use trajectory that involved greater levels of processing beyond simply drying and storing them for later consumption.

In terms of the nut density maps, hickory and walnut tend to be nearly ubiquitous throughout the structure's floor (figure 11.11). The densest concentrations of these nuts, however, occur in the southern corner of the structure, defined as Cluster 1. Acorn is more restricted in its distribution, concentrated in the southern corner of the house, in same area as the high density hickory and walnut units. These patterns confirm the concentration of nutshell in this portion of Structure 35.

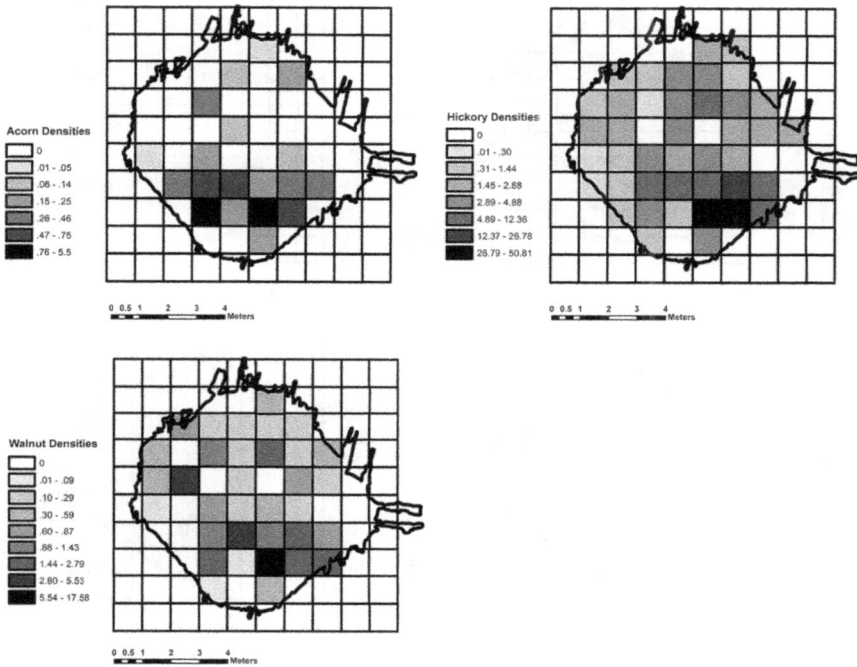

FIGURE 11.11. *GIS map of Structure 35 plotting relative densities of nutshell (acorn, hickory, and walnut) (density calculated as nutshell counts divided by soil volume per unit).*

As with hickory and walnut, corn kernels and cupules were also fairly ubiquitous in their distribution throughout the house floor (figure 11.12); the highest densities of cupules and kernels also occur in the southern corner of the house. Beans were less abundant and their distribution more restricted, with two concentrations in the northern and southern corners (see figure 11.12); the southern corner (Cluster 1) yields the highest density value for beans. Finally, bottle gourd rind fragments were identified in great abundance along the structure floor (see figure 11.12). The density map does not reveal a clear pattern in the same way as the PCA or the box plot/outlier analysis. However, the units with the densest concentration of bottle gourd rind fragments occur in the west-central portion of the house floor, which overlaps with Cluster 3, as defined in the PCA and box plot analysis.

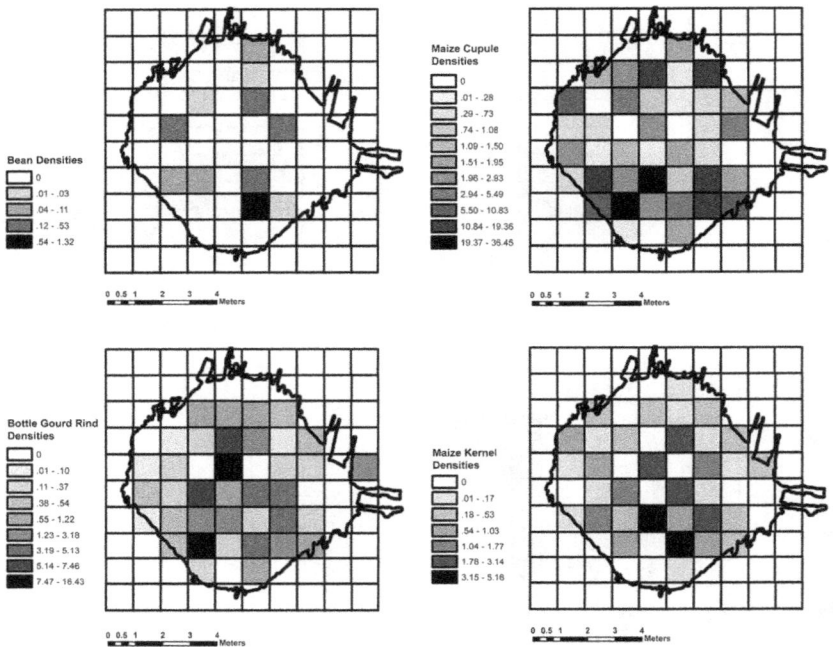

FIGURE II.12. *GIS map of Structure 35 plotting relative densities of cultigens (bean, corn kernels, corn cupules, and bottle gourd rind fragments) (density calculated as seed counts divided by soil volume per unit).*

INTERPRETATIONS BASED ON THE SPATIAL ANALYSIS

Based on the analyses presented above, we offer an interpretation of the spatial layout of subsistence-based activities in Structure 35. Three clusters were defined based on the PCA and confirmed by the box plot analysis. The GIS-based density analysis reveals that the distribution of plant taxa was not restricted to any specific cluster; rather, many taxa were distributed widely throughout the structure floor, requiring the identification of high-density units. The wide distribution of taxa throughout the floor of the structure is to be expected if the structure's residents relaxed their cleaning routines in expectation of imminent abandonment. Moreover, if any plants were stored or hung from the roof beams, the collapse of these beams would have led to a broader distribution of plants throughout the structure floor.

Cluster 1 is located in the southern corner of the structure and is composed of nutshell, corn, bean, and some sumac. The presence of great quantities of nutshell (not nutmeats or whole nuts) indicates significant nut processing in the southern corner of the structure. The fact that outliers of both corn kernels and cupules also occur in this cluster suggest that corn processing occurred here as well. The presence of cupules indicates that people were engaged in shelling corn in this area of the structure. That so many corn kernels also occur there indicate either that (1) shelling had not yet been completed (the kernels had not been removed and stored elsewhere) or (2) this was a two-stage process, with shelling followed by grinding or soaking, which was either planned or underway. Regardless, these data tell us that the southern corner of the structure was likely a locus of food processing and preparation.

Cluster 2, in the northern corner, is made almost exclusively of high densities of fruit seeds, with modest amounts of corn, nuts, and bottle gourd fragments (as these taxa are ubiquitous). With the exception of a sumac outlier also occurring in Cluster 1, all the fruit outliers are restricted to Cluster 2. We interpret this cluster as an area of dried fruit storage. After collecting fresh fruits, we surmise that the structure's residents dried and stored these fruits, possibly hanging them from the building rafters. When the house burned, and the roof collapsed, these fruits would have fallen to the floor amidst the general food processing debris composed of corn and nuts.

Located in the west-central portion of the house, Cluster 3 is composed of bottle gourd seeds and rind fragments, with rind fragments five times more frequent than seeds. The definition of Cluster 3 is based on the PCA and the box plot analysis; the GIS-based density analysis did not provide clear confirmation of this cluster, because of the sheer ubiquity of the bottle gourd fragments throughout the structure. It bears repeating that bottle gourd remains were littered along the entire floor of the structure. The densest concentration of these remains, however, can be found near the western corner. The amount of bottle gourd identified in this structure is quite rare, especially for an open-air site. It is clear that Structure 35 offers unique preservation conditions for this plant. Bottle gourds are commonly thought to function as liquid storage containers. Given the high densities of seeds and rind near the western corner, we suggest that bottle gourds were also hung from the rafters, possibly filled with liquids or in the process of being dried for manufacture into liquid storage containers or ladles. When the beams collapsed during the structure's burning, the gourds fell to the floor (some also probably fell prior to the collapse of the beams). At impact, the gourds broke and fragments likely scattered across the floor; this would explain the high ubiquity of bottle gourd fragments throughout the floor, coupled with the higher densities in the western corner.

It is interesting that these clusters are all located away from the structure opening/vestibule in the eastern corner. The area of the structure directly inside the doorway was kept clear of food processing activities, food/liquid storage, and food refuse. Instead these locales were placed along the walls tangent to the opening and along the opposite (western) corner.

In summary, the unique preservation circumstances and abandonment context of Structure 35 have allowed for a spatial analysis of plant-related activities on the house floor. This study provides a rare look into household activity space and how/where foods were processed and stored within living space. We have identified three clusters that we interpret as representing (1) a processing locale for corn and nuts in the southern corner of the house, just to the left of the vestibule entrance, (2) an area of dried fruit storage in the northern corner of the structure, to the right of the house entrance (probably stored in or hanging from the roof beams), and (3) an area of possible liquid storage and/or gourd curing near the western corner of the structure. This area is denoted by the high density of bottle gourd remains in that corner; bottle gourds were likely strung up from the rafters and came crashing down when the beams collapsed during the fire that incinerated the structure.

CONCLUSION

Although spatial analysis has gained momentum in archaeobotany over the last two decades, it continues to be underrepresented in the literature. When archaeobotanists do approach this topic, they choose one of two approaches—either assigning a priori spatial categories based on other archaeological data sets, followed by an analysis of the plant data, or using exploratory analysis of the plant data as a starting point for determining the spatial categories. In terms of exploratory approaches to spatial analysis, our literature review reveals some commonalities in terms of how archaeobotanists analyze their data quantitatively. We highlight three of these quantitative approaches: (1) multivariate statistics such as PCA, (2) box plot analysis to search for outliers, the contexts of which are plotted onto a map, and (3) GIS-based density analysis. These three quantitative methods were employed to examine the distribution of plant remains on the floor of a Late Qualla Cherokee house structure that was burned to the ground, leaving the primary activity spaces on the house floor undisturbed at the time of abandonment. All three statistical techniques yielded similar patterning, allowing for the identification of three clusters which we interpreted as areas of food processing and storage. The results of the case study demonstrate the effectiveness of these techniques for the spatial analysis of archaeobotanical data. By outlining the use of these techniques, alongside a demonstration of their interpretative strength, we hope that spatial analysis will become more common in the archaeobotanical literature.

ACKNOWLEDGMENTS

We foremost acknowledge Tasha Benyshek for her careful work at directing the excavations at Ravensford, in addition to her assistance in delineating which flotation samples were clearly associated with the floor contexts from Structure 35. We also thank Gregory Wilson and Dana Bardolph for providing comments on the manuscript, and Lana Martin and Alexia Smith for suggesting additional source material. Thanks also to Mac Marston, Christina Warinner, and Jade d'Alpoim Guedes for organizing the SAA session for which this chapter was written, and for their careful editing of the manuscript. Finally, we thank the anonymous reviewers for their comments.

12

Intersite Variation
within Archaeobotanical
Charred Assemblages

A Case Study Exploring
the Social Organization of
Agricultural Husbandry in
Iron Age and Roman Britain

CHRIS J. STEVENS

Less than 200 years ago, four-fifths of the world's working population was engaged in agriculture in one form or another (Grigg 1985:137). Prior to industrialization, the organization and scheduling of sowing, harvesting, processing, storage, and consumption of crops in cereal-growing communities shaped almost every aspect of people's lives. The annual cycles of such events determined the timing of both work and festivals through the year. They thus played an integral role in structuring political and economic systems, from settlement patterns (Stone 1996; Trigger 1968:62) to cosmological and ideological beliefs (Frazer 1912; Wilkinson and Stevens 2003:226–28).

For many societies, the basis of agricultural production lies within smaller social units, often united through kinship. These kinship units serve to reduce the uncertainties and risks that small-scale, non-market-based agricultural production may face (Bennett and Kanel 1983). At its most basic level, the household is the primary structuring principle of many past societies, embodying relations of consumption and production (Forster 1984; Hammel 1984; Netting et al. 1984; Segalen 1986:1; Stone et al. 1990; Wilk and Netting 1984). How families are integrated into larger social networks is vital to understanding the decisions made concerning agricultural production. In addition, it is important to understand what factors, other than purely environmental ones, might influence such choices (Lees 1983).

DOI: 10.5876/9781607323167.c012

Since the 1960s, the application of systematic flotation to archaeological excavations has led to an increase in the quantities of archaeobotanical data available for analysis. Using this large corpus of data, Knörzer (1971) recognized that charred assemblages from cereal-growing communities in northern Europe predominately contain three basic elements. Aside from wood fuel, they contain cereal grains, cereal chaff, and seeds of wild weeds from ancient fields. Unlike other forms of preservation, charred assemblages could then be seen to almost exclusively contain the by-products of cereal agriculture.

Along with other evidence such as storage structures, tools associated with harvesting and tillage, field systems, millstones, and quernstones, charred assemblages provide a major line of evidence for agricultural practice. These data sources are potentially reflective of the organization of agricultural activities both at the household and at broader levels of social organization. It is fundamental for the archaeobotanist to find pragmatic, interpretive methods for untangling the intricate threads of evidence that tie charred material to households and wider social structures through past agricultural practices.

The exploration of chronological and spatial variation among sites is key to understanding these relationships. As agriculture plays an important role in the formation of past societies, then it follows that any variation within the evidence for it, seen across time and space, must echo variation within socioeconomic, political, and religious systems.

With the growing body of data, charred assemblages from sites within a number of regions across the world have been examined with respect to variation between them and their relationship to agriculture and society. A few such studies from the Near East, Europe, South America, and China are briefly described below to illustrate the diversity of intersite approaches to relating charred assemblages to farming practices.

Studies of variation with respect to grain size and the incidence of tough and brittle rachis fragments, both indicators of domestication, have been carried out for Near Eastern sites (Fuller 2007b). Such studies help document early gathering of cereals, their cultivation, and their eventual domestication. A study of the charred assemblages from Early Neolithic sites across the Near East and Europe helped chart the spread of early farmers and the crops and weeds that accompanied them, recording where crops were lost and new weeds gained (Coward et al. 2008). A study of charcoal assemblages from sites in Iran also showed the value of intersite analysis in the examination of population change and its effects on selective deforestation during the fourth to second millennia BC (Miller 1985).

A further study in northeast England by van der Veen (1992a) distinguished two groups of sites. The first group contained cultivated emmer and was dominated by seeds of annual weed species associated with nitrogen-rich soils; this group was interpreted as being composed of communities that farmed more intensively. The second group contained predominately spelt wheat and these assemblages were dominated by seeds of perennial species associated with less fertile soils. These sites were seen as farming less intensively and more extensively.

In South America, Christine Hastorf (1990) has studied settlements in the Andean central highlands, measuring carbon isotopic values relating to the consumption of C_3 and C_4 plants in addition to macrobotanical analysis. Broad consistency in bone isotopic chemistry and macrobotanical assemblages led her to conclude that Inka rule had direct effects on production and consumption at the level of individual households.

The combination of Geographic Information Systems (GIS) along with charred remains relating to crop-processing activities has also proved a successful approach to the study of Neolithic and Early Bronze Age settlements in the Ying valley, China (Zhang et al. 2010). Zhang found strong geographic patterning in how farmers along the valley processed their crops, with closely situated settlements often demonstrating very similar patterns.

CHARRED ASSEMBLAGES AS A MEANS OF EXAMINING SOCIAL ORGANIZATION

The often rich, charred assemblages from Iron Age Britain (700 BC to AD 43), collected from a large number of excavated sites, provide an excellent data set from which to study farming communities cultivating hulled wheats (i.e., emmer and spelt) and hulled barley (figure 12.1). Furthermore, the continuation of this data set into the Romano-British period (AD 43 to 410) allows us to study the impact of Romanization upon these communities.

The examination of the charred assemblages from British Iron Age and Roman sites has shown that a great deal of disparity exists in the proportions of chaff, grain, and weed seeds at different sites. These differences were first noted by Jones (1985), but similar patterns have since been recorded and studied in Britain by others, including van der Veen (1990, 1991), Jones and Nye (1991), Palmer and Jones (1991), Jones (1993), G. Campbell (2000), Stevens (2003a, 2003b), van der Veen and Jones (2006), and Fuller and Stevens (2009). Although these authors have generally agreed on the patterns seen within this data set, they have proposed different hypotheses to explain these patterns and their relationships to crop processing.

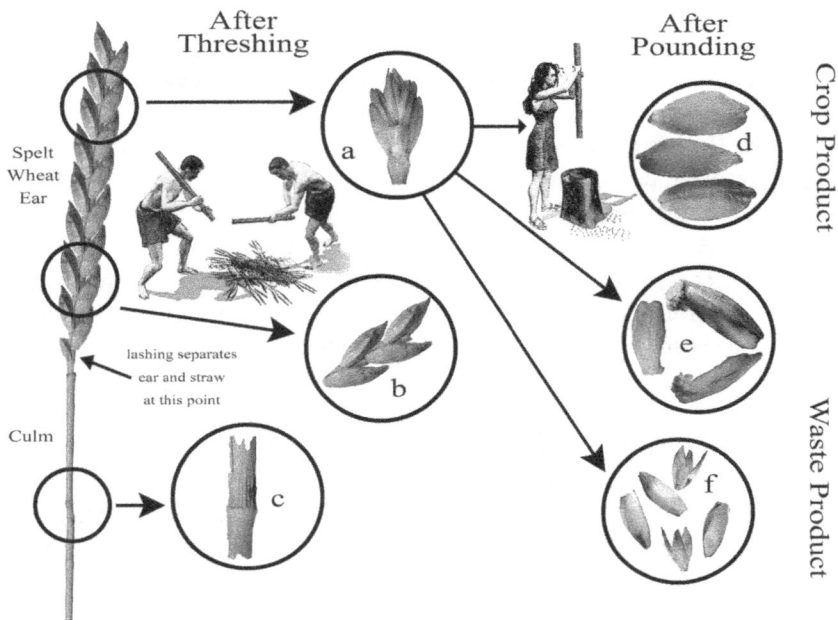

FIGURE 12.1. *The breaking of spelt wheat ears into spikelets by threshing and the breaking of spikelets by pounding to release the grain from the glumes: (a) spikelet; (b) incompletely broken ear or partially threshed ear. These may be rethreshed, stored for animal fodder or as a famine food, or potentially, if only the straw is removed, stored for human consumption; (c) culm nodes usually removed by raking, winnowing, and coarse sieving; (d) free-grains of spelt wheat; (e) glume bases (two still joined = a spikelet fork); (f) paleas and lemmas (light chaff).*

CONSUMER-PRODUCER MODELS

Studies by Martin Jones (Jones 1985, 1996; Jones and Nye 1991) have attributed the patterns seen between sites as due to differences between producers and consumers. Jones (Jones 1985; Jones and Nye 1991) examined charred assemblages from the hillfort at Danebury, five sites in the Thames valley of England, a reasonably large nucleated settlement at Ashville (Muir and Roberts 1999; Parrington 1978), a probable smaller settlement at Mount Farm, and three smaller settlements closer to the floodplain: Clayton Pike (Miles et al. 2007), Smith's Field (Allen 1981), and Mingies Ditch (Allen and Robinson 1993).

Rather than a generally homogenous distribution of grain, chaff, and weed seeds, a distinctive pattern emerged from the analysis of material at these sites.

Although sites were rich in cereal grains, others were richer in chaff and weed seeds (see Marston, chapter 9, this volume, figure 9.2). This pattern followed settlement location to some extent, with sites on the drier gravel terraces richer in grain, whereas those close to the floodplain were richer in weeds and chaff. The hillfort at Danebury, however, showed a distinctively mixed pattern. Jones attributed the differences in the charred assemblages as reflecting differences in the sites' past roles in production and consumption. From his own observations of traditional cereal-growing communities, where grain often covered every surface, he reasoned that within producer settlements grain would be readily wasted, leading to grain-rich assemblages. Given that the grain-rich settlements were situated in locations more suited to arable farming, he interpreted them as cereal producers. Conversely, in sites receiving grain he suggested crops would be more carefully processed, with grain less readily wasted, leading to assemblages richer in weed seeds and chaff. That settlements with charred assemblages richer in weed seeds and chaff were recovered from sites less suited for arable farming on the floodplain led Jones (1985) to interpret them as pastoralist consumers.

PROCESSING SCHEDULES AND STORAGE

This model was challenged based on the observation that other sites with high amounts of weed seeds and chaff were clearly involved in farming. Stevens (2003a) developed an alternative model that explained the differences in the proportion of grain, chaff, and weed seeds as resulting from the stage at which crops (predominately hulled wheats—spelt and emmer—but with some hulled barley) were stored.

The following sections demonstrate the use of three statistical ratios (see Marston, chapter 9, this volume, for further discussion of such measures) to reanalyze Jones's data (1985), as well as additional sites in the Upper Thames. These ratios, adapted from van der Veen (1992a), G. Jones (1984, 1987), and Hillman (1981, 1984a, 1984b), have led scholars to different conclusions regarding production, storage, and processing. The sites are summarized in table 12.1, along with comments relating to their size, interpretations of the probable processing stage at which crops were stored, and whether crops may have been dehusked en masse as they were taken from storage.

The Ratio of Glume Bases to Estimated Grains of Hulled Wheat

Hillman (1981, 1984a) proposed that farmers residing in wetter climates store hulled wheats in the spikelet. This is because the short number of predictable

TABLE 12.1. Sites, settlement type, size, and interpretative patterns of charred assemblages discussed in the text

Site	Site Notes	Storage As	After-Storage Processing	References
UPPER THAMES VALLEY (LOWLANDS)				
Abingdon	Large Enclosed (Oppida)	Semi-clean spikelets	Mixed. Some grain-rich, most glume-rich	Stevens 1996
Claydon Pike	Small, paddocks, dispersed	Sheaves/ears	Probably small scale	M. K. Jones 1984b
Lechlade	Small, paddocks?	Sheaves/ears	Small scale (grain-rich LBA storage pit)	Stevens 2003a
Mingies Ditch	Small enclosed floodplain	Sheaves/ears	Probably small scale, glume-rich	Jones 1993
Yarnton	Small dispersed, unenclosed	Sheaves/ears	Small scale, glume/weed-rich	Stevens 1996, 2011
Ashville	Little to no evidence, large unenclosed	Semi-clean spikelets	Large scale, grain-rich	Jones 1978; M. K. Jones 1984b
Mount Farm	Paddocks, small dispersed	Semi-clean spikelets	Large scale, grain-rich	M. K. Jones 1984b
Whitehorse Road	Small, unenclosed	Semi-clean spikelets	Large scale, but fewer grain-rich	Letts 1993
WESSEX, UPLANDS AND HILLFORTS				
Danebury, Hampshire	Hillfort	Semi-clean spikelets	Mainly large scale, grain-rich	Jones and Nye 1991
Maiden Castle, Dorset	Hillfort	Semi-clean spikelets in Early Iron Age; sheaves/ears in Middle Iron Age	Mainly small scale/less obvious period division	Palmer and Jones 1991
Battlesbury, Wilshire	Hillfort (pits outside)	Semi-clean spikelets	Some indication of larger scale	Clapham and Stevens 2008
Weston Down Hampshire	Small settlement	Mixed	Small-scale mainly glume-rich	Stevens 2007

continued on next page

TABLE 12.1—*continued*

Site	Site Notes	Storage As	After-Storage Processing	References
West of Scotland Lodge, Wiltshire	Small settlement	Sheaves/ears? But some rich in larger weed seeds only.	Small-scale mainly glume-rich	Leivers and Stevens 2008
Lains Farm, Hampshire	Small settlement	Semi-clean spikelets occasional sheaves/ears	Very mixed: some larger, some small scale.	Monk and Fasham 1980
Rollright Stones	Small enclosed (banjo?)	Semi-clean spikelets	Large scale, grain-rich	Moffett 1988
Asheldham, Essex	Hillfort	Semi-clean spikelets	Large scale, probably mainly burnt stores	Murphy 1991

dry days restricts the time available after harvest for dehusking the spikelets before the crops need to be safely stored. In addition, storage as spikelets also provides increased protection to the grains from fungal or insect attack (Nesbitt and Samuel 1996:40). Further based on the analysis of the burnt contents of storage pits (Ballantyne 2004; M. Jones 1984a), it is probable that in Iron Age Britain hulled wheats were stored as whole spikelets.

Each spikelet has two glumes and on average two grains. Therefore a higher ratio of glume bases to the estimated number of hulled wheat grains implies that the charred assemblage contains dehusking waste (figures 12.1 and 12.2).

If crops are stored in the spikelet, then such dehusking would only be conducted after storage and therefore the charred waste can be attributed to the processing of crops taken from storage. For a number of the sites (e.g., Yarnton) this is clearly the case, with the majority of the sample richer in glumes than estimated hulled wheat grains (figures 12.3 and 12.4).

That many of the samples can be related to the charring of waste from the processing of crops as they are taken from storage should come as no surprise. Of all the various taphonomic routes that lead to the formation of individual charred samples (see Gallagher, chapter 2, this volume), it is those that most frequently result in the charring of plant material in the settlement itself that will make the greatest contribution to the archaeobotanical record. The routine processing of whole spikelets taken from storage would likely be conducted 365 days of the year within the settlement where, as Hillman (1981)

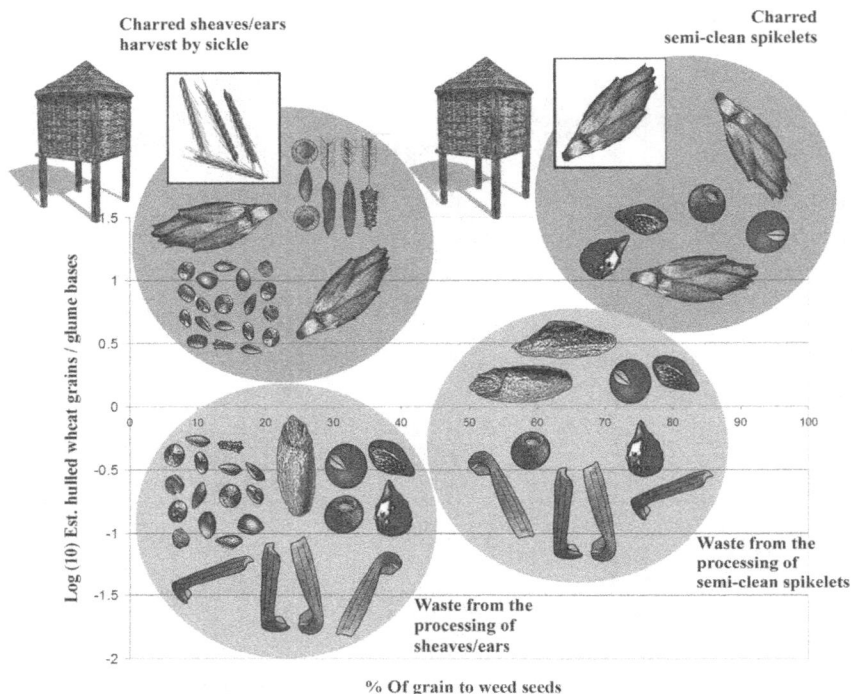

FIGURE 12.2. *Relationships of samples plotted according to the proportion of grain to weed seeds against the logarithmic (base 10) values of estimated hulled wheat grains divided by glume bases to processing waste and the stored crop. The x-axis crosses the y-axis at a ratio of 10 grains to each glume base.*

notes, waste is often amalgamated and discarded straight into the fire. In contrast, if crops are fully processed following the harvest, the waste produced is generated in the field and, even if brought to back to the settlement for use as fuel, may only be present on the site for a few weeks around harvest time (Stevens 2003b). For hulled wheats, the by-products from these early processing stages are less likely to become charred, as they are often used for fodder or animal bedding rather than for fuel (D'Andrea and Haile 2002).

Alternative taphonomic pathways to preservation, such as the accidental burning of stores or the destruction of crops during drying or parching, are likely to be much rarer in comparison to those generated by routine processing. In general, charred assemblages appear to relate to the deliberate charring of

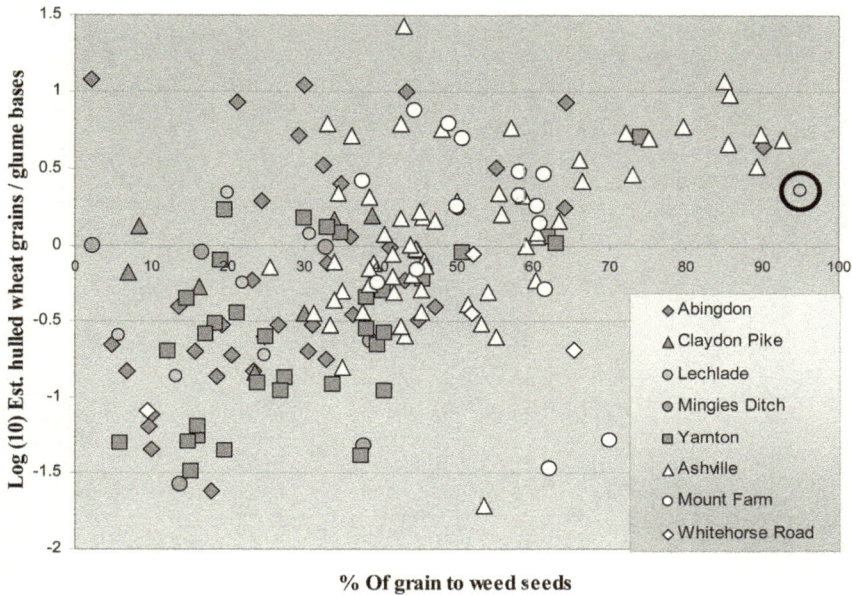

FIGURE 12.3. *Samples from the Upper Thames valley, plotted according to the proportion of estimated hulled wheat grains to glume bases and grain to weed seeds. The sites include those studied by Jones (1985, 1993) and Stevens (2003b). The circled sample is an assemblage from a Late Bronze Age storage pit at Lechlade (Stevens 2003a).*

the processing waste generated within the preparation of daily meals, rather than accidents, which explains why cereals are so common in charred assemblages compared to other plant material. However, this is not to say that accidental charring of grain stores does not occur. In the case of two Iron Age hillforts, Danebury and Wandlebury, cited above, as well as a smaller settlement at Lechlade, the excavation of the contents of storage pits clearly revealed charred spikelets burnt in situ (Ballantyne 2004; M. K. Jones 1984a; Stevens 2003a). Samples from these pits are much richer in grain than glumes (figures 12.3 and 12.4), a fact that is in keeping with the charring of the crop product rather than the waste from its processing.

The more glume-rich assemblages from sites such as Yarnton can be interpreted as resulting from the charring of routine processing waste of crops taken from storage, but it does raise the question of the interpretation of sites with more grain than glume-rich assemblages. For example, the grain-rich type site of Ashville clearly has a majority of assemblages richer in grain than

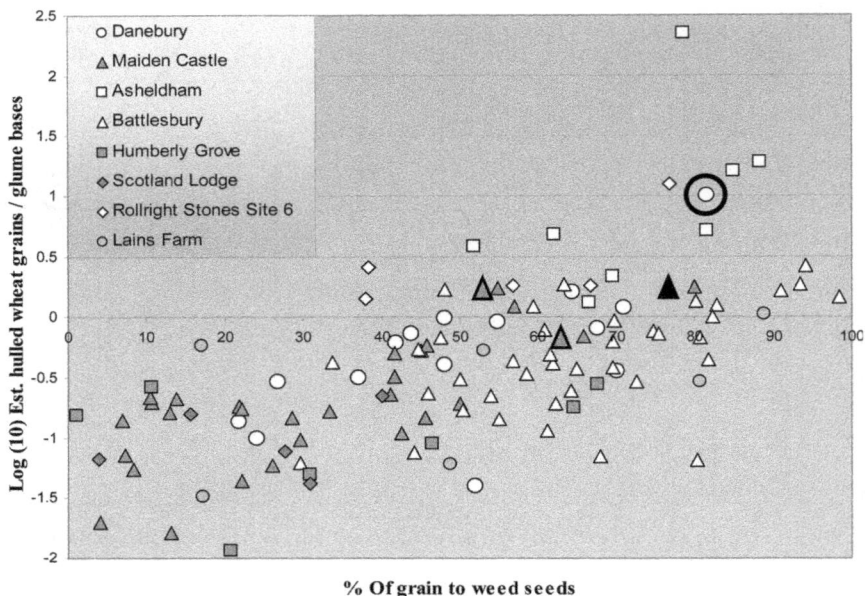

FIGURE 12.4. *Samples from Wessex and Essex (Asheldham) plotted according to the proportion of estimated hulled wheat grains to glume bases and grain to weed seeds. The circled sample is the assemblage from the storage pit at Danebury (Stevens 2003a).*

glumes. But if such assemblages were the result of the accidental charring of either processed grain or unpounded spikelets (as recently suggested by van der Veen and Jones [2006]), then it would imply that almost every assemblage from Ashville is the result of an accident, and only a small minority resulting from routine processing waste. Given that the excavations at Ashville revealed what appears to be a relatively typical Iron Age settlement (Parrington 1978), the apparent absence of charred waste from routine processing requires further explanation.

Experimental tests have demonstrated that glume survival by charring is poor relative to that of grain (Boardman and Jones 1990), especially following deposition. These same experiments also demonstrated that preservation is best when charring occurs in reduced oxygen environments. As such, material charred in situ from storage pits presents an ideal preservation environment, in that there is limited oxygen and the material is relatively undisturbed. Yet turning to the example given above, where charred spikelets were recovered from a storage pit (number 1078) at Danebury, these at best produced only one glume for every two grains (as also seen for Lechlade, figure 12.3), whereas on average this ratio was reduced to one glume per 10 grains (figure 12.3; see Stevens 2003b:figure 4).

Further work has shown that the bias toward the preservation of grains compared to glumes may be quite extreme. Silica skeletons of glume bases rarely survive in the archaeological record, but rich deposits of spelt glumes containing identifiable grains, identifiable charred glume bases, and silica skeletons of glumes allowed Robinson and Straker (1991) to demonstrate just how many glume bases were lost in comparison to those that survived. Further, burnt ears of emmer wheat from a hillfort in southwest England produced flotation samples in which not a single glume survived (Ede 1999).

Given that many of the assemblages from grain-rich sites are still richer in glume bases than deposits from storage pits, where we know whole spikelets were originally charred, it is quite probable that these assemblages also were once much richer in glumes, especially where deposits were not burnt in situ. Thus, most of the grain-rich assemblages can still be attributable to routine waste (figure 12.2; Stevens 2003b).

The Ratio of Weed Seeds to Grain

The ratio of grain to weed seeds has been proposed as an indicator of whether crop product or crop waste is present (van der Veen 1992a:82; 2007a:table 6; van der Veen and Jones 2006:table 2). However, it is clear that some assemblages, such as at Yarton, are richer in weed seeds (figure 12.3), whereas others, such as at Battlesbury, are richer in grain (figure 12.4); yet based on the high proportion of glume bases to grain, both sites appear to contain waste from dehusking rather than charred crop product.

One explanation for this pattern comes from examining crop-processing sequences. As weed seeds are gradually removed at various stages of crop-processing, the ratio of weed seeds to grain within the crop declines (figure 12.5; Stevens 2003b).

If processing waste (from routine processing after storage), is the dominant form of charred remains represented in most samples, then variation in the ratio of weed seeds to crop grain may reflect the number of processing stages the waste has undergone. If crops were stored largely unprocessed, then the waste from all the remaining stages would contain high numbers of weed seeds, but if they were stored in a more processed state, then the waste would contain far fewer weed seeds compared to the grain, as weed seeds are also lost during dehusking.

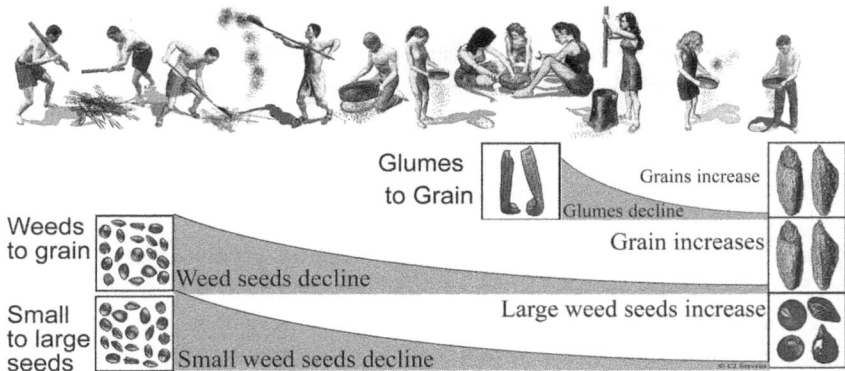

FIGURE 12.5. *The changing ratios of glumes to grain, weed seeds to grain, and small weed seeds to large weed seeds in the crop and processing waste for hulled wheats. Variation in the order of some of these actions has been noted by some authors; contrary to Hillman (1981, 1984a, 1984b), and following D'Andrea and Haile (2002) and Samuel (1999), handsorting has been placed before pounding and followed by a winnowing event.*

The Proportion of Small, Large, and Intermediate–Sized Weed Seeds

The ratio of large to small and intermediate weed seeds can be used to test the hypothesis that different stages of storage are responsible for grain-rich or weed-rich assemblages. There are several species that produce free (i.e., non-headed) seeds that are similar in size and weight to spikelets and grains. Because these seeds mimic the grains of the crop, they are difficult to remove and indeed their very survival in the field is often dependant on being resown with the crop. Such seeds have to be removed by hand sorting, a process that is time-consuming and generally only conducted as crops are taken from storage (see D'Andrea and Haile 2002; Hillman 1981, 1984a; G. Jones 1984; Jones 1987; Samuel 1999). As smaller weed seeds are removed by earlier sieving and winnowing events, the ratio of large to small weed seeds will increase through the processing sequence (figure 12.5).

If all crops in the Iron Age were stored at a single processing stage, then this ratio should remain broadly consistent whether it is the stored crop that is charred or the amalgamated waste from the processing of this stored crop. However, clear intersite patterning emerges, with waste including earlier processing stages and dominated by small weed seeds characterizing the samples from one group of sites, whereas the assemblages from the second group of sites do not appear to contain this waste, being dominated by large weed seeds (figures 12.6 and 12.7).

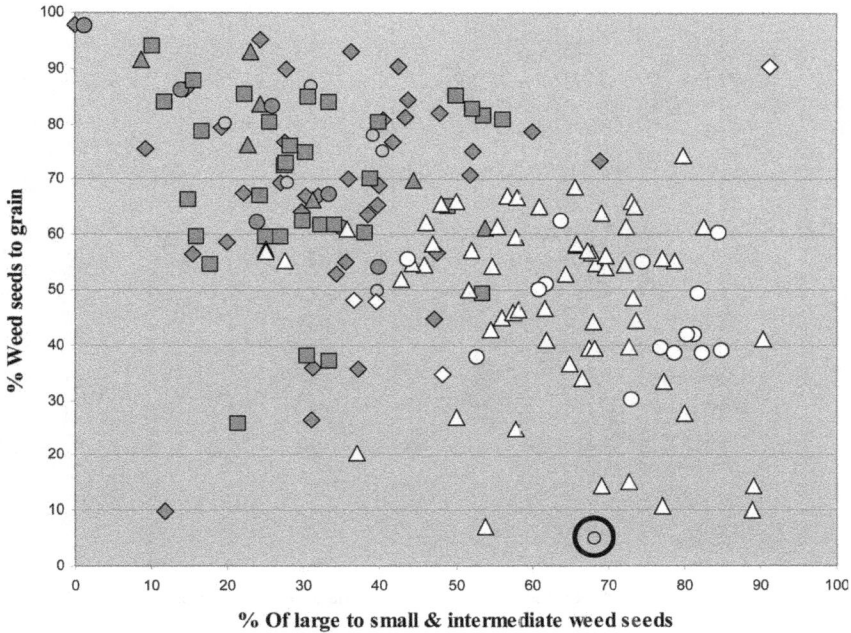

FIGURE 12.6. *Samples from Upper Thames valley. The proportion of weed seeds to grain is plotted against the proportion of large to small weed seeds (see figure 12.3 for the key). The circled sample is the storage pit at Lechlade (Stevens 2003a).*

The crop-processing model thus predicts that by using the ratios of grain-to-weed seeds and large-to-small weed seeds it is possible to interpret variation among sites as evidence for crop storage at different stages of processing (figures 12.8).

Storage as Sheaves or Storage as Semi-Clean Spikelets
The differences seen by Jones can then be interpreted as relating not to producers and consumers, but as to how crops were stored (Stevens 2003b). For one group of sites, those that were rich in small weed seeds, barley rachises, and culm nodes, storage appears to be in the form of sheaves or partially threshed ears (i.e., after the straw had been removed; Stevens 2003b), although for the other group of sites, those rich in grain and larger weed seeds, the mode of storage is interpreted as being in the form of semi-clean spikelets.

The possibility that cereal crops in the Iron Age were stored as partially threshed ears is supported by observations from experimental processing. In

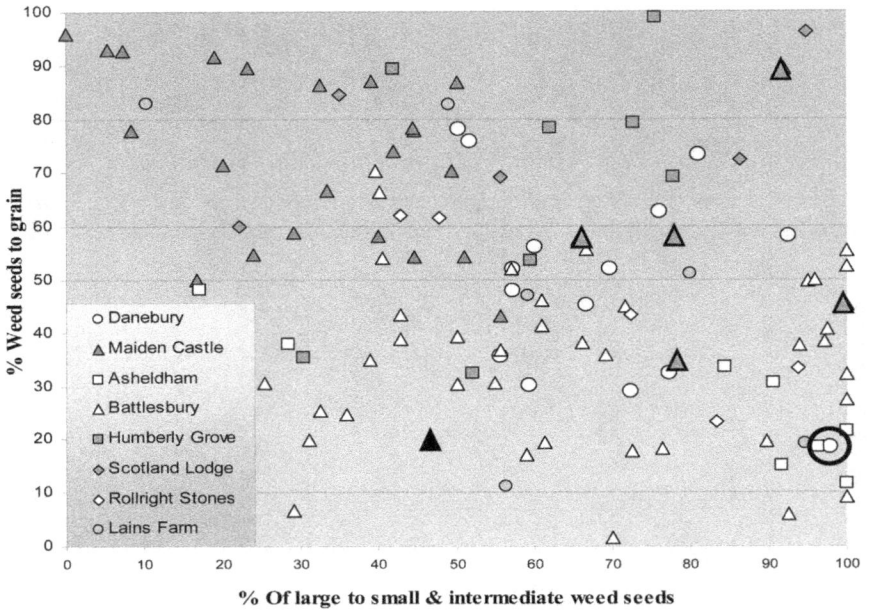

FIGURE 12.7. *Samples from Wessex and Essex (Asheldham). The proportion of weed seeds to grain is plotted against the proportion of large to small weed seeds (see figure 12.3 for the key). The circled sample is the storage pit at Danebury. The darker triangles are the EIA samples from Maiden Castle, the black from the Romano-British period.*

these experiments, the straw of spelt wheat is relatively easy to lift off by hand after the first threshing, but a number of threshings may be needed to break up ears. This attribute of hulled wheat has also been noted during ethnographic work in Spain, where, due to their semi-fragile rachis, the ears often break from the base above the third rachis node, leaving one to two sterile spikelets at the top of the straw (Peña-Chocarro 1996). In the same study areas, it is recorded that einkorn "ears were separated from the straw [for thatching, basketry, etc.] by beating them against a threshing sledge or the ground. After lashing, the heads were threshed with a threshing sledge fitted with discs in order to break them into spikelets" (Peña-Chocarro 1996:137). Similar observations regarding einkorn have been recorded for mountainous communities in Morocco where sheaves are beaten to separate the ears from the straw (Peña-Chocarro et al. 2009).

Along with ethnographic work (D'Andrea and Haile 2002:190; Peña-Chocarro 1996), experience with the processing of hulled wheats grown in

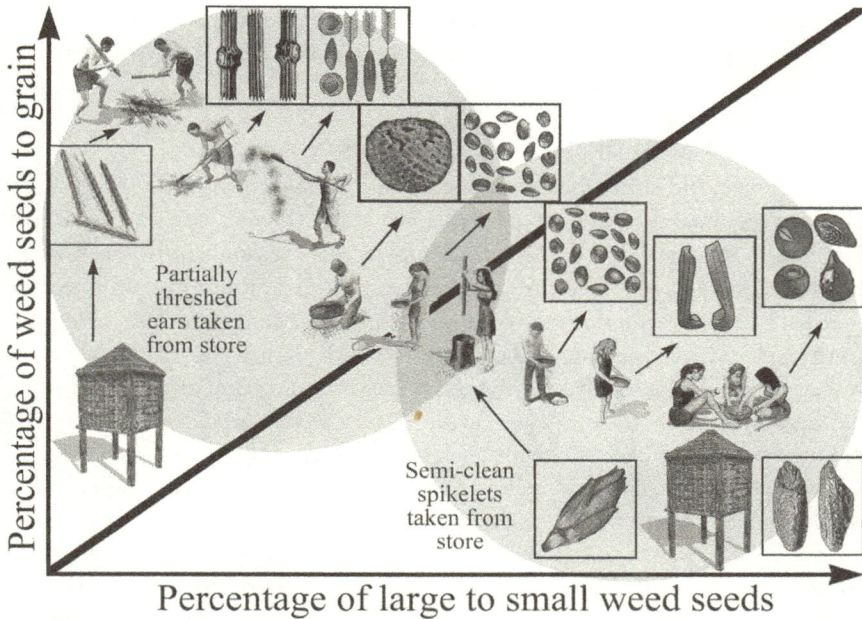

FIGURE 12.8. *Relationship of samples plotted according to the proportion of weed seeds to grain against the proportion of large to small weed seeds showing the relationship to processing waste and the stored crop. Note that the traditional Hillman (1981, 1984a, 1984b) processing model has been followed in this illustration.*

Britain demonstrate that both the method of threshing and the moisture content of the crop will greatly affect the degree to which full breakage occurs during threshing, and hence, the number of times a crop must be threshed in order to shatter the vast majority of ears into individual spikelets. For example, D'Andrea and Haile (2002:190) record that in particularly wet years two or more threshings were required. For emmer, Hillman (1984b:125) also notes that crops may need to be rethreshed if they are damp or unripe.

Hillman (1981, 1984a) cited climatic variation as a determining factor in deciding when crops were stored. He observed that Turkish villages on the drier Anatolia plain stored hulled wheats as fully dehusked grain, but settlements in the mountains stored grain as semi-clean spikelets. Farmers occupying regions of the world with few consecutive rain-free days sometimes stored crops as sheaves (Hillman 1981, 1984a). It is probable not only that the number of rain-free days determines such patterns, but also that wetter climates will increase the number of times a crop needs to be threshed. The moisture content of spikelets may also determine how easily they are dehusked, possibly also dictating the necessity of parching (Hillman 1984b:129; see also Nesbitt and Samuel 1996).

Household Versus Inter-Household Organization

Given that the sites discussed here are all located within the same broad climatic region, a further explanation is needed as to why such significant differences in storage exist. Harvest time represents a seasonal bottleneck when demands on labor resources are at their highest (Grantham 1994; Stone et al. 1990). The greater the number of processing stages that must be carried out, the greater the need to pool and organize labor. Thus, intersite differences may reflect the scale of agricultural organization, with one group of sites displaying patterns of household-level organization and the second displaying communal organization, where the ability to draw on a larger body of labor is due to the existence of large extended households or is accomplished through kinship, residential, or the centralized organization of labor.

It is still, however, noted that for many sites storing crops as semi-clean spikelets, glume chaff appears higher in relation to grain (figures 12.3 and 12.4; Stevens 2003b:figures 4 and 5). This can potentially be attributed to the mass processing of grain taken from storage where more grain might be wasted, "producing patterns similar to those suggested for manorial farmsteads by Hillman (1984a), and 'producer' sites by M. Jones (1985)" (Stevens 2003b:73). Such increased waste of grain might occur through the processing of spikelets in bulk, as might be the case for larger extended households. This is because a greater number of unpounded spikelets remain intact in the waste or through increased incidental charring of spikelets during routine parching.

Although not clarified in the original model, the observation above raises the possibility of detecting not only the organization of labor prior to storage but also following storage (see table 12.1). Although households may join forces to harvest and thresh a crop, it does not necessarily follow that they will store it communally. For individuals occupying dispersed farms, even though the harvest might be brought to a central threshing floor, after processing the resultant crop might then be divided to be stored and processed on a small scale within each individual homestead.

RELATING THESE PATTERNS TO SETTLEMENT AND STORAGE

Given potential differences in the availability of labor between sites, it might be reasoned that the archaeobotanical patterns described above could be

TABLE 12.2. Summary of the model proposed by Stevens (2003b) and Fuller and Stevens (2009): Variations in the three key ratios discussed in the text and their interpretation in terms of processing and organization of labor

Pre-Storage Organization	Storage As	Archaeobotanical Evidence	Potential Communal Storage?	Post-Storage Organization	Archaeobotanical Evidence
Small scale	Sheaves/ears	High numbers small weed seeds	Yes	Large scale	High grain, low glumes
Small scale	Sheaves/ears	High numbers small weed seeds	No	Small scale	High glumes, low grain
Large Scale	Semi-cleanspikelets	High grain and large weed seeds	Yes	Large scale	High grain, low glumes
Large Scale	Semi-cleanspikelets	High grain and large weed seeds	No	Small scale	High glumes, low grain
Large Scale	Clean Grain	Grain plus few large weed seeds	Yes	n/a	Mainly grain, few glumes

linked with evidence for the size of populations at individual sites or evidence for larger-scale organization of interrelated sites. As stated above, although labor might be organized on a broader scale at certain sites, this evidence does not imply that the entire crop would be stored at one location or that such sites would necessarily have evidence for larger-scale storage. However, if the proportion of estimated hulled wheat grains to glumes is related to the scale of post-storage processing, then evidence for both increased population and grain storage might be expected at grain-rich sites (table 12.2).

RELATIONSHIP TO SETTLEMENT PATTERNS

Looking at these case study sites, a few patterns emerge (table 12.1; figures 12.3–12.7; see also Fuller and Stevens 2009). Among the larger settlements, three of the four hillforts along with Ashville appear to have been storing crops in a relatively processed state and processing them in bulk following storage. Several of the samples from Asheldham Camp, however, probably came from a burnt granary (Murphy 1991). For these larger sites, it appears that the basic unit of production extends beyond that of the small nuclear household.

Of considerable interest is that the large hillfort at Maiden Castle, in contrast to the other three hillforts, only contains grain-rich samples during the earliest phase of Iron Age occupation (figures 12.4 and 12.7), and likewise Abingdon, which develops into a Late Iron Age *oppidum* (town), also exhibits relatively few grain-rich samples (figures 12.3 and 12.6). Although Abingdon appears to have been storing crops in a relatively unprocessed form, a number of the samples are rich in grain relative to glumes, perhaps suggesting some bulk processing as crops were taken from storage (figure 12.3).

Of the smaller dispersed settlements, many of the Upper Thames valley sites, such as Yarnton, Claydon Pike, Mingies Ditch, and Lechlade, were dominated by small weed seeds and glumes, which is suggestive of small-scale, household production (figures 12.3 and 12.6). However, Mount Farm, Whitehorse Stone (in Oxford), and Rollright Stones Site 6 (situated more in the upland hillfort zone) had samples more indicative of the storage of semi-clean spikelets.

The remaining three smaller sites (Lains Farm, Weston Down, and West of Scotland Lodge) all had slightly mixed patterns (figures 12.4 and 12.7) indicative of both larger- and smaller-scale processing. These mixed patterns suggest either that relationships within production changed from household to inter-household and back again, or that households at these sites participated in communal operations as well as conducting their own smaller operations at the household level.

Although the relationship between settlement pattern and the patterns seen in the charred assemblages is far from clear, there is some correspondence. Many of the weed-rich assemblages are associated with small, dispersed settlements, such as Yarnton. This conforms to the interpretation that these settlements operated relatively independently and on a small scale, with the storage of partially threshed ears. That the *oppidum* at Abingdon appears to have such organization is perhaps best explained by the fact it begins as a more dispersed settlement and so, potentially, as small households organizing agricultural subsistence on a an individual family-by-family basis (Allen 1993). The hillfort at Maiden Castle is something more of an anomaly in that it appears to shift from larger-scale processing in the Early Iron Age to small household organization during the Middle Iron Age, which is discussed further below.

That grain-rich assemblages are found on some of the larger sites is in keeping with the theory that ties of residence and possibly also kinship enabled these communities to organize and pool labor for processing on a much grander scale, both before and following harvest.

This brings us to those settlements that are smaller, but with assemblages dominated by grain and so characteristic of larger-scale processing following harvest and storage. In part, such patterns may be explained by cooperation between such settlements and other nearby settlements, whereas the mixed patterns seen might reflect fluctuations in the size of households or the strength of such cooperation.

ALTERNATIVE EXPLANATIONS

Two alternative reinterpretations of the original data as presented by Jones have been proposed by Gill Campbell (2000) and Marijke van der Veen (van der Veen 2007a, 2007b; van der Veen and Jones 2006). G. Campbell (2000) suggests that glume chaff may be absent on grain-rich sites because it was being routinely used as animal fodder rather than fuel. However, glume waste would have no intrinsic value as fodder unless mixed with grain, and often it is the waste from the earlier processing stages, which is richer in grain, that is used as fodder (see D'Andrea and Haile 2002). As such, it seems unlikely that grain-rich waste would be used as fuel with glume-rich waste used for fodder, as suggested by the hypothesis. The hypothesis would also fail to account for the differences seen in the ratio of large-to-small weed seeds.

The second theory proposed by van der Veen and Jones (2006), in reinterpreting the data from Jones's original sites, is that grain-rich assemblages arise from accidental charring of either clean grain or spikelets: occurring, for example, during the drying of a crop prior to storage or during the parching of the crop prior to dehusking. Such accidents they see as more likely occurring in places where grain is handled on a large scale. As such their conclusion, but not their reasoning, is similar to the model outlined above, in which grain-rich assemblages are associated with large-scale cereal production involving many people, and weed- and chaff-rich assemblages with small-scale organization at a household level.

Many of the problems with this model have been addressed above. The first is the misplaced association that "the grain-rich samples were commonly found in one particular type of site, i.e., the hillforts of central-southern England" (van der Veen 2007a:981). Although this association holds true to an extent, of the three original "grain-rich" type sites, only Danebury is a hillfort, and while Ashville is a fairly large settlement, Mount Farm is unlikely to be much more than a relatively small farmstead, although it may have comprised multiple households. As has been demonstrated for Maiden Castle, not all hillforts appear to display such patterns.

The second issue, as discussed at the beginning of this chapter, is the clear patterns that emerge, in particular with the ratios of glumes to estimated grains of hulled wheat. The model of van der Veen and Jones (2006) would imply that for some sites (e.g., Ashville) nearly every assemblage is the result of an accident, with few resulting from routine dehusking waste.

Finally, this model cannot account for the differences seen within the ratio of large-to-small weed seeds. If charred assemblages are generated through either the charring of semi-clean spikelets (the crop product) or through the charring of weed seeds removed during the processing of this crop, then this ratio should be more or less the same for both the waste and the burnt crop product. Variation in this ratio occurs, causing distinct separation between the two groups of sites, making chance accidents an unlikely explanation.

CONCLUSIONS

The study of charred assemblages makes an important contribution to the understanding of the economic and social organization of past societies. The implications of such studies and even the interpretation of such assemblages can be seen to be a matter of debate. Both Stevens (2003b) and van der Veen and Jones (2006) agree, however, that such questions are best explored through the continued application of simple ratios to new sites on a sample-by-sample basis.

The application of such ratios here and within Fuller and Stevens (2009) shows clear potential for further study and improvement of crop-processing models. Such application indicates that the original model (Stevens 2003a) still seems to provide a better explanation for intersite differences in grain, chaff, and weed seed distributions among Iron Age and Roman sites in Britain than the relationship of such assemblages to increased accidental charring when grain is handled on a large scale, as advocated by van der Veen and Jones (2006).

PART IV

Integration of Paleoethnobotanical Data

13

Peopling the Environment

*Interdisciplinary Inquiries
into Socioecological Systems
Incorporating Paleoclimatology
and Geoarchaeology*

TIMOTHY C. MESSNER AND
GARY E. STINCHCOMB

In recent decades scholars from the geological and social sciences have begun unraveling the inherently complex effects of human behavior on the environment and how climatically driven changes influence human lifeways. The objective of this chapter is to highlight (1) the state of intellectual inquiry into ancient socioecological systems and (2) the contributions of an emerging interdisciplinary approach that draws from the geological, biological, and social sciences and involves such fields as archaeobotany, geoarchaeology, and paleoclimatology (Craig et al. 2010; Liu et al. 2007a; Liu et al. 2007b; Stinchcomb et al. 2011; van der Leeuw and Redman 2002). For the purpose of this chapter we focus on human-environmental relationships during the most recent millennial-scale Holocene climatic change event—the Medieval Warming Period (MWP, ca. AD 800–1300) through the Little Ice Age (LIA, ca. AD 1300–1800) in northeastern North America. However, the approaches and interpretations presented here are pertinent to scholars working in many regions of the world over multiple timeframes.

SOCIOECOLOGICAL SYSTEMS AND INTERDISCIPLINARY COLLABORATION

Nearly a half-century ago anthropological inquiry began to focus on understanding the relationship between ancient peoples and their environment. These early studies highlighted the importance of the natural

DOI: 10.5876/9781607323167.c013

world in shaping culture (Steward 1955, 1959) as well as how cultural practices figure into larger ecosystem dynamics (Rappaport 1968). Today, archaeologists and geoscientists increasingly recognize the importance of ancient anthropogenic influences upon the environment (Dean 2010; Fisher et al. 2009; Gremillion and Piperno 2009a; Munoz and Gajewski 2010; Redman 1992, 1999; Redman et al. 2004; Rick and Erlandson 2008; Ruddiman 2003). Researchers use various terms and concepts to explain the principles and perspectives involved in these human-induced environmental modifications, including *anthropogenic ecology, socionatural archaeology, historical ecology, niche construction,* and *domesticated landscapes* (Crumley 1994; Fish 2010; Minnis 2010; Smith 2007a, 2007b; Terrell et al. 2003). A common goal of each of these approaches is to understand how people either intentionally or inadvertently alter their environment while promoting or ensuring a resource base.

People can cause severe ecological impacts on the environment. For instance, Foster et al. (2003:78) point out that ancient land-use practices related to agriculture, forestry, anthropogenic fire, and the manipulation of animal populations had widespread, irreversible effects on terrestrial and aquatic ecosystems (Dupouey et al. 2002; Ekdahl et al. 2004; Staland et al. 2010). Recent debates over the validity of using *Anthropocene* to describe an epoch of human influence on the environment highlights the intensity with which people have shaped the earth's global processes. Although most see the nineteenth century as the beginning of this era (Castro et al. 2007; Ellis 2011; Steffen et al. 2007; Zalasiewicz et al. 2011), some geologists argue that widespread ancient farming practices and deforestation as early as 8,000 years ago influenced greenhouse gas trends and thus climate on a global scale (Kaplan et al. 2009; Kaplan et al. 2011; Nevle et al. 2011; Ruddiman 2003; Ruddiman and Ellis 2009; Ruddiman et al. 2008). As these studies suggest, archaeology offers valuable insight into the history of human influence on the environment.

Just as people possess the ability to shape their environment, rapid climate change can cause the restructuring of environments and, potentially, human lifeways. Paleoenvironmental reconstructions show that climate changes may have had far-reaching effects on ancient societies and environments across the globe and throughout prehistory (Anderson et al. 2007; deMenocal 2001; Munoz et al. 2010). Paleoenvironmental/paleoclimatic studies use data from tropical oceans, monsoons, glaciers, and ice caps to model past changes in the Inter-Tropical Convergence Zone, the North Atlantic Oscillation, the El Niño-Southern Oscillation, and other atmospheric teleconnections. Results from these studies demonstrate that climates have fluctuated drastically over the last 11,700 calendar years (Cronin 2010). Palynological analyses—in conjunction with marine and ice-core records—indicate that during the Holocene climate changed abruptly roughly every 1,500 years throughout North America and possibly the world (Bond et al. 1997; Viau et al. 2002). More recent studies suggest that regionally variable rapid climate changes occurred at centennial and decadal timescales (Wanner et al. 2008). Together, these studies suggest that such climate change events restructure environments, which can change human lifeways.

INTERDISCIPLINARY APPROACHES TO SOCIOECOLOGICAL SYSTEMS

Although the science of socioecological systems (i.e., human-environment or coupled human and natural systems) is founded in ecological anthropology, environmental geography, and human ecology, it also moves beyond these disciplines in that it recognizes that the natural world consists of a multitude of interdependent relationships between living organisms and their abiotic world (Liu et al. 2007a; Liu et al. 2007b).

As figure 13.1 illustrates, each variable within a socioecological system has multiple interdependencies. For example, although climate governs the distribution and composition of land cover as well as the formation of landforms, people can also play an integral role in shaping the structure of these systems (e.g., Constante et al. 2011; Nevle et al. 2011; Novak et al. 2010; Röpke et al. 2011; Staland et al. 2010). The degree of anthropogenic influence on the natural world depends on factors related to the sociocultural and climatic context. For instance, the socioeconomic and political structure of a society can dictate the type of resource management strategy used, as well as the intensity of its application. Human influence on land cover is therefore case-dependent and subject to change due to sociocultural and/or climatic drivers. Thus, socioecological systems appear more like a complex "web of interaction" (Liu et al. 2007b:639) than a linear cause-and-effect relationship. In fact, reciprocal effects, thresholds, legacy effects, and resilience often define these connections. For this reason, examining the complex interconnections between ancient people and their environments requires an approach that provides an understanding of the spheres of interaction between variables within a stable and/or dynamic ecological system. As we will demonstrate in the following case study, archaeobotany, terrestrial paleoclimatology, and geomorphology complement each other in their ability to describe feedback between variables within socioecological systems.

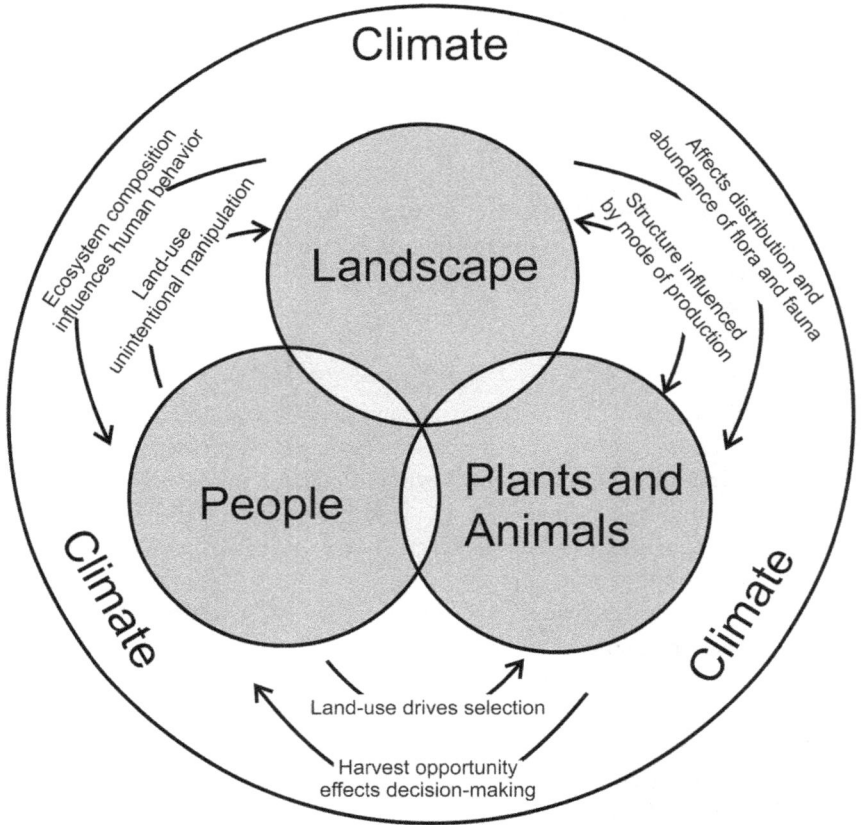

FIGURE 13.1. *Socioecological system analyses recognize the need to understand the link between social and natural systems. The interlocking circles signify the presence of reciprocal interactions between variables. The outer arrows describe these connections when guided by natural processes. The inner arrows discuss the influence people have on natural systems. Coherent interdisciplinary approaches that merge the geo- and social sciences provide a greater understanding of the interaction (i.e., patterns and processes, feedback and linkages) between ancient natural and cultural processes than do unilateral inquiries.*

CASE STUDY: INTERDISCIPLINARY APPROACHES TO NORTHEAST LATE HOLOCENE ENVIRONMENTAL HISTORY

Our case study focuses on the late Holocene archaeology of central New York, southern Ontario, northern Pennsylvania, and portions of New England. Researchers note linguistic, ethnic, and sociocultural diversity within this region (Chilton 2008; Crawford and Smith 1996; Engelbrecht 1999, 2003; Hart and Brumbach 2009; Smith and Crawford 2002; Stewart 1994). For instance, at least two distinct language groups (Iroquoian and Algonquian) were present, suggesting a degree of sociocultural variability. Even within these language groups, scholars recognized traces of ethnic diversity expressed by ceramic motifs (Hart and Engelbrecht 2012). Maize-based agriculture became the dominant subsistence strategy, yet its adoption and the degree of population reliance upon it differed throughout the region (Hart and Lovis 2013; Messner 2011). Architecture and household composition also changed through time. Some groups formed large multifamilial residences by the thirteenth century AD (Hart 2000), whereas others maintained small, unfortified hamlets late into prehistory. Alongside these changes in settlement and subsistence were noted climatic changes. We focus specifically on the Medieval Warming Period and Little Ice Age as an opportunity to highlight the complex interplay between people, plants, and landscapes set within a period of climate change.

The data used in these analyses are drawn from ethnographic and ethnohistoric accounts, macrobotanical and microfossil (pollen, phytoliths, and charcoal) analyses, isotope geochemistry, and geomorphology. Independently, these methods provide insight into changing conditions within the socioecological system (e.g., vegetation and landforms). But when integrated (either spatio-temporally, as demonstrated here, or through systems modeling, e.g., Parker et al. 2003), these data sets reveal insights into the relationship between system components—for example, the timing and extent of anthropogenic deforestation and concomitant increases in sedimentation.

DATA AND METHODS

The Ethnohistoric and Ethnographic Record

European colonists, naturalists, and anthropologists recorded elements of early colonial Native American life. These studies depict the complex plant-based knowledge system in place at the onset of European colonization. Integral to this analysis are descriptions of techniques and technologies people used to manipulate their environment, the scale at which this was accomplished, and environmental responses to these manipulations.

Archaeobotany

Macrobotanical and microfossil research has expanded our understanding of ancient subsistence economies as well as the degree to which people relied upon domesticated plants (Smith 2001b). The following case study uses previously published direct dates on macro- and microbotanical remains to assess (1) when food-producing economies emerged in the region and (2) periods of crop intensification. Because food production often requires a degree of environmental management/manipulation, archaeobotanical data examine the influence a particular subsistence strategy or change in its application had on socioecological systems.

Ancient Forests and Fields

To detect and assess the influence and potential scale of anthropogenic influence resulting from land use (food-production and habitation) on ancient forests of the Northeast, researchers have used several different proxies. During early historic times, land surveyors often marked/recorded property lines using conspicuous trees. When compiled from surveyor's notebooks, these records of *witness trees* (also referred to as *bearing* or *warrant trees*) provide insight into precolonial forest structure. Scholars compare this information to the expected forest structure under "natural" succession in areas adjacent to known archaeological resources. If the recorded composition differs from that associated with natural processes, anthropogenic forces likely contributed to the anomalous arboreal pattern (Abrams and Ruffner 1995; Black et al. 2006 ; Foster et al. 2010). Dendrochronology of fire scars located on old-growth species also provide site-specific evidence of presumed anthropogenic burning (Buell et al. 1954; Ruffner and Abrams 2002). Palynological studies reveal evidence of anthropogenic perturbations in the form of "disturbance indicator species" (such as *Ambrosia, Artemisia,* Brassicaceae, Caryophyllaceae, *Chenopodium, Plantago,* Poaceae, *Polygonum, Pteridum, Ranunculus, Rumex,* and *Urtica*) and/or counterintuitive arboreal compositions based upon presumed "natural" succession (Clark and Royall 1995; Munoz and Gajewski 2010). To confirm that people, as opposed to natural processes, caused these environmental modifications, each of the researchers cited in this section cross-referenced their findings with previously recorded archaeological evidence.

Phytoliths in C$_3$-Dominated Ecosystems

Short cell phytoliths (silica bodies formed inside the epidermal cells of grass leaves) serve as taxonomic and photosynthetic pathway indicators (Twiss 1992). The majority of eastern North America is characterized by C$_3$-dominated vegetation (figure 13.2; Cerling and Quade 1993). Thus tracking the presence of short cell C$_4$ grasses through a soil profile can provide insight into changing ecological conditions present at or adjacent to archaeological sites.

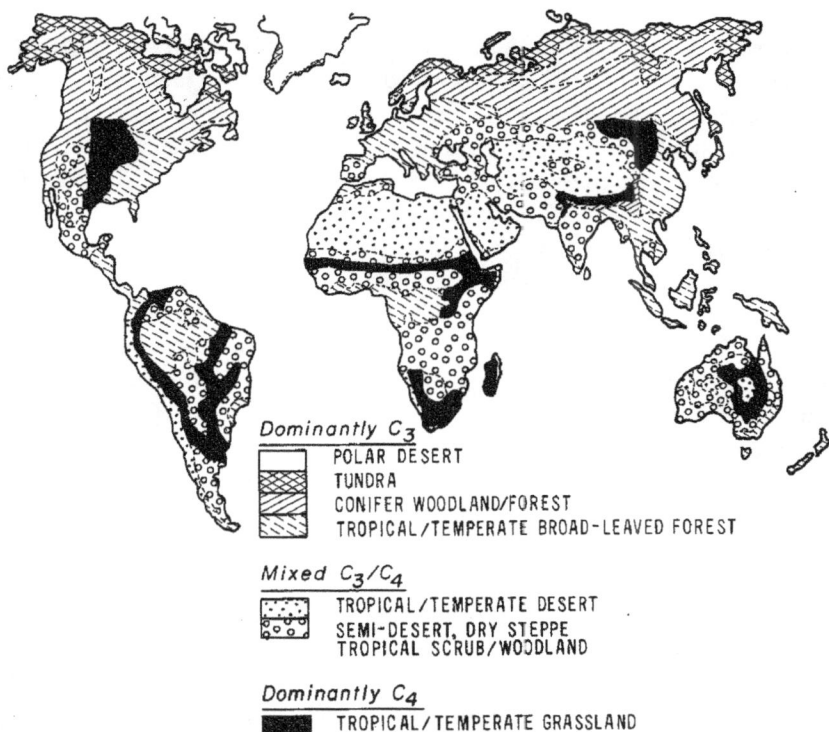

FIGURE 13.2. *The worldwide distribution of C3- and C4-dominated ecosystems. From Cerling and Quade (1993:219), reproduced/modified by permission of American Geophysical Union.*

Isotope Geochemistry

The carbon isotopic composition of soil organic matter ($\delta^{13}C_{SOM}$) partly reflects the $\delta^{13}C$ of the overlying plant community (Nadelhoffer and Fry 1988). As such, $\delta^{13}C_{SOM}$ from soil and archaeological samples have been used as a paleoenvironmental and paleoclimatic proxy (Baker et al. 2000; Beach et al. 2009; Beach et al. 2011; Boutton, Archer, et al. 1998; Cerling et al. 1993; Cordova et al. 2011; Cyr et al. 2011; Driese et al. 2005; Driese et al. 2008; Huang et al. 2001; Kelly et al. 1993; Nordt et al. 1994; Nordt et al. 2002; Nordt et al. 2007; Nordt et al. 2008; Runge 2002; Sedov et al. 2003; Springer et al. 2010; Stinchcomb et al. 2011; Webb et al. 2004; Wright et al. 2009). The utility of $\delta^{13}C_{SOM}$ is partly based on the fact that plants have a broad range in $\delta^{13}C$ values resulting from ^{13}C discrimination during photosynthesis along one of three pathways: C_3, C_4, CAM (see Warinner, chapter 14, this volume for a detailed explanation of this distinction; also Farquhar et al. 1980; Hatch 1987; Nobel 1994). We exclude CAM plants because they are largely desert succulents and not relevant to this research. C_3 plants discriminate against ^{13}C more than C_4 plants due to enzyme-based kinetic isotope effects imposed during CO_2 fixation (Boutton 1996; Cerling et al. 1993; Ehleringer et al. 2000; Farquhar et al. 1989). This discrimination during photosynthesis leads to unique ranges of $\delta^{13}C$ values for the two plant types: C_3 values generally fall between −20‰ and −37‰ and C_4 between −9‰ and −16‰ (Buchmann et al. 1996; Ehleringer 1993; Kohn 2010). The unique $\delta^{13}C$ ranges have allowed researchers to differentiate between the two plant types. This is particularly useful because several studies have shown external environmental conditions drive the distribution of C_3 and C_4 plants along a landscape.

A number of studies have investigated the causes of $\delta^{13}C$ variation specific to C_3 and C_4 plants (Farquhar et al. 1982; Schulze et al. 1996; Stewart et al. 1995). External environmental conditions including light, temperature, salinity, and moisture availability can influence C_3 and C_4 photosynthesis and the plant $\delta^{13}C$ value (Ehleringer et al. 1993; Ehleringer and Monson 1993; Farquhar et al. 1989 ; Farquhar et al. 1982). As an example, Stewart et al. (1995) and Schulze et al. (1996) have shown that moisture availability, which is related to precipitation and evapotranspiration, can influence the $\delta^{13}C$ value in both C_3 and C_4 plants. Favorable conditions promoting C_4 plant distribution include ample light, increased availability of O_2, decreased availability of CO_2, low availability of H_2O, low availability of N, and high leaf temperatures (see Wynn and Bird 2008 and references therein).

A growing body of research shows that some carbon isotopic fractionation occurs during soil organic matter turnover (Balesdent et al. 1993; Dijkstra et al. 2006; Garten et al. 2000; Millard et al. 2010; Nadelhoffer and Fry 1988). Organic matter turnover, especially respiration through soil microbes, can result in a heavier $\delta^{13}C_{SOM}$ value relative to litter and root inputs (Millard et al. 2010), thus complicating the use of $\delta^{13}C_{SOM}$ as a paleoclimate proxy. Though soil respiration can result in heavier $\delta^{13}C_{SOM}$ with depth, studies have also shown that the disequilibrium of $\delta^{13}C_{SOM}$ at the surface and with depth may be related to recent changes in the relative abundance of C_3 and C_4 vegetation (Boutton, Nordt, and Kuehn 1998; Dzurec et al. 1985).

To account for potential influences from soil respiration, Beach et al. (2011) chose an increase greater than 3‰ in the $\delta^{13}C_{SOM}$ relative to the overlying vegetation $\delta^{13}C$ as a threshold reflecting actual vegetation change and not microbial decomposition. As a result, this method constrains the identification of vegetation change to only large-magnitude shifts in $\delta^{13}C_{SOM}$ through time. Multiproxy investigations that include both phytolith and $\delta^{13}C_{SOM}$ have also been used to determine the influence of C_4 plants on the archaeological and environmental record (Stinchcomb et al. 2011; Stinchcomb et al. 2013).

Alluvial Geomorphology

Climate change and land use can modify stream behavior and floodplain development. The logical basis for studying and understanding these interactions is either implicitly or explicitly based on the channel stability model (Lane 1955). In a simplified form of Lane's (1955) model, channel stability is illustrated as a dynamic balance between water discharge and sediment load. Because channels and their respective floodplains are often linked (Nanson and Croke 1992), changes in channel stability will affect the floodplain. Land use and climate affect the distribution of land cover and precipitation, and therefore have a direct influence on stream discharge, sediment load, and floodplain development through time. This is the basic model researchers use to explain prehistoric and historic interactions between climate, land use, and streams and their respective floodplains (James 2013).

Secular changes in floodplain sedimentation rates have also been used to infer alluvial response to climate change. Schuldenrein (2003) documented fluctuating sedimentation rates along the Middle Delaware River valley during the Holocene possibly related to "moist-dry" cycles (Wendland and Bryson 1974). Stewart et al. (1991) observed increased floodplain sedimentation and decreased landscape stability during the mid-Holocene at several sites along the Delaware River, suggesting warm-dry (Hypsithermal) climate conditions as the forcing mechanism.

Historic hydrological studies clearly show the impact human land use has had on stream systems throughout eastern North America. One of the earliest systematic studies of historic land use in eastern North America focused on the Piedmont province (Trimble 1974). This study showed how historic agricultural practices, specifically reductions in upland land cover, resulted in an increase in sediment delivery to the valley bottoms. More recent research has shown that a widespread legacy of floodplain sediment deposited immediately upstream from mill-dams (the "slackwater effect") is evident throughout eastern North America (Walters and Merritts 2008). Historical hydrologic studies of the Northeast also demonstrate a correlation between anthropogenic reductions in forest cover and hydrological system alterations (Pastore et al. 2010). However, most, if not all these studies discount or de-emphasize the possibility of prehistoric land use impacting the adjacent floodplains and streams.

Data Integration and Interpretation

Ethnohistoric documents describe land-use strategies related to food production at the time of European arrival. For instance, Doolittle (2000) notes that throughout the Northeast, Native groups created small hills or mounds upon which to cultivate their crops. The scale with which these fields were created varied. Accounts from southern New England range from groups of small mounds to "about thirty acres, which must include over 80,000 hills" (Delabarre and Wilder 1920:213). Day (1953), in his study of prehistoric Northeast agricultural practices, also describes the common use of fire as a tool in forest management.

These ethnohistoric descriptions provide insight into the ecological composition of successional fallowing systems. This information can guide interpretations of archaeobotanical and palynological data sets. For example, some writers report that Native peoples often burned off weeds in fallow fields before tilling the soil (Doolittle 2000:136), whereas others Maxwell 1910:83) note the colonization of fallow tracts by "broom grass" (a common name for C_4 panicoid grasses of the *Andropogon* genus[1]). As with all ethnographic analogies, it is difficult to determine how old these practices were, but the description of periodic burning and its ecological responses nevertheless provides insight into past fallowing ecology. As described in further detail below, palynological, phytolith, and isotope geochemistry studies in the Northeast all confirm the presence of grasses associated with anthropogenic "old field" ecosystems. Thus, not only do documentary sources depict a substantial degree of anthropogenic land-cover modification throughout segments of eastern North America, they also enhance our ability to more fully interpret paleoenvironmental data.

Archaeobotanical Evidence of Food Production

Currently, a *Cucurbita* sp. (gourd) specimen from Maine marks the earliest evidence for cultivated plants in the Northeast, circa 3700 BC (Petersen and Asch Sidell 1996). The *Cucurbita* find establishes the presence of translocal interactions between the Northeast and the American mid-continent beginning as early as the mid-Holocene. Interaction networks also resulted in the introduction of maize agriculture in central New York circa 300 BC (Hart, Brumbach, and Lusteck 2007), and phytoliths recovered from ceramic cooking residues substantiate a long history of maize utilization in the region (Hart et al. 2003; Thompson et al. 2004).

By AD 500 the interaction between people and their subsistence base appears to have changed, namely by an increased consumption of maize. Isotopic studies of human bone begins to reflect a C_4-enriched diet (Katzenberg et al. 1995) and macrobotanical maize becomes more common in the archaeobotanical record. By AD 800, with the onset of the MWP, macrobotanical maize becomes ubiquitous throughout much of the interior Northeast (Asch Sidell 2008). These data raise questions about the ecological influence of agricultural practices, as well as how the environment might have affected production.

The Environmental Impact of Late Holocene Food Production

Determining whether or not, and the degree to which, ancient people's land-use practices influenced forest structure in the Northeast has been a heavily debated topic. Over the last half-century researchers have challenged the previously widespread notion that historic forests were unaffected by anthropogenic processes (Day 1953; Oyuela-Caycedo 2010). To date, both qualitative (Abrams and Nowacki 2008; Day 1953) and quantitative efforts (Clark and Royall 1995, 1996) have changed our perception of the anthropogenic forces acting upon Northeast forests.

Fire, for instance, provided people with a means of deliberately sculpting their environment via the removal or promotion of specific successional cycles (Day 1953; Delcourt and Delcourt 2004; Delcourt et al. 1998; Dorney and Dorney 1989; Foster et al. 2002; Guyette et al. 2002). In the Northeast, several studies confirm the presence of periodic burning over the last two millennia in areas situated adjacent to archaeological sites (Clark and Royall 1995, 1996; Munoz and Gajewski 2010). According to Munoz and Gajewski (2010), the palynological record in segments of the Northeast suggests that anthropogenically modified areas exhibited increased frequencies of particulate charcoal beginning at AD 1100, whereas charcoal records taken from sites some distance removed from mapped archaeological occupations decrease after AD 1000. The act of periodic burning resulted in an "old-field" successional stage dominated by shade-intolerant annuals, grasses, and more xeric tolerant trees (Abrams and Nowacki 2008; Munoz and Gajewski 2010:975). According to these findings, people used fire to actively manage their environment by removing forest cover for habitation and food production. The act of repeated periodic burning ultimately influenced ecological succession.

One recent terrestrial paleoclimatological study that illustrates clearly anthropogenically influenced vegetation changes in this region focuses on the MWP-LIA. Munoz and Gajewski (2010) compiled palynological and particulate charcoal data spanning the last 2,000 years across the Northeast.

To strengthen their argument, they calibrated their findings against a frequency distribution of archaeologically derived radiocarbon ages from which they extrapolated land-use intensity. In doing so, they identified five locations where anthropogenic processes resulted in environmental restructuring. Pollen records from these sites exhibited an increase in the frequency of *Quercus* (oak, a fire-tolerant, warm-dry species) and *Pinus* (pine, a shade intolerant taxa with tolerance to periodic burning) during the cooler-wetter climates of the late Holocene. Researchers argue that this phenomenon could not have resulted from climate alone (Munoz and Gajewski 2010:975). Instead, this study demonstrates that anthropogenic processes caused this anomalous patterning in arboreal taxa.

Recent studies of phytoliths isolated from alluvial soils and sediments in the Northeast have helped to refine our understanding of grasses present in the region during the last 2,000 years. In addition to C_3 Pooideae taxa, phytoliths from the C_4 Chloridoideae and Panicoideae grasses fluctuate in number during this period but steadily increase over the ~500 years prior to European colonization (Stinchcomb et al. 2011). Although an increase in C_4 grasses during the MWP could be attributed to climate, their persistence and increased frequency during the LIA likely relates to greater areas of cleared forest resulting from human settlement and maize-based agriculture. According to ethnohistoric, archaeobotanical, and paleoclimatological studies, anthropogenic influences on forest succession commonly result in "old field" settings, where shade-intolerant herbs and grasses colonize abandoned and fallowed fields (Asch Sidell 2008; Doolittle 2000; Munoz and Gajewski 2010). As Stinchcomb et al.'s (2011) findings demonstrate, phytolith assemblages present in alluvial soils serve not only as proxies for in situ vegetation composition (via soil A horizons) and basinwide input (C horizons; Nordt 2001), they also chronicle changes in vegetation associated with land use on both these scales (Piperno 2006b). In the Northeast, a correlation between increasing frequencies of grass phytoliths, archaeological sites, and macrobotanical remains of maize further strengthens the argument that land use contributed to the restructuring of biomass during the late Holocene (Stinchcomb et al. 2011).

Coupling isotope geochemistry findings with additional lines of paleoenvironmental inquiry (e.g., phytoliths, pollen, sedimentation indices, etc.) strengthens interpretations of $\delta^{13}C_{SOM}$ values. For instance, in a study of late Holocene floodplain development in eastern North America, Stinchcomb et al. (2011) discovered a $\delta^{13}C_{SOM}$ enrichment that coincided with an increase in the number of C_4 grass phytoliths and the presence of maize macrobotanicals. The timing of this enrichment coincided with a regional increase in

warm climate
(↔ C$_4$)

climate(T&P)

/ / / / dry climate
(↟ C$_4$)

(A)

(B)

closed canopy
(↓C$_4$)

open canopy
(↟ C$_4$)

land-use &
farming (↟ C$_4$)

fire (↟ C$_4$)

less flooding (↓ C$_4$)

(C)

microbial
decomposition
(apparent↟ C$_4$)

(D)

more flooding (↟C$_4$)

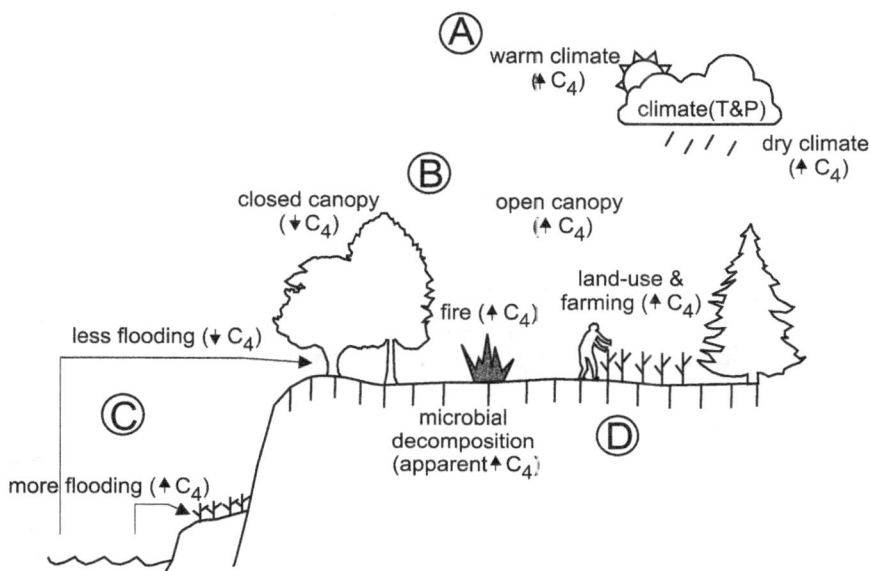

FIGURE 13.3. *Potential influences on the δ^{13}C soil organic matter (SOM) values from floodplain sites in the Northeast United States. A–C depict processes conducive to the establishment of early succession species such as C$_4$ grasses. (A) Climate: temperature, precipitation, and the seasonal distribution of moisture. (B) Vegetation dynamics: canopy effects, fire, land use (e.g., farming). (C) Alluvial dynamics: frequency of flooding and overbank deposition. (D) Soil dynamics: microbial decomposition of SOM creates an apparent increase in C$_4$ grasses.*

terrestrial sedimentation (further discussed below), suggesting that indigenous Woodland farmers had a pronounced impact on their surrounding hydrologic system in eastern North America. Springer et al. (2010) also examined δ^{13}C$_{calcite}$ from a West Virginia speleothem deposit and discovered an enrichment in δ^{13}C thought to reflect anthropogenic disturbance-related changes in the above-ground biomass. Further supporting this interpretation, a similar δ^{13}C$_{SOM}$ enrichment was also recorded in alluvium of the overlying watershed. These examples illustrate how, through the use of interdisciplinary inquiries, changes in δ^{13}C$_{SOM}$ during the late Holocene can be shown to relate to simultaneous influences of anthropogenic, biological, climatic, and geomorphological processes (figure 13.3).

Forest clearance had a lasting effect on alluvial hydrology in the Northeast. Early fluvial geomorphic studies suggested that observed increases in late

Holocene floodplain sedimentation may be the result of aboriginal land use, but these works provide little direct evidence to support this hypothesis (Alexander and Prior 1971; Gooding 1971; Nelson 1966; Scully and Arnold 1981; Thieme 2001; Vento et al. 1989). A recent study conducted along the Delaware River in northeast Pennsylvania, however, demonstrates an increased period of sedimentation that predates the MWP-LIA transition (Stinchcomb et al. 2011). This period of heightened sedimentation corresponds with increased prehistoric site density, higher archaeobotanical maize frequencies, and archaeological evidence of prolonged sedentism, leading researchers to interpret prehistoric land use as responsible for the widespread increase in sedimentation during the late Holocene (Stinchcomb et al. 2011).

Climatic Influence upon Socioecological Systems

Although parts of the Northeast experienced a long history of maize-based food production, this "long history" does not signify a homogenous, unchanging mode-of-production with a uniform effect upon the environment. Rather, for over a millennium people cultivated plants and tended economic mast-producing trees, yet the majority of the terrestrial paleoclimatological and geomorphological evidence of anthropogenic disturbance occurs during the middle MWP, ~1000 years after the emergence of food-producing economies.

In Europe, farming societies during the late Holocene prospered due to the ameliorating climates of the MWP (Engelbrecht 2003:24; Fagan 2008). Climate may also have influenced the escalation of food-producing economies in the Northeast (Hasenstab 1990:16). Speleothem calcite $\delta^{18}O$ data from West Virginia show a pronounced enrichment during the MWP (Hardt et al. 2010). This has been interpreted as a shift toward summer-dominant precipitation. When plotted against a cumulative probability curve of 98, pooled and directly dated maize ages (Stinchcomb et al. 2011), there is a visual correlation between increased summer precipitation and maize frequencies (figure 13.4). Along with increasing temperatures, this transition toward wetter summer months may have increased maize yields per plant or plot among the prehistoric farmers of the Northeast.

Further questions emerge as one begins to consider the climatic deterioration associated with the LIA. During the fourteenth to seventeenth centuries the climatic irregularities of the LIA impacted societies of the Northern Hemisphere. In Northern Europe, climate irregularities caused crop failures, which led to malnourishment, leaving people vulnerable to disease in overcrowded settlements (Fagan 2002). However, not all peoples uniformly experienced cataclysmic effects of climate change and anthropogenic environmental

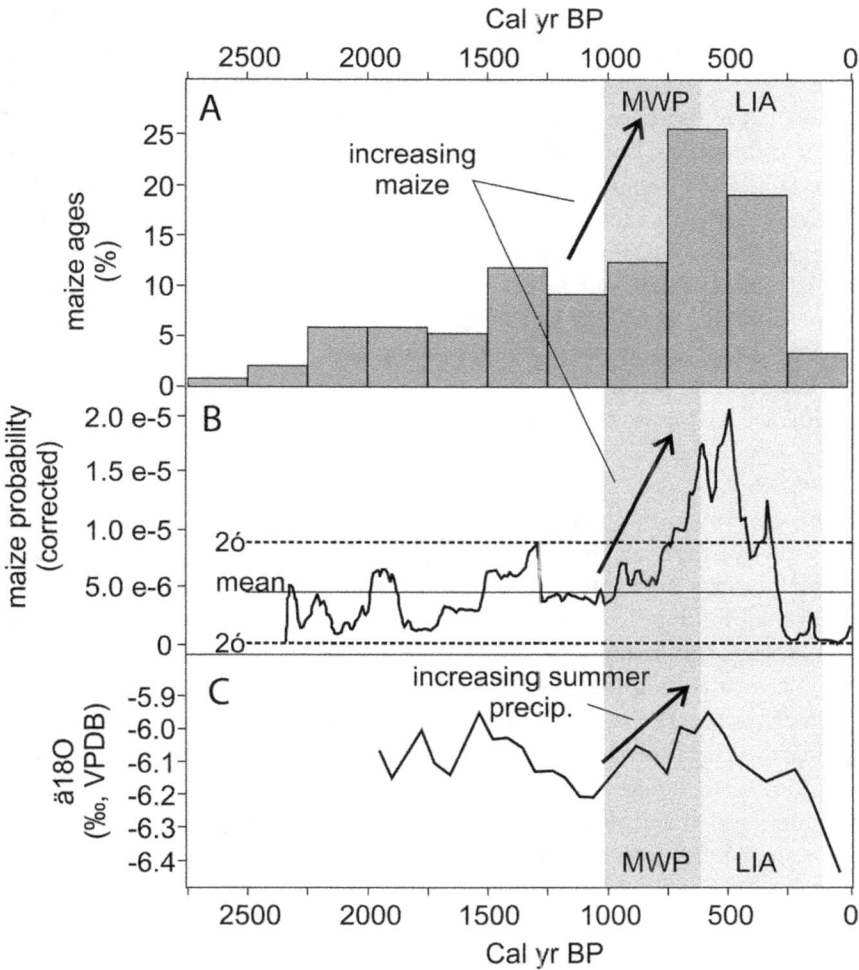

Figure 13.4. *Late Holocene maize and paleoclimate time-series for the Northeast United States. (A) Frequency distribution of pooled maize ages from eastern North America. (B) Cumulative probability curve of maize ages corrected for taphonomic bias using methods from Surovell et al. (2009). Note the coherence between the frequency (A) and probability (B), suggesting that taphonomic bias has little influence on the secular variations in maize frequency. (C) δ¹⁸O from West Virginia speleothem showing secular changes interpreted as changes in seasonal precipitation. Heavier (less negative) values reflect a dominance of summer precipitation, whereas lighter (more negative) values reflect a trend towards winter-dominated precipitation (after Hardt et al. 2010).*

deterioration, as recently popularized (e.g., Diamond 1997, 2005). Rather, the degree to which climate influences people's lives depends upon geography, history, subsistence economy, and access to resource-rich loci (Anderson et al. 2007:13; Hassan 2009:40), as well as kinship, ideology, and perceptions of threat and scarcity (Bollig and Schulte 1999; Briggs et al. 2006; Petterson 1988). Given projected population levels and increased sedentism during the end of the MWP, it seems likely that the onset of the cooler and wetter LIA may have influenced sociocultural dynamics of Northeast small-scale societies to some degree (Wykoff 1988). For instance, Custer (1996) suggests that the onset of the Little Ice Age likely had a negative affect on agricultural productivity as it reduced the number of frost-free growing days. A reduction in maize yields and conflict over arable land may help explain increased archaeological indices of violence during this era (Custer 1996:308).

Discussion

The environmental history of the late Holocene Northeast demonstrates the utility of merging the geological and social sciences to gain insight into "coupled human and natural systems" (Liu et al. 2007a; Liu et al. 2007b). By integrating findings from archaeobotany, terrestrial paleoclimatology, and geomorphology, the linkages (legacy effects, thresholds, and resilience) between variables comprising the socioecological system become apparent. For example, archaeology shows us that much of the Northeast was heavily populated during the late Holocene (Peros et al. 2010) and that people occupied most locations on a semipermanent basis (Engelbrecht 2003). The ethnohistoric literature and archaeobotanical findings indicate that these people practiced maize-based agriculture. The combination of permanent settlements and intensive subsistence strategies left a lasting imprint (legacy effect) upon the region's forests, rivers and streams.

In the Northeast, this environmental signature becomes apparent ca. AD 1100–1500 (MWP-LIA) when the combined effect of heightened sociocultural complexity, increased sedentism, and high population numbers reliant on maize-based agriculture forced the natural environment's ability to absorb anthropogenic input past a critical threshold. The science of socioecological systems makes an invaluable contribution to our understanding of the patterns and processes characterized within these human-environmental systems. In the Northeast, it took approximately 1,000 years to intensify maize production, and these processes ultimately had an effect upon forests, fields, rivers, and streams. Researchers also report similar findings during the Neolithic transition in southeastern Europe and south India (Fuller and Korisettar 2004; Willis and Bennett 1994). Based on this patterning in resiliency, certain natural systems may tolerate a level of human input at which natural processes continue unabated. Once the level of input crossed a threshold, however, feedback from anthropcgenic forces resulted in landscape modifications. These examples demonstrate the nonlinearity of coupled human/natural systems—that is, agriculture alone does not necessarily result in a land-use legacy. Rather, it is the combined effect of sociocultural and environmental variables that ultimately seem to have the greatest influence on natural and cultural systems.

This example speaks to the inherent complexity of socioecological systems and the need for future inquiry into the range of diversity within human-environment dynamics from varied global and temporal contexts. Processes and outcomes of human-environmental interactions vary according to time, geography, and any one of the components responsible for their composition. For example, archaeobotanical evidence of cultivation in the American Northeast, southern Europe, and south India predates paleoenvironmental indications of anthropogenic disturbance (but see Mullins et al. 2011), whereas Pearsall (2007:210) notes that the reverse is true for the forested environments of the Central and South American neotropics. There, paleoenvironmental disturbance indicators are the earliest evidence of prehistoric agriculture (Bush and Colinvaux 1994; Dull 2004; Goman and Byrne 1998; Islebe et al. 1996; Piperno et al. 1991a, 1991b; Piperno and Jones 2003; Piperno et al. 2007; Pohl et al. 2007).

CONCLUSIONS

The use of an interdisciplinary approach facilitates understanding the complex relationships between people, the environment, and climate in the ancient past. As the Northeast case study demonstrates, paleoethnobotany offers insights into when, where, and how people used plants as well as the level or degree to which people intervened in their lifecycles. Terrestrial paleoclimatology examines vegetation dynamics and isotope systems at local, regional, and global scales, and, in addition to other geological data, serves as a proxy for changing patterns in temperature, precipitation, and seasonality. Because climate influences environmental composition (i.e., vegetation, soils, and sediments), it also has the potential to affect human behavior. Geomorphology can determine how landscapes respond to climate, vegetation, and land use, and in turn, how landscapes influence human behavior and ecosystem composition. When viewed through a socioecological lens, which merges the geological, social, and biological sciences, data collected by these disciplines enables researchers to improve their understanding of the relationships between variables in coupled human-natural systems.

The era of conducting Holocene paleoenvironmental reconstructions, or contemporary ecological studies, without incorporating archaeological data or considering the historical legacies of ancient people is rapidly coming to an end (Fish 2010:386). As we demonstrate here, interdisciplinary analyses should attempt to mirror the systemic relationship between people, plants, climate, and landscapes. Only through collaborative efforts, which leave room for additional synergistic inquiries (e.g., zooarchaeology, paleolimnology, etc.), can scholars work toward understanding the spheres of interaction between each of the variables comprising socioecological systems.

ACKNOWLEDGMENTS

Thanks to all the contributors for their helpful comments on earlier drafts of this chapter and to the editors for their hard work in producing this volume.

NOTE

1. Common names can be unreliable especially when extrapolating from early historic documents.

14

Paleodietary reconstruction can provide great insights into social and environmental processes of the past. Three principal lines of research are typically applied to the investigation of ancient diet: paleoethnobotany, zooarchaeology, and stable isotope analysis. A fourth approach, ancient DNA analysis, has recently emerged and offers great promise for increased taxonomic resolution and the identification of genes under natural and artificial selection (see Wales et al., chapter 15, this volume). From microscopy to mass spectrometry to molecular biology, archaeologists have at their fingertips a diverse range of tools to make inferences about ancient diet from the atomic to the macroscopic level. However, although such a wealth of tools is available, relatively few studies employ more than one approach. With a special emphasis on stable isotope analysis and paleoethnobotany, this chapter seeks to demonstrate the benefits of a multidisciplinary approach and to explore how the combined efforts of each discipline can contribute to a more complete understanding of ancient diet.

PARTNERS IN INFERENCE

Paleoethnobotany and stable isotope analysis represent distinctive but complementary approaches to paleodietary reconstruction. Each approach has its own advantages and disadvantages, its own benefits, biases, and limitations. The key to effective paleodietary

DOI: 10.5876/9781607323167.c014

reconstruction is to know when and how to use each method separately and in combination. This may seem obvious, but disciplinary boundaries and differences in education and training frequently lead to the two approaches being employed independently with little collaboration or communication between the two disciplines. Although synthetic studies may cite research from both disciplines in the analysis of a larger research question, data obtained in one area are not often used to refine the analytical parameters of the other.

For example, while stable isotope studies may consult paleoethnobotanical references to affirm the presence of a particular plant taxon, the larger ecological reconstruction provided by paleobotanical studies does not often factor into any refinement of the input parameters employed in stable isotope models. This practice stands in contrast to the close relationship between stable isotope analysis and zooarchaeology, where local studies of isotopic variability among ancient animal food resources is commonplace (e.g., Bösl et al. 2006). There seems to be a prevailing assumption that while animal resources are isotopically diverse and therefore require local isotopic characterization, plant isotopic variability is fully predictable from established models and requires no further characterization beyond C_3, C_3/C_4, or $C_3/C_4/CAM$.

A common sentiment expressed in stable isotope introductory texts is that paleoethnobotany describes the menu, whereas only stable isotope analysis can reveal the meal. This statement oversimplifies and misrepresents both disciplines, at once underestimating the power of quantitative methods in paleoethnobotany and overstating the quantitative precision of stable isotope analysis. Rather than acting as antagonists, the two disciplines have much to gain by working together and drawing upon one another's strengths. The preceding chapters in this book have analyzed in detail the strengths and weaknesses of using a paleoethnobotanical approach to address various paleodietary questions. In this chapter, I focus on stable isotope-based paleodietary analysis and attempt to provide a balanced view on its advantages and limitations, and how it can be productively used in combination with botanical data to yield a better understanding of the past.

FROM THE GROUND UP: THE THEORY
BEHIND STABLE ISOTOPE ANALYSIS

The basis of stable isotope analysis is grounded in familiar territory for paleoethnobotanists: plants. In order to understand how stable isotope analysis works, one must first look to the carbon and nitrogen cycles and the foundational role played by plants.

CARBON CYCLE

Carbon is a fundamental building block of life that first enters the biological portion of the carbon cycle during photosynthesis (figure 14.1).

During this process, plants take up inorganic carbon dioxide from the air and, through a serious of enzymatic reactions fueled by sunlight, convert it into a host of high-energy carbon-based molecules that both feed (e.g., sugars, starches) and support (e.g., cellulose) the plant (Post et al. 1990). All of the carbon present in a plant comes from carbon dioxide, and in this sense plants are literally made out of thin air.

There are two principal forms of photosynthesis, C_3 and C_4, which differ both in anatomy and physiology, as well as in energy efficiency (Bender 1971; Farquhar et al. 1989; Sage 2004). A third photosynthetic adaptation, Crassulacean acid metabolism (CAM), is similar to C_4 photosynthesis and is found among cacti and succulents (Bender et al. 1973; Griffiths 1992; Osmund et al. 1973). C_3 photosynthesis is the original form of photosynthesis, and it evolved at a time when the carbon dioxide content of the atmosphere was much higher, and the oxygen content much lower, than it is today. C_4 photosynthesis evolved independently more than 40 times in grasses, sedges, and some dicots in response to the rising oxygen content of the atmosphere, and in particular to the stresses of heat and aridity (Sage 2004). CAM photosynthesis arose multiple times in response to the extreme heat and aridity of desert environments (Cushman 2001). Today, approximately 82 percent of the world's species of terrestrial plants are C_3, 15 percent are CAM, and 3 percent are C_4 (Griffiths 1992; Sage 2004). Among economic plants, C_3 plants dominate; however, C_4 crops include some of the world's most important agricultural staples, including maize, millet, sorghum, and sugarcane. CAM plants take a distant third among economic plants; however, some notable CAM domesticates include agave, pineapple, vanilla, and many species of cactus.

Of relevance for stable isotope analysis, the enzymes used to capture and "fix" atmospheric carbon differ between the two main types of photosynthesis. In C_3 photosynthesis, carbon is fixed directly by the enzyme ribulose-1,5-bisphosphate carboxylase oxygenase (RuBisCO), whereas C_4 photosynthesis uses an intermediate enzyme called phosphoenolypyruvate carboxylase (PEPC) to fix carbon before delivering it to RuBisCO. Both enzymes are less efficient at fixing $^{13}CO_2$ than $^{12}CO_2$, and as a result plant tissues contain proportionally less ^{13}C than is present in the atmosphere. However, C_3 photosynthesis more strongly discriminates against $^{13}CO_2$ than does C_4 photosynthesis. The relative isotopic difference between C_3 and C_4 plants, expressed in per mil (i.e., one tenth of a percent, ‰) relative to a geological standard (VPDB),

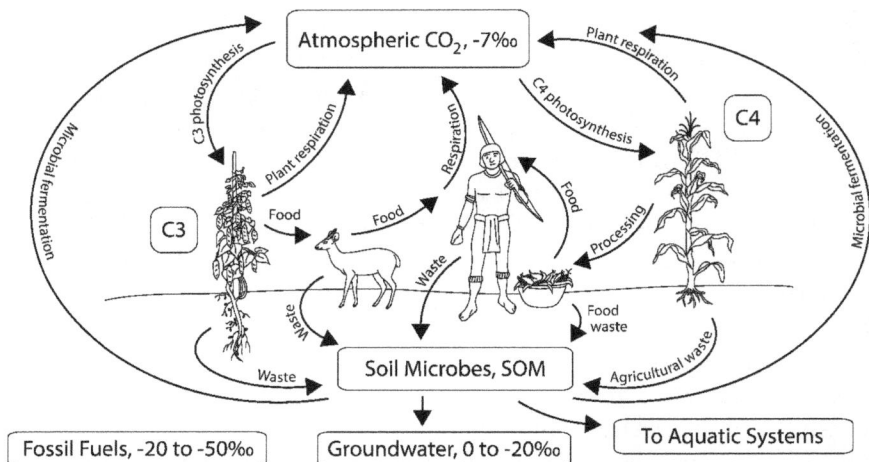

FIGURE 14.1. *Simplified terrestrial carbon isotopic cycle. Carbon enters the biological portion of the cycle during photosynthesis. Typical carbon isotopic values for C₃ plants range from −21 to −36‰, whereas C₄ plants range from −8 to −14‰. Waste products either return to the atmosphere directly via respiration or are deposited in the soil as soil organic matter (SOM). Bacteria further break down the waste and release carbon back into the atmosphere via fermentation. Remaining carbon enters sediments and groundwater and either proceeds to fossil fuel formation or enters freshwater or oceanic aquatic systems. Limestone deposits, which precipitate from aquatic systems, typically have a carbon isotopic value near 0‰. Each arrow in the diagram represents a step in which isotopic fractionation may occur. Carbon isotopic values are reported in per mil (‰) relative to a geologic standard (VPDB).*

is large and the ranges are non-overlapping.[1] Carbon stable isotope analysis essentially works by tracing this fundamental difference in ^{13}C content up the food chain while making dietary inferences along the way.

The biochemical mechanisms of C_3 and C_4 photosynthesis were first elucidated in the 1950s and 1960s (Bassham et al. 1950 ; Craig 1953, 1954; Hatch and Slack 1966, 1967), and soon the groundwork (Bender 1971; DeNiro 1985; Downton 1975; Edwards and Walker 1983; Schoeninger and DeNiro 1984; Smith and Epstein 1971; Vogel et al. 1978) was being laid for the first archaeological studies of the late 1970s and early 1980s (e.g., Ambrose and DeNiro 1986b; Bender et al. 1981; Burleigh and Brothwell 1978; Chisholm et al. 1982; DeNiro and Epstein 1977; Schoeninger et al. 1983; Tauber 1981; van der Merwe and Vogel 1978; Vogel and van der Merwe 1977). Subsequent field studies and animal feeding experiments focused on better describing the relationship between the isotopic values of diet and those measured for animal tissues such as meat, milk, fat, hair, bioapatite, and bone collagen (DeNiro and Epstein 1978; Howland et al. 2003; Metges et al. 1990; Passey et al. 2005; Sealy et al. 1987; Sponheimer et al. 2003; Tieszen and Fagre 1993b; Vogel et al. 1978; Warinner and Tuross 2009, 2010; Wright 1994). A general pattern of isotopic enrichment, or a relative increase in the proportion of tissue ^{13}C, was observed along food chains, and this was attributed to complex processes involved in animal energy metabolism and protein synthesis (Ambrose and Norr 1993; Clementz et al. 2007; Jim et al. 2004; Krueger and Sullivan 1984; Lee-Thorp et al. 1989; Passey et al. 2005; Tieszen and Fagre 1993b). Formal carbon isotope-based paleodietary models began to emerge (Clementz et al. 2009; Hedges 2003; Kellner and Schoeninger 2007; Phillips and Koch 2002; Schwarcz 1991, 2000), and further adjustments were made to account for additional modifying factors, including the systematic isotopic depletion of atmospheric carbon caused by industrial pollution (Leavitt and Long 1986; Marino and McElroy 1991; Suess 1955; van der Merwe 1989).

NITROGEN CYCLE

Unlike their processing of carbon, plants cannot acquire nitrogen directly from inorganic sources (figure 14.2). Instead, they rely on soil bacteria to fix atmospheric nitrogen for them. Decaying plant and animal matter, urine, manure, and synthetic nitrogen fertilizers also provide ready sources of bioavailable nitrogen. Nitrogen is taken up from the soil by the roots of plants where it is later converted into the amino acids that form the building blocks of proteins. These proteins, especially in the form of enzymes, are essential for the plant to grow and thrive, and nitrogen restriction leads to slowed growth, metabolic insufficiency, and eventually death.

With respect to nitrogen, plants may be classed into two categories: legumes and non-legumes (Virginia and Delwiche 1982). Legumes, which include important cultigens such as beans, clover, and alfalfa, produce specialized root nodules that house symbiotic nitrogen-fixing bacteria for the plant. Legumes are thus adapted to survive in nitrogen-poor soils where external sources of nitrogen may be insufficient for sustaining non-leguminous plant growth. The idea that legumes derive their nitrogen from symbiotic bacteria, whereas other plants incorporate nitrogen from more diverse sources, including soil bacteria, animal waste products, and decaying plant matter, is the basis of the presumed isotopic difference between leguminous and non-leguminous plants (Delwiche et al. 1979; DeNiro and Epstein 1981). Once consumed, this

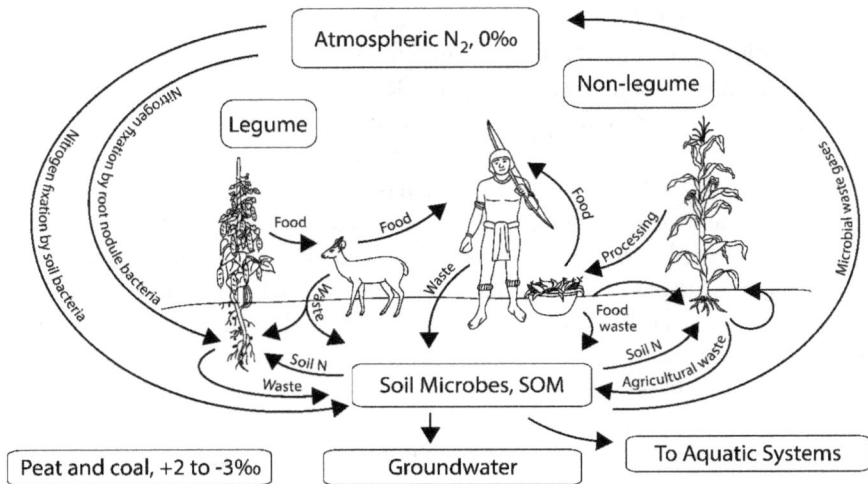

FIGURE 14.2. *Simplified terrestrial nitrogen isotopic cycle. Nitrogen enters the biological portion of the nitrogen cycle when bacteria fix atmospheric nitrogen in the soil. Plants that produce specialized root nodules to house nitrogen-fixing bacteria are called legumes. Little or no isotopic fractionation occurs during bacterial nitrogen fixation. Once absorbed by plant roots, nitrogen is subject to metabolic processes that change the isotopic values of biological nitrogen. Within plants, typical nitrogen isotopic values range from −5 to +18‰. Nitrogen wastes are deposited in the soil as soil organic matter (SOM). This biological nitrogen can then be reabsorbed by plant roots or further broken down by soil microbes into waste gases, or it may enter freshwater or oceanic aquatic systems. Each arrow in the diagram represents a step in which isotopic fractionation may occur. Nitrogen isotopic values are reported in per mil (‰) relative to atmospheric nitrogen (AIR).*

difference is maintained and passed up the food chain, with the relative proportion of ^{15}N further increasing at each trophic level through complex processes of animal metabolism. Nitrogen stable isotope analysis is used to infer dietary protein sources by employing known patterns of trophic level isotopic enrichment within food chains to interpret human or animal tissue isotopic values (Post 2002; Robinson 2001).

Investigation of plant nitrogen sources began in earnest during the Green Revolution as researchers sought to improve farming efficiency through scientific technology. After nitrogen isotopes were found to substantially vary among natural substances (Hoering 1955, 1956), a number of studies began focusing on nitrogen isotopic variability in soil and among leguminous and non-leguminous plants (Delwiche and Steyn 1970; Delwiche et al. 1979; Meints et al. 1975; Rennie et al. 1976; Shearer and Kohl 1988; Shearer et al. 1974; Steyn and Delwiche 1970; Wada et al. 1975). Subsequent research on animals revealed that the proportion of heavier nitrogen isotopes tended to increase as one went up the food chain, suggesting that nitrogen isotopes could serve as a trophic level indicator (DeNiro and Epstein 1981; Minagawa and Wada 1984; Schoeninger and DeNiro 1984). These observations were quickly applied to the study of ancient human populations, where they were used to infer sources of paleodietary protein (Ambrose and DeNiro 1986b; Chisholm et al. 1982, 1983; DeNiro and Epstein 1981; Farnsworth et al. 1985; Schoeninger et al. 1983; Schwarcz et al. 1985; Sealy and van der Merwe 1985, 1986, 1988; Tauber 1981; Walker and DeNiro 1986).

As with carbon stable isotope analysis, subsequent studies focused on better describing the relationship between the isotopic values of diet and those measured for various animal tissues and waste products (reviewed in Kelly 2000; see also Sponheimer et al. 2003; and Warinner and Tuross 2009, 2010). The stepwise pattern of isotopic enrichment observed along food chains was ascribed to isotopic fractionation occurring during digestion and the metabolic processes of protein synthesis and waste excretion (Ambrose 1991; Ambrose and DeNiro 1986a; Sealy et al. 1987; Sponheimer et al. 2003; Steele and Daniel 1978). Today, a number of formal nitrogen isotope-based dietary models are in use (McCutchan et al. 2003; Phillips and Koch 2002; Post 2002).

ONGOING AREAS OF RESEARCH

Forty years after its emergence, carbon and nitrogen isotope-based paleodietary analysis is a mature discipline, and its methods are widely applied to a variety of archaeological questions and contexts (reviewed in Lee-Thorp 2008). Nevertheless, many uncertainties and ambiguities remain that complicate straightforward interpretation of isotopic data. The actual biochemical processes that cause isotopic enrichment are still poorly understood in animal models, let alone in humans, leaving us with an essentially black-box understanding of isotopic inputs and outputs, but little knowledge of the mechanisms by which isotopic enrichment and partitioning occur within living systems (e.g., see discussions in Hedges and Reynard 2007). In addition, it has long been acknowledged that bulk isotopic analysis of whole tissues masks significant isotopic differences among substructures (e.g., the germ, endosperm, and endocarp of a seed) and individual nutrients (e.g., carbohydrates, proteins, lipids, and fiber), which also have differential digestive capacities and efficiencies, as well as different metabolic uses (DeNiro and Epstein 1977;

Focken and Becker 1998; Marino and DeNiro 1987; Pinnegar and Polunin 1999; Tieszen and Fagre 1993a; Warinner and Tuross 2009). Together, these metabolic uncertainties mean that complex diets and various ontological and physiological states may result in unexpected isotopic outcomes (Fuller et al. 2005; Sponheimer et al. 2003; Warinner and Tuross 2010).

Complex environmental factors also pose serious difficulties. With respect to carbon, for example, isotopic models assume perfect atmospheric mixing, which has been shown to be untrue in closed canopy forests (van der Merwe and Medina 1991), and even species within the same environment have been shown to react differently to systematic changes in isotopic composition of atmospheric carbon (e.g., Francey 1981; Freyer and Belacy 1983). In addition, environmental factors such as temperature and aridity can influence the $\delta^{13}C$ of plants by altering carbon fixation efficiency rates, thereby tying the carbon isotopic ratios of plants to climatic cycles (McCarroll et al. 2009; McCarroll and Loader 2004; Treydte et al. 2001). Some taxa are also known to systematically differ from plant isotopic averages. Maize, for example, is consistently isotopically heavier than the C_4 average (DeNiro and Hastorf 1985; Tieszen and Fagre 1993a), and among C_3 plants, grasses and non-grasses have different isotopic averages (van der Merwe 1989).

With respect to nitrogen, climate (Ambrose 1991; Ambrose and DeNiro 1987; Heaton et al. 1986; Szpak et al. 2013) and anthropogenic amendments (Bateman et al. 2005; Bogaard et al. 2007; Commisso and Nelson 2008) have been shown to impact the $\delta^{15}N$ values of plants. Furthermore, systematic isotopic differences among plant parts (e.g., grain and chaff) have also been observed (Bogaard et al. 2007). In addition, it has long been cautioned by botanists (though often ignored by archaeologists) that legumes grown in fertile soils may isotopically resemble non-leguminous plants, with little or no isotopic distinction observed between the two groups (e.g., Delwiche et al. 1979; Warinner et al. 2013). Finally, industrial fertilizers and pollution have substantially distorted the nitrogen cycle in contemporary agricultural and natural environments (Freyer and Aly 1974; Hastings et al. 2009; Shearer et al. 1974), making it difficult to reconstruct pre-industrial isotopic ecology using modern analogues. Attempts to disambiguate these problems by measuring the $\delta^{15}N$ of ancient plants directly (e.g., DeNiro and Epstein 1981) were abandoned when the values were shown to be taphonomically altered (DeNiro and Hastorf 1985). Carbonized archaeobotanical remains, however, have proven more resistant to isotopic diagenesis and there is now renewed interest in their investigation (Aguilera et al. 2008; Bogaard et al. 2007; DeNiro and Hastorf 1985).

Aquatic resource exploitation also poses considerable challenges to isotopic researchers as aquatic food webs are far more complex than their terrestrial counterparts. The rate of carbon exchange between the atmosphere and bodies of water is variable, depending on water depth and mixing, and different reservoir turnover rates have been measured for the Pacific, Atlantic, and Indian Oceans (Stuiver et al. 1983). Aquatic systems additionally derive carbon from mineral sources, such as submerged calcium carbonate deposits, which differ in isotopic composition from atmospheric carbon (Butcher et al. 1992). The nitrogen isotopic values of some aquatic plants can vary seasonally by as much as the equivalent of one trophic level due to alterations in the solubility of nitrogen compounds driven by changes in water temperature (Carvalho et al. 2007). Freshwater vertebrate and invertebrate resources have been shown to vary enormously in $\delta^{13}C$ and $\delta^{15}N$ for reasons that are not well understood (Post 2002), and marine resources vary greatly in $\delta^{15}N$ as a function of the origin and length of their food chains (Keegan and DeNiro 1988; Richards and Hedges 1999; Schoeninger and DeNiro 1984).

Finally, current paleodietary models are highly simplified and cannot accommodate many known sources of isotopic variability. Inferring backward from a single isotopic measurement to a paleodietary interpretation contingent on multiple varying parameters leads to unresolvable issues of equifinality (Peterson et al. 1986; Phillips and Gregg 2001; Phillips et al. 2005; Post 2002). Although some studies (e.g., Clementz et al. 2009) attempt to overcome this problem by analyzing multiple tissues (e.g., bone collagen and enamel apatite) and multiple isotopes (e.g., $\delta^{13}C$ and $\delta^{15}N$), there is no unified mathematical formula or straightforward way to combine these lines of evidence, and all interpretation involves a degree of subjectivity.

A BALANCED VIEW: STRENGTHS AND WEAKNESSES OF STABLE ISOTOPE-BASED PALEODIETARY ANALYSIS

The above-mentioned complications primarily affect fine-scale and quantitative isotopic interpretations in which small isotopic discrepancies between or within populations are argued to reflect certain and specific dietary differences. Stable isotope-based paleodietary analysis is at best only semiquantitative, and the robusticity of current stable isotope models to accurately parse such fine isotopic differences has not yet been established. However, despite all of the unknowns and uncertainties, stable isotope-based paleodietary analysis has proven itself to be a robust method for characterizing past subsistence strategies at a broad scale. Under the right conditions, C_4 consumers can be readily distinguished from non-C_4 consumers (e.g., Barton et al. 2009), farmers can be distinguished from fisher-gatherers (e.g., Richards et al. 2003), and agriculturalists can be distinguished from pastoralists (e.g., Ambrose and DeNiro 1986b). There are limits, however, to stable isotope-based inference, even at a broad scale. The following comparative case studies illustrate the successes and nonsuccesses of a stable isotope-based approach in investigating paleodietary questions.

CASE STUDY 1: THE SPREAD OF MAIZE IN EASTERN NORTH AMERICA

Tracking the timing and tempo of the adoption of maize as a dietary staple across prehistoric eastern North America is the classic success story of carbon stable isotope analysis (Lee-Thorp 2008; Schoeninger 2009). Throughout the twentieth century, there was considerable interest in the history of maize agriculture in North America (Buikstra and Milner 1991; Whiting 1944). Accounts of the mysterious rise and fall of the "Mound Builders" of the American mid-continent inspired both amateur and professional archaeologists to excavate numerous mounds in the Mississippi valley, and subsequent generations of archaeologists and physical anthropologists argued bitterly over the role that maize cultivation played in the development of what later came to be known as the Woodland and Mississippian cultures (Cohen and Armelagos 1984; Goodman et al. 1984; Harn 1978; Lallo et al. 1978). The question achieved even greater significance as it became embroiled in anthropological debates over factors contributing to the rise of complex societies (Braun and Plog 1982; Goldstein 1981; Griffin 1967; Peebles and Kus 1977).

Throughout the 1960s and 1970s, characterizing the spread and intensity of maize agriculture posed numerous difficulties. Macrobotanical remains were rare and sporadically found. Once found, archaeologists could only date the ancient maize specimens by association (e.g., Ritchie 1969) because radiocarbon dating methods of the time required sample sizes too large for direct dating. Accelerator mass spectrometry (AMS) radiocarbon dating, which can analyze samples as small as a few milligrams, would not become available to archaeologists until the mid-1980s (Creel and Long 1986), and it was not until the 1990s, following improvements in fine-meshed screens and flotation techniques, that recovery of maize macrobotanical remains was sufficient to allow longitudinal radiocarbon studies (Little 2002).

At the end of the 1970s, however, the recently formulated principles of stable isotope analysis promised to dramatically expand testing opportunities by providing a method for the direct investigation of human remains, which were amply available for nearly every site and time period. Importantly, it had been known that prior to the introduction of maize, eastern North America consisted of an almost entirely C_3 environment; thus, the transition to a C_4 staple, maize, was expected to cause a major isotopic shift. In 1977, Vogel and van der Merwe published a seminal proof-of-concept paper in *American Antiquity* that demonstrated the efficacy of stable isotope analysis for identifying both the presence of maize agriculture and its intensity in prehistoric New York State. They quickly followed with an expanded study including sites from Illinois to West Virginia and found clear evidence for a rapid transition to maize agriculture after AD 600 (van der Merwe and Vogel 1978).

Subsequent research has further contextualized the transition to maize agriculture in eastern North America, both geographically and temporally (e.g., Bender et al. 1981; Buikstra and Milner 1991; Greenlee 2006; Hart and Lovis 2013; Rose 2008; Stinchcomb et al. 2011). Remaining inconsistencies, such as the occasional discovery of small macrobotanical maize finds at sites with no isotopic evidence for maize consumption, were later reconciled when animal experiments determined that low-level C_4 consumption may not be detectable by isotopic analysis of bone collagen because of threshold effects (see Lee-Thorp 2008). Despite modifications to Vogel and van der Merwe's initial interpretations, carbon stable isotope analysis has proven to be a powerful and enduring tool for identifying maize-dominated subsistence strategies throughout eastern North America.

CASE STUDY 2: THE ORIGIN OF MAIZE AGRICULTURE IN MESOAMERICA

Stable isotope analysis has met with more equivocal success in the elucidation of the origins of maize agriculture in Mesoamerica. In recent years, a growing body of microbotanical evidence (phytoliths, pollen, and starch) for Archaic period maize cultivation and processing has pushed back the proposed origins of maize domestication to before 6500 BC (Piperno et al. 2009; Ranere et al. 2009). Archaeological evidence for sedentism and intensive maize agriculture, however, lags several millennia behind and only becomes widespread ca. 1000 BC during the Middle Formative period. To explain this pattern, Hugh Iltis (2000) and others (Smalley and Blake 2003; Webster et al. 2005) have suggested that maize was originally domesticated by seasonally mobile horticulturalists for the sugary juice of its stalk and only later under different selective pressures developed the large cob and numerous grains that make it the agricultural dietary staple we are familiar with today. Characterizing the timing and tempo of this transition, from an early minor crop to the dietary staple of subsequent complex societies, has proven both challenging and controversial, and since the 1980s, several studies have attempted to use stable isotope analysis to clarify the transition.

DeNiro and Epstein (1981) were the first study to apply stable isotope analysis to the problem of maize domestication in Mesoamerica. Building on the methodological successes of Vogel and van der Merwe in eastern North America, DeNiro and Epstein turned to the Tehuacan Valley of Puebla, Mexico, a region once believed to be the ancestral homeland of maize (MacNeish 1967). Within the valley, numerous rockshelters containing archaeological deposits spanning more than 10,000 years had been excavated. Significant finds included a primitive maize cob (later directly dated to 3540 BC) and human remains dated by association to stratigraphic layers spanning 6800 BC to AD 1540 (Byers 1967; B. Smith 2005). DeNiro and Epstein measured bone collagen $\delta^{13}C$ from 12 individuals: 10 from periods of known maize agriculture and 2 predating 1000 BC (DeNiro and Epstein 1981:table 1). All individuals exhibited high collagen $\delta^{13}C$ values, although the earliest skeleton, dated to the El Regio period ca. 6800–5000 BC, was lower (−13.3‰) than the average after 5000 BC (−6.3 ± 0.3‰).[2] Later reanalysis of the data by Farnsworth et al. (1985) concluded that the isotopic evidence supported a Coxcatlan period (ca. 5000–3500 BC) emergence of maize agriculture.

However, it is difficult to know how to interpret these data. Unlike eastern North America, the Tehuacan Valley is not a C_3 environment. As one might expect for the purported homeland of a C_4 domesticate, it is a hot and dry environment supporting an abundance of C_4 grasses and CAM plants. The use of carbon stable isotopes to identify dietary reliance on maize in the Tehuacan Valley assumes that Archaic period foragers and horticulturalists selectively consumed C_3 plants and did not utilize CAM and other C_4 resources in sufficient quantity to obscure an isotopic trend announcing the introduction of maize as a dietary staple. Macrobotanical evidence from the rockshelters (Smith 1986; Smith 1967), however, indicates that highland Archaic foragers and horticulturalists used many CAM and C_4 taxa (including *Setaria* grasses, amaranth, prickly pear cactus, and agave, among others), and wild CAM and C_4 plants would also have been available to local fauna (including cottontail rabbits, jackrabbits, and now extinct species of horse and antelope), and therefore indirectly to humans. The El Regio isotopic value could signify either a moderate degree of maize consumption or a diet rich in wild C_4 and CAM plants. Because no Tehuacan skeletons clearly predating the period of maize domestication have been found, it is not possible to establish the baseline $\delta^{13}C$ of a non-maize-consuming Tehuacan forager for comparison. Finally, the entire isotopic argument for an El Regio/Coxcatlan transition rests problematically on the measurement of a single sample.

Subsequent attempts to isotopically characterize the origins of maize agriculture in Mesoamerica moved away from the mixed C_4/CAM environments of the highlands and focused instead on investigating the expansion of maize agriculture into C_3-dominated tropical regions in Panama and coastal Soconusco in Mexico. In Panama, elevated human collagen $\delta^{13}C$ values (−14‰) have been measured at the site of Cerro Mangote during the period 5000–2500 BC, and in Soconusco very high (−9.8‰) and moderately high (−18‰) human collagen $\delta^{13}C$ values have been found at several sites spanning the period 2700–1000 BC (Blake et al. 1992; Chisholm and Blake 2006; Norr 1991, 1995).

Although Smalley and Blake (2003) have argued that these values are evidence for dietary maize reliance, this interpretation is complicated by the fact that all of these individuals were recovered from either coastal or estuarine sites with evidence for aquatic resource consumption (Blake et al. 1992; Chisholm and Blake 2006; Norr 1991, 1995; Voorhies 1976). Because mean $\delta^{13}C$ of Middle American marine and estuarine fish and shellfish is more enriched than that of terrestrial C_3 plants, elevated collagen $\delta^{13}C$ cannot be assumed a priori to result from increased C_4 plant consumption. Nitrogen isotopic ratios, which have been used to distinguish exploitation of terrestrial and marine resources in North American and European populations (e.g., Richards et al. 2003; Salamón et al. 2008; Schoeninger et al. 1983), are of less use in Mesoamerica, where there is a high degree of isotopic scatter in the $\delta^{15}N$ of fish and shellfish (Chisholm and Blake 2006; Keegan and DeNiro 1988), and coastal and noncoastal populations show little isotopic differentiation (see discussion in Warinner 2010). Although some degree of maize consumption at these sites is probable, given archaeobotanical evidence for minor maize processing at contemporaneous sites in Panama (Piperno et al. 2000), Tabasco (Pohl et al. 2007), and northern South America (Zarrillo et al. 2008), determination of maize consumption or status as a dietary staple cannot be made on the basis of current stable isotope evidence.

In total, only 23 individuals predating 1000 BC have been analyzed for $\delta^{13}C$ and $\delta^{15}N$ in Mesoamerica and lower Central America. Of these, 19 have yielded elevated collagen $\delta^{13}C$ values, but all were recovered from either mixed C_4/CAM environments or coastal/estuarine sites where aquatic resource exploitation complicates isotopic interpretation of maize consumption. Given the isotopically complicated ecology of Mesoamerica, it is difficult to apply stable isotope analysis effectively to the study of emergent maize agriculture. Unless more early human samples become available and isotopic models of greater complexity are developed, stable isotope analysis will only be able to play a limited role in elucidating the early history of agriculture in Mesoamerica.

LESSONS LEARNED

The above case studies illustrate the contextualized nature of isotopic data. Stable isotope analysis cannot directly determine ancient diet, but rather it is a tool that can be used to discriminate between a limited number of options arrived at by other means using paleoethnobotanical, zooarchaeological, ethnohistorical, ethnographic, or archaeological evidence. In many cases, isotopic ecology is too complex and poorly defined, food resources are too isotopically moderate, and human behaviors are too poorly understood for analysts to draw definitive paleodietary conclusions. This is why so many studies conclude with the disappointingly vague finding that the population of interest consumed a mixed diet of plant and animal resources. Stable isotope analysis is most robust when the paleodietary hypothesis is clear and well-defined, the dietary alternatives are isotopically distinct, and the sampling strategy affords a comparative approach across time or space. When these conditions are met, powerful paleodietary inferences may be made.

NEW DIRECTIONS IN COLLABORATIVE ISOTOPIC-PALEOETHNOBOTANICAL RESEARCH

Throughout its history, stable isotope analysis has reached several plateaus during which basic assumptions underwent reevaluation and new questions were formulated. The first plateau occurred at the end of the 1980s when insufficient understanding of isotopic partitioning during metabolism, newly discovered climatic sources of isotopic variability, and problems of apatite taphonomy reached a fevered pitch (Sillen et al. 1989). The subsequent call for increased basic research and experimentation in model systems led to many important discoveries and advancements that infused the isotopic research of the 1990s. Today, isotopic research finds itself at another plateau, and again there is an urgent need for basic research, this time focusing on regional isotopic ecology.

In a recent review of the field, Lee-Thorp (2008) called for a more intensive and broader effort to improve our understanding of the natural distribution of isotopes within ecosystems rather than focusing simply on global distributions. As stable isotope analysis is applied to more regions and contexts, it has become increasingly apparent that many of our basic assumptions about plant isotopic ecology are in need of reevaluation and refinement (Szpak et al. 2013; Warinner et al. 2013). Some required adjustments are relatively minor, involving the correction of misclassified C_3/C_4 taxa (e.g., epazote, see discussion in Warinner 2010) and the empirical determination of the C_3/C_4 status and frequency of understudied indigenous wild and cultivated plant resources (e.g., Llano 2009; Warinner et al. 2013). Other adjustments, however, involve a fundamental rethinking of isotopic categories.

This process of reevaluation may necessarily undermine some previous isotopic inferences, but it also offers the opportunity to explore potential insights offered by isotopic parameters that were previously ignored. Szpak et al. (2013), for example, found correlations between plant $\delta^{13}C$ and altitude in the Andes, whereas Araus et al. (2001) has demonstrated a clear relationship between aridity, wheat yield, and $\delta^{13}C$ in modern agricultural fields. Although inconvenient for conventional forms of isotopic inference, this relationship opens up new opportunities for investigating ancient growing conditions and irrigation practices by measuring the $\delta^{13}C$ of archaeological grain. Further research in other ecological zones and among other plant types, such as legumes and tubers, is urgently needed.

In light of widespread isotopic evidence for improbably high levels of meat consumption among farming communities, Dürrwächter et al. (2006) likewise revisited assumptions regarding the $\delta^{15}N$ of crop plants and suggested that isotopically enriched crops or fodder may be responsible for some of the high collagen $\delta^{15}N$ values observed in Neolithic linear pottery culture (LBK) populations. Subsequent experiments by Bogaard et al. (2007) demonstrated that the long-term manuring of fields can indeed result in trophic-level increases in the $\delta^{15}N$ of cereals compared to control plots. The implications of such findings are far-reaching and have particular significance for ancient diets consisting of cultivated crops and wild meat resources (Warinner et al. 2013). In addition, for both farming and non-farming societies, climatic factors such as precipitation must be considered when making paleodietary inferences because water stress tends to increase the $\delta^{15}N$ of plants (e.g., Szpak et al. 2013).

The decoupling of $\delta^{15}N$ values and meat consumption will likely force the reevaluation of previous estimates of meat consumption in many studies, but it will also allow alternative explanations for previous isotopic enigmas (figure 14.3), such as the nitrogen isotopic similarities between Maya maize farmers and large cats (Wright 2006) and between Neanderthals and hyenas (Richards and Schmitz 2008; Richards and Trinkaus 2009), as well as the

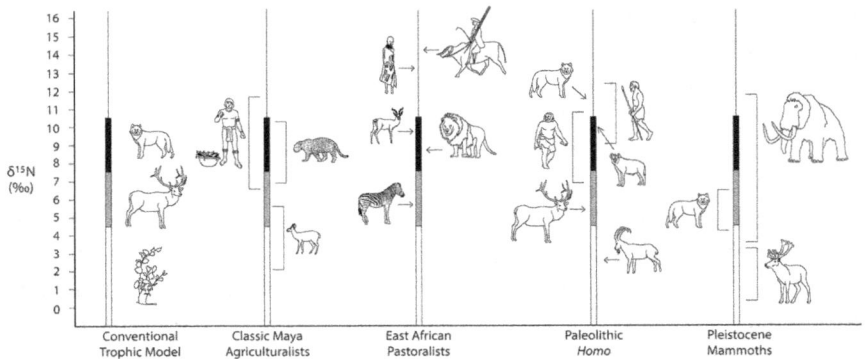

FIGURE 14.3. *Examples of archaeological datasets that do not conform to a conventional nitrogen isotopic model. Along a food chain, nitrogen isotopic values are expected to increase by approximately 3‰ with each trophic level step. The expected ranges of nitrogen isotopic values for plants, herbivores, and carnivores are marked in white, gray, and black, respectively. The actual nitrogen isotopic values measured from four different archaeological food chains are plotted alongside the modeled trophic levels. Unexplained patterns, such as the clustering of Maya maize farmers with large cats, the higher nitrogen isotopic values observed in humans and Grant's gazelle than lions, and the range of mammoth nitrogen isotopic values spanning three trophic levels, suggest that current models fail to capture the isotopic complexity of many wild and anthropogenic ecosystems. (Data collected from Ambrose and DeNiro 1986a, 1986b; Clementz et al. 2009; Gerry 1993; Iacumin et al. 2000; Richards and Schmitz 2008; Richards and Trinkaus 2009; White et al. 2004; and Wright 1994, 1997, 2006.*[3]

higher δ^{15}N values found among African pastoralists than for lions (Ambrose and DeNiro 1986a, 1986b) and the ~9‰ range of δ^{15}N observed among mammoths (Clementz et al. 2009; Iacumin et al. 2000). New means are required to investigate nitrogen isotope variability within past human foodwebs, and carbonized macrobotanical remains are poised to become an important substrate for this analysis.

The need for future collaboration between stable isotope analysts and paleoethnobotanists is strong and growing. Collaboration with zooarchaeologists led to significant gains in the 1990s and 2000s, but we are once again at an impasse, this time at a more fundamental level. Forty years of isotopic research has taught us that isotopic data only have meaning within a well-defined context. It is time to take a closer look at the base of the human food web and start building from the ground up.

ACKNOWLEDGMENTS

I thank my fellow editors for their close and constructive readings of this chapter, as well as the numerous colleagues and students who have helped me think through these issues. Finally, I thank the authors in this volume, as well as all of the participants in our 2010 and 2011 SAA symposia, without whom this book would not have been possible.

NOTES

1. Depending on environmental conditions, CAM plants may isotopically resemble either C_4 or C_3 plants, with C_4-like values dominating under hot, arid conditions (Winter and Holtum 2002; O'Leary 1988).

2. This average includes only samples with a C/N of 2.8–3.6 (see DeNiro 1985). Note that the original publication (DeNiro and Epstein 1981) reports incorrect C/N values that were later revised in an erratum (DeNiro and Epstein 1986).

3. Maya human ($n = 31$) and felid (*Felis* spp., $n = 3$) data are from the site of Dos Pilas; red brocket deer (*Mazama americana*; $n = 4$) are from sites throughout the Southern Maya Lowlands. East African pastoralists include historic period Turkana ($n = 7$; mean value shown) and Griqua ($n = 12$; mean value shown). Modern African fauna are from Kenya and Tanzania; differences in herbivore nitrogen isotopic values may in part be due to the fact that Grant's gazelle (*Gazella granti*) are non-obligate drinkers, whereas zebras (*Equus burchelli*) are obligate drinkers. Paleolithic *Homo* include Neanderthals ($n = 3$) and anatomically modern humans ($n = 6$) dating from 25,000 to 35,000 BP. Fauna (*Cervus elaphus*, *Canis lupus*, *Capra* sp., and Hyaeninae) are from Middle Paleolithic deposits in the Kleine Feldhofer Grotte. Pleistocene mammoth (*Mammuthus primigenius*, $n = 37$), reindeer (*Rangifer tarandus*, $n = 21$), and gray wolf (*Canis lupus*, $n = 5$) are from Siberia and Beringia.

15

Ancient Biomolecules from Archaeobotanical Remains

NATHAN WALES,
KENNETH ANDERSEN, AND
ENRICO CAPPELLINI

The term *ancient biomolecules* describes the suite of organic substances that, after the death of a living system, can still provide meaningful information when analyzed with molecular methods. Despite the action of biotic and abiotic diagenetic processes, these molecules can be identified and characterized using analytical procedures accounting for the chemical peculiarities of ancient biomolecules.

Ancient genetic evidence is one of the most frequently analyzed types of ancient biomolecular data, principally because it facilitates the reconstruction of evolutionary and selection dynamics, as well as past genetic diversity. In a living eukaryotic cell, most genetic information is coded on a set of DNA molecules in the cell nucleus: the chromosomes, present in two copies (diploid) or a multiple of two (i.e., tetraploid or hexaploid for four or six copies, respectively). The remaining portion of DNA, minor in terms of sequence length, but present in hundreds or even thousands of copies per cell, is located in specific organelles, principally the mitochondria and chloroplasts (figure 15.1). DNA's double-stranded structure provides molecular stability but is incompatible with most cellular functions. Instead, RNA, the transcribed version of DNA, is involved in a wider range of processes and reactions thanks to its single-stranded structure and more hydrophilic properties. For example, messenger RNA (mRNA) serves as the "working copy" of DNA by defining the correct sequence of amino acids to be

DOI: 10.5876/9781607323167.c015

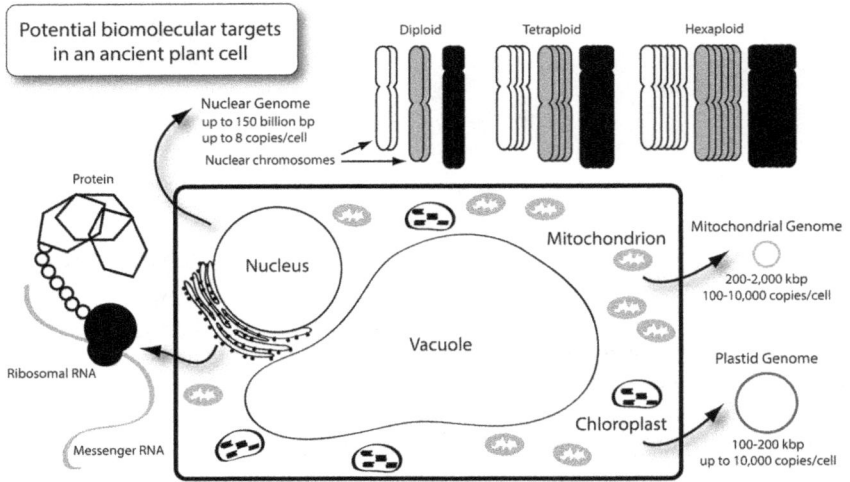

FIGURE 15.1. *Potential biomolecular targets in an ancient plant cell. Nuclear DNA (nuDNA), organized as sets of chromosomes within the cell nucleus, contains the majority of an organism's genome. Some organelles, notably mitochondria and chloroplasts, have their own DNA sequences in short circular molecules. These portions of the genome do not recombine during sexual reproduction and are frequently used in ancient DNA research. Illustration by Christina Warinner.*

assembled in protein synthesis. In addition, ribosomal RNA (rRNA) has a structural role in the ribosomes, the catalytic ribo-proteic complexes where protein building takes place. RNA usually degrades faster than DNA, but in specific contexts, like seeds, RNA can be stored and preserved for long periods. Proteins represent a direct expression of encoded genetic information, and they perform several roles in the cell, including catalysis, regulation and signaling, and structural functions.

By investigating genetic data from time points in the past, researchers can achieve resolutions far exceeding those obtained relying exclusively on modern samples. The sequencing of ancient DNA (aDNA) fragments has opened the field of archaeogenetics and provided fundamental contributions to the advancement of knowledge in several disciplines, including archaeology, human evolution, molecular ecology, and paleontology.

EARLY EVIDENCE FROM NUCLEIC ACIDS

Although the first efforts to extract and characterize aDNA were conducted on animal samples (Higuchi et al. 1984), it was immediately clear that archaeobotanical remains could also preserve ancient biomolecules. Rollo (1985) pioneered the recovery of ancient nucleic acids from plants by characterizing fragments of rRNA up to 10 bases in length from cress (*Lepidium sativum*) seeds dating to 1400 BC from Thebes, Egypt. Rollo et al. (1987) later isolated aDNA from other archaeological specimens, including Peruvian maize (*Zea mays*) kernels dated to AD 800 and Italian grape (*Vitis vinifera*) seeds from the first to fourth centuries BC. Subsequently, the same group announced they had successfully amplified 1,000-year-old maize DNA using the then-new polymerase chain reaction (PCR) (Rollo et al. 1988).

The scientific aim of research conducted in this early phase was to produce aDNA-based evidence to augment existing data on the origin and movement of crop species through time, plant breeding, domestication, and, in general, human-directed plant evolution, with direct information on the organization of genomes of progenitor species. It is often not clear, for example, how many domestication events were involved in each crop's past, how geographically dispersed those events were, or how domestication trajectories interacted with one another. These questions may be highly complex because many crops underwent genetic transformation when human populations were already organized in culturally defined sedentary societies and engaging in long-distance trade.

The work by Goloubinoff, Pääbo, and Wilson (1993) arguably represents the first clear example where aDNA extracted from archaeobotanical remains helped answer archaeological inquiries. After amplifying and sequencing a 300 base pair (bp) fragment of the nuclear gene encoding alcohol dehydrogenase 2 (*Adh2*), the authors reconstructed two ancient alleles from Peruvian maize dated to 4,700 ± 500 years old. The two versions of the gene were found to be more related to modern alleles than to each other, leading the authors to argue that the maize gene pool must be several million years old, vastly predating the domestication era and thereby indicating that landraces of maize must stem from several wild ancestral populations. However, the analysis of multiple genetic markers in modern maize and wild teosinte indicates a single maize domestication event occurred in southern Mexico about 9,000 years ago (Matsuoka et al. 2002). Introgression of teosinte alleles in the ancient maize gene pool could be explained by gene flow between maize and wild *Zea mays* subspecies early in maize's domestication (van Heerwaarden et al. 2011).

Investigation of aDNA also contributed to the reconstruction of the elaborate series of genetic modifications that occurred during the domestication of wheat, one of the first crops and one of the most important food sources for humans today. Cultivation triggered a proliferation of wheat species with new genetic transformations, notably polyploidy—the addition of extra sets of chromosomes in living cells. Based upon the observation of morphological features of plant remains commonly recovered from archaeological sites, conventional archaeobotanical techniques can be used to discriminate species and varieties of glume wheats (Hillman et al. 1996). For grains from naked wheats, however, this approach does not always allow confident assessments of species or ploidy-level, thus making it impossible to distinguish hexaploids, such as common bread wheat (*Triticum aestivum*), from tetraploids, such as pasta wheat (*Triticum durum*), from seeds alone. This serious limitation hinders our ability to appreciate the dynamics of human interaction underpinning the diffusion of different wheats.

Comparisons of nucleotide sequence polymorphisms in ancient samples, however, can serve as a reliable method for examining the genotypes of archaeological remains. For example, a series of studies distinguished between four motifs of the A, B, D, and G wheat genomes using PCR on a short fragment of the leader regions of high molecular weight glutenin (Allaby et al. 1997; Brown et al. 1993; Brown et al. 1994; Brown et al. 1998; Schlumbaum et al. 1998). In most of these cases the ancient materials analyzed were charred, as is commonly the case for archaeobotanical wheat remains, and collected from temperate/warm geographic areas. These conditions are not ideal for DNA preservation and consequently biomolecular recovery was, not surprisingly, difficult and sporadic.

In the early days of aDNA research, overambitious claims were presented and shortly afterwards discredited. These studies include reports on plant DNA successfully recovered from Miocene leaves and fossil material dated between 17 and 40 million years ago (Golenberg et al. 1990; Poinar et al. 1993; Soltis et al. 1992). Even today, researchers occasionally report pre-Pleistocene DNA (Panieri et al. 2010), though careful consideration of such studies generally identifies gross shortcomings. The need to define the physical characteristics of aDNA opened a rigorous and painstaking phase of biological (Pääbo et al. 1989; Poinar et al. 1996) and analytical chemistry observations (McCobb et al. 2001; O'Donoghue, Brown, et al. 1994, 1996; O'Donoghue, Clapham, et al. 1996), and the potential of aDNA research was shown to be greatly challenged by the phenomenon of contamination, the presence of PCR inhibitors, and DNA degradation linked to the age, thermal history, and to some degree, geographic origin of the sample.

The remainder of this chapter describes the methodological improvements introduced to expand the boundaries of biomolecular research and the achievements of the last 10 years in several research areas, including paleoecology, paleoethnobotany, plant evolution, and the reconstruction of the past movements of cultivated species. We describe which plant remains are most frequently studied in aDNA investigations, as well as the best practices and procedures to collect them during fieldwork. Keeping in mind paleoethnobotanical interests, the analytical methodologies adopted, including their limits and obstacles, are explained to illustrate what kinds of information can be recovered and which scientific questions are possible to address using this approach. We also consider the tremendous growth DNA sequencing technology has undergone in the last few years, because aDNA research capitalized upon, and in some cases led, the high-throughput next-generation sequencing revolution. Finally, perspectives for future research on ancient biomolecules other than DNA from plants are illustrated. For further details on ancient plant biomolecules, we recommend consulting review publications that report and integrate the major advancements in aDNA research and provide an exhaustive collection of references (Brown 1999; Gilbert and Willerslev 2007; Gugerli et al. 2005; Palmer, Smith, and Allaby 2012; Schlumbaum et al. 2008).

IN THE FIELD: SOURCES OF PLANT ADNA AND HOW TO COLLECT THEM

Suitable Sources of Plant aDNA

Although it is important for a paleoethnobotanist to have a general grasp of the issues and goals in aDNA research, one of the most important concerns is whether a given site might yield plant aDNA and, in turn, what archaeological questions those data may answer. The range of archaeological plant materials suitable for the recovery of ancient biomolecules is fortuitously quite broad. During a plant's life, virtually every cell contains copies of nuclear, mitochondrial, and plastid DNA, as well as a large complement of proteins and other biomolecules, including RNA and lipids. After death, however, decomposition of the organism, as well as biotic and abiotic taphonomic processes, progressively degrade the organic components of the plant. Nonetheless, fragments of nucleic acids can often be collected and analyzed thousands of years later, depending on the depositional environment.

Macroscopic botanical remains, including seeds, fruits, grains, branches, and roots, are frequently used as source material for ancient biomolecular analyses. If DNA within a specimen is well preserved, the amount required for DNA analysis can be as small as a single seed. However, multiple seeds are always recommended for replicate studies. For larger plant tissues like branches and maize cobs, a mass of approximately 200 mg is generally sufficient for most analyses. Waterlogged and desiccated plant remains tend to yield endogenous DNA more often than charred remains because the heating process damages biomolecules. Totally carbonized samples are very unlikely to yield aDNA; however, partially charred remains have been investigated in numerous studies (e.g., Allaby et al. 1997; Brown et al. 1998; Bunning et al. 2012; Manen et al. 2003).

Much less is known about biomolecular preservation in microscopic botanical remains. Although some researchers report positive results from extracting aDNA from microbotanicals, the techniques have not been thoroughly tested and are arguably still in the experimental phase. Tanaka et al. (2010) report finding aDNA trapped inside 1,100-year-old rice phytoliths. Future research will need to determine whether aDNA can routinely be found within phytoliths, or if contamination may be to blame in this unusual case. Pollen, on the other hand, has on several occasions been reported to yield aDNA (Magyari et al. 2011; Paffetti et al. 2007; Parducci et al. 2005). For instance, Paffetti et al. (2007) isolated aDNA from pollen grains recovered from Venice lagoon sediments, thereby allowing them to assess changes in *Fagus* spp. composition over the last 45,000 years. Future research will determine whether similar studies can provide data on related archaeological questions. Similarly, although at a shallower time depth, studies on temporal genetic variation can utilize plant material available in herbarium collections. Such materials provide an easily accessible historical record of species, varietals, and lineages that may now be extinct or rare for investigating questions on crop dispersal routes and origins (Palmer, Smith, and Allaby 2012, Warriner et al. 2014).

An alternate approach investigates aDNA associated with substrates such as soil, lake, and anthropogenic sediments, including coprolites (desiccated feces). Such samples—often collectively referred to as "dirt" DNA—contain a mixture of plant remains and genetic material from diverse species (see Messner and Stinchcomb, chapter 13, this volume). Importantly, "dirt" DNA can be detected in samples devoid of microfossils and macrofossils, thereby complementing morphological studies by detecting species that otherwise remain unseen. This approach has been tested on coprolites to understand plant components of past human diets (Poinar et al. 2001; Rasmussen et al. 2009). Ancient DNA-based archaeobotanical studies of anthropogenic sediments are so far absent; however, similar research on animal aDNA in sediments from a Norse Greenlandic settlement (ca. AD 1000–1400) provided insights into temporal changes in the relative abundances of domesticated animals (Hebsgaard et al. 2009). Special precautions are required when studying aDNA associated with sediments at unfrozen sites; researchers must carefully consider whether DNA movement via leaching has led to contamination of older sedimentary layers with more recently deposited DNA (Andersen et al. 2012; Haile et al. 2007). In addition to sediments, it is sometimes possible to isolate DNA adhering to artifacts, as has been reported for Classical and Hellenistic Greek shipwreck amphoras (Foley et al. 2012).

Although all botanical remains initially contain biomolecules, some environmental factors—temperature and humidity being the most important (Lindahl 1993)—limit what is actually preserved, so the geographic location and climate of the excavation site is crucial for aDNA preservation. Generally, nucleic acid degradation proceeds faster at higher temperature and humidity. Even under freezing conditions, DNA molecules will spontaneously break if given enough time. In other words, even under the best possible conditions, DNA molecules in all organic remains will eventually fragment to such a degree that geneticists cannot recover any useful data (Allentoft et al. 2012). The question "How old is too old?" is challenging to answer because it depends on the context of each specimen. Authenticated plant chloroplast DNA (cpDNA) that may date to more than 450,000 years ago has been found in silty ice at the bottom of Greenlandic glacier ice (Willerslev et al. 2007) and in 300,000–400,000-year-old Siberian permafrost sediments (Lydolph et al. 2005; Willerslev et al. 2003). Although humidity increases the rate of hydrolytic DNA damage, research on marine (waterlogged) sediments indicates that permanently anoxic environments retard extracellular DNA degradation, extending the time window available to studies of ancient genetics (Corinaldesi et al. 2011). For example, lake sediments have yielded plant cpDNA from 11,000-year-old spruce (*Picea abies*) seeds and cone scales (Magyari et al. 2011) as well as nuclear DNA (nuDNA) from 4,000-year-old apple (*Malus* sp.) seeds (Schlumbaum et al. 2012).

How to Collect Plant aDNA Samples

To overcome the difficulties posed by sample contamination and degradation, precautions must be taken from the beginning of the research, ideally when the sample is found and collected in the field. Although most aDNA research has been conducted on animal remains, several of the procedures adopted to collect zooarchaeological remains apply equally well to the sampling of archaeobotanical macrofossils.

It is strongly recommended to isolate macrobotanical remains in situ, while wearing disposable plastic inspection gloves and using DNA-free disposable tools, such as sterile scalpels and forceps (figure 15.2). Alternatively, excavation

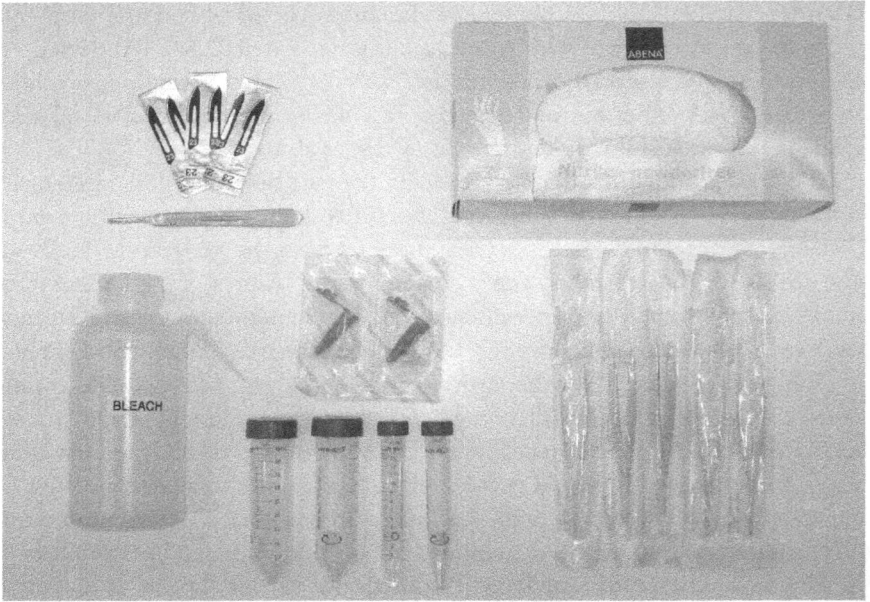

Figure 15.2. *Recommended plant aDNA collection toolkit. In order to properly collect and transport plant aDNA samples, archaeologists are encouraged to have the following supplies on hand: sterile sealable plastic bags, disposable gloves, disposable forceps, scalpels, and sterile vials, ranging in volume from 1.5 mL to 50 mL. Ten percent dilutions of commercial bleach (approx. 0.5% NaOCl) in water can be made in the field to decontaminate field implements like trowels. Dissolvable bleach tablets are a convenient way to transport bleach to areas where liquid bleach is not readily available. Careful collection of archaeobotanical remains using this kit will minimize the risk of modern DNA contamination.*

tools can be washed in a 10 percent commercial bleach solution and allowed to air dry. Tools may also be irradiated with 260 nm UV light (Willerslev and Cooper 2005), and sealed in sterile sealable bags until use. In order to limit introducing exogenous DNA into samples, any washing, drying, or direct handling should be avoided (Bollongino et al. 2008). Ideally, supplementary control samples should be taken from the surrounding sediments for use as "negative" controls of in situ contamination (Anderson-Carpenter et al. 2011; Gilbert et al. 2008; Haile et al. 2009).

Altering the depositional environment in which the sample has been preserved can accelerate DNA degradation. Some evidence suggests that aDNA in animal bones can degrade faster once excavated if not handled appropriately

(Pruvost et al. 2008). Although similar tests for plant aDNA have yet to be undertaken, "fresh" samples are still preferred over samples excavated in past field seasons. Contaminant DNA from modern organisms further complicates the situation because modern DNA is ubiquitously present and can swamp out the low quantities of endogenous DNA in ancient samples. Thus, in the field, samples intended for aDNA analysis should ideally be placed in sterile sealable plastic bags or vials and stored in a cool, dry place with minimal temperature fluctuations. Specimens from wet contexts should not be stored with excessive water in the vial and should be curated in a refrigerator.

A key question for many paleoethnobotanists is whether macrobotanical remains collected via flotation are suitable for aDNA studies. The answer mostly depends on the state of degradation of the sample. Most botanical remains collected this way are charred, and DNA is damaged when subjected to high heat. However, in some cases aDNA has successfully been extracted from morphologically well-preserved ancient seeds collected using traditional flotation methods (Cappellini et al. 2010). A more serious issue with flotation is the likelihood of DNA contamination from modern sources. Flotation of sediment samples is often conducted outdoors in the vicinity of living plants and with water taken from nearby lakes or streams. Given the ubiquitous nature of DNA-bearing pollen, it is impossible to determine whether a DNA molecule is endogenous to a specimen or if it recently became associated with it in the flotation machine. To minimize this issue, flotation of excavated soil for aDNA samples should be performed in a freshly cleaned laboratory, isolated from modern plant specimens. Dry sieving sediment samples may also provide a reasonable alternative to flotation in some circumstances.

IN THE ANCIENT DNA LABORATORY: SEQUENCING aDNA WHILE DEALING WITH DEGRADATION, CONTAMINATION, AND REACTION INHIBITION

Ancient DNA research has recently matured to the point that geneticists can reconstruct complete genomes from limited remains of prehistoric organisms and deceased humans, including the woolly mammoth (Miller et al. 2008), Neanderthal (Green et al. 2010), Denisova hominin (Reich et al. 2010), a human Paleo-Eskimo (Rasmussen et al. 2010), and an Australian Aborigine (Rasmussen et al. 2011). Ancient DNA studies have benefitted immensely from the recent developments in DNA sequencing techniques. However, the technology that made these exciting developments possible, the polymerase chain reaction (PCR), still remains central to studies of aDNA. Theoretically PCR can start from a single DNA molecule and, through exponential growth, yield millions or even billions of DNA copies that can then be detected and measured by a range of instruments. This process works through the enzymatic activity of DNA polymerases, which double the number of copies of the target sequence in each PCR cycle. The drawback associated with this powerful approach is the co-amplification of the same DNA target sequence from any contaminant source accidentally introduced in the PCR solution. By its nature, aDNA is always present in a limited number of copies and thus extremely vulnerable to contamination.

Ancient DNA poses several challenges different from those encountered when studying modern DNA, although many of the molecular methods used are similar. Prior to PCR amplification of aDNA, while the number of copies of the ancient DNA molecules is still very limited, extensive safeguards are required. The successful recovery of authentic DNA from degraded samples requires clean laboratories that must meet a variety of strict requirements, including physical separation from buildings where molecular work is conducted, nightly irradiation with UV light, and filtered ventilation with positive air flow to prevent modern DNA from entering the facility (Fulton 2012). A clean laboratory must carry an extensive supply of DNA-free disposable tools, filtered pipette tips, and molecular biology-grade reagents. While in the clean laboratory, researchers should ideally wear full body suits, disposable gloves, and facemasks to limit the chances of sample contamination during sample preparation (figure 15.3).

It should be noted that despite these precautions, traces of domesticated plants and animals are occasionally observed in PCR reactions that do not contain sample DNA. It is believed that this form of contamination primarily occurs during the industrial production of microbiology reagents, as biological products from a variety of species are added to the growth media of microbial producers of PCR reagents. Fortunately, treatment of PCR reagents with a heat-liable dsDNase (an enzyme that degrades contaminant double-stranded DNA molecules and then can be subsequently heat inactivated before adding sample DNA to the PCR), has been shown to destroy more than 99 percent of contaminant molecules, effectively reducing the problem (Champlot et al. 2010).

The setup of extraction and PCR negative controls is also an important precaution measure that allows detection of laboratory contamination (e.g., Hofreiter et al. 2001; Knapp et al. 2012; Willerslev and Cooper 2005). Nevertheless, the possibility of exogenous DNA entering samples in the field,

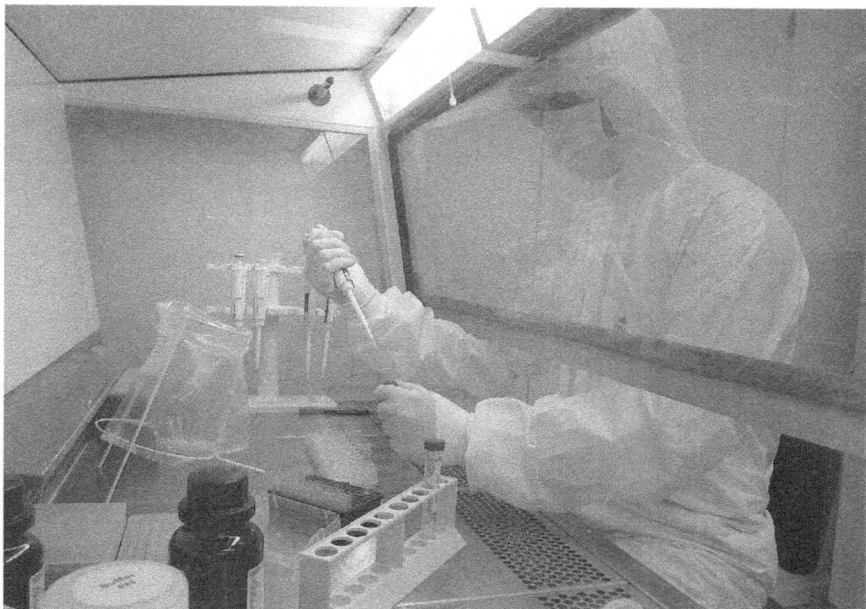

FIGURE 15.3. *Clean laboratory for plant aDNA research. All pre-amplification steps on aDNA must be performed in a dedicated facility designed to prevent modern DNA from contaminating the laboratory. Researchers need to wear full body suits with hoods, facemasks, and disposable gloves. DNA extractions should be performed under a flowhood using filtered pipette tips and molecular biology-grade reagents.*

during the handling of samples, or in laboratory reagents (Leonard et al. 2007) can never be entirely eliminated. Ultimately, the replication of results in an independent laboratory is the best authentication criterion available.

MOLECULAR METHODS IN aDNA

Before the nucleotide sequence of DNA molecules can be analyzed, the DNA must be extracted, purified, PCR amplified, and read. Several alternative DNA extraction methods to remove PCR inhibitors and yet maintain high DNA yields have been developed (e.g., Kistler 2012); for a review see Campos et al. (2009). Considering the low copy number of aDNA molecules in archaeological remains, losses occurring in the pre-PCR phase are more relevant than when working with modern DNA. Nevertheless, in most cases sufficient amounts of high-purity aDNA can be recovered from degraded samples by binding and washing the DNA on silica as suggested by Höss and Pääbo (1993). Several commercial kits based on this approach are available (e.g., Qiagen QIAquick PCR Purification Kit).

Some compounds inadvertently co-extracted with DNA can interfere with the PCR reaction. This effect arises as a result of such inhibitors inactivating or slowing down the DNA polymerase, competitively binding with the DNA templates, or simply overwhelming the PCR solution and preventing reagents from interacting. Ancient botanical remains, in particular, often contain an especially complicated cocktail of soil and plant chemicals, dominated by humic acids, which inhibit enzymatic reactions (Baar et al. 2011; Matheson et al. 2010). Substances in charred botanical remains can act as inhibitors as well (Banerjee and Brown 2002). This is an added problem for charred macrobotanical remains, as the process of charring further reduces DNA quantity. These inhibiting effects can often be partially overcome by applying bovine serum albumin (BSA) to the PCR reaction to reduce the interaction of the co-extracted inhibitors with DNA polymerase, prolonging the extension step in each PCR cycle to compensate for the reduction in enzymatic efficiency (Baar et al. 2011), or by using DNA polymerases designed to resist inhibition (Monroe et al. 2013). These modifications, in combination with an increased number of PCR cycles, significantly improve the DNA amplification yield for many recalcitrant samples, including ancient ones.

Until recently, aDNA investigations relied upon conventional PCR amplification of a few target segments of DNA, with each target generally between 100 and 200 bp in length (figure 15.4a). After piecing together overlapping segments, even the most noteworthy studies failed to cover more than a few thousand bp of aDNA sequences (Krause et al. 2006). In stark contrast, recent PCR-based "high-throughput" DNA sequencing platforms (e.g., the Roche GS-FLX, Illumina Genome Analyzer/HiSeq, and Life Technologies SOLiD series) now allow for the sequencing of millions to hundreds of billions of bases per experiment. Although each platform requires samples to be prepared following a different protocol, each begins by ligating double-stranded DNA oligomers of known sequence, called adapters, to each double stranded DNA molecule extracted from a sample, generating what is conventionally known as a DNA library (figure 15.4b) (also see Rizzi et al. 2012). The adapters at the ends of each DNA library molecule function as primer binding-sites for amplification of the entire DNA library, rather than a specific short DNA target as in conventional PCR. These solutions were originally developed to sequence DNA from single samples; however, the inclusion of sample-specific nucleotide-tags in the adapters can be used to assign a distinctive index to

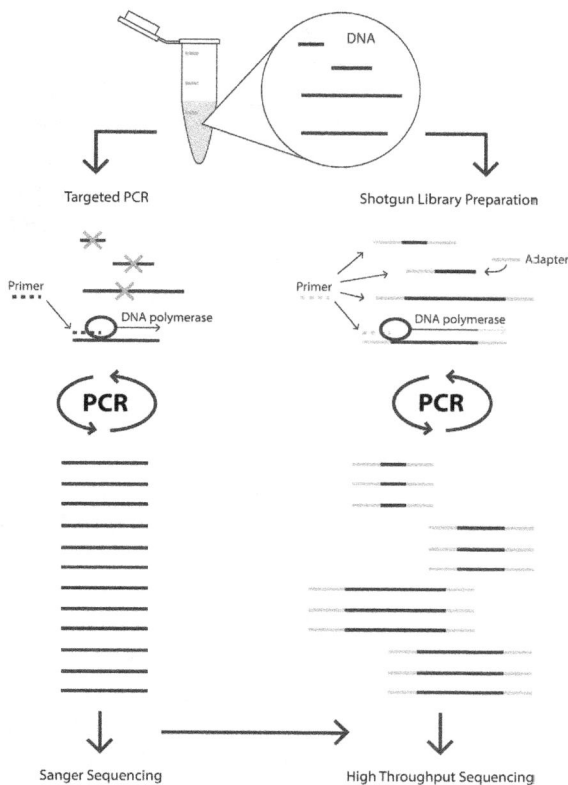

FIGURE 15.4. *Comparison of targeted sequencing of a single template versus shotgun sequencing of a pool of extracted DNA fragments in a sample. In the former case, a specific DNA target locus (for example, a portion of the chloroplast* rbcL *gene) is enriched by PCR amplification using primers (dashed black line) complementary to DNA sequences flanking the DNA target. Only the targeted DNA is sequenced, either by Sanger sequencing technology or by high-throughput sequencing, and all other non-targeted DNA fragments are lost. Typically, Sanger sequencing is used if only one species is targeted, whereas high-throughput "deep" sequencing can be performed on environmental samples, where targeted DNA from a range of species may be present. In shotgun sequencing, a library is prepared by ligating nucleotide adapters (gray lines) to all DNA fragments in a sample. The adapters act as universal primer-binding sites during PCR (dashed gray line), resulting in the amplification/enrichment of the entire DNA library at once. Once the library is created, a high-throughput sequencing platform determines the nucleotide sequences of the millions (or billions) of different DNA fragments in the library. Shotgun sequencing is typically used for whole genome sequencing or whole metagenome sequencing. For both targeted deep sequencing and shotgun high-throughput sequencing, an optional index tag can be included in the primer to identify interexperiment contamination or facilitate the pooling of multiple samples into one sequencing reaction. Illustration by Christina Warinner.*

different samples, allowing the simultaneous processing of hundreds of samples in a single sequencing run (Binladen et al. 2007).

One of the few drawbacks observed in the pioneering phase of aDNA high-throughput sequencing was that a majority of DNA recovered was exogenous, chiefly stemming from microorganisms accumulating in samples after deposition (Poinar et al. 2006). For example, in one experiment on 3,300-year-old charred cereal grains, less than 1 percent of the DNA sequences matched cereal genomes (Bunning et al. 2012). To combat this problem, target enrichment steps have been developed to selectively recover particular portions of chromosomes or entire organelle genomes. DNA sequence capture kits are based on the hybridization between target DNA sequences and custom-designed probes. Magnetic beads, bound to the probes, enable researchers to isolate sequences of interest and discard all others (Maricic et al. 2010; Schuenemann et al. 2011). Currently, the application of "in-solution" capture techniques on aDNA extracts from plants is still in the experimental phase but has been successfully applied to 700–1,000-year-old maize cobs and kernels from Chile and Arizona (Ávila-Arcos et al. 2011). In effect, this process makes high-throughput sequencing of aDNA more efficient, driving down research costs even further. If targeted capture is not feasible for a given experiment, quantitative-PCR experiments may be used in a prescreening step to help identify the least contaminated samples in a collection, thereby maximizing the amount of useful sequencing data that will be obtained from conventionally prepared libraries (Wales et al. 2012). It should be noted that although high-throughput sequencing has led to a dramatic drop in cost per sequenced base, experiments based on this approach require elaborate infrastructures for both data storage and bioinformatical analyses of large data sets.

The newest wave of sequencing technology, the "third generation" (e.g., Helicos HeliScope, Pacific BioSciences RS II, and upcoming Oxford Nanopore GridION), enables the characterization of DNA samples without any amplification steps. This approach avoids biases that may be introduced during PCR, and therefore should give a more accurate representation of the molecules in a sample. These platforms are now becoming commercially available for molecular biology and have already been successfully applied to aDNA (Orlando et al. 2011).

It is important to recognize that sequence databases of modern DNA provide the foundation for all aDNA studies. Such data allow researchers to design probes and primers to isolate areas of interest, and differentiate between phenotypes, varietals, and lineages. As expected, most plant aDNA research has focused on plants very well characterized in genetic databases, such as cereals and some fruits. Conversely, if a species is underrepresented in genetic databases, aDNA will not be able to answer archaeological questions until the database is expanded.

PLANT ADNA

GENETIC LOCI FOR ANALYSES

Plants differ from animals at the genetic level in a number of ways, but notably for having three discrete genomes: nuclear (nuDNA), mitochondrial (mtDNA), and chloroplast (cpDNA). The nuclear genome is by far the largest of the three and provides the genetic code for most of the phenotypic and developmental traits of the organism. However, aDNA research has largely been restricted to the study of organelle DNA (mtDNA and cpDNA) since, initially, these genomes exist in high copy numbers within the cell. In plant cells the number of organelles and genome copies per organelle varies and depends on the plant species, cell type, and developmental stage of the tissue (Lutz et al. 2011). Diploid organisms have two copies of their nuclear genome per cell, whereas the number of cpDNA genomes can be as high as 10,000 copies per cell in a tobacco (*Nicotina tabacum*) leaf (Lutz et al. 2011). Unlike nuDNA, both mtDNA and cpDNA are inherited without recombination and are generally inherited maternally in angiosperms and paternally in gymnosperms.

Geneticists focus on a number of features to identify and compare different ancient plant samples. Since the mid-1990s, a number of plant aDNA studies have analyzed microsatellites, noncoding regions of the genome with strings of repetitive patterns often consisting of repeated units of one to six nucleotides in length (e.g., Manen et al. 2003; O'Donoghue, Clapham, et al. 1996; Raniello and Procaccini 2002). The number of repeated units can differ between species or cultivars, and genetic testing after PCR can determine the number of repeats in a given specimen. In a similar manner, single nucleotide polymorphisms (SNPs) can be used to differentiate lineages and some phenotypic traits. In this case, geneticists identify positions in the genome that have different nucleotides for different individuals. After mapping the variation of SNPs, researchers can address the phylogenetic relationships among individuals and between populations. When such studies include aDNA, it is possible to learn about the genetic history of a species across space and time, which is a fundamental goal in paleoethnobotanical research on domestication trajectories and prehistoric transportation routes of domesticated plants.

A peculiar issue in plant aDNA is ploidy level, the number of nuclear chromosome copies in a cell. Most non-domesticated plants are diploid, with two copies of each chromosome in all somatic cells. Domestication has led to some plants being tetraploid or even hexaploid, as additional pairs of chromosomes can lead to desirable phenotypic changes, including enlarged fruits. As previously mentioned, the ploidy level of ancient domesticates has been a key question for paleoethnobotanists. Due to DNA degradation, it is not possible to count chromosomes in ancient samples, as is done with karyotyping in living cells. However, as discussed in the introduction to this chapter, it can be possible to identify genetic markers of different ploidy levels, as has been done for wheats.

For certain bulk samples, researchers may be interested in measuring the biodiversity of organisms—including plants—within an environmental sample. Genetic meta-barcoding is a relatively new approach that allows geneticists to answer these types of questions. Genetics-based taxonomic identifications (Hollingsworth et al. 2009) rely on sequence variation and are most easily achieved with long DNA sequences. Because aDNA is highly fragmented, the sequence length becomes a limiting factor for taxonomic identification. As a result, barcoding markers developed for species identification of modern specimens are not suitable for ancient materials. In aDNA studies a compromise is reached: researchers focus on short variable DNA sequences flanked by conserved regions for primer binding. For angiosperm and gymnosperm plant species, such barcoding markers have been identified in the *mat*K, *trn*L, and *rbc*L genes, which are all part of the chloroplast genome (Poinar et al. 1998; Taberlet et al. 2007).

Another aspect that influences the choice of markers in aDNA studies is that the three different genomes present in plants evolve at different rates. The low mutation rate of the mitochondrial genome in plants makes it unsuitable for fine taxonomic differentiation; instead, the chloroplast genome is most commonly used in ancient DNA studies of plants. Although many macrofossils can be identified to species level based on morphology, cpDNA markers generally only allow taxonomic identification at the genus or family level. After amplifying and sequencing the ~50–140 bp *trn*L fragment, geneticists can unambiguously assign 20 percent of plant specimens to the level of species, 41 percent to genus, and 79 percent to the family level (Taberlet et al. 2007). Meta-barcoding is now routinely used in DNA-based diet studies and for paleoecological reconstruction based on aDNA. This approach opens up a new frontier in archaeogenetics, and, after further research, will likely prove to be an invaluable technique for studying a wide array of paleoethnobotanical samples.

What Can Be Learned from Studying Ancient Plant DNA?

Despite the numerous caveats posed by aDNA research, there are in fact many ways in which aDNA from paleoethnobotanical samples can yield crucial data. The central strength of plant aDNA research is that genetic loci can provide higher analytical resolution than most morphological characteristics. Specific morphological (i.e., phenotypic) traits represent the expression of different genetic profiles. Characterization of these markers, plus unexpressed neutral ones in non-coding regions of the genome, allow higher resolution in comparative studies. Access to the paleogenomes of progenitor species can provide evidence of selection in genes linked to domestication and may shed light on the region of domestication and prehistoric human contact routes. A number of noteworthy applications for paleoethnobotany are described below, but it should be recognized that plant aDNA data are also used for many other inquiries, including phylogeny, paleoecology, and domestication processes (Palmer, Smith, and Allaby 2012).

An obvious goal for every archaeologist is to learn as much about the archaeological finds as possible. For archaeobotanical remains, macroscopic and microscopic analyses usually provide sufficient detail. Anomalous or sensational finds warrant deeper investigation, especially when morphological traits are ambiguous. Genetic analyses, such as the barcoding discussed above, can help identify botanical remains to taxonomic groups. It is similarly possible to detect plant aDNA when macroscopic remains are too fragmentary or distorted for visual inspection, such as in coprolites. Poinar et al. (2001) amplified *rbc*L genetic markers from 2,000-year-old human coprolites to determine the plant species consumed by Native American individuals. Microscopic analysis of the same coprolites found one species not recovered using aDNA, but failed to observe six other species detected by aDNA. This demonstrates that by combining traditional methods with genetic analyses, researchers can attain a more comprehensive understanding of important archaeological questions.

Genetic markers can also be used to identify varietal lineages of domesticates, surpassing what is possible with morphological attributions. For example, it is now possible to differentiate between hundreds of modern grape cultivars using a large SNP database (Myles et al. 2011). This database will soon be tested using ancient samples, but lower-resolution tests have already been conducted on ancient grape seeds using microsatellites (Cappellini et al. 2010). After determining the use of different cultivars in the past, one can better understand past human preferences, ancient trade routes, and migration patterns. An exciting example of human selection as seen through aDNA comes from two-row barley found at the Egyptian site Qasr Ibrim (Palmer et al. 2009). Despite having the more primitive phenotype, the 3,000-year-old barley has the genetic signature of six-row barley with a nonfunctional version of the gene responsible for growing six grains. Given this confounding discovery, researchers suggest that farmers at Qasr Ibrim chose to propagate the aberrant two-row variety, perhaps due to its ability to handle water stress better than six-row barley. Genome rearrangements observed in archaeological cotton (*Gossypium* sp.) from Qasr Ibrim have also been interpreted as resulting from adaptation to local aridity (Palmer, Clapham, et al. 2012).

Another application of plant aDNA in paleoethnobotany is inferring ancient phenotypic traits. In living species, genetic markers can be associated with different characteristics. If these traits are not visible in archaeobotanical remains, genetic analyses may be the only option. For example, the domestication of maize required a number of important changes from the progenitor teosinte. Jaenicke-Després et al. (2003) extracted aDNA from maize cobs dating between 660 and 4,400 years old, with a focus on three genes that affect the phenotype of the plants. They demonstrated that some phenotypic traits, including an unbranched plant architecture, were present in maize by 4,000 years ago. Other characteristics, such as starch quality, were still under selection 2,000 years ago.

Finally, aDNA can also be used to investigate ancient plant pathogens. Under the right circumstances, traces of microorganisms responsible for plant diseases and their DNA can be preserved along with the remains of the plant they infected, potentially for thousands of years. So far, this branch of inquiry remains mostly untested. However, it has been shown that DNA from potato blight oomycete (*Phytophthora infestans*) can be recovered from potato (*Solanum tuberosum*) specimens that have been stored in herbaria for over 150 years (Ristaino et al. 2001). Using such an approach on archaeobotanical remains, it could be possible to test hypotheses of agricultural demise due to pathogens.

ANCIENT BIOMOLECULES FROM PLANTS: NOT JUST ADNA

PROTEINS

Although DNA is the most informative source of molecular information, other biomolecules can also be analyzed from ancient biological samples. Their analysis in ancient samples can produce evidence to clarify specific aspects of archaeological or ethnobotanical interest that are otherwise impossible to address using aDNA alone. In plants, for example, the protein component represents an important indicator of seed and grain quality. As already suggested over two decades ago by Brown et al. (1993), ancient DNA studies will not be able to provide much information on the nutritional value of the grain, as this is determined by the quality and quantity of the seed proteins.

Pioneering studies on archaeological cereal seeds (Derbyshire et al. 1977; Shewry et al. 1982) suggested that the investigation of proteins from ancient grains could aid in understanding plant domestication, but this work was hampered by the prevailing technology of the time. The recent availability of mass spectrometry (MS)-based protein sequencing and the adoption of high-throughput "shotgun proteomics" strategies have provided the resolution and sensitivity required to confidently and reproducibly sequence protein traces from ancient samples. For instance, the application of mass spectrometry has enabled the identification of ancient bone proteins (Nielsen-Marsh et al. 2002; Nielsen-Marsh et al. 2005) and protein remains in archaeological garments and ceramics (Hollemeyer et al. 2008; Solazzo et al. 2008). A preliminary report describes MS-based protein sequencing from archaeological grape (*Vitis vinifera*) seeds (Cappellini et al. 2010). Results demonstrate that at least the most abundant storage proteins from archaeological seeds can be identified with high confidence. The study also describes the typologies of chemical damage affecting ancient protein residues. Although we are still unable to address any specific archaeological question, this work starts to clarify the chemical characteristics of a new category of potentially useful ancient biomolecules from plants, as it was necessary to do for aDNA approximately 10 to 20 years ago.

RNA

Researchers have recently demonstrated that it is possible to recover RNA from ancient plant samples (Callaway 2010; Fordyce et al. 2013). Although all cells in an organism usually share the same genome(s) (DNA), their total molecular composition and function varies according to the tissue to which they belong, the organism's developmental phase, and the cell's metabolism. The transcriptome, the entirety of RNA molecules in a tissue, is consequently influenced by environmental conditions and correspondingly varies in both qualitative and quantitative aspects. Messenger RNA (mRNA) represents the transcribed version of protein-coding sequences in genes. Mature seeds contain long-lived mRNAs that can survive desiccation and remain active in dry quiescent embryos, ready to trigger protein synthesis during the early phases of germination (Bønsager et al. 2007; Rajjou et al. 2004). In a way, seeds have evolved to function as "time capsules" and under optimal conditions can store genetic information over extended periods. Questions that have so far been out of the scope of aDNA research, such as gene expression and regulation in response to environmental factors including climate, drought, or pathogens, could be approached with RNA data. For example, seed-specific mRNA expression patterns are known to vary in modern seeds according to irrigation practices (Grimplet et al. 2007). Ancient RNA research is in its infancy, in large part due to the widespread assumption that RNA does not preserve for long periods of time. RNA is far more fragile than DNA, but it has been shown nonetheless that ancient RNA can be reproducibly extracted from some plant samples, as has been achieved for a set of 723-year-old maize kernels from Arizona (Fordyce et al. 2013). These findings are further supported by well-documented cases of viability of some ancient plant tissues. The germination of a 2000-year-old date palm (*Phoenix dactylifera*) seed and the in vitro regeneration of plants from 30,000-year-old *Silene stenophylla* fruit tissues found in permafrost could have only been possible if RNA had survived (Sallon et al. 2008; Yashina et al. 2012). Future research will determine the extent to which ancient RNA can shed light on paleoethnobotanical questions.

FUTURE PERSPECTIVES

The future for biomolecular investigations of ancient plant remains looks promising. Considering the successes of the first ancient human and animal genome sequencing projects, it is not unreasonable to expect that the first complete genome of an ancient plant will soon be released. The progressive diffusion of second- and third-generation DNA sequencing platforms will ultimately enable geneticists to reliably determine longer and more complicated genetic traits from more samples. These technologies, in combination with refined sample preparation techniques, will allow access to highly degraded archaeobotanical materials so far considered off-limits.

It is more challenging to envisage all the scientific implications of these technical improvements. Assuredly, the "classic" questions of plant aDNA investigations will remain key avenues of inquiry. Clarifying the evolution, selection, and fixation of domestication syndrome traits on stronger experimental evidence will allow a more accurate reconstruction of domestication processes. In the future, these questions could also be tackled at a higher level (i.e., systems biology) by exploring interactions within an extended network of genes. Ancient DNA investigation already succeeded in the characterization of lost alleles (Römpler et al. 2006), and the extension of this approach to multiple target genes will allow the reconstruction of phenotypic traits of ancient plants. Using such knowledge, researchers could characterize the nutritional and organoleptic properties of ancient agricultural products, providing a more vivid depiction of plant exploitation in the past and clearer relationships with extant crops.

These methods may even allow the discovery and resurrection of biomolecules that are currently extinct. Genetic variation, lost in the past to pursue selection of desired agronomic traits, could be identified and eventually reintroduced in modern plants in order to increase biodiversity and impart resistance to environmental stress factors. Likewise, ancient alleles that are not present in living organisms could code for protein isoforms with biochemical properties of possible applicative interest, as recently suggested for mammoth hemoglobin (Yuan et al. 2011). These fascinating possibilities confer ancient archaeobotanical remains a clear value as a genetic resource in addition to their crucial archaeological importance.

ACKNOWLEDGMENTS

This chapter is dedicated to Professor Franco Ugo Rollo, who passed away in September 2014. Prof. Rollo was the first to identify preserved nucleic acids in plant remains. His work in the 1980s and early 1990s ensured that biomolecular archaeobotany developed into the rigorous and respected discipline that it has now become.

Financial support for N.W. is provided by the American-Scandinavian Foundation. E.C. is supported by the European Union with a Marie Curie Intra European Fellowship (Grant No. 237227) and by a Danish Council for Independent Research "Sapere Aude" award (10-081390) allotted to Prof. M. Thomas P. Gilbert. The Danish National Research Foundation supports the Center for GeoGenetics. The authors thank Prof. M. Thomas P. Gilbert, John M. Marston, Jade d'Alpoim Guedes, and Christina Warinner for their helpful comments on the manuscript. The authors are especially grateful to Christina Warinner for illustrating figures 15.1 and 15.4 and for inviting them to contribute to this volume.

16

*A Landscape Context
for Paleoethnobotany*

The Contribution of Aerial
and Satellite Remote Sensing

JESSE CASANA

At first glance, aerial and satellite remote sensing technologies would seem to offer few contributions to paleoethnobotanical research. Although these data sets constitute unparalleled resources for documenting the regional distribution and dynamic changes in plant communities today, planes and satellites are only a few decades old and the images they collect cannot be used to directly detect ancient plants. Moreover, dramatic changes in climate, patterns of land use, and the resultant distribution of vegetation over the Holocene mean that any measure of modern vegetation may have little resemblance to past landscapes. In the lowlands of the Yucatan Peninsula, areas now covered by dense rainforest were home to expansive agricultural fields during the Classic Maya period (AD 250–900). In southern Mesopotamia, areas now covered by extensive marshlands were intensively irrigated agricultural fields in the Uruk period (3800–3100 BC) when the world's first cities emerged there. Fundamentally, satellite remote sensing data show us the landscape of the last few decades.

There are nonetheless numerous insights that satellite and aerial remote sensing can provide to paleoethnobotanical research, primarily in offering a landscape context for analysis of ancient plant remains and interpretation of past agricultural strategies. Following an overview of currently available remote sensing resources, this chapter offers a review of several ways in which satellite and aerial remote sensing can support

DOI: 10.5876/9781607323167.c016

paleoethnobotany, including the direct detection of ancient agricultural fields and water management systems, the mapping of environmental contexts within which ancient settlements were located, and the modeling of complex, landscape-scale vegetation responses to variable climate regimes and land use practices. I conclude with suggestions for potential future directions for these emerging areas of research.

REMOTE SENSING RESOURCES FOR ARCHAEOLOGY

Archaeological remote sensing has made use of a dizzying variety of imagery and data sets since the earliest studies were undertaken more than a century ago using balloon photographs, and several recent books offer introductions to the topic (Bewley and Raczkowski 2000; Comer and Harrower 2013; Conolly and Lake 2006; Cowley et al. 2010; Johnson 2006; Parcak 2009). Although the availability of imagery resources is constantly growing, there are several important resources that have historically been used by archaeologists and that are primarily discussed in this chapter. Table 16.1 summarizes the general characteristics of these image resources and notes their strengths and weaknesses as applied to archaeological problems. In general, the main variables of optical imagery concern an image's spatial resolution, or the size of the ground surface represented by one pixel, and its spectral resolution, or the portion of the light spectrum an image records. Another major variable is sometimes termed temporal resolution, referring to when an image was acquired and/or how frequently the same part of the earth's surface was imaged by the same sensor. Some studies increasingly utilize detailed topographic data, which are also collected by various satellite and aerial sensors.

For many archaeological applications, an image of high spatial resolution is essential because the features we hope to detect are quite small and thus do not appear on coarser satellite photos. Simple, black-and-white aerial photographs or declassified CORONA satellite images (essentially just aerial photos taken from space) are often the most valuable, because they were frequently acquired before the mechanization of agriculture, the growth of urban areas, and the damming of river valleys obscured or destroyed many archaeological sites and features around the world (Casana et al. 2012; Cowley et al. 2010). On the other hand, multispectral satellite images derived from Landsat, SPOT, ASTER, or other satellites have rather coarse spatial resolution, ranging from 60 m in Landsat's thermal infrared bands to SPOT's 10-m panchromatic (black and white) band. Yet the ability of these sensors to document wavelengths of light across the visible and infrared spectrum enable them to

TABLE 16.1. Overview of aerial and satellite remote sensing data sets commonly employed by archaeologists

	Spatial Resolution	Spectral Resolution	Date	Cost	Strengths	Weaknesses
Historic aerial photography	< 1–5 m	black and white	1910s–present	Free to Low	Can be useful for recognition of archaeological features because it predates modern land use; stereo images enable 3D viewing.	Often difficult to locate images and frequently unavailable; may be problematic to work with due to lack of metadata.
Declassified satellite photography (CORONA, Gambit, etc.)	2 m	black and white	1960s–1970s	Low	Older images provide near global coverage of good spatial resolution predating much development. Stereo capabilities of imagery enable 3D viewing.	Panoramic camera format makes orthorectification challenging. Low spectral resolution prevents some applications.
Civilian multispectral satellites (Landsat, SPOT, Aster, Hyperion)	10–30 m	visible, near infrared, far infrared/ thermal	1970s–present	Free	A long history of global coverage, offering robust spectral resolution, making these images ideal for environmental and other mapping applications.	Coarse spatial resolution renders images ineffective for direct detection of many cultural features.
Multispectral aircraft scanners (TIMS, Daedalus, Terrahawk)	< 1–5 m	visible, near infrared, far infrared/ thermal	1980s–present	High	Combines high spatial resolution of air photos with spectral resolution of civilian satellites.	Very expensive to acquire because planes must be tasked; recent images may postdate development.

continued on next page

TABLE 16.1—*continued*

	Spatial Resolution	Spectral Resolution	Date	Cost	Strengths	Weaknesses
Commerical high-resolution (Quickbird, IKONOS, GeoEye)	1 m or better	visible and near infrared	1999–present	High	Provides very high resolution imagery of entire globe; easily viewed through Google and other online resources.	Incorporating into GIS or mapping operation requires purchase of imagery. Recent images may postdate development.
Vegetation monitoring (AVHRR and MODIS)	250 m–1 km	visible and near infrared	1978–present	Free	Excellent resource for mapping landscape changing dynamics due to high spectral and temporal resolution.	Extremely coarse spatial resolution makes direct detection of most cultural features impossible.
SRTM	90 m	N/A	2000	Free	Global, pre-processed elevation data set is easy to acquire and incorporate into GIS applications.	Low spatial resolution often obscures cultural features with topographic expression.
LiDAR	0.1–1 m	N/A	1990s–present	High	Very high spatial resolution maps both vegetation canopies and underlying ground surface.	Processing data is difficult; acquisition is very costly.

map regional-scale variability in vegetation, soils, and geology better than any other resource. Landsat images record the reflected radiation of the earth's surface in up to 7 distinct bands, whereas ASTER images divide this same spectral range into 15 bands. Experimental "hyperspectral" sensors, like that employed on NASA's Hyperion satellite, record more than 200 distinct wavelengths of light in visible and near-infrared spectra. Analysis of how certain minerals, plants, or land use patterns reflect across a variety of light spectra enable remote sensing scientists to distinguish them on multispectral imagery, and these same techniques enable some archaeological sites and features to be more readily recognized in these images than in other, higher resolution images. The greater frequency with which multispectral satellite images were collected makes them very useful in tracking land use and vegetation change at regional scales. Even images at very coarse spatial resolution such as the Moderate Resolution Imaging Spectroradiometer (MODIS) at 250 m or the Advanced Very High Resolution Radiometer (AVHRR) at 1 km can be a great aid to reconstructing plant environments because they provide daily coverage of the entire globe, enabling detailed analysis of vegetation response to climatic variability or anthropogenic forces. Some of the best image data for archaeological applications has been acquired by aircraft-borne scanners that collect images of high spatial and spectral resolution, although acquisition of such imagery can be extremely costly. In some contexts, agricultural features such as canals may be detected by their topographic expression using freely available Shuttle Radar Topography Mission (SRTM) or other similar data sets. There is also growing interest among archaeologists in using high-resolution topographic data sets such as LiDAR (Light Detection And Ranging) to discover and map archaeological landscape features (Cowley and Opitz 2013). Because some of the low-frequency light wave emitted by LiDAR sensors penetrates tree canopies and other vegetation, the technology can produce extremely high-resolution (< 0.1 m) topographic maps and reveal features obscured by forests and vegetation. Unfortunately, LiDAR requires the flight of specialized aircraft and is thus extremely expensive to acquire, making it beyond the reach of most archaeologists.

DIRECT DETECTION OF ANCIENT FIELD SYSTEMS

The most straightforward and yet often underutilized way in which satellite and aerial remote sensing can provide support for interpretation of ancient agricultural practices is through the direct detection of archeological field systems and related features. The ability to see where cultivation was taking place in the past does not provide direct evidence as to what crops were being cultivated, but it provides an essential tool for understanding the spatiality of ancient agricultural practice and a powerful complement to more traditional paleoethnobotanical research.

Since the early twentieth century, archaeologists working in the British Isles have relied on aerial photographs to document ancient agricultural fields across the region (e.g., Bowen 1963; Bradford 1957; Crawford and Keiller 1928). Wilson's (1982) summary of such features provides a useful overview of how many of these field systems appear in conventional aerial photography, as well as how they can be approximately dated. The rich record of ancient fields preserved in the British landscape is primarily evident as field boundary features, even in cases where later field systems have been overlaid on top of them (Gleason 1994). The soil composition of field boundaries is often very different than that of the cultivated fields that they demarcate if cultivation continues for long periods of time (decades or centuries) and field boundaries remain stable. Cultivated fields are repeatedly plowed, fertilized and cleared of large stones; on field boundaries, plowing does not occur, native plants, trees, or hedges are allowed to grow, and stones cleared from fields are piled on these boundaries. These differing histories result in soil on boundaries that differs in moisture content and composition, which in turn can affect the health of vegetation that grows on it. Subtle differences in soil color or in plant growth are not evident in all aerial images, because variable soil moisture, ground cover, and lighting conditions at the time that aerial images were acquired can significantly impact the visibility of field boundaries. In many cases, historic aerial images or even declassified satellite images (e.g., Fowler and Fowler 2005) are particularly useful in documenting ancient field boundaries because modern land use practices, involving mechanized plowing and irrigation, often rapidly obscure these features. Under especially good conditions, as in the very arid summer of 1996, many field boundaries were particularly easy to recognize from the air, and a dedicated series of reconnaissance missions were flown by the Royal Commission on the Historical Monuments of England to document them (Featherstone et al. 1999). However, many fields in Britain and elsewhere in northern Europe are clearly visible under many conditions, even on modern, high-resolution commercial satellite imagery, such as the extensive systems of fields that can be seen surrounding Stonehenge in southern England (figure 16.1). Study of these field systems from the air spawned an entire lexicon dedicated to describing their variable morphologies and exploring their historic and social contexts (Bowen 1963). In some cases the morphology of field systems alone can provide an approximate date, as with

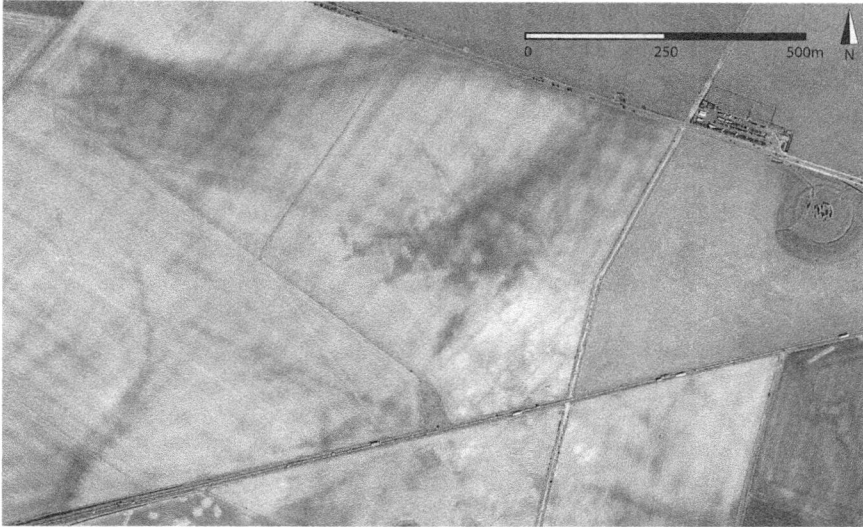

FIGURE 16.1. *A Quickbird satellite image from 2006 at 70-cm resolution showing extensive systems of ancient fields, likely dating to the first millennium BC, just west of Stonehenge, UK (at far right of image). Map data ©2006 Digital Globe, Google Earth.*

the "coaxial" fields that date to the Bronze Age (e.g., Johnston 2005) or the "ridge and furrow" systems that are generally medieval (e.g., Demidowicz 2005). In other cases, the date of ancient field boundaries can be deduced by their association with archaeological sites or other dated archaeological features, as well as by the way in which they are cut by progressively more recent field boundaries and roadways.

The basic strategies employed in the study of English and northern European field systems have been successfully replicated in Mediterranean regions, where the history of cultivation is both longer and more intensive.

Among the most studied features in the region are Roman centuriated fields, field systems laid out by surveyors along an orthogonal grid system (Dilke 1971). The large square plots contained in the system, usually at a standard size, were generally given to retiring military officers as a pension. The rockier soils found in many Mediterranean regions have led to the formation of large clearance walls along field boundaries as farmers were forced to move stones out of cultivated tracks. These boundaries and the farmed parcels they demarcate changed gradually over time as land changed hands among owners and across generations. Nonetheless, portions of the original

Roman grid system are often preserved in fragments across the landscape, as the initial ownership of adjoining plots led to distinct paths of ownership subsequently. In addition, roadways and informal routes sometimes developed between centuriated plots, and these roads can also lead to preservation of the boundaries. In many cases around the Mediterranean region changing land use patterns over recent decades, particularly since World War II, have resulted in the disappearance of long-preserved Roman and medieval fields, but they remain detectable on historic aerial photography and satellite imagery (Bescoby 2006; Stoker 2010).

A recent study of centuriated field systems in Catalonia, Spain, demonstrates how careful analysis of the orientation of preserved fields as evidenced on historic aerial imagery can be used to map a changing landscape history for the region (Palet and Orengo 2011). In this case, an original network of roads that predates the Roman period seems to have been preserved, but whatever cultivated landscapes existed there originally were largely erased. A system of orthogonal centuriated fields was then imposed at the same time that a new city was laid out on the coast. This eventually gave way to a system of radial fields surrounding small villages in the medieval period.

In some cases, the presence of these sorts of field boundaries can demonstrate the existence of intensive agriculture in areas that saw little or no cultivation historically. In western Syria, for example, all intensive agricultural production extending back to the early Holocene was likely restricted to lowland plains and river valleys, leaving upland areas largely uncultivated until the late first millennium BC (Casana 2007). Then from around 300 BC–AD 650, uplands experienced a relatively short episode of intensive cultivation, resulting in good preservation of ancient field systems but also triggering large-scale soil erosion (Casana 2008).

Centuriated fields are visible in valleys, as in figure 16.2a, illustrating an area just east of Homs, Syria. Small rectilinear fields, demarcated largely by stone clearance mounds, can be found in many upland areas, and these are also effectively documented by analysis of declassified CORONA satellite imagery (figure 16.2b; Casana et al. 2012; Philip et al. 2005).

Today, many of the field clearance walls and cairns or stone piles made within cultivated fields of Roman or late Roman date have been removed to make way for modern agriculture, but they are clearly visible in historic imagery from the 1960s (Philip and Bradbury 2010). As in Europe, it is not possible to determine precisely what was being cultivated in these fields, but most evidence from the region points to a mixed agricultural economy focused on cereals, olives, and grapes, along with fruit and nut orchards and garden crops.

FIGURE 16.2. *A declassified CORONA satellite image from March 1969 showing (top) centuriated fields in a lowland plain southeast of Homs, Syria, probably dating to the first century AD, and (bottom) small, rectilinear fields marked by stone clearance walls and cairns in basaltic uplands west of Homs, probably also dating to the Roman period. Image courtesy of CORONA Atlas of the Middle East, University of Arkansas/US Geological Survey.*

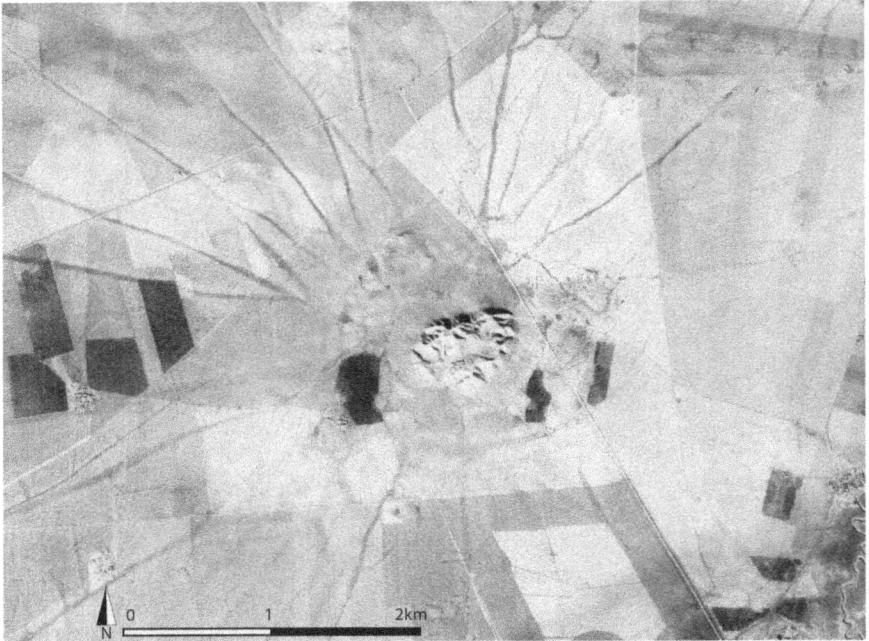

FIGURE 16.3. *Radial system of ancient roadways or "hollow ways" surrounding Tell Brak in northeastern Syria, visible on a declassified CORONA satellite image from 1968. These features, dating to the third millennium BC, probably demarcate ancient field boundaries. Image courtesy of CORONA Atlas of the Middle East, University of Arkansas/US Geological Survey.*

Further to the east, in northern Mesopotamia, many archaeological sites, particularly large mounded tells dating to the Early Bronze Age (third millennium BC) are surrounded by radial systems of ancient roadways, commonly termed *hollow ways* in archaeological literature (figure 16.3).

First documented in aerial photography (Van Liere and Lauffray 1954), they have been most thoroughly mapped using CORONA satellite imagery (Ur 2003; Wilkinson et al. 2010). These features are hypothesized to have been formed by the frequent movement of people and herds of animals between settlements and rangelands (Wilkinson 1993). Although not field boundaries in the ordinary sense, hollow ways likely formed because traffic was constrained on either side by cultivated fields. As herds reached the edge of the cultivated zone, dominated by dry-farmed cereals, they would disperse and the hollow ways would terminate. Hollow ways therefore are particularly valuable in reconstructing the extent of ancient agricultural systems in this region because they demarcate the edge of intensively cultivated fields during the third millennium BC (Wilkinson et al. 2007; Wilkinson et al. 2010). Recent discoveries of similar features over a much wider region and spanning several millennia may indicate the existence of similar agricultural strategies where hollow ways are found (Casana 2013).

While conventional aerial and satellite photography remains a powerful resource for discovery and mapping of ancient field systems, recent studies have explored the potential of high-resolution aircraft-mounted sensors to reveal more subtle features that are otherwise invisible. Analysis of Daedalus multispectral images has proven particularly valuable in a number of studies (e.g., Challis et al. 2009; Powlesland et al. 2006) because many field boundaries are evident in near-infrared or thermal image bands but cannot be recognized in the visible light spectrum. Ancient field boundaries also often have topographic expression seen in subtle ridges and depressions that sometimes mark their edges, caused by the accumulation of stones and soil on uncultivated boundaries or the gullies that form at the edge of plowed zones. A number of studies have successfully employed the use of LiDAR to document field boundaries with even very small topographic relief (e.g., Bewley et al. 2005). Such a technique has proven particularly powerful in mapping ancient fields located in areas now covered by forest or dense vegetation, areas where traditional aerial photography would be unlikely to reveal much of interest (figure 16.4). In the Franche-Comté and Meurthe-et-Moselle regions of northeastern France, medieval and Roman fields with associated settlements and other installations have been discovered below dense forest cover that would make recognition of such features otherwise nearly impossible (Devereux et al. 2005; Georges-Leroy et al. 2009).

A study in the coastal region of Mauguio in southern France has achieved similarly good results (Poirier et al. 2013), as has a study at the site of Jezreel, Israel (Ebeling et al. 2012), suggesting that LiDAR will become an increasingly powerful tool in Mediterranean environments.

Similar techniques have been employed in the New World, as at the Maya site of Caracol, Belize, where extensive systems of terraced agricultural fields have been documented using LiDAR in areas now covered by rainforest (Chase et al. 2011). Elsewhere in the Maya lowlands, field systems characterized by rectilinear ridges have also been documented using conventional aerial photography in areas cleared of forest for modern agriculture (Siemens and Puleston 1972). The dense forest found throughout much of the region continues to be a challenge to studies of pre-European-contact agriculture, although

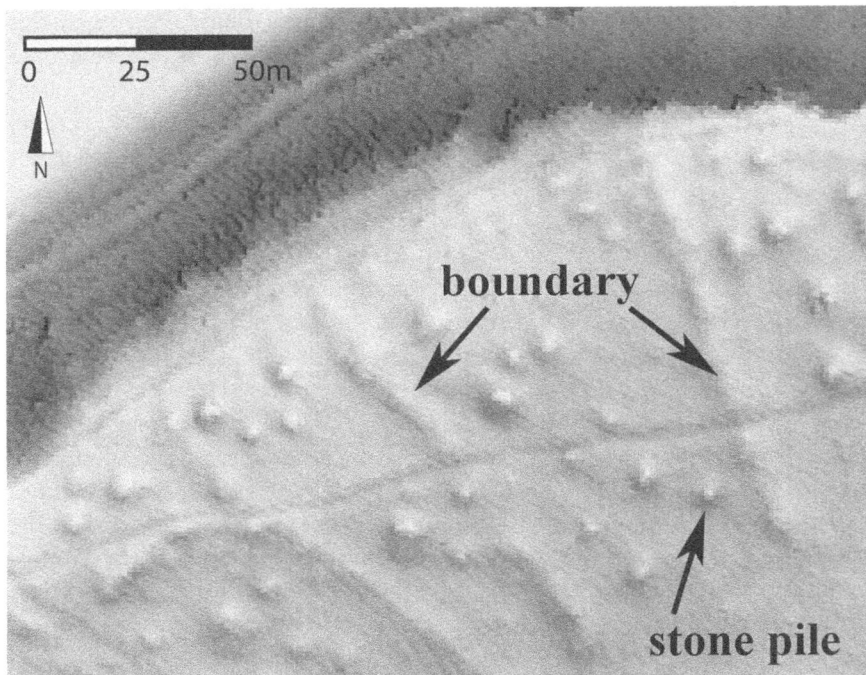

FIGURE 16.4. *LiDAR data showing medieval field systems below dense forest cover in northeastern France. Image credit: Rachel Opitz.*

a system of rotating cultivation or swidden agriculture that was practiced in some parts of the New World would likely leave little evidence behind, certainly not much that would be detectable in remote sensing data sets. During times when agricultural production was intensified, in periods of peak population densities and political organization, agricultural field systems are more likely to be visible in remote sensing data.

In the Andes, extensive prehistoric field systems are preserved in many areas and the sparse vegetation of high deserts enables easy recognition of field systems in aerial and satellite imagery. In the Altiplano, a high plateau in the Andes bordering modern Peru and Bolivia and centered around Lake Titicaca, extensive remains of field systems can be documented through remote sensing (Erickson 2000). In the low-lying marsh zones on the shores of the shallow lake, countless oblong, raised fields are found preserved adjacent to and submerged by the lake, dating largely to the Tiwanaku period (AD 500–1100). On the steep slopes surrounding the lake basin, systems of terracing dating to this period and later are also preserved. The existence of these two distinct approaches to agricultural sustainability likely helped communities cope with the highly variable environmental conditions in the region.

Further to the south, remarkable systems of ridged fields have been documented in coastal regions in central Chile. These fields, dating to the period from around AD 1200–1600, are argued to have been an agricultural technology imported from the north, perhaps from the Lake Titicaca region itself, owing to the obvious parallels between them and the raised fields of the central Andes (Dillehay et al. 2007). It is thought that these fields were dedicated to growing potatoes, tubers, and beans, the staple crops of pre-European South American agriculture. These fields appear clearly on satellite imagery, even appearing in modern commercial QuickBird or IKONOS satellite images visible through GoogleEarth, and thus one would expect many other such features to be visible throughout the region.

WATER MANAGEMENT FEATURES

Water management features related to ancient agricultural production, particularly those involving irrigation, are frequently detectable in satellite imagery or aerial photography. Areas suitable for intensive irrigation in the distant past are also generally good places for modern irrigation projects and, across the globe, such initiatives have sadly destroyed remnants of ancient systems. Fortunately, many ancient irrigation networks can be detected on historic satellite imagery or aerial photography, and these resources have proved critical to their documentation in recent years. For example, in the Khuzistan region of southwestern Iran, extensive networks of ancient irrigation canals are visible on CORONA satellite images from the 1960s, crossing vast areas of the plain (figure 16.5).

These systems are difficult to date directly, but their close association with settlements of the Parthian and Sassanian periods (ca. 200 BC–AD 650) suggests they are contemporary (Alizadeh et al. 2004). Like ancient field boundaries, what crops were being cultivated in these areas cannot be directly inferred from the preserved irrigation network, but they nonetheless attest to a substantial increase in intensive agricultural production in the region during a specific historic period. They also reveal a sophisticated understanding of hydraulic engineering that served as a model for the institution of a new irrigation project in the same region beginning in the 1970s (Kouchoukos 2001). Today, most of these features have been obscured or destroyed by modern land use (Casana 2013). Similarly, in the Orontes valley of western Syria and

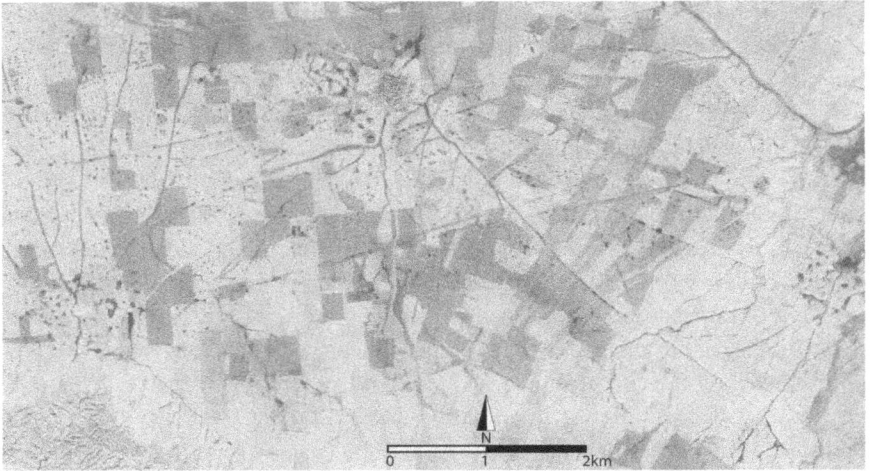

FIGURE 16.5. *Irrigation channels in Khuzistan Province, southwest Iran, visible on a 1966 CORONA satellite image. These massive features, probably dating to the Parthian and Sassanian periods (150 BC–AD 600) have been destroyed by modern irrigation in the region. Image courtesy of CORONA Atlas of the Middle East, University of Arkansas/US Geological Survey.*

southern Turkey, major irrigation canals can be seen on CORONA imagery from the 1960s throughout the river basin (Casana 2003, 2013). Interestingly, most low-lying plains of the river valley were submerged below permanent or seasonal marshland during recent centuries, until they were mechanically drained in the 1950s–1960s as part of nationally sponsored irrigation projects. It is likely that some of the ancient systems visible in the region similarly drained ancient marshlands, and thus reconstructing the history of marsh formation and drainage is critical to a broader reconstruction of the plant communities and environments in which ancient people subsisted.

In intensively irrigated zones, such as southern Mesopotamia, various networks of ancient irrigation crosscut one another with such dizzying complexity that peeling apart their relative age represents a serious challenge to archaeologists. Several recent studies have relied on the topographic expression of these features to aid in their mapping because larger canals possess sizable levees or upcast mounds that are easily detectable in remote sensing data sets. Hritz and Wilkinson (2006) utilize relatively low-spatial-resolution digital elevation data derived from the Shuttle Radar Topography Mission (SRTM), a global, 90-m digital elevation model (DEM) produced by a radar carried aboard the Space Shuttle in 2000 and now widely relied upon as a standard basemap. Despite the coarse spatial resolution of the data, many of the largest canal features were successfully mapped. As higher-resolution digital elevation data become available, particularly as derived from historic stereo images such as CORONA (Casana and Cothren 2008), more detailed analyses of these canal networks will likely prove possible.

In many arid regions of the world where cultivation took place in the past, water management features are also evident in high-resolution aerial and satellite imagery, often in the form of stone walls and check dams that are part of runoff systems of agriculture. In order to take full advantage of very sparse rainfall, ancient people often built systems of stone walls, sometimes running for miles across the landscape, that were carefully designed to channel surface runoff into small fields. By concentrating precipitation that falls over large areas into small plots, agriculture can often be supported in regions that would otherwise be far too arid to sustain human settlement. In the Libyan desert, systems of runoff farming dating to the Roman period are abundant and well-preserved, as the region saw little settlement following the fourth century AD (Gilbertson and Hunt 1996). The existence of these fields implies the presence of a very different agricultural landscape than is found in the region today, and helps to contextualize paleoethnobotanical studies in the area (Barker 2002). Similarly, extensive systems of runoff farming have been documented in the Hadramawt region of Yemen, where current rainfall is insufficient to support even this type of desert agriculture (Harrower 2008). Harrower's (2010) innovative study of these systems relies on detailed topographic data and surface flow modeling to determine how successful the runoff systems found in the region might have been under different rainfall conditions in the past.

Ancient irrigation features in the Americas have received less attention than those in the Old World, but such features can often be detected using a variety of remote sensing data sets. In central Mexico, a classic study, perhaps the first to explore the value of infrared imagery in archaeology, successfully documented canals surrounding Teotihuacán (Gumerman and Neely 1972). Water management features related to irrigation agriculture have now been documented in aerial and satellite imagery in many parts of Mexico and the Andean highlands (e.g., Lane 2009). Similar small canal networks are also known throughout much of the arid American Southwest where they have been well-documented using historic aerial photos from the 1930s (Friedman et al. 2003). Many of these canals have now been obscured by modern land use, and in many areas deep sedimentation resulting from the imposition of European farming technologies buried irrigation networks (Damp et al. 2002).

A debate continues as to the exact date of the canals, with some scholars arguing they postdate European settlement in the region, but most research now suggests that the canals attest to a phase of intensive cultivation that was contemporary with the expansion of Puebloan settlements during the early second millennium AD.

THE ENVIRONMENTAL CONTEXTS OF AGRICULTURE

Numerous studies have used remote sensing data sets to document environmental or other features that offer indirect evidence for ancient agricultural strategies. One example comes from Pournelle's (2007) study of southern Mesopotamia, in which she argues that the earliest urban centers of the fourth millennium BC emerged not within a farmed, agricultural hinterland as had been argued by generations of archaeologists, but rather within marshy, deltaic environments. Since the pioneering work of Robert McCormick Adams (1981), archaeologists have believed that early Mesopotamian cities relied on a patchwork of resources including irrigated cereal and garden agriculture along rivers and canals, sheep and goat pastoralism in hinterlands, and exploitation of rich marsh environments to the south of the urban heartland (e.g., Algaze 2001). Based on analysis of geomorphic features visible in CORONA satellite imagery from the 1960s, Pournelle argues instead that these cities were built on islands surrounded by deltaic marsh. If proven correct, the theory would radically alter our idea of cultivation and subsistence in the world's first cities. On the other hand, it is possible that the marsh-related features Pournelle has documented formed relatively recently, and thus may postdate occupation at the sites in question. Expanding marshland is known to have formed from subsidence or sinking of the Tigris-Euphrates delta, a result of increased sedimentation during the later Holocene, and could also have been influenced by changes in fluvial discharge. Nonetheless, Pournelle's work offers an example of how analysis of remote sensing-derived environmental data can be essential to properly interpreting ancient landscapes.

In a similar case, Sever and Irwin's (2003) widely cited research relies on remote sensing data sets, particularly those derived from multispectral Landsat imagery, to document the environments surrounding ancient Maya settlements in the Petén region of Guatemala. The area is now dominated by seasonal and permanent swamps known as *bajos* within which there are few places suitable for permanent settlement and little opportunity for agricultural production. A long-standing debate in the region surrounds the extent to which slash-and-burn or swidden agricultural practices that dominated early centuries of Maya history in the region were replaced by more intensive cultivation strategies as populations peaked in the Late Classic period (AD 650–800). Research using multispectral image data enabled Sever and Irwin to map the extent of the bajos. They were then able to identify topographic rises within the swamps using high-resolution (5-m) STAR *3i* topographic data, collected using a specialized aircraft sensor similar to LiDAR. Though comparison with previously documented site locations and ground truthing a sample of the features, all elevated islands within the bajos were then shown to have been occupied during the Late Classic period, and many of these islands were connected by ancient causeways or canals that were found on Landsat and high-resolution commercial IKONOS imagery. Results suggest that bajos landscapes were indeed intensively cultivated by Late Classic Maya communities. Research by geomorphologists and archaeologists working in the region now confirms remote sensing-based interpretations, having found conclusive evidence that the bajos were likely transformed into agrarian landscapes during this period (Dunning et al. 2002). Emerging work with LiDAR imagery, like that discussed above (Chase et al. 2011), will likely contribute to growing understanding of agricultural activities in the region.

MODELING LANDSCAPE PHENOLOGY

A variety of multispectral satellite sensors offer the opportunity to conduct more sophisticated analyses of the regional distribution in plant communities as well as to document intra- and interannual variability in vegetation, what is sometimes termed *landscape phenology*. Most of these approaches utilize a Normalized Differential Vegetation Index (NDVI) to represent plant health. Photosynthesis in most plants causes them to absorb much of the red spectrum of light (650–750 nm), whereas the cellular structure of the healthy vegetation results in reflection of most near infrared (NIR) light (750–1400 nm). This differential effect of growing vegetation can be highlighted by computing a simple ratio between red and infrared wavelengths according to the following formula: NDVI = (NIR − red)/(NIR + red). Many satellite sensors can produce NDVI data, as long as they record reflectance in both the red and near infrared spectra, but sensors with high temporal resolution (i.e., those offering many readings of the same area over time) can illustrate seasonal growth and dormancy cycles for plants, and these can in turn be used to build characterizations of different regional plant communities and the health of those communities under different environmental conditions (Weier and Herring 2000). The very high temporal resolution of some satellite sensors, particularly the AVHRR and MODIS, offer the capability to analyze cycles of plant growth and the effects that climate variability and anthropogenic activities have had on vegetation over the past several decades. In the case of AVHRR, the satellite provides only very coarse spatial resolution at 1 km, but has collected daily images of the entire globe since 1978. Processing these data sets can be challenging for non-specialists and they contain many errors and artifacts that must be cleaned through processing, but corrected versions are available (Tucker et al. 2005).

Even at very low spatial resolution, AVHRR data provide us with an unparalleled view of the response of vegetation to differing climatic regimes and land use practices. A study by Kouchoukos (2001) demonstrates how these data can be used to classify land use and land cover patterns in southern Mesopotamia into a variety of categories based on cycles of plant growth that are in turn related to differing irrigation and rainfall regimes. As part of a NASA-funded project at the University of Arkansas's Center for Advanced Spatial Technologies, we use a similar approach to explore patterns of vegetation growth across the northern Fertile Cresent, a zone extending from the eastern Mediterranean to northern Iraq.

We start with a normalized data set provided by Tucker et al. (2005) in which NDVI values are produced in 8×8-km cells for every 15-day period from 1981 to 2006. We then compute an average NDVI value for each cell in each 15-day period of the year to produce a picture of mean annual plant growth cycles. The resultant data set, essentially a 24-band raster image of NDVI values, illustrate different regional trends in seasonal greening and plant growth, as related to precipitation, temperature, and land use. The raster image is then processed with a standard classification algorithm, categorizing all 8×8-km cells into one of 14 distinct classes, each with a unique pattern of plant growth (figure 16.6). These classes correspond fairly well to a more qualitative assessment of different plant communities, with coastal mountains, irrigated plains, semiarid desert steppe, and other regions appearing quite clearly, but offer a far more detailed view of differences among subregions. Archaeological sites located within these differing vegetated landscapes can then be evaluated to look for systematic differences in the types of plants and animals that ancient residents exploited or relied upon. For example, in the Orontes valley region of the northern Levant, results show two spikes in plant growth annually, essentially offering two harvests each year. Areas on the fringe of the desert, by contrast, show a high spike in annual greening once per year, with conditions close to those in the central, hyperarid desert during summer months. Viewing these data across the 25-year period included in our analysis shows that

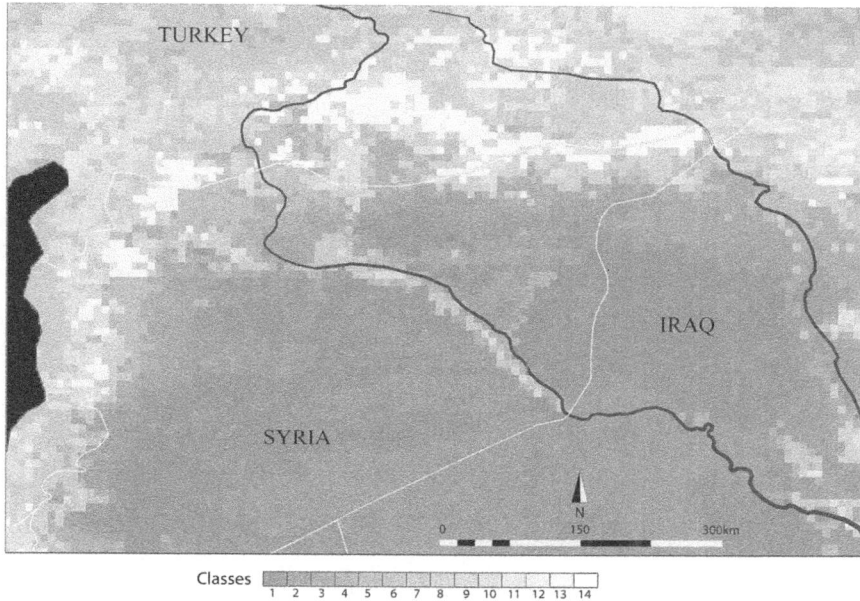

FIGURE 16.6. *Map illustrating 14 distinct vegetation classes in the northern Fertile Crescent, based on analysis of mean NDVI values showing seasonal variability in plant growth, as controlled by climate and land use. Cells are 8×8 km, derived from AVHRR data from 1981–2006. Image credit: Brian Bunker.*

there are also significant differences in plant greening under differing climate regimes, for example with highly variable greening evident in steppe areas along the northern fringe of the Syrian desert. Such high variability in marginal steppe zones would surely have been a key factor to ancient residents, as agricultural production must have been less reliable on a year-to-year basis in these areas as compared to other regions (figure 16.7).

It is difficult for standard classification methods to capture the complexity of a multidimensional data set like that produced by a long-time series of AVHRR and MODIS imagery, but more sophisticated methods for classifying data, such as the segmentation approach taken by Bunker (2013), offer many additional possibilities for evaluating trends in vegetation health and agricultural patterns.

Of course, remote sensing data show only the modern distribution of plant communities, and the ancient landscape may have been substantially different as a result of climate change, deforestation, soil erosion and landscape

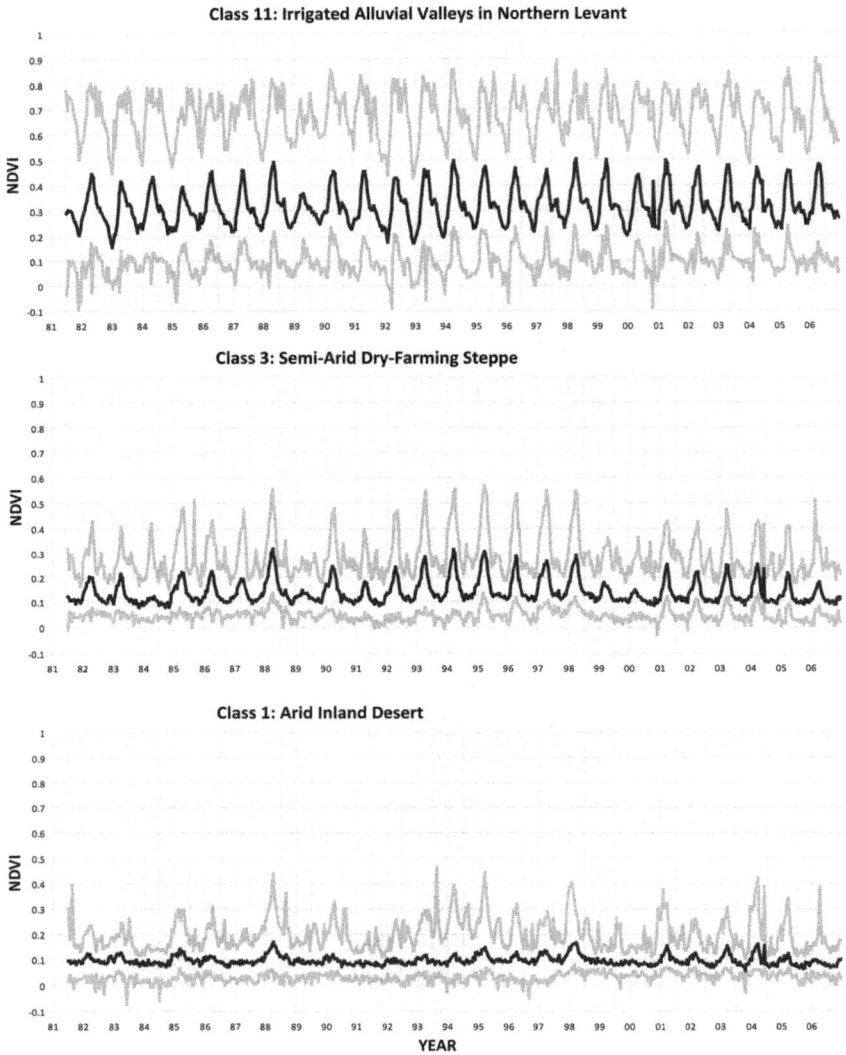

FIGURE 16.7. *NDVI values from 1981 to 2006 for three distinct vegetation classes as illustrated in Figure 16.6. Data reflect greening cycles for vegetation in the irrigated Orontes River valley (A), the dry-farmed steppe in eastern Syria (B), and the arid inland desert (C). Dark center lines in graphs represent mean values, with maximum and minimum values for the class indicated in gray. Image credit: Brian Bunker.*

transformations, importation of modern crops and invasive species, and other processes. However, exploring the various classes of modern plant community distribution in the region enables us to establish a baseline for modern mean conditions, as well as a picture of how the landscape responded to recent droughts or periods of higher precipitation. These extreme conditions can then be used to better evaluate the possible impacts of past climate change, evidenced through a variety of paleoclimatic indicators. These data also provide a powerful complement to the type of statistical analyses of faunal and botanical remains undertaken by Smith and Munro (2009).

FUTURE DIRECTIONS

This brief review of the role that archaeological remote sensing plays in building a landscape context for paleoethnobotanical research has highlighted recent work in a number of areas including detection and mapping of ancient agricultural field systems and water management features, analysis of the environments within which archaeological sites are located, and modeling vegetation dynamics as a means both to explore the spatial distribution of various plant communities and to suggest how past climate change might have affected these distributions. Across much of the globe, such studies remain in their infancy, but with the growing availability of remote sensing data sets and the increasing ease with which these images can be processed and analyzed, we can expect many new discoveries in coming years. For example, across much of eastern North America, little attention has been paid to prehistoric field systems, but those few that have been documented, such as the ridged field systems dating to the Late Woodland period in central Wisconsin (Gartner 1999), could potentially be detected on aerial or satellite imagery. In the intensively cultivated river valleys of Asia, including the Indus, Yangtze, and Yellow river valleys, little work has been done to document ancient agriculture fields via remote sensing, but many of the same methods described here could have great potential in those regions. Similarly, the application of LiDAR and other high-resolution airborne sensors has immense possibilities for the documentation of more subtle features or those that are obscured by vegetation, as in the Amazon Basin, Central Europe, and Sub-Saharan Africa. Ongoing research in these and other regions of the world will undoubtedly continue to provide an invaluable context for paleoethnobotanical research in the years to come.

PART V

Interpretation

17

*Human Behavioral Ecology
and Paleoethnobotany*

KRISTEN J. GREMILLION

At the core of human behavioral ecology (HBE) lies
the principle that Darwinian evolutionary theory has
something important to say about human decision
making. Humans, like other animals, have been shaped
over millennia of natural selection to behave in ways
that, overall and in the long term, help them to survive and potentially raise reproductively successful offspring (Smith and Winterhalder 1992; Winterhalder
and Goland 1997). Unlike other animals, humans have
a degree of behavioral flexibility that allows them to
adjust to virtually any environment. They also have culture, a system of social transmission of information that
does much of the work that individual learning and
somatic adaptations must do in other animals (Boyd
and Richerson 1985, 1995; Flinn 1997; Richerson and
Boyd 2005). These characteristics are frequently invoked
to point out the unsuitability of evolutionary models of
human behavior. However, plasticity of behavior and
cumulative social learning (and the cognitive mechanisms that support them) are themselves evolved traits.
The complexity and great variability of human behavior
across space and time is therefore nonrandom, and can
be at least partly understood in terms of broad, species-
specific biases in decision making.

Why paleoethnobotanists themselves have not more
often turned to HBE for assistance in formulating and
testing hypotheses is not entirely clear. Most applications of human behavioral ecology to questions about
past human-plant relationships have emerged from a

DOI: 10.5876/9781607323167.c017

broader interest in evolutionary theory and subsistence change, without necessarily being informed by the technical expertise of trained paleoethnobotanists. These same specialists may avoid HBE for a variety of reasons, some historical and some ideological or theoretical. Applications of HBE highlight the difficulty of reconstructing past plant use and environments from material remains (see discussion of methodological issues below). In many respects, however, HBE is at no particular methodological disadvantage as compared to strict empiricism or more traditional kinds of hypothesis testing.

My goal here is to demonstrate, through discussion of several case studies, that HBE has contributed to the advancement of paleoethnobotanical knowledge. First, I outline the research strategy of HBE and discuss how it deploys models to increase understanding of past phenomena. I describe the foraging models that have most frequently been used in conjunction with paleoethnobotanical findings—prey choice, patch choice, the marginal value theorem, and variations on the central place foraging model. I also discuss models that move beyond efficiency maximization by considering situations in which reducing risk might be the preferred goal. Finally, I present case studies selected from the published literature in which paleoethnobotanical evidence plays a crucial role in the application or testing of specific models.

THE RESEARCH STRATEGY OF HUMAN BEHAVIORAL ECOLOGY

Evolutionary ecology can be defined simply as the study of "evolution and adaptive design in ecological context" (Smith and Winterhalder 1992:3). Behavioral ecology specifically asks "why certain patterns of behavior have emerged and continue to persist and looks to their socioecological context in seeking answers" (Bird and O'Connell 2006:144). The framework of HBE is set up to investigate adaptation (which does not automatically brand it as "adaptationist"; Potochnik 2009). It proposes causal relationships between behavioral choices and natural selection acting on phenotypic variation. The mechanism of inheritance need not be specified, as long as offspring tend to resemble their parents more than they resemble a randomly selected individual. HBE is therefore fully compatible with the acknowledgment of human agency and creativity; it simply recognizes that these phenomena are not unconstrained by evolutionary history. Nor does its application preclude the acknowledgment of biases in the transmission of cultural traits that can produce decidedly nonadaptive complexes of behaviors and beliefs (Richerson and Boyd 1992). HBE is a specialized field that studies behavioral adaptation without making the claim that all behavior is adaptive.

The employment of HBE models is regarded with enthusiasm by some archaeologists and with considerable skepticism by others. HBE arouses suspicion that theoretical models are forcing interpretations in a particular direction by assuming economic rationality and material causality (Smith 2009a, 2011a; Zeder 2012; Zeder and Smith 2009). Some believe that HBE entails genetic determinism, or dehumanization and denial of agency, or that humans have broken free of the constraints imposed on other animal species by evolutionary history. It is not my intention to mount a full-fledged defense of HBE. Readers interested in the details of this ongoing debate are invited to consult the many publications that touch on it (Bettinger 2006; Winterhalder 2002; Winterhalder and Kennett 2006). However, because many of the criticisms of it are based on misconceptions about its goals and epistemological claims, I offer a brief discussion of the justification for the use of models as research tools. I then move on to a consideration of some frequently used HBE models and their application to questions of paleoethnobotanical significance.

THE STRATEGY OF MODELING IN HBE: RATIONALE AND LIMITATIONS

Why Models are Useful in HBE

It is important to keep in mind that HBE as a theoretical perspective is not coeval with the practice of modeling, nor should it be conflated with any particular model, such as the diet breadth model of optimal foraging theory (Bird and O'Connell 2006:144). Although HBE uses models to connect data and theory, to generate hypotheses, and to organize thinking (Winterhalder 2002), in principle it is not tied to any particular set of methods. In practice, HBE models are usually founded on microeconomic principles such as optimization, efficiency maximization, and risk minimization (Bird and O'Connell 2006; Smith and Winterhalder 1992; Winterhalder and Goland 1997; Winterhalder and Kennett 2006; Winterhalder and Smith 2000). These variables have a logical relationship to fitness: efficiency translates into savings of time or energy that can be invested in other fitness-enhancing activities, such as mating; risk avoidance increases probability of survival in variable environments. Optimization balances tradeoffs between alternative choices so as to meet needs at the lowest possible cost, whether in time, energy, or risk.

Models are intentionally simplified representations of real-world phenomena that seek to preserve the effects of key variables while reducing nonessential details (Winterhalder 2002). The benefits of a model-based research strategy are many, and have been discussed in detail elsewhere (Beatty 1980; Godfrey-Smith 2006; Odenbaugh 2005; Winterhalder 2002). Models can be used heuristically (to organize thinking, define research problems, and develop plans for data collection) or can be mobilized to formulate and test hypotheses (Winterhalder 2002). Building a model requires the researcher to make assumptions explicit and to assign specific costs and benefits to different behavioral options (Winterhalder and Goland 1997). The payoff of all this work is that even when the model fails to make accurate predictions, we can systematically examine the points at which it is vulnerable. This process can reveal unexpected relationships or raise new questions to be pursued (Winterhalder 2002).

Limitations and Pitfalls

Like any research strategy, HBE has limitations; pushed beyond its limits, it will yield results that are unhelpful at best. Models are tools for learning about the real world and can yield only limited insights without explicit testing against data. Testing often takes the form of a comparison of predictions and observations, but can also evaluate the model's internal logic, assumptions, or how well it conforms to theory (Winterhalder 2002). The models themselves are neither true nor false; it is more appropriate to regard them in terms of goodness of fit to the empirical case at hand (Odenbaugh 2005). One must be vigilant against the temptation to reify the models themselves (as if they were templates for behavior) or to tinker with them until they produce the desired result. A good rule of thumb is to change models only in ways that make them more testable, not less so (Bell 1981).

Foraging Theory and Optimization

Optimal foraging theory, which includes a family of models developed within evolutionary ecology, is an important toolbox for the investigation of plant use from an HBE perspective. The diet breadth (or prey choice) and patch choice models were the first to be developed in ecology (Winterhalder 2002). Other popular foraging models predict the optimal use of space—for example, in which resource patches to forage (the patch choice model) and how long to stay in each patch (the marginal value theorem). For a thorough discussion of these models and their archaeological applications see Bettinger (1991). Diet breadth and marginal value have both been applied fruitfully to questions about the use of plant resources, although explicit tests of the models are rare due in part to the challenge of reconstructing subsistence behavior from paleoethnobotanical data (see discussion of methodological issues below). The central place foraging model, which traces relationships between travel distance, load characteristics, and economic efficiency, has been useful in studies of logistical foraging for plant resources. Similar microeconomic concepts inform applications of linear programming to model optimal solutions to food choice in past environments. More recently, investigators have turned to foraging models that consider the impact of environmental variability on food choice.

HBE AND THE PALEOETHNOBOTANICAL RECORD: METHODOLOGICAL ISSUES

The models and methods of HBE are relevant to paleoethnobotany because the interactions between humans and plants have a long evolutionary history that has been shaped by natural and sociocultural environments (Gremillion 1996a, 2002b; Gremillion and Piperno 2009a, 2009b). Dietary adaptations and the occupation and use of landscapes are the kinds of interactions of greatest interest to prehistorians. However, HBE can just as readily be applied to questions about other uses of plants. Choices of plant medicines and construction materials, for example, are likely to have effects on the survival and social success of the individuals who make them, leading to the differential accumulation of traditions regarding these aspects of plant use.

HBE bridges existing data and general theory by positing causal relationships between key variables such as food choice, settlement patterns, resource distributions, and the population dynamics of human and plant populations. Researchers have sometimes turned to HBE as a source of explanations for paleoethnobotanical patterns, such as the origins of food production or a shift to a more varied diet, that have already been well documented archaeologically or historically (e.g., see Barlow 2002, 2006; Bettinger et al. 1997; Broughton et al. 2010; Denham and Barton 2006; Gardner 1997; Gremillion 1996a, 1998; Gremillion and Piperno 2009a; Piperno 2006a; Piperno and Pearsall 1998a; Stiner et al. 2000). In this interpretive mode of application, well-confirmed models are extended to propose an explanation for a previously unexplained pattern (Winterhalder 2002). The models may be quantitative, taking the form of simulations using realistic estimated values, or qualitative assessments of the direction and relative magnitude of observed historical changes as instantiations of the modeled relationships. Perhaps less frequently, the researcher takes an evaluative stance, testing the model by developing hypotheses, making predictions, and collecting or analyzing the relevant data (Winterhalder 2002). The test may be of the model's assumptions (e.g., that crop yields decline over time as a function of soil fertility) as well as hypotheses derived from the model (such as the frequency and timing of village relocation and the corresponding distribution of artifacts across a landscape). Whatever the initial stimulus for or direction of the research, evaluation of model and data is an ongoing process.

A number of methodological issues impact all archaeological applications of HBE and its models. One of the key benefits of the modeling strategy is especially challenging for archaeologists, namely the exploration of mismatches between model and data as a way to isolate and probe important relationships between variables. It can be difficult to determine why predictions fail because there are many parameters that are vulnerable to inaccuracy (Gremillion 2002b). Neither the behavior nor the environmental context are directly observable, but rather have to be reconstructed from fragmentary evidence. Another potential snag is that foraging models predict individual decisions contingent on immediate environmental circumstances, whereas the archaeological record often represents cumulative decisions of many individuals over long periods of time (Grayson and Delpech 1998). Testing requires us to assume that these aggregations of material remains adequately reflect trends in food choice.

Application of HBE to paleoethnobotanical data has lagged behind similar work in zooarchaeology. One reason for this pattern is the difficulty of accurately reconstructing plant use from material remains. Zooarchaeologists have developed methodological tools that permit them to reduce data derived from bone assemblages in ways that allow models to be tested without too much loss of information. One example of this trend is the use of mammal body size as a proxy for resource ranking (Broughton 1994a, 1994b; Grayson and Cannon 1999), which obviates the need for detailed calculations of energy content and procurement costs for each prey type in order to predict optimal diet breadth. Researchers have also developed ratios of large-bodied to small-bodied prey and of fast-moving to slow-moving animals in order to assess diet optimization (Stiner et al. 2000). No comparable methods exist for plant foods. In part, this situation reflects the fragmentary nature of the archaeobotanical record and the difficulty of estimating food quantity or subsistence importance from plant remains. There is much more variation between plants in anatomical and chemical characteristics that have nutritional significance than there is among vertebrates. For this reason, there is no equivalent of the body size proxy to use for ranking plant resources; costs and benefits must be calculated experimentally or from ethnographic data for each taxon (Grayson and Cannon 1999). Several studies have addressed the definition of plant resources by grouping them into economic or ecological categories such as domesticates, highly ranked versus low-ranked seed producers, underground plant parts, or mast.

CASE STUDIES

In order to illustrate how HBE can be put to work to enhance understanding of paleoethnobotanical data, I describe a number of case studies. I have selected them to be reasonably representative of the variety of models and modes of application currently in use. However, this discussion necessarily eliminates important details that the interested reader can find in the original publications. There are also many excellent studies that cannot be summarized in this brief chapter; I cite these at appropriate points to direct the interested reader.

I begin with research that seeks optimal solutions to the problem of acquiring plant resources. These studies pose questions about which plant foods should be targeted and (in some cases) how much they should contribute to human diets under specific environmental conditions. Studies of resource depression, in which human harvesting depletes a plant (or animal) population, have been particularly useful in interpreting the archaeological record of changes in diet breadth. A second set of applications focuses on the problem of central place foraging, asking how far people should travel to collection sites and what size and quality of load they should bring back to a central place. These studies have important implications for how we interpret archaeobotanical data.

Diet Optimization

One of the most persistent questions in paleoethnobotanical research is why people in the past chose to collect, consume, and even produce some plant foods while apparently ignoring others. To explore the implications of these choices, researchers have frequently turned to the diet breadth model (hereafter, DBM). This is a very simple and robust model that predicts which prey items a forager will pursue on encounter under different conditions of prey density. The forager in the model encounters a potential prey item and faces a decision: whether to pursue (or harvest) it or continue searching for something better (more highly ranked in the amount of energy gained per unit time spent in pursuit and handling). All else being equal, the best option would be to wait for the top-ranked food item, say a large mammal. But doing so entails added costs of continuing the food quest, accumulating additional costs without reaping any benefits. If that favored food item is rare, so much time is spent searching for it that the forager can do better by being less selective than she can by continuing the search. The optimal solution is to pursue the animal (or harvest the plant) only if doing so will yield a higher average rate of return than continuing to search for something more profitable. Thus the model predicts that as higher-ranked resources decline in abundance, diet breadth will increase to admit less profitable items in rank order until the point at which adding the next item will actually reduce the average return rate for foraging despite the savings in search costs. The optimum diet breadth is that which yields the best average return rate possible by managing this tradeoff between search costs and pursuit costs (Bettinger 1991; Kelly 1995; Pyke et al. 1977; Stephens and Krebs 1986).

Diet Choice and Plant Husbandry

It may seem odd that so many applications of foraging theory in archaeology have been inspired by questions about the origins and economics of farming (Barlow 2002, 2006; Denham and Barton 2006; Foster 2003; Gremillion 2002a; Gremillion and Piperno 2009a; Keegan 1986; Kennett et al. 2006; Piperno 2006a; Piperno and Pearsall 1998a; Winterhalder and Goland 1993, 1997; Winterhalder and Kennett 2006). Yet the robusticity and generality of the DBM allow it to be extended to accommodate resources that are managed or produced rather than harvested. Efforts to do so have generated some creative approaches to modifying the DBM and have yielded significant insights into the economics and evolutionary significance of plant husbandry.

Gremillion (1996b, 1998, 2002a, 2002b, 2004) has used the DBM as a platform from which to examine the rise of seed crop cultivation in eastern North America, specifically in the uplands along the western slope of the Appalachians in eastern Kentucky. Here, rockshelters with excellent conditions for plant preservation have yielded some of the earliest and most comprehensive collections of plant remains from the Archaic (8000–1000 BC) and Woodland (1000 BC–AD 400) periods. Paleoethnobotanical research has indicated that storage and consumption of small starchy and oily seeds (including goosefoot, *Chenopodium berlandieri* Moq.; marshelder, *Iva annua* L., and maygrass, *Phalaris caroliniana* Walt.), many of which show morphological signs of domestication, intensified after ca. 1000 BC. This change seems puzzling in an environment generally rich in mast from hickory, oak, chestnut, butternut, and walnut, the refuse of which is common in archaeological middens. By comparison to these nuts, which can be quite profitable, seeds seem like an inefficient choice for an optimal diet. In a series of publications, Gremillion (1993, 1994, 1996b, 1998) addressed this apparent contradiction by exploring the consequences of changing forest composition for optimal diet choice. For example, the DBM predicts that an increase in abundance of hickory, oak, and chestnut yields under a regime of anthropogenic burning would have led to a narrow focus on the highest-ranked of these important plant resources, namely hickory, at the expense of the more costly acorn (Gremillion 1998). She suggests that this ecological factor partly explains the drop in representation of acorn shell on archaeological sites after the appearance of seed crops, but that the nutritional similarity of starchy seeds and acorns might have caused them to swap roles. The latter hypothesis was shown to be unlikely following a subsequent analysis of the interactions between abundance, nutrient content, and processing costs using linear programming; however, the same analysis supported the plausibility of acorn and other nuts coming into use from time to time when hickory was scarce (Gremillion 2002b). Gremillion (2004) also considered the costs of processing plant foods and the impact of technology on their return rates, concluding that whereas some nuts could offer high return rates with improved technology, the profitability of small seeds was consistently constrained by the time-consuming tasks of winnowing, pounding, and cooking. One insight to emerge from this analysis is that stored seeds would have had a much higher rank during the winter, when other foods were scarce, especially in years when mast yields were low. Small seeds are relatively cheap to harvest and need not have interfered with collection of other foods; processing could have been postponed until winter or spring, when energy was scarce and time was freed from many competing activities (Gremillion 2004).

Piperno and Pearsall (1998a) and Piperno (Gremillion and Piperno 2009a; Piperno 2006a) put the DBM to work in a similar way, using it to propose explanations for the increasing importance of tuber crops in the Neotropics. They propose changes in human diets accompanying the Pleistocene-Holocene transition. Late Pleistocene large-game populations diminished as savannah-scrub was replaced by seasonal wet-dry forests. With the decline in abundance of these top-ranked resources, human diets expanded to include foods previously ignored, such as tubers. These newly adopted resources were concentrated in dense patches, which had two important consequences: low handling costs and an abundance sufficient to support human population growth. Here, as in Gremillion's work, the DBM is used as an interpretive framework to explain the first steps toward food production as a response to environmental change.

The DBM can help to make sense of switches between specialization on one or a few resources and a more eclectic diet. However, it assumes that the profitability (resource rank) of a given plant food remains stable as it is being harvested. Barlow, in her study of Fremont maize farming, takes into account the diminishing returns characteristic of agriculture (Barlow 2002, 2006). The archaeological culture of the Great Basin of the United States known as Fremont is distinctive in showing great spatial variability in the economic importance of maize agriculture within a mixed foraging-farming economy. Barlow assesses the return rates that might be expected from Fremont maize cultivation, using data from Latin American traditional agricultural systems as a source of estimates. She finds that maize yields follow a diminishing returns curve over time (i.e., the rate of increase in yield falls off as more labor is invested). For this reason, Fremont people had little incentive to invest heavily in maize. Instead, low to moderate investments in maize cultivation would have made economic sense, but only if game and highly ranked wild plant foods became scarce. These results indicate that maize farming is not a single resource type; instead, higher levels of investment can cause return rates to decline even as yields increase. The combined predictions of the DBM and the diminishing returns curve for agricultural investment help to make sense of the variability in Fremont agriculture. Barlow's use of models in this study argues against the idea that agriculture is either so highly productive that it will outrank foraging for wild foods, or so unproductive that it should be adopted only in the most dire shortages. Fremont populations chose a flexible strategy that allowed for casual maize farming as an occasional supplement to reduced availability of preferred wild foods.

The DBM and other deterministic models of diet optimization make predictions from the standpoint of an individual; however, foragers and their resources also interact at the population level in a dynamic way. In order to evaluate the claim that human populations inevitably increase when they adopt agriculture, Winterhalder and Goland (1993) designed a simulation model that included a predator and several prey items with various return rates and densities. They wanted to know how forager populations would respond after declines in foraging efficiency caused them to turn to a relatively low-ranked plant resource (such as the small starchy seeds from which many a domesticate has originated). Whether or not the forager population grew turned out to be highly dependent upon the sustainability of the newly adopted plant, a function of its density and its rate of increase. Under the assumption that once resources enter the optimal diet, they are harvested in proportion to their density, it is easy to see how even the most modest of plant foods might become a staple. Dependence is even more likely if the plant population is able to rebound rapidly under predation and resist depletion. Under these conditions, even a low-ranking plant food can dominate human diets and cause an increase in human population. However, a resource similar in rank but slow to reproduce and not particularly abundant might remain at consistent, and low, levels of use for long periods without sponsoring human population growth.

Resource Depression and Niche Construction

One of the key insights of the DBM is that adding low-ranked resources makes the best of a bad situation—a decline in the availability of the most profitable foods—by maintaining the highest possible level of efficiency under new conditions. When human predation is the cause of that decline, it is known as "resource depression." The prevalence of this phenomenon has become increasingly evident with the application of HBE to archaeology. Broughton et al. (2010) have argued convincingly that resource depression is a powerful mode of niche construction, the process by which organisms modify their own environment in ways that influence the survival and reproductive success of their descendants as well as themselves. They illustrate this point with a case study from the prehistoric Sacramento Valley of California, in which zooarchaeological evidence of resource depression is paralleled by the intensification of acorn and small seed use as indicated by the archaeobotanical record. This historical pattern is consistent with the prediction of the DBM that diet breadth will expand as more highly ranked resources are depleted. Further empirical support for this interpretation is drawn from human skeletal remains, which provide evidence of interpersonal violence, reduced stature, and skeletal pathologies associated with inadequate nutrition.

Broughton et al. (2010) also find a relationship between resource depression in the Mimbres region of southern New Mexico and the intensification of agriculture. Archaeological evidence of subsistence intensification in this region comes from the bone chemistry of jackrabbits (which here indicates elevated consumption of maize), settlement shifts to favor alluvial settings, and increased investment in grinding stone technology. These changes parallel closely the decline in foraging efficiency documented by zooarchaeological data. Here the application of HBE makes sense of a correlation between bone chemistry, settlement, and technology that might otherwise go unexplained. These findings serve as an independent test of Barlow's (2002) hypothesized relationship between declining foraging efficiency and investment in agriculture.

Niche construction (Laland et al. 2000; Smith 2007a) can also have a positive effect on the plant environment, creating the opposite of resource depression: productivity enhancement. Denham and Barton (2006) make this point in their discussion of the beginnings of root crop cultivation in New Guinea. They argue that dispersal of cuttings by human groups served to enrich certain patches, permitting increased residence time as predicted by the marginal value theorem. In the near absence of relevant archaeobotanical data, foraging models help researchers to focus on causal hypotheses that are consistent with ecological theory without depending exclusively upon ethnographic analogies.

Linear Programming

Some of the first applications of foraging theory to questions about plant resource use in the past experimented with linear programming as a method for estimating optimal diet. Linear programming is used in microeconomic research to determine how a consumer can satisfy specified needs under certain constraints at the lowest possible cost (for a concise and lucid description of the method, see Bettinger 2009). The assumptions, constraints, formulas, and results are discussed in detail in the original publications. Unlike the HBE models that use energy as a currency, linear programming can set up an array of nutrient constraints (e.g., minimal requirements for vitamin C) and can even incorporate non-food needs (such as construction materials). Input can be manipulated readily to facilitate study of how variables interact. For example, if starchy seeds are not part of the optimal diet, what happens if processing costs are modified? Or if hickory yields are low? The precision of linear programming is appealing, but archaeological data are too poorly resolved at present to allow testing at the same level of detail (interested readers are invited to consult Belovsky 1987; Gardner 1992; Keene 1979, 1981, 1985; Reidhead 1976, 1980 for further details).

CENTRAL PLACE FORAGING AND FIELD PROCESSING

Perhaps some of the most paleoethnobotanically relevant research to emerge from HBE concerns the economics of plant food harvesting under the constraints of travel to and from a central place. Logistical foraging couples residential stability with access to diverse, spatially separated resource patches. When travel and transport of foodstuffs is involved, travel time and constraints on the size and value of the load brought back to camp are likely to have a significant effect on efficiency, and thus food choice. Modeling of field processing and how it affects return rates has yielded important insights into the composition of the archaeobotanical record and the inferences made from it.

The central place foraging (CPF) model was first developed to explore the effects of round-trip travel from a home base (Orians and Pearson 1979). Its central prediction is that greater travel distances (hence costs) require increasingly profitable resource "packages"; eventually package quality cannot keep up with travel costs, at which point the forager is predicted to switch to a patch closer to home. Jones and Madsen (1989) used CPF theory to predict maximum transport distances (MTDs) for a varied set of Great Basin plant resources. To do this, they used estimates of basket size (based on ethnographic collections), nutrient characteristics of plant resources (and grasshoppers) from experimental data, and realistic values for travel times and speeds of a human forager. Their results allowed them to predict which resources are unlikely to be found on an archaeological site located at great distance from a suitable growing habitat. Jones and Madsen acknowledge that their estimates failed to include variables that might make a significant difference to MTDs, such as processing costs and load weight.

In a subsequent publication, Rhode (1990) argued that most of these MTDs were artificially high. He suggests that actual transport distances are likely to have been much lower than the predicted maxima due to constraints that were not factored into Jones and Madsen's model. For example, costs of relocating an entire family rather than an individual might make a distant target less tempting than the predicted MTD suggests. Furthermore, most of the resources analyzed could have been found within several kilometers of any documented archaeological site in the region, so that in practice the MTD has little relevance to actual foraging decisions. Without discounting the value of Jones and Madsen's predictions, Rhode was able to explain the large gap between the actual maximum distances that people were willing to go (determined by ethnographic and archaeological evidence) and the maxima predicted from consideration of travel costs and nutrient content alone. Rhode's version improved the accuracy of predictions because it included more realistic parameters. However, it is easy to see how realistic models begin to erode the utility of modeling itself by introducing complexity that approaches that of the real-world situation of interest.

Of particular relevance to paleoethnobotany are studies of the effects field processing has on load quality (Bettinger et al. 1997; Metcalfe and Barlow 1992). Processing at the collection sites takes time that might otherwise be spent gathering, but also increases the value of a load by removing parts that create bulk without providing calories (such as nutshells or chaff from seed heads). This model assumes that processing back at the base camp will be done at no cost to the foragers, whose goal is to deliver the highest-quality basketload possible given the round-trip travel distance they must cover. Should a forager fill her basket and return, or spend time removing inedible parts before returning home? The model of optimal load processing (Metcalfe and Barlow 1992) predicts that the greater the increase in utility of the load with time spent processing, the shorter the distance at which processing is worthwhile. If shelling nuts is fast and allows the forager to return home with a basketload of (fully edible) nutmeats, then it is worth doing even for a short trip. A plant food whose profitability increases at a lower rate with processing time should be transported intact at the same distance; the extra time spent simply does not pay off unless the costs of transport are also high.

Barlow and Metcalfe (1996) tested this model by comparing two plant resources of the Great Basin: pinyon and pickleweed. Pickleweed refuse is often found in considerable quantities at archaeological sites, despite its low return rates. This is so because removal of chaff and other low-utility parts does virtually nothing to improve pickleweed return rates; the collected plants would have been transported only short distances and returned to camp intact. In contrast, pinyon seeds from distant locations were probably shelled in the field to compensate for transportation costs by bringing back a food-rich packet; although important dietarily, they would have been consumed at the base camp without leaving behind any refuse to document their importance. The economics of long-distance collecting thus have important implications for the composition of the archaeobotanical record: there may be a bias against plant resources that have been heavily field processed.

RISK

Although paleoethnobotanists have shown a great deal of interest in risk as a factor in subsistence decisions, particularly in agricultural systems, there have been relatively few attempts to develop risk-based HBE models for use in archaeology. Winterhalder and Goland (1997) discuss one ecological model that predicts diet choice as a compromise between maximizing return rates and minimizing risk. Following on the work of Caraco (1981) and others, they explored the implications of the Z-score model for food choice. Unlike the diet breadth model, the Z-score model is stochastic in nature; it makes the assumption that decisions have variable rather than determined outcomes. The model recognizes that two options can have identical average return rates, but very different amounts of variance around the mean. The optimal choice is usually to choose the less variable, thus less risky option; only when there is a likelihood of failing to achieve some critical minimum required reward does it pay to opt for high variance (figure 17.1). A bird in the hand may be worth two in the bush—but not if one bird is not enough to keep you alive.

Winterhalder and Goland (1997) discuss the implications of the Z-score model for agricultural origins, making the point that risk is likely to be especially high for transitional forager-farmers. Dependence on high-yielding domesticates is likely to lead to either unsustainable population growth (if the domesticates are high in rank) or restricted dietary diversity (if low in rank). Marston (2011) uses the Z-score model as a starting point for his analysis of modes of risk reduction at the Anatolian site of Gordion. He argues that both diversification and intensification are viable strategies for risk reduction

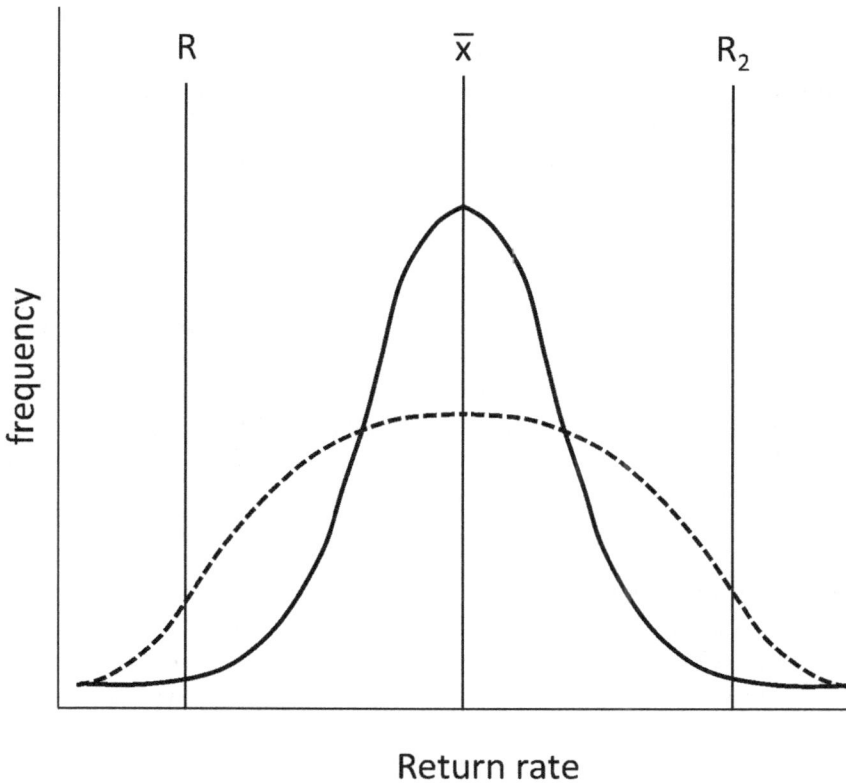

FIGURE 17.1. *Graphical rendering of the Z-score model. The solid line represents the distribution of outcomes for a subsistence strategy that has relatively low variance. The dashed line represents the distribution of outcomes for a strategy with higher variance. Both strategies have the same mean rate of return. When a population's required minimum is well below the average (at line R), risk (defined as the probability of a shortfall) is virtually nil for the low-variance curve. In contrast, when requirements are as high as R_2, only the higher variance option offers a chance of avoiding a shortfall (Winterhalder 1986; Winterhalder and Goland 1997).*

and develops archaeological criteria that indicate their use. Marston's work is unusual and innovative in that he goes beyond manipulation of models to closely examine the archaeobotanical record (as well as other categories of remains) for evidence of risk management. His findings make a strong case for the value of paleoethnobotanical data for testing and extending behavioral ecology models.

SUMMARY AND CONCLUSIONS

Human behavioral ecology, applied judiciously and with respect for the limitations of models, has great potential to advance knowledge of the paleo-ethnobotanical record and the past behaviors that shaped it. The case studies presented here illustrate that potential, as do many others that have been published in recent years (see for example Elston and Zeanah 2002; Foster 2003; Gremillion 2002a; Kennett et al. 2006; Zeanah 2004). HBE models of diet choice have grounded phenomena such as resource depression and logistical collection of plant foods in evolutionary theory by identifying and exploring their implications for economic efficiency. Although the potential of the simplest HBE models, such as the diet breadth model, has not yet been exhausted, it is encouraging to see that archaeologists are moving beyond them into simulations of human-plant population ecology (Winterhalder et al. 2010), the adaptation of foraging models to address the origins of food production (Gremillion 2004; Piperno 2006a), exploration of the intersection of foraging theory and niche construction (Broughton et al. 2010), and consideration of risk minimization as a powerful factor affecting plant use (Marston 2011). A particularly important challenge is presented by the expansion of HBE models to incorporate social variables such as the gendered division of labor (Elston and Zeanah 2002; Zeanah 2004).

My hope is that younger scholars will build on these advances, develop their own models and ecological variables, and begin to explore human adaptation to the plant world beyond nutrition. Choice of plants for construction (Marston 2009) and medicine, landscape modification, and agricultural techniques and traditions can also be modeled in ecological context. Economic efficiency and risk avoidance both have reasonably well-understood relationships to survival and the likelihood of passing on genetic and cultural information to others, but other currencies are possible and will no doubt be explored. I expect the development of models that are more realistic, incorporating nutritional constraints, gendered division of labor, and social inequality. Realism is likely to be further enhanced by experimental studies of crop yields and plant food processing. Despite claims to the contrary (Smith 2011a; Zeder 2009, 2012; Zeder and Smith 2009), there is every indication that the modeling strategy of HBE will continue to advance knowledge and understanding of the intricate and complex interactions between human populations and the plant resources on which they depend (Winterhalder and Smith 2000).

18

Documenting Human
Niche Construction in the
Archaeological Record

Bruce D. Smith

Indigenous landscape management practices and
the alterations in vegetation that result from them
often leave little material evidence to be uncovered
by archaeologists. (Anderson 1999:88)

The term *human niche construction* provides a useful
general heading for the broad and diverse category of
different activities carried out by human societies that
result in modification of their surrounding environment. Developed in evolutionary biology and ecology
over the past three decades, niche construction theory
addresses what was recognized as a basic flaw in the
general concept of adaptation—namely that organisms
do not simply adapt to their selective environments but
in fact play an active role in shaping them: "Organisms
do not adapt to their environment; they construct
them out of the bits and pieces of the external world"
(Lewontin 1983:280; Odling-Smee et al. 2003:16).

As a result, Odling-Smee et al. (2003) argue that
niche construction should be considered, after natural selection, as a second major aspect of evolution
because it introduces feedback into the evolutionary
process and can significantly modify the selection pressures operating on organisms, their descendants, and
on unrelated populations. This in turn can change the
direction, rate, and dynamics of the evolutionary process. Although dam construction by beavers (*Castor*
spp.) is perhaps the most obvious, and certainly the
most frequently cited, example of nonhuman niche

DOI: 10.5876/9781607323167.c018

construction, environmental modification by a diverse array of other species has been documented (Odling-Smee et al. 2003).

Within the broader context of niche construction theory and the recognition that all organisms modify, in different ways and to different degrees, their surrounding ecosystems, humans stand out as the "ultimate niche constructors" or "ecosystem engineers" (Jones et al. 1997; Odling-Smee et al. 2003).[1] Over the past half-century researchers in a variety of disciplines and using a wide range of alternative terms have recognized and documented various forms of human niche construction by preindustrial societies across most of the world's environments, from tropical forests to semiarid savannahs (see Smith 2011b:table 1). Given this long history of documenting human ecological engineering by diverse foraging and farming societies worldwide, it is somewhat surprising that the concept of niche construction has as yet not been incorporated into very many explanatory frameworks of cultural evolution (see Smith 2007a, 2011c), and the majority of archaeologists interested in hunter-gatherers have only recently begun to reassess their theoretical models and to actively consider the role of environmental enhancement in hunter-gatherer lifeways (e.g., Lightfoot et al. 2013).

Human niche construction can be both inadvertent and deliberate, and when deliberate it is most often carried out to restructure biotic communities and food webs in ways that increase both the abundance and predictability of the species of plants and animals that human societies rely on for food and other raw materials (Smith 2011a). Domesticated plants and animals and the world's diverse agricultural economies that are based on them represent the most obvious general way in which human societies have modified the earth's ecosystems more to their liking over the past 10,000 years (Smith 2007a; Smith and Zeder 2013), and the landscape changes associated with agriculture as niche construction have been the subject of excellent and exhaustive regional syntheses such as those of William Doolittle (2000) and William Denevan (2003).

More recently, landmark regional-scale considerations of niche-construction efforts by smaller-scale societies with more limited, if any, reliance on domesticates have been published for the West Coast (Anderson 2005) and Northwest Coast (Deur and Turner 2005) regions of North America, and the Great Basin of North America has long been the focus of research on human niche construction (e.g., Fowler 2000; Fowler and Rhode 2011; Steward 1933). Such broader-scale syntheses of human manipulation of wild species of plants and animals by nonagricultural societies, along with the more numerous accounts of human management of specific wild species or species groups, when taken together, provide a modern baseline data set of human niche construction activities. It is this pool of niche construction descriptions that can be searched for potential archaeological indicators of past efforts by human societies to reshape ecosystems more to their liking. As indicated by the opening quotation from Kat Anderson, finding evidence of past human niche construction, however, is a difficult undertaking.

In this chapter I approach the considerable challenges facing anyone interested in looking for evidence of human management of wild plants in the archaeological record by outlining four different strategies of human niche construction that target specific plant species and species groups in specific ways, paying particular attention to their potential archaeological markers. I then address the more complicated challenge of recognizing and interpreting archaeological evidence for broader-spectrum efforts by small-scale human societies to generally change ancient vegetation communities. In the case of both focused and more diffuse forms of human ecosystem engineering, compiling a reference class of present-day and recent past descriptions of human niche construction is relatively straightforward. However, it is currently challenging to identify ways in which such human efforts to "improve" their local environments might be recognized in the archaeological record. In general the challenge involves first being able to distinguish between natural and anthropogenic causation in shaping local environments, and second being able to differentiate between human modification of vegetation communities associated with enhancement of wild resource species as distinct from those specifically associated with cultivation of domesticated crops.

The vast majority of available descriptions of efforts by human societies to reshape their "natural environment" involve plant species and species groups, rather than animals. The simple explanation for this is that, given their stationary nature, wild plants are much more feasible and more predictable targets for successful management than wild animals. Human efforts to increase the abundance and harvest predictability of wild animal species primarily involve either indirect habitat improvement through modification of vegetation communities (see below), or structural modifications to the landscape designed to predictably constrain animals in time and space for killing (e.g., drive lines and fish weirs; Smith 2011a, 2013).

Ironically, while fish weirs and drive lines, kites, and fences have a relatively good probability of being preserved in the archaeological record, evidence for human niche construction targeting wild plant species is much more difficult to confidently identify and accurately characterize, for a number of reasons. Management of wild plants is often carried out by small-scale societies, for example, which leave a relatively light footprint on the landscape, and their manipulation of vegetation communities frequently both mimics and is obscured by similar natural processes (e.g., fires, windfalls, colonization of open areas by early successional species, climate-driven changes in biotic communities). Deliberate human alteration of vegetation communities must also be ongoing in order to sustain the imposed modifications—otherwise natural succession sequences can in large measure erase the anthropogenic environments in a few decades or less. In addition, management of wild plant species, when compared to domesticates, is not so obviously reflected in morphological changes in the plants themselves, thus removing a key archaeological marker of human manipulation (Lepofsky and Lertzman 2008; Smith 2011a).

In spite of these difficulties, efforts to identify human niche construction involving wild plant species and species groups in the archaeological record are increasing, sometimes with remarkable success (e.g., D'Andrea et al. 2006; Doolittle et al. 2004). Along with such well-focused analysis and interpretation of specific archaeological case studies of past human management of particular species of wild plants, conference proceedings having a much broader consideration of human niche construction are also appearing (e.g., Dean 2010; Kendal et al. 2011), along with impressive regional-scale considerations of past patterns of human plant management and ecosystem engineering (e.g., Lepofsky and Lertzman 2008).

Lepofsky and Lertzman's (2008) regional synthesis of ancient plant management in the Northwest Coast of North America underscores an important aspect of the search for archaeological markers of human niche construction involving wild plants—that it can't be limited to analysis of archaeobotanical assemblages alone. Physical changes to the landscape can provide indications of human manipulation of plant communities, as can analysis of soils and a variety of different environmental records, including charcoal, pollen, and phytolith profiles.

STRUCTURAL CHANGES TO THE LANDSCAPE, SOIL MOISTURE, AND HUMAN MANAGEMENT OF WILD PERENNIAL ROOT AND BASAL ROSETTE CROPS

Underscoring the importance of non-archaeobotanical markers, physical modification of the landscape in the form of relocating soil and rocks provides clear archaeological evidence in a number of different environmental settings for the deliberate and sustained enhancement of plots of perennial wild plants having starch-rich underground storage organs (roots, rhizomes, culms) and basal rosettes or stems. In a frequently cited example of substantial labor investment in landscape modification to expand and enhance populations of wild root crops, for example, Owens Valley Paiute groups in the Great Basin area of California constructed an irrigation system that carried and dispersed water across extensive tracts of swampy low-lying floodplain meadows adjacent to the Owens River (Fowler 2000; Fowler and Rhode 2011; Lawton et al. 1976). These irrigation efforts were designed to enhance and expand natural stands of bulbous hydrophytic food plant species, including blue dicks or purplehead brodiaea (*Dichelostemma capitatum* ssp. *capitatum*), chufa flat sedge (*Cyperus esculentus*), and possibly spikerush (*Eleocharis* spp.). Construction and subsequent removal of temporary diversion dams along some of the tributary creeks of the Owens River called for a substantial amount of labor on an annual basis. Feeder ditches up to 6.5 km long carried nutrient rich, early summer mountain runoff from dams to the river valley plots (Steward 1933). No efforts were made at planting, tilling, or tending either the wild root crops of these water meadows or the adjacent downstream stands of wild seed plants (including sunflower, chenopod, and lovegrass) that also benefited from the irrigation efforts. Unfortunately, it is probably not possible to determine how far back in time these labor-intensive water management practices were carried out (Fowler 2000).

In the absence of preserved evidence of the feeder ditches and dam structures, however, there would be little if anything in the archaeological record to indicate deliberate human enhancement and expansion of these naturally occurring mixed stands of wild root and seed crops. Any observed increase in the size or abundance of roots recovered from processing or storage contexts, for example, or an increase in earth ovens or processing technology, or even soil profile indications of an expansion of the extent of the water meadow root "gardens," would be difficult to attribute to human niche construction efforts, as opposed to the default alternative of the past existence of naturally occurring higher seasonal watertable levels. Dendrochronological records indicating reduced regional precipitation and stream flow in the same time frame as evidence for water meadow expansion could support an argument for human ecosystem engineering, but otherwise there would appear to be little to indicate the efforts made by the Owens Valley Paiute to increase the yield and reliability of an important wild plant resource.

Physical modification of the landscape also provides the clearest evidence to date for the efforts made by small-scale societies along the Northwest Coast of North America to both expand and enhance the saturated soil habitats of indigenous wild root crops (Deur 2005). In contrast to the Owens Valley

Idealized Salt Marsh Cross-Section

a. Prior to Garden Rockwork Construction

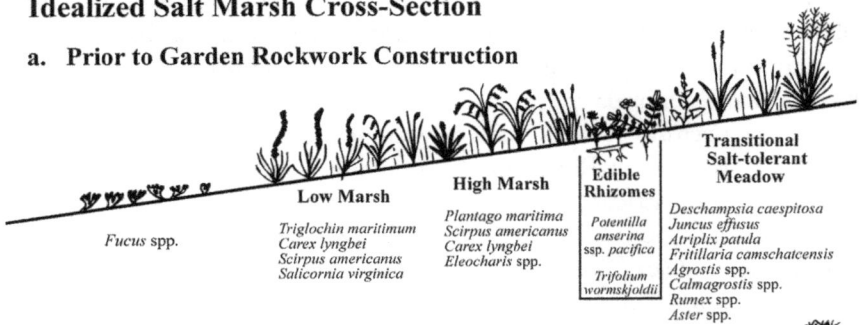

Transitional
Salt-tolerant
Meadow

Edible
Rhizomes

High Marsh

Low Marsh

Fucus spp.

Triglochin maritimum
Carex lyngbei
Scirpus americanus
Salicornia virginica

Plantago maritima
Scirpus americanus
Carex lyngbei
Eleocharis spp.

Potentilla
anserina
ssp. *pacifica*

Trifolium
wormskjoldii

Deschampsia caespitosa
Juncus effusus
Atriplix patula
Fritillaria camschatcensis
Agrostis spp.
Calmagrostis spp.
Rumex spp.
Aster spp.

b. With Intact Garden Rockwork

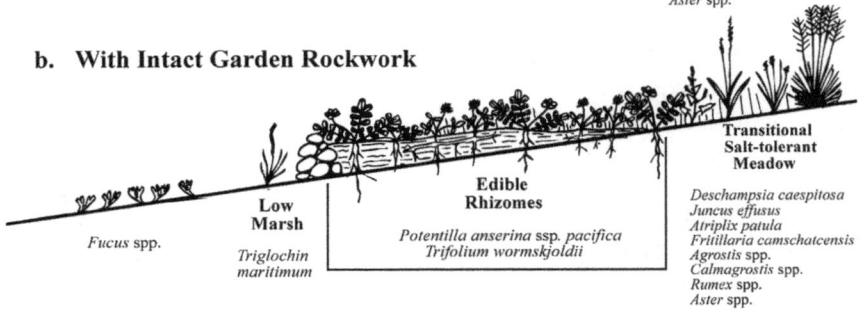

Transitional
Salt-tolerant
Meadow

Edible
Rhizomes

Low
Marsh

Fucus spp.

Triglochin
maritimum

Potentilla anserina ssp. *pacifica*
Trifolium wormskjoldii

Deschampsia caespitosa
Juncus effusus
Atriplix patula
Fritillaria camschatcensis
Agrostis spp.
Calmagrostis spp.
Rumex spp.
Aster spp.

FIGURE 18.1. *Profile of root garden construction (from Deur 2005:313).*

Paiute, Northwest Coast ecosystem engineering focused not on water delivery systems, but on the artificial expansion of the habitat zone of a number of estuarine food plant species, including springbank clover (*Trifolium worm-skjoldii*), pacific silverweed (*Potentilla anserine* ssp. *pacificia*), northern rice-root lily (*Fritillaria camschatcensis*), and Nootka lupine (*Lupinus nootkatensis*), which all produce dense concentrations of long and thin starchy roots and rhizomes. These species have a narrow range of distribution within the tidal column in undisturbed high salt marsh estuarine settings. Northwest Coast societies expanded this narrow habitat zone downslope by constructing rock and wood reinforcing walls, and backfilling with soil to reduce water depth to that required by the target species (figure 18.1).

Within these extended "garden plots" the soil was periodically churned, creating a texturally diverse soil while also mixing in the most recent deposits of fresh organic matter. Churning also increased the porosity of the soil, thereby encouraging the growth of the larger, longer, and straighter roots so highly prized by Northwest Coast societies. Along with churning the soil, human management of these expanded cultivation areas also involved sustained weeding of grasses and other unwanted invaders throughout the growing season, and the vegetative replanting of root fragments and small plants at the time of harvest in order to ensure future abundant yields.

In addition to the construction of downslope retaining walls, there are at least two other potential archaeological markers of such wild root crop "garden plots." The presence of longer, straighter, and larger rhizomes in archaeobotanical assemblages would provide strong evidence for the existence of such gardens, and when preserved, the altered soils themselves would provide indications of the location and size of such reclaimed marshland zones. Dating of retaining walls or soils could also potentially allow determination of the time depth of wild root crop cultivation (Deur 2005).

The Southwest United States provides another example of human niche construction directed toward increasing the yield of a wild perennial crop: *Agave* spp., the leaves and basal rosettes of which were important sources of both raw material and food for Southwestern indigenous societies. As is the case on the Northwest Coast and the Great Basin, modification to the physical landscape provides the clearest archaeological evidence of human encouragement of this species. Rock mulching laid out in rectangular grid patterns by Hohokam maize agriculturalists between ca. AD 600–1350 have been identified in hundreds of locations within the Phoenix, Tonto, and Tucson Basins. Designed to capture rainfall, retain surface runoff, and reduce evaporation, these features substantially increase soil moisture levels (Doolittle et al. 2004). Although still far below what would have been needed to grow maize or other domesticated crop plants, the increase in soil moisture resulting from these rock grid features was significant in terms of supporting indigenous perennials such as agave that could withstand seasonal moisture shortfalls.

Situated on the broad cobble and boulder terraces adjacent to the alluvial plain of the Gila River in southern Arizona, the Safford valley grid features are among the best-documented examples of this form of niche construction (Doolittle et al. 2004). Rock lines forming squares roughly 10 m on a side and forming grid clusters covering an area of 82 ha were situated within 1 km on either side of Spring Wash, a tributary of the Gila River. It is estimated that this rock grid system could have supported an estimated 44,500 agave plants at any one time. Small "offsets" or "pups" of mature parent plants were likely initially collected from relatively distant stands and transplanted to the prepared rock grid mulch fields. Once established, mature plants within the rock grids could produce all the pups needed for the perpetuation of the cultivated stands of wild agave.

A series of roasting pits situated along Spring Wash and several other tributaries transecting the rock grid areas yielded agave processing tools along with both monocot tissue compatible with agave and cf. agave leaf base fragments, providing solid archaeological markers of agave processing, and representing, in isolation, potential evidence for agave management. If enough roasting pits and associated processing tools and agave remains were recovered from a particular location, a plausible argument could be developed for large-scale and sustained human management of agave, even in the absence of any associated mulching features.

Structural modifications of the landscape associated with soil moisture management efforts can on occasion also provide good archaeological evidence for human enhancement of other wild perennial and annual species having economic importance. In Kuk swamp in the highlands of New Guinea, for example, complex drainage canals associated with the cultivation of tree crops (e.g., banana) have been dated as far back as 7,000 BP (Denham et al. 2003). Artificial walls or "bunds" dating as early as 7,700 BP and designed to retain floodwaters and thereby expand the natural habitat of wild and early cultivated rice crops have also been documented in the Yangtze delta region of China (Zong et al. 2007).

TRANSPLANTATION ORCHARDS OF
PERENNIAL FRUIT-BEARING SPECIES

Targeting a different category of perennial wild plants, this form of human niche construction involves digging up seedlings or young fruit-bearing trees or bushes that are found scattered across the landscape and transplanting them in anthropogenic disturbed habitat openings in closer proximity to human settlements, and in much greater density than they occur in the wild. This general practice of transplanting long-lived species, especially those bearing fruit, adjacent to settlements allowed for easier harvesting and shorter travel time. It would also have strengthened perceptions of ownership of the resources, reduced unwanted harvesting of crops by human and nonhuman interlopers, and facilitated the monitoring and harvesting of fruits, berries, and other plant parts as they matured (Doolittle 2000; Gremillion 2011).

Eastern North America provides a good example of the key aspects of this transplantation strategy. It is not surprising that the peach (*Prunus persica*), for example, was quickly adopted when introduced by Europeans, given its key similarities to native wild trees that were already subject to transplantation and tending by indigenous societies (Gremillion 1996a). Species targeted for such transplantation share three key characteristics: they are weedy colonizers and require a minimum of labor investment for transplantation or tending; they mature rapidly, bearing fruit within ca. 3–5 years; and they are perennials with life spans of several decades or more, ensuring a sustained harvest of fruit each year with minimal maintenance.

A dozen or more native fruit-bearing trees of the Eastern Woodlands of North America meet these criteria, flourishing in open sunny forest edges and clearings: (e.g., honeylocust (*Gleditsia triacanthos*), elderberry (*Sambucus canadensis*), mulberry (*Morus rubra*), hackberry (*Celtis occidentalis*), sugarberry (*Celtis laevigata*), hawthorn (*Crataegus* spp.), plum and cherry (*Prunus* spp.), and persimmon (*Diospyros virginiana*), all of which were potential targets for transplantation (Gremillion 2011). Early historical accounts mention plums, peaches, persimmons, beautyberry, and red mulberry, among other species, growing in "orchards" adjacent to old Indian settlements (Hammett 1992).

Many early historical accounts in the Eastern Woodlands of North America also describe a variety of different berry crops growing in "old fields" around Indian settlements. Kris Gremillion (2011) lists wild strawberry (*Fragaria virginiana*), groundcherry (*Physalis* spp.), and *Rubus* species (dewberry and blackberry) as often observed thriving in open areas adjacent to settlements, with understory shrubs that produced edible fruits such as blueberry and cranberry (*Vaccinium* spp.), serviceberry (*Amelanchier alnifolia*), and huckleberry (*Gaylussacia* spp.) recorded as commonly present in overgrown fields. Similarly, Doolittle (2000) summarizes early European descriptions from the Northeast of raspberry and strawberries growing close to settlements, with accounts often mentioning their abundance in overgrown fallow fields, and occasional reports of transplanting. In addition to perennial fruit and berry crops, there are a wide variety of other economically important plants, from cattails to cacao that are documented as having been targeted for transplantation across a range of different environments (Atron 1993; McNeil 2009; Smith 2011a, 2011b).

As is the case with other general strategies of human niche construction targeting wild plant species, recognizing transplantation in the archaeological record—especially distinguishing it from simple harvesting of "naturally occurring" plants—is a difficult challenge. Does a significant increase in the representation of perennial fruit-bearing species in archaeobotanical assemblages, for example, reflect the creation of orchards or simply indicate any number of other alternatives (e.g., shifts in biotic community composition, human harvesting strategies or priorities, or storage and processing methods)?

Transplantation of parthenocarpic fig trees (*Ficus carica*) in proximity to 11,000-year-old settlements in the Jordan Valley has recently been proposed, providing the oldest potential evidence for transplantation of a fruit-bearing species (Kislev et al. 2006). Witness tree records obtained within a decade or two of abandonment of Native American settlements in the Southeast United States, prior to the reestablishment of an overstory canopy, have also shown higher than expected frequencies of fruit-bearing trees, indicating either transplantation or selective culling (Foster et al. 2004). Unfortunately, such rare species characteristics as parthenocarpy in figs, as well as witness tree records (obtained in the brief temporal window prior to re-establishment of the overstory canopy), or volcanic ash deposits enshrining entire orchards are of limited use as archaeological markers of transplantation of economically important plant species. Pollen analysis targeting samples recovered from archaeological contexts, in contrast, does appear to hold some potential for documenting the transplantation of economically important perennials by past societies worldwide. At the SGang Gway Midden site in British Columbia, for example, six samples from a 13-cm sequence of litter and shell midden debris provided a record of the vegetation composition within the village, and based on the high amounts of rose family pollen, Hebda et al. (2005) suggest that fruit-producing members of the rose family such as salmonberry and perhaps Pacific crabapple may have been grown in the village. Similarly, using pollen samples taken from several Jomon period sites in Japan, Kitagawa and Yasuda (2004, 2008) document an increase in abundance of pollen from two economically important tree species—chestnut (*Castanea* spp.) and horse chestnut (*Aesculus* spp.)—beginning at ca. 7,000–4,500 BP, suggesting selective encouragement and perhaps transplantation by Jomon groups.

SELECTIVE IN SITU ENCOURAGEMENT OF PERENNIAL FRUIT AND NUT-BEARING SPECIES

Human management of mature fruit trees, along with slow to mature nut-bearing species, focuses on in situ encouragement rather than transplantation, and most often takes the form of selective culling of competing trees both for building material and firewood, and during general vegetation clearance in the creation of mosaic patches and edge areas.

In Eastern North America, for example, Hammett (1992, 1997) outlines a general pattern of landscape management by indigenous pre-European societies that has settlements and their adjacent small gardens encircled by two resource catchment zones—an adjacent area of actively cultivated and fallow fields, orchards, and berry patches, surrounded by a wooded zone containing mast, nut-, and fruit-bearing trees as well as trees for construction and firewood, along with white-tailed deer and other prey species. Nishida (1983) describes a similar abstract catchment zone pattern for Japan.

Selective retention of overstory nut- and mast-bearing trees during field clearance results in their scattered distribution in the close-in zone of active and fallow fields. In outlying forest zones their relative abundance is increased by selective culling of competitors, resulting in larger and higher yielding nut- and mast-bearing trees (Hammett 1992, 1997; Yarnell 1964, 1982). Delcourt et al. (1998) suggest that such patterns of management of Eastern North American forests have considerable time depth. As settlements and their concentric resource catchment zones were periodically relocated throughout forest zones of North America, they would have left behind a legacy of fallow-cycle vegetation communities that were substantially enriched in forest species of economic value in comparison to their composition prior to clearing (Black et al. 2006; Wykoff 1991).

Encouragement of mature nut- and fruit-bearing trees and the selective culling of competing species has also been documented in a number of different past and present-day low-latitude tropical forest environments (Atron 1993; Cosgrove 1996; Posey 1985; Posey and Balee 1989), as well as in temperate forest and more open environments. Catherine Fowler (2000), for example, documents the clearing away of vegetation from piñon trees in the Great Basin, as well as "knocking" branches and pinching growth tips to encourage additional cone development. In Japan, Kitagawa and Yasuda's (2004, 2008) analysis of pollen samples from Jomon period sites, as well as prior studies showing an increase in the size of nuts, provide evidence of selective encouragement of both chestnut (*Castanea* spp.) and horse chestnut (*Aesculus* spp.) as early as 5,000 BP, and Nishida (1983) outlines broader patterns of management of "wild" plants in contemporary villages in rural Japan. Similarly, in Africa, D'Andrea et al. (2006) provide a compelling and broadly based argument for late Holocene arboriculture involving oil palm (*Elaeis guineensis*).

In situ management and manipulation of long-lived perennials also, of course, includes those species that can be harvested for raw material rather than food. A variety of different species in different parts of the world are coppiced and pollarded (pruned) to maintain them in a physiologically young state (figure 18.2), producing new growth each year to be used for firewood and a range of manufactured items, including baskets (Anderson

FIGURE 18.2. *Evidence of coppicing is sometimes well preserved in wetland sites, like this woven panel or hurdle laid down as part of a footpath through a marsh in the Somerset Levels of South West England. Photograph by John Coles and courtesy of EXARC.*

1999; Fowler 2000; Haas and Schweingruber 1994; Thiébault 2006; Turner et al. 2009).

The recovery of uniformly sized and straight branches from archaeological contexts could provide a useful marker of coppicing in the archaeological record.

Pollen profiles in general hold the potential for providing evidence of selective human culling and a resultant shift in species composition of forest biomes toward economically valuable species, particularly in those situations in which multiple profiles indicate variation in forest cover across a relatively small region (e.g., Jacomet et al. 2004). In addition, changes in the relative abundance of other forest species can also, in theory, reflect human efforts at arboreal engineering. Munson (1986), for example, has argued that in middle Holocene faunal assemblages in Eastern North America, a shift in the relative abundance away from a closed canopy species of squirrel (*Sciurus carolina*) toward an open habitat species (*Sciurus niger*), indicates human efforts to increase the abundance and yield of nut- and mast-bearing trees. With all of these potential markers of arboreal manipulation, however, the challenge remains one of being able to recognize human engineering against a background of alternative natural causes in shaping forest composition and diversity.

SEASONAL SOWING OF PIONEERING WILD ANNUALS IN UNOCCUPIED HABITATS

As floodwaters recede on a predictable annual basis along the margins of rivers and lakes in many different world environments, the unoccupied bare areas that are exposed represent an optimum opportunity for colonization by early succession annual seed plants. Small-scale human societies can, through the simple practice of broadcast sowing of harvested seed, fill up these empty habitat patches by establishing new stands of "wild" seed-bearing plants of economic value.

As spring floodwaters receded along the lower Mississippi River, for example, Natchez women and children are described in the early 1700s as scattering the seeds of a plant called *choupichoul* (cf. *Chenopodium berlandieri*) along newly exposed sandbank margins (Smith 2006). Following seed dispersal, the planters casually pushed sand over the seeds with their feet. No other investment of labor was involved. Such broadcast sowing onto open sandbank situations could have created large and very productive wild stands of this and other economically important annual seed plants: e.g., marshelder (*Iva annua*), sunflower (*Helianthus annuus*), erect knotweed (*Polygonum erectum*), and cucurbits (*Lagenaria secaria, Cucurbita pepo* ssp. *ovifera*).

In another well documented example, Castetter and Bell (1951) describe Cocopa societies of the lower Colorado River as broadcast sowing in "décrue" fashion (i.e., following the drop in water level of a body of water), seeds that they had harvested the previous fall on thin, muddy, nutrient rich river-bank soils exposed by receding spring floodwaters. These floodplain plots, which were up to 50–100 m wide and could extend several kilometers along the river, received no further attention prior to harvest, and included any of five different identified species. Three of these were historic-period introductions of Eurasian origin, whereas two species of panic grass (*Panicum*) were indigenous and known to have been grown at least as far back as 1541, suggesting the possibility that this human environmental modification or "semicultivation" of grasses may have preceded maize-bean-squash agriculture in the region. Although involving different plant species, and located in very different environmental settings, the Natchez and Cocopa case study examples of décrue sowing of annual seed crops are similar in that human niche construction efforts in both situations took advantage of naturally occurring and predictable open areas that held the additional dual benefits of high groundwater levels for early seedling growth and fertile soils due to nutrient-rich annual floodwaters. Numerous other examples of broadcast sowing of wild seed-bearing annuals by small-scale societies can be found in different ecosystem settings, from the Great Basin in North America (Fowler 2000; Fowler and Rhode 2011) to Sub-Saharan Africa (Harlan 1992).

No compelling archaeological indicators have as yet been identified for such broadcast sowing of annual seed plants. The recovery of large numbers of seeds from settlements in river valley or lake margin settings—above what might be expected from harvesting of natural stands—might suggest décrue planting, as would the occurrence of species outside of their documented geographical distribution. In either case, however, it would be necessary to rule out alternative causes.

GENERAL MODIFICATION OF VEGETATION COMMUNITIES

Although the human niche construction strategies discussed above target specific categories of plants, in specific ways, and are designed to increase the abundance of these species in the environment, small-scale human societies also carry out more generalized efforts to alter the overall composition of vegetation communities. This is done in order to increase the relative abundance of a range of early successional stage plants that provide a source of food for either humans or for animals that play a role in human economies, at the expense of other species of plants of lesser economic value. This overall modification of vegetation communities is directed toward disrupting the reproductive rate of the slowly growing "climax" vegetation (excepting those of economic value), enhancing the short-term productivity of early successional stage plants, and increasing in-patch diversity (e.g., Jacomet et al. 2004; Smith 2011a). In contrast to the variety of different efforts that are directed toward selectively enhancing individual plants or clusters of plants of known location, general strategies for shaping vegetation communities represent more diffuse efforts designed to result in larger-scale patterns of modification. Such general efforts to modify vegetation communities appear to be the primary way in which human societies attempt to increase biomass levels of animal species of economic importance (Mellars 1976; Smith 2011a).

Fire has long been an effective, low-cost, and frequently employed way for small-scale societies to reshape vegetation communities in ways that increase the abundance of a variety of animal and plant species that are important food resources. Controlled and moderate-impact burning of open grassland and shrub communities as well as forest environments creates and maintains a mosaic of small patches of habitat at different stages of regeneration (e.g., Anderson 2005; Bird et al. 2005; Bliege Bird et al. 2008; Delcourt and Delcourt 2004; Frawley and O'Connor 2010; Laris 2002; Sheuyange et al. 2005; Smith 2009b; Stephens et al. 2007).

Once "cleansed" by fire, the resultant vegetation patches at early stages of regeneration, and the edge or interface zones between them, support higher biomass levels of plant and animal species of economic importance to humans than do later successional communities. Across a broad range of environments, the food plants used by humans (and other species) often have a competitive advantage early in a successional sequence, but subsequently decline in abundance over time.

Charcoal, pollen, and fire-scar tree-ring records from a worldwide range of environments have been cited in a steady stream of studies documenting the widespread practice of deliberate burning of vegetation by human societies throughout the Holocene (e.g., Akeret et al. 1999; Allen et al. 2008; Bliege Bird et al. 2008; Clark and Royall 1995; Dean 2004 ; Delcourt and Delcourt 2004; Delcourt et al. 1998; Dorney and Dorney 1989; Huang et al. 2006; Lepofsky and Lertzman 2008; Russell 1983; Sullivan 1996 ; Turner 1999; Vale 2002; Weiser and Lepofsky 2009; Williams 2002; Zong et al. 2007). In recent years, increasingly sophisticated analyses of fire records that combine different approaches and multiple data sets are steadily improving our ability to establish the scale and frequency of past burn episodes (e.g., Evett and Cutrell 2011; LaBelle et al. 2011). As a result, it may in the future be possible to distinguish with greater confidence not only between natural and human caused fires, but between anthropogenic fires associated with management of wild resources and those related to clearing for domesticated crops.

CONCLUSIONS

Identifying evidence of past human niche construction will remain a difficult challenge. The brief overview presented here represents an initial framework of expectation in the continuing search for archaeological markers of different forms of human management of wild plant resources. Within any biotic community, those wild plant species that are the most obvious likely targets of focused human manipulation can be identified, if present (e.g., perennial fruit or nut-bearing species, perennial plants having starch-rich underground storage organs, and annual pioneering seed plants). At the same time, the form that more general efforts at vegetation modification will likely take can be anticipated (e.g., an extended record of moderate impact, localized mosaic burn patterns). Identifying the archaeological signatures of these strategies of human niche construction will not be easy, but the search is just beginning.

NOTE

1. Although some evolutionary ecologists draw a fine distinction between the concepts of *niche construction* and *ecological engineering*, the two terms can in general be used interchangeably, and for our purposes can be considered to have essentially the same meaning (Odling-Smee et al. 2003).

19

Paleoethnobotanical
Analysis, Post-Processing

Shanti Morell-Hart

*In our enthusiasm for subsistence, we forgot
about food. People don't eat species, they eat meals.*
(Sherratt 1991:221)

Paleoethnobotanists, like many other archaeological specialists, are often found in the uncomfortable
position of straddling two domains: hard sciences
and humanistic studies. We are left feeling as though
our methodologies and statistical approaches must
be as rigorous as those found in our sister sciences—
botany, ecology, forestry, and the like—but that our
research questions must also be strongly humanistic
in nature, addressing interpretive frameworks and
cultural perspectives. Ours is not the only field with
such struggles (psychology, economics, and sociology
come to mind), but the nature of our data is rather
unique, encompassing material traces related to virtually every other discipline.

Beyond broader troubles related to the scope and
aims of archaeology in the North American tradition,
students of the 1980s and 1990s were raised on tales
of the struggles between theoretical approaches cat-
egorized as *processual* or *postprocessual*, (Binford 1989;
Chippindale 1993; Flannery 1982; Kohl 1993; Shanks
and Hodder 1995; Trigger 2006) in spite of a multitude
of hybrids and variants that did not fit easily into one or
the other. A few brave scholars tried to bridge the two
worlds (Earle 1991; Preucel 1991; Watson 1991; Weiner
1995; Yoffee and Sherratt 1993), viewing processual hard

DOI: 10.5876/9781607323167.c019

scientists and postprocessual humanists to be compatible in their broad aims if not their specific pursuits. However, for an entire generation of archaeologists-in-training, our academic parents were fighting, and divorce seemed inevitable. Meanwhile, paleoethnobotany carried on, drawing inspiration from each but largely staying outside the quarrel. For those of us who sought refuge in this discipline, there seemed a straightforwardness to the data and the narratives, in spite of known sampling and preservation issues. Working with statisticians gave us confidence (even when the statisticians sometimes looked on dubiously) and problem-oriented approaches gave us purpose. What happened at Easter Island? How were our most important crops domesticated? What transformations, natural and cultural, were related to climate change? There were so many critical questions to be answered. Yet it was often difficult to convince field directors to follow methodologies supportive of significant data returns; to gather and store large quantities of dirt on the project dime.

Today, paleoethnobotanical interpretations consider a variety of questions from a multitude of standpoints. The work of other contributors to this volume demonstrates the full potential of approaches labeled *processual*; other approaches termed *postprocessual* are the focus of this chapter and others, although neither realm is perfectly discrete. Many of us find ourselves trying to remain true to the empirical rigor imparted by years of processual endeavor, but also the ideas imparted by years of critical approaches, reflexive methodologies, and considerations of meaning. Such interpretive tools have come to us from both inside anthropology (e.g., Geertz 1973; Sahlins 1976) and outside of it (e.g., Bourdieu 1977; Foucault 1984; Giddens 1979).

Our attempts to maximize all sorts of theoretical resources have led us to develop attendant methodologies, with varied and interesting results. In this chapter, I outline some of the approaches labeled processual and postprocessual, and some of the intentions and implications of these perspectives in paleoethnobotany. I then focus on two theoretical pools that I have found especially useful in my own work: linguistic- and practice-based approaches. Although not perfectly suited to every botanical puzzle, I have found them to be enormously helpful when digesting my own data set. I illustrate how I implemented this type of modeling by providing a few brief examples from sites in Northwestern Honduras. I address the potential of linguistic- and practice-based perspectives in macro- and microbotanical analysis of artifacts and places and in the interpretation of plant assemblages. Such postprocessual approaches seek to incorporate meaning while remaining committed to the basic scientific arguments often viewed as rooted firmly within the processual domain.

A MOSAIC OF APPROACHES

Our views of the underlying frameworks for human society and its doings channel the very questions we ask of plant remains and the methodologies we employ. Paleoethnobotanical data have been used in discourse on social change, ethnicity, plant taphonomic processes, diet and subsistence, plant-use practices, crop origins, and evolution of agricultural systems, among many other topics. Traditional retrospectives, with some exceptions (e.g., Preucel 1991), have tended to divide fundamental archaeological approaches into "processual" and "postprocessual" pools. Such approaches, in paleoethnobotany, can similarly be divided, although as with the broader field of archaeology they do not cleave perfectly into one category or the other. Below, I outline a few examples of each sort of approach.

PROCESSUAL APPROACHES

How were landscapes managed? What diverse subsistence strategies were employed by ancient societies? What was the relative importance of various plant resources? What were the processes of domestication and their associated plants, implements, and areas of activity? What were the environmental and ecological implications of various ethnobotanical practices? What activity areas and tool uses can be identified through paleoethnobotanical analysis? Such processual questions make the most of ongoing studies of identification, classification, and categorizations of various plant remains, while saying meaningful things about human behaviors and the complexity of human-plant interactions.

Discussions of plant resources vis-à-vis optimality models (e.g., Bettinger 1991; Binford 1980; Reddy 1994) view the natural landscape sometimes as a benevolent set of potential assets and sometimes as a malevolent force to battle. Nutritional information and demography estimates may be approximated from paleoethnobotanical remains, while diachronic studies address questions of what emerges from long-term contact between human populations and the environment (e.g., Day 1993; McAnany and Yoffee 2009). In a move away from more static conceptions of both ecology and anthropology, some authors (e.g., Gleason 1994; Hastorf and Popper 1988; Jones 1941) address the dynamic nature of human-plant interactions. In their view, the trajectory of the surrounding ecology is strongly intertwined with that of the human subjects who simultaneously control plant resources and are subject to the availability of them. These resources are often assessed for their relative importance and availability (e.g., Lentz 1991, 2001; Smith 1998).

Some authors interpret paleoethnobotanical specimens in terms of the practices associated with individual species and the relative importance of specific plant foods (Dennell 1976; Hastorf 1988; Jones 1983a). Often, authors examine patterns of deforestation and reforestation (McNeil 2003; Piqué and Barceló 2002) and periods of occupation and abandonment (Johnston et al. 2001). In a similar vein, some scholars address the need to pursue a broader landscape approach when using macrobotanical remains (Gleason 1994; Jones 1985) and even advocate "the removal of the barrier between 'site' and 'environment'" (Jones 1985:123). Many authors have complicated the dichotomy between "wild" and "domesticated" landscapes and associated ethnobotanical practices (Crane 1996; Lentz 1991, 2001; Piqué and Barceló 2002; Reed 1999; Sheets 1982).

In the study of the distribution of foodways across various contexts, features, and implements, paleoethnobotanists have made an impressive set of contributions. Bozarth and Guderjan (2004), using phytolith data, identified the deliberate deposit of food-related taxa in ritual contexts. Other authors have linked specific features with plants and foodstuffs (Balme and Beck 2002; Brown and Gerstle 2002; Haaland 2007; Hard et al. 1996; Lyons and D'Andrea 2003), or linked specific artifacts with plants and activities (Fullagar et al. 2008; Kealhofer et al. 1999; Pearsall et al. 2004; Perry 2001; Piperno et al. 2004). Specific anatomical portions of macrobotanical specimens, along with models of taphonomic processes, have provided clues to locations of processing activities and hierarchies of settlement (Hastorf 1988; Jones 1987; Portillo et al. 2009). Contexts and practices have even been identified by proxy, in studies addressing irrigation and phytolith morphology (Rosen and Weiner 1994), crop processing, and methods of crop sowing, tending, manuring, and rotation (Bogaard et al. 2001; Bogaard et al. 1999).

In paleoethnobotany, such approaches marked as processual have significant overlap with those marked as postprocessual, even where seemingly disparate. Both types of studies start from the same building blocks—botanical data and an interest in social realms—even where the specific questions are dissimilar. The attention to ecology, taxonomy, formation processes, and subsistence has been complemented by attention to social constructions and meanings of ethnobotanical practices. In essence, postprocessual approaches, though making use of the same sorts of data sets, ask different questions.

POSTPROCESSUAL APPROACHES

Postprocessual perspectives first began to coalesce in the Martin Jones article "Archaeobotany beyond Subsistence Reconstruction" (Jones 1985). As noted by Jones and others, much of the work of paleoethnobotany has been strongly intertwined with studies of subsistence, diet, and foodways. For this reason, I draw postprocessual applications of paleoethnobotany from a combination of paleoethnobotanical literature and foodways scholarship. I cluster these studies under several broad themes—(1) construction of the "edible," (2) ingredients and cuisine, (3) politics and power, (4) identity, aesthetics, and embodiment, and (5) meanings and semiotics—although there are also many other potential categories. Anthropological literature must be taken with a grain of salt, however, given the critical examination of the use of ethnographic models for paleoethnobotanical purposes (G. Jones 1984). Such models, helpful though they are in directing research and interpretation, cannot serve as direct and perfect analogs irrespective of region and time period.

In considering what is "edible," food is more than a biological given: it is a social construction, molded by individual tastes and preferences. Edible/inedible classifications are dynamic and historically contextualized: "the boundary between 'natural' inedibles and the cultural binarity of edible/inedible is a fuzzy one," subject to immediate social context and current identity of the consumer (Falk 1991:759,761). For this reason, what is potentially edible is not always regarded as food (Falk 1991:759; Farrington and Urry 1985:145; Fischler 1980:940; Soler 1997:55), and furthermore, what is considered "food" is not always entirely edible. Paleoethnobotanical pursuit of these topics has focused on the macrobotanical paucity of certain resources marked as nutritionally valuable (e.g., Miksicek et al. 1981) and broader dietary and social implications.

In pursuit of "cuisine," many authors have drawn structural analogies between ingredients and *langue*, cuisine and *parole* (Barthes 1997; Counihan and Van Esterik 1997; Douglas 1997; Soler 1997; Weismantel 1988). Lévi-Strauss, in formulating his triangle of Raw, Cooked, and Rotted, states that "the cooking of a society is a language in which it unconsciously translates its structure—or else resigns itself, still unconsciously, to revealing its contradictions" (1997:35). Mary Douglas, in the study of her own family's meal planning, pursues syntagmatic relations and the "meaning" of foods, addressing "the degree to which a family uses symbolic structures which are available from the wider social system" (1997:43). In a more elaborate approach, Mary Weismantel views foods as both symbols and indices (1988). Through her work among the Zumbagua, she draws distinctions between food "paradigms" which are relational to other systems, and food "syntagms" which are relational to other items on a plate. Paleoethnobotanists have incorporated similar themes, in studies of daily life and ethnobotanical practice (Gumerman 1994; Jacomet 2009; Johannessen 1993). I return to many of these interpretations further on.

Closely tied to the structuration and transformation of cuisine is the structuration and transformation of politics. From household to community to region, social power is negotiated in the kitchen. As Sutton (2001:5) has noted, "anthropological work has produced a broad consensus that food is about commensality—eating to make friends—and competition—eating to make enemies." Echoing these sentiments, Counihan and Van Esterik note that "[food] is a central pawn in political strategies of states and households. Food marks social differences, boundaries, bonds, and contradictions. Eating is an endlessly evolving enactment of gender, family, and community relationships" (Counihan and Van Esterik 1997:1). When addressing political aspects of food, popular topics have included feasting (Dietler and Hayden 2001), food production (Farrington and Urry 1985; Hamilakis 1996), food distribution (Powers and Powers 1984:73), personal obligation (Shack 1969), reciprocity (Meigs 1997), the interplay between food, subjectivity and familial relationships (Lupton 1994), gastro-politics (Appadurai 1981), acculturation (Allison 1991; Young 1971), and differentiation of class (Bourdieu 1984; Bray 2003; Gumerman 1994; Mennell 1997). Paleoethnobotanists that have drawn from these studies have explored social stratification and inequality (Crader 1990; Crane 1996; Frink 2007; Kelertas 1997; Morehart and Eisenberg 2010) and political economy (van der Veen and Jones 2006).

People at least partially define themselves through the plants they use and the foodstuffs they consume. Communities differentiate themselves from their neighbors in multiple aspects, from tools to food. In some cases, entire social groups use food to define themselves vis-à-vis the "other" as has happened across the globe from historic Papua New Guinea to ancient Europe (Fischler 1988; Hesse 1990; Janik 2003; Kahn 1986; Sutton 2001:5). Foodways are tied to the formation of identity (Allison 1991; Appadurai 1981; Barthes 1997), including gender (Barthes 1997; Bynum 1997), and may be deliberately manifested (Allison 1991; Weismantel 1988). Food may be commemorative (Barthes 1997; Hamilakis 1999), and specific plants and foodstuffs may connect people to their heritage through the practice of cooking recipes of forebears (similar to Sutton 2001). Some authors have addressed the embodiment of tastes and the elaboration of foodstuffs prized for certain flavors they possess (Fischler 1988). Such studies may be closely tied to aesthetics (Arnold 1999; Fischler 1980; Sherratt 1987). Tastes, as Farrington and Urry argue (1985:154), could even be responsible for the first practices of cultivation, instead of the more common "staple crop" arguments. Through the tools of paleoethnobotany specifically, various authors have illustrated identity and personhood as tied to foodways (Boenke 2007; Crown 2000; Franklin 2001; Janik 2003).

Finally, the semiotics of food, although alluded to in the course of many other studies, is only explicitly emphasized in several. Weismantel (1988:7), claims that, overall, "it is because they are ordinarily immersed in everyday practice in a material way that foods, abstracted as symbols from this material process, can condense in themselves a wealth of ideological meanings." The meanings of foods are varied and encompass many of the themes elaborated above. In some cases, certain foods have been shown to act as semiotic substitutes when the ideal ingredients are not available (Adolph 2009). In paleoethnobotany, when considering the semiotic character of plant use, most authors have highlighted symbolic ethnobotany and ritualized practice (Bozarth and Guderjan 2004; Brown and Gerstle 2002; Lentz et al. 2005; Morehart et al. 2005).

Paleoethnobotanical methodologies have enriched studies of foodways, just as foodways literature has enriched paleoethnobotanical interpretation. Together, they represent a varied tapestry of contributions to anthropological endeavor. Some of these contributions could be grouped under the heading "processual" and others under the heading "postprocessual." However, in combining the strengths of these various approaches, the actual labels become subsumed under broader questions. It is in the pursuit of inclusivity that I turn to bodies of literature that might potentially encompass both.

LINGUISTIC- AND PRACTICE-BASED APPROACHES

Theories of practice bridge such apparently dichotomous areas as subjectivism and objectivism, symbolic studies and material studies, theory and research, structure and agency, microanalysis and macroanalysis (Bourdieu and Wacquant 1992; Giddens 1979). This middle ground is staked out through the study of practice. *Practice*, in this sense, comprises "regulated improvisation," the dynamic mediation between the internal and the external (Bourdieu 1977, 1990; similarly to Giddens 1979:56). It is that which subjects do, make, maintain, and transform, and is neither entirely effect nor entirely activity, as it encompasses both routinized habits and acts that fall within varying degrees of consciousness (Bourdieu 1977, 1990; Giddens 1979).

Foodways, a dominant aspect of daily life, are constructed through layers of practice and in turn formulate future practice. They are transformed and reified through daily and ritual activities that are themselves governed by prior activities involving food. As noted above, foodways are part belief and part custom. For this reason, they influence both *doxa* (a sort of coalescing of cultural logics) and *habitus* (the embodied "taken-for-granteds" of daily practice). The practices and ingredients involved in a meal depend on fields (the place of position-takings), both social and physical, which are in turn dependent on them.

In thinking about the ways that past plant activities were patterned, transformed, and maintained, theories of practice have proven quite helpful. However, in order to understand how certain foods and food practices were patterned or anomalous within *specific* contexts and spaces, and how these patterns and anomalies transformed over time, understanding modes of enactments becomes critical. For this reason, I turn to perspectives that incorporate language, since the interplay between practice and doxa (Bourdieu 1990) is roughly analogous to the interplay between paradigm and syntagm, text and context, and even space and place (following de Certeau 1984).

As previously noted, linguistic approaches are not new to studies of food (Douglas 1997; Leach 1964; Lehrer 1972; Lévi-Strauss 1997; Weismantel 1988), nor even to archaeological studies of foodways and ethnobotanical practice (E. Campbell 2000; Parker Pearson 2003; Wetterstrom 1978). However, I wished to stretch such models to consider foodways as locutionary acts, explore the dialectical relationship of foodways with various contexts, and elaborate practices of discourse. I wanted to be able to interweave structuration (though not structuralism) and practice, over the long(er) *durée* and at several sites, while incorporating various types of contextual factors.

I started with a very basic Saussurean model (explained clearly and at greater length by Chandler 1994) which is schematically outlined in figure 19.1. As shown in this illustration, the paradigm is essentially a set of similarly classified elements within a category. It is the vertical set of possible options for each category along the axis of substitution (Chandler 1994). The syntagmatic axis can be defined as the horizontal placement of elements (spatial, temporal, or associative), along the axis of positioning (Chandler 1994). Basically, it marks how the elements of the paradigm combine, in different ways, in a dynamic interplay between different contexts, timing, and availability. The syntagmatic associations are, essentially, "what goes with what," as conditioned by particular situations.

Following the Saussurean model, I consider the paradigms as the sets of possible options, concepts, or activities guided by practices as they unfold along the syntagmatic axis. I consider the syntagms as the sets of associations formed through the selection of options, concepts, or activities from the limited paradigmatic axis. As context, syntagm, and paradigm interact, they result in a set of syntagmatic consequences, a sort of "time-line" or collection of interdependent elements. In this matrix, the dynamic interplay between paradigm

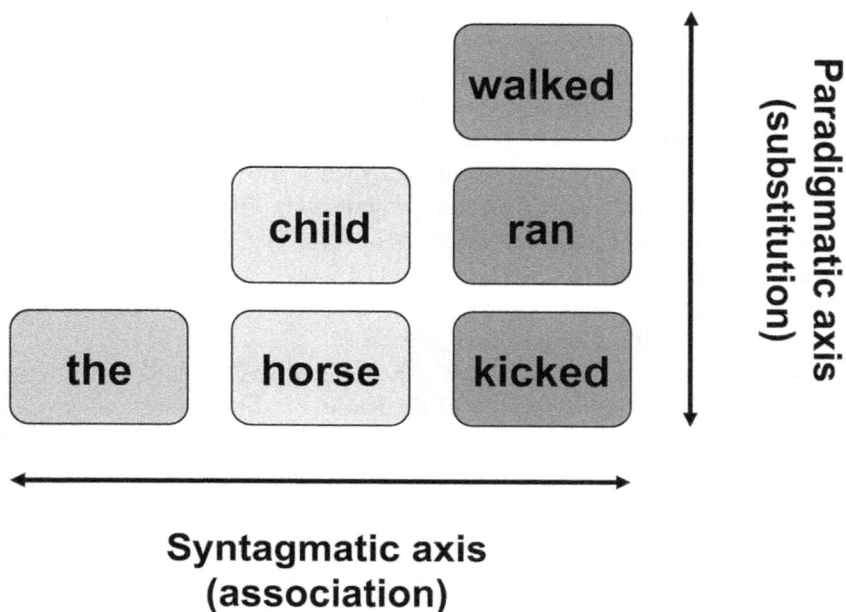

walked

child **ran**

the **horse** **kicked**

Paradigmatic axis
(substitution)

**Syntagmatic axis
(association)**

FIGURE 19.1. *Articulation of the paradigmatic axis with the syntagmatic axis in language.*

and syntagm is both producer and product of practice. Transformations, either in relations between elements or in the available paradigmatic subset, can produce changes in the other. The options taken during the course of a speech act can be likened to the cognitive concept of *chaîne opératoire* (Schlanger 1994), although in this case, grammar is only manifested in-practice. This differs from traditional Saussurean approaches in which the grammatical template is used as a sort of yardstick against which individual speech acts are measured.

Linguistic concepts can be translated for studies of foodways in several aspects. We can begin with a lexicon of possibilities—the entire population of nutritionally available foods including fruits, seeds, animals, insects, and even human beings. From this nutritionally available population are drawn the paradigms of *culturally* available foods. Cultural perceptions and constructions of paradigmatic elements of food are highly fluid, evident even in the changes to categories of food within the past 50 years in the United States (consider the fall of jello salads and the rise of heirloom vegetables).

As with other cultural dimensions, the ways that archaeologists formulate paradigms of food may be quite different from the paradigms of the culture under study. This is partially due to methodology. In archaeological research of foodways, the relevant data sets are usually farmed out to different specialists (e.g., the zooarchaeologist, the paleoethnobotanist, the spatial analyst) and partitioned into different segments of reports (e.g., plants, fish, animals, geography). Essentially, the data become typed based on ecofact or artifact form. There are functional divisions, as well, such as those found in nutritional analyses: divisions into carbohydrates, proteins, fats, vitamins, minerals, and water. There are also categorical mixtures of form *and* function: staples, proteins, condiments, vegetables. However partitioned, the paradigms that we as archaeologists formulate directly impact the study, whether in pursuit of caloric yields or cultural conceptions of edibles.

The syntagmatic axes of foodways are also highly fluid and at least partially dependent on the perspective of the researcher. Such factors as scheduling, seasonality, agricultural production, cultural preferences, personal tastes, ritual values, and so on all have enormous impact on syntagmatic associations within foodways. These associations exist between foods and tools, foods and practices, foods and other foods, foods and spaces, and foods and contexts, among others. For example, acorns may be boiled in baskets but not roasted in firepits, consumed daily but never for feasts, ground but not cut, eaten with meat but not with roots, and so on. Each instance of association, when aggregated with others, provides a possible pattern of associations that helps to define the syntagmatic axis.

When stretching the Saussurean model to understand a culinary "speech act," I borrow from Mary Douglas (1997) to construct a schematic that has to do with a set of items on a plate. I consider what might be a meal, in this case for a Southeastern Mesoamerican household of the precontact period (figure 19.2).

This model represents an atemporal set of syntagms. That is, the elements are associated not by temporal ordering (the verb comes after the noun comes after the article) but rather through principles of combination (certain things fit with others, but are not necessarily in a particular order). In the same way that you probably wouldn't say "the horse ran" to describe a child's soccer game, you wouldn't serve only snack foods and call it a meal. In expanding this to a set of speech acts, over the course of a day, the combinations would likely vary. In the same way that you wouldn't say "the ran ran" you probably wouldn't serve a full meal as a between-meal snack.

Certain elements fit with other elements along the syntagmatic axis, but all are context-contingent. This context is complicated by long and short arcs of practice, immediate surroundings, the targeted listener/consumer, the history

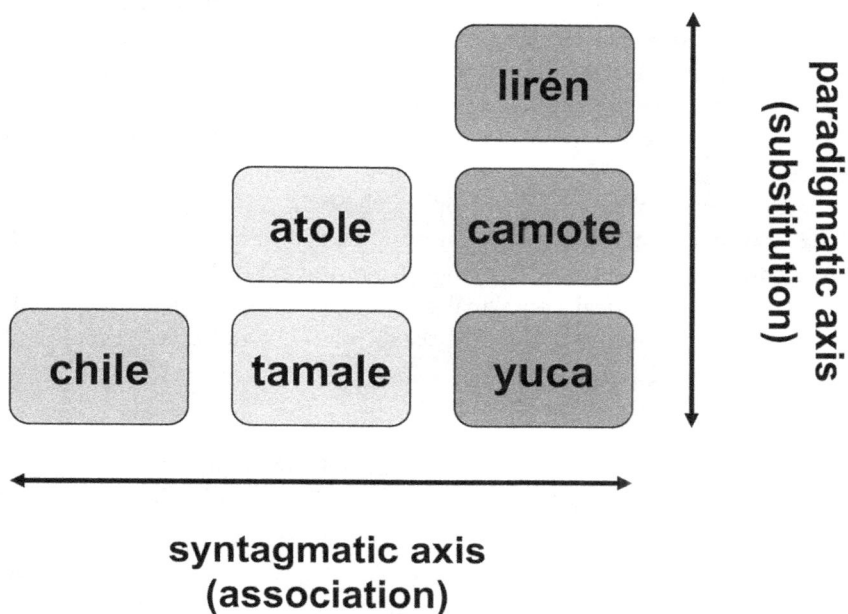

FIGURE 19.2. *Very hypothetical example of a precontact "meal" in Southeastern Mesoamerica.*

of the speaker/cook, and so on. Incorporating these additional factors is what I see as the domain of practice theory. This is not a novel approach: studies of linguistics since at least the late 1970s have incorporated elements of practice in fields such as emergent grammar (e.g., Hanks 1990) and conversational discourse analysis (e.g., Goffman 1979). If we look at a particular dish, such as *atole*, certain elements will be present: maize *masa*, water, and salt. Perhaps this particular dish is usually served with chile. Perhaps this dish is served with chile for breakfast, but without chile for lunch. Perhaps this dish is, on a daily basis, served only for breakfast and lunch, and never for dinner. Perhaps this dish is served almost every day of the year, except for particular feast or fast days. Already the *atole*, a relatively common and simple maize gruel, is in need of a complicated flowchart, a set of algorithms, a Venn diagram, or all of the above, to describe its relationship to other foods.

"Grammars" of foodways—the articulated paradigms and syntagms—are instantiated, maintained, transformed, and reiterated through the daily practice that is in turn shaped by these "grammars." Such iterations and reiterations, through daily meals and feasts, can result in the innovation of foodways and the production of novel forms of recipes, practice, process, and performance. The linguistic model, when applied to foodways, is not meant to represent *the* grammar, but rather *a* grammar. It is mean to be a sort of "average" of knowledge, a range of possible practices, or a pattern as it becomes manifest under particular conditions.

These idealized schematics are complicated by the addition of actual things, places, and actions, especially when interpreting paleoethnobotanical data sets. I turn now to examples from four sites in Northwestern Honduras to try to piece together a historical, contextual perspective on foodways that views ethnobotanical habits not as a "finished set of rules" but rather a "repertoire of possibilities" (Stahl 2002:832).

CASE STUDIES FROM NORTHWESTERN HONDURAS

In previous work (Morell-Hart 2011), I considered syntagms in terms of associations between elements, and paradigms in terms of possible substitutions of elements within a set. For example, can we see evidence of "staple carbohydrates" (root crops and maize combined) or are "root crop foods" categorically separate from "maize foods"? What might indicate paradigmatic substitution, in terms of replacing available elements within a particular category of food (e.g., consuming maize in place of root crops if they are interchangeable as "staple carbohydrates")? Furthermore, over time, how do syntagmatic relationships change, interwoven as they are with transformations in ecology and society (e.g., the disappearance of certain root crops as maize becomes culturally favored)? Finally, what are possible syntagmatic recombinations of foodstuffs at particular places and times (e.g., the pairing of maize with ritual contexts), and what are the syntagmatic reassociations of foodstuffs, given differing combinations of ingredients over time (e.g., shifts from staple carbohydrate combinations to maintaining separate "maize" and "root crop" dishes)? In the subsequent sections, I provide sketches of my approach to several of these questions, borrowing heavily from practice theorists and linguistic models. I make use of data from four sites in Northwestern Honduras: Los Naranjos, Cerro Palenque, Currusté, and Puerto Escondido.

Artifacts and Plants as Syntagms

How can we identify the associations and disassociations between specific artifacts and ethnobotanical practices? To draw comparisons, I made use of

TABLE 19.1. Artifact categories and number of analyzed samples associated with each

Artifact category	Number of samples	Site(s) where recovered
Obsidian biface tool	1	Cerro Palenque
Obsidian flake fragments	2	Los Naranjos
Obsidian retouched flakes	4	Los Naranjos, Cerro Palenque, Puerto Escondido
Obsidian blade fragments	10	Los Naranjos, Puerto Escondido, Cerro Palenque
Ceramic vessel sherds	4	Cerro Palenque

microbotanical remains (phytoliths and starch grains) recovered from four kinds of obsidian artifacts and ceramic vessels. I present only the results from sonicated effluvium, and not results from adhering sediment (included in the broader set of sitewide results in Morell-Hart 2011). I look at 21 artifacts in total: sherds from four ceramic vessels, one obsidian biface tool, two obsidian flake fragments, four obsidian retouched flakes, and fragments of 10 obsidian blades (table 19.1). These vessels and implements were recovered from three of the four sites in my study, the exception being Currusté, where I did not have access to artifacts. Although admittedly not an exhaustive analysis of hundreds of implements, this preliminary sketch does reveal some interesting results and prospective working hypotheses.

I began by looking individually at each taxon recovered from artifacts (in starch grain and/or phytolith form) and considering associated artifact types and relative abundances of microbotanical remains. I then explored the relative abundances of taxa, as related to each individual artifact. Turning to broader artifact classes, I identified the differences and similarities between artifact classes and then within artifact classes, comparing ceramic vessels to obsidian implements, and then comparing different types of obsidian implements with each other. In each case, I looked at the richness (total number of species) and relative abundances of taxa associated with each artifact class or artifact type. Finally, I explored the stronger associations between taxa and particular artifact types through ubiquity measures. I compared the results of each of these analyses to previous expectations and analogies, looking for possible paradigmatic substitutions and syntagmatic associations of Southeastern Mesoamerican foodways. What I present here is a brief summary of some of these results.

First, the obsidian artifacts appear to have been predominantly multiuse. At least 26 different taxa were recovered from obsidian artifacts (table 19.2). Every taxon recovered from artifacts, with the exception of squash *(Cucurbita* sp.), was recovered from the obsidian implements. It appears as though, almost across the board, obsidian artifacts were used for cutting and slicing woody, fibrous things, including grasses, bromeliads, palm leaves, and wood.

Relative abundances of taxa varied from artifact to artifact. However, woody species dominated most assemblages, whether ceramic or obsidian, with the exception of four blades from Los Naranjos. Panicoid grasses and palm species were also frequently represented, irrespective of artifact class, though always much less abundant than the woody phytoliths. This is at least partially a function of the better preservation and identification of these species, and may or may not reflect percentages of actual uses.

In terms of previous expectations, even given the paucity of diagnostic starch grains, I was pleasantly surprised by the overall richness and abundance of recovered microremains. This diversity has been signaled in ethnographic and historic narratives, as well as prior work at other sites in Southeastern Mesoamerica. The great abundance and ubiquity of wood, though surprising, should perhaps have been anticipated by these same narratives. As relative abundances occur within a closed array (always totaling 100%), the woody materials were bound to dominate each artifact's assemblage. For this reason, although some root crops and maize microremains were recovered, their abundance seemed relatively low as compared to prior expectations.

It is somewhat surprising that there were not more differentiated uses for particular obsidian artifacts, considering the diversity of forms. In terms of syntagmatic associations, with the exception of the Los Naranjos blades, there are no broad regularities of use associated with a particular obsidian artifact type. In terms of paradigmatic substitutions, however, there may be some observable patterns. Although palm, wood, and grass microremains are most common and abundant across obsidian artifact types, at the level of individual artifacts, the remaining taxa are much more constrained, and appear to be "substituted" with other taxa, depending on the artifact. Bromeliaceae, Chloridoideae, Euphorbiaceae, arrowroot *(Maranta* sp.), and Pooideae grass species are associated only with obsidian blade fragments, whereas lirén *(Calathea* sp.) is associated only with a single obsidian flake fragment, and manioc *(Manihot esculenta)* only with a retouched flake. The remaining unknown phytoliths were found in association with only one or two artifact types. Interestingly, given these results, it appears as though potential food species are, in a sense, paradigmatically "swapped out" for each other, depending on the tool, although this may be partially attributed to sampling size.

Table 19.2. Phytolith and starch grain taxa recovered from artifact samples, by artifact category

Ceramic sherd interiors	Obsidian biface	Obsidian blade fragments	Obsidian flake fragments	Retouched obsidian flakes
Arecaceae sp.	Arecaceae sp.	Arecaceae sp.	Arecaceae sp.	Arecaceae sp.
Cucurbita sp.	Panicoideae sp.	Arecaceae sp. B	*Calathea* sp.	Chloridoideae sp.
Panicoideae sp.	unknown phytolith 3	Bromeliaceae sp.	Panicoideae sp.	*Manihot esculenta*
unknown phytolith 2	unknown starch	Chloridoideae sp.	unknown phytolith 2	Marantaceae sp.
unknown starch	unknown woody sp.	Euphorbiaceae sp.	unknown starch	Panicoideae sp.
unknown woody sp.		*Maranta* sp.	unknown woody sp.	unknown phytolith 1
Zea mays leaf		Marantaceae sp.		unknown phytolith 14
Zea mays cob				
		Panicoideae sp.		unknown phytolith 2
		Pooideae sp.		unknown phytolith 3
		unknown fiber		unknown phytolith scutiform
		unknown phytolith 11		unknown starch
		unknown phytolith 12		unknown storage
		unknown phytolith 16		unknown vascular
		unknown phytolith 2		unknown woody sp.
		unknown phytolith 3		*Zea mays* leaf
				Zea mays starch
		unknown starch		
		unknown starch 1		
		unknown woody sp.		
		Zea mays leaf		
		Zea mays cob		
		Zea mays starch grain		

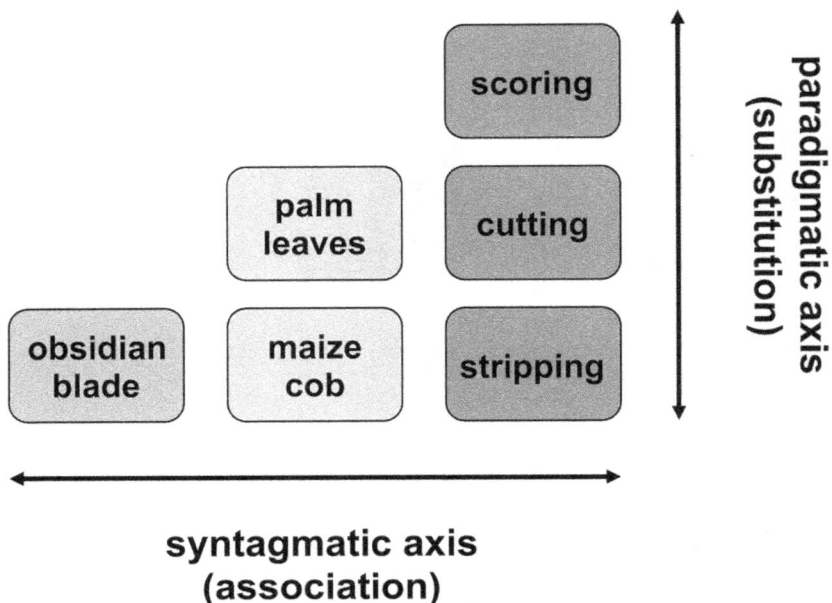

FIGURE 19.3. *One set of potential syntagmatic associations and paradigmatic substitutions related to obsidian blades.*

Syntagmatic relationships could have existed between one taxon and others, and one artifact and particular taxa. However, few syntagmatic associations are noted between artifact types, or even artifact classes. Many artifacts appear to have been multiuse, incorporating both food and non-food elements, although all these elements may be incorporated in the course of normal culinary practice (figure 19.3).

Overall, in this preliminary analysis of artifact samples, we see the linked fates of practices, artifacts, and taxa in each object biography. To use an imperfect analogy, people may use a single pocketknife for a whole variety of things, from cutting into a motor oil container to slicing an apple. These "pocket knives" of the past, however, seem to have been more freely shared between people, as they were less durable and tended to be stored together (shown in situ at Joya de Cerén [Sheets 2002]), rather than stored individually with a single person. For this reason, the non-discrete uses of various tools may actually be linked to discrete activities carried out by multiple individuals. Such syntagmatic associations, however, would be very difficult to identify through paleoethnobotanical means.

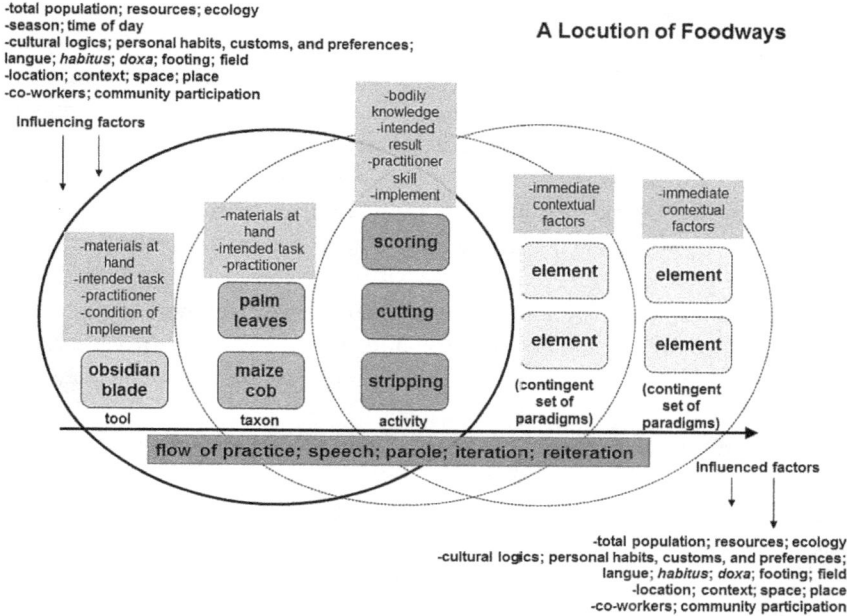

A Locution of Foodways

-total population; resources; ecology
-season; time of day
-cultural logics; personal habits, customs, and preferences; langue; *habitus*; *doxa*; footing; field
-location; context; space; place
-co-workers; community participation

Influencing factors

-bodily knowledge
-intended result
-practitioner skill
-implement

-materials at hand
-intended task
-practitioner

-materials at hand
-intended task
-practitioner
-condition of implement

scoring

palm leaves

cutting

maize cob

stripping

obsidian blade

tool

taxon

activity

-immediate contextual factors

element

element

(contingent set of paradigms)

-immediate contextual factors

element

element

(contingent set of paradigms)

flow of practice; speech; parole; iteration; reiteration

Influenced factors

-total population; resources; ecology
-cultural logics; personal habits, customs, and preferences; langue; *habitus*; *doxa*; footing; field
-location; context; space; place
-co-workers; community participation

FIGURE 19.4. *An example of a "locution" of foodways.*

Elsewhere (Morell-Hart 2011), I used similar approaches when considering questions related to spatiality, materiality, and historical ecology. Through such studies of spaces, places, and botanical assemblages, and studies of artifacts similar to those presented here, we can pursue transient substitutions and associations as well as permeable cultural logics. Future research could broaden this base to incorporate other factors including environmental histories, hydrological transformations, oral histories, and public policy, in order to better contextualize and frame the data as well as direct interpretation.

BROAD SCHEMATICS AND COMPLEMENTARY STUDIES

Although I am still undergoing the process of fully articulating all of the elements in my own research, an idealized model of foodways may look something like what I illustrate in figure 19.4.

In this broad schematic, the first two sets of paradigms are given—things that have actually been recovered in association with each other ("tool" and "taxon"). The next set of paradigms ("activity") is hypothesized, drawn from analogous ethnographies and ethnohistories. This locutionary moment is encircled to indicate a snippet of "speech"; a single defined act. Subsequent circles indicate contingent future, continued, or broader locutionary moments. The instantiation of particular associations impacts the contingent sets of paradigms. That is, the next set of paradigms might include "discard of stripped maize cob" and "storage of stripped maize cob as cleaning implement," but only if a maize cob were stripped during the course of the prior locutionary moment. Each act is dependent on broader context (including resources, season, *habitus*, etc.) and may shift over time or pattern differently at greater scales. There are also immediate contextual factors that have influence over the "speech acts" of tool use and the longer series of speech acts. However, broad and immediate contextual factors are also influenced *by* such enactments.

How many contextual factors can we identify? We can track climate, both locally and regionally, through the use of oxygen isotopes, sediment cores, and pollen profiles. We can have a sense of practice through analogous examples in ethnographic and ethnohistoric literature. What is more difficult is teasing out factors that are strongly codependent. Calculations of demography, for example, would be much informed by studies of nutrition and subsistence, but those studies would also be much informed by calculations of demography.

Overall, what does such a schematic reveal? Though far from complete, it reveals a set of potential relationships and a possible grammar of tool use. It presents a set of factors and conditions that may be further explored through the incorporation of other studies, both archaeological and analogical. By reviewing the evidence in this way, we are able to compare these various taxa to the broad paradigms of expected plants. However, the combination of items recovered also reflects syntagmatic relations of foodways: the residues of daily residential practices. These practices likely include procurement from cultivated and fallow maize fields (subsequent to a large set of crop-production practices), weeding and/or expedient use of plants as fuel, home gardening, the disposal of hearth materials near residential structures, and potential ritual or medicinal activity. These practical combinations are analogous to a set of continuous "speech acts," subject to ecological diversity and historically contextualized in the *longue durée* of Northwestern Honduran activities. Such "speech acts," though granting us insight into the daily lives of precontact peoples, require further community-level comparisons and short-term plant use histories in order to better socially and historically contextualize the two axes of foodways.

FINAL THOUGHTS

In a busy kitchen, the location of each activity defines, and is defined by, both *habitus* and *doxa*: the unstated habits in terms of how the food is prepared and the unstated beliefs in what constitutes a particular dish or meal. These loci are also defined by the movement of particular objects and ingredients suitable to the task at hand, just as these objects and ingredients are selected based on the intended locus. Each culinary "field" is defined by the materials, space, and activities carried out there, in the same way that each culinary field helps to define these elements and each of these elements serves to define the others. In a busy kitchen, for example, salads are prepared in certain places, by certain people, using certain ingredients and techniques, at certain times of the day and on certain days of the week, following certain beliefs as to what constitutes a salad, where and how it is prepared, when it is prepared, and who prepares it. It is this metaphor that I have extended into the past, though considering *atoles* (maize gruels) more often than salads.

Anthony Giddens claims that all social activity is necessarily situated in "three intersecting moments of difference: temporally, paradigmatically (invoking structure which is present only in its instantiation) and spatially" (Giddens 1979:54). My approach is similarly practice-based, linguistically oriented, historically contextualized, and spatially focused. It is also engaged with a qualified materiality, as the transitory nature of food (if not culinary equipment) introduces an additional complexity. Food occupies a sort of liminal space; it exists as practice and material. It is both paradigm and syntagm, ingestible and action. It can be icon, index, and symbol, or all three in overlap.

Illuminating paradigmatic substitutions and syntagmatic relations allows us to address various sorts of questions. What adaptations do people make in their foodways as responses to external and internal factors (shifting to novel food resources, for example)? What are the paradigmatic substitutions in terms of available elements within a particular category of food (consuming maize in place of root crops, for example)? Over time, what syntagmatic relationships change, interwoven as they are with transformations in ecology and society (the disappearance of certain root crops, for example)? What are the syntagmatic recombinations in terms of foodstuffs in a particular place and time, and what are the syntagmatic reassociations in terms of combinations of foodstuffs over time (the pairing of maize with ritual contexts, for example)? What can such investigations reveal about underlying cultural understandings and overt compromises in ancient societies (e.g., the pursuit of particular tastes or the rejection of certain foods, even during famine periods)? Broadly, what can concepts of substitutions and associations reveal about human resilience and cultural transformation?

Traditionally segregated "processual" and "postprocessual" approaches, when re-combined, contribute to such integrative modeling. The incredible potential of paleoethnobotany lies partially in the way that it can accommodate a multitude of approaches in the pursuit of a multitude of goals. The pursuit of these goals ultimately contributes to the multitude of approaches, as archaeologists are able to witness the unfolding of practice over time, and paleoethnobotanists, particularly, can approach the complex relationship between humans and plants over the *longue durée*. There is hardly one program for everyone. Our objectives, methods, and pools of thought overlap others in complicated ways. We are left with something of a salad bowl, where perhaps some people will pick out the carrots, and other people are allergic to the glazed pecans, but everyone has a seat at the table and a share of the meal.

Abbo, Shahal, Inbar Zezak, Efrat Schwartz, Simcha Lev-Yadun, and Avi Gopher. 2008. "Experimental Harvesting of Wild Peas in Israel: Implications for the Origins of Near East Farming." *Journal of Archaeological Science* 35 (4): 922–29. http://dx.doi.org/10.1016/j.jas.2007.06.016.

Abrams, Marc D., and Gregory J. Nowacki. 2008. "Native Americans as Active and Passive Promoters of Mast and Fruit Trees in the Eastern USA." *The Holocene* 18 (7): 1123–37. http://dx.doi.org/10.1177/0959683608095581.

Abrams, Marc D., and Charles M. Ruffner. 1995. "Physiographic Analysis of Witness-Tree Distribution (1765–1798) and Present Forest Cover through North Central Pennsylvania." *Canadian Journal of Forest Research* 25 (4): 659–68. http://dx.doi.org/10.1139/x95-073.

Acs, Peter, Thomas Wilhalm, and Klaus Oeggl. 2005. "Remains of Grasses Found with the Neolithic Iceman 'Ötzi'." *Vegetation History and Archaeobotany* 14 (3): 198–206. http://dx.doi.org/10.1007/s00334-005-0014-x.

Adams, Karen R. 1994. "A Regional Synthesis of *Zea mays* in the Prehistoric American Southwest." In *Corn and Culture in the Prehistoric New World*, edited by Sissel Johannessen and Christine Ann Hastorf, 273–302. Boulder, CO: Westview Press.

Adams, Karen R., and Robert E. Gasser. 1980. "Plant Microfossils from Archaeological Sites: Research Considerations, and Sampling Techniques and Approaches." *Kiva* 45:293–300.

DOI: 10.5876/9781607323167.c020

Adams, Robert McCormick. 1981. *Heartland of Cities: Surveys of Ancient Settlement and Land Use on the Central Floodplain of the Euphrates.* Chicago: University of Chicago Press.

Adolph, Andrea. 2009. *Food and Femininity in Twentieth-Century British Women's Fiction.* Farnham, UK: Ashgate Publishing Company.

Aguilera, Mònica, José Luis Araus, Jordi Voltas, Maria Oliva Rodríguez-Ariza, Fernando Molina, Núria Rovira, Ramon Buxó, and Juan Pedro Ferrio. 2008. "Stable Carbon and Nitrogen Isotopes and Quality Traits of Fossil Cereal Grains Provide Clues on Sustainability at the Beginnings of Mediterranean Agriculture." *Rapid Communications in Mass Spectrometry* 22 (11): 1653–63. http://dx.doi.org/10.1002/rcm.3501.

Akeret, Örni, Jean Nicolas Haas, Urs Leuzinger, and Stefanie Jacomet. 1999. "Plant Macrofossils and Pollen in Goat/Sheep Faeces from the Neolithic Lake-Shore Settlement Arbon Bleiche 3, Switzerland." *The Holocene* 9 (2): 175–82. http://dx.doi.org/10.1191/095968399666631581.

Akers, Brian P., Juan Francisco Ruiz, Alan Piper, and Carl A. P. Ruck. 2011. "A Prehistoric Mural in Spain Depicting Neurotropic *Psilocybe* Mushrooms?" *Economic Botany* 65 (2): 121–8. http://dx.doi.org/10.1007/s12231-011-9152-5.

Albert, Rosa M., Ruth Shahack-Gross, Dan Cabanes, Ayelet Gilboa, Simcha Lev-Yadun, Marta Portillo, Ilan Sharon, Elisabetta Boaretto, and Steve Weiner. 2008. "Phytolith-Rich Layers from the Late Bronze and Iron Ages at Tel Dor (Israel): Mode of Formation and Archaeological Significance." *Journal of Archaeological Science* 35 (1): 57–75. http://dx.doi.org/10.1016/j.jas.2007.02.015.

Aldenderfer, Mark S., and Roger K. Blashfield. 1984. *Cluster Analysis. Quantitative Applications in the Social Sciences No. 44.* Beverly Hills: Sage Publications.

Alexa. 2011. "Site Overview: wikipedia.org." Accessed November 26. http://www.alexa.com/siteinfo/wikipedia.org?range=5y&size=large&y=t.

Alexander, Charles S., and Jean Cutler Prior. 1971. "Holocene Sedimentation Rates in Overbank Deposits in the Black Bottom of the Lower Ohio River, Southern Illinois." *American Journal of Science* 270 (5): 361–72. http://dx.doi.org/10.2475/ajs.270.5.361.

Algaze, Guillermo. 2001. "Initial Social Complexity in Southwestern Asia: The Mesopotamian Advantage." *Current Anthropology* 42 (2): 199–233. http://dx.doi.org/10.1086/320005.

Alizadeh, Abbas, Nicholas Kouchoukos, Tony J. Wilkinson, Andrew M. Bauer, and Marjan Mashkour. 2004. "Human-Environment Interactions on the Upper Khuzestan Plains, Southwest Iran: Recent Investigations." *Paléorient* 30 (1): 69–88. http://dx.doi.org/10.3406/paleo.2004.4773.

Allaby, Robin G., Kerry O'Donoghue, Robert Sallares, Martin K. Jones, and Terence A. Brown. 1997. "Evidence for the Survival of Ancient DNA in Charred Wheat Seeds from European Archaeological Sites." *Ancient Biomolecules* 1 (2): 119–29.

Allen, Craig D., R. Scott Anderson, Renata B. Jass, Jamie L. Toney, and Christopher H. Baisan. 2008. "Paired Charcoal and Tree-Ring Records of High-Frequency Holocene Fire from Two New Mexico Bog Sites." *International Journal of Wildland Fire* 17 (1): 115–30. http://dx.doi.org/10.1071/WF07165.

Allen, Susan E. 2005. "A Living Landscape: The Palaeothnobotany of Sovjan, Albania." Unpublished PhD diss. Department of Archaeology, Boston University, Boston.

Allen, Tim G. 1981. "Smiths Field, Hardwich with Yelford." *Council for British Archaeology Group IX Newsletter* 11:112–46.

Allen, Tim G. 1993. "Abingdon, Abingdon Vineyard 1992: Area 2 and 3, the Early Defences." *South Midlands Archaeology* 23:64–6.

Allen, Tim G., and Mark Robinson. 1993. *The Prehistoric Landscape and Iron Age Enclosed Settlement at Mingies Ditch. Thames Valley Landscapes: The Windrush Valley.* Vol. 2. Oxford: Oxford Archaeology.

Allentoft, Morten E., Matthew Collins, David Harker, James Haile, Charlotte L. Oskam, Marie L. Hale, Paula F. Campos, Jose A. Samaniego, M. T. P. Gilbert, E. Willerslev, Guojie Zhang, R. Paul Scofield, Richard N. Holdaway, and Michael Bunce. 2012. "The Half-Life of DNA in Bone: Measuring Decay Kinetics in 158 Dated Fossils." *Proceedings of the Royal Society B: Biological Sciences* 279 (1748): 4724–33. http://dx.doi.org/10.1098/rspb.2012.1745.

Allison, Anne. 1991. "Japanese Mothers and Obentōs: The Lunch-Box as Ideological State Apparatus." *Anthropological Quarterly* 64 (4): 195–208. http://dx.doi.org /10.2307/3317212.

Alonso, Natàlia, Emili Junyent, Angel Lafuente, and Joan B. López. 2008. "Plant Remains, Storage and Crop Processing inside the Iron Age Fort of Els Vilars D'arbeca (Catalonia, Spain)." *Vegetation History and Archaeobotany* 17 (S1 Suppl. 1): S149–58. http://dx.doi.org/10.1007/s00334-008-0163-9.

Alonso, Natàlia, and D. López. 2005. "Esclerocios de *Cenococcum geophilum* Fr. en Yacimientos Protohistóricos del Nordeste Peninsular." *Avances en arqueometría* 6:213–21.

Ambrose, Stanley. 1991. "Effects of Diet, Climate and Physiology on Nitrogen Isotope Abundances in Terrestrial Foodwebs." *Journal of Archaeological Science* 18 (3): 293–317. http://dx.doi.org/10.1016/0305-4403(91)90067-Y.

Ambrose, Stanley, and Michael DeNiro. 1986a. "The Isotopic Ecology of East African Mammals." *Oecologia* 69 (3): 395–406. http://dx.doi.org/10.1007/BF00377062.

Ambrose, Stanley, and Michael DeNiro. 1986b. "Reconstruction of African Human Diet Using Bone-Collagen Carbon and Nitrogen Isotope Ratios." *Nature* 319 (6051): 321–24. http://dx.doi.org/10.1038/319321a0.

Ambrose, Stanley, and Michael DeNiro. 1987. "Bone Nitrogen Isotope Composition and Climate." *Nature* 325 (6101): 201. http://dx.doi.org/10.1038/325201a0.

Ambrose, Stanley, and Lynette Norr. 1993. "Experimental Evidence for the Relationship of the Carbon Isotope Ratios of Whole Diet and Dietary Protein to Those of Bone Collagen and Carbonate." In *Prehistoric Human Bone: Archaeology at the Molecular Level*, edited by Joseph B. Lambert and Gisela Grupe, 1–38. New York: Springer-Verlag. http://dx.doi.org/10.1007/978-3-662-02894-0_1.

Andersen, Kenneth, Karen Lise Bird, Morten Rasmussen, James Haile, Henrik Breuning-Madsen, Kurt H. Kjaer, Ludovic Orlando, M. Thomas P. Gilbert, and Eske Willerslev. 2012. "Meta-Barcoding of 'Dirt' DNA from Soil Reflects Vertebrate Biodiversity." *Molecular Ecology* 21 (8): 1966–79. http://dx.doi.org/10.1111/j.1365-294X.2011.05261.x.

Anderson, David G., Kirk A. Maasch, Daniel H. Sandweiss, and Paul A. Mayewski. 2007. "Climate and Culture Change: Exploring Holocene Transitions." In *Climate Change and Cultural Dynamics: A Global Perspective on Mid-Holocene Transitions*, edited by David G. Anderson, Kirk A. Maasch, and Daniel H. Sandweiss, 1–23. Amsterdam: Academic Press. http://dx.doi.org/10.1016/B978-012088390-5.50006-6.

Anderson, M. Kat. 1999. "The Fire, Pruning, and Coppice Management of Temperate Ecosystems for Basketry Material by California Indian Tribes." *Human Ecology* 27 (1): 79–113. http://dx.doi.org/10.1023/A:1018757317568.

Anderson, M. Kat. 2005. *Tending the Wild*. Berkely: University of California Press.

Anderson, Seona, and Füsün Ertuğ-Yaras. 1996. "Fuel, Fodder and Faeces: An Ethnographic and Botanical Study of Dung Fuel Use in Central Anatolia." *Environmental Archaeology* 1 (1): 99–109. http://dx.doi.org/10.1179/env.1996.1.1.99.

Anderson, Soren H. 1986. "Mesolithic Dug-Outs and Paddles from Tybrind Vig, Denmark." *Acta Archaeologica* 57:87–106.

Anderson-Carpenter, Lynn L., Jason S. McLachlan, Stephen T. Jackson, Melanie Kuch, Candice Y. Lumibao, and Hendrik N. Poinar. 2011. "Ancient DNA from Lake Sediments: Bridging the Gap between Paleoecology and Genetics." *BMC Evolutionary Biology* 11 (1): 30. http://dx.doi.org/10.1186/1471-2148-11-30.

Anthony, David W., Dorcas Brown, E. Brown, A. Goodman, Alexander Kokhlov, P. Kosintsev, Pavel Kuznetsov, Oleg Mochalov, Eileen Murphy, D. Peterson, A. Pike-Tay, L. Popova, Arlene Miller Rosen, N. Russel, and Allison Weisskopf. 2005. "The Samara Valley Project: Late Bronze Age Economy and Ritual in the Russian Steppes." *Eurasia Antiqua* 11:395–417.

Aplin, David M., and Vernon H. Heywood. 2008. "Do Seed Lists Have a Future?" *Taxon* 57 (3): 1–3.

Appadurai, Arjun. 1981. "Gastro-Politics in Hindu South Asia." *American Ethnologist* 8 (3): 494–511. http://dx.doi.org/10.1525/ae.1981.8.3.02a00050.

Araus, José Luis, Gustavo Ariel Slafer, Ignacio Romagosa, and Miquel Molist. 2001. "Estimated Wheat Yields During the Emergence of Agriculture Based on the Carbon Isotope Discrimination of Grains: Evidence from a 10th Millennium BP Site on the Euphrates." *Journal of Archaeological Science* 28 (4): 341–50. http://dx.doi .org/10.1006/jasc.2000.0569.

Arnold, Bettina. 1999. "'Drinking the Feast': Alcohol and the Legitimation of Power in Celtic Europe." *Cambridge Archaeological Journal* 9 (01): 71–93. http://dx.doi.org /10.1017/S0959774300015213.

Arobba, Daniele, Rosanna Caramiello, and Angiolo del Lucchese. 2003. "Archaeo-botanical Investigations in Liguria: Preliminary Data on the Early Iron Age at Monte Trabocchetto (Pietra Ligure, Italy)." *Vegetation History and Archaeobotany* 12 (4): 253–62. http://dx.doi.org/10.1007/s00334-003-0022-7.

Asch, David L., and Nancy Asch Sidell. 1988. "Archaeological Plant Remains: Applications to Stratigraphic Analysis." In *Current Paleoethnobotany: Analytical Methods and Cultural Interpretations of Archaeological Plant Remains*, edited by Christine A. Hastorf and Virginia S. Popper, 86–96. Chicago: University of Chicago Press.

Asch Sidell, Nancy. 2008. "The Impact of Maize-Based Agriculture on Prehistoric Plant Communities in the Northeast." In Current Northeast Paleoethnobotany II, edited by John P. Hart, 29–52. Bulletin Series 512. Albany: New York State Museum.

Asouti, Eleni, and Dorian Q Fuller. 2013. "A Contextual Approach to the Emergence of Agriculture in Southwest Asia: Reconstructing Early Neolithic Plant-Food Production." *Current Anthropology* 54 (3): 299–345. http://dx.doi.org/10.1086/670679.

Atahan, P., F. Itzstein-Davey, D. Taylor, J. Dodson, J. Qin, H. Zheng, and A. Brooks. 2008. "Holocene-Aged Sedimentary Records of Environmental Changes and Early Agriculture in the Lower Yangtze, China." *Quaternary Science Reviews* 27 (5–6): 556–70. http://dx.doi.org/10.1016/j.quascirev.2007.11.003.

Atalay, Sonya, and Christine A. Hastorf. 2006. "Food, Meals, and Daily Activities: Food Habitus at Neolithic Catalhoyuk." *American Antiquity* 71 (2): 283–319. http:// dx.doi.org/10.2307/40035906.

Atchison, Jennifer, and Richard Fullagar. 1998. "Starch Residues on Pounding Implements from Jimnium Rock-Shelter." In *A Closer Look: Recent Australian Studies of Stone Tools*, edited by R. Fullagar, 109–26. Sydney: Archaeological Computing Laboratory, The University of Sydney.

Atchison, Jennifer, Lesley Head, and Richard Fullagar. 2005. "Archaeobotany of Fruit Seed Processing in a Monsoon Savanna Environment: Evidence from the Keep River Region, Northern Territory, Australia." *Journal of Archaeological Science* 32 (2): 167–81. http://dx.doi.org/10.1016/j.jas.2004.03.022.

Atron, Scott. 1993. "Itza Maya Tropical Agro-Forestry." *Current Anthropology* 34 (5): 633–700. http://dx.doi.org/10.1086/204212.

Ávila-Arcos, María C., Enrico Cappellini, J. Alberto Romero-Navarro, Nathan Wales, J. Víctor Moreno-Mayar, Morten Rasmussen, Sarah L. Fordyce, Rafael Montiel, Jean-Philippe Vielle-Calzada, Eske Willerslev, and M. Thomas P. Gilbert. 2011. "Application and Comparison of Large-Scale Solution-Based DNA Capture-Enrichment Methods on Ancient DNA." *Scientific Reports* 1:74. http://dx.doi.org/10.1038/srep00074.

Baar, Claudia, Marc d'Abbadie, Alexandra Vaisman, Mercedes E. Arana, Michael Hofreiter, Roger Woodgate, Thomas A. Kunkel, and Philipp Holliger. 2011. "Molecular Breeding of Polymerases for Resistance to Environmental Inhibitors." *Nucleic Acids Research* 39 (8): e51. http://dx.doi.org/10.1093/nar/gkq1360.

Badenhuizen, N. P. 1965. "Occurrence and Development of Starch in Plants." In *Starch: Chemistry and Technology*, edited by Roy L. Whistler and Eugene F. Paschall, 65–100. New York: Academic Press.

Badenhuizen, N. P. 1969. *The Biogenesis of Starch Granules in Higher Plants.* New York: Appleton-Century-Crofts.

Bailey, J. M., and W. J. Whelan. 1961. "Physical Properties of Starch: I. Relationship between Iodine Stain and Chain Length." *Journal of Biological Chemistry* 236 (4): 969–73.

Bailey, R. W., and J. C. Macrae. 1973. "Hydrolysis of Intact Leaf Starch Grains by Glucamylase and Alpha-Amylase." *FEBS Letters* 31 (2): 203–4. http://dx.doi.org/10.1016/0014-5793(73)80103-6.

Baker, Herbert G., and Irene Baker. 1979. "Starch in Angiosperm Pollen Grains and Its Evolutionary Significance." *American Journal of Botany* 66 (5): 591–600. http://dx.doi.org/10.2307/2442509.

Baker, Richard G., Glen G. Fredlund, Rolfe D. Mandel, and E. A. Bettis. 2000. "Holocene Environments of the Central Great Plains: Multi-Proxy Evidence from Alluvial Sequences, Southeastern Nebraska." *Quaternary International* 67:75–88. http://dx.doi.org/10.1016/S1040-6182(00)00010-0.

Balesdent, Jerome, Cyril Girardin, and Andre Mariotti. 1993. "Site-Related δ^{13}C of Tree Leaves and Soil Organic-Matter in a Temperate Forest." *Ecology* 74 (6): 1713–21. http://dx.doi.org/10.2307/1939930.

Ball, Terry, John S. Gardner, and Jack D. Brotherson. 1996. "Identifying Phytoliths Produced by the Inflorescence Bracts of Three Species of Wheat (*Triticum monococcum* L., *T. dicoccon* Schrank., and *T. aestivum* L.) Using Computer-Assisted Image and Statistical Analyses." *Journal of Archaeological Science* 23 (4): 619–32. http://dx.doi.org/10.1006/jasc.1996.0058.

Ball, Terry, L. Vrydaghs, I. Van Den Hauwe, J. Manwaring, and E. De Langhe. 2006. "Differentiating Banana Phytoliths: Wild and Edible *Musa acuminata* and *Musa balbisiana.*" *Journal of Archaeological Science* 33 (9): 1228–36. http://dx.doi.org/10.1016/j.jas.2005.12.010.

Ballantyne, Rachel. M. 2004. "A Cross-Disciplinary Investigation of Iron Age Pit Deposition." In *Evaluation Survey and Excavation at Wandlebury Ringwork, Cambridgeshire*, edited by Charles French, 53–57. Cambridge: Proceedings of Cambridge Antiquarian Society.

Balme, Jane, and Wendy E. Beck. 2002. "Starch and Charcoal: Useful Measures of Activity Areas in Archaeological Rockshelters." *Journal of Archaeological Science* 29 (2): 157–66. http://dx.doi.org/10.1006/jasc.2001.0700.

Banerjee, Monica, and Terence A. Brown. 2002. "Preservation of Nuclear but Not Chloroplast DNA in Archaeological Assemblages of Charred Wheat Grains." *Ancient Biomolecules* 4 (2): 59–63. http://dx.doi.org/10.1080/135861021000010659.

Barker, Graeme. 1995. *A Mediterranean Valley: Landscape Archaeology and Annales History in the Biferno Valley*. London: Leicester University Press.

Barker, Graeme. 2002. "A Tale of Two Deserts: Contrasting Desertification Histories on Rome's Desert Frontiers." *World Archaeology* 33 (3): 488–507. http://dx.doi.org/10.1080/0043824012010749 5.

Barlow, K. Renee. 2002. "Predicting Maize Agriculture among the Fremont: An Economic Comparison of Farming and Foraging in the American Southwest." *American Antiquity* 67 (1): 65–88. http://dx.doi.org/10.2307/2694877.

Barlow, K. Renee. 2006. "A Formal Model for Predicting Agriculture among the Fremont." In *Behavioral Ecology and the Transition to Agriculture*, edited by Douglas J. Kennett, and Bruce Winterhalder, 87–102. Berkeley: University of California Press.

Barlow, K. Renee, and Duncan Metcalfe. 1996. "Plant Utility Indices: Two Great Basin Examples." *Journal of Archaeological Science* 23 (3): 351–71. http://dx.doi.org/10.1006/jasc.1996.0033.

Barthes, Roland. 1997. "Toward a Psychosociology of Contemporary Food Consumption." In *Food and Culture: A Reader*, 1st ed., edited by Carole Counihan and Penny Van Esterik, 20–27. New York: Routledge.

Barton, Huw. 2005. "The Case of Rainforest Foragers: The Starch Record at Niah Cave, Sarawak." *Asian Perspective* 44 (1): 56–72. http://dx.doi.org/10.1353/asi.2005.0005.

Barton, Huw. 2006. "Testing for Contamination on Tool Edges." In *Ancient Starch Research*, edited by Robin Torrence and Huw Barton, 192–94. Walnut Creek, CA: Left Coast Press.

Barton, Huw. 2007. "Starch Residues on Museum Artefacts: Implications for Determining Tool Use." *Journal of Archaeological Science* 34 (10): 1752–62. http://dx.doi .org/10.1016/j.jas.2007.01.007.

Barton, Huw, and Peter J. Matthews. 2006. "Taphonomy." In *Ancient Starch Research*, edited by Robin Torrence and Huw Barton, 75–94. Walnut Creek, California: Left Coast Press.

Barton, Huw, Robin Torrence, and Richard Fullagar. 1998. "Clues to Stone Tool Function Re-Examined: Comparing Starch Grain Frequenceies on Used and Unused Obsidian Artefacts." *Journal of Archaeological Science* 25 (12): 1231–38. http:// dx.doi.org/10.1006/jasc.1998.0300.

Barton, Loukas. 2003. "Early Food Production in China's Western Loess Plateau." Unpublished PhD diss., University of California Davis, Davis.

Barton, Loukas, Seth D. Newsome, Fa-Hu Chen, Hui Wang, Thomas P. Guilderson, and Robert L. Bettinger. 2009. "Agricultural Origins and the Isotopic Identity of Domestication in Northern China." *Proceedings of the National Academy of Sciences of the United States of America* 106 (14): 5523–28. http://dx.doi.org/10.1073/pnas.0809960106.

Bassham, James A., Andrew A. Benson, and Melvin Calvin. 1950. "The Path of Carbon in Photosynthesis." *Journal of Biological Chemistry* 185 (2): 781–87.

Bateman, Alison S., Simon D. Kelly, and Timothy D. Jickells. 2005. "Nitrogen Isotope Relationships between Crops and Fertilizer: Implications for Using Nitrogen Isotope Analysis as an Indicator of Agricultural Regime." *Journal of Agricultural and Food Chemistry* 53 (14): 5760–65. http://dx.doi.org/10.1021/jf050374h.

Baxter, Michael J. 1994. *Exploratory Multivariate Analysis in Archaeology*. Edinburgh: Edinburgh University Press.

Baxter, Michael J. 2003. *Statistics in Archaeology*. London: Arnold.

Beach, Tim, Sheryl Luzzadder-Beach, Nicholas Dunning, John Jones, Jon Lohse, Tom Guderjan, Steve Bozarth, Sarah Millspaugh, and Tripti Bhattacharya. 2009. "A Review of Human and Natural Changes in Maya Lowland Wetlands over the Holocene." *Quaternary Science Reviews* 28 (17–18): 1710–24. http://dx.doi.org/10 .1016/j.quascirev.2009.02.004.

Beach, Tim, Sheryl Luzzadder-Beach, Richard Terry, Nicholas Dunning, Stephen Houston, and Thomas Garrison. 2011. "Carbon Isotopic Ratios of Wetland and Terrace Soil Sequences in the Maya Lowlands of Belize and Guatemala." *Catena* 85 (2): 109–18. http://dx.doi.org/10.1016/j.catena.2010.08.014.

Beattie, Owen, Brian Apland, Erik W. Blake, James A. Cosgrove, Sarah Gaunt, Sheila Greer, Alexander P. Mackie, Kjerstin E. Mackie, Dan Straathof, Valerie Thorp, and Peter M. Troffe. 2000. "The Kwädạy Dän Ts'ínchị Discovery from a Glacier in British Columbia." *Journal Canadien d'Archéologie* 24 (1): 129–47.

Beatty, John. 1980. "Optimal-Design Models and the Strategy of Model Building in Evolutionary Biology." *Philosophy of Science* 47 (4): 532–61. http://dx.doi.org/10 .1086/288955.

Beaudoin, Alwynne, and Mel A. Reasoner. 1992. "Evaluation of Differential Pollen Deposition and Pollen Focussing from Three Holocene Intervals in Sediments from Lake O'hara, Yoho National Park, British Columbia, Canada: Intra-Lake Variability in Pollen Percentages, Concentrations, and Influx." *Review of Palaeobotany and Palynology* 75 (1–2): 103–31. http://dx.doi.org/10.1016/0034-6667(92)90152-7.

Beck, Wendy E. 1989. "The Taphonomy of Plants." In *Plants in Australian Archaeology, Tempus*, vol. 1, edited by Wendy E. Beck, Anne Clarke, and Lesley Head, 31–53. Birsbane: University of Queensland Anthropology Museum.

Beentje, Henk J. 2010. *The Kew Plant Glossary: An Illustrated Dictionary of Plant Terms.* Kew: Royal Botanic Gardens.

Behre, Karl-Ernst. 2008. "Collected Seeds and Fruits from Herbs as Prehistoric Food." *Vegetation History and Archaeobotany* 17 (1): 65–73. http://dx.doi.org/10.1007 /s00334-007-0106-x.

Belitz, Hans-Dietler, Werner Grosche, and Peter Schieberle. 2009. *Food Chemistry.* 4th ed. New York: Springer-Verlag.

Bell, James A. 1981. "Scientific Method and the Formulation of Testable Computer Simulation Models." In *Simulations in Archaeology*, edited by Jeremy A. Sabloff, 51–64. Albuquerque: University of New Mexico Press.

Belovsky, Gary E. 1987. "Hunter-Gatherer Foraging: A Linear Programming Approach." *Journal of Anthropological Archaeology* 6 (1): 29–76. http://dx.doi.org/10 .1016/0278-4165(87)90016-X.

BeMiller, James N., and Roy L. Whistler. 2009. *Starch: Chemistry and Technology.* New York: Academic Press.

Bender, Margaret M. 1971. "Variations in $^{13}C/^{12}C$ Ratios of Plants in Relation to Pathway of Photosynthetic Carbon Dioxide Fixation." *Phytochemistry* 10 (6): 1239–44. http://dx.doi.org/10.1016/S0031-9422(00)84324-1.

Bender, Margaret M., David A. Baerreis, and Raymond L. Steventon. 1981. "Further Light on Carbon Isotopes and Hopewell Agriculture." *American Antiquity* 46 (2): 346–53. http://dx.doi.org/10.2307/280213.

Bender, Margaret M., I. Rouhani, H. M. Vines, and C. C. Black, Jr. 1973. "$^{13}C/^{12}C$ Ratio Changes in Crassulacean Acid Metabolism Plants." *Plant Physiology* 52 (5): 427–30.

Bennett, John. W., and Don Kanel. 1983. "Agricultural Economic Anthropology: Confrontation and Accommodation." In *Economic Anthropology: Topics and Theories*, edited by Sutti Ortiz, 201–48. Monographs in Economic Anthropology no. 1. London: Society for Economic Anthropology.

Benz, Bruce F., Lorenza López Mestas C, and Jorge Ramos de la Vega. 2006.
"Organic Offerings, Paper, and Fibers from the Huitzilapa Shaft Tomb, Jalisco,
Mexico." *Ancient Mesoamerica* 17 (02): 283–96. http://dx.doi.org/10.1017/S0956
536106060196.

Beresford-Jones, David G., Katherine Johnson, Alexander G. Pullen, Alexander J. E.
Pryor, Jiri Svoboda, and Martin K. Jones. 2010. "Burning Wood or Burning Bone?
A Reconsideration of Flotation Evidence from Upper Palaeolithic (Gravettian)
Sites in the Moravian Corridor." *Journal of Archaeological Science* 37 (11): 2799–811.
http://dx.doi.org/10.1016/j.jas.2010.06.014.

Beresford-Jones, David G., Oliver Whaley, Carmela Alarcón Ledesma, and Lauren
Cadwallader. 2011. "Two Millennia of Changes in Human Ecology: Archaeobo-
tanical and Invertebrate Records from the Lower Ica Valley, South Coast Peru."
Vegetation History and Archaeobotany 20 (4): 273–92.

Berg, Björn, and Charles McClaugherty. 2008. *Plant Litter: Decomposition, Humus
Formation, Carbon Sequestration.* 2nd ed. Berlin: Springer. http://dx.doi.org/10.1007
/978-3-540-74923-3.

Bescoby, D. J. 2006. "Detecting Roman Land Boundaries in Aerial Photographs
Using Radon Transforms." *Journal of Archaeological Science* 33 (5): 735–43. http://
dx.doi.org/10.1016/j.jas.2005.10.012.

Bettinger, Robert L. 1991. *Hunter-Gatherers: Archaeological and Evolutionary Theory.*
New York: Plenum. http://dx.doi.org/10.1007/978-1-4899-0658-8.

Bettinger, Robert L. 2006. "Agriculture, Archaeology, and Human Behavioral Ecology." In *Behavioral Ecology and the Transition to Agriculture*, edited by Douglas J.
Kennett and Bruce Winterhalder, 304–22. Berkeley: University of California Press.

Bettinger, Robert L. 2009. *Hunter-Gatherer Foraging: Five Simple Models.* Clinton
Corners, New York: Eliot Werner.

Bettinger, Robert L., Ripan Malhi, and Helen McCarthy. 1997. "Central Place
Models of Acorn and Mussel Processing." *Journal of Archaeological Science* 24 (10):
887–99. http://dx.doi.org/10.1006/jasc.1996.0168.

Bewley, R. H., S. P. Crutchley, and C. A. Shell. 2005. "New Light on an Ancient
Landscape: Lidar Survey in the Stonehenge World Heritage Site." *Antiquity* 79
(305): 636–47.

Bewley, Robert H., and Wlodzimierz Raczkowski, eds. 2000. *Aerial Archaeology:
Developing Future Practice.* Amsterdam: IOS Press.

Bezic, Ana. 2009. "Building Çatalhöyük: Towards an Archaeology of the Instant at
the Neolithic Site in Turkey." PhD diss., Department of Anthropology, Stanford
University.

Biliaderis, Costas G. 2009. "Structural Transitions and Related Physical Properties of Starch." In *Starch: Chemistry and Technology*, edited by James N. BeMiller, and Roy L. Whistler, 293–372. New York: Academic Press. http://dx.doi.org/10.1016/B978-0-12-746275-2.00008-2.

Binford, Lewis R. 1980. "Willow Smoke and Dogs' Tails: Hunter-Gatherer Settlement Systems and Archaeological Site Formation." *American Antiquity* 45 (1): 4–20. http://dx.doi.org/10.2307/279653.

Binford, Lewis R. 1989. *Debating Archaeology*. San Diego: Academic Press.

Binladen, Jonas, M. Thomas P. Gilbert, Jonathan P. Bollback, Frank Panitz, Christian Bendixen, Rasmus Nielsen, and Eske Willerslev. 2007. "The Use of Coded PCR Primers Enables High-Throughput Sequencing of Multiple Homolog Amplification Products by 454 Parallel Sequencing." *PLoS ONE* 2 (2): e197. http://dx.doi.org/10.1371/journal.pone.0000197.

Bird, Douglas W., Rebecca Bliege Bird, and Christopher H. Parker. 2005. "Aboriginal Burning Regimes and Hunting Strategies in Australia's Western Desert." *Human Ecology* 33 (4): 443–64. http://dx.doi.org/10.1007/s10745-005-5155-0.

Bird, Douglas W., and James F. O'Connell. 2006. "Behavioral Ecology and Archaeology." *Journal of Archaeological Research* 14 (2): 143–88. http://dx.doi.org/10.1007/s10814-006-9003-6.

Birks, Hilary H. 1980. "Plant Macrofossils in Quaternary Lake Sediments." *Archiv fuer Hydrobiologie* 15:1–60.

Birks, Hilary H. 2001. "Plant Macrofossils." In *Tracking Environmental Change Using Lake Sediments*, Volume 3: Terrestrial, Algal, and Siliceous Indicators, edited by John P. Smol, H. John B. Birks, and William M. Last, 49–74. Dordt, Netherlands: Springer.

Birks, Hilary H. 2007. "Plant Macrofossil Introduction." In *Encyclopedia of Quaternary Science*, edited by Scott A. Elias, 2266–88. Oxford: Elsevier. http://dx.doi.org/10.1016/B0-44-452747-8/00215-5.

Birks, H., and B. John. 1974. "Numerical Zonations of Flandrian Pollen Data." *New Phytologist* 73 (2): 351–58. http://dx.doi.org/10.1111/j.1469-8137.1974.tb04769.x.

Birks, H. John B., Joy Deacon, and Sylvia Peglar. 1975. "Pollen Maps for the British Isles 5000 Years Ago." *Proceedings of the Royal Society B* 189 (1094): 87–105. doi:10.1098/rspb.1975.0044.

Birks, H. John B., and A. David Gordon. 1985. *Numerical Methods in Quaternary Pollen Analysis*. London: Academic Press.

Black, Bryan A., Charles M. Ruffner, and Marc D. Abrams. 2006. "Native American Influences on the Forest Composition of the Allegheny Plateau, Northwest

Pennsylvania." *Canadian Journal of Forest Research* 36 (5): 1266–75. http://dx.doi
.org/10.1139/x06-027.

Blake, Michael. 2006. "Dating the Initial Spread of *Zea mays*." In *Histories of Maize:
Multidisciplinary Approaches to the Prehistory, Linguistics, Biogeography, Domestication, and Evolution of Maize*, edited by John E. Staller, Robert H. Tykot, and Bruce
F. Benz, 55–72. New York: Elsevier. http://dx.doi.org/10.1016/B978-012369364-8
/50256-4.

Blake, Michael, Brian S. Chisholm, John E. Clark, Barbara Voorhies, and Michael W.
Love. 1992. "Prehistoric Subsistence in the Soconusco Region." *Current Anthropology* 33 (1): 83–94. http://dx.doi.org/10.1086/204038.

Blanshard, J. M. V. 1987. "Starch Granule Structure and Function: A Physicochemi-
cal Approach." In *Starch: Properties and Potential*, edited by T. Galliard, 16–54. John
Wiley and Sons, Inc.

Bliege Bird, Rebecca, Douglas W. Bird, Brian F. Codding, Christopher H. Parker,
and J. H. Jones. 2008. "The 'Fire Stick Farming' Hypothesis: Australian Aboriginal
Foraging Strategies, Biodiversity, and Anthropogenic Fire Mosaics." *Proceedings of
the National Academy of Sciences USA* 105: 14796–801.

Boardman, Sheila, and Glynis E. M. Jones. 1990. "Experiments on the Effects of
Charring on Cereal Plant Components." *Journal of Archaeological Science* 17 (1): 1–11.
http://dx.doi.org/10.1016/0305-4403(90)90012-T.

Bocek, Barbara. 1986. "Rodent Ecology and Burrowing Behavior: Predicted Effects
on Archaeological Site Formation." *American Antiquity* 51 (3): 589–602. http://
dx.doi.org/10.2307/281754.

Boenke, Nicole. 2007. "Human Excrement from a Prehistoric Salt Mine: A Window
onto Daily Life." In *The Archaeology of Food and Identity*, edited by Katheryn C.
Twiss, 50–68. Carbondale, IL: Center for Archaeological Investigations, Southern
Illinois University.

Bogaard, Amy. 2004. *Neolithic Farming in Central Europe. An Archaeobotanical Study
of Crop Husbandry Practices*. London: Routledge.

Bogaard, Amy, Michael Charles, Katheryn C. Twiss, Andrew Fairbairn, Nurcan
Yalman, Dragana Filipovic, G. Arzu Demirergi, Füsun Ertuğ, Nerissa Russell,
and Jennifer Henecke. 2009. "Private Pantries and Celebrated Surplus: Storing
and Sharing Food at Neolithic Catalhoyuk, Central Anatolia." *Antiquity* 83 (321):
649–68.

Bogaard, Amy, T. H. E. Heaton, P. Poulton, and I. Merbach. 2007. "The Impact of
Manuring on Nitrogen Isotope Ratios in Cereals: Archaeological Implications for
Reconstruction of Diet and Crop Management Practices." *Journal of Archaeological
Science* 34 (3): 335–43. http://dx.doi.org/10.1016/j.jas.2006.04.009.

Bogaard, Amy, Glynis Jones, and Mike Charles. 2005. "The Impact of Crop Process-ing on the Reconstruction of Crop Sowing Time and Cultivation Intensity from Archaeobotanical Weed Evidence." *Vegetation History and Archaeobotany* 14 (4): 505–9. http://dx.doi.org/10.1007/s00334-005-0061-3.

Bogaard, Amy, Glynis Jones, Mike Charles, and John G. Hodgson. 2001. "On the Archaeobotanical Inference of Crop Sowing Time Using the FIBS Method." *Jour-nal of Archaeological Science* 28 (11): 1171–83. http://dx.doi.org/10.1006/jasc.2000.0621.

Bogaard, Amy, Carol Palmer, Glynis Jones, Mike Charles, and John G. Hodgson. 1999. "A FIBS Approach to the Use of Weed Ecology for the Archaeobotanical Recognition of Crop Rotation Regimes." *Journal of Archaeological Science* 26 (9): 1211–24. http://dx.doi.org/10.1006/jasc.1998.0364.

Bohrer, Vorsila L., and Karen R. Adams. 1977. *Ethnobotanical Techniques and Approaches at Salmon Ruin, New Mexico.* Portales: Eastern New Mexico University.

Boivin, Nicole, and Dorian Q Fuller. 2009. "Shell Middens, Ships and Seeds: Explor-ing Coastal Subsistence, Maritime Trade and the Dispersal of Domesticates in and around the Ancient Arabian Peninsula." *Journal of World Prehistory* 22 (2): 113–80. http://dx.doi.org/10.1007/s10963-009-9018-2.

Bojňanský, Vit, and A. Fargašová. 2007. *Atlas of Seeds and Fruits of Central and East-European Flora: The Carpathian Mountains Region.* Dordrecht: Springer.

Bökönyi, Sándor, Lorenzo Costantini, and J. Fitt. 1993. "The Farming Economy." In *Fourth Century B.C. Magna Graecia: A Case Study*, edited by M. Gualtieri, 295–307. Partille, Sweden: Paul Åstroms Forlag.

Bollig, Michael, and Anja Schulte. 1999. "Environmental Change and Pastoral Perceptions: Degradation and Indigenous Knowledge in Two African Pastoral Communities." *Human Ecology* 27 (3): 493–514. http://dx.doi.org/10.1023/A:1018783725398.

Bollongino, Ruth, Anne Tresset, and Jean-Denis Vigne. 2008. "Environment and Excavation: Pre-Lab Impacts on Ancient DNA Analyses." *Comptes Rendus. Palévol* 7 (2–3): 91–98. http://dx.doi.org/10.1016/j.crpv.2008.02.002.

Bond, Gerard, William Showers, Maziet Cheseby, Rustry Lotti, Peter Almasi, Peter deMenocal, Paul Priore, Heidi Cullen, Irka Hajdas, and Georges Bonani. 1997. "A Pervasive Millennial-Scale Cycle in North Atlantic Holocene and Glacial Cli-mates." *Science* 278 (5341): 1257–66. http://dx.doi.org/10.1126/science.278.5341.1257.

Bønsager, Birgit C., Christine Finnie, Peter Roepstorff, and Birte Svensson. 2007. "Spatio-Temporal Changes in Germination and Radical Elongation of Barley Seeds Tracked by Proteome Analysis of Dissected Embryo, Aleurone Layer, and Endosperm Tissues." *Proteomics* 7 (24): 4528–40. http://dx.doi.org/10.1002/pmic.200700766.

Borojevic, Ksenija. 2011. "Interpreting, Dating, and Reevaluating the Botanical Assemblage from Tell Kedesh: A Case Study of Historical Contamination." *Journal of Archaeological Science* 38 (4): 829–42. http://dx.doi.org/10.1016/j.jas.2010.11.005.

Borojevic, Ksenija, Warren E. Steiner, Jr., Rainer Gerisch, Chiara Zazzaro, and Cheryl Ward. 2010. "Pests in an Ancient Egyptian Harbor." *Journal of Archaeological Science* 37 (10): 2449–58. http://dx.doi.org/10.1016/j.jas.2010.04.013.

Borowski, Christine. 2011. "Enough Is Enough." *Journal of Experimental Medicine* 208 (7): 1337. http://dx.doi.org/10.1084/jem.20111061.

Bortenschlager, Sigmar, and Klaus Oeggl, eds. 2000. *The Iceman and His Natural Environment: Palaeobotanical Results*. Berlin: Springer. http://dx.doi.org/10.1007/978-3-7091-6758-8.

Bösl, C., G. Grupe, and J. Peters. 2006. "A Late Neolithic Vertebrate Food Web Based on Stable Isotope Analyses." *International Journal of Osteoarchaeology* 16 (4): 296–315. http://dx.doi.org/10.1002/oa.834.

Bottema, Sytze. 1984. "The Composition of Modern Charred Seed Assemblages." In *Plants and Ancient Man: Studies in Palaeoethnobotany*, edited by Willem van Zeist and W. A. Casparie, 207–12. Rotterdam: A.A. Balkema.

Bourdieu, Pierre. 1977. *Outline of a Theory of Practice*. Cambridge: Cambridge University Press. http://dx.doi.org/10.1017/CBO9780511812507.

Bourdieu, Pierre. 1984. *Distinction: A Social Critique of the Judgment of Taste*. Cambridge: Harvard University Press.

Bourdieu, Pierre. 1990. *The Logic of Practice*. Cambridge: Polity Press.

Bourdieu, Pierre, and Loïc J. D. Wacquant. 1992. *An Invitation to Reflexive Sociology*. Chicago: University of Chicago Press.

Boutin, Paul. 2010. "The Age of Music Piracy Is Officially Over." Wired Magazine. Accessed November 26, 2011. http://www.wired.com/2010/11/st_essay_nofreebird/.

Boutton, Thomas W. 1996. "Stable Carbon Isotope Ratios of Soil Organic Matter and Their Use as Indicators of Vegetation and Climate Change." In *Mass Spectrometry of Soils*, edited by Thomas W. Boutton and S. Yamasaki, 47–82. New York: Marcel Dekker.

Boutton, Thomas W., Steven R. Archer, Andrew J. Midwood, Stephen F. Zitzer, and Roland Bol. 1998. "Delta C-13 Values of Soil Organic Carbon and Their Use in Documenting Vegetation Change in a Subtropical Savanna Ecosystem." *Geoderma* 82 (1–3): 5–41. http://dx.doi.org/10.1016/S0016-7061(97)00095-5.

Boutton, Thomas W., Lee C. Nordt, and D. D. Kuehn. 1998. "Late Quaternary Vegetation and Climate Change in the North American Great Plains." In *Proceedings of an International Symposium on Isotope Techniques in the Study of Past and Current Environmental Changes in the Hydrosphere and the Atmosphere*, 653–62." International Atomic Energy Agency, Vienna.

Bowen, H. C. 1963. *Ancient Fields: A Tentative Analysis of Vanishing Earthworks and Landscapes*. London: British Association for the Advancement of Science.

Boyadjian, Célia Helena C., Sabine Eggers, and Karl J. Reinhard. 2007. "Dental Wash: A Problematic Method for Extracting Microfossils from Teeth." *Journal of Archaeological Science* 34:1622–28.

Boyd, Robert, and Peter J. Richerson. 1985. *Culture and the Evolutionary Process*. Chicago: University of Chicago Press.

Boyd, Robert, and Peter J. Richerson. 1995. "Why Does Culture Increase Human Adaptability?" *Ethology and Sociobiology* 16 (2): 125–43. http://dx.doi.org/10.1016/0162-3095(94)00073-G.

Bozarth, Steven R., and Thomas H. Guderjan. 2004. "Biosilicate Analysis of Residue in Maya Dedicatory Cache Vessels from Blue Creek, Belize." *Journal of Archaeological Science* 31 (2): 205–15. http://dx.doi.org/10.1016/j.jas.2003.08.002.

Braadbaart, Freek, and Pim F. Bergen. 2005. "Digital Imaging Analysis of Size and Shape of Wheat and Pea Upon Heating under Anoxic Conditions as a Function of the Temperature." *Vegetation History and Archaeobotany* 14 (1): 67–75. http://dx.doi.org/10.1007/s00334-004-0050-y.

Braadbaart, Freek, J. J. Boon, H. Veld, P. David, and P. F. van Bergen. 2004. "Laboratory Simulations of the Transformation of Peas as a Result of Heat Treatment: Changes of the Physical and Chemical Properties." *Journal of Archaeological Science* 31 (6): 821–33. http://dx.doi.org/10.1016/j.jas.2003.12.001.

Braadbaart, Freek, and I. Poole. 2008. "Morphological, Chemical and Physical Changes During Charcoalification of Wood and Its Relevance to Archaeological Contexts." *Journal of Archaeological Science* 35 (9): 2434–45. http://dx.doi.org/10.1016/j.jas.2008.03.016.

Braadbaart, Freek, and Patti J. Wright. 2007. "Changes in Mass and Dimensions of Sunflower (*Helianthus annuus* L.) Achenes and Seeds Due to Carbonization." *Economic Botany* 61 (2): 137–53. http://dx.doi.org/10.1663/0013-0001(2007)61[137:CIMADO]2.0.CO;2.

Braadbaart, Freek, Patti J. Wright, J. van der Horst, and J. J. Boon. 2007. "A Laboratory Simulation of the Carbonization of Sunflower Achenes and Seeds." *Journal of Analytical and Applied Pyrolysis* 78 (2): 316–27. http://dx.doi.org/10.1016/j.jaap.2006.07.007.

Bradford, John. 1957. *Ancient Landscapes: Studies in Field Archaeology*. London: Bell.

Brantingham, Jeffery P., Todd A. Surovell, and Nicole M. Waguespack. 2007. "Modeling Post-Depositional Mixing of Archaeological Deposits." *Journal of Anthropological Archaeology* 26 (4): 517–40. http://dx.doi.org/10.1016/j.jaa.2007.08.003.

Braun, David P., and Stephen Plog. 1982. "Evolution of 'Tribal' Social Networks: Theory and Prehistoric North American Evidence." *American Antiquity* 47 (3): 504–25. http://dx.doi.org/10.2307/280232.

Bray, Tamara L. 2003. "Inka Pottery as Culinary Equipment: Food, Feasting, and Gender in Imperial State Design." *Latin American Antiquity* 14 (1): 3–28. http://dx.doi.org/10.2307/972232.

Briggs, John M., Katherine A. Spielmann, Hoski Schaafsma, Keith W. Kintigh, Melissa Kruse, Kari Morehouse, and Karen Schollmeyer. 2006. "Why Ecology Needs Archaeologists and Archaeology Needs Ecologists." *Frontiers in Ecology and the Environment* 4 (4): 180–88. http://dx.doi.org/10.1890/1540-9295(2006)004[0180:WENAAA]2.0.CO;2.

Brock, Fiona, Thomas Higham, Peter Ditchfield, and Christopher Bronk Ramsey. 2010. "Current Pretreatment Methods for AMS Radiocarbon Dating at the Oxford Radiocarbon Accelerator Unit (ORAU)." *Radiocarbon* 52 (1): 103–12.

Brombacher, Christoph. 1997. "Archaeobotanical Investigations of Late Neolithic Lakeshore Settlements (Lake Biel, Switzerland)." *Vegetation History and Archaeobotany* 6 (3): 167–86. http://dx.doi.org/10.1007/BF01372569.

Brooks, Robert R., and Dieter Johannes. 1990. *Phytoarchaeology*. Historical, Ethno- and Economic Botany Series. Vol. 3. Portland, OR: Dioscorides Press.

Broström, Anna, Shinya Sugita, Marie-José Gaillard, and Petter Pilesjo. 2005. "Estimating the Spatial Scale of Pollen Dispersal in the Cultural Landscape of Southern Sweden." *The Holocene* 15:252–62.

Broughton, Jack M. 1994a. "Declines in Mammalian Foraging Efficiency During the Late Holocene, San Francisco Bay, California." *Journal of Anthropological Archaeology* 13 (4): 371–401. http://dx.doi.org/10.1006/jaar.1994.1019.

Broughton, Jack M. 1994b. "Late Holocene Resource Intensification in the Sacramento Valley, California: The Vertebrate Evidence." *Journal of Archaeological Science* 21 (4): 501–14. http://dx.doi.org/10.1006/jasc.1994.1050.

Broughton, Jack M., Michael D. Cannon, and Eric J. Bartelink. 2010. "Evolutionary Ecology, Resource Depression, and Niche Construction Theory: Applications to Central California Hunter-Gatherers and Mimbres-Mogollon Agriculturalists." *Journal of Archaeological Method and Theory* 17 (4): 371–421. http://dx.doi.org/10.1007/s10816-010-9095-7.

Brown, Linda A., and Andrea Gerstle. 2002. "Structure 10: Feasting and Village Festivals." In *Before the Volcano Erupted: The Ancient Ceren Village*, edited by Payson D. Sheets, 97–103. Austin: University of Texas Press.

Brown, Stephen A., and Dexter French. 1977. "Specific Adsorption of Starch Oligosaccharides in the Gel Phase of Starch Granules." *Carbohydrate Research* 59 (1): 203–12. http://dx.doi.org/10.1016/S0008-6215(00)83306-6.

Brown, Terence A. 1999. "How Ancient DNA May Help in Understanding the Origin and Spread of Agriculture." *Philosophical Transactions of the Royal Society of London. Series B, Biological Sciences* 354 (1379): 89–98. http://dx.doi.org/10.1098/rstb.1999.0362.

Brown, Terence A., Robin G. Allaby, Keri A. Brown, and Martin K. Jones. 1993. "Biomolecular Archaeology of Wheat: Past, Present and Future." *World Archaeology* 25 (1): 64–73. http://dx.doi.org/10.1080/00438243.1993.9980228.

Brown, Terence A., Robin G. Allaby, Keri A. Brown, Kerry O'Donoghue, and Robert Sallares. 1994. "DNA in Wheat Seeds from European Archaeological Sites." *Experientia* 50 (6): 571–75. http://dx.doi.org/10.1007/BF01921727.

Brown, Terence A., Robin G. Allaby, Robert Sallares, and Glynis E. M. Jones. 1998. "Ancient DNA in Charred Wheats: Taxonomic Identification of Mixed and Single Grains." *Ancient Biomolecules* 2 (2): 185–93.

Brown, Terence A., and Keri Brown. 2011. *Biomolecular Archaeology: An Introduction.* Malden, MA: Wiley-Blackwell. http://dx.doi.org/10.1002/9781444392449.

Brunning, Richard, and Conor McDermott. 2013. "Trackways and Roads across the Wetlands." In *The Oxford Handbook of Wetland Archaeology*, edited by Francesco Menotti and Aidan O'Sullivan, 360–84. Oxford: Oxford University Press.

Bruno, Maria C. 2006. "A Morphological Approach to Documenting the Domestication of *Chenopodium* in the Andes." In *Documenting Domestication: New Genetic and Archaeological Paradigms*, edited by Melinda A. Zeder, Daniel G. Bradley, Eve Emshwiller, and Bruce D. Smith, 32–45. Berkeley: University of California Press.

Bryant, Vaughn M., Jr. 1978. "Palynology: A Useful Method for Determining Paleo-Environment." *Texas Journal of Science* 30:25–42.

Bryant, Vaughn M., Jr. 1989. "Botanical Remains in Archaeological Sites." In *Interdisciplinary Workshop on the Physical-Chemical-Biological Processes Affecting Archaeological Sites*, edited by Christopher C. Mathewson, 85–115. Environmental Impact Research Program Contract Report E11–89–1. U.S. Army Corps of Engineers, Washington, DC.

Bryant, Vaughn M., and Glenna W. Dean. 2006. "Archaeological Coprolite Science: The Legacy of Eric O. Callen (1912–1970)." *Palaeogeography, Palaeoclimatology, Palaeoecology* 237 (1): 51–66. http://dx.doi.org/10.1016/j.palaeo.2005.11.032.

Bryant, Vaughn M., Jr., and Stephen A. Hall. 1993. "Archaeological Palynology in the United States: A Critique." *American Antiquity* 58 (2): 277–86. http://dx.doi.org/10.2307/281970.

Bryant, Vaughn M., Jr., and Richard G. Holloway. 1983. "The Role of Palynology in Archaeology." In *Advances in Archaeological Method and Theory*, vol. 6, edited by Michael B. Schiffer, 191–223. New York: Academic Press.

Bryant, Vaughn M., Jr., and Richard G. Holloway. 1996. "New Frontiers in Palynology: Archaeological Palynology." In *Palynology: Principles and Applications*, vol. 3, edited by J. Jansonius and D. C. McGregor, 913–17. American Association of Stratigraphic Palynologists Foundation.

Bryant, Vaughn M., Jr., Richard G. Holloway, John G. Jones, and David L. Carlson. 1994. "Pollen Preservation in Alkaline Soils of the American Southwest." In *Sedimentation of Organic Particles*, edited by Alfred Traverse, 47–58. Cambridge: Cambridge University Press. http://dx.doi.org/10.1017/CBO9780511524875.005.

Bryant, Vaughn M., Jr., and Don P. Morris. 1986. "Uses of Ceramic Vessels and Grinding Implements: The Pollen Evidence." In *Archaeological Investigations at Antelope House*, edited by Don P. Morris, 489–500. Washington, DC: National Park Service, U. S. Department of the Interior.

Bryant, Vaughn M., Jr., and Robert E. Murry, Jr. 1982. "Preliminary Analysis of Amphora Contents." In *Yassi Ada, Volume I: A Seventh-Century Byzantine Shipwreck*, edited by George F. Bass, and Frederick H. van Doorninck, Jr., 327–31. College Station: Texas A&M University Press.

Buchmann, N., J. R. Brooks, K. D. Rapp, and J. R. Ehleringer. 1996. "Carbon Isotope Composition of C4 Grasses Is Influenced by Light and Water Supply." *Plant, Cell & Environment* 19 (4): 392–402. http://dx.doi.org/10.1111/j.1365-3040.1996.tb00331.x.

Buell, Murray F., Helen F. Buell, and John A. Small. 1954. "Fire in the History of Mettler's Woods." *Bulletin of the Torrey Botanical Club* 81 (3): 253–55. http://dx.doi.org/10.2307/2481817.

Buikstra, Jane E., and George R. Milner. 1991. "Isotopic and Archaeological Interpretations of Diet in the Central Mississippi Valley." *Journal of Archaeological Science* 18 (3): 319–29. http://dx.doi.org/10.1016/0305-4403(91)90068-Z.

Bunker, Brian. 2013. "Classification of Satellite Time Series-Derived Land Surface Phenology Focused on the Northern Fertile Crescent." MA Thesis, Department of Geosciences, University of Arkansas, Fayetteville.

Bunning, Sandra L., Glynis E. M. Jones, and Terence A. Brown. 2012. "Next Generation Sequencing of DNA in 3300-Year-Old Charred Cereal Grains." *Journal of Archaeological Science* 39 (8): 2780–84. http://dx.doi.org/10.1016/j.jas.2012.04.012.

Bunting, M. Jane, Richard Tipping, and Jane Downes. 2001. ""Anthropogenic" Pollen Assemblages from a Bronze Age Cemetery at Linga Fiold, West Mainland, Orkney." *Journal of Archaeological Science* 28 (5): 487–500. http://dx.doi.org/10.1006/jasc.2000.0607.

Burkill, H. M. 2004. *The Useful Plants of West Tropical Africa*. Vol. 6. Kew: Royal Botanical Gardens.

Burleigh, Richard, and Don R. Brothwell. 1978. "Studies on Amerindian Dogs, 1: Carbon Isotopes in Relation to Maize in the Diet of Domestic Dogs from Early Peru and Ecuador." *Journal of Archaeological Science* 5 (4): 355–62. http://dx.doi.org/10.1016/0305-4403(78)90054-7.

Burov, Grigory M. 2001. "Ancient Wooden Objects and Structures in Oxbow Peat Bogs of the European Northeast (Russia)." In *Enduring Records: The Environmental and Cultural Heritage of Wetlands*, edited by Barbara A. Purdy, 214–32. Oxford: Oxbow Books.

Bush, Mark B., and Paul A. Colinvaux. 1994. "Tropical Forest Disturbance: Palaeoecological Records from Darien, Panama." *Ecology* 75 (6): 1761–68. http://dx.doi.org/10.2307/1939635.

Butcher, Samuel S., Robert J. Charlson, Gordon H. Orians, and Gordon V. Wolfe, eds. 1992. *Global Biogeochemical Cycles*. San Diego: Academic Press Limited.

Buttrose, M. S. 1962. "The Influence of Environment on the Shell Structure of Starch Granules." *Journal of Cell Biology* 14 (2): 159–167. http://dx.doi.org/10.1083/jcb.14.2.159.

Bye, Robert A. 1986. "Voucher Specimens in Ethnobiological Studies and Publications." *Journal of Ethnobiology* 6:1–8.

Byers, Douglas S. 1967. *The Prehistory of the Tehuacan Valley*. Austin: University of Texas Press.

Bynum, Carol Walker. 1997. "Fast, Feast, and Flesh: The Religious Significance of Food to Medieval Women." In *Food and Culture: A Reader*, 1st ed., edited by Carole Counihan and Penny Van Esterik, 138–58. New York: Routledge.

Cabanes, Dan, Carolina Mallol, Isabel Expósito, and Javier Baena. 2010. "Phytolith Evidence for Hearths and Beds in the Late Mousterian Occupations of Esquilleu Cave (Cantabria, Spain)." *Journal of Archaeological Science* 37 (11): 2947–57. http://dx.doi.org/10.1016/j.jas.2010.07.010.

Cabanes, Dan, Steve Weiner, and Ruth Shahack-Gross. 2011. "Stability of Phytoliths in the Archaeological Record: A Dissolution Study of Modern and Fossil Phytoliths." *Journal of Archaeological Science* 38 (9): 2480–90. http://dx.doi.org/10.1016/j.jas.2011.05.020.

Cahill, Jane, Karl Reinhard, David Tarler, and Peter Warnock. 1991. "Scientists Examine Remains of Ancient Bathroom." *Biblical Archaeology Review* 17 (3): 64–69.

Callaway, Ewen. September 2010. "Taking Molecular Snaps of Ancient Crops." *Nature News* (September 13). doi:10.1038/news.2010.464.

Campbell, Ewan. 2000. "The Raw, the Cooked and the Burnt." *Archaeological Dialogues* 7 (02): 184–98. http://dx.doi.org/10.1017/S1380203800001744.

Campbell, Gill. 2000. "Plant Utilisation: The Evidence from Charred Plant Remains." In *The Danebury Environs Programme: The Prehistory of a Wessex Landscape*, vol. 1, edited by Barry W. Cunliffe, 45–59. Oxford: Institute of Archaeology.

Campbell, Ian D. 1999. "Quaternary Pollen Taphonomy: Examples of Differential Redeposition and Differential Preservation." *Palaeogeography, Palaeoclimatology, Palaeoecology* 149 (1–4): 245–56. http://dx.doi.org/10.1016/S0031-0182(98)00204-1.

Campbell, Ian D., and Gail L. Chmura. 1994. "Pollen Distribution in the Atchafalaya River, U.S.A." *Palynology* 18 (1): 55–65. http://dx.doi.org/10.1080/01916122.1994.9989439.

Campos, P., E. Willerslev, M. Thomas, and P. Gilbert. 2009. "Isolation of DNA from Ancient Samples." In *Handbook of Nucleic Acid Purification*, edited by Dongyou Liu, 449–70. Boca Raton: CRC Press. http://dx.doi.org/10.1201/9781420070972.ch19.

Canti, Matthew, Stephen Carter, Donald Davidson, and Susan Limbrey. 2006. "Problems of Unscientific Method and Approach in 'Archaeological Soil and Pollen Analysis of Experimental Floor Deposits; with Special Reference to Butser Ancient Farm, Hampshire, UK' by R. I. Macphail, G. M. Cruise, M. Allen, J. Linderholm, and P. Reynolds." *Journal of Archaeological Science* 33 (2): 295–98. http://dx.doi.org/10.1016/j.jas.2005.07.001.

Canti, Matthew G. 2003. "Earthworm Activity and Archaeological Stratigraphy: A Review of Products and Processes." *Journal of Archaeological Science* 30 (2): 135–48. http://dx.doi.org/10.1006/jasc.2001.0770.

Caple, C., and D. Dungworth. 1997. "Investigations into Waterlogged Burial Environments." In *Archaeological Sciences 1995*, edited by A. Sinclair, E. Slater, and J. Gowlett, 233–40. Oxford: Oxbow Books.

Cappellini, Enrico, M. Thomas P. Gilbert, Filippo Geuna, Girolamo Fiorentino, Allan Hall, Jane Thomas-Oates, Peter D. Ashton, David A. Ashford, Paul Arthur, Paula F. Campos, Johan Kool, Eske Willerslev, and Matthew J. Collins. 2010. "A Multidisciplinary Study of Archaeological Grape Seeds." *Naturwissenschaften* 97 (2): 205–17. http://dx.doi.org/10.1007/s00114-009-0629-3.

Cappers, René T. J. 1993. "Seed Dispersal by Water: A Contribution to the Interpretation of Seed Assemblages." *Vegetation History and Archaeobotany* 2 (3): 173–86. http://dx.doi.org/10.1007/BF00198588.

Cappers, René T. J. 1995. "A Palaeoecological Model for the Interpretation of Wild Plant Species." *Vegetation History and Archaeobotany* 4 (4): 249–57. http://dx.doi.org/10.1007/BF00235756.

Cappers, René T. J. 2006. *Roman Foodprints at Berenike: Archaeobotanical Evidence of Subsistence and Trade in the Eastern Desert of Egypt*. Los Angeles: Cotsen Institute of Archaeology, University of California.

Cappers, René T. J., Renée M. Bekker, and Judith E. A. Jans. 2006. *Digitale Zade-natlas Van Nederland/Digital Seed Atlas of the Netherlands*. Groningen: Barkhuis Publishing and Groningen University Library.

Cappers, René T. J., S. Bottema, and H. Woldring. 1998. "Problems in Correlating Pollen Diagrams of the Near East: A Preliminary Report." In *The Origins of Agriculture and Crop Domestication: The Harlan Symposium*, edited by A. B. Damania, J. Valkoun, G. Willcox, and C. O. Qualset, 160–69. Aleppo, Syria: ICARDA.

Cappers, René T. J., Reinder Neef, and Renée M. Bekker. 2009. *Digital Atlas of Economic Plants*. 3 vols. Eelde, Netherlands: Barkhuis Publishing.

Caraco, Thomas. 1981. "Energy Budgets, Risk, and Foraging Preferences in Dark-Eyed Juncos (*Junco hyemalis*)." *Behavioral Ecology and Sociobiology* 8 (3): 213–17. http://dx.doi.org/10.1007/BF00299833.

Carter, Joseph Coleman. 2006. *Discovering the Greek Countryside at Metaponto*. Ann Arbor: University of Michigan Press.

Carter, Roger L. 2007. "Advancement of Digital Photography and Related Technologies Timetable." In *Focal Encyclopedia of Photography: Digital Imaging, Theory and Applications, History and Science*, edited by Michael R. Peres, 15–22. Boston: Elsevier/Focal Press. http://dx.doi.org/10.1016/B978-0-240-80740-9.50010-6.

Carvalho, M. C., K. Hayashizaki, and H. Ogawa. 2007. "Environment Determines Nitrogen Content and Stable Isotope Composition in the Sporophyte of *Undaria pinnatifida* (Harvey) Suringar." *Journal of Applied Phycology* 20 (5): 245–53.

Casana, Jesse. 2003. "The Archaeological Landscape of Late Roman Antioch." In *Culture and Society in Late Roman Antioch*, edited by J. A. R. Huskinson and B. Sandwell, 102–25. Oxford: Oxbow.

Casana, Jesse. 2007. "Structural Transformations in Settlement Systems of the Northern Levant." *American Journal of Archaeology* 111 (2): 195–221. http://dx.doi.org/10.3764/aja.111.2.195.

Casana, Jesse. 2008. "Mediterranean Valleys Revisited: Linking Soil Erosion, Land Use and Climate Variability in the Northern Levant." *Geomorphology* 101 (3): 429–42. http://dx.doi.org/10.1016/j.geomorph.2007.04.031.

Casana, Jesse. 2013. "Radial Route Systems and Agro-Pastoral Strategies in the Fertile Crescent: New Discoveries from Western Syria and Southwestern Iran." *Journal of Anthropological Archaeology* 32 (2): 257–73. http://dx.doi.org/10.1016/j.jaa.2012.12.004.

Casana, Jesse, and Jackson Cothren. 2008. "Stereo Analysis, Dem Extraction and Orthorectification of CORONA Satellite Imagery: Archaeological Applications from the Near East." *Antiquity* 82 (317): 732–49.

Casana, Jesse, Jackson Cothren, and Tuna Kalayci. 2012. "Swords into Ploughshares: Archaeological Applications of CORONA Satellite Imagery in the Near East." *Internet Archaeology* 32 (2). http://intarch.ac.uk/journal/issue32/casana_index.html.

Castetter, Edward Franklin, and Willis Harvey Bell. 1951. *Yuman Indian Agriculture: Primitive Subsistence on the Lower Colorado and Gila Rivers.* Inter-Americana Series 2. Albuquerque: University of New Mexico Press.

Castiglioni, Elisabetta. 2005. "Analisi Archeobotaniche su Campioni di San Candido." In *Littamum: Una Mansio Nel Noricum,* edited by Lorenzo Dal Ri, and Stefano di Stefano, 523–37. BAR International Series 1462. Oxford: British Archaeological Reports.

Castro, Maria Clara, Chris Michael Hall, Delphine Patriarche, Patrick Goblet, and Brian Robert Ellis. 2007. "A New Noble Gas Paleoclimate Record in Texas—Basic Assumptions Revisited." *Earth and Planetary Science Letters* 257 (1–2): 170–87. http://dx.doi.org/10.1016/j.epsl.2007.02.030.

Cerling, Thure E., and Jay Quade. 1993. "Stable Carbon and Oxygen Isotopes in Soil Carbonates." In *Climate Change in Continental Isotopic Records,* edited by P. K. Smart, K. C. Lohmann, J. McKenzie, and S. Savin, 217–31. Geophysical Monograph no. 78. Washington, DC: American Geophysical Union. http://dx.doi.org /10.1029/GM078p0217.

Cerling, Thure E., Yang Wang, and Jay Quade. 1993. "Expansion of C_4 Ecosystems as an Indicator of Global Ecological Change in the Late Miocene." *Nature* 361 (6410): 344–45. http://dx.doi.org/10.1038/361344a0.

Challis, Keith, Mark Kincey, and Andy J. Howard. 2009. "Airborne Remote Sensing of Valley Floor Geoarchaeology Using Daedalus ATM and CASI." *Archaeological Prospection* 16 (1): 17–33. http://dx.doi.org/10.1002/arp.340.

Champlot, Sophie, Camille Berthelot, Mélanie Pruvost, E. Andrew Bennett, Thierry Grange, and Eva-Maria Geigl. 2010. "An Efficient Multistrategy DNA Decontamination Procedure of PCR Reagents for Hypersensitive PCR Applications." *PLoS ONE* 5 (9): e13042. http://dx.doi.org/10.1371/journal.pone.0013042.

Chandler, Daniel. 1994. "Semiotics for Beginners." Accessed April 25, 2001. http:// www.aber.ac.uk/media/Documents/S4B/semiotic.html.

Chandler-Ezell, Karol, Deborah M. Pearsall, and James A. Zeidler. 2006. "Root and Tuber Phytoliths and Starch Grains Document Manioc (*Manihot esculenta*), Arrowroot (*Maranta arundinacea*), and Llerén (*Calathea* sp.) at the Real Alto Site, Ecuador." *Economic Botany* 60 (2): 103–20. http://dx.doi.org/10.1663/0013 -0001(2006)60[103:RATPAS]2.0.CO;2.

Charles, Michael. 1998. "Fodder from Dung: The Recognition and Interpretation of Dung-Derived Plant Material from Archaeological Sites." *Environmental Archaeology* 1 (1): 111–22. http://dx.doi.org/10.1179/env.1996.1.1.111.

Charles, Mike, and Amy Bogaard. 2001. "Third Millennium BC Charred Plant Remains from Tell Brak." In *Excavations at Tell Brak Volume 2: Nagar in the Third Millennium BC*, edited by David Oates, Joan Oates, and Helen McDonald, 301–26. Cambrdige: McDonald Institute for Archaeological Research and the British School of Archaeology in Iraq.

Charles, Mike, Amy Bogaard, Glynis Jones, John Hodgson, and Paul Halstead. 2002. "Towards the Archaeobotanical Identification of Intensive Cereal Cultivation: Present-Day Ecological Investigation in the Mountains of Asturias, Northwest Spain." *Vegetation History and Archaeobotany* 11 (1–2): 133–42. http://dx.doi.org/10.1007/s003340200015.

Charles, Michael, C. Hoppé, G. Jones, A. Bogaard, and J. G. Hodgson. 2003. "Using Weed Functional Attributes for the Identification of Irrigation Regimes in Jordan." *Journal of Archaeological Science* 30 (11): 1429–41. http://dx.doi.org/10.1016/S0305-4403(03)00038-4.

Charles, M., G. Jones, and J. G. Hodgson. 1997. "FIBS in Archaeobotany: Functional Interpretation of Weed Floras in Relation to Husbandry Practices." *Journal of Archaeological Science* 24 (12): 1151–61. http://dx.doi.org/10.1006/jasc.1997.0194.

Chase, Arlen F., Diane Z. Chase, John F. Weishampel, Jason B. Drake, Ramesh L. Shrestha, K. Clint Slatton, Jaime J. Awe, and William E. Carter. 2011. "Airborne LiDAR, Archaeology, and the Ancient Maya Landscape at Caracol, Belize." *Journal of Archaeological Science* 38 (2): 387–98. http://dx.doi.org/10.1016/j.jas.2010.09.018.

Chen, H. L., K. A. Jakes, and D. W. Foreman. 1998. "Preservation of Archaeological Textiles through Fibre Mineralization." *Journal of Archaeological Science* 25 (10): 1015–21. http://dx.doi.org/10.1006/jasc.1997.0286.

Chen, Tao, Yan Wu, Yongbing Zhang, Bo Wang, Yaowu Hu, Changsui Wang, and Hongen Jiang. 2012. "Archaeobotanical Study of Ancient Food and Cereal Remains at the Astana Cemeteries, Xinjiang, China." *PLoS ONE* 7 (9): e45137. http://dx.doi.org/10.1371/journal.pone.0045137.

Chernoff, Miriam C. 1988. "The Archaeobotanical Material from Tel El Ifshar: A Diachronic Study of Agriculture Strategies During the Third and Second Millennia B.C.E." Unpublished PhD. diss., Brandeis University, Waltham, MA.

Chernoff, Miriam C., and Samuel M. Paley. 1998. "Dynamics of Cereal Production at Tell El Ifshar, Israel During the Middle Bronze Age." *Journal of Field Archaeology* 25 (4): 397–416. http://dx.doi.org/10.1179/009346998792005289.

Cheshire, M. V. 1979. *Nature and Origin of Carbohydrates in Soils*. London: Academic Press.

Cheshire, M. V., M. P. Greaves, and C. M. Mundie. 1974. "Decomposition of Soil Polysaccharide." *Journal of Soil Science* 25 (4): 483–98. http://dx.doi.org/10.1111/j.1365-2389.1974.tb01143.x.

Cheshire, M. V., C. M. Mundie, and H. Shepherd. 1969. "Transformation of ^{14}C Glucose and Starch in Soil." *Soil Biology & Biochemistry* 1 (2): 117–30. http://dx.doi.org/10.1016/0038-0717(69)90002-9.

Chilton, Elizabeth S. 2008. "So Little Maize, So Much Time: Understanding Maize Adoption in New England." In *Current Northeast Ethnobotany II*, edited by John P. Hart, 53–58. Bulletin Series 512. Albany: New York State Museum.

Chippindale, Christopher. 1993. "Ambition, Deference, Discrepancy, Consumption: The Intellectual Background to a Post-Processual Archaeology." In *Archaeological Theory: Who Sets the Agenda*, edited by N. Yoffee, 27–36. Cambridge, UK: Cambridge University Press. http://dx.doi.org/10.1017/CBO9780511720277.004.

Chisholm, Brian S., and Michael Blake. 2006. "Diet in Prehistoric Soconusco." In *Histories of Maize in Mesoamerica: Multidisciplinary Approaches*, edited by John E. Staller, Robert H. Tykot, and Bruce F. Benz, 161–72. Burlington, MA: Associated Press.

Chisholm, Brian S., D. Erle Nelson, and Henry P. Schwarcz. 1982. "Stable-Carbon Isotope Ratios as a Measure of Marine Versus Terrestrial Protein in Ancient Diets." *Science* 216 (4550): 1131–32. http://dx.doi.org/10.1126/science.216.4550.1131.

Chisholm, Brian S., D. Erle Nelson, and Henry P. Schwarcz. 1983. "Marine and Terrestrial Protein in Prehistoric Diets on the British Columbia Coast." *Current Anthropology* 24 (3): 396–98. http://dx.doi.org/10.1086/203018.

Christenson, Andrew L. 1980. "Change in the Human Food Niche in Response to Population Growth." In *Modeling Prehistoric Subsistence Economies*, edited by Timothy Earle and Andrew L. Christenson, 31–72. New York: Academic Press.

Ciaraldi, Marina. 2000. "Drug Preparation in Evidence? An Unusual Plant and Bone Assemblage from the Pompeian Countryside, Italy." *Vegetation History and Archaeobotany* 9 (2): 91–98. http://dx.doi.org/10.1007/BF01300059.

Clapham, Alan J., and Chris J. Stevens. 2008. "Charred Plant Remains." In *An Iron Age Settlement Outside Battlesbury Hillfort, Warminster and Sites Along the Southern Range Road, Salisbury*, edited by Chris Ellis, and Andrew B. Powell, 93–102. Report no. 22. Salisbury: Wessex Archaeology.

Clark, Geoffrey A., and C. Russell Stafford. 1982. "Quantification in American Archaeology: A Historical Perspective." *World Archaeology* 14 (1): 98–119. http://dx.doi.org/10.1080/00438243.1982.9979852.

Clark, James S., and P. Dan Royall. 1995. "Transformation of a Northern Hardwood Forest by Aboriginal (Iroquois) Fire: Charcoal Evidence from Crawford Lake, Ontario, Canada." *The Holocene* 5 (1): 1–9. http://dx.doi.org/10.1177/095968369500500101.

Clark, James S., and P. Dan Royall. 1996. "Local and Regional Sediment Charcoal Evidence for Fire Regmines in Presettlement North-Eastern North America." *Journal of Ecology* 84 (3): 365–82. http://dx.doi.org/10.2307/2261199.

Clementz, Mark T., K. Fox-Dobbs, P. V. Wheatley, P. L. Koch, and D. F. Doak. 2009. "Revisiting Old Bones: Coupled Carbon Isotope Analysis of Bioapatite and Collagen as an Ecological and Palaeoecological Tool." *Geological Journal* 44 (5): 605–20. http://dx.doi.org/10.1002/gj.1173.

Clementz, Mark T., Paul L. Koch, and Cathy A. Beck. 2007. "Diet Induced Differences in Carbon Isotope Fractionation between Sirenians and Terrestrial Ungulates." *Marine Biology* 151 (5): 1773–84. http://dx.doi.org/10.1007/s00227-007-0616-1.

Cleveland, William S. 1994. *The Elements of Graphing Data*. Murray Hill, NJ: AT&T Bell Laboratories.

Cohen, Mark N., and George J. Armelagos, eds. 1984. *Paleopathology at the Origins of Agriculture*. Orlando: Academic Press.

Coles, Bryony, and J. M. Coles. 1989. *People of the Wetlands: Bogs, Bodies, and Lake-Dwellers*. New York: Thames & Hudson.

Colledge, Sue. 1998. "Identifying Pre-Domestication Cultivation Using Multivariate Statistics." In *The Origins of Agriculture and Crop Domestication: The Harlan Symposium*, edited by A. B. Damania, J. Valkoun, G. Willcox, and C. O. Qualset, 121–31. Aleppo, Syria: ICARDA.

Colledge, Sue. 2001. *Plant Exploitation on Epipalaeolithic and Early Neolithic Sites in the Levant*. BAR International Series 986. Oxford: British Archaeological Reports.

Colledge, Sue, James Conolly, and Stephen Shennan. 2004. "Archaeobotanical Evidence for the Spread of Farming in the Eastern Mediterranean." *Current Anthropology* 45 (S4): S35–58. http://dx.doi.org/10.1086/422086.

Comer, Douglas C., and Michael J. Harrower. 2013. *Mapping Archaeological Landscapes from Space*. New York: Springer. http://dx.doi.org/10.1007/978-1-4614-6074-9.

Commisso, R. G., and D. Erle Nelson. 2008. "Correlation between Modern Plant δ15N Values and Activity Areas of Medieval Norse Farms." *Journal of Archaeological Science* 35 (2): 492–504. http://dx.doi.org/10.1016/j.jas.2007.05.012.

Connelly, Thomas J., and William J. Cannon. 1999. "Comments on 'America's Oldest Basketry.'" *Radiocarbon* 41:309–13.

Conolly, James, and Mark Lake. 2006. *Geographical Information Systems in Archaeology*. Cambridge: Cambridge University Press. http://dx.doi.org/10.1017/CBO9780511807459.

Constante, Ana, José Luis Peña, Arsenio Muñoz, and Jesús Picazo. 2011. "Climate and Anthropogenic Factors Affecting Alluvial Fan Development During the Late Holocene in the Central Ebro Valley, Northeast Spain." *The Holocene* 21 (2): 275–86. http://dx.doi.org/10.1177/0959683610378873.

Cordova, Carlos E., William C. Johnson, Rolfe D. Mandel, and Michael W. Palmer. 2011. "Late Quaternary Environmental Change Inferred from Phytoliths and

Other Soil-Related Proxies: Case Studies from the Central and Southern Great Plains, USA." *Catena* 85 (2): 87–108. http://dx.doi.org/10.1016/j.catena.2010.08.015.

Corinaldesi, C., M. Barucca, G. M. Luna, and A. Dell'Anno. 2011. "Preservation, Origin and Genetic Imprint of Extracellular DNA in Permanently Anoxic Deep-Sea Sediments." *Molecular Ecology* 20 (3): 642–54. http://dx.doi.org/10.1111/j.1365 -294X.2010.04958.x.

Corner, Edred J. H. 1976. *The Seeds of Dicotyledons.* 2 vols. Cambridge: Cambridge University Press.

Cortella, A. R., M. L. Pochettino, A. Manzo, and G. Raviña. 2001. "*Erythroxylum coca*: Microscopical Identification in Powdered and Carbonized Archaeological Material." *Journal of Archaeological Science* 28 (8): 787–94. http://dx.doi.org/10.1006 /jasc.2000.0575.

Cosgrove, Richard. 1996. "Origin and Development of Australian Aboriginal Tropical Rainforest Culture: A Reconsideration." *Antiquity* 70:900–912.

Costantini, Lorenzo, and John Giorgi. 2001. "Charred Plant Remains of the Archaic Period from the Forum and Palatine." *Journal of Roman Archaeology* 14:239–48.

Counihan, Carole, and Penny Van Esterik. 1997. "Introduction." In *Food and Culture: A Reader*, 1st ed., edited by Carole Counihan and Penny Van Esterik, 1–9. New York: Routledge.

Coward, Fiona, Stephen Shennan, Sue Colledge, James Conolly, and Mark Collard. 2008. "The Spread of Neolithic Plant Economies from the Near East to Northwest Europe: A Phylogenetic Analysis." *Journal of Archaeological Science* 35 (1): 42–56. http://dx.doi.org/10.1016/j.jas.2007.02.022.

Cowley, David, and Rachel S. Opitz, eds. 2013. *Interpreting Archaeological Topography: Lasers, 3D Data, Observation, Visualisation and Applications.* Oxford: Oxbow Books.

Cowley, David, Robin A. Standring, and Matthew J. Abicht, eds. 2010. *Landscapes through the Lens: Aerial Photographs and Historic Environment.* Oxford: Oxbow Books.

Crader, Diana C. 1990. "Slave Diet at Monticello." *American Antiquity* 55 (4): 690–717. http://dx.doi.org/10.2307/281246.

Craig, Harmon. 1953. "The Geochemistry of the Stable Carbon Isotopes." *Geochimica et Cosmochimica Acta* 3 (2–3): 53–92. http://dx.doi.org/10.1016/0016-7037(53)90001-5.

Craig, Harmon. 1954. "Carbon–13 in Plants and the Relationships between Carbon–13 and Carbon–14 Variations in Nature." *Journal of Geology* 62 (2): 115–49. http://dx.doi .org/10.1086/626141.

Craig, Nathan, Mark S. Aldenderfer, Paul Baker, and Catherine Rigsby. 2010. "Terminal Archaic Settlement Pattern and Land Cover Change in the Rio Ilave, Southwestern Lake Titicaca Basin, Peru." In *The Archaeology of Anthropogenic*

Environments, edited by Rebecca M. Dean, 35–53. Carbondale: Southern Illinois University Center for Archaeological Investigations.

Crane, Cathy J. 1996. "Archaeobotanical and Palynological Research at a Late Pre-classic Maya Community, Cerros, Belize." In *The Managed Mosaic: Ancient Maya Agriculture and Resource Use*, edited by Scott L. Fedick, 262–77. Salt Lake City: University of Utah Press.

Crawford, Gary W. 1983. *Paleoethnobotany of the Kameda Peninsula Jomon. Anthropological Papers 73. Museum of Anthropology*. Ann Arbor: University of Michigan.

Crawford, Gary W. 1997. "Anthropogenesis in Prehistoric Northeastern Japan." In *People, Plants, and Landscapes: Studies in Paleoethnobotany*, edited by Kristin J. Gremillion, 86–103. Tuscaloosa: University of Alabama Press.

Crawford, Gary W. 2006. "East Asian Plant Domestication." In *Archaeology of Asia*, edited by Miriam T. Stark, 77–95. Oxford: Blackwell.

Crawford, Gary W. 2009. "Agricultural Origins in North China Pushed Back to the Pleistocene-Holocene Boundary." *Proceedings of the National Academy of Sciences of the United States of America* 106 (18): 7271–72. http://dx.doi.org/10.1073/pnas.0903375106.

Crawford, Gary W. 2011. "Gary W. Crawford, University of Toronto." Accessed October 30, 2011. http://profgarycrawford.ca/.

Crawford, Gary W., and David G. Smith. 1996. "Migration in Prehistory: Princess Point and the Northern Iroquoian Case." *American Antiquity* 61 (4): 782–90. http://dx.doi.org/10.2307/282018.

Crawford, Osbert Guy Stanhope, and Alexander Keiller. 1928. *Wessex from the Air*. Oxford: The Clarendon Press.

Creel, Darrell, and Austin Long. 1986. "Radiocarbon Dating of Corn." *American Antiquity* 51 (4): 826–36. http://dx.doi.org/10.2307/280869.

Cronin, Thomas M. 2010. *Paleoclimates: Understanding Climate Change Past and Present*. New York: Columbia University Press.

Crown, Patricia L. 2000. "Women's Role in Changing Cuisine." In *Women and Men in the Prehispanic Southwest: Labor, Power, and Prestige*, edited by Patricia L. Crown, 221–66. Santa Fe: School of American Research Press.

Crowther, Alison. 2005. "Starch Residues on Undecorated Lapita Pottery from Anir, New Ireland." *Archaeology in Oceania* 41:62–66.

Crowther, Alison, Michael Haslam, Nikki Oakden, Dale Walde, Julio Mercader. 2014. "Documenting Contamination in Ancient Starch Laboratories," *Journal of Archaeological Science* 49: 90–104.

Crumley, Carole L. 1994. "Historical Ecology: A Multidimensional Ecological Orientation." In *Historical Ecology: Cultural Knowledge and Changing Landscapes*, edited by Carole L. Crumley, 1–16. Santa Fe: School of American Research Press.

Cummings, Linda Scott, and Ann Magennis. 1997. "A Phytolith and Starch Record of Food and Grit in Mayan Human Tooth Tartar." In *Primer Encuentro Europeo Sobre El Estudio de Fitolitos*, edited by A. Pinilla, J. Juan-Tresserras, and M. J. Machado, 211–18. Madrid: Graficas Fersan.

Currie, Chris. 2005. *Garden Archaeology*. York: Council for British Archaeology.

Cushman, John C. 2001. "Crassulacean Acid Metabolism: A Plastic Photosynthesis Adaptation to Arid Environments." *Plant Physiology* 127 (4): 1439–48. http://dx.doi .org/10.1104/pp.010818.

Custer, Jay F. 1996. *Prehistoric Cultures of Eastern Pennsylvania. Anthropological Series Number 7*. Harrisburg: Pennsylvania Historical and Museum Commission.

Cyr, Howard, Calla McNamee, Leslie Amundson, and Andrea Freeman. 2011. "Reconstructing Landscape and Vegetation through Multiple Proxy Indicators: A Geoarchaeological Examination of the St. Louis Site, Saskatchewan, Canada." *Geoarchaeology: An International Journal* 26 (2): 165–88. http://dx.doi.org/10.1002/gea.20345.

d'Alpoim Guedes, Jade, and Jiang Ming. 2011. "Xinjian Baodun Yizhi 2009 Niandu Kaogu Shijue Fuxuan Jieguo Fenxi Baogao" (Report on the Results of the Flotation from the 2009 Excavations at the Site of Baodun in Xinjin). Chengdu Kaogu Faxian 2009, 67–81.

D'Andrea, A. Catherine. 2008. "T'ef (*Eragrostis tef*) in Ancient Agricultural Systems of Highland Ethiopia." *Economic Botany* 62 (4): 547–66. http://dx.doi.org /10.1007/s12231-008-9053-4.

D'Andrea, A. Catherine. 2010. *Early State Development in Northern Ethiopia. Eastern Tigrai Archaeological Project Year 3: Final Report to the ARCCH*. Authority for Research and Conservation of Cultural Heritage, Addis Ababa.

D'Andrea, A. Catherine, and Mitiku Haile. 2002. "Traditional Emmer Processing in Highland Ethiopia." *Journal of Ethnobiology* 22:197–217.

D'Andrea, A. C., M. Klee, and J. Casey. 2001. "Archaeobotanical Evidence for Pearl Millet (*Pennisetum glaucum*) in Sub-Saharan West Africa." *Antiquity* 75 (288): 341–48.

D'Andrea, A. Catherine, Amanda L. Logan, and Derek J. Watson. 2006. "Oil Palm and Prehistoric Subsistence in Tropical Africa." *Journal of African Archaeology* 4 (2): 195–222. http://dx.doi.org/10.3213/1612-1651-10072.

Damp, Jonathan E., Stephen A. Hall, and Susan J. Smith. 2002. "Early Irrigation on the Colorado Plateau near Zuni Pueblo, New Mexico." *American Antiquity* 67 (4): 665–76. http://dx.doi.org/10.2307/1593797.

Davis, E. Mott, and Al B. Wesolowsky. 1975. "The Izum: A Simple Water Separation Device." *Journal of Field Archaeology* 2:271–73.

Day, Gordon M. 1953. "The Indian as an Ecological Factor in the Northeastern Forest." *Ecology* 34 (2): 329–46. http://dx.doi.org/10.2307/1930900.

Day, Petra. 1993. "Preliminary Results of High-Resolution Palaeoecological Analyses at Star Carr, Yorkshire." *Cambridge Archaeological Journal* 3 (1): 129–33. http://dx.doi.org/10.1017/S0959774300000755.

de Certeau, Michel. 1984. *The Practice of Everyday Life*. Berkeley: University of California Press.

de Moulins, Dominique. 2007. "The Weeds from the Thatch Roofs of Medieval Cottages from the South of England." *Vegetation History and Archaeobotany* 16 (5): 385–98. http://dx.doi.org/10.1007/s00334-006-0035-0.

de Wet, J. M. J., J. R. Harlan, and D. E. Brink. 1986. "Reality of Infraspecific Taxonomic Units in Domesticated Cereals." In *Infraspecific Classification of Wild and Cultivated Plants*, edited by B. T. Styles, 211–22. Oxford: Clarendon Press.

Dean, Glenna W. 2006. "The Science of Coprolite Analysis: The View from Hinds Cave." *Palaeogeography, Palaeoclimatology, Palaeoecology* 237 (1): 67–79. http://dx.doi.org/10.1016/j.palaeo.2005.11.029.

Dean, J. 2004. "Anthropogenic Environmental Change in the Southwest as Viewed from the Colorado Plateau." In *The Archaeology of Global Change: The Impact of Humans on Their Environment*, edited by Charles L. Redman, Steven R. James, Paul R. Fish, and J. Daniel Rogers, 191–207. Washington, DC: Smithsonian Books.

Dean, Rebecca M., ed. 2010. *The Archaeology of Anthropogenic Environments*. Carbondale: Southern Illinois University.

Del Pilar Babot, Maria. 2003. "Starch Grain Damage as an Indicator of Food Processing." In *Phytolith and Starch Research in the Australian-Pacific-Asian Regions: The State of the Art*, edited by D. M. Hart, and L. A. Wallis, 69–81. Canberra: Pandanus Press.

Del Pilar Babot, Maria, and Maria C. Apella. 2003. "Maize and Bone: Residues of Grinding in Northwestern Argentina." *Archaeometry* 45 (1): 121–32. http://dx.doi.org/10.1111/1475-4754.00099.

Delabarre, Edmund B., and Harris H. Wilder. 1920. "Indian Corn-Hills in Massachusetts." *American Anthropologist* 22 (3): 203–25. http://dx.doi.org/10.1525/aa.1920.22.3.02a00010.

Delcourt, P. A., O. K. Davis, and R. C. Bright. 1979. *Bibliography of Taxonomic Literature for the Identification of Fruits, Seeds, and Vegetative Plant Fragments. Publication 1328*. Tennessee: Environmental Sciences Division, Oak Ridge National Laboratory.

Delcourt, Paula A., and Hazel R. Delcourt. 1980. "Pollen Preservation and Quaternary Environmental History in the Southeastern United States." *Palynology* 4 (1): 215–31. http://dx.doi.org/10.1080/01916122.1980.9939209.

Delcourt, Paul A., and Hazel R. Delcourt. 2004. *Prehistoric Native Americans and Ecological Change: Human Ecosystems in Eastern North America since the*

Pleistocene. Cambridge: Cambridge University Press. http://dx.doi.org/10.1017/
CBO9780511525520.

Delcourt, Paul A., Hazel R. Delcourt, Cecil R. Ison, William E. Sharp, and Kristen J.
Gremillion. 1998. "Prehistoric Human Use of Fire, the Eastern Agricultural Com-
plex, and Appalachian Oak-Chestnut Forests: Paleoecology of Cliff Palace Pond,
Kentucky." *American Antiquity* 63 (2): 263–78. http://dx.doi.org/10.2307/2694697.

Delhon, Claire, Lucie Martin, Jacqueline Argant, and Stéphanie Thiébault. 2008.
"Shepherds and Plants in the Alps: Multi-Proxy Archaeobotanical Analysis of
Neolithic Dung from 'La Grande Rivoire' (Isère, France)." *Journal of Archaeological
Science* 35 (11): 2937–52. http://dx.doi.org/10.1016/j.jas.2008.06.007.

Delorit, Richard J. 1970. *Illustrated Taxonomy Manual of Weed Seeds*. River Falls, Wisconsin: Agronomy Publications.

Delwiche, Constant C., and Pieter L. Steyn. 1970. "Nitrogen Isotope Fractionation in
Soils and Microbial Reactions." *Environmental Science & Technology* 4 (11): 929–35.
http://dx.doi.org/10.1021/es60046a004.

Delwiche, Constant C., P. J. Zinke, C. M. Johnson, and R. A. Virginia. 1979. "Nitrogen Isotope Distribution as a Presumptive Indicator of Nitrogen-Fixation."
Botanical Gazette (Chicago, Ill.) 140 (S1): S65–69. http://dx.doi.org/10.1086/337037.

deMenocal, Peter B. 2001. "Cultural Responses to Climate Change During the Late
Holocene." *Science* 292 (5517): 667–73. http://dx.doi.org/10.1126/science.1059827.

Demidowicz, George. 2005. *Ridge and Furrow Survey (King's Norton)*. Birmingham:
Birmingham and Warwickshire Archaeological Society.

Denevan, William M. 2003. *Cultivated Landscapes of Native Amazonia and the Andes*.
Oxford: Oxford University Press.

Denham, Tim. 2005. "Envisaging Early Agriculture in the Highlands of New
Guinea: Landscapes, Plants and Practices." *World Archaeology* 37 (2): 290–306.
http://dx.doi.org/10.1080/00438240500095447.

Denham, Tim, and Huw Barton. 2006. "The Emergence of Agriculture in New
Guinea: A Model of Continuity from Pre-Existing Foraging Practices." In *Behav-
ioral Ecology and the Transition to Agriculture*, edited by Douglas J. Kennett, and
Bruce Winterhalder, 237–64. Berkeley: University of California Press.

Denham, Tim, S. B. Haberle, C. Lentfer, R. Fullagar, J. Field, M. Therin, N. Porch,
and B. Winsborough. 2003. "Origins of Agriculture at Kuk Swamp in the Highlands of New Guinea." *Science* 301 (5630): 189–93. http://dx.doi.org/10.1126/science
.1085255.

DeNiro, Michael. 1985. "Postmortem Preservation and Alteration of in Vivo Bone-
Collagen Isotope Ratios in Relation to Paleodietary Reconstruction." *Nature* 317
(6040): 806–9. http://dx.doi.org/10.1038/317806a0.

DeNiro, Michael, and Samuel Epstein. 1977. "Mechanism of Carbon Isotope Fractionation Associated with Lipid-Synthesis." *Science* 197 (4300): 261–63. http://dx.doi.org/10.1126/science.327543.

DeNiro, Michael, and Samuel Epstein. 1978. "Influence of Diet on Distribution of Carbon Isotopes in Animals." *Geochimica et Cosmochimica Acta* 42 (5): 495–506. http://dx.doi.org/10.1016/0016-7037(78)90199-0.

DeNiro, Michael, and Samuel Epstein. 1981. "Influence of Diet on the Distribution of Nitrogen Isotopes in Animals." *Geochimica et Cosmochimica Acta* 45 (3): 341–51. http://dx.doi.org/10.1016/0016-7037(81)90244-1.

DeNiro, Michael, and Samuel Epstein. 1986. "Erratum." *Geochimica et Cosmochimica Acta* 50 (2): 329. http://dx.doi.org/10.1016/0016-7037(86)90181-X.

DeNiro, Michael, and Christine A. Hastorf. 1985. "Alteration of $^{15}N/^{14}N$ and $^{13}C/^{12}C$ Ratios of Plant Matter During the Initial Stages of Diagenesis: Studies Utilizing Archaeological Specimens from Peru." *Geochimica et Cosmochimica Acta* 49 (1): 97–115. http://dx.doi.org/10.1016/0016-7037(85)90194-2.

Dennell, Robert W. 1974. "Botanical Evidence for Prehistoric Crop Processing Activities." *Journal of Archaeological Science* 1 (3): 275–84. http://dx.doi.org/10.1016/0305-4403(74)90027-2.

Dennell, Robin W. 1976. "The Economic Importance of Plant Resources Represented on Archaeological Sites." *Journal of Archaeological Science* 3 (3): 229–47. http://dx.doi.org/10.1016/0305-4403(76)90057-1.

Derbyshire, E., N. Harris, D. Boulter, and E. M. Jope. 1977. "The Extraction, Composition and Intra-Cellular Distribution of Protein in Early Maize Grains from an Archaeological Site in N.E. Arizona." *New Phytologist* 78 (2): 499–504. http://dx.doi.org/10.1111/j.1469-8137.1977.tb04856.x.

DeTore, Kathryn, and Rebecca E. Bria. 2012. "iArchaeology: Explorations in in-Field Digital Data Collection." Paper presented at the 77th Annual Meeting of the Society for American Archaeology, Memphis, TN.

Deur, Douglas. 2005. "Tending the Garden, Making the Soil: Northwest Coast Estuarine Gardens as Engineered Environments." In *Keeping It Living: Traditions of Plant Use and Cultivation on the Northwest Coast of North America*, edited by Douglas Deur and Nancy Turner, 296–330. Seattle: University of Washington Press.

Deur, Douglas, and Nancy Turner, eds. 2005. *Keeping It Living: Traditions of Plant Use and Cultivation on the Northwest Coast of North America*. Seattle: University of Washington Press.

Devereux, B. J., G. S. Amable, P. Crow, and A. D. Cliff. 2005. "The Potential of Airborne Lidar for Detection of Archaeological Features under Woodland Canopies." *Antiquity* 79 (305): 648–60.

Dezendorf, Caroline. 2013. "The Effects of Food Processing on the Archaeological Visibility of Maize: An Experimental Study of Carbonization of Lime-Treated Maize Kernels." *Ethnobiology Letters* 4 (0): 12–20. http://dx.doi.org/10.14237/ebl .4.2013.10.

di Lernia, Savino, Isabella Massamba N'siala, and Anna Maria Mercuri. 2012. "Saharan Prehistoric Basketry. Archaeological and Archaeobotanical Analysis of the Early-Middle Holocene Assemblage from Takarkori (Acacus Mts., SW Libya)." *Journal of Archaeological Science* 39 (6): 1837–53. http://dx.doi.org/10.1016/j.jas.2012 .01.026.

Di Piazza, Anne. 1998. "Archaeobotanical Investigations of an Earth Oven in Kiribati, Gilbert Islands." *Vegetation History and Archaeobotany* 7 (3): 149–54. http://dx.doi .org/10.1007/BF01374003.

Diamant, Steven. 1979. "A Short History of Archaeological Sieving at Franchthi Cave, Greece." *Journal of Field Archaeology* 6 (2): 203–17. http://dx.doi.org/10.1179 /009346979791489366.

Diamond, Jared. 1997. *Guns, Germs and Steel: The Fates of Human Societies.* New York: W.W. Norton & Company.

Diamond, Jared. 2005. *Collapse: How Societies Choose to Fail or Succeed.* New York: Penguin Group.

Dickau, Ruth, Anthony J. Ranere, and Richard G. Cooke. 2007. "Starch Grain Evidence for the Preceramic Dispersals of Maize and Root Crops into Tropical Dry and Humid Forests of Panama." *Proceedings of the National Academy of Sciences of the United States of America* 104 (9): 3651–56. doi: 10.1073/pnas.0611605104.

Dickinson, D. B. 1968. "Rapid Starch Synthesis Associated with Increased Respiration in Germinating Lily Pollen." *Plant Physiology* 43 (1): 1–8. http://dx.doi.org /10.1104/pp.43.1.1.

Dickson, James H., Klaus Oeggl, and Linda L. Handley. 2003. "The Iceman Reconsidered." *Scientific American* 288 (5): 70–79. http://dx.doi.org/10.1038/scientific american0503-70.

Dickson, James H., Michael P. Richards, Richard J. Hebda, Petra J. Mudie, Owen Beattie, Susan Ramsay, Nancy J. Turner, Bruce J. Leighton, John M. Webster, Niki R. Hobischak, Gail S. Anderson, Peter M. Troffe, and Rebecca J. Wigen. 2004. "Kwäday Dän Ts'ìnchì, the First Ancient Body of a Man from a North American Glacier: Reconstructing His Last Days by Intestinal and Biomolecular Analyses." *Holocene* 14 (4): 481–86. http://dx.doi.org/10.1191/0959683604hl742rp.

Diehl, Michael W. 2005. "Morphological Observations on Recently Recovered Early Agricultural Period Maize Cob Fragments from Southern Arizona." *American Antiquity* 70 (2): 361–75. http://dx.doi.org/10.2307/40035708.

Diehl, Michael W., and Jennifer A. Waters. 2006. "Aspects of Optimization and Risk in the Early Agricultural Period in Southeastern Arizona." In *Behavioral Ecology and the Transition to Agriculture*, edited by Douglas J. Kennett and Bruce Winterhalder, 63–86. Berkeley: University of California Press.

Dietler, Michael, and Brian Hayden. 2001. *Feasts: Archaeological and Ethnographic Perspectives on Food, Politics, and Power*. Smithsonian Books.

Digital Photography Review. 2005. "Kodak's Digital Sales Overtake Film." http://www.dpreview.com/articles/6085531672/kodaksales.

Dijkstra, Paul, Ayaka Ishizu, Richard Doucett, Stephen C. Hart, Egbert Schwartz, Oleg V. Menyailo, and Bruce A. Hungate. 2006. "C–13 and N–15 Natural Abundance of the Soil Microbial Biomass." *Soil Biology & Biochemistry* 38 (11): 3257–66. http://dx.doi.org/10.1016/j.soilbio.2006.04.005.

Dilke, Oswald Ashton Wentworth. 1971. *The Roman Land Surveyors: An Introduction to the Agrimensores*. New York: David and Charles.

Dillehay, Tom D., Mario Pino Quivira, Renée Bonzani, Claudia Silva, Johannes Wallner, and Carlos Le Quesne. 2007. "Cultivated Wetlands and Emerging Complexity in South-Central Chile and Long Distance Effects of Climate Change." *Antiquity* 81 (314): 949–60.

Dimbleby, Geoffrey W. 1978. *Plants and Archaeology*. 2nd ed. Atlantic Highlands, NJ: Humanities Press.

Dimbleby, Geoffrey W. 1985. *The Palynology of Archaeological Sites*. London: Academic Press.

Dincauze, Dena Ferran. 2000. *Environmental Archaeology: Principles and Practice*. Cambridge: Cambridge University Press. http://dx.doi.org/10.1017/CBO9780511607837.

Doolittle, William E. 2000. *Cultivated Landscapes of Native North America*. Oxford: Oxford University Press.

Doolittle, William E., James Neely, Paul R. Fish, and Karen R. Adams. 2004. *Safford Valley Grids: Prehistoric Cultivation in the Southern Arizona Desert*. Tucson: University of Arizona Press.

Dorney, Cheryl H., and John R. Dorney. 1989. "An Unusual Oak Savanna in Northeastern Wisconsin: The Effect of Indian-Caused Fire." *American Midland Naturalist* 122 (1): 103–13. http://dx.doi.org/10.2307/2425687.

Douglas, Mary. 1997. "Deciphering a Meal." In *Food and Culture: A Reader*, 1st ed., edited by Carole Counihan and Penny Van Esterik, 36–54. New York: Routledge.

Downton, W. J. S. 1975. "Occurrence of C4 Photosynthesis among Plants." *Photosynthetica* 9 (1): 96–105.

Doyon-Bernard, S. J. 1990. "From Twining to Triple Cloth: Experimentation and Innovation in Ancient Peruvian Weaving (ca. 5000–400 B.C.)." *American Antiquity* 55 (1): 68–87. http://dx.doi.org/10.2307/281493.

Drennan, Robert D. 2009. *Statistics for Archaeologists: A Commonsense Approach.* 2nd ed. New York: Springer. http://dx.doi.org/10.1007/978-1-4419-0413-3.

Driese, Steven G., Zheng-Hua Li, and Sally P. Horn. 2005. "Late Pleistocene and Holocene Climate and Geomorphic Histories as Interpreted from a 23,000 14C Yr B.P. Paleosol and Floodplain Soils, Southeastern West Virginia, USA." *Quaternary Research* 63 (2): 136–49. http://dx.doi.org/10.1016/j.yqres.2004.10.005.

Driese, Steven G., Zheng-Hua Li, and Larry D. McKay. 2008. "Evidence for Multiple, Episodic, Mid-Holocene Hypsithermal Recorded in Two Soil Profiles Along an Alluvial Floodplain Catena, Southeastern Tennessee, USA." *Quaternary Research* 69 (2): 276–91. http://dx.doi.org/10.1016/j.yqres.2007.12.003.

Dueppen, Stephen A. 2012. *Egalitarian Revolution in the Savanna: The Origins of a West African Political System.* London: Equinox Pub. Ltd.

Duffus, C. M. 1979. "Carbohydrate Metabolism and Cereal Grain Development." In *Recent Advances in the Biochemistry of Cereals,* edited by D. L. Laidman and R. G. Wyn Jones, 209–38. London: Academic Press.

Dull, Robert A. 2004. "An 8000-Year Record of Vegetation, Climate, and Human Disturbance from the Sierra de Apaneca, El Salvador." *Quaternary Research* 61 (2): 159–67. http://dx.doi.org/10.1016/j.yqres.2004.01.002.

Duncan, Neil A. 2010. "Paleoethnobotany of Buena Vista: A Case Study of Ritual Feasting in Late Preceramic Peru." Unpublished PhD diss., Department of Anthropology, University of Missouri, Columbia.

Dunning, Nicholas P., Sheryl Luzzadder-Beach, Timothy Beach, John G. Jones, Vernon Scarborough, and T. Patrick Culbert. 2002. "Arising from the Bajos: The Evolution of a Neotropical Landscape and the Rise of Maya Civilization." *Annals of the Association of American Geographers* 92 (2): 267–83. http://dx.doi.org/10.1111/1467-8306.00290.

Dupouey, J. L., E. Dambrine, J. D. Laffite, and C. Moares. 2002. "Irreversible Impact of Past Land Use on Forest Soils and Biodiversity." *Ecology* 83 (11): 2978–84. http://dx.doi.org/10.1890/0012-9658(2002)083[2978:IIOPLU]2.0.CO;2.

Dürrwächter, Claudia, Oliver E. Craig, Matthew J. Collins, Joachim Burger, and Kurt W. Alt. 2006. "Beyond the Grave: Variability in Neolithic Diets in Southern Germany?" *Journal of Archaeological Science* 33 (1): 39–48. http://dx.doi.org/10.1016/j.jas2005.06.009.

Dzurec, R. S., T. W. Boutton, M. M. Caldwell, and B. N. Smith. 1985. "Carbon Isotope Ratios of Soil Organic-Matter and Their Use in Assessing Community

Composition Changes in Curlew Valley, Utah." *Oecologia* 66 (1): 17–24. http://dx.doi.org/10.1007/BF00378547.

Earle, Timothy K. 1991. "Toward a Behavioral Archaeology." In *Processual and Postprocessual Archaeologies: Multiple Ways of Knowing the Past*, edited by Robert W. Preucel, 83–95. Carbondale: Southern Illinois University Press.

Eastwood, Warren J., Neil Roberts, and Henry F. Lamb. 1998. "Paleoecological and Archaeological Evidence for Human Occupance in Southwest Turkey: The Beyşehir Occupation Phase." *Anatolian Studies* 48:69–86. http://dx.doi.org/10.2307/3643048.

Ebeling, Jennie R., Norma Franklin, and Ian Cipin. 2012. "Jezreel Revealed in Laser Scans: A Preliminary Report of the 2012 Survey Season." *Near Eastern Archaeology* 75 (4): 232–39.

Ebersbach, Renate. 2013. "Houses, Households, and Settlements: Architecture and Living Spaces." In *The Oxford Handbook of Wetland Archaeology*, edited by Francesco Menotti and Aidan O'Sullivan, 284–301. Oxford: Oxford University Press.

Ede, Joy. 1999. "The Charred Seeds," in "Excavations at Ham Hill, Montacute, Somerset 1994 and 1998," edited by J. McKinley. *Proceedings of the Somerset Archaeology and Natural History Society* 142: 116–124 (77–137).

Edwards, Gerald E., and David A. Walker. 1983. *C3, C4: Mechanism, and Cellular and Environmental Regulation, of Photosynthesis*. Oxford: Blackwell Scientific Publications.

Ehleringer, James R. 1993. "Carbon and Water Relations in Desert Plants: An Isotopic Perspective." In *Stable Isotopes and Plant Carbon-Water Relations*, edited by James R. Ehleringer, Anthony E. Hall, and Graham D. Farquhar, 155–72. New York: Academic Press. http://dx.doi.org/10.1016/B978-0-08-091801-3.50018-0.

Ehleringer, James R., Nina Buchmann, and Lawrence B. Flanagan. 2000. "Carbon Isotope Ratios in Belowground Carbon Cycle Processes." *Ecological Applications* 10 (2): 412–22. http://dx.doi.org/10.1890/1051-0761(2000)010[0412:CIRIBC]2.0.CO;2.

Ehleringer, James R., Anthony E. Hall, and Graham D. Farquhar. 1993. *Stable Isotopes and Plant Carbon-Water Relations*. San Diego: Academic Press.

Ehleringer, James R., and Russell K. Monson. 1993. "Evolutionary and Ecological Aspects of Photosynthetic Pathway Variation." *Annual Review of Ecology and Systematics* 24 (1): 411–39. http://dx.doi.org/10.1146/annurev.es.24.110193.002211.

Ekdahl, Erik J., Jane L. Teranes, Thomas P. Guilderson, Charles L. Turton, John H. McAndrews, Chad A. Wittkop, and Eugene F. Stoermer. 2004. "Prehistorical Record of Cultural Eutrophication from Crawford Lake, Canada." *Geology* 32 (9): 745–48. http://dx.doi.org/10.1130/G20496.1.

Elbaum, Rivka, Steve Weiner, Rosa M. Albert, and Michael Elbaum. 2003. "Detection of Burning of Plant Materials in the Archaeological Record by Changes in the Refractive Indices of Siliceous Phytoliths." *Journal of Archaeological Science* 30 (2): 217–26. http://dx.doi.org/10.1006/jasc.2002.0828.

Ellenberg, Heinz. 1979. "Zeigerwerte de Gefässpflanzen mitteleuropas." *Scripta Geobotanica* 9:1–122.

Ellis, Erle C. 2011. "Anthropogenic Transformation of the Terrestrial Biosphere." *Philosophical Transactions of the Royal Society* 369 (1938): 1010–35. http://dx.doi.org/10.1098/rsta.2010.0331.

Elston, Robert G., and David W. Zeanah. 2002. "Thinking Outside the Box: A New Perspective on Diet Breadth and Sexual Division of Labor in the Prearchaic Great Basin." *World Archaeology* 34 (1): 103–30. http://dx.doi.org/10.1080/0043824022013 4287.

Emslie, Steven D., Jim I. Mead, and Larry Coats. 1995. "Split-Twig Figurines in Grand Canyon, Arizona: New Discoveries and Interpretations." *Kiva* 61 (2): 145–73.

Engelbrecht, William E. 1999. "Iroquoian Ethnicity and Archaeological Taxa." In *Taming the Taxonomy: Toward a New Understanding of Great Lakes Archaeology*, edited by Ronald F. Williams, and Christopher M. Watts, 51–60. Toronto: Eastend Books.

Engelbrecht, William E. 2003. *Iroquoia: The Development of a Native World*. Syracuse: Syracuse University Press.

Erdtman, Gunner. 1969. *Handbook of Palynology: Morphology, Taxonomy, Ecology*. Lund: Universitetsfori.

Erickson, Clark L. 2000. "The Lake Titicaca Basin: A Precolumbian Built Landscape." In *An Imperfect Balance: Landscape Transformations in the Precolumbian Americas*, edited by David Lewis Lentz, 311–56. New York: Columbia University Press.

Erlandson, Jon M., and T. K. Rockwell. 1987. "Radiocarbon Reversals and Stratigraphic Discontinuities: The Effects of Natural Formation Processes on Coastal California Archaeological Site." In *Natural Formation Processes and the Archaeological Record*, edited by D. T. Nash and M. D. Petraglia, 51–73. Oxford: British Archaeological Reports.

Ernst, Michaela, and Stefanie Jacomet. 2006. "The Value of the Archaeobotanical Analysis of Desiccated Plant Remains from Old Buildings: Methodological Aspects and Interpretation of Crop Weed Assemblages." *Vegetation History and Archaeobotany* 15 (1): 45–56. http://dx.doi.org/10.1007/s00334-005-0077-8.

Esau, Katherine. 1965. *Vascular Differentiation in Plants*. New York: Holt, Rinehart, and Winston.

Eubanks, Mary W. 1999. *Corn in Clay: Maize Paleoethnobotany in Pre-Columbian Art*. Gainesville: University Press of Florida.

Everitt, Brian, Sabine Landau, and Morven Leese. 2001. *Cluster Analysis.* New York: Oxford University Press.

Evers, A. D. 1971. "Scanning Electron Microscopy of Wheat Starch. III. Granule Development in the Endosperm." *Stärke* 23 (5): 157–62. http://dx.doi.org/10.1002/star.19710230502.

Evers, A. D. 1979. "Cereal Starches and Proteins." In *Food Microscopy*, edited by John G. Vaughan, 139–91. London: Academic Press.

Evett, Rand, and Rob Cutrell. 2011. "Phytolith Evidence for the Extent and Nature of Paleo-Grasslands in Quiroste Valley, Central California." Paper presented at the 76th Annual Meeting of the Society for American Archaeology, Sacramento, CA.

Faegri, Knut, and Johannes Iversen. 1975. *Textbook of Pollen Analysis.* New York: Hafner Press.

Faegri, Knut, Peter Emil Kaland, and Knut Krzywinski. 1989. *Textbook of Pollen Analysis.* 4th ed. Chichester, England: Wiley.

Fagan, Brian. 2002. *The Little Ice Age: How Climate Made History 1300–1850.* New York: Basic Books.

Fagan, Brian. 2008. *The Great Warming: Climate Change and the Rise and Fall of Civilizations.* New York: Bloomsbury Press.

Fahmy, A. G. 2008. "Diversity of Lobate Phytoliths in Grass Leaves from the Sahel Region, West Tropical Africa: Tribe Paniceae." *Plant Systematics and Evolution* 270 (1–2): 1–23. http://dx.doi.org/10.1007/s00606-007-0597-z.

Fahmy, Ahmed Gamal-El-Din, and Carlos Magnavita. 2006. "Phytoliths in a Silo: Micro-Botanical Evidence from Zilum (Lake Chad Basin), NE Nigeria (c. 500 Cal BC)." *Journal of Biological Sciences* 6 (5): 824–32. http://dx.doi.org/10.3923/jbs.2006.824.832.

Fairbairn, Andrew. 2007. "Seeds from the Slums: Archaeobotanical Investigations at Mountain Street, Ultimo, Sydney, New South Wales." *Australian Archaeology* 64:1–8.

Fairbairn, Andrew, Eleni Asouti, Julie Near, and Danièle Martinoli. 2002. "Macro-Botanical Evidence for Plant Use at Neolithic Çatalhöyük, South-Central Anatolia, Turkey." *Vegetation History and Archaeobotany* 11 (1–2): 41–54. http://dx.doi.org/10.1007/s003340200005.

Falk, Pasi. 1991. "Homo Culinarius: Towards an Historical Anthropology of Taste." *Social Sciences Information. Information Sur les Sciences Sociales* 30 (4): 757–90. http://dx.doi.org/10.1177/053901891030004008.

Fannon, John E., Richard J. Hauber, and James N. BeMiller. 1992. "Surface Pores of Starch Granules." *Cereal Chemistry* 69 (3): 284–88.

Farnsworth, Paul, James E. Brady, Michael J. DeNiro, and Richard S. MacNeish. 1985. "A Re-Evaluation of the Isotopic and Archaeological Reconstructions of Diet in the Tehuacan Valley." *American Antiquity* 50 (1): 102–16. http://dx.doi.org/10.2307/280636.

Farquhar, Graham D., James R. Ehleringer, and K. T. Hubick. 1989. "Carbon Isotope Discrimination and Photosynthesis." *Annual Review of Plant Physiology and Plant Molecular Biology* 40 (1): 503–37. http://dx.doi.org/10.1146/annurev.pp.40.060189.002443.

Farquhar, Graham D., M. H. O'Leary, and J. A. Berry. 1982. "On the Relationship between Carbon Isotope Discrimination and the Inter-Cellular Carbon-Dioxide Concentration in Leaves." *Australian Journal of Plant Physiology* 9 (2): 121–37. http://dx.doi.org/10.1071/PP9820121.

Farquhar, Graham D., S. Caemmerer, and J. A. Berry. 1980. "A Biochemical Model of Photosynthetic CO_2 Assimilation in Leaves of C3 Species." *Planta* 149 (1): 78–90. http://dx.doi.org/10.1007/BF00386231.

Farrington, Ian S., and James Urry. 1985. "Food and the Early History of Cultivation." *Journal of Ethnobiology* 5 (2): 143–57.

Featherstone, Roger, Peter Horne, David Macleod, and Robert Bewley. 1999. "Aerial Reconnaissance over England in Summer 1996." *Archaeological Prospection* 6 (2): 47–62. http://dx.doi.org/10.1002/(SICI)1099-0763(199906)6:2<47::AID-ARP113>3.0.CO;2-Y.

Fischler, Claude. 1980. "Food Habits, Social Change and the Nature/Culture Dilemma." *Social Sciences Information. Information Sur les Sciences Sociales* 19 (6): 937–53. http://dx.doi.org/10.1177/053901848001900603.

Fischler, Claude. 1988. "Food, Self and Identity." *Social Sciences Information. Information Sur les Sciences Sociales* 27 (2): 275–92. http://dx.doi.org/10.1177/053901888027002005.

Fish, Paul R. 2010. "Anthropogenic Environments: An Americanist Perspective." In *The Archaeology of Anthropogenic Environments*, edited by Rebecca M. Dean, 380–92. Carbondale: Center for Archaeological Investigations.

Fish, Suzanne K. 1994. "Archaeological Palynology of Gardens and Fields." In *The Archaeology of Garden and Field*, edited by Naomi F. Miller and Kathryn L. Gleason, 44–69. Philadelphia: University of Pennsylvania Press.

Fisher, Christopher T., J. Brett Hill, and Gary M. Feinman, eds. 2009. *The Archaeology of Environmental Change: Socionatural Legacies of Degradation and Resilience.* Tuscon: University of Arizona Press.

Fishkis, Olga, Joachim Ingwersen, and Thilo Streck. 2009. "Phytolith Transport in Sandy Sediment: Experiments and Modeling." *Geoderma* 151 (3–4): 168–78. http://dx.doi.org/10.1016/j.geoderma.2009.04.003.

Flad, Rowan, Timothy J. Horsley, Jade d'Alpoim Guedes, He Kunyu, Gwen Bennett, Pochan Chen, Li Shuicheng, Jiang Zhanghua. 2013. "Survey, Excavation, and Geophysics at Sonjiaheba—A Small Bronze Age Site in the Chengdu Plain." *Asian Perspectives* 52:119–44.

Flad, Rowan, Shuicheng Li, Xiaohong Wu, and Zhijun Zhao. 2010. "Early Wheat in China: Results from New Studies at Donghuishan in the Hexi Corridor." *The Holocene* 20 (6): 955–65. http://dx.doi.org/10.1177/0959683609358914.

Flannery, Kent V. 1982. "The Golden Marshalltown: A Parable for the Archeology of the 1980s." *American Anthropologist* 84 (2): 265–78. http://dx.doi.org/10.1525/aa.1982 .84.2.02a00010.

Flannery, Kent V. 1986. *Guilá Naquitz: Archaic Foraging and Early Agriculture in Oaxaca, Mexico*. Orlando: Academic Press.

Flinn, Mark. 1997. "Culture and the Evolution of Social Learning." *Evolution and Human Behavior* 18 (1): 23–67. http://dx.doi.org/10.1016/S1090-5138(96)00046-3.

Florian, M.-L. E. 1987. "The Underwater Environment." In *Conservation of Marine Archaeological Objects*, edited by Colin Pearson, 1–20. London: Butterworths.

Focken, Ursula, and K. Becker. 1998. "Metabolic Fractionation of Stable Carbon Isotopes: Implications of Different Proximate Compositions for Studies of the Aquatic Food Webs Using $\delta 13C$ Data." *Oecologia* 115 (3): 337–43. http://dx.doi .org/10.1007/s004420050525.

Fogelin, Lars. 2007. "Inference to the Best Explanation: A Common and Effective Form of Archaeological Reasoning." *American Antiquity* 72 (4): 603–25. http:// dx.doi.org/10.2307/25470436.

Foley, Brendan P., Maria C. Hansson, Dimitris P. Kourkoumelis, and Theotokis A. Theodoulou. 2012. "Aspects of Ancient Greek Trade Re-Evaluated with Amphora DNA Evidence." *Journal of Archaeological Science* 39 (2): 389–98. http://dx.doi.org /10.1016/j.jas.2011.09.025.

Foley, Jonathan A., Ruth DeFries, Gregory P. Asner, Carol Barford, Gordon Bonan, Stephen R. Carpenter, F. Stuart Chapin, Michael T. Coe, Gretchen C. Daily, Holly K. Gibbs, Joseph H. Helkowki, Tracey Holloway, Erica A. Howard, Christopher J. Kucharik, Chad Monfreda, Jonathan A. Patz, I. Colin Prentice, Navin Ramankutty, and Peter K. Snyder. 2005. "Global Consequences of Land Use." *Science* 309 (5734): 570–74. http://dx.doi.org/10.1126/science.1111772.

Ford, Anabel. 2008. "Dominant Plants of the Maya Forest and Gardens of El Pilar: Implications for Paleoenvironmental Reconstructions." *Journal of Ethnobiology* 28 (2): 179–99.

Ford, Richard I. 1979. "Paleoethnobotany in American Archaeology." In *Advances in Archaeological Method and Theory*, vol. 2, edited by M. B. Schiffer, 285–336. New York: Academic Press.

Ford, Richard I. 1994. "Corn Is Our Mother." In *Corn and Culture in the Prehistoric New World*, edited by Sissel Johannessen and Christine Ann Hastorf, 513–26. Boulder, CO: Westview Press.

Ford, Richard I. 2003. "Foreword." In *People and Plants in Ancient Eastern North America*, edited by Paul E. Minnis, xii–xvi. Washington, DC: Smithsonian Institution Press.

Ford, Richard I. 2004. "Foreword." In *People and Plants in Ancient Western North America*, edited by Paul E. Minnis, x–xiv. Washington, DC: Smithsonian Institution Press.

Ford, Richard I., and Volney N. Jones. 1974. "Job's Tears, *Coix lachryma-jobi* L., Beads from the West Ridge-Gibraltar Site, Southeastern Michigan." *Michigan Archaeologist* 20:105–11.

Fordyce, Sarah L., Maria C. Ávila-Arcos, Morten Rasmussen, Enrico Cappellini, J. Alberto Romero-Navarro, Nathan Wales, David E. Alquezar-Planas, Steven Penfield, Terence A. Brown, Jean-Philippe Vielle-Calzada, Rafael Montiel, Tina Jørgensen, Nancy Odegaard, Michael Jacobs, Bernardo Arriaza, Thomas F. G. Higham, Christopher Bronk Ramsey, Eske Willerslev, and M. Thomas P. Gilbert. 2013. "Deep Sequencing of RNA from Ancient Maize Kernels." *PLoS ONE* 8 (1): e50961. http://dx.doi.org/10.1371/journal.pone.0050961.

Forster, Brian L. 1984. "Family Structure and the Generations of Thai Social Exchange Networks." In *Households: Comparative and Historical Studies of the Domestic Group*, edited by Robert McC. Netting, Richard R. Wilk, and Eric J. Arnould, 84–105. Berkeley: University of California Press.

Foster, David R., Susan Clayden, David A. Orwig, Brian Hall, and Sylvia Barry. 2002. "Oak, Chestnut and Fire: Climatic and Cultural Controls of Long-Term Forest Dynamics in New England, USA." *Journal of Biogeography* 29 (10–11): 1359–79. http://dx.doi.org/10.1046/j.1365-2699.2002.00760.x.

Foster, David R., Frederick Swanson, John Aber, Ingrid Burke, Nicholas Brokaw, David Tilman, and Alan Knapp. 2003. "The Importance of Land-Use Legacies to Ecology and Conservation." *Bioscience* 53 (1): 77–88. http://dx.doi.org/10.1641/0006-3568(2003)053[0077:TIOLUL]2.0.CO;2.

Foster, H. Thomas, II. 2003. "Dynamic Optimization of Horticulture among the Muscogee Creek Indians of the Southeastern United States." *Journal of Anthropological Archaeology* 22 (4): 411–24. http://dx.doi.org/10.1016/S0278-4165(03)00062-X.

Foster, H. Thomas, II, Bryan A. Black, and Marc D. Abrams. 2004. "A Witness Tree Analysis of the Effects of Native American Indians on the Pre-European Settlement Forests in East-Central Alabama." *Human Ecology* 32 (1): 27–47. http://dx.doi.org/10.1023/B:HUEC.0000015211.98991.9c.

Foster, Thomas, Virginia Dale, and Lisa Olsen. 2010. "Environmental Management and Policy Using Ecological Indicators Derived from Archaeological and Historical Data." In *The Archaeology of Anthropogenic Environments*, edited by Rebecca M. Dean, 321–40. Carbondale: Center for Archaeological Investigations, Southern Illinois University.

Foucault, Michel. 1984. "Space, Knowledge and Power." In *The Foucault Reader*, edited by Paul Rainbow, 239–56. New York: Pantheon Books.

Fowler, Catherine S. 2000. "We Live by Them." In *Biodiversity and Native America*, edited by Paul Minnis and W. Elisens, 99–132. Norman: University of Oklahoma Press.

Fowler, Catherine S., and Don D. Fowler, eds. 2008. *The Great Basin: People and Place in Ancient Times*. Santa Fe: School for Advanced Research Press.

Fowler, Catherine S, and David Rhode. 2011. "Plant Foods and Foodways among the Great Basin's Indigenous Peoples." In *Subsistence Economies of Indigenous North American Societies*, edited by Bruce D. Smith, 233–70. Lanham, MD: Rowman and Littlefield.

Fowler, Kent D., Haskel J. Greenfield, and Leonard O. van Schalkwyk. 2004. "The Effects of Burrowing Activity on Archaeological Sites: Ndondondwane, South Africa." *Geoarchaeology: An International Journal* 19 (5): 441–70. http://dx.doi.org /10.1002/gea.20005.

Fowler, Martin J. F., and Yvonne M. Fowler. 2005. "Detection of Archaeological Crop Marks on Declassified CORONA KH–4B Intelligence Satellite Photography of Southern England." *Archaeological Prospection* 12 (4): 257–64. http://dx.doi.org /10.1002/arp.266.

Francey, R. J. 1981. "Tasmanian Tree Rings Belie Suggested Anthropogenic $^{13}C/^{12}C$ Trends." *Nature* 290 (5803): 232–35. http://dx.doi.org/10.1038/290232a0.

Franklin, Maria. 2001. "The Archaeological Dimensions of Soul Food: Interpreting Race, Culture, and Afro-Virginian Identity." In *Race and the Archaeology of Identity*, edited by Randall H. McGuire, 88–107. Salt Lake City: University of Utah Press.

Frawley, Susan, and Sue O'Connor. 2010. "A 40,000 Year Wood Charcoal Record from Carpenter's Gap 1: New Insights into Palaeovegetation Change and Indigenous Foraging Strategies in the Kimberley, Western Australia." In *Altered Ecologies: Fire, Climate and Human Influence on Terrestrial Landscapes*, edited by Simon G. Haberle, Janelle Stevenson, and Matthew Prebble, 257–79. Canberra: Australian National University.

Frazer, James G. 1912. *The Great Golden Bough, a Study in Magic and Religion. Part V: Spirits in the Corn and the Wild*. 3rd ed. London: Macmillan and Co.

Fredlund, Glen G., and Larry T. Tieszen. 1994. "Modern Phytolith Assemblages from the North American Great Plains." *Journal of Biogeography* 21 (3): 321–35. http://dx.doi.org/10.2307/2845533.

French, Dexter. 1975. "Chemistry and Biochemistry of Starch." In *Biochemistry of Carbohydrates*, edited by W. J. Whelan, 267–335. London: Butterworths.

French, Dexter. 1984. "Organization of Starch Granules." In *Starch: Chemistry and Technology*, edited by Roy L. Whistler, James N. BeMiller, and Eugene F. Paschall, 183–247. London: Academic Press.

French, David H. 1971. "An Experiment in Water-Sieving." *Anatolian Studies* 21:59–64.

Frey-Wyssling, A. 1940. "Die Optik der Starkekorner." *Berichte der schweizerischen botanischen Gesellschaft* 50:321–36.

Freyer, H. D., and A. I. M. Aly. 1974. "Nitrogen–15 Variations in Fertilizer Nitrogen." *Journal of Environmental Quality* 3 (4): 405–6. http://dx.doi.org/10.2134/jeq1974.004 72425000300040023x.

Freyer, H. D., and N. Belacy. 1983. " $^{13}C/^{12}C$ Records in Northern Hemispheric Trees During the Past 500 Years: Anthropogenic Impact and Climatic Super-Positions." *Journal of Geophysical Research-Oceans and Atmospheres* 88 (Nc11): 6844–52.

Friedman, Richard A., John R. Stein, and Taft Blackhorse, Jr. 2003. "A Study of a Pre-Columbian Irrigation System at Newcomb, New Mexico." *Journal of GIS in Archaeology* 1:4–10.

Frink, Lisa. 2007. "Storage and Status in Precolonial and Colonial Coastal Western Alaska." *Current Anthropology* 48 (3): 349–74. http://dx.doi.org/10.1086/512997.

Friskopp, Johan, and Göran Isacsson. 1984. "A Quantitative Microradiographic Study of Mineral Content of Supragingival and Subgingival Dental Calculus." *Scandinavian Journal of Dental Research* 92:25–32.

Fritz, Gayle J. 1984. "Identification of Cultigen Amaranth and Chenopod from Rockshelter Sites in Northwest Arkansas." *American Antiquity* 49 (3): 558–72. http://dx.doi.org/10.2307/280360.

Fritz, Gayle J. 2005. "Paleoethnobotanical Methods and Applications." In *Handbook of Archaeological Methods*, edited by Herbert D. G. Maschner and Christopher Chippindale, 773–834. Walnut Creek, CA: Altamira Press.

Fritz, Gayle J. 2007. "Pigweeds for the Ancestors: Cultural Identities and Archaeobotanical Identification Methods." In *The Archaeology of Food and Identity*, edited by Katheryn C. Twiss, 288–307. Carbondale, IL: Center for Archaeological Investigations, Southern Illinois University.

Fritz, Gayle J., Karen R. Adams, Glen E. Rice, and John L. Czarzasty. 2009. "Evidence for Domesticated Amaranth (*Amaranthus*) from a Sedentary Period Hohokam House Floor at Las Canopas." *Kiva* 75:393–418.

Fritz, Gayle J., and Neal H. Lopinot. 2003. "Native Crops at Early Cahokia: Comparing Domestic and Ceremonial Contents." In *People, Plants, and Animals: Archaeological Studies of Human-Environment Interactions in the Midcontinent, Essays in Honor of Leonard W. Blake*, edited by R.E. Warren. *Illinois Archaeology* 15&16:90–111.

Fritz, Gayle J., and Bruce D. Smith. 1988. "Old Collections and New Technology: Documenting the Domestication of *Chenopodium* in Eastern North America." *Midcontinental Journal of Archaeology* 13 (1): 3–27.

Fullagar, Richard, Judith Field, Tim Denham, and Carol Lentfer. 2006. "Early and Mid-Holocene Tool-Use and Processing of Taro (*Colocasia esculenta*), Yam (*Dioscorea* sp.) and Other Plants at Kuk Swamp in the Highlands of Papua New Guinea." *Journal of Archaeological Science* 33 (5): 595–614. http://dx.doi.org/10.1016/j.jas.2005.07.020.

Fullagar, Richard, Judith Field, and Lisa Kealhofer. 2008. "Grinding Stones and Seeds of Change: Starch and Phytoliths as Evidence of Plant Food Processing." In *New Approaches to Old Stones: Recent Studies of Ground Stone Artifacts*, edited by Yorke M. Rowan and Jennie R. Ebeling, 159–72. London: Equinox Publishing.

Fuller, Benjamin T., James L. Fuller, Nancy E. Sage, David A. Harris, Tamsin C. O'Connell, and Richard E. M. Hedges. 2005. "Nitrogen Balance and $\delta^{15}N$: Why You're Not What You Eat During Nutritional Stress." *Rapid Communications in Mass Spectrometry* 19 (18): 2497–506. http://dx.doi.org/10.1002/rcm.2090.

Fuller, Dorian Q. 2000. "The Emergence of Agricultural Societies in South India: Botanical and Archaeological Perspectives." Unpublished PhD diss., Department of Archaeology, Cambridge University, Cambridge.

Fuller, Dorian Q. 2006. "Agricultural Origins and Frontiers in South Asia: A Working Synthesis." *Journal of World Prehistory* 20 (1): 1–86. http://dx.doi.org/10.1007/s10963-006-9006-8.

Fuller, Dorian Q. 2007a. "Archaeological Science in Field Training." In *From Concepts of the Past to Practical Strategies: The Teaching of Archaeological Field Techniques*, edited by Peter Ucko, Qin Ling, and Jane Hubert, 183–205. London: Saffron Books.

Fuller, Dorian Q. 2007b. "Contrasting Patterns in Crop Domestication and Domestication Rates: Recent Archaeobotanical Insights from the Old World." *Annals of Botany* 100 (5): 903–24. http://dx.doi.org/10.1093/aob/mcm048.

Fuller, Dorian Q. 2007c. "Portable Archaeobotany I: Bucket Flotation." http://www.youtube.com/watch?v=NbkfeoB4zBg. Accessed October 30, 2011.

Fuller, Dorian Q. 2011. "Archaeobotany in the Field." http://sites.google.com/site/archaeobotany/. Accessed October 30.

Fuller, Dorian Q, and Emma L. Harvey. 2006. "The Archaeobotany of Indian Pulses: Identification, Processing and Evidence for Cultivation." *Environmental Archaeology* 11 (2): 219–46. http://dx.doi.org/10.1179/174963106x123232.

Fuller, Dorian Q, and Ravi Korisettar. 2004. "The Vegetational Context of Early Agriculture in South India." *Man and Environment* XXIX (1): 7–27.

Fuller, Dorian Q, L. Qin, Y. F. Zheng, Z. J. Zhao, X. Chen, L. A. Hosoya, and G. P. Sun. 2009. "The Domestication Process and Domestication Rate in Rice: Spikelet Bases from the Lower Yangtze." *Science* 323 (5921): 1607–10.

Fuller, Dorian Q, and Chris J. Stevens. 2009. "Agriculture and the Development of Complex Societies: An Archaeobotanical Agenda." In *From Foragers to Farmers: Papers in Honour of Gordon C. Hillman*, edited by Andy Fairbairn and Ehud Weiss, 37–57. Oxford: Oxbow Books.

Fuller, Dorian Q, P.C. Venkatasubbaihah, and R. Korisettar, and . 2001. "The Beginning of Agriculture in the Kunderu River Basin: Evidence from Archaeological Survey and Archaeobotany." *Bulletin of the Indian Archaeological Society* 31:1–8.

Fuller, Dorian Q, and Steven A. Weber. 2005. "Formation Processes and Paleoethnobotanical Interpretation in South Asia." *Journal of Interdisciplinary Studies in History and Archaeology* 2 (1): 91–114.

Fuller, Dorian Q, and H. Zhang. 2007. "A Preliminary Report of the Survey Archaeobotany of the Upper Ying Valley (Henan Province)." In *Dengfeng Wangchenggang Yizhi de Faxian Yu Yanjiu (2002–2005) [Archaeological Discovery and Research at the Wangchenggang Site in Dengfeng (2002–2005)]*, edited by the School of Archaeology and Museology in Peking University and Henan Provincial Institute of Cultural Relics and Archaeology, 916–58. Zhengzhou, China: Elephant Press.

Fulton, Tara L. 2012. "Setting up an Ancient DNA Laboratory." In *Ancient DNA: Methods and Protocols*, edited by Beth Shapiro and Michael Hofreiter, 1–11. Humana Press. http://dx.doi.org/10.1007/978-1-61779-516-9_1.

Gallagher, Daphne. 2010. "Farming Beyond the Escarpment: Society, Environment, and Mobility in Precolonial Southeastern Burkina Faso." Unpublished PhD diss., Department of Anthropology, University of Michigan.

Galliard, T. 1987. "Starch Availability and Utilization." In *Starch: Properties and Potential*, edited by T. Galliard, 1–15. John Wiley and Sons, Inc.

Galliard, T., and P. Bowler. 1987. "Morphology and Composition of Starch." In *Starch: Properties and Potential*, edited by T. Galliard, 55–78. John Wiley and Sons, Inc.

Gardner, Paul S. 1992. "Diet Optimization Models and Prehistoric Subsistence Change in the Eastern Woodlands." PhD diss., Department of Anthropology, University of North Carolina, Chapel Hill.

Gardner, Paul S. 1997. "The Ecological Structure and Behavioral Implications of Mast Exploitation Strategies." In *People, Plants, and Landscapes: Studies in Paleoethnobotany*, edited by Kristen J. Gremillion, 161–78. Tuscaloosa: University of Alabama Press.

Garfinkel, Simson I. 2008. "Wikipedia and the Meaning of Truth. MIT Technology Review." Accessed September 28, 2013. http://www.technologyreview.com/review /411041/wikipedia-and-the-meaning-of-truth/.

Garten, C. T., Jr., L. W. Cooper, W. M. Post, III, and P. J. Hanson. 2000. "Climate Controls on Forest Soil C Isotope Ratios in the Southern Appalachian Mountains." *Ecology* 81 (4): 1108–19. http://dx.doi.org/10.1890/0012-9658(2000)081[1108:CCOFS C]2.0.CO;2.

Gartner, William G. 1999. "Late Woodland Landscapes of Wisconsin: Ridged Fields, Effigy Mounds and Territoriality." *Antiquity* 73 (281): 671–83.

Gasser, Robert E., and E. Charles Adams. 1981. "Aspects of Deterioration of Plant Remains in Archaeological Sites: The Walpi Archaeological Project." *Journal of Ethnobiology* 1:182–92.

Gauch, Hugh G. 1982. *Multivariate Analysis in Community Ecology*. Cambridge: Cambridge University Press. http://dx.doi.org/10.1017/CBO9780511623332.

Geertz, Clifford. 1973. "Deep Play: Notes on the Balinese Cockfight." In *The Interpretation of Cultures*, edited by Clifford Geertz, 412–53. New York: Basic Books.

Geib, Phil R., and Susan J. Smith. 2008. "Palynology and Archaeological Inference: Bridging the Gap between Pollen Washes and Past Behavior." *Journal of Archaeological Science* 35 (8): 2085–101. http://dx.doi.org/10.1016/j.jas.2008.01.011.

GenBank. 2011. "What Is Genbank?" Accessed November 26, 2011. http://www.ncbi .nlm.nih.gov/genbank/.

Georges-Leroy, Murielle, Jérôme Bock, Etienne Dambrine, and Jean-Luc Dupouey. 2009. "Le Massif Forestier, Objet Pertinent pour la Recherche Archéologique: L'exemple du Massif Forestier de Haye (Meurthe-et-Moselle)." *Revue Geographique de l'Est* 49:2–3.

Gerry, John. 1993. "Diet and Status among the Classic Maya: An Isotopic Perspective." PhD Thesis, Department of Anthropology, Harvard University.

Ghosh, Ruby, Ashalata D'Rozario, and Subir Bera. 2006. "Can Palynomorphs Occur in Burnt Ancient Potsherds? An Experimental Proof." *Journal of Archaeological Science* 33 (10): 1445–51. http://dx.doi.org/10.1016/.jas.2006.01.015.

Giddens, Anthony. 1979. *Central Problems in Social Theory: Action, Structure, and Contradiction in Social Analysis*. Berkeley: University of California Press.

Giesecke, Thomas, and Sonia L. Fontana. 2008. "Revisiting Pollen Accumulation Rates from Swedish Lake Sediments." *The Holocene* 18 (2): 293–305. http://dx.doi .org/10.1177/0959683607086767.

Gilbert, M., D. L. Jenkins, A. Gotherstrom, N. Naveran, J. J. Sanchez, M. Hofreiter, P. F. Thomsen, J. Binladen, T. F. G. Higham, R. M. Yohe, R. Parr, L. S. Cummings, and E. Willerslev. 2008. "DNA from Pre-Clovis Human Coprolites in

Oregon, North America." *Science* 320 (5877): 786–89. http://dx.doi.org/10.1126/science.1154116.

Gilbert, M. Thomas P., and Eske Willerslev. 2007. "Ancient Plant DNA." In *Encyclopedia of Quaternary Science*, edited by Scott A. Elias, 1574–81. Oxford: Elsevier.

Gilbertson, D. D., and C. O. Hunt. 1996. "Romano-Lybian Agriculture: Walls and Floodwater Farming." In *Farming the Desert: The UNESCO Lybian Valleys Archaeological Survey*, edited by Graeme Barker, 191–225. London: UNESCO

Gleason, Kathryn L. 1994. "To Bound and to Cultivate: An Introduction to the Archaeology of Gardens and Fields." In *The Archaeology of Garden and Field*, edited by Naomi F. Miller and Kathryn L. Gleason, 1–24. Philadelphia: University of Pennsylvania Press.

Godfrey-Smith, Peter. 2006. "The Strategy of Model-Based Science." *Biology and Philosophy* 21 (5): 725–40. http://dx.doi.org/10.1007/s10539-006-9054-6.

Goffman, Erving. 1979. "Footing." *Semiotica* 25 (1–2): 1–30. http://dx.doi.org/10.1515/semi.1979.25.1-2.1.

Goldberg, Paul, and Richard Macphail. 2003. "Short Contribution: Strategies and Techniques in Collecting Micromorphology Samples." *Geoarchaeology: An International Journal* 18 (5): 571–78. http://dx.doi.org/10.1002/gea.10079.

Goldstein, Lynne. 1981. "One-Dimensional Archaeology and Multidimensional People: Spatial Organization and Mortuary Analysis." In *The Archaeology of Death*, edited by Robert Chapman, Ian Kinnes, and Klavs Randsborg, 53–69. Cambridge: Cambridge University Press.

Golenberg, Edward M., David E. Giannasi, Michael T. Clegg, Charles J. Smiley, Mary Durbin, David Henderson, and Gerard Zurawski. 1990. "Chloroplast DNA Sequence from a Miocene *Magnolia* Species." *Nature* 344 (6267): 656–58. http://dx.doi.org/10.1038/344656a0.

Goloubinoff, P. Svante Pääbo, and Allan C. Wilson. 1993. "Evolution of Maize Inferred from Sequence Diversity of an *Adh2* Gene Segment from Archaeological Specimens." *Proceedings of the National Academy of Sciences of the United States of America* 90:1997–2001.

Goman, Michelle, and Roger Byrne. 1998. "A 5000-Year Record of Agriculture and Troical Forest Clearance in the Tuxtlas, Veracruz, Mexico." *The Holocene* 8 (1): 83–89. http://dx.doi.org/10.1191/095968398670396093.

Good, Irene. 2001. "Archaeological Textiles: A Review of Current Research." *Annual Review of Anthropology* 30 (1): 209–26. http://dx.doi.org/10.1146/annurev.anthro.30.1.209.

Gooding, Ansel M. 1971. "Postglacial Alluvial History in Upper Whitewater Basin, Southeastern Indiana, and Possible Regional Relationships." *American Journal of Science* 271 (4): 389–401. http://dx.doi.org/10.2475/ajs.271.4.389.

Goodman, Alan H., J. Lallo, George J. Armelagos, and J. C. Rose. 1984. "Health Changes at Dickson Mounds, Illinois (AD 950–1300)." In *Paleopathology at the Origins of Agriculture*, edited by Mark N. Cohen, and George J. Armelagos, 271–305. New York: Academic Press.

Google. 2011. Search by Images. Google press release. Accessed December 11. http://www.google.com/insidesearch/features/images/searchbyimage.html.

Gorham, L. Dillon, and Vaughn M. Bryant. 2001. "Pollen, Phytoliths, and Other Microscopic Plant Remains in Underwater Archaeology." *International Journal of Nautical Archaeology* 30 (2): 282–98.

Grabowski, Radoslaw. 2011. "Changes in Cereal Cultivation During the Iron Age in Southern Sweden: A Compilation and Interpretation of the Archaeobotanical Material." *Vegetation History and Archaeobotany* 20 (5): 479–94. http://dx.doi.org/10.1007/s00334-011-0283-5.

Graham, Philip, and Alexia Smith. 2013. "A Day in the Life of an Ubaid Household: Archaeobotanical Investigations at Kenan Tepe, Southeastern Turkey." *Antiquity* 87 (336): 405–17.

Grantham, George. 1994. "Economic History and the History of Labour Markets." In *Labour Market Evolution: The Economic History of Market Integration, Wage Flexibility and the Employment Relation*, edited by George Grantham and Mary MacKinnon, 1–26. London: Routledge. http://dx.doi.org/10.4324/9780203021774.ch1.

Gratten, D. W. 1987. "Waterlogged Wood." In *Conservation of Marine Archaeological Objects*, edited by Colin Pearson, 55–67. London: Butterworths.

Grayson, Donald K., and Michael D. Cannon. 1999. "Human Paleoecology and Foraging Theory in the Great Basin." In *Models for the Millennium: The Current Status of Great Basin Anthropological Research*, edited by C. Beck, 141–51. Salt Lake City: University of Utah Press.

Grayson, Donald K., and Françoise Delpech. 1998. "Changing Diet Breadth in the Early Upper Palaeolithic of Southwestern France." *Journal of Archaeological Science* 25 (11): 1119–29. http://dx.doi.org/10.1006/jasc.1998.0339.

Green, Francis J. 1979. "Phosphatic Mineralization of Seeds from Archaeological Sites." *Journal of Archaeological Science* 6 (3): 279–84. http://dx.doi.org/10.1016/0305-4403(79)90005-0.

Green, Richard E., Johannes Krause, Adrian W. Briggs, Tomislav Maricic, Udo Stenzel, Martin Kircher, Nick Patterson, Heng Li, Weiwei Zhai, Markus Hsi-Yang Fritz, Nancy F. Hansen, Eric Y. Durand, Anna-Sapfo Malaspinas, Jeffrey D.

Jensen, Tomas Marques-Bonet, Can Alkan, Kay Prüfer, Matthias Meyer, Hernán A. Burbano, Jeffrey M. Good, Rigo Schultz, Ayinuer Aximu-Petri, Anne Butthof, Barbara Höber, Barbara Höffner, Madlen Siegemund, Antje Weihmann, Chad Nusbaum, Eric S. Lander, Carsten Russ, Nathaniel Novod, Jason Affourtit, Michael Egholm, Christine Verna, Pavao Rudan, Dejana Brajkovic, Željko Kucan, Ivan Gušic, Vladimir B. Doronichev, Liubov V. Golovanova, Carles Lalueza Fox, Marco de la Rasilla, Javier Fortea, Antonio Rosas, Ralf W. Schmitz, Philip L. F. Johnson, Evan E. Eichler, Daniel Falush, Ewan Birney, James C. Mullikin, Montgomery Slatkin, Rasmus Nielsen, Janet Kelso, Michael Lachmann, David Reich, and Svante Pääbo. 2010. "A Draft Sequence of the Neandertal Genome." *Science* 328 (5979): 710–22. http://dx.doi.org/10.1126/science.1188021.

Greenacre, Michael. 2007. *Correspondence Analysis in Practice*. Boca Raton, FL: Chapman and Hall. http://dx.doi.org/10.1201/9781420011234.

Greenlee, D. M. 2006. "Dietary Variation and Prehistoric Maize Farming in the Middle Ohio Valley." In *Histories of Maize: Multidisciplinary Approaches to the Prehistory, Linguistics, Biogeography, Domestication, and Evolution of Maize*, edited by John E. Staller, Robert H. Tykot, and Bruce F. Benz, 215–33. San Diego: Academic Press. http://dx.doi.org/10.1016/B978-012369364-8/50268-0.

Greig, James. 1994. "Pollen Analyses of Latrine Fills from Archaeological Sites in Britain: Results and Future Potential." In *Aspects of Archaeological Palynology: Methodology and Applications*, edited by Owen K. Davis, 101–14. Contributions Series, Number 29. Houston, TX: American Association of Stratigraphic Palynologists Foundation.

Gremillion, Kristen J. 1993. "Plant Husbandry at the Archaic/Woodland Transition: Evidence from the Cold Oak Shelter, Kentucky." *Midcontinental Journal of Archaeology* 18:161–89.

Gremillion, Kristen J. 1994. "The Archaic/Woodland Transition and Early Farming in Eastern Kentucky." *Proceedings of the Southeastern Archaeological Conference*. Lexington, Kentucky.

Gremillion, Kristen J. 1996a. "Diffusion and Adoption of Crops in Evolutionary Perspective." *Journal of Anthropological Archaeology* 15 (2): 183–204. http://dx.doi.org/10.1006/jaar.1996.0007.

Gremillion, Kristen J. 1996b. "Early Agricultural Diet in Eastern North America: Evidence from Two Kentucky Rockshelters." *American Antiquity* 61 (3): 520–36. http://dx.doi.org/10.2307/281838.

Gremillion, Kristen J. 1997. *People, Plants, and Landscapes: Studies in Paleoethnobotany*. Tuscaloosa: University of Alabama Press.

Gremillion, Kristen J. 1998. "Changing Roles of Wild and Cultivated Plant Resources among Early Farmers of Eastern Kentucky." *Southeastern Archaeology* 17:140–57.

Gremillion, Kristen J. 2002a. "Central Place Foraging and Food Production in Eastern Kentucky." In *Foraging Theory and Thetransition to Agriculture*, edited by Douglas J. Kennett and Bruce Winterhalder, 41–62. Berkeley: University of California Press.

Gremillion, Kristen J. 2002b. "Foraging Theory and Hypothesis Testing in Archaeology: An Exploration of Methodological Problems and Solutions." *Journal of Anthropological Archaeology* 21 (2): 142–64. http://dx.doi.org/10.1006/jaar.2001.0391.

Gremillion, Kristen J. 2004. "Seed Processing and the Origins of Food Production in Eastern North America." *American Antiquity* 69 (2): 215–33. http://dx.doi.org/10 .2307/4128417.

Gremillion, Kristen J. 2006. "Central Place Foraging and Food Production on the Cumberland Plateau, Eastern Kentucky." In *Behavioral Ecology and the Transition to Agriculture*, edited by Douglas J. Kennett and Bruce Winterhalder, 41–62. Berkeley: University of California Press.

Gremillion, Kristen J. 2011. "The Role of Plants in Southeastern Subsistence Economies." In *Subsistence Economies of Indigenous North American Societies*, edited by Bruce D. Smith, 387–400. Lanham, MD: Rowman and Littlefield.

Gremillion, Kristen J., and Dolores R. Piperno. 2009a. "Human Behavioral Ecology, Phenotypic (Developmental) Plasticity, and Agricultural Origins: Insights from the Emerging Evolutionary Synthesis." *Current Anthropology* 50 (5): 615–19. http:// dx.doi.org/10.1086/605360.

Gremillion, Kristen J., and Dolores R. Piperno. 2009b. "Rethinking the Origins of Agriculture: A Reply." *Current Anthropology* 50 (5): 709–11. http://dx.doi.org/10 .1086/605684.

Gremillion, Kristen J., and Kristen D. Sobolik. 1996. "Dietary Variability among Prehistoric Forager-Farmers of Eastern North America." *Current Anthropology* 37 (3): 529–39. http://dx.doi.org/10.1086/204515.

Gremillion, Kristen J., Jason Windingstad, and Sarah C. Sherwood. 2008. "Forest Opening, Habitat Use, and Food Production on the Cumberland Plateau, Kentucky: Adaptive Flexibility in Marginal Settings." *American Antiquity* 73 (3): 387–411.

Griffin, James B. 1967. "Eastern North American Archaeology: A Summary." *Science* 156 (3772): 175–91. http://dx.doi.org/10.1126/science.156.3772.175.

Griffiths, H. 1992. "Carbon Isotope Discrimination and the Integration of Carbon Assimilation Pathways in Terrestrial CAM Plants." *Plant, Cell & Environment* 15 (9): 1051–62. http://dx.doi.org/10.1111/j.1365-3040.1992.tb01655.x.

Grigg, David. 1985. *An Introduction to Agricultural Geography*. London: Routledge.

Grimplet, Jerome, Laurent G. Deluc, Richard L. Tillett, Matthew D. Wheatley, Karen A. Schlauch, Grant R. Cramer, and John C. Cushman. 2007. "Tissue-Specific mRNA Expression Profiling in Grape Berry Tissues." *BMC Genomics* 8 (1): 187. http://dx.doi.org/10.1186/1471-2164-8-187.

Grömer, Karina, and Daniela Kern. 2010. "Technical Data and Experiments on Corded Ware." *Journal of Archaeological Science* 37 (12): 3136–45. http://dx.doi.org/10.1016/j.jas.2010.07.015.

Guarino, Carmine, and Rosaria Sciarrillo. 2004. "Carbonized Seeds in a Protohistoric House: Results of Hearth and House Experiments." *Vegetation History and Archaeobotany* 13 (1): 65–70. http://dx.doi.org/10.1007/s00334-003-0026-3.

Gugerli, Felix, Laura Parducci, and Rémy J. Petit. 2005. "Ancient Plant DNA: Review and Prospects." *New Phytologist* 166 (2): 409–18. http://dx.doi.org/10.1111/j.1469-8137.2005.01360.x.

Guggenberger, Georg, Edward T. Elliott, Serita D. Frey, Johan Six, and Keith Paustian. 1999. "Microbial Contributions to the Aggregation of a Cultivated Grassland Soil Amended with Starch." *Soil Biology & Biochemistry* 31 (3): 407–19. http://dx.doi.org/10.1016/S0038-0717(98)00143-6.

Gumerman, George. 1994. "Feeding Specialists: The Effect of Specialization on Subsistence Variation." In *Paleonutrition: The Diet and Health of Prehistoric Americans*, edited by Kristin D. Sobolik, 80–97. Occasional Paper 22. Carbondale: Center for Archaeological Investigation, Southern Illinois University.

Gumerman, George J., and James A. Neely. 1972. "An Archaeological Survey of the Tehuacan Valley, Mexico: A Test of Color Infrared Photography." *American Antiquity* 37 (4): 520–27. http://dx.doi.org/10.2307/278958.

Gustafsson, Stefan. 2000. "Carbonized Cereal Grains and Weed Seeds in Prehistoric Houses—an Experimental Perspective." *Journal of Archaeological Science* 27 (1): 65–70. http://dx.doi.org/10.1006/jasc.1999.0441.

Guyette, R. P., R. M. Muzika, and D. C. Dey. 2002. "Dynamics of an Anthropogenic Fire Regime." *Ecosystems (New York, N.Y.)* 5 (5): 472–86.

Haaland, Randi. 2007. "Porridge and Pot, Bread and Oven: Food Ways and Symbolism in Africa and the Near East from the Neolithic to the Present." *Cambridge Archaeological Journal* 17 (02): 165–82. http://dx.doi.org/10.1017/S0959774307000236.

Haas, Jean Nicholas, and Fritz Hans Schweingruber. 1994. "Wood-Anatomical Evidence of Pollarding in Ash Stems from the Valais, Switzerland." *Dendrochronologia* 11:35–43.

Hageman, Jon B., and David J. Goldstein. 2009. "An Integrated Assessment of Archaeobotanical Recovery Methods in the Neotropical Rainforest of Northern

Belize: Flotation and Dry Screening." *Journal of Archaeological Science* 36 (12): 2841–52. http://dx.doi.org/10.1016/j.jas.2009.09.013.

Haile, James, Duane G. Froese, Ross D. E. MacPhee, Richard G. Roberts, Lee J. Arnold, Alberto V. Reyes, Morten Rasmussen, Rasmus Nielsen, Barry W. Brook, Simon Robinson, M. Thomas P. Gilbert, Kasper Munch, Jeremy J. Austin, Alan Cooper, Ian Barnes, Per Möller, and Eske Willerslev. 2009. "Ancient DNA Reveals Late Survival of Mammoth and Horse in Interior Alaska." *Proceedings of the National Academy of Sciences of the United States of America* 106 (52): 22352–57. http://dx.doi.org/10.1073/pnas.0912510106.

Haile, James, Richard Holdaway, Karen Oliver, Michael Bunce, M. T. P. Gilbert, R. Nielsen, K. Munch, S. Y. W. Ho, B. Shapiro, and E. Willerslev. 2007. "Ancient DNA Chronology within Sediment Deposits: Are Paleobiological Reconstructions Possible and Is DNA Leaching a Factor?" *Molecular Biology and Evolution* 24 (4): 982–89. http://dx.doi.org/10.1093/molbev/msm016.

Hald, Mette Marie. 2010. "Distribution of Crops at Late Early Bronze Age Titriş Höyük, Southeast Anatolia: Towards a Model for the Identification of Consumers of Centrally Organised Food Distribution." *Vegetation History and Archaeobotany* 19 (1): 69–77. http://dx.doi.org/10.1007/s00334-009-0223-9.

Hald, Mette Marie, and Michael Charles. 2008. "Storage of Crops During the Fourth and Third Millennia B.C. at the Settlement Mound of Tell Brak, Northeast Syria." *Vegetation History and Archaeobotany* 17 (S1): S35–41. http://dx.doi.org/10.1007/s00334-008-0154-x.

Hally, D. J. 1981. "Plant Preservation and the Content of Paleobotanical Samples: A Case Study." *American Antiquity* 46 (4): 723–42. http://dx.doi.org/10.2307/280102.

Hamdy, R. 2007. "Plant Remains from the Intact Garlands Present at the Egyptian Museum in Cairo." In *Fields of Change: Progress in African Archaeobotany*, edited by René T. J. Cappers, 115–26. Groningen, Netherlands: Barkhuis.

Hamilakis, Yannis. 1996. "Wine, Oil and the Dialectics of Power in Bronze Age Crete: A Review of the Evidence." *Oxford Journal of Archaeology* 15 (1): 1–32. http://dx.doi.org/10.1111/j.1468-0092.1996.tb00071.x.

Hamilakis, Yannis. 1999. "Food Technologies/Technologies of the Body: The Social Context of Wine and Oil Production and Consumption in Bronze Age Crete." *World Archaeology* 31 (1): 38–54. http://dx.doi.org/10.1080/00438243.1999.9980431.

Hammel, E. A. 1984. "On the **** of Studying Household Form and Function." In *Households: Comparative and Historical Studies of the Domestic Group*, edited by Robert McC. Netting, Richard R. Wilk, and Eric J. Arnould, 29–43. Berkeley: University of California Press.

Hammett, Julia E. 1992. "Ethnohistory of Aboriginal Landscapes in the Southeastern United States." *Southern Indian Studies* 41:1–50.

Hammett, Julia E. 1997. "Interregional Patterns of Land Use and Plant Management in Native North America." In *People, Plants and Landscapes*, edited by Kristen J. Gremillion, 195–216. Tuscaloosa: University of Alabama Press.

Hanks, William F. 1990. *Referential Practice: Language and Lived Space among the Maya*. Chicago: University of Chicago Press.

Hanssen, E., E. Dodt, and E. G. Niemann. 1953. "Bestimmung von Korngrösse, Kornoberfläche und Korngewicht bei pflanzlichen Stärken." *Kolloid Zeitschrift* 130 (1): 19–31. http://dx.doi.org/10.1007/BF01519791.

Hansson, Ann-Marie. 1994. "Grain-Paste, Porridge and Bread. Ancient Cereal-Based Food." *Laborative Arkeologi: Journal of Nordic Archaeological Science* 7:5–20.

Haour, Anne K. Manning, N. Arazi, O. Gosselain, N. S. Guèye, D. Keita, A. Livingstone Smith, K. MacDonald, A. Mayor, S. McIntosh, and R. Vernet, eds. 2010. *African Pottery Roulettes Past and Present: Techniques, Identification and Distribution*. Oxford: Oxbow Books.

Hard, Robert J., Raymond P. Mauldin, and Gerry R. Raymond. 1996. "Mano Size, Stable Carbon Isotope Ratios, and Macrobotanical Remains as Multiple Lines of Evidence of Maize Dependence in the American Southwest." *Journal of Archaeological Method and Theory* 3 (3): 253–318. http://dx.doi.org/10.1007/BF02229401.

Hardt, Ben, Harold D. Rowe, Gregory S. Springer, Hai Cheng, and R. Lawrence Edwards. 2010. "The Seasonality of East Central North American Precipitation Based on Three Coeval Holocene Speleothems from Southern West Virginia." *Earth and Planetary Science Letters* 295:342–48.

Harlan, Jack R. 1975. *Crops and Man*. 1st ed. Madison: American Society of Agronomy.

Harlan, Jack R. 1992. *Crops and Man*. 2nd ed. Madison: American Society of Agronomy.

Harlan, Jack R., and J. M. J. de Wet. 1971. "Toward a Rational Classification of Cultivated Plants." *Taxon* 20 (4): 509–17. http://dx.doi.org/10.2307/1218252.

Harlan, Jack R., and J. M. J. de Wet. 1973. "On the Quality of Evidence for Origin and Dispersal of Cultivated Plants [and Comments and Reply]." *Current Anthropology* 14 (1/2): 51–62. http://dx.doi.org/10.1086/201406.

Harn, Alan D. 1978. "Mississippian Settlement Patterns in the Central Illinois River Valley." In *Mississippian Settlement Patterns*, edited by Bruce D. Smith, 233–68. New York: Academic Press.

Harrower, Michael J. 2008. "Mapping and Dating Incipient Irrigation in Wadi Sana, Hadramawt (Yemen)." *Proceedings of the Seminar for Arabian Studies* 38:187–202.

Harrower, Michael J. 2010. "Geographic Information Systems (GIS) Hydrological Modeling in Archaeology: An Example from the Origins of Irrigation in

Southwest Arabia (Yemen)." *Journal of Archaeological Science* 37 (7): 1447–52. http://dx.doi.org/10.1016/j.jas.2010.01.004.

Hart, Diane M. 2003. "The Influence of Soil Fauna on Phytolith Distribution in an Australian Soil." In *Phytolith and Starch Research in the Austalian-Pacific-Asian Regions: The State of the Art*, edited by Diane M. Hart, and Lynley A. Wallis, 83–91. Terra Australis 19. Canberra: Pandanus Books.

Hart, Diane M., and G. S. Humphreys. 1997. "The Mobility of Phytoliths in Soils; Pedological Considerations." In *The State-of-the-Art of Phytoliths in Soils and Plants*, edited by Ascensión Pinilla, J. Juan-Tresserras, and Maria José Machado, 93–100. Madrid: Centro de Ciencias Medioambientales, Consejo Superior de Investigaciones Científicas.

Hart, John P., ed. 1999. *Current Northeast Paleoethnobotany*. Albany: New York State Museum.

Hart, John P. 2000. "New Dates from Classic New York Sites: Just How Old Are Those Longhouses?" *North American Archaeologist* 60:1–22.

Hart, John P. 2008. *Current Northeast Paleoethnobotany II*. Albany: New York State Museum.

Hart, John P., and Hetty Jo Brumbach. 2009. "On Pottery Change and Northern Iroquoian Origins: An Assessment from the Finger Lakes Region of Central New York." *Journal of Anthropological Archaeology* 28 (4): 367–81. http://dx.doi.org/10.1016/j.jaa.2009.07.001.

Hart, John P., Hetty Jo Brumbach, and Robert Lusteck. 2007. "Extending the Phytolith Evidence for Early Maize (*Zea mays* ssp. *mays*) and Squash (*Cucurbita* sp.) in Central New York." *American Antiquity* 72 (3): 563–83. http://dx.doi.org/10.2307/40035861.

Hart, John P., and William E. Engelbrecht. 2012. "Northern Iroquoian Ethnic Evolution: A Social Network Analysis." *Journal of Archaeological Method and Theory* 19 (2): 322–49. http://dx.doi.org/10.1007/s10816-011-9116-1.

Hart, John P., and William A. Lovis. 2013. "Reevaluating What We Know About the Histories of Maize in Northeastern North America: A Review of Current Evidence." *Journal of Archaeological Research* 21 (2): 175–216. http://dx.doi.org/10.1007/s10814-012-9062-9.

Hart, John P., William A. Lovis, Janet K. Schulenberg, and Gerald R. Urquhart. 2007. "Paleodietary Implications from Stable Carbon Isotope Analysis of Experimental Cooking Residues." *Journal of Archaeological Science* 34 (5): 804–13. http://dx.doi.org/10.1016/j.jas.2006.08.006.

Hart, John P., and R. G. Matson. 2009. "The Use of Multiple Discriminant Analysis in Classifying Prehistoric Phytolith Assemblages Recovered from Cooking

Residues." *Journal of Archaeological Science* 36 (1): 74–83. http://dx.doi.org/10.1016
/j.jas.2008.07.011.

Hart, John P., Robert G. Thompson, and Hetty Jo Brumbach. 2003. "Phytolith Evidence for Early Maize (*Zea mays*) in the Northern Finger Lakes Region of New York." *American Antiquity* 68 (4): 619–40. http://dx.doi.org/10.2307/3557065.

Harvey, Emma, Dorian Q Fuller, R. K. Mohanty, and Basanta Mohanta. 2006. "Early Agriculture in Orissa: Some Archaeobotanical Results and Field Observations." *Man and Environment* 31 (2): 21–32.

Harvey, Emma L., and Dorian Q Fuller. 2005. "Investigating Crop Processing Using Phytolith Analysis: The Example of Rice and Millets." *Journal of Archaeological Science* 32 (5): 739–52. http://dx.doi.org/10.1016/j.jas.2004.12.010.

Hasenstab, Robert J. 1990. "Agriculture, Warfare, and Tribalization in the Iroquois Homeland of New York: A G.I.S. Analysis of Late Woodland Settlement." Unpublished PhD diss., University of Massachusetts, Amherst.

Haslam, Michael. 2004. "The Decomposition of Starch Grains in Soils: Implications for Archaeological Residue Analyses." *Journal of Archaeological Science* 31 (12): 1715–34. http://dx.doi.org/10.1016/j.jas.2004.05.006.

Hassan, Fekri A. 2009. "Human Agency, Climate Change, and Culture: An Archaeological Perspective." In *Anthropology & Climate Change: From Encounters to Actions*, edited by Susan A. Crate and Mark Nuttall, 39–69. Walnut Creek: Left Coast Press.

Hastings, M. G., J. C. Jarvis, and E. J. Steig. 2009. "Anthropogenic Impacts on Nitrogen Isotopes of Ice-Core Nitrate." *Science* 324 (5932): 1288. http://dx.doi.org/10.1126/science.1170510.

Hastorf, Christine A. 1983. "Prehistoric Agricultural Intensification and Political Development in the Jauja Region of Central Peru". Unpublished PhD diss., University of California, Los Angeles.

Hastorf, Christine A. 1988. "The Use of Paleoethnobotanical Data in Prehistoric Studies of Crop Production, Processing, and Consumption." In *Current Paleoethnobotany: Analytical Methods and Cultural Interpretations of Archaeological Plant Remains*, edited by Christine A. Hastorf and Virginia S. Popper, 119–44. Chicago: University of Chicago Press.

Hastorf, Christine A. 1990. "The Effect of the Inka State on Sausa Agricultural Production and Crop Consumption." *American Antiquity* 55 (2): 262–90. http://dx.doi.org/10.2307/281647.

Hastorf, Christine A. 1991. "Gender, Space, and Food in Prehistory." In *Engendering Archaeology: Women and Prehistory*, edited by Joan M. Gero and Margaret W. Conkey, 132–59. Oxford: Blackwell.

Hastorf, Christine A. 1999. "Recent Research in Paleoethnobotany." *Journal of Archaeological Research* 7 (1): 55–103. http://dx.doi.org/10.1007/BF02446085.

Hastorf, Christine A., and Virginia S. Popper, eds. 1988. *Current Paleoethnobotany: Analytical Methods and Cultural Interpretations of Archaeological Plant Remains.* Chicago: University of Chicago Press.

Hastorf, Christine A., and Melanie F. Wright. 1998. "Interpreting Wild Seeds from Archaeological Sites: A Dung Charring Experiment from the Andes." *Journal of Ethnobiology* 18 (2): 221–27.

Hatch, Marshall D. 1987. "C4 Photosynthesis: A Unique Blend of Biochemistry, Anatomy, and Ultrastructure." *Biochimica et Biophysica Acta* 895 (2): 81–106. http://dx.doi.org/10.1016/S0304-4173(87)80009-5.

Hatch, M. D., and C. R. Slack. 1966. "Photosynthesis by Sugarcane Leaves: A New Carboxylation Reaction and the Pathway of Sugar Formation." *Biochemical Journal* 101:103–11.

Hatch, M. D., and C. R. Slack. 1967. "Further Studies on a New Pathway of Photosynthetic Carbon Dioxide Fixation in Sugar-Cane and Its Occurrence in Other Plant Species." *Biochemical Journal* 102:417–22.

Hather, Jon G. 1993. *An Archaeobotanical Guide to the Identification of Roots and Tubers. Volume 1: Europe and South West Asia.* Oxford: Oxbow Books.

Hather, Jon G. 1994. *Tropical Archaeobotany: Applications and New Developments.* London: Routledge.

Hather, Jon G. 2000. *Archaeological Parenchyma.* London: Archetype.

Hättenschwiler, Stephan, Alexei V. Tiunov, and Stefan Scheu. 2005. "Biodiversity and Litter Decomposition in Terrestrial Ecosystems." *Annual Review of Ecology Evolution and Systematics* 36 (1): 191–218. http://dx.doi.org/10.1146/annurev.ecolsys.36.112904.151932.

Hays-Gilpin, Kelley, and Michelle Hegmon. 2005. "The Art of Ethnobotany: Depictions of Maize and Other Plants in the Prehistoric Southwest." In *Engaged Anthropology: Research Essays on North American Archaeology, Ethnobotany, and Museology,* edited by Michelle Hegmon, and B. Sunday Eiselt, 89–113. Ann Arbor: University of Michigan, Museum of Anthropology.

Heaton, Tim H. E., John C. Vogel, Gertrud von la Chevallerie, and Gill Collett. 1986. "Climatic Influence on the Isotopic Composition of Bone Nitrogen." *Nature* 322 (6082): 822–23. http://dx.doi.org/10.1038/322822a0.

Hebda, Richard J., Marlow G. Pellatt, Rolf W. Mathewes, Daryl W. Fedje, and Steven Acheson. 2005. "Vegetation History of Anthony Island, Haida Gwaii, and Its Relationship to Climate Change and Human Settlement." In *Haida Gwaii: Human History and Environment from the Time of Loon to the Time of the Iron*

People, edited by Daryl W. Fedje and Rolf W. Mathewes, 59–76. Vancouver: University of British Columbia Press.

Hebsgaard, Martin B., M. Thomas P. Gilbert, Jette Arneborg, Patricia Heyn, Morten E. Allentoft, Michael Bunce, Kasper Munch, Charles Schweger, and Eske Willerslev. 2009. "'The Farm beneath the Sand'—an Archaeological Case Study on Ancient 'Dirt' DNA." *Antiquity* 83 (320): 430–44.

Hedges, Richard E. M. 2003. "On Bone Collagen: Apatite-Carbonate Isotopic Relationships." *International Journal of Osteoarchaeology* 13 (1–2): 66–79. http://dx.doi.org/10.1002/oa.660.

Hedges, Richard E. M., and Linda M. Reynard. 2007. "Nitrogen Isotopes and the Trophic Level of Humans in Archaeology." *Journal of Archaeological Science* 34 (8): 1240–51. http://dx.doi.org/10.1016/j.jas.2006.10.015.

Heiss, Andreas G., Werner Kofler, and Klaus Oeggl. 2005. "The Ulten Valley in South Tyrol, Italy: Vegetation and Settlement History of the Area, and Macrofossil Record from the Iron Age Cult Site of St. Walburg." *Palyno-Bulletin* 1 (1–2): 63–72.

Heiss, Andreas G., and Klaus Oeggl. 2009. "The Plant Macro-Remains from the Iceman Site (Tisenjoch, Italian–Austrian Border, Eastern Alps): New Results on the Glacier Mummy's Environment." *Vegetation History and Archaeobotany* 18 (1): 23–35. http://dx.doi.org/10.1007/s00334-007-0140-8.

Helbaek, Hans. 1953. "Appendix I." In *Early Rome I: Stratigraphic Researches in the Forum Romanum and Along the Sacra Via*, edited by Einar Gjerstad, 155–282. Acta Institui Romani Regni Sueciae, Series 40, vol. 8. Lund, Sweden: C. W. K. Gleerup.

Helbaek, Hans. 1960. "Cereals and Weed Grasses in Phase A." In *Excavations in the Plain of Antioch*, vol. 1, edited by Robert J. Braidwood and Linda S. Braidwood, 99–118. Chicago: University of Chicago Press.

Helbaek, Hans. 1967. "Appendix II: Agricoltura Preistorica a Luni Sul Mignone in Etruria." In *Luni Sul Mignone: E Problemi Della Preistoria D'italia*, edited by Carl Eric Östenberg, 279–282. Acta Institui Romani Regni Sueciae, Series in 40, vol. 25. Lund, Sweden: C. W. K. Gleerup.

Helbaek, Hans. 1969. "Plant Collecting, Dry Farming and Irrigation Agriculture in Prehistoric Deh Luran." In *Prehistory and Human Ecology of the Deh Luran Plain: An Early Village Sequence from Khuzistan, Iran*, edited by Frank Hole, Kent V. Flannery, and James A. Neely, 383–428. Ann Arbor: University of Michigan.

Henry, Amanda G. 2010. "Plant Foods and the Dietary Ecology of Neandertals and Modern Humans." Unpublished PhD diss., Department of Anthropology, The George Washington University, Washington, DC.

Henry, Amanda G., Alison S. Brooks, and Dolores R. Piperno. 2011. "Microfossils in Calculus Demonstrate Consumption of Plants and Cooked Foods in Neanderthal

Diets (Shanidar III, Iraq; Spy I and II, Belgium)." *Proceedings of the National Academy of Sciences of the United States of America* 108 (2): 486–91. http://dx.doi.org /10.1073/pnas.1016868108.

Henry, Amanda G., Holly F. Hudson, and Dolores P. Piperno. 2009. "Changes in Starch Grain Morphologies from Cooking." *Journal of Archaeological Science* 36 (3): 915–22. http://dx.doi.org/10.1016/j.jas.2008.11.008.

Henry, Amanda G., and Dolores P. Piperno. 2008. "Using Plant Microfossils from Dental Calculus to Recover Human Diet: A Case Study from Tell Al-Raqa'i, Syria." *Journal of Archaeological Science* 35 (7): 1943–50. http://dx.doi.org/10.1016/j .jas.2007.12.005.

Hesse, Brian C. 1990. "Pig Lovers and Pig Haters: Patterns of Palestinian Pork Production." *Journal of Ethnobiology* 10 (2): 195–225.

Higuchi, Russell, Barbara Bowman, Mary Freiberger, Oliver A. Ryder, and Allan C. Wilson. 1984. "DNA Sequences from the Quagga, an Extinct Member of the Horse Family." *Nature* 312 (5991): 282–84. http://dx.doi.org/10.1038/312282a0.

Hill, M. O., and H. G. Gauch, Jr. 1980. "Detrended Correspondence Analysis: An Improved Ordination Technique." *Vegetatio* 42 (1–3): 47–58. http://dx.doi.org /10.1007/BF00048870.

Hillman, Gordon C. 1981. "Reconstructing Crop Husbandry Practices from Charred Remains of Crops." In *Farming Practice in British Prehistory*, edited by R. Mercer, 123–62. Edinburgh: Edinburgh University Press.

Hillman, Gordon C. 1984a. "Interpretation of Archaeological Plant Remains: The Application of Ethnographic Models from Turkey." In *Plants and Ancient Man: Studies in Palaeoethnobotany*, edited by Willem van Zeist and W. A. Casparie, 1–41. Rotterdam: A.A. Balkema.

Hillman, Gordon C. 1984b. "Traditional Husbandry and Processing of Archaic Cereals in Recent Times: Part I: The Glume Wheats." *Bulletin on Sumerian Agriculture* 1:114–52.

Hillman, Gordon C. 1985. "Traditional Husbandry and Processing of Archaic Cereals in Recent Times. Part 2: The Free-Threshing Cereals." *Bulletin on Sumerian Agriculture* 2:1–31.

Hillman, Gordon C. 1986. "Plant Foods in Ancient Diet: The Archaeological Role of Palaeofaces in General and Lindow Man's Gut Contents in Particular." In *Lindow Man: The Body in the Bog*, edited by I. M. Stead, J. B. Bourke, and Don R. Brothwell, 99–115. Ithaca: Cornell University Press.

Hillman, Gordon C. 1989. "Late Palaeolithic Plant Foods from Wadi Kubbaniya in Upper Egypt: Dietary Diversity, Infant Weaning, and Seasonality in a Riverine Environment." In *Foraging and Farming: The Evolution of Plant Exploitation*, edited by David R. Harris and Gordon C. Hillman, 207–39. London: Unwin Hyman.

Hillman, Gordon C., Ewa Madeyska, and Jon Hather. 1989. "Wild Plant Foods and Diet at Late Paleolithic Wadi Kubbaniya: The Evidence from Charred Remains." In *The Prehistory of Wadi Kubbaniya Volume 2: Stratigraphy, Paleoeconomy, and Environment*, edited by Fred Wendorf, Romuald Schild, and Angela E. Close, 162–242. Dallas: Southern Methodist University Press.

Hillman, Gordon C., Sarah Mason, Dominique de Moulins, and Mark Nesbitt. 1996. "Identification of Archaeological Remains of Wheat: The 1992 London Workshop." *Circaea* 12 (2): 195–209.

Hjelmqvist, H. 1977. "Appendix 2: Economic Plants of the Italian Iron Age from Monte Irsi." In *Monte Irsi, Southern Italy: The Canadian Excavations in the Iron Age and Roman Sites 1971–1972*, edited by Alastair Small. BAR Supplementary Series 20. Oxford: British Archaeological Reports.

Hoebler, C., A. Karinthi, M. F. Devaux, F. Guillon, D. J. G. Gallant, B. Bouchet, C. Melegari, and J. L. Barry. 1998. "Physical and Chemical Transformations of Cereal Food During Oral Digestion in Human Subjects." *British Journal of Nutrition* 80 (05): 429–36. http://dx.doi.org/10.1017/S0007114598001494.

Hoering, Thomas. 1955. "Variations of Nitrogen–15 Abundance in Naturally Occurring Substances." *Science* 122 (3182): 1233–34. http://dx.doi.org/10.1126/science.122.3182.1233.

Hoering, Thomas. 1956. "Variations in the Nitrogen Isotope Abundance." In *Natural Processes in Geologic Settings: Proceedings of the Second Conference*. Nuclear Science Series no. 19, pub. 400, 39–44. Washington, D.C.: National Academy of Sciences-National Research Council Publications.

Hofreiter, Michael, David Serre, Hendrik N. Poinar, Melanie Kuch, and Svante Pääbo. 2001. "Ancient DNA." *Nature Reviews Genetics* 2 (5): 353–59. http://dx.doi.org/10.1038/35072071.

Holden, Timothy G. 1986. "Preliminary Report on the Detailed Analyses of the Macroscopic Remains from the Gut of Lindow Man." In *Lindow Man: The Body in the Bog*, edited by I. M. Stead, J. B. Bourke, and Don R. Brothwell, 116–25. Ithaca: Cornell University Press.

Hollemeyer, Klaus, Wolfgang Altmeyer, Elmar Heinzle, and Christian Pitra. 2008. "Species Identification of Oetzi's Clothing with Matrix-Assisted Laser Desorption/Ionization Time-of-Flight Mass Spectrometry Based on Peptide Pattern Similarities of Hair Digests." *Rapid Communications in Mass Spectrometry* 22 (18): 2751–67. http://dx.doi.org/10.1002/rcm.3679.

Hollenbach, Kandace D., and Renee B. Walker. 2010. "Documenting Subsistence Change During the Pleistocene/Holocene Transition: Investigations of Paleoethnobotanical and Zooarchaeological Data from Dust Cave, Alabama." In *Integrating Zooarchaeology and Paleoethnobotany. A Consideration of Issues, Methods, and*

Cases, edited by Amber M. VanDerwarker and Tanya M. Peres, 227–44. New York: Springer. http://dx.doi.org/10.1007/978-1-4419-0935-0_10.

Holliday, Vance T. 2004. *Soils in Archaeological Research*. New York: Oxford University Press.

Hollingsworth, Peter M., Laura L. Forrest, John L. Spouge, Mehrdad Hajibabaei, and Sujeevan Ratnasingham, Michelle van der Bank, Mark W. Chase, Robyn S. Cowan, David L. Erickson, Aron J. Fazekas, Sean W. Graham, Karen E. James, Ki-Joong Kim, W. John Kress, Harald Schneider, Jonathan van AlphenStahl, Spencer C.H. Barrett, Cassio van den Berg, Diego Bogarin, Kevin S. Burgess, Kenneth M. Cameron, Mark Carine, Juliana Chacón, Alexandra Clark, James J. Clarkson, Ferozah Conrad, Dion S. Devey, Caroline S. Ford, Terry A.J. Hedderson, Michelle L. Hollingsworth, Brian C. Husband, Laura J. Kelly, Prasad R. Kesanakurti, Jung Sung Kim, Young-Dong Kim, Renaud Lahaye, Hae-Lim Lee, David G. Long, Santiago Madriñán, Olivier Maurin, Isabelle Meusnier, Steven G. Newmaster, Chong-Wook Park, Diana M. Percy, Gitte Petersen, James E. Richardson, Gerardo A. Salazar, Vincent Savolainen, Ole Seberg, Michael J. Wilkinson, Dong-Keun Yi, and Damon P. Little. 2009. "A DNA Barcode for Land Plants." *Proceedings of the National Academy of Sciences of the United States of America* 106 (31): 12794–97. doi: 10.1073/pnas.0905845106.

Holloway, Richard G. 1989. "Experimental Mechanical Pollen Degradation and Its Application to Quaternary Age Deposits." *Texas Journal of Science* 41 (2): 131–45.

Horrocks, M. 2005. "A Combined Procedure for Recovering Phytoliths and Starch Residues from Soils, Sedimentary Deposits and Similar Materials." *Journal of Archaeological Science* 32 (8): 1169–75. http://dx.doi.org/10.1016/j.jas.2005.02.014.

Horrocks, Mark, Geoff Irwin, Martin Jones, and Doug Sutton. 2004. "Starch Grains and Xylem Cells of Sweet Potato (*Ipomoea batatas*) and Bracken (*Pteridium esculentum*) in Archaeological Deposits from Northern New Zealand." *Journal of Archaeological Science* 31 (3): 251–58. http://dx.doi.org/10.1016/S0305-4403(03) 00018-9.

Hosch, Sabine, and Petra Zibulski. 2003. "The Influence of Inconsistent Wet-Sieving Procedures on the Macroremain Concentration in Waterlogged Sediments." *Journal of Archaeological Science* 30 (7): 849–57. http://dx.doi.org/10.1016/S0305-4403 (02)00263-7.

Höss, Matthias, and Svante Pääbo. 1993. "DNA Extraction from Pleistocene Bones by a Silica-Based Purification Method." *Nucleic Acids Research* 21 (16): 3913–14. http://dx.doi.org/10.1093/nar/21.16.3913.

Hovsepyan, Roman, and George Willcox. 2008. "The Earliest Finds of Cultivated Plants in Armenia: Evidence from Charred Remains and Crop Processing

Residues in Pisé from the Neolithic Settlements of Aratashen and Aknashen."
Vegetation History and Archaeobotany 17 (S1): S63–71. http://dx.doi.org/10.1007
/s00334-008-0158-6.

Howland, M. R., L. T. Corr, S. M. M. Young, V. Jones, S. Jim, N. J. Van Der Merwe, A.
D. Mitchell, and R. P. Evershed. 2003. "Expression of the Dietary Isotope Signal in
the Compound-Specific δ¹³C Values of Pig Bone Lipids and Amino Acids." *International Journal of Osteoarchaeology* 13 (1–2): 54–65. http://dx.doi.org/10.1002/oa.658.

Hritz, Carrie, and Tony J. Wilkinson. 2006. "Using Shuttle Radar Topography to
Map Ancient Water Channels in Mesopotamia." *Antiquity* 80 (308): 415–24.

Huang, Chun Chang, Jiangli Pang, Chen Shu'e, Hongxia Su, Jia Han, Yanfeng
Cao, Wenyu Zhao, and Zhihai Tan. 2006. "Charcoal Records of Fire History in
the Holocene Loess-Soil Sequences over the Southern Loess Plateau of China."
Paleogeography, Paleoclimate, Paleoecology 239 (1–2): 28–44. http://dx.doi.org/10
.1016/j.palaeo.2006.01.004.

Huang, Y., F. A. Street-Perrott, S. E. Metcalfe, M. Brenner, M. Moreland, and K. H.
Freeman. 2001. "Climate Change as the Dominant Control on Glacial-Interglacial
Variations in C–3 and C–4 Plant Abundance." *Science* 293 (5535): 1647–51. http://
dx.doi.org/10.1126/science.1060143.

Hubbard, R. N. L. B. 1980. "Development of Agriculture in Europe and the Near
East: Evidence from Quantitative Studies." *Economic Botany* 34 (1): 51–67. http://
dx.doi.org/10.1007/BF02859554.

Hubbard, R. N. L. B., and A. al Azm. 1990. "Quantifying Preservation and Distortion in Carbonized Seeds and Investigating the History of Friké Production."
Journal of Archaeological Science 17 (1): 103–6. http://dx.doi.org/10.1016/0305
-4403(90)90017-Y.

Hubbard, R. N. L. B., and A. Clapham. 1992. "Quantifying Macroscopic Plant
Remains." *Review of Palaeobotany and Palynology* 73 (1–4): 117–32. http://dx.doi
.org/10.1016/0034-6667(92)90050-Q.

Humphreys, G. S. et al. 2003. "Phytoliths as Indicators of Process in Soils." *Phytolith
and Starch Research in the Australian-Pacific-Asian Regions: The State of the Art*. Canberra, ACT: Pandanus Books, 93–104.

Hunt, Harriet V., Marc Vander Linden, Xinyi Liu, Giedre Motuzaite-Matuzeviciute,
Sue Colledge, and Martin K. Jones. 2008. "Millets across Eurasia: Chronology and
Context of Early Records of the Genera *Panicum* and *Setaria* from Archaeological
Sites in the Old World." *Vegetation History and Archaeobotany* 17 (S1): S5–18. http://
dx.doi.org/10.1007/s00334-008-0187-1.

Hunter, Andre A., and Brian R. Gassner. 1998. "Evaluation of the Flote-Tech
Machine-Assisted Flotation System." *American Antiquity* 63 (1): 143–56. http://
dx.doi.org/10.2307/2694781.

Iacumin, P., V. Nikolaev, and M. Ramigni. 2000. "C and N Stable Isotope Measurements on Eurasian Fossil Mammals, 40,000 to 10,000 Years BP: Herbivore Physiologies and Palaeoenvironmental Reconstruction." *Palaeogeography, Palaeoclimatology, Palaeoecology* 163 (1–2): 33–47. http://dx.doi.org/10.1016/S0031-0182(00)00141-3.

Iltis, Hugh H. 2000. "Homeotic Sexual Translocations and the Origin of Maize (*Zea mays*, Poaceae): A New Look at an Old Problem." *Economic Botany* 54 (1): 7–42. http://dx.doi.org/10.1007/BF02866598.

Inside Wood. 2004. "Inside Wood." Accessed August 23, 2013. http://insidewood.lib.ncsu.edu/search.

Ionescu, Daniel. 2011. "Kindle E-Books Top Print Book Sales on Amazon." *PC World*. http://www.techhive.com/article/228242/Kindle_E_Books_Top_Print_Books_Sales_on_Amazon.html.

Iriarte, José. 2003. "Assessing the Feasibility of Identifying Maize through the Analysis of Cross-Shaped Size and Three-Dimensional Morphology of Phytoliths in the Grasslands of Southeastern South America." *Journal of Archaeological Science* 30 (9): 1085–94. http://dx.doi.org/10.1016/S0305-4403(02)00164-4.

Islebe, Gerald A., Henry Hooghiemstra, Mark Brenner, Jason H. Curtis, and David A. Hodell. 1996. "A Holocene Vegetation History from Lowland Guatemala." *The Holocene* 6 (3): 265–71. http://dx.doi.org/10.1177/095968369600600302.

Jackson, Jeremy B. C., Michael X. Kirby, Wolfgang H. Berger, Karen A. Bjorndal, Louis W. Botsford, Bruce J. Bourque, Roger H. Bradbury, Richard Cooke, Jon Erlandson, James A. Estes, Terence P. Hughes, Susan Kidwell, Carina B. Lange, Hunter S. Lenihan, John M. Pandolfi, Charles H. Peterson, Robert S. Steneck, Mia J. Tegner, and Robert R. Warner. 2001. "Historical Overfishing and the Recent Collapse of Coastal Ecosystems." *Science* 293 (5530): 629–37. http://dx.doi.org/10.1126/science.1059199.

Jacomet, Stefanie. 2007. "Neolithic Plant Economies in the Northern Alpine Foreland from 500–3500 cal BC." In *The Origins and Spread of Domestic Plants in Southwest Asia and Europe*, edited by Sue Colledge and James Conolly, 221–58. Walnut Creek, CA: Left Coast Press.

Jacomet, Stefanie. 2009. "Plant Economy and Village Life in Neolithic Lake Dwellings at the Time of the Alpine Iceman." *Vegetation History and Archaeobotany* 18 (1): 47–59. http://dx.doi.org/10.1007/s00334-007-0138-2.

Jacomet, Stefanie. 2013. "Analyses of Plant Remains from Waterlogged Archaeological Sites." In *The Oxford Handbook of Wetland Archaeology*, edited by Francesco Menotti and Aidan O'Sullivan, 497–514. Oxford: Oxford University Press.

Jacomet, Stefanie, and Christoph Brombacher. 2005. "Reconstructing Intra-Site Patterns in Neolithic Lakeshore Settlements: The State of Archaeobotanical Research and Future Prospects." *Proceedings of the International Conference on Wetland Econo-mies and Societies 10–13 March 2004.* Collectio Archæologica 3:69–94. Chronos, Zurich.

Jacomet, Stefanie, and Angela Kreuz. 1999. *Archäobotanik: Aufgaben, Methoden und Ergebnisse Vegetations- und Agrargeschichtlicher Forschungen.* Stuttgart: Eugen Ulmer.

Jacomet, Stefanie, Urs Leuzinger, and Jörg Schibler. 2004. *Die Jungsteinzeitliche Seeufersiedlung Arbon Bleiche 3.* Departement für Erziehung und Kultur des Kantons Thurgau, Kanton Thurgau.

Jacquat, C., and D. Martinoli. 1999. "*Vitis vinifera* L.: Wild or Cultivated? Study of the Grape Pips Found at Petra, Jordan; 150 BC–AD 40." *Vegetation History and Archaeobotany* 8 (1–2): 25–30. http://dx.doi.org/10.1007/BF02042839.

Jaenicke-Després, Viviane, Ed S. Buckler, Bruce D. Smith, M. Thomas P. Gilbert, Alan Cooper, John Doebley, and Svante Pääbo. 2003. "Early Allelic Selection in Maize as Revealed by Ancient DNA." *Science* 302 (5648): 1206–8. http://dx.doi .org/10.1126/science.1089056.

James, L. Allan. 2013. "Legacy Sediment: Definitions and Processes of Episodi-cally Produced Anthropogenic Sediment." *Anthropocene* 2 (October): 16–26. DOI: 10.1016/j.ancene.2013.04.001.

Jamieson, Ross W., and Meredith B. Sayre. 2010. "Barley and Identity in the Spanish Colonial *Audiencia* of Quito: Archaeobotany of the 18th Century San Blas Neigh-borhood in Riobamba." *Journal of Anthropological Archaeology* 29 (2): 208–18. http:// dx.doi.org/10.1016/j.jaa.2010.02.003.

Jane, Jay-lin. 2009. "Structural Features of Starch Granules II." In *Starch: Chemistry and Technology*, edited by James N. BeMiller, and Roy L. Whistler, 193–236. San Diego, CA: Academic Press.

Jane, Jay-lin, and James J. Shen. 1993. "Internal Structure of the Potato Starch Gran-ule Revealed by Chemical Gelatinization." *Carbohydrate Research* 247:279–90.

Jane, Jay-lin, L. Shen, L. Wang, and C. C. Maningat. 1992. "Preparation and Proper-ties of Small-Particle Corn Starch." *Cereal Chemistry* 69:280–83.

Janik, Liliana. 2003. "Changing Paradigms: Food as a Metaphor for Cultural Identity among Prehistoric Fisher-Gatherer-Hunter Communities of Northern Europe." In *Food, Culture and Identity in the Neolithic and Early Bronze Age*, edited by Mike Parker Pearson, 113–25. BAR International Series 1117. London: British Archaeo-logical Reports.

Jarman, H. N., J. Anthony Legge, and J. A. Charles. 1972. "Retrieval of Plant Remains from Archaeological Sites by Froth Flotation." In *Papers in Economic History*, edited by Eric S. Higgs, 39–48. Cambridge: Cambridge University Press.

Jenkins, Emma. 2009. "Phytolith Taphonomy: A Comparison of Dry Ashing and Acid Extraction on the Breakdown of Conjoined Phytoliths Formed in *Triticum durum.*" *Journal of Archaeological Science* 36 (10): 2402–7. http://dx.doi.org/10.1016/j.jas.2009.06.028.

Jenkins, Emma, Khalil Jamjoum, and Sameeh Al Nuimat. 2011. "Irrigation, and Phytolith Formation: An Experimental Study." In *Water, Life, and Civilisation: Climate, Environment, and Society in the Jordan Valley*, edited by Steven Mithen and Emily Black, 347–72. Cambridge: Cambridge University Press. http://dx.doi.org/10.1017/CBO9780511975219.021.

Jensen, Hans Arne. 1998. *Bibliography on Seed Morphology.* Rotterdam: A. A. Balkema.

Jiang, Hongen, Xiao Li, and Chengsen Li. 2007. "Cereal Remains from Yanghai Tomb in Turpan, Xinjiang and Their Palaeoenvironmental Significance." *Journal of Palaeogeography* 9 (5): 551–58.

Jim, Susan, Stanley H. Ambrose, and Richard P. Evershed. 2004. "Stable Carbon Isotopic Evidence for Differences in the Dietary Origin of Bone Cholesterol, Collagen and Apatite: Implications for Their Use in Palaeodietary Reconstruction." *Geochimica et Cosmochimica Acta* 68 (1): 61–72. http://dx.doi.org/10.1016/S0016-7037(03)00216-3.

Johannessen, Sisel. 1988. "Plant Remains and Culture Change: Are Paleoethnobotanical Data Better Than We Think?" In *Current Paleoethnobotany: Analytical Methods and Cultural Interpretations of Archaeological Plant Remains*, edited by Christine A. Hastorf and Virginia S. Popper, 145–66. Chicago: University of Chicago Press.

Johannessen, Sissel. 1993. "Food, Dishes, and Society in the Mississippi Valley." In *Foraging and Farming in the Eastern Woodlands*, edited by C. Margaret Scarry, 182–205. Gainesville, FL: University of Florida Press.

Johnson, Donald L. 1989. "Subsurface Stone Lines, Stone Tools, Artifact Manuport Layers, and Biomantles Produced by Bioturbation Via Pocket Gophers (*Thomonys bottae*)." *American Antiquity* 54 (2): 370–89. http://dx.doi.org/10.2307/281712.

Johnson, Jay K. 2006. *Remote Sensing in Archaeology an Explicitly North American Perspective.* Tuscaloosa: University of Alabama Press.

Johnston, Kevin J., Andrew J. Breckenridge, and Barbara C. Hansen. 2001. "Paleoecological Evidence of an Early Postclassic Occupation in the Southwestern Maya Lowlands: Laguna Las Pozas, Guatemala." *Latin American Antiquity* 12 (2): 149–66. http://dx.doi.org/10.2307/972053.

Johnston, Robert. 2005. "Pattern without a Plan: Rethinking the Bronze Age Coaxial Field Systems on Dartmoor, Southwest England." *Oxford Journal of Archaeology* 24 (1): 1–21. http://dx.doi.org/10.1111/j.1468-0092.2005.00222.x.

Jolliffe, I. T. 2002. *Principal Components Analysis.* New York: Springer.

Jones, Clive G., John H. Lawton, and Moshe Shachak. 1997. "Positive and Negative Effects of Organisms as Physical Ecosystem Engineers." *Ecology* 78 (7): 1946–57. http://dx.doi.org/10.1890/0012-9658(1997)078[1946:PANEOO]2.0.CO;2.

Jones, C. R. 1940. "The Production of Mechanically Damaged Starch in Milling as a Governing Factor in the Diastatic Activity of Flour." *Cereal Chemistry* 17:133–69.

Jones, Glynis E. M. 1983a. "The Ethnoarchaeology of Crop Processing: Seeds of a Middle-Range Methodology." *Archaeological Review from Cambridge* 2 (2): 17–26.

Jones, Glynis E. M. 1983b. "The Use of Ethnographic and Ecological Models in the Interpretation of Archaeological Plant Remains: Case Studies from Greece." Unpublished PhD diss., Cambridge University.

Jones, Glynis E. M. 1984. "Interpretation of Archaeological Plant Remains: Ethnographic Models from Greece." In *Plants and Ancient Man: Studies in Paleoethnobotany*, edited by Willem van Zeist and W. A. Casparie, 43–61. Rotterdam, Netherlands: AA Balkema.

Jones, Glynis E. M. 1987. "A Statistical Approach to the Archaeological Identification of Crop Processing." *Journal of Archaeological Science* 14 (3): 311–23. http://dx.doi.org/10.1016/0305-4403(87)90019-7.

Jones, Glynis E. M. 1991. "Numerical Analysis in Archaeobotany." In *Progress in Old World Palaeoethnobotany*, edited by Willem van Zeist, Krystyna Wasylikowa, and Karl-Ernst Behre, 63–80. Rotterdam: A.A. Balkema.

Jones, Glynis E. M. 1998. "Wheat Grain Identification—Why Bother?" *Environmental Archaeology* 2 (1): 29–34. http://dx.doi.org/10.1179/env.1997.2.1.29.

Jones, Glynis E. M. 2002. "Weed Ecology as a Method for the Archaeobotanical Recognition of Crop Husbandry Practices." *Acta Palaeobotanica* 42:185–94.

Jones, Glynis E. M., Amy Bogaard, Michael Charles, and John G. Hodgson. 2000. "Distinguishing the Effects of Agricultural Practices Relating to Fertility and Disturbance: A Functional Ecological Approach in Archaeobotany." *Journal of Archaeological Science* 27 (11): 1073–84. http://dx.doi.org/10.1006/jasc.1999.0543.

Jones, Glynis E. M., Amy Bogaard, Michael Charles, and John G. Hodgson. 2001. "Erratum: Distinguishing the Effects of Agricultural Practices Relating to Fertility and Disturbance: A Functional Ecological Approach in Archaeobotany." *Journal of Archaeological Science* 28 (11): 1257. http://dx.doi.org/10.1006/jasc.2001.0765.

Jones, Glynis E. M., Michael Charles, Amy Bogaard, and John G. Hodgson. 2010. "Crops and Weeds: The Role of Weed Functional Ecology in the Identification of Crop Husbandry Methods." *Journal of Archaeological Science* 37 (1): 70–77. http://dx.doi.org/10.1016/j.jas.2009.08.017.

Jones, Glynis E. M., Michael Charles, Amy Bogaard, John G. Hodgson, and Carol Palmer. 2005. "The Functional Ecology of Present-Day Arable Weed Floras and Its Applicability for the Identification of Past Crop Husbandry." *Vegetation History and Archaeobotany* 14 (4): 493–504. http://dx.doi.org/10.1007/s00334-005-0081-z.

Jones, Glynis E. M., and Paul Halstead. 1995. "Maslins, Mixtures and Monocrops: On the Interpretation of Archaeobotanical Crop Samples of Heterogeneous Composition." *Journal of Archaeological Science* 22 (1): 103–14. http://dx.doi.org/10.1016/S0305-4403(95)80168-5.

Jones, Glynis E. M., and Peter Rowley-Conwy. 2007. "On the Importance of Cereal Cultivation in the British Neolithic." In *The Origins and Spread of Domestic Plants in Southwest Asia and Europe*, edited by Sue Colledge and James Conolly, 391–419. Walnut Creek, CA: Left Coast Press.

Jones, Glynis E. M., Soultana M. Valamoti, and Michael Charles. 2000. "Early Crop Diversity: A "New" Glume Wheat from Northern Greece." *Vegetation History and Archaeobotany* 9 (3): 133–46. http://dx.doi.org/10.1007/BF01299798.

Jones, Julie, Heather Tinsley, and Richard Brunning. 2007. "Methodologies for Assessment of the State of Preservation of Pollen and Plant Macrofossil Remains in Waterlogged Deposits." *Environmental Archaeology* 12 (1): 71–86. http://dx.doi.org/10.1179/174963107x172769.

Jones, Kevin T., and David B. Madsen. 1989. "Calculating the Cost of Resource Transportation: A Great Basin Example." *Current Anthropology* 30 (4): 529–34. http://dx.doi.org/10.1086/203780.

Jones, Martin K. 1978. "The Plant Remains." In *The Excavation of an Iron Age Settlement, Bronze Age Ring-Ditches and Roman Features at Ashville Trading Estate, Abingdon (Oxfordshire), 1974–76*, edited by M. Parrington, 93–110. Report no. 28. York: Council for British Archaeology Research.

Jones, Martin K. 1984a. "The Plant Remains." In *Danebury: An Iron Age Hillfort in Hampshire. Volume 2: The Excavations, 1969–1978: The Finds*, edited by Barry W. Cunliffe, 483–95. Report no. 52. York: Council For British Archaeology Research.

Jones, Martin K. 1984b. "The Ecological and Cultural Implications of Carbonised Seed Assemblages from Selected Archaeological Contexts in Southern Britain." Unpublished D.Phil. Thesis, University of Oxford, Oxford.

Jones, Martin K. 1985. "Archaeobotany Beyond Subsistence Reconstruction." In *Beyond Domestication in Prehistoric Europe: Investigations in Subsistence Archaeology and Social Complexity*, edited by Graeme Barker and Clive Gamble, 107–28. London: Academic Press.

Jones, Martin K. 1993. "The Carbonised Plant Remains." In *The Prehistoric and Iron Age Enclosed Settlement at Mingies Ditch, Hardwick-with-Yelford, Oxon*, edited by Tim G. Allen, and Mark A. Robinson, 120–23. Thames Valley Landscapes: The Windrush Valley, vol. 2. Oxford: Oxford Archaeology Unit and Oxford University Committee for Archaeology.

Jones, Martin K. 1996. "Plant Exploitation." In *The Iron Age in Britain and Ireland: Recent Trends*, edited by Timothy C. Champion and John R. Collis, 29–40. Sheffield: Sheffield Academic Press.

Jones, Martin K., and Sandra Nye. 1991. "The Plant Remains." In *Danebury: An Iron Age Hillfort in Hampshire. Volume 5: The Excavations, 1979–1988: The Finds*, edited by Barry W. Cunliffe, 439–46. Research Report 73. London: Council for British Archaeology.

Jones, Volney H. 1936. "The Vegetal Remains of Newt Kash Hollow Shelter." In *Rock Shelters in Menifee County, Kentucky*, edited by William S. Webb and W. D. Funkhouser, 147–65. Lexington, KY: University of Kentucky.

Jones, Martin K. 1941. "The Nature and Status of Ethnobotany." *Chronica Botanica* 6 (10): 219–21.

Jongman, R. H., C. J. F. ter Braak, and O. F. R. van Tongeren. 1987. *Data Analysis and Community and Landscape Ecology*. Wageningen: Pudoc.

Joshi, S. R., G. D. Sharma, and R. R. Mishra. 1993. "Microbial Enzyme Activities Related to Litter Decomposition near a Highway in a Sub-Tropical Forest of North East India." *Soil Biology & Biochemistry* 25 (12): 1763–70. http://dx.doi.org /10.1016/0038-0717(93)90181-A.

Juan-Tresserras, J., C. Lalueza, R. M. Albert, and M. Calvo. 1997. "Identification of Phytoliths from Prehistoric Human Dental Remains from the Iberian Peninsula and the Balearic Islands." In *Primer Encuentro Europeo Sobre El Estudio de Fitolitos*, edited by A. Pinilla, J. Juan-Tresserras, and M. J. Machado, 197–203. Madrid: Graficas Fersan.

Juggins, S., and N. Cameron. 2010. "Diatoms and Archaeology." In *The Diatoms*, edited by J. P. Smol, and Eugene F. Stoermer, 514–22. 2nd ed. Cambridge: Cambridge University Press.

Kadane, Joseph B. 1988. "Possible Statistical Contibutions to Paleoethnobotany." In *Current Paleoethnobotany: Analytical Methods and Cultural Interpretations of Archaeological Plant Remains*, edited by Christine A. Hastorf and Virginia S. Popper, 206–14. Chicago: University of Chicago Press.

Kahn, Miriam. 1986. *Always Hungry, Never Greedy*. Cambridge: Cambridge University Press.

Kajale, M. D. 1991. "Current Status of Indian Palaeoethnobotany: Introduced and Indigenous Food Plants with a Discussion of the Historical and Evolutionary Development of Indian Agricultural Systems in General." In *New Light on Early Farming*, edited by Jane M. Renfrew, 155–89. Edinburgh: University Press.

Kaplan, Jed O., Kristen M. Krumhardt, Erle C. Ellis, William F. Ruddiman, Carsten Lemmen, and Kess Klein Goldewijk. 2011. "Holocene Carbon Emissions as a Result of Anthropogenic Land Cover Change." *The Holocene* 21 (5): 775–91.

Kaplan, Jed O., Kristen M. Krumhardt, and Niklaus Zimmermann. 2009. "The Prehistoric and Preindustrial Deforestation of Europe." *Quaternary Science Reviews* 28 (27–28): 3016–34. http://dx.doi.org/10.1016/j.quascirev.2009.09.028.

Kaplan, Lawrence, Mary B. Smith, and Lesley Sneddon. 1990. "The Boylston Street Fishweir: Revisited." *Economic Botany* 44 (4): 516–28. http://dx.doi.org/10.1007/BF02859788.

Kapp, Ronald O. 1969. *How to Know Pollen and Spores*. William C. Dubuque, Iowa: Brown.

Kapp, Ronald O., Owen K. Davis, and James E. King. 2000. *Ronald O. Kapp's Pollen and Spores*. 2nd ed. College Station, TX: American Association of Stratigraphic Palynologists Foundation.

Karkanas, Panagiotis. 2010. "Preservation of Anthropogenic Materials under Different Geochemical Processes: A Mineralogical Approach." *Quaternary International* 214 (1–2): 63–69. http://dx.doi.org/10.1016/j.quaint.2009.10.017.

Katzenberg, M. Anne, Henry P. Schwarcz, Martin Knyf, and F. Jerome Melbye. 1995. "Stable Isotope Evidence for Maize Horticulture and Paleodiet in Southern Ontario." *American Antiquity* 60 (2): 335–50. http://dx.doi.org/10.2307/282144.

Kealhofer, Lisa, and Dolores R. Piperno. 1998. *Opal Phytoliths in Southeast Asian Flora*. Smithsonian Contributions to Botany 88.

Kealhofer, Lisa, Robin Torrence, and Richard Fullagar. 1999. "Integrating Phytoliths within Use-Wear/Residue Studies of Stone Tools." *Journal of Archaeological Science* 26 (5): 527–46. http://dx.doi.org/10.1006/jasc.1998.0332.

Keegan, William F. 1986. "The Optimal Foraging Analysis of Horticultural Production." *American Anthropologist* 88 (1): 92–107. http://dx.doi.org/10.1525/aa.1986.88.1.02a00060.

Keegan, William F., and Michael J. DeNiro. 1988. "Stable Carbon- and Nitrogen-Isotope Ratios of Bone Collagen Used to Study Coral-Reef and Terrestrial Components of Prehistoric Bahamian Diet." *American Antiquity* 53 (2): 320–36. http://dx.doi.org/10.2307/281022.

Keene, Arthur S. 1979. "Economic Optimization Models and the Study of Hunter-Gatherer Subsistence Settlement Systems." In *Transformations, Mathematical Approaches to Culture Change*, edited by Colin Renfrew and Kenneth L. Cooke, 369–404. New York: Academic Press.

Keene, Arthur S. 1981. "Optimal Foraging in a Non-Marginal Environment." In *Hunter-Gatherer Foraging Strategies: Ethnographic and Archaeological Analyses*, edited by Bruce Winterhalder and Eric Alden Smith, 171–93. Chicago: University of Chicago Press.

Keene, Arthur S. 1985. "Constraints on Linear Programming Applications in Archaeology." In *For Concordance in Archaeological Analysis: Bridging Data Structure,*

Quantitative Technique and Theory, edited by Christopher Carr, 239–73. Kansas City, MO: Westport.

Keepax, Carole. 1975. "Scanning Electron Microscopy of Wood Replaced by Iron Corrosion Products." *Journal of Archaeological Science* 2 (2): 145–50. http://dx.doi .org/10.1016/0305-4403(75)90033-3.

Kelertas, Kristina A. 1997. "Agricultural Food Systems and Social Inequality: The Archaeobotany of Late Neolithic and Early Bronze Age Thy, Denmark." Unpublished PhD diss., Interdepartmental Graduate Program in Archaeology, University of California, Los Angeles.

Kellner, Corina M., and Margaret J. Schoeninger. 2007. "A Simple Carbon Isotope Model for Reconstructing Prehistoric Human Diet." *American Journal of Physical Anthropology* 133 (4): 1112–27. http://dx.doi.org/10.1002/ajpa.20618.

Kelly, Eugene F., Caroline Yonker, and Bruno Marino. 1993. "Stable Carbon Isotope Composition of Paleosols: An Application to Holocene." In *Climate Change in Continental Isotopic Records*, edited by Peter K. Swart, Kyger C. Lohmann, Judith A. McKenzie, and S. Savin, 233–39. Washington, D.C.: American Geophysical Union. http://dx.doi.org/10.1029/GM078p0233.

Kelly, Jeffrey F. 2000. "Stable Isotopes of Carbon and Nitrogen in the Study of Avian and Mammalian Trophic Ecology." *Canadian Journal of Zoology* 78 (1): 1–27. http:// dx.doi.org/10.1139/z99-165.

Kelly, Robert L. 1995. *The Foraging Spectrum*. Washington, D. C.: Smithsonian Institution Press.

Kelso, Gerald K., Frederica R. Dimmick, David H. Dimmick, and Tonya B. Largy. 2006. "An Ethnopalynological Test of Task-Specific Area Analysis: Bay View Stable, Cataumet, Massachusetts." *Journal of Archaeological Science* 33 (7): 953–60. http://dx.doi.org/10.1016/j.jas.2005.11.002.

Kelso, Gerald K., Stephen A. Mrozowski, Douglas Currie, Andrew C. Edwards, Marley R. Brown III, Audrey J. Horning, Gregory J. Brown, and Jeremiah R. Dandoy. 1995. "Differential Pollen Preservation in a Seventheenth-Century Refuse Pit, Jamestown Island, Virginia." *Historical Archaeology* 29 (2): 43–54.

Kelso, Gerald K., Duncan Ritchie, and Nicole Misso. 2000. "Pollen Record Preservation Processes in the Salem Neck Sewage Plant Shell Midden (19-ES–471), Salem, Massachusetts, U.S.A." *Journal of Archaeological Science* 27 (3): 235–40. http://dx.doi .org/10.1006/jasc.1999.0454.

Kelso, Gerald K., and Allen M. Solomon. 2006. "Applying Modern Analogs to Understand the Pollen Content of Coprolites." *Palaeogeography, Palaeoclimatology, Palaeoecology* 237 (1): 80–91. http://dx.doi.org/10.1016/j.palaeo.2005.11.036.

Kendal, Jeremy R., J. Jamshid, J. Tehrani, and F. John Odling-Smee. 2011. "Human Niche Construction—Papers of a Theme Issue." *Philosophical Transactions of the Royal Society of London. Series B, Biological Sciences* 366:785–92.

Kennett, Douglas J., Barbara Voorhies, and Dean Martorana. 2006. "An Ecological Model for the Origins of Maize-Based Food Production on the Pacific Coast of Southern Mexico." In *Behavioral Ecology and the Transition to Agriculture*, edited by Douglas J. Kennett and Bruce Winterhalder, 103–36. Berkeley: University of California Press.

Kennett, Douglas J., and Bruce Winterhalder, eds. 2006. *Behavioral Ecology and the Transition to Agriculture*. Berkeley: University of California Press.

Kenward, H. K., A. R. Hall, and A. K. C. Jones. 1980. "A Tested Set of Techniques for the Extraction of Plant and Animal Macrofossils from Waterlogged Archaeological Deposits." *Science and Archaeology* 22:3–15.

King, James E., Walter E. Klippel, and Rose Duffield. 1975. "Pollen Preservation and Archaeology in Eastern North America." *American Antiquity* 40 (2): 180–90. http://dx.doi.org/10.2307/279613.

Kislev, Mordechai, Anat Hartmann, and Ofer Bar-Yosef. 2006. "Early Domesticated Fig in the Jordan Valley." *Science* 312 (5778): 1372–74. http://dx.doi.org/10.1126/science.1125910.

Kislev, Mordechai E. 1997. "Early Agriculture and Paleoecology of Netiv Hagdud." In *An Early Neolithic Village in the Jordan Valley*, edited by Ofer Bar-Yosef, and Avi Gopher, 209–36. Cambridge, MA: Peabody Museum of Archaeology and Ethnology, Harvard University.

Kistler, Logan. 2012. "Ancient DNA Extraction from Plants." *Methods in Molecular Biology* 840: 71–79.

Kitagawa, Junko, and Yoshinori Yasuda. 2004. "The Influence of Climatic Change on Chestnut and Horse Chestnut Preservation around Jomon Sites in Northeastern Japan." *Quaternary International* 123–25:89–103. http://dx.doi.org/10.1016/j.quaint.2004.02.011.

Kitagawa, Junko, and Yoshinori Yasuda. 2008. "Development and Distribution of Castanea and Aesculus Culture During the Jomon Period in Japan." *Quaternary International* 184 (1): 41–55. http://dx.doi.org/10.1016/j.quaint.2007.09.014.

Klinge, JoAnna, and Patricia Fall. 2010. "Archaeobotanical Inference of Bronze Age Land Use and Land Cover in the Eastern Mediterranean." *Journal of Archaeological Science* 37 (10): 2622–29.

Knapp, H. 2006. *Samenatlas. Teil 1: Caryophyllaceae. Teil 2: Ranunculaceae.* Vienna: Mitteilungen der Kommission für Quartärforschung. Österreichischen Akademie der Wissenschaften.

Knapp, H. 2010. *Samenatlas. Teil 3: Fabaceae. Teil 4: Hyperiaceae.* Vienna: Mitteilungen der Kommission für Quartärforschung. Österreichischen Akademie der Wissenschaften.

Knapp, Michael, Andrew C. Clarke, K. Ann Horsburgh, and Elizabeth A. Matisoo-Smith. 2012. "Setting the Stage—Building and Working in an Ancient DNA Laboratory." *Annals of Anatomy-Anatomischer Anzeiger* 194 (1): 3–6. http://dx.doi .org/10.1016/j.aanat.2011.03.008.

Knörzer, Karl-Heinz. 2000. "3000 Years of Agriculture in a Valley of the High Himalayas." *Vegetation History and Archaeobotany* 9 (4): 219–22. http://dx.doi.org /10.1007/BF01294636.

Knörzer, K. H. 1971. "Urgeschichtliche Unkräuter im Rheinland Ein Beitrag zur Entstehungsgeschichte der Segetalgesellschaften." *Vegetatio* 23 (3–4): 89–111.

Kohl, Philip L. 1993. "Limits to a Post-Processual Archaeology (or, the Dangers of a New Scholasticism)." In *Archaeological Theory: Who Sets the Agenda,* edited by Norman Yoffee, 13–19. Cambridge: Cambridge University Press. http://dx.doi.org /10.1017/CBO9780511720277.002.

Kohn, Matthew J. 2010. "Carbon Isotope Compositions of Terrestrial C3 Plants as Indicators of (Paleo)Ecology and (Paleo)Climate." *Proceedings of the National Academy of Sciences of the United States of America* 107 (46): 19691–95. http://dx.doi .org/10.1073/pnas.1004933107.

Korstanje, M. Alejandra, and Patricia Cuenya. 2010. "Ancient Agriculture and Domestic Activities: A Contextual Approach Studying Silica Phytoliths and Other Microfossils in Soils." *Environmental Archaeology* 15 (1): 43–63. http://dx.doi .org/10.1179/146141010X12640787648739.

Kosina, R. 1984. "Morphology of the Crease of Wheat Caryopses and Its Usability for the Identification of Some Species. A Numerical Approach." In *Plants and Ancient Man: Studies in Palaeoethnobotany,* edited by W. van Zeist and W. A. Casparie, 177–91. Rotterdam: Balkema.

Kouchoukos, Nicholas. 2001. "Satellite Images and near-Eastern Landscapes." *Near Eastern Archaeology* 64 (1–2): 80–91.

Kozáková, Radka, Petr Pokorný, Jan Havrda, and Vlasta Jankovská. 2009. "The Potential of Pollen Analyses from Urban Deposits: Multivariate Statistical Analysis of a Data Set from the Medieval City of Prague, Czech Republic." *Vegetation History and Archaeobotany* 18 (6): 477–88. http://dx.doi.org/10.1007 /s00334-009-0217-7.

Krause, Johannes, Paul H. Dear, Joshua L. Pollack, Montgomery Slatkin, Helen Spriggs, Ian Barnes, Adrian M. Lister, Ingo Ebersberger, Svante Pääbo, and Michael Hofreiter. 2006. "Multiplex Amplification of the Mammoth

Mitochondrial Genome and the Evolution of Elephantidae." *Nature* 439 (7077): 724–27. http://dx.doi.org/10.1038/nature04432.

Kreuz, Angela, Elena Marinova, Eva Schäfer, and Julian Wiethold. 2005. "A Comparison of Early Neolithic Crop and Weed Assemblages from the Linearbandkeramik and the Bulgarian Neolithic Cultures: Differences and Similarities." *Vegetation History and Archaeobotany* 14 (4): 237–58. http://dx.doi.org/10.1007/s00334-005-0080-0.

Kreuz, Angela, and Eva Schäfer. 2002. "A New Archaeobotanical Database Programme." *Vegetation History and Archaeobotany* 11 (1–2): 177–80. http://dx.doi.org/10.1007/s003340200019.

Krueger, Harold W., and Charles H. Sullivan. 1984. "Models for Carbon Isotope Fractionation between Diet and Bone." In *Stable Isotopes in Nutrition*, edited by Judith R. Turnlund and Phyllis E. Johnson, 205–20. Washington, DC: American Chemical Society. http://dx.doi.org/10.1021/bk-1984-0258.ch014.

Kubiak-Martens, Lucyna. 1999. "The Plant Food Component of the Diet at the Late Mesolithic (Ertebolle) Settlement at Tybrind Vig, Denmark." *Vegetation History and Archaeobotany* 8 (1–2): 117–27. http://dx.doi.org/10.1007/BF02042850.

Kunth, C. 1826. "Examen Botanique." In *Catalogue Raisonne et Historique de Antiquités Découverte en Egypte*, edited by J. Passalaqua, 227–28. Paris: Musées Nationaux.

LaBelle, Jason, Jason Sibold, and Laurie Huckaby. 2011. "Glass Beads, Conical Lodges, and Fire Scars: Native American Occupation of the Colorado Front Range." Paper presented at the 76th Annual Meeting of the Society for American Archaeology, Sacramento, CA.

Laland, Kevin N., John Odling-Smee, and Marcus W. Feldman. 2000. "Niche Construction, Biological Evolution, and Cultural Change." *Behavioral and Brain Sciences* 23 (1): 131–75. http://dx.doi.org/10.1017/S0140525X00002417.

Lallo, John W., Jerome R. Rose, and George J. Armelagos. 1978. "Paleoepidemiology of Infectious Disease in the Dickson Mounds Population." *Medical College of Virginia Quartely* 14:17–23.

Lalueza Fox, Carles, Jordi Juan, and Rosa M. Albert. 1996. "Phytolith Analysis on Dental Calculus, Enamel Surface, and Burial Soil: Information About Diet and Paleoenvironment." *American Journal of Physical Anthropology* 101 (1): 101–13. http://dx.doi.org/10.1002/(SICI)1096-8644(199609)101:1<101::AID-AJPA7>3.0.CO;2-Y.

Lalueza Fox, Carles, A. Pérez-Pérez, and Jordi Juan. 1994. "Dietary Information through the Examination of Plant Phytoliths on the Enamel Surface of Human Dentition." *Journal of Archaeological Science* 21 (1): 29–34. http://dx.doi.org/10.1006/jasc.1994.1005.

Lamb, Jenna, and Thomas H. Loy. 2005. "Seeing Red: The Use of Congo Red Dye to Identify Cooked and Damaged Starch Grains in Archaeological Residues." *Journal of Archaeological Science* 32 (10): 1433–40. http://dx.doi.org/10.1016/j.jas.2005.03.020.

Lane, Chad S., Sally P. Horn, Zachary P. Taylor, and Claudia I. Mora. 2009. "Assessing the Scale of Prehistoric Human Impact in the Neotropics Using Stable Carbon Isotope Analyses of Lake Sediments: A Test Case from Costa Rica." *Latin American Antiquity* 20 (1): 120–33.

Lane, E. W. 1955. "The Importance of Fluvial Geomorphology in Hydraulic Engineering." *Proceedings of the ASCE* 81:1–17.

Lane, Kevin. 2009. "Engineered Highlands: The Social Organization of Water in the Ancient North-Central Andes (AD 1000–1480)." *World Archaeology* 41 (1): 169–90. http://dx.doi.org/10.1080/00438240802655245.

Lange, A. Gustaaf. 1990. *De Horden near Wijk Bij Duurstede.* Plant Remains from a Native Settlement at the Roman Frontier: A Numerical Approach. *Nederlandse Oudheden 13. Kromme Rijn Projekt 3.* Amersfoort: Rijksdienst voor het Oudheidkundig Bodermonderzoek.

Lansky, S., M. Kooi, and T. J. Schoch. 1949. "Properties of the Fractions and Linear Subfractions from Various Starches." *Journal of the American Chemical Society* 71 (12): 4066–75. http://dx.doi.org/10.1021/ja01180a056.

Laris, Paul. 2002. "Burning the Seasonal Mosaic: Preventative Burning Strategies in the Wooded Savanna of Southern Mali." *Human Ecology* 30 (2): 155–86. http://dx.doi.org/10.1023/A:1015685529180.

Lawlor, Elizabeth Jane. 1995. "Archaeological Site-Formation Processes Affecting Plant Remains in the Mojave Desert." Unpublished PhD diss., Department of Anthropology, University of California, Riverside.

Lawton, Harry W., Philip J. Wilke, Mary DeDecker, and William M. Mason. 1976. "Agriculture among the Paiute of Owens Valley." *Journal of California Anthropology* 3:13–50.

Leach, Edmund R. 1964. "Anthropological Aspects of Language: Animal Categories and Verbal Abuse." In *New Directions in the Study of Language*, edited by Eric H. Lenneberg, 151–65. Cambridge, MA: MIT Press.

Leach, H. W., and T. J. Schoch. 1961. "Structure of the Starch Granule II: Action of Various Amylases on Granular Starches." *Cereal Chemistry* 38:34–46.

Leavitt, Steven W., and Austin Long. 1986. "Trends of $^{13}C/^{12}C$ Ratios in Pinyon Tree Rings of the American Southwest and the Global Carbon-Cycle." *Radiocarbon* 28 (2A): 376–82.

Lebreton, Vincent, Erwan Messager, Laurent Marquer, and Josette Renault-Miskovsky. 2010. "A Neotaphonomic Experiment in Pollen Oxidation and Its

Implications for Archaeopalynology." *Review of Palaeobotany and Palynology* 162 (1): 29–38. http://dx.doi.org/10.1016/j.revpalbo.2010.05.002.

Lee, Gyoung-Ah. 2012. "Taphonomy and Sample Size Estimation in Paleoethnobotany." *Journal of Archaeological Science* 39 (3): 648–55. http://dx.doi.org/10.1016/j.jas.2011.10.025.

Lee, Gyoung-Ah, Gary W. Crawford, Li Liu, and Xingcan Chen. 2007. "Plants and People from the Early Neolithic to Shang Periods in North China." *Proceedings of the National Academy of Sciences of the United States of America* 104 (3): 1087–92. http://dx.doi.org/10.1073/pnas.0609763104.

Lee-Thorp, Julia A. 2008. "On Isotopes and Old Bones." *Archaeometry* 50 (6): 925–50. http://dx.doi.org/10.1111/j.1475-4754.2008.00441.x.

Lee-Thorp, Julia A., Judith C. Sealy, and Nikolaas J. van der Merwe. 1989. "Stable Carbon Isotope Ratio Differences between Bone Collagen and Bone Apatite, and Their Relationship to Diet." *Journal of Archaeological Science* 16 (6): 585–99. http://dx.doi.org/10.1016/0305-4403(89)90024-1.

Lees, S. H. 1983. "Environmental Hazards and Decision Making: Another Perspective from Human Ecology." In *Economic Anthropology: Topics and Theories*, edited by Sutti Ortiz, 183–99. Monographs in Economic Anthropology, no. 1. London: Society for Economic Anthropology.

Lehrer, Adrienne. 1972. "Cooking Vocabularies and the Culinary Triangle of Levi-Strauss." *Anthropological Linguistics* 14 (5): 155–71.

Leivers, Mathew, and Chris J. Stevens. 2008. "The Middle Bronze Age to Romano-British Periods." In *Archaeology on the A303 Stonehenge Improvement*, edited by Matt Leivers and Chris Moore, 34–54. Salisbury: Wessex Archaeology.

Lelievre, J. 1974. "Starch Damage." *Stärke* 26 (3): 85–88. http://dx.doi.org/10.1002/star.19740260305.

Lennstrom, Heidi A., and Christine A. Hastorf. 1992. "Testing Old Wives' Tales in Palaeoethnobotany: A Comparison of Bulk and Scatter Sampling Schemes from Pancán, Peru." *Journal of Archaeological Science* 19 (2): 205–29. http://dx.doi.org/10.1016/0305-4403(92)90050-D.

Lennstrom, Heidi A., and Christine A. Hastorf. 1995. "Interpretation in Context: Sampling and Analysis in Paleoethnobotany." *American Antiquity* 60 (4): 701–21. http://dx.doi.org/10.2307/282054.

Lentfer, Carol, Michael Therin, and Robin Torrence. 2002. "Starch Grains and Environmental Reconstruction: A Modern Test Case from West New Britain, Papua New Guinea." *Journal of Archaeological Science* 29 (7): 687–98. http://dx.doi.org/10.1006/jasc.2001.0783.

Lentz, David L. 1991. "Maya Diets of the Rich and Poor: Paleoethnobotanical Evidence from Copan." *Latin American Antiquity* 2 (3): 269–87. http://dx.doi.org/10.2307/972172.

Lentz, David L. 2001. "Diets under Duress: Paleoethnobotanical Evidence from the Late Classic Maya Site of Aguateca." Paper presented at the Society for American Archaeology Annual Meetings, New Orleans, LA.

Lentz, David L., and Brian Hockaday. 2009. "Tikal Timbers and Temples: Ancient Maya Agroforestry and the End of Time." *Journal of Archaeological Science* 36 (7): 1342–53. http://dx.doi.org/10.1016/j.jas.2009.01.020.

Lentz, David L., Jason Yaeger, Cynthia Robin, and Wendy Ashmore. 2005. "Pine, Prestige and Politics of the Late Classic Maya at Xunantunich, Belize." *Antiquity* 79 (305): 573.

Leonard, Jennifer A., Orin Shanks, Michael Hofreiter, Eva Kreuz, Larry Hodges, Walt Ream, Robert K. Wayne, and Robert C. Fleischer. 2007. "Animal DNA in PCR Reagents Plagues Ancient DNA Research." *Journal of Archaeological Science* 34 (9): 1361–66. http://dx.doi.org/10.1016/j.jas.2006.10.023.

Lepofsky, Dana, and Ken Lertzman. 2008. "Documenting Ancient Plant Management in the Northwest of North America." *Botany* 86 (2): 129–45. http://dx.doi.org/10.1139/B07-094.

Lepofsky, Dana, and Natasha Lyons. 2003. "Modeling Ancient Plant Use on the Northwest Coast: Towards an Understanding of Mobility and Sedentism." *Journal of Archaeological Science* 30 (11): 1357–71. http://dx.doi.org/10.1016/S0305-4403(03)00024-4.

Lepš, Jan, and Petr Šmilauer. 2003. *Multivariate Analysis of Ecological Data Using Canoco.* Cambridge: Cambridge University Press. http://dx.doi.org/10.1017/CBO9780511615146.

Letts, John. 1993. "The Charred Plant Remains." In "Excavations at Whitehouse Road, Oxford 1992," by Andrew Mudd. *Oxoniensia* 58:33–85 (71–78).

Lévi-Strauss, Claude. 1997. "The Culinary Triangle." In *Food and Culture: A Reader*, 1st ed., edited by Carole Counihan and Penny Van Esterik, 28–35. New York: Routledge.

Lewontin, Richard C. 1983. "Gene, Organism, and Environment." In *Evolution from Molecules to Men*, edited by D. S. Bendall, 273–85. Cambridge: Cambridge University Press.

Li, MingQi, XiaoYan Yang, Hui Wang, Qiang Wang, Xin Jia, and QuanSheng Ge. 2010. "Starch Grains from Dental Calculus Reveal Ancient Plant Foodstuffs at Chenqimogou Site, Gansu Province." *Science China Earth Sciences* 53 (5): 694–99.

Lieverse, Angela R. 1999. "Diet and the Aetiology of Dental Calculus." *International Journal of Osteoarchaeology* 9 (4): 219–32. http://dx.doi.org/10.1002/(SICI)1099 -1212(199907/08)9:4<219::AID-OA475>3.0.CO;2-V.

Lightfoot, Kent, Rob Cuthrell, Chuck Striplen, and Mark Hylkema. 2013. "Rethinking the Study of Landscape Management Practices among Hunter-Gatherers in North America." *American Antiquity* 78 (2): 285–301. http://dx.doi.org/10.7183/0002 -7316.78.2.285.

Limp, W. Fredrick. 1974. "Water Separation and Flotation Processes." *Journal of Field Archaeology* 1 (3/4): 337–42. http://dx.doi.org/10.2307/529302.

Lindahl, Tomas. 1993. "Instability and Decay of the Primary Structure of DNA." *Nature* 362 (6422): 709–15. http://dx.doi.org/10.1038/362709a0.

Liphschitz, Nili, Ram Gophna, Moshe Hartman, and Gideon Biger. 1991. "The Beginning of Olive (*Olea europaea*) Cultivation in the Old World: A Reassessment." *Journal of Archaeological Science* 18 (4): 441–53. http://dx.doi.org/10.1016/0305 -4403(91)90037-P.

Little, Elizabeth A. 2002. "Kautantouwit's Legacy: Calibrated Dates on Prehistoric Maize in New England." *American Antiquity* 67 (1): 109–18. http://dx.doi.org /10.2307/2694880.

Liu, Jianguo, Thomas Dietz, Stephen R. Carpenter, Marina Alberti, Carl Folke, Emilio Moran, Alice N. Pell, Peter Deadman, Timothy Kratz, Jane Lubchenco, Elinor Ostrom, Zhiyun Ouyang, William Provencher, Charles L. Redman, Stephen H. Schneider, and William W. Taylor. 2007a. "Complexity of Coupled Human and Natural Systems." *Science* 317 (5844): 1513–16. http://dx.doi.org/10.1126 /science.1144004.

Liu, Jianguo, Thomas Dietz, Stephen R. Carpenter, Carl Folke, Marina Alberti, Charles L. Redman, Stephen H. Schneider, Elinor Ostrom, Alice N. Pell, Jane Lubchenco, William W. Taylor, Zhiyun Ouyang, Peter Deadman, Timothy Kratz, and William Provencher. 2007b. "Coupled Human Natural Systems." *Ambio* 36 (8): 639–49. http://dx.doi.org/10.1579/0044-7447(2007)36[639:CHANS]2.0.CO;2.

Llano, C. 2009. "Photosynthetic Pathways, Spatial Distribution, Isotopic Ecology, and Implications for Pre-Hispanic Human Diets in Central-Western Argentina." *International Journal of Osteoarchaeology* 19 (2): 130–43. http://dx.doi.org/10.1002/oa.1051.

Logan, Amanda L. 2012. "A History of Food without History: Food, Trade, and Environment in West-Central Ghana in the Second Millennium A.D." Unpublished PhD diss., Department of Anthropology, University of Michigan.

Londo, J. P., Y. C. Chiang, K. H. Hung, T. Y. Chiang, and B. A. Schaal. 2006. "Phylogeography of Asian Wild Rice, *Oryza rufipogon*, Reveals Multiple Independent Domestications of Cultivated Rice, *Oryza sativa*." *Proceedings of the National*

Academy of Sciences of the United States of America 103 (25): 9578–83. http://dx.doi
.org/10.1073/pnas.0603152103.

Lopinot, Neal H. 1984. *Archaeobotanical Formation Processes and Late Middle Archaic
Human-Plant Interrelationships in the Midcontinental U.S.A.* Carbondale: Southern
Illinois University, Department of Anthropology.

Lopinot, Neal H., and David Eric Brussell. 1982. "Assessing Uncarbonized Seeds
from Open-Air Sites in Mesic Environments: An Example from Southern Illinois." *Journal of Archaeological Science* 9 (1): 95–108. http://dx.doi.org/10.1016
/0305-4403(82)90009-7.

Lopinot, Neil H., and William I. Woods. 1993. "Wood Overexploitation and the
Collapse of Cahokia." In *Foraging and Farming in the Eastern Woodlands*, edited by
C. Margaret Scarry, 206–31. Gainesville: University Press of Florida.

Lotze, Heike K. 2010. "Historical Reconstruction of Human-Induced Changes
in US Estuaries." *Oceanography and Marine Biology—an Annual Review* 48 (48):
267–338. http://dx.doi.org/10.1201/EBK1439821169-c5.

Loy, Tom, and Huw Barton. 2006. "Post-Excavation Contamination and Measures
for Prevention." In *Ancient Starch Research*, edited by Robin Torrence and Huw
Barton, 165–67. Walnut Creek, California: Left Coast Press.

Loy, Thomas H. 1994. "Methods in the Analysis of Starch Residues on Prehistoric
Stone Tools." In *Tropical Archaeobotany: Applications and New Developments*, edited
by Jon G. Hather, 86–114. London: Routledge.

Loy, Thomas H., Matthew Spriggs, and Stephen Wickler. 1992. "Direct Evidence for
Human Use of Plants 28,000 Years Ago: Starch Residues on Stone Artefacts from
the Northern Solomon Islands." *Antiquity* 66:898–912.

Lupton, Deborah. 1994. "Food, Memory and Meaning: The Symbolic and Social
Nature of Food Events." *Sociological Review* 42 (4): 664–85. http://dx.doi.org
/10.1111/j.1467-954X.1994.tb00105.x.

Lutz, Kerry, Wenqin Wang, Anna Zdepski, and Todd Michael. 2011. "Isolation and
Analysis of High Quality Nuclear DNA with Reduced Organellar DNA for Plant
Genome Sequencing and Resequencing." *BMC Biotechnology* 11 (1): 54. http://
dx.doi.org/10.1186/1472-6750-11-54.

Lydolph, Magnus C., Jonas Jacobsen, Peter Arctander, M. T. P. Gilbert, D. A. Gilich-
insky, A. J. Hansen, E. Willerslev, and L. Lange. 2005. "Beringian Paleoecology
Inferred from Permafrost-Preserved Fungal DNA." *Applied and Environmental
Microbiology* 71 (2): 1012–17. http://dx.doi.org/10.1128/AEM.71.2.1012-1017.2005.

Lynch, D. L., and L. J. Cotnoir. 1956. "The Influence of Clay Minerals on the Breakdown of Certain Organic Substrates." *Proceedings—Soil Science Society of America*
20 (3): 367–70. http://dx.doi.org/10.2136/sssaj1956.03615995002000030019x.

Lyons, Diane, and A. Catherine D'Andrea. 2003. "Griddles, Ovens, and Agricultural Origins: An Ethnoarchaeological Study of Bread Baking in Highland Ethiopia." *American Anthropologist* 105 (3): 515–30. http://dx.doi.org/10.1525/aa.2003.105.3 .515.

MacNeish, Richard S. 1967. "A Summary of the Subsistence." In *Prehistory of the Tehuacan Valley*, vol. 1, edited by Douglas S. Byers, 201–11. Austin: University of Texas Press.

Macphail, Richard I., G. M. Cruise, Michael J. Allen, and Johan Linderholm. 2006. "A Rebuttal of the Views Expressed in "Problems of Unscientific Method and Approach in Archaeological Soil and Pollen Analysis of Experimental Floor Deposits; with Special Reference to Butser Ancient Farm, Hampshire, UK by R. I. Macphail, G. M. Cruise, M. Allen, J. Linderholm and P. Reynolds" by Matthew Canti, Stephen Carter, Donald Davidson, and Susan Limbrey." *Journal of Archaeological Science* 33 (2): 299–305. http://dx.doi.org/10.1016/j.jas.2005.07.002.

Macphail, Richard I., G. M. Cruise, Michael J Allen, Johan Linderholm, and Peter Reynolds. 2004. "Archaeological Soil and Pollen Analysis of Experimental Floor Deposits; with Special Reference to Butser Ancient Farm, Hampshire, UK." *Journal of Archaeological Science* 31 (2): 175–91. http://dx.doi.org/10.1016/j.jas.2003.07.005.

Madeja, Jacek, Agnieszka Wacnik, Agata Zyga, Elzbieta Stankiewicz, Ewa Wypasek, Witold Guminski, and Krystyna Harmata. 2009. "Bacterial Ancient DNA as in Indicator of Human Presence in the Past: Its Correlation with Palynological and Archaeological Data." *Journal of Quaternary Science* 24 (4): 317–21. http://dx.doi .org/10.1002/jqs.1237.

Madella, Marco, Martin K. Jones, P. Echlin, A. Powers-Jones, and M. Moore. 2009. "Plant Water Availability and Analytical Microscopy of Phytoliths: Implications for Ancient Irrigation in Arid Zones." *Quaternary International* 193 (1–2): 32–40. http://dx.doi.org/10.1016/j.quaint.2007.06.012.

Madella, Marco, and Debora Zurro, eds. 2007. *Plants, People, and Places: Recent Studies in Phytolith Analysis*. Oxford: Oxbow Books.

Madsen, Torsten. 1988. "Multivariate Statistics and Archaeology." In *Multivariate Archaeology. Numerical Approaches in Scandinavian Archaeology*, edited by Torsten Madsen, 7–27. Jutland Archaeological Society Publications Aarhus University Press Aarhus.

Magyari, Enikö K., Ágnes Major, Miklós Bálint, Judit Nédli, Mihaály Braun, István Rácz, and Laura Parducci. 2011. "Population Dynamics and Genetic Changes of *Picea abies* in the South Carpathians Revealed by Pollen and Ancient DNA Analyses." *BMC Evolutionary Biology* 11 (1): 66. http://dx.doi.org/10.1186/1471 -2148-11-66.

Makarewicz, Cheryl A., Nathan B. Goodale, Philip Rassmann, Chantel White, Holly Miller, Jihad Haroun, Eric Carlson, Alexis Pantos, Matthew Kroot, Seiji Kadowaki, Ak sel Casson, James T. Williams, Anne E. Austin, and Benjamin Fabre. 2006. "El-Hemmeh: A Multi-Period Pre-Pottery Neolithic Site in the Wadi El-Hasa, Jordan." *Eurasian Prehistory* 4 (1–2): 183–220.

Maloney, Bernard K. 1994. "The Prospects and Problems of Using Palynology to Trace the Origin of Agriculture: The Case of Southeast Asia." In *Tropical Archaeobotany: Applications and New Developments*, edited by John G. Hather, 139–71. London: Routledge.

Manen, J. F., L. Bouby, O. Dalnoki, P. Marinval, M. Turgay, and A. Schlumbaum. 2003. "Microsatellites from Archaeological *Vitis vinifera* Seeds Allow a Tentative Assignment of the Geographical Origin of Ancient Cultivars." *Journal of Archaeological Science* 30 (6): 721–29. http://dx.doi.org/10.1016/S0305-4403(02)00244-3.

Mangafa, Maria, and Kostas Kotsakis. 1996. "A New Method for the Identification of Wild and Cultivated Charred Grape Seeds." *Journal of Archaeological Science* 23 (3): 409–18. http://dx.doi.org/10.1006/jasc.1996.0036.

Manning, Katie, Ruth Pelling, Tom Higham, Jean-Luc Schwenniger, and Dorian Q Fuller. 2011. "4500-Year Old Domesticated Pearl Millet (*Pennisetum glaucum*) from the Tilemsi Valley, Mali: New Insights into an Alternative Cereal Domestication Pathway." *Journal of Archaeological Science* 38 (2): 312–22. http://dx.doi.org/10.1016/j.jas.2010.09.007.

Margaritis, Evi, and Martin Jones. 2006. "Beyond Cereals: Crop Processing and *Vitis vinifera* L. Ethnography, Experiment and Charred Grape Remains from Hellenistic Greece." *Journal of Archaeological Science* 33 (6): 784–805. http://dx.doi.org/10.1016/j.jas.2005.10.021.

Maricic, Tomislav, Mark Whitten, and Svante Pääbo. 2010. "Multiplexed DNA Sequence Capture of Mitochondrial Genomes Using PCR Products." *PLoS ONE* 5 (11): e14004. http://dx.doi.org/10.1371/journal.pone.0014004.

Marino, Bruno D., and Michael J. DeNiro. 1987. "Isotopic Analysis of Archaeobotanicals to Reconstruct Past Climates: Effects of Activities Associated with Food Preparation on Carbon, Hydrogen and Oxygen Isotope Ratios of Plant Cellulose." *Journal of Archaeological Science* 14 (5): 537–48. http://dx.doi.org/10.1016/0305-4403(87)90037-9.

Marino, Bruno D., and Michael B. McElroy. 1991. "Isotopic Composition of Atmospheric CO_2 Inferred from Carbon in C_4 Plant Cellulose." *Nature* 349 (6305): 127–31. http://dx.doi.org/10.1038/349127a0.

Mariotti Lippi, Marta, Tiziana Gonnelli, and Pasquino Pallecchi. 2011. "Rice Chaff in Ceramics from the Archaeological Site of Sumhuram (Dhofar, Southern Oman)."

Journal of Archaeological Science 38 (6): 1173–79. http://dx.doi.org/10.1016/j.jas.2010 .09.028.

Märkle, Tanja, and Manfred Rosch. 2008. "Experiments on the Effects of Carbonization on Some Cultivated Plant Seeds." *Vegetation History and Archaeobotany* 17 (S1): S257–63. http://dx.doi.org/10.1007/s00334-008-0165-7.

Marston, John M. 2009. "Modeling Wood Acquisition Strategies from Archaeological Charcoal Remains." *Journal of Archaeological Science* 36 (10): 2192–200. http:// dx.doi.org/10.1016/j.jas.2009.06.002.

Marston, John M. 2010. "Evaluating Risk, Sustainability, and Decision Making in Agricultural and Land-Use Strategies at Ancient Gordion." Unpublished PhD diss., Interdepartmental Graduate Program in Archaeology, University of California, Los Angeles.

Marston, John M. 2011. "Archaeological Markers of Agricultural Risk Management." *Journal of Anthropological Archaeology* 30 (2): 190–205. http://dx.doi.org /10.1016/j.jaa.2011.01.002.

Marston, John M. 2012a. "Agricultural Strategies and Political Economy in Ancient Anatolia." *American Journal of Archaeology* 116 (3): 377–403. http://dx.doi.org/10 .3764/aja.116.3.0377.

Marston, John M. 2012b. "Reconstructing the Functional Use of Wood at Phrygian Gordion through Charcoal Analysis." In *The Archaeology of Phrygian Gordion, the Royal City of Midas*, edited by C. Brian Rose, 47–54. Philadelphia: University of Pennsylvania Museum Press.

Martin, A. C. 1946. "The Comparative Internal Morphology of Seeds." *American Midland Naturalist* 36 (3): 513–660. http://dx.doi.org/10.2307/2421457.

Martin, Alexander C., and William D. Barkley. 1961. *Seed Identification Manual*. Berkeley: University of California Press.

Matheson, Carney D., Carli Gurney, Neal Esau, and Ryan Lehto. 2010. "Assessing PCR Inhibition from Humic Substances." *Open Enzyme Inhibition Journal* 3:38–45.

Matsumoto, Naoyuki, Tamotsu Hoshino, Goro Yamada, Akira Kawakami, and Yuko Takada-Hoshino. 2010. "Sclerotia of *Typhula ishikariensis* Biotype B (Typhulaceae) from Archaeological Sites (4000 to 400 BP) in Hokkaido, Northern Japan." *American Journal of Botany* 97 (3): 433–37. http://dx.doi.org/10.3732/ajb.0900133.

Matsuoka, Yoshihiro, Yves Vigouroux, Major M. Goodman, Jesus Sanchez G., Edward Buckler, and John Doebley. 2002. "A Single Domestication for Maize Shown by Multilocus Microsatellite Genotyping." *Proceedings of the National Academy of Sciences of the United States of America* 99 (9): 6080–84. http://dx.doi .org/10.1073/pnas.052125199.

Matthews, Wendy. 2010. "Geoarchaeology and Taphonomy of Plant Remains and Microarchaeological Residues in Early Urban Environments in the Ancient Near

East." *Quaternary International* 214 (1–2): 98–113. http://dx.doi.org/10.1016/j
.quaint.2009.10.019.

Maunsell, John. 2010. "Announcement Regarding Supplemental Material." *Journal of
Neuroscience* 30 (32): 10599–600.

Mauquoy, D., and B. Van Geel. 2007. "Mire and Peat Macros." In *Encyclopedia of
Quaternary Science*, edited by S. Elias, 2315–36. Oxford: Elsevier. http://dx.doi
.org/10.1016/B0-44-452747-8/00229-5.

Maxwell, H. 1910. "The Use and Abuse of Forests by the Virginia Indians." *William
and Mary College Quarterly Historical Magazine* 19 (2): 73–103. http://dx.doi.org
/10.2307/1921261.

McAnany, Patricia Ann, and Norman Yoffee, eds. 2009. *Questioning Collapse: Human
Resilience, Ecological Vulnerability and the Aftermath of Empire*. Cambridge: Cambridge University Press. http://dx.doi.org/10.1017/CBO9780511757815.

McBrearty, S. 1990. "Consider the Humble Termite: Termites as Agents of Post-
Depositional Disturbance at African Archaeological Sites." *Journal of Archaeological Science* 17 (2): 111–43. http://dx.doi.org/10.1016/0305-4403(90)90054-9.

McCarroll, Danny, Mary H. Gagen, Neil J. Loader, Iain Robertson, Kevin J. Anchu-
kaitis, Sietse Los, Giles H. F. Young, Risto Jalkanen, Andreas Kirchhefer, and John
S. Waterhouse. 2009. "Correction of Tree Ring Stable Carbon Isotope Chronolo-
gies for Changes in the Carbon Dioxide Content of the Atmosphere." *Geochimica
et Cosmochimica Acta* 73 (6): 1539–47. http://dx.doi.org/10.1016/j.gca.2008.11.041.

McCarroll, Danny, and Neil J. Loader. 2004. "Stable Isotopes in Tree Rings." *Quaternary Science Reviews* 23 (7–8): 771–801. http://dx.doi.org/10.1016/j.quascirev
.2003.06.017.

McClung de Tapia, Emily, Javier González Vázquez, Judith Zurita Noguera, and
Emilio Ibarra Morales. 1996. *La Domesticación Prehispánica de* Amaranthus.
Mexico City: Universidad Nacional Autónoma de México, Instituto de Investiga-
ciones Antropológicas.

McCobb, Lucy M. E., Derek E. G. Briggs, Wendy J. Carruthers, and Richard
P. Evershed. 2003. "Phosphatisation of Seeds and Roots in a Late Bronze Age
Deposit at Potterne, Wiltshire, UK." *Journal of Archaeological Science* 30 (10):
1269–81. http://dx.doi.org/10.1016/S0305-4403(03)00016-5.

McCobb, Lucy M. E., Derek E. G. Briggs, Richard P. Evershed, Allan R. Hall, and
Richard A. Hall. 2001. "Preservation of Fossil Seeds from a 10th Century AD Cess
Pit at Coppergate, York." *Journal of Archaeological Science* 28 (9): 929–40. http://
dx.doi.org/10.1006/jasc.2000.0617.

McConnell, Kathleen, and Sue O'Connor. 1997. "40,000 Year Record of Food Plants
in the Southern Kimberley Ranges, Western Australia." *Australian Archaeology*
45:20–31.

McCutchan, James H., William M. Lewis, Carol Kendall, and Claire C. McGrath. 2003. "Variation in Trophic Shift for Stable Isotope Ratios of Carbon, Nitrogen, and Sulfur." *Oikos* 102 (2): 378–90. http://dx.doi.org/10.1034/j.1600-0706.2003.12098.x.

McGill, Robert, John W. Tukey, and Wayne A. Larsen. 1978. "Variations of Box Plots." *American Statistician* 32:12–6.

McMeekin, Dorothy. 1992. "Representations on Pre-Columbian Spindle Whorls of the Floral and Fruit Structure of Economic Plants." *Economic Botany* 46 (2): 171–80. http://dx.doi.org/10.1007/BF02930633.

McNeil, Cameron, ed. 2009. *Chocolate in Mesoamerica: A Cultural History of Cacao.* Gainesville: University Press of Florida. http://dx.doi.org/10.5744/florida/97808 13029535.001.0001.

McNeil, Cameron L. 2003. *Paleobotanical Research at Copan.* Honduras: Foundation for the Advancement of Mesoamerican Studies, Inc.

McParland, Laura C., Margaret E. Collinson, Andrew C. Scott, Gill Campbell, and Robyn Veal. 2010. "Is Vitrification in Charcoal a Result of High Temperature Burning of Wood?" *Journal of Archaeological Science* 37 (10): 2679–87. http://dx.doi .org/10.1016/j.jas.2010.06.006.

Meigs, Anna S. 1997. "Food as a Cultural Construction." In *Food and Culture: A Reader*, 1st ed., edited by Carole Counihan and Penny Van Esterik, 95–106. New York: Routledge.

Meints, V. W., L. V. Boone, and L. T. Kurtz. 1975. "Natural [15]N Abundance in Soil, Leaves, and Grain as Influenced by Long Term Additions of Fertilizer N at Several Rates." *Journal of Environmental Quality* 4 (4): 486–90. http://dx.doi.org/10 .2134/jeq1975.00472425000400040013x.

Mellars, Paul A. 1976. "Fire Ecology, Animal Populations, and Man." *Proceedings of the Prehistoric Society* 4:15–45.

Mennell, Stephen. 1997. "On the Civilizing of Appetite." In *Food and Culture: A Reader*, 1st ed., edited by Carole Counihan and Penny Van Esterik, 315–37. New York: Routledge.

Menotti, Francesco. 2012. *Wetland Archaeology and Beyond: Theory and Practice.* Oxford: Oxford University Press. http://dx.doi.org/10.1093/oxfordhb/978019957 3493.001.0001.

Messner, Timothy C. 2008. *Woodland Period People and Plant Interactions: New Insights from Starch Grain Analysis.* Philadelphia, PA: Temple University.

Messner, Timothy C. 2011. *Acorns and Bitter Roots: Starch Grain Research in the Prehistoric Eastern Woodlands.* Tuscaloosa: University of Alabama Press.

Messner, Timothy C., and Bill Schindler. 2010. "Plant Processing Strategies and Their Affect Upon Starch Grain Survival When Rendering *Peltandra virginica*

(L.) Kunth, Araceae Edible." *Journal of Archaeological Science* 37 (2): 328–36. http://dx.doi.org/10.1016/j.jas.2009.09.044.

Metcalfe, Duncan, and K. Renee Barlow. 1992. "A Model for Exploring the Optimal Trade-Off between Field Processing and Transport." *American Anthropologist* 94 (2): 340–56. http://dx.doi.org/10.1525/aa.1992.94.2.02a00040.

Metges, C., K. Kempe, and H. L. Schmidt. 1990. "Dependence of the Carbon-Isotope Contents of Breath Carbon Dioxide, Milk, Serum and Rumen Fermentation Products on the $\delta^{13}C$ Value of Food in Dairy Cows." *British Journal of Nutrition* 63 (02): 187–96. http://dx.doi.org/10.1079/BJN19900106.

Michel, J. B., Y. K. Shen, A. P. Aiden, A. Veres, M. K. Gray, J. P. Pickett, D. Hoiberg, D. Clancy, P. Norvig, J. Orwant, S. Pinker, M. A. Nowak, and E. Lieberman Aiden. 2011. "Quantitative Analysis of Culture Using Millions of Digitized Books." *Science* 331 (6014): 176–82. http://dx.doi.org/10.1126/science.1199644.

Miksicek, Charles H. 1987. "Formation Processes of the Archaeological Record." In *Advances in Archaeological Method and Theory*, vol. 10, edited by Michael B. Schiffer, 211–47. New York: Academic Press.

Miksicek, Charles H., Kathryn J. Elsesser, Ingrid A. Wuebber, Karen Olsen Bruhns, and Norman Hammond. 1981. "Rethinking Ramon—a Comment on Reina and Hill Lowland Maya Subsistence." *American Antiquity* 46 (4): 916–19. http://dx.doi.org/10.2307/280117.

Miles, David, Simon Palmer, Alex Smith, and Grace Jones. 2007. *Iron Age and Roman Settlement in the Upper Thames Valley: Cotswold Water Park Excavations at Claydon Pike and Other Sites within the Cotswold Water Park*. Thames Valley Landscapes Monograph, no. 26. Oxford: University School of Archaeology and Oxford Archaeology.

Millard, Peter, Andrew J. Midwood, John E. Hunt, Margaret M. Barbour, and David Whitehead. 2010. "Quantifying the Contribution of Soil Organic Matter Turnover to Forest Soil Respiration, Using Natural Abundance $\delta^{13}C$." *Soil Biology & Biochemistry* 42 (6): 935–43. http://dx.doi.org/10.1016/j.soilbio.2010.02.010.

Miller, Melanie J., José M. Capriles, and Christine A. Hastorf. 2010. "The Fish of Lake Titicaca: Implications for Archaeology and Changing Ecology through Stable Isotope Analysis." *Journal of Archaeological Science* 37 (2): 317–27. http://dx.doi.org/10.1016/j.jas.2009.09.043.

Miller, Naomi F. 1984. "The Use of Dung as Fuel: An Ethnographic Example and an Archaeological Application." *Paléorient* 10 (2): 71–79. http://dx.doi.org/10.3406/paleo.1984.941.

Miller, Naomi F. 1985. "Paleoethnobotanical Evidence for Deforestation in Ancient Iran: A Case Study of Urban Malyan." *Journal of Ethnobiology* 5:1–21.

Miller, Naomi F. 1988. "Ratios in Paleoethnobotanical Analysis." In *Current Paleo-ethnobotany: Analytical Methods and Cultural Interpretations of Archaeological Plant Remains*, edited by Christine A. Hastorf and Virginia S. Popper, 72–96. Chicago: University of Chicago Press.

Miller, Naomi F. 1989. "What Mean These Seeds: A Comparative Approach to Archaeological Seed Analysis." *Historical Archaeology* 23 (2): 50–59.

Miller, Naomi F. 1996. "Seed Eaters of the Ancient Near East: Human or Herbivore?" *Current Anthropology* 37 (3): 521–28. http://dx.doi.org/10.1086/204514.

Miller, Naomi F. 1997. "Farming and Herding Along the Euphrates: Environmental Constraint and Cultural Choice (Fourth to Second Millennia B.C.)." *MASCA Research Papers in Science and Archaeology* 14:123–32.

Miller, Naomi F. 1999. "Seeds, Charcoal and Archaeological Context: Interpreting Ancient Environment and Patterns of Land Use." *TÜBA-AR* 2:15–27.

Miller, Naomi F. 2000. "Plant Forms in Jewellery from the Royal Cemetery at Ur." *Iraq* 62:149–55.

Miller, Naomi F. 2010a. *Archaeobotany Questionnaire Preliminary Results. MASCA Ethnobotanical Lab Report 49.* University of Pennsylvania Museum.

Miller, Naomi F. 2010b. *Botanical Aspects of Environment and Economy at Gordion, Turkey.* Philadelphia: University of Pennsylvania Museum.

Miller, Naomi F. 2011a. "Archaeobotanical Methodology: Results of an Archaeo-botany Questionnaire." *SAA Archaeological Record* 11 (4): 8–10.

Miller, Naomi F. 2011b. "Managing Predictable Unpredictability: The Question of Agricultural Sustainability at Gordion." In *Sustainable Lifeways: Cultural Persistence in an Ever-Changing Environment*, edited by Naomi F. Miller, Katherine M. Moore, and Kathleen Ryan, 310–24. Philadelphia: University of Pennsylvania Museum Press.

Miller, Naomi F. 2013. "Symbols of Fertility and Abundance in the Royal Cemetery at Ur, Iraq." *American Journal of Archaeology* 117 (1): 127–33. http://dx.doi.org/10.3764/aja.117.1.0127.

Miller, Naomi F., and Kathryn L. Gleason. 1994. "Fertilizer in the Identification and Analysis of Cultivated Soil." In *The Archaeology of Garden and Field*, edited by Naomi F. Miller and Kathryn L. Gleason, 25–43. Philadelphia, Pennsylvania: University of Pennsylvania Press.

Miller, Naomi F., and John M. Marston. 2012. "Archaeological Fuel Remains as Indicators of Ancient West Asian Agropastoral and Land-Use Systems." *Journal of Arid Environments* 86:97–103. http://dx.doi.org/10.1016/j.jaridenv.2011.11.021.

Miller, Naomi F., and Tristine Lee Smart. 1984. "Intentional Burning of Dung as Fuel: A Mechanism for the Incorporation of Charred Seeds into the Archeological Record." *Journal of Ethnobiology* 4:15–28.

Miller, Naomi F., Melinda A. Zeder, and Susan R. Arter. 2009. "From Food and Fuel to Farms and Flocks: The Integration of Plant and Animal Remains in the Study of the Agropastoral Economy at Gordion, Turkey." *Current Anthropology* 50 (6): 915–24. http://dx.doi.org/10.1086/606035.

Miller, Webb, Daniela I. Drautz, Aakrosh Ratan, Barbara Pusey, Ji Qi, Arthur M. Lesk, Lynn P. Tomsho, Michael D. Packard, Fangqing Zhao, Andrei Sher, Alexei Tikhonov, Brian Raney, Nick Patterson, Kerstin Lindblad-Toh, Eric S. Lander, James R. Knight, Gerard P. Irzyk, Karin M. Fredrikson, Timothy T. Harkins, Sharon Sheridan, Tom Pringle. and Stephan C. Schuster. 2008. "Sequencing the Nuclear Genome of the Extinct Woolly Mammoth." *Nature* 456 (7220): 387–90. http://dx.doi.org/10.1038/nature07446.

Minagawa, Masao, and Eitaro Wada. 1984. "Stepwise Enrichment of ^{15}N Along Food-Chains: Further Evidence and the Relation between $\delta^{15}N$ and Animal Age." *Geochimica et Cosmochimica Acta* 48 (5): 1135–40. http://dx.doi.org/10.1016/0016-7037(84)90204-7.

Minnis, Paul. 2010. "Ancient Anthropogenic Ecology: Beyond the Past." In *The Archaeology of Anthropogenic Environments*, edited by R. M. Dean, 373–79. Carbondale: Center for Archaeological Investigations, Southern Illinois University.

Minnis, Paul E. 1981. "Seeds in Archaeological Sites: Sources and Some Interpretive Problems." *American Antiquity* 46 (1): 143–52. http://dx.doi.org/10.2307/279993.

Minnis, Paul E. 2003. *People and Plants in Ancient Eastern North America*. Washington, DC: Smithsonian Institution Press.

Minnis, Paul E. 2004. *People and Plants in Ancient Western North America*. Washington, DC: Smithsonian Institution Press.

Moffett, Lisa. 1988. "Charred Seeds and Crop Remains from the Iron Age Enclosure." In *The Rollright Stones: Megaliths, Monuments, and Settlement in the Prehistoric Landscape*, edited by George H. Lambrick, 103–5. Archaeological Report 6. London: English Heritage.

Monckton, S. G. 2002. "Plant Remains." In *The Excavations of San Giovanni di Ruoti: Vol. 3: The Faunal and Plant Remains*, edited by Michael R. MacKinnon, 201–6. Toronto: University of Toronto Press.

Monk, Michael. 2007. *Environmental Sampling: Guidelines for Archaeologists. Compiled by the Environmental Sub-Committee*. Dublin: Institute of Archaeologists of Ireland.

Monk, M. A., and J. Peter Fasham. 1980. "Carbonised Plant Remains from Two Iron Age Sites in Central Hampshire." *Proceedings of the Prehistoric Society* 46:321–44.

Monroe, Cara, Colin Grier, and Brian M. Kemp. 2013. "Evaluating the Efficacy of Various Thermo-Stable Polymerases against Co-Extracted PCR Inhibitors in

Ancient DNA Samples." *Forensic Science International* 228 (1–3): 142–53. http://
dx.doi.org/10.1016/j.forsciint.2013.02.029.

Moore, Andrew M. T., Gordon C. Hillman, and Anthony J. Legge. 2000. *Village on
the Euphrates: From Foraging to Farming at Abu Hureyra.* London: Oxford University Press.

Moore, Peter D., and Judith A. Webb. 1978. *An Illustrated Guide to Pollen Analysis.*
New York: Wiley.

Moore, Peter D., Judith A. Webb, and Margaret E. Collinson. 1991. *Pollen Analysis.*
2nd ed. Oxford: Blackwell Scientific Publications.

Morehart, Christopher T., and Dan T. A. Eisenberg. 2010. "Prosperity, Power, and
Change: Modeling Maize at Postclassic Xaltocan, Mexico." *Journal of Anthropological Archaeology* 29 (1): 94–112.

Morehart, Christopher T., David L. Lentz, and Keith M. Prufer. 2005. "Wood of the
Gods: The Ritual Use of Pine (*Pinus* spp.) by the Ancient Lowland Maya." *Latin
American Antiquity* 16 (3): 255–74. http://dx.doi.org/10.2307/30042493.

Morell-Hart, Shanti. 2011. "Paradigms and Syntagms of Ethnobotanical Practice in
Pre-Hispanic Northwestern Honduras." PhD diss., Anthropology, University of
California, Berkeley.

Morris, Lesley R., Ronald J. Ryel, and Neil E. West. 2010. "Can Soil Phytolith
Analysis and Charcoal Be Used as Indicators of Historic Fire in the Pinyon-Juniper and Sagebrush Steppe Ecosystem Types of the Great Basin Desert, USA?" *The
Holocene* 20 (1): 105–14. http://dx.doi.org/10.1177/0959683609348858.

Moss, Madonna L. 2013. "Fishing Traps and Weirs on the Northwest Coast of North
America: New Approaches and New Insights." In *The Oxford Handbook of Wetland
Archaeology,* edited by Francesco Menotti and Aidan O'Sullivan, 323–37. Oxford:
Oxford University Press. http://dx.doi.org/10.1093/oxfordhb/9780199573493.013
.0020.

Moss, Madonna L., Jon M. Erlandson, and Robert Stuckenrath. 1990. "Wood Stake
Weirs and Salmon Fishing on the Northwest Coast: Evidence from Southeast
Alaska." *Canadian Journal of Archaeology* 14:143–58.

Motta, Laura. 2002. "Planting the Seed of Rome." *Vegetation History and Archaeobotany* 11 (1–2): 71–78. http://dx.doi.org/10.1007/s003340200008.

Moulherat, Christophe, Margareta Tengberg, Jérôme-F. Haquet, and Benoît Mille.
2002. "First Evidence of Cotton at Neolithic Mehrgarh, Pakistan: Analysis of
Mineralized Fibres from a Copper Bead." *Journal of Archaeological Science* 29 (12):
1393–401. http://dx.doi.org/10.1006/jasc.2001.0779.

Mrozowski, Stephen A., Maria Franklin, and Leslie Hunt. 2008. "Archaeobotanical Analysis and Interpretations of Enslaved Virginian Plant Use at Rich Neck
Plantation (44WB52)." *American Antiquity* 73 (4): 699–728.

Muir, Jeff, and Mark Roberts. 1999. *Excavations at Wyndyke Furlong, Abingdon, Oxfordshire, 1994*. Oxford: Oxford Archaeological Unit.

Mulholland, Susan. 1989. "Phytolith Shape Frequencies in North Dakota Grasses: A Comparison to General Patterns." *Journal of Archaeological Science* 16 (5): 489–511. http://dx.doi.org/10.1016/0305-4403(89)90070-8.

Mullins, H. T., W. P. Patterson, M. A. Teece, and A. W. Burnett. 2011. "Holocene Climate and Environmental Change in Central New York (USA)." *Journal of Paleolimnology* 45 (2): 243–56. http://link.springer.com/article/10.1007%2Fs10933 -011-9495-z#page-1.

Munoz, Samuel E., and Konrad Gajewski. 2010. "Distinguishing Prehistoric Human Influence on Late-Holocene Forests in Southern Ontario, Canada." *The Holocene* 20 (6): 967–81. http://dx.doi.org/10.1177/0959683610362815.

Munoz, Samuel E., Konrad Gajewski, and Matthew C. Peros. 2010. "Synchronous Environmental and Cultural Change in the Prehistory of the Northeastern United States." *Proceedings of the National Academy of Sciences of the United States of America* 107 (51): 22008–13. http://dx.doi.org/10.1073/pnas.1005764107.

Munson, Patrick. 1986. "Hickory Silviculture: A Subsistence Revolution in the Pre-history of Eastern North America." Paper presented at the Conference on Emergent Horticultural Economies of the Eastern Woodlands, Carbondale, Illinois.

Munson, Patrick J. 1984. *Experiments and Observations on Aboriginal Wild Plant Food Utilization in Eastern North America*. Indianapolis: Indiana Historical Society.

Murphy, Peter. 1991. "Cereals and Crop Weeds," in "Asheldham Camp—an Early Iron Age Hill Fort: The 1985 Excavations," by Owen Bedwin. *Essex Archaeology and History* 22:13–37 (31–35).

Murray, Shawn Sabrina. 2005. "The Rise of African Rice Farming and the Economic Use of Plants in the Upper Middle Niger Delta (Mali)." Unpublished PhD diss., Department of Anthropology, University of Wisconsin-Madison, Madison.

Myles, Sean, Adam R. Boyko, Christopher L. Owens, Patrick J. Brown, Fabrizio Grassi, Mallikarjuna K. Aradhya, Bernard Prins, Andy Reynolds, Jer-Ming Chia, Doreen Ware, Carlos D. Bustamante, and Edward S. Buckler. 2011. "Genetic Structure and Domestication History of the Grape." *Proceedings of the National Academy of Sciences of the United States of America* 108 (9): 3530–35. http://dx.doi.org /10.1073/pnas.1009363108.

Nadelhoffer, K. J., and B. Fry. 1988. "Controls on Natural Nitrogen–15 and Carbon–13 Abundances in Forest Soil Organic-Matter." *Soil Science Society of America Journal* 52 (6): 1633–40. http://dx.doi.org/10.2136/sssaj1988.03615995005200060024x.

Nanson, G. C., and J. C. Croke. 1992. "A Genetic Classification of Floodplains." *Geomorphology* 4 (6): 459–86. http://dx.doi.org/10.1016/0169-555X(92)90039-Q.

National Science Foundation. 2011a. "Dissemination and Sharing of Research Results." Accessed December 11, 2011. http://www.nsf.gov/bfa/dias/policy/dmp.jsp.

National Science Foundation. 2011b. Senior Archaeology Award Info. Accessed December 11, 2011. http://www.nsf.gov/sbe/bcs/arch/senior.jsp.

Neef, Reinder. 1990. "Introduction, Development and Environmental Implications of Olive Culture: The Evidence from Jordan." In *Man's Role in the Shaping of the Eastern Mediterranean Landscape*, edited by S. Bottema, G. Entjes-Nieborg, and W. van Zeist, 295–306. Rotterdam: A.A. Balkema.

Neef, Reinder, René T. J. Cappers, Renée M. Bekker, and Loutfy Boulos. 2012. *Digital Atlas of Economic Plants in Archaeology*. Groningen: Barkhuis and Groningen University Library.

Neff, Hector, Deborah M. Pearsall, John G. Jones, Bárbara Arroyo, Shawn K. Collins, and Dorothy E. Friedel. 2006. "Early Maya Adaptive Patterns: Mid-Late Holocene Paleoenvironmental Evidence from Pacific Guatemala." *Latin American Antiquity* 17 (3): 287–315. http://dx.doi.org/10.2307/25063054.

Nelson, J. G. 1966. "Man and Geomorphic Process in the Chemung River Valley, New York and Pennsylvania." *Annals of the Association of American Geographers* 56 (1): 24–32. http://dx.doi.org/10.1111/j.1467-8306.1966.tb00541.x.

Nesbitt, Mark. 2006. *Identification Guide for Near Eastern Grass Seeds*. London: Institute of Archaeology, University College London.

Nesbitt, Mark, Sue Colledge, and Mary Anne Murray. 2003. "Organisation and Management of Seed Reference Collections." *Environmental Archaeology* 8: 77–84.

Nesbitt, Mark, and James Greig. 1989. "A Bibliography for the Archaeobotanical Identification of Seeds from Europe and the Near East." *Circaea* 7 (1): 11–30.

Nesbitt, Mark, Rory P. H. McBurney, Melanie Broin, and Henk J. Beentje. 2010. "Linking Biodiversity, Food and Nutrition: The Importance of Plant Identification and Nomenclature." *Journal of Food Composition and Analysis* 23 (6): 486–98. http://dx.doi.org/10.1016/j.jfca.2009.03.001.

Nesbitt, Mark, and Delwen Samuel. 1996. "From Staple Crop to Extinction? The Archaeology and History of the Hulled Wheats." In *Hulled Wheats: Proceedings of the First International Workshop on Hulled Wheats, 21–22 July 1995, Castelvecchio Pascoli, Tuscany, Italy*, edited by Stefano Padulosi, Karl Hammer, and Joachim Heller, 41–101. International Plant Genetic Resources Institute, Rome.

Netting, Robert McC., Richard R. Wilk, and Eric J. Arnould. 1984. "Introduction: Comparative and Historical Studies of the Domestic Group." In *Households: Comparative and Historical Studies of the Domestic Group*, edited by Robert McC. Netting, Richard R. Wilk, and Eric J. Arnould, xiii–xxxviii. Berkeley: University of California Press.

Neumann, Katharina. 1999. "Charcoal from West African Savanna Sites: Questions of Identification and Interpretation." In *The Exploitation of Plant Resources in Ancient Africa*, edited by Marijke van der Veen, 205–19. New York: Kluwer Academic. http://dx.doi.org/10.1007/978-1-4757-6730-8_17.

Neumann, Katharina, Ann Butler, and Stefanie Kahlheber, eds. 2003. *Food, Fuel and Fields: Progress in African Archaeobotany*. Köln: Heinrich-Barth-Institut.

Nevle, R. J., D. K. Bird, W. F. Ruddiman, and R. A. Dull. 2011. "Neotropical Human-Landscape Interactions, Fire, and Atmospheric CO_2 During European Conquest." *The Holocene* 21 (5): 853–64.

Newsom, Lee A., and Barbara A. Purdy. 1990. "Florida Canoes: A Maritime Heritage from the Past." *Florida Anthropologist* 43:164–80.

Newsom, S. W. B., and Peggy Shaw. 1997a. "Airborne Particles from Latex Gloves in the Hospital Environment." *European Journal of Surgery Supplement* 579:31–33.

Newsom, S. W. B., and M. Shaw. 1997b. "A Survey of Starch Particle Counts in the Hospital Environment in Relation to the Use of Powdered Latex Gloves." *Occupational Medicine* 47 (3): 155–58. http://dx.doi.org/10.1093/occmed/47.3.155.

Newsome, J. 1988. "Late Quaternary Vegetational History of the Central Highlands of Sumatra. I: Present Vegetation and Modern Pollen Rain." *Journal of Biogeography* 15 (2): 363–86. http://dx.doi.org/10.2307/2845418.

Nielsen-Marsh, Christina M., Peggy H. Ostrom, Hasand Gandhi, Beth Shapiro, Alan Cooper, Peter V. Hauschka, and Matthew J. Collins. 2002. "Sequence Preservation of Osteocalcin Protein and Mitochondrial DNA in Bison Bones Older Than 55 ka." *Geology* 30 (12): 1099–102. http://dx.doi.org/10.1130/0091-7613(2002)030<1099:SPOOPA>2.0.CO;2.

Nielsen-Marsh, Christina M., Michael P. Richards, Peter V. Hauschka, Jane E. Thomas-Oates, Erik Trinkaus, Paul B. Pettitt, Ivor Karavanic, Hendrik Poinar, and Matthew J. Collins. 2005. "Osteocalcin Protein Sequences of Neanderthals and Modern Primates." *Proceedings of the National Academy of Sciences of the United States of America* 102 (12): 4409–13. http://dx.doi.org/10.1073/pnas.0500450102.

Nikon Corporation. 2006. "Nikon Prepares to Strengthen Digital Line-up for 2006." Nikon Press Release. Accessed November 26, 2011. http://www.nikon.co.uk/press_room/releases/show.aspx?rid=201 (site discontinued).

Nilsson, Siwert T., and Joseph Praglowski, eds. 1992. *Erdtman's Handbook of Palynology*. 2nd ed. Copenhagen: Munksgaard.

Nishida, Masaki. 1983. "The Emergence of Food Production in Neolithic Japan." *Journal of Anthropological Archaeology* 2 (4): 305–22. http://dx.doi.org/10.1016/0278-4165(83)90012-0.

Nixon, Sam, Mary Anne Murray, and Dorian Q Fuller. 2011. "Plant Use at an Early Islamic Merchant Town in the West African Sahel: The Archaeobotany of Essouk-Tadmakka (Mali)." *Vegetation History and Archaeobotany* 20 (3): 223–39. http://dx.doi.org/10.1007/s00334-010-0279-6.

Nobel, Park S. 1994. *Remarkable Agaves and Cacti.* New York: Oxford University Press.

Nordt, Lee C. 2001. "Stable Carbon and Oxygen Isotopes in Soils." In *Earth Sciences and Archaeology*, edited by Paul Goldberg, Vance T. Holliday, and C. Reid Ferring, 419–48. New York: Kluwer Academic/Plenum Publishers. http://dx.doi.org/10.1007/978-1-4615-1183-0_15.

Nordt, Lee C., Thomas W. Boutton, Charles T. Hallmark, and Michael R. Waters. 1994. "Late Quaternary Vegetation and Climate Changes in Central Texas Based on the Isotopic Composition of Organic-Carbon." *Quaternary Research* 41 (1): 109–20. http://dx.doi.org/10.1006/qres.1994.1012.

Nordt, Lee C., Thomas W. Boutton, John S. Jacob, and Rolfe D. Mandel. 2002. "C-4 Plant Productivity and Climate-CO2 Variations in South-Central Texas During the Late Quaternary." *Quaternary Research* 58 (2): 182–88. http://dx.doi.org/10.1006/qres.2002.2344.

Nordt, Lee C., Joseph von Fischer, and Larry L. Tieszen. 2007. "Late Quaternary Temperature Record from Buried Soils of the North American Great Plains." *Geology* 35 (2): 159–62. http://dx.doi.org/10.1130/G23345A.1.

Nordt, Lee C., Joseph von Fischer, Larry L. Tieszen, and J. Tubbs. 2008. "Coherent Changes in Relative C4 Plant Productivity and Climate During the Late Quaternary in the North American Great Plains." *Quaternary Science Reviews* 27 (15–16): 1600–11. http://dx.doi.org/10.1016/j.quascirev.2008.05.008.

Norr, Lynette. 1991. "Nutritional Consequences of Prehistoric Subsistence Strategies in Lower Central America." Unpublished PhD diss., Department of Anthropology, University of Illinois, Urbana-Champaign.

Norr, Lynette. 1995. "Interpreting Dietary Maize from Bone Stable Isotopes in the American Tropics: The State of the Art." In *Archaeology in the Lowland American Tropics*, edited by P. Stahl, 198–223. New York: Cambridge University Press. http://dx.doi.org/10.1017/CBO9780511521188.010.

Novak, Jan, Libor Petr, and Václav Treml. 2010. "Late-Holocene Human-Induced Changes to the Extent of Alpine Areas in the East Sudetes, Central Europe." *The Holocene* 20 (6): 895–905. http://dx.doi.org/10.1177/0959683610365938.

O'Leary, Marion H. 1988. "Carbon Isotopes in Photosynthesis." *Bioscience* 38 (5): 328–36. http://dx.doi.org/10.2307/1310735.

O'Donoghue, Kerry, Terence A. Brown, James F. Carter, and Richard P. Evershed. 1994. "Detection of Nucleotide Bases in Ancient Seeds Using Gas Chromatography/Mass Spectrometry and Gas Chromatography/Mass Spectrometry/Mass Spectrometry." *Rapid Communications in Mass Spectrometry* 8 (7): 503–8. http://dx.doi.org/10.1002/rcm.1290080702.

O'Donoghue, Kerry, Terence A. Brown, James F. Carter, and Richard P. Evershed. 1996. "Application of High Performance Liquid Chromatography/Mass Spectrometry with Electrospray Ionization to the Detection of DNA Nucleosides in Ancient Seeds." *Rapid Communications in Mass Spectrometry* 10 (5): 495–500. http://http://10.1002 /(SICI)1097-0231(19960331)10:5%3C495::AID-RCM492%3E3.0.CO;2-D.

O'Donoghue, Kerry, Alan J. Clapham, Richard P. Evershed, and Terence A. Brown. 1996. "Remarkable Preservation of Biomolecules in Ancient Radish Seeds." *Proceedings of the Royal Society B: Biological Sciences* 263 (1370): 541–47. http://dx.doi. org/10.1098/rspb.1996.0082.

Odenbaugh, Jay. 2005. "Idealized, Inaccurate but Successful: A Pragmatic Approach to Evaluating Models in Theoretical Ecology." *Biology and Philosophy* 20 (2–3): 231–55. http://dx.doi.org/10.1007/s10539-004-0478-6.

Odling-Smee, F. John, Kevin N. Laland, and Marcus W. Feldman. 2003. *Niche Construction: The Neglected Process in Evolution.* Princeton: Princeton University Press.

Oeggl, Klaus. 2009. "The Significance of the Tyrolean Iceman for the Archaeobotany of Central Europe." *Vegetation History and Archaeobotany* 18 (1): 1–11. http://dx.doi .org/10.1007/s00334-008-0186-2.

Oeggl, Klaus, Werner Kofler, Alexandra Schmidl, James H. Dickson, Eduard Egarter-Vigl, and Othmar Gaber. 2007. "The Reconstruction of the Last Itinerary of 'Ötzi,' the Neolithic Iceman, by Pollen Analyses from Sequentially Sampled Gut Extracts." *Quaternary Science Reviews* 26 (7–8): 853–61. http://dx.doi.org/10.1016 /j.quascirev.2006.12.007.

Ollendorf, Amy L. 1987. "Archaeological Implications of a Phytolith Study at Tel Miqne (Ekron), Israel." *Journal of Field Archaeology* 14 (4): 453–63. http://dx.doi .org/10.1179/jfa.1987.14.4.453.

Olsen, K. M., and B. A. Schaal. 1999. "Evidence on the Origin of Cassava: Phylogeography of *Manihot esculenta*." *Proceedings of the National Academy of Sciences of the United States of America* 96 (10): 5586–91. http://dx.doi.org/10.1073/pnas.96.10 .5586.

Orians, Gordon H., and Nolan E. Pearson. 1979. "On the Theory of Central Place Foraging." In *Analysis of Ecological Systems*, edited by D. J. Horn, B. R. Stairs, and R. D. Mitchell, 155–77. Columbus: Ohio State University Press.

Orlando, Ludovic, Aurelien Ginolhac, Maanasa Raghavan, Julia Vilstrup, Morten Rasmussen, Kim Magnussen, Kathleen E. Steinmann, Philipp Kapranov, John F. Thompson, Grant Zazula, Duane Froese, Ida Moltke, Beth Shapiro, Michael Hofreiter, Khaled A.S. Al-Rasheid, M. Thomas P. Gilbert, and Eske Willerslev. 2011. "True Single-Molecule DNA Sequencing of a Pleistocene Horse Bone." *Genome Research* 21 (10): 1705–19. http://dx.doi.org/10.1101/gr.122747.111.

Osmund, C. B., W. G. Allaway, B. G. Sutton, J. H. Troughton, O. Queiroz, U. Lüttge, and K. Winter. 1973. "Carbon Isotope Discrimination in Photosynthesis of CAM Plants." *Nature* 246 (5427): 41–42. http://dx.doi.org/10.1038/246041a0.

Oyuela-Caycedo, Augusto. 2010. "The Forest as a Fragmented Archaeological Artifact." In *The Archaeology of Anthropogenic Environments*, edited by Rebecca M. Dean, 75–94. Carbondale: Center for Archaeological Investigations, Southern Illinois University.

Pääbo, Svante, Russell G. Higuchi, and Allan C. Wilson. 1989. "Ancient DNA and the Polymerase Chain Reaction: The Emerging Field of Molecular Archaeology." *Journal of Biological Chemistry* 264 (17): 9709–12.

Paap, Norbert. 1983. "Economic Plants in Amsterdam: Qualitative and Quantitative Analysis." In *Integrating the Subsistence Economy. Symposia of the Association for Environmental Archaeology No. 4. BAR International Series 181*, edited by Martin Jones, 315–25. Oxford: British Archaeological Reports.

Paffetti, Donatella, Cristina Vettori, David Caramelli, Cristiano Vernesi, Martina Lari, Arturo Paganelli, Ladislav Paule, and Raffaello Giannini. 2007. "Unexpected Presence of *Fagus orientalis* Complex in Italy as Inferred from 45,000-Year-Old DNA Pollen Samples from Venice Lagoon." *BMC Evolutionary Biology* 7 (Suppl 2): S6. http://dx.doi.org/10.1186/1471-2148-7-S2-S6.

Palet, Josep Maria, and Hèctor A. Orengo. 2011. "The Roman Centuriated Landscape: Conception, Genesis, and Development as Inferred from the Ager Tarraconensis Case." *American Journal of Archaeology* 115 (3): 383–402. http://dx.doi.org/10.3764/aja.115.3.0383.

Palmer, Carol, and Martin K. Jones. 1991. "Plant Resources." In *Maiden Castle, Excavations and Field Survey 1985–6*, edited by Niall M. Sharples, 129–38. Archaeological Report no. 19. London: English Heritage.

Palmer, Sarah A., Alan J. Clapham, Pamela Rose, Fábio O. Freitas, Bruce D. Owen, David Beresford-Jones, Jonathan D. Moore, James L. Kitchen, and Robin G. Allaby. 2012. "Archaeogenomic Evidence of Punctuated Genome Evolution in *Gossypium*." *Molecular Biology and Evolution* 29 (8): 2031–38. http://dx.doi.org/10.1093/molbev/mss070.

Palmer, Sarah A., Jonathan D. Moore, Alan J. Clapham, Pamela Rose, and Robin G. Allaby. 2009. "Archaeogenetic Evidence of Ancient Nubian Barley Evolution from Six to Two-Row Indicates Local Adaptation." *PLoS ONE* 4 (7): e6301. http://dx.doi.org/10.1371/journal.pone.0006301.

Palmer, Sarah A., Oliver Smith, and Robin G. Allaby. 2012. "The Blossoming of Plant Archaeogenetics." *Annals of Anatomy* 194 (1): 146–56. http://dx.doi.org/10.1016/j.aanat.2011.03.012.

Panieri, G., S. Lugli, V. Manzi, M. Roveri, B. C. Schreiber, and K. A. Palinska. 2010. "Ribosomal RNA Gene Fragments from Fossilized Cyanobacteria Identified in Primary Gypsum from the Late Miocene, Italy." *Geobiology* 8 (2): 101–11. http://dx.doi.org/10.1111/j.1472-4669.2009.00230.x.

Parcak, Sarah H. 2009. *Satellite Remote Sensing for Archaeology*. London: Routledge.

Parducci, L., Y. Suyama, M. Lascoux, and K. D. Bennett. 2005. "Ancient DNA from Pollen: A Genetic Record of Population History in Scots Pine." *Molecular Ecology* 14 (9): 2873–82. http://dx.doi.org/10.1111/j.1365-294X.2005.02644.x.

Parker, Dawn C., Steven M. Manson, Marco A. Janssen, Matthew J. Hoffmann, and Peter Deadman. 2003. "Multi-Agent Systems for the Simulation of Land-Use and Land-Cover Change: A Review." *Annals of the Association of American Geographers* 93 (2): 314–37. http://dx.doi.org/10.1111/1467-8306.9302004.

Parker Pearson, Mike. 2003. "Food, Culture and Identity: An Introduction and Overview." In *Food, Culture and Identity in the Neolithic and Early Bronze Age*, edited by Mike Parker Pearson, 1–30. Oxford: British Archaeological Reports International Series.

Parrington, Michael, ed. 1978. *The Excavation of an Iron Age Settlement, Bronze Age Ring Ditches and Roman Features at Ashville Trading Estate, 1974–76*. Abingdon, Oxfordshire: Council for British Archaeology.

Passey, Benjamin H., Todd F. Robinson, Linda K. Ayliffe, Thure E. Cerling, Matt Sponheimer, M. Denise Dearing, Beverly L. Roeder, and James R. Ehleringer. 2005. "Carbon Isotope Fractionation between Diet, Breath CO_2, and Bioapatite in Different Mammals." *Journal of Archaeological Science* 32 (10): 1459–70. http://dx.doi.org/10.1016/j.jas.2005.03.015.

Pastore, Christopher L., Mark B. Green, Daniel J. Bain, Andrea Muñoz-Hernandez, Charles J. Vörösmarty, Jennifer Arrigo, Sara Brandt, Jonathan M. Duncan, Francesca Greco, Hyojin Kim, Sanjiv Kumar, Michael Lally, Anthony J. Parolari, Brian Pellerin, Nira Salant, Adam Schlosser, and Kake Zalzal. 2010. "Tapping Environmental History to Recreate America's Colonial Hydrology." *Environmental Science & Technology Feature* 44 (23): 8798–803. http://dx.doi.org/10.1021/es102672c.

Pauketat, Timothy R., Lucretia S. Kelly, Gayle J. Fritz, Neal H. Lopinot, Scott Elias, and Eve Hargrave. 2002. "The Residues of Feasting and Public Ritual at Early Cahokia." *American Antiquity* 67 (2): 257–79. http://dx.doi.org/10.2307/2694566.

Pauly, Daniel. 1995. "Anecdotes and the Shifting Baseline Syndrome of Fisheries." *Trends in Ecology & Evolution* 10 (10): 430. http://dx.doi.org/10.1016/S0169-5347(00)89171-5.

Peacock, Evan. 1993. "Reconstructing the Black Belt Environment Using Leaf Impressions in Daub." *Southeastern Archaeology* 12 (2): 148–54.

Pearsall, Deborah M. 1979. "The Application of Ethnobotanical Techniques to the Problem of Subsistence in the Ecuadorian Formative." Unpublished PhD diss., Department of Anthropology, University of Illinois, Urbana-Champaign.

Pearsall, Deborah M. 1983. "Evaluating the Stability of Subsistence Strategies by Use of Paleoethnobotanical Data." *Journal of Ethnobiology* 3 (2): 121–37.

Pearsall, Deborah M. 1988. "Interpreting the Meaning of Macroremain Abundance: The Impact of Source and Context." In *Current Paleoethnobotany: Analytical Methods and Cultural Interpretations of Archaeological Plant Remains*, edited by Christine A. Hastorf and Virginia S. Popper, 97–118. Chicago: University of Chicago Press.

Pearsall, Deborah M. 1989. *Paleoethnobotany: A Handbook of Procedures.* 1st ed. San Diego: Academic Press.

Pearsall, Deborah M. 2000. *Paleoethnobotany: A Handbook of Procedures.* 2nd ed. San Diego: Academic Press.

Pearsall, Deborah M. 2004. *Plants and People in Ancient Ecuador: The Ethnobotany of the Jama River Valley.* Case Studies in Archaeology. Belmont, CA: Wadsworth/ Thomson Learning.

Pearsall, Deborah M. 2007. "Modeling Prehistoric Agriculture through the Palaeoenvironmental Record: Theoretical and Methodological Issues." In *Rethinking Agriculture: Archaeological and Ethnoarchaeological Perspectives*, edited by Tim Denham, Jose Iriarte, and Luc Vrydaghs, 210–30. Walnut Creek: Left Coast Press.

Pearsall, Deborah M. 1982. "Phytolith Analysis: Applications of a New Paleoethnobotanical Technique in Archaeology." *American Anthropologist* 84 (4): 862–71. http://dx.doi.org/10.1525/aa.1982.84.4.02a00100.

Pearsall, Deborah M., Karol Chandler-Ezell, and James A. Zeidler. 2004. "Maize in Ancient Ecuador: Results of Residue Analysis of Stone Tools from the Real Alto Site." *Journal of Archaeological Science* 31 (4): 423–42. http://dx.doi.org/10.1016/j.jas .2003.09.010.

Pearsall, Deborah M., and Dolores R. Piperno, eds. 1993. *Current Research in Phytolith Analysis: Applications in Archaeology and Paleoecology.* Philadelphia: University of Pennsylvania Press.

Pearsall, Deborah M., and Michael K. Trimble. 1984. "Identifying Past Agricultural Activity through Soil Phytolith Analysis: A Case Study from the Hawaiian Islands." *Journal of Archaeological Science* 11 (2): 119–33. http://dx.doi.org/10.1016 /0305-4403(84)90047-5.

Peebles, Christopher S., and Susan M. Kus. 1977. "Some Archaeological Correlates of Ranked Societies." *American Antiquity* 42 (3): 421–48. http://dx.doi.org/10.2307 /279066.

Peña-Chocarro, Leonor. 1996. "In Situ Conservation of Hulled Wheat Species: The Case of Spain." In *Hulled Wheats: Proceedings of the First International Workshop on*

Hulled Wheats, 21–22 July 1995, Castelvecchio Pascoli, Tuscany, Italy, edited by Stefano Padulosi, Karl Hammer, and Joachim Heller, 128–46. Rome: International Plant Genetic Resources Institute.

Peña-Chocarro, Leonor, Lydia Zapata Peña, Jesús Emilio González-Urquijo, and Jose Ibáñez Estévez Juan. 2009. "Einkorn (*Triticum monococcum* L) Cultivation in Mountain Communities of the Western Rif (Morocco): An Ethnoarchaeological Project." In *From Foragers to Farmers: Papers in Honour of Gordon C. Hillman*, edited by Andy Fairbairn and Ehud Weiss, 103–11. Oxford: Oxbow Books.

Pendleton, Michael W. 1983. "A Comment Concerning "Testing Flotation Recovery Rates"." *American Antiquity* 48 (3): 615–16. http://dx.doi.org/10.2307/280570.

Peres, Tanya M. 2010. "Methodological Issues in Zooarchaeology." In *Integrating Zooarchaeology and Paleoethnobotany: A Consideration of Issues, Methods, and Cases*, edited by Amber M. VanDerwarker and Tanya M. Peres, 15–36. Berlin: Springer. http://dx.doi.org/10.1007/978-1-4419-0935-0_2.

Peres, Tanya M., Amber M. VanDerwarker, and Christopher A. Pool. 2010. "The Farmed and the Hunted: Integrating Floral and Faunal Data from Tres Zapotes, Veracruz." In *Integrating Zooarchaeology and Paleoethnobotany: A Consideration of Issues, Methods, and Cases*, edited by Amber M. VanDerwarker and Tanya M. Peres, 281–308. Berlin: Springer. http://dx.doi.org/10.1007/978-1-4419-0935-0_12.

Pérez, Serge, Paul M. Baldwin, and Daniel J. Gallant. 2009. "Structural Features of Starch Granules I." In *Starch: Chemistry and Technology*, edited by James N. BeMiller, and Roy L. Whistler, 149–92. San Diego, CA: Academic Press.

Pérez, Serge, and Eric Bertoft. 2010. "The Molecular Structures of Starch Components and Their Contribution to the Architecture of Starch Granules: A Comprehensive Review." *Stärke* 62 (8): 389–420. http://dx.doi.org/10.1002/star .201000013.

Peros, Matthew C., Samuel E. Munoz, Konrad Gajewski, and André E. Viau. 2010. "Prehistoric Demography of North America Inferred from Radiocarbon Data." *Journal of Archaeological Science* 37 (3): 656–64. http://dx.doi.org/10.1016/j.jas.2009 .10.029.

Perry, Linda. 2001. "Prehispanic Subsistence in the Middle Orinoco Basin: Starch Analyses Yield New Evidence." PhD diss., Department of Anthropology, Southern Illinois University at Carbondale, Carbondale, IL.

Perry, Linda. 2004. "Starch Analyses Reveal the Relationship between Tool Type and Function: An Example from the Orinoco Valley of Venezuela." *Journal of Archaeological Science* 31 (8): 1069–81. http://dx.doi.org/10.1016/j.jas.2004.01.002.

Perry, Linda. 2007. "Starch Remains, Preservation Biases and Plant Histories: An Example from Highland Peru." In *Rethinking Agriculture: Archaeological and*

Ethnoarchaeological Perspectives, edited by José Iriarte and Luc Vrydaghs, 241–55. Left Coast Press.

Perry, Linda, Ruth Dickau, Sonia Zarrillo, Irene Holst, Deborah M. Pearsall, Dolores Piperno, Mary Jane Berman, Richard G. Cooke, Kurt Rademaker, Anthony J. Ranere, J. Scott Raymond, Daniel H. Sandweiss, Franz Scaramelli, Kay Tarble, and James Zeidler. 2007. "Starch Fossils and the Domestication and Dispersal of Chili Peppers (*Capsicum* spp. L.) in the Americas." *Science* 315 (5814): 986–88. http://dx.doi.org/10.1126/science.1136914.

Petersen, James B., and Nancy Asch Sidell. 1996. "Mid-Holocene Evidence of *Cucurbita* sp. From Central Maine." *American Antiquity* 61 (4): 685–98. http://dx.doi.org /10.2307/282011.

Peterson, Bruce J., Robert W. Howarth, and Robert H. Garritt. 1986. "Sulfur and Carbon Isotopes as Tracers of Salt-Marsh Organic Matter Flow." *Ecology* 67 (4): 865–74. http://dx.doi.org/10.2307/1939809.

Peterson, Sarah E. 2009. "Retrieval of Materials with Water Separation Machines." *Instap Archaeological Excavation Manual 1*. Philadelphia: INSTAP Academic Press.

Petterson, J. S. 1988. "The Reality of Perception: Demonstrable Effects of Perceived Risk in Goiania, Brazil." *Practicing Anthropology* 10 (3–4): 8–12.

Philip, Graham, Maamoun Abdulkarim, Paul Newson, Anthony Beck, David Bridgland, Maryam Bshesh, Andrew Shaw, Rob Westaway, and Keith Wilkinson. 2005. "Settlement and Landscape Development in the Homs Region, Syria: Report on Work Undertaken During 2001–2003." *Levant* 37 (1): 21–42. http:// dx.doi.org/10.1179/lev.2005.37.1.21.

Philip, Graham, and Jennie Bradbury. 2010. "Pre-Classical Activity in the Basalt Landscape of the Homs Region, Syria: Implications for the Development of 'Sub-Optimal' Zones in the Levant During the Chalcolithic-Early Bronze Age." *Levant* 42 (2): 136–69. http://dx.doi.org/10.1179/175638010X12797237885659.

Phillips, Donald L., and Jillian W. Gregg. 2001. "Uncertainty in Source Partitioning Using Stable Isotopes." *Oecologia* 127 (2): 171–79. http://dx.doi.org/10.1007/s004420 000578.

Phillips, Donald L., and Paul L. Koch. 2002. "Incorporating Concentration Dependence in Stable Isotope Mixing Models." *Oecologia* 130 (1): 114–25.

Phillips, Donald L., Seth D. Newsome, and Jillian W. Gregg. 2005. "Combining Sources in Stable Isotope Mixing Models: Alternative Methods." *Oecologia* 144 (4): 520–27. http://dx.doi.org/10.1007/s00442-004-1816-8.

Pinnegar, J. K., and N. V. C. Polunin. 1999. "Differential Fractionation of $\delta^{13}C$ and $\delta^{15}N$ among Fish Tissues: Implications for the Study of Trophic Interactions." *Functional Ecology* 13 (2): 225–31. http://dx.doi.org/10.1046/j.1365-2435.1999.00301.x.

Piperno, Dolores R. 1985. "Phytolith Taphonomy and Distributions in Archaeological Sediments from Panama." *Journal of Archaeological Science* 12 (4): 247–67. http://dx.doi.org/10.1016/0305-4403(85)90032-9.

Piperno, Dolores R. 1988. *Phytolith Analysis: An Archaeological and Geological Perspective*. San Diego: Academic Press.

Piperno, Dolores R. 1991. "The Status of Phytolith Analysis in the American Tropics." *Journal of World Prehistory* 5 (2): 155–91. http://dx.doi.org/10.1007/BF00974678.

Piperno, Dolores R. 1995. "Plant Microfossils and Their Application in the New World Tropics." In *Archaeology in the Lowland American Tropics: Current Analytical Methods and Recent Applications*, edited by Peter W. Stahl, 130–53. Cambridge: Cambridge University Press. http://dx.doi.org/10.1017/CBO9780511521188.007.

Piperno, Dolores R. 2006a. "The Origins of Plant Cultivation and Domestication in the Neotropics: A Behavioral Ecology Perspective." In *Behavioral Ecology and the Transition to Agriculture*, edited by Douglas J. Kennett and Bruce Winterhalder, 137–66. Berkeley: University of California Press.

Piperno, Dolores R. 2006b. *Phytoliths: A Comprehensive Guide for Archaeologists and Paleoecologists*. Lanham, MD: AltaMira Press.

Piperno, Dolores R. 2009. "Identifying Crop Plants with Phytoliths (and Starch Grains) in Central and South America: A Review and an Update of the Evidence." *Quaternary International* 193 (1–2): 146–59. http://dx.doi.org/10.1016/j.quaint.2007.11.011.

Piperno, Dolores R., Mark B. Bush, and Paul A. Colinvaux. 1991a. "Palaeoecological Perspectives on Human Adaptation in Central Panama, I: The Pleistocene." *Geoarchaeology: An International Journal* 6 (3): 201–26. http://dx.doi.org/10.1002/gea.3340060301.

Piperno, Dolores R., Mark B. Bush, and Paul A. Colinvaux. 1991b. "Palaeoecological Perspectives on Human Adaptation in Central Panama, II: The Holocene." *Geoarchaeology: An International Journal* 6 (3): 227–50. http://dx.doi.org/10.1002/gea.3340060302.

Piperno, Dolores R., and Tom D. Dillehay. 2008. "Starch Grains on Human Teeth Reveal Early Broad Crop Diet in Northern Peru." *Proceedings of the National Academy of Sciences of the United States of America* 105 (50): 19622–27. http://dx.doi.org/10.1073/pnas.0808752105.

Piperno, Dolores R., and Irene Holst. 1998. "The Presence of Starch Grains on Prehistoric Stone Tools from the Humid Neotropics: Indications of Early Tuber Use and Agriculture in Panama." *Journal of Archaeological Science* 25 (8): 765–76. http://dx.doi.org/10.1006/jasc.1997.0258.

Piperno, Dolores R., and John G. Jones. 2003. "Paleoecological and Archaeological Implications of a Late Pleistocene/Early Holocene Record of Vegetation and Climate from the Pacific Coastal Plain of Panama." *Quaternary Research* 59 (1): 79–87. http://dx.doi.org/10.1016/S0033-5894(02)00021-2.

Piperno, Dolores R., J. E. Moreno, Jose Iriarte, Irene Holst, M. Lachniet, John G. Jones, A. J. Ranere, and R. Castanzo. 2007. "Late Pleistocene and Holocene Environmental History of the Iguala Valley, Central Balsas Watershed of Mexico." *Proceedings of the National Academy of Sciences of the United States of America* 104 (29): 11874–81. http://dx.doi.org/10.1073/pnas.0703442104.

Piperno, Dolores R., and Deborah M. Pearsall. 1998a. *The Origins of Agriculture in the Lowland Neotropics.* San Diego: Academic Press.

Piperno, Dolores R., and Deborah M. Pearsall. 1998b. *The Silica Bodies of Tropical American Grasses: Morphology, Taxonomy, and Implications for Grass Systematics and Fossil Phytolith Identification.* Smithsonian Contributions to Botany, no. 85.

Piperno, Dolores R., Anthony J. Ranere, Irene Holst, and Patricia Hansell. 2000. "Starch Grains Reveal Early Root Crop Horticulture in the Panamanian Tropical Forest." *Nature* 407 (6806): 894–97. http://dx.doi.org/10.1038/35038055.

Piperno, Dolores R., Anthony J. Ranere, Irene Holst, José Iriarte, and Ruth Dickau. 2009. "Starch Grain and Phytolith Evidence for Early Ninth Millennium B.P. Maize from the Central Balsas River Valley, Mexico." *Proceedings of the National Academy of Sciences of the United States of America* 106 (13): 5019–24. http://dx.doi.org/10.1073/pnas.0812525106.

Piperno, Dolores R., Ehud Weiss, Irene Holst, and Dani Nadel. 2004. "Processing of Wild Cereal Grains in the Upper Palaeolithic Revealed by Starch Grain Analysis." *Nature* 430 (7000): 670–73. http://dx.doi.org/10.1038/nature02734.

Piqué, Raquel, and Juan A. Barceló. 2002. "Firewood Management and Vegetation Changes: A Statistical Analysis of Charcoal Remains from North-East Iberian Peninsula Holocenic Sites." In *Charcoal Analysis: Methodological Approaches, Paleoecological Results and Wood Uses*, edited by Stéphanie Thiébault, 1–8. Oxford: British Archaeological Reports.

Piwowar, Heather. 2010. "Supplementary Materials Is a Stopgap for Data Archiving." Accessed November 26, 2011. http://researchremix.wordpress.com/2010/08/13/supplementary-materials-is-a-stopgap-for-data-archiving/.

Pohl, Mary E. D., Dolores R. Piperno, Kevin O. Pope, and John G. Jones. 2007. "Microfossil Evidence for Pre-Columbian Maize Dispersals in the Neotropics from San Andres, Tabsco, Mexico." *Proceedings of the National Academy of Sciences of the United States of America* 104 (16): 6870–75. http://dx.doi.org/10.1073/pnas.0701425104.

Poinar, Hendrik N., Raul J. Cano, and George O. Poinar, Jr. 1993. "DNA from an Extinct Plant." *Nature* 363 (6431): 677. http://dx.doi.org/10.1038/363677a0.

Poinar, Hendrik N., Michael Hofreiter, W. Geoffrey Spaulding, Paul S. Martin, B. Artur Stankiewicz, Helen Bland, Richard P. Evershed, Göran Possnert, and Svante Pääbo. 1998. "Molecular Coproscopy: Dung and Diet of the Extinct Ground Sloth *Nothrotheriops shastensis.*" *Science* 281 (5375): 402–6. http://dx.doi.org/10.1126/science.281.5375.402.

Poinar, Hendrik N., Matthias Hoss, Jeffrey L. Bada, and Svante Pääbo. 1996. "Amino Acid Racemization and the Preservation of Ancient DNA." *Science* 272 (5263): 864–66. http://dx.doi.org/10.1126/science.272.5263.864.

Poinar, Hendrik N., Melanie Kuch, Kristin D. Sobolik, Ian Barnes, Artur B. Stankiewicz, and Tomasz Kuder, W. Geofferey Spaulding, Vaughn M. Bryant, Alan Cooper, and Svante Pääbo. 2001. "A Molecular Analysis of Dietary Diversity for Three Archaic Native Americans." *Proceedings of the National Academy of Sciences of the United States of America* 98 (8): 4317–22. http://dx.doi.org/10.1073/pnas.061014798.

Poinar, Hendrik N., Carsten Schwarz, Ji Qi, Beth Shapiro, Ross D. E. MacPhee, Bernard Buigues, Alexei Tikhonov, Daniel H. Huson, Lynn P. Tomsho, Alexander Auch, Markus Rampp, Webb Miller, and Stephan C. Schuster. 2006. "Metagenomics to Paleogenomics: Large-Scale Sequencing of Mammoth DNA." *Science* 311 (5759): 392–94. http://dx.doi.org/10.1126/science.1123360.

Poirier, Nicolas, Rachel S. Opitz, Laure Nuninger, and Krištof Ostir. 2013. "LiDAR in Mediterranean Agricultural Landscapes: Reassessing Land Use in the Mauguio." In *Interpreting Archaeological Topography: Lasers, 3D Data, Observation, Visualisation and Applications*, edited by David Cowley and Rachel S. Opitz, 184–96. Oxford: Oxbow Books.

Popper, Virginia S. 1988. "Selecting Quantitative Measurements in Paleoethnobotany." In *Current Paleoethnobotany: Analytical Methods and Cultural Interpretations of Archaeological Plant Remains*, edited by Christine A. Hastorf and Virginia S. Popper, 53–71. Chicago: University of Chicago Press.

Popper, Virginia S., and Christine A. Hastorf. 1988. "Introduction." In *Current Paleoethnobotany: Analytical Methods and Cultural Interpretations of Archaeological Plant Remains*, edited by Christine A. Hastorf and Virginia S. Popper, 1–16. Chicago: University of Chicago Press.

Porter, H. K., and R. V. Martin. 1952. "Preparation of Radioactive Starch, Glucose and Fructose from $C^{14}O_2$." *Journal of Experimental Botany* 3 (3): 326–36. http://dx.doi.org/10.1093/jxb/3.3.326.

Portillo, Marta, Rosa M. Albert, and Donald O. Henry. 2009. "Domestic Activities and Spatial Distribution in Ain Abū Nukhayla (Wadi Rum, Southern Jordan):

The Use of Phytoliths and Spherulites Studies." *Quaternary International* 193 (1–2): 174–83. http://dx.doi.org/10.1016/j.quaint.2007.06.002.

Posey, Darrell A. 1985. "Indigenous Management of Tropical Forest Ecosystems: The Kayapo Indians of the Brazilian Amazon." *Agroforestry Systems* 3 (2): 139–58. http://dx.doi.org/10.1007/BF00122640.

Posey, Darrell A., and William Balee, eds. 1989. *Resource Management in Amazonia.* New York: New York Botanical Garden.

Post, David. 2002. "Using Stable Isotopes to Estimate Trophic Position: Models, Methods, and Assumptions." *Ecology* 83 (3): 703–18. http://dx.doi.org/10.1890 /0012-9658(2002)083[0703:USITET]2.0.CO;2.

Post, Wilfred M., Tsung-Hung Peng, William R. Emanuel, Anthony W. King, Virginia H. Dale, and Donald L. DeAngelis. 1990. "The Global Carbon-Cycle." *American Scientist* 78 (4): 310–26.

Potochnik, Angela. 2009. "Optimality Modeling in a Suboptimal World." *Biology and Philosophy* 24 (2): 183–97. http://dx.doi.org/10.1007/s10539-008-9143-9.

Pournelle, Jennifer R. 2007. "KLM to CORONA: A Bird's-Eye View of Cultural Ecology and Early Mesopotamian Urbanization." In *Settlement and Society: Essays Dedicated to Robert McCormick Adams*, edited by Elizabeth C. Stone, 29–62. Los Angeles: Cotsen Institute of Archaeology, University of California.

Powers, William K., and Marla M. N. Powers. 1984. "Metaphysical Aspects of an Ogalala Food System." In *Food in the Social Order: Studies of Food and Festivities in Three American Communities*, edited by Mary Douglas, 40–96. New York: Russell Sage Foundation.

Powers-Jones, Alix H., and Joannne Padmore. 1993. "The Use of Quantitative Methods and Statistical Analyses in the Study of Opal Phytoliths." In *Current Research in Phytolith Analysis: Applciations in Archaeology and Paleoecology. MASCA Research Papers in Science and Archaeology 10*, edited by Deborah M. Pearsall and Dolores R. Piperno, 47–56. Philadelphia: University of Pennsylvania.

Powlesland, Dominic, James Lyall, Guy Hopkinson, Danny Donoghue, Maria Beck, Aidan Harte, and David Stott. 2006. "Beneath the Sand—Remote Sensing, Archaeology, Aggregates and Sustainability: A Case Study from Heslerton, the Vale of Pickering, North Yorkshire, UK." *Archaeological Prospection* 13 (4): 291–99. http://dx.doi.org/10.1002/arp.297.

Preiss, Jack. 2009. "Biochemistry and Molecular Biology of Starch Biosynthesis." In *Starch: Chemistry and Technology*, edited by James N. BeMiller, and Roy L. Whistler, 83–148. San Diego, CA: Academic Press. http://dx.doi.org/10.1016 /B978-0-12-746275-2.00004-5.

Preucel, Robert W. 1991. "The Philosophy of Archaeology." In *Processual and Postprocessual Archaeologies: Multiple Ways of Knowing the Past*, edited by Robert Preucel, 17–29. Carbondale: Center of Archaeological Investigations, South Illinois University.

Prior, J., and K. L. Alvin. 1983. "Structural Changes on Charring Woods of *Dichrostachys* and *Salix* from South Africa." *IAWA Bulletin* 4 (4): 197–206. http://dx.doi.org/10.1163/22941932-90000782.

Pruvost, Mélanie, Reinhard Schwarz, Virginia Bessa Correia, Sophie Champlot, Thierry Grange, and Eva-Maria Geigl. 2008. "DNA Diagenesis and Palaeogenetic Analysis: Critical Assessment and Methodological Progress." *Palaeogeography, Palaeoclimatology, Palaeoecology* 266 (3–4): 211–19. http://dx.doi.org/10.1016/j.palaeo.2008.03.041.

Pyke, G. H., H. R. Pulliam, and E. L. Charnov. 1977. "Optimal Foraging: A Selective Review of Theory and Tests." *Quarterly Review of Biology* 52 (2): 137–54. http://dx.doi.org/10.1086/409852.

Rajjou, Loïc, Karine Gallardo, Isabelle Debeaujon, Joël Vandekerckhove, Claudette Job, and Dominique Job. 2004. "The Effect of Alpha-Amanitin on the *Arabidopsis* Seed Proteome Highlights the Distinct Roles of Stored and Neosynthesized mRNAs During Germination." *Plant Physiology* 134 (4): 1598–613. http://dx.doi.org/10.1104/pp.103.036293.

Ramsay, Jennifer H. 2010. "Trade or Trash: An Examination of the Archaeobotanical Remains from the Harbour at Caesarea Maritima, Israel." *International Journal of Nautical Archaeology* 39:376–82. http://dx.doi.org/10.1111/j.1095-9270.2010.00267.x.

Ranere, Anthony J., Dolores R. Piperno, Irene Holst, Ruth Dickau, and José Iriarte. 2009. "The Cultural and Chronological Context of Early Holocene Maize and Squash Domestication in the Central Balsas River Valley, Mexico." *Proceedings of the National Academy of Sciences of the United States of America* 106 (13): 5014–18. http://dx.doi.org/10.1073/pnas.0812590106.

Raniello, Raffaella, and Gabriele Procaccini. 2002. "Ancient DNA in the Seagrass *Posidonia oceanica*." *Marine Ecology Progress Series* 227:269–73. http://dx.doi.org/10.3354/meps227269.

Rappaport, Roy A. 1968. *Pigs for the Ancestors*. New Haven: Yale University Press.

Rasmussen, Morten, Linda Scott Cummings, M. T. P. Gilbert, V. Bryant, C. Smith, D. L. Jenkins, and E. Willerslev. 2009. "Response to Comment by Goldberg et al. on 'DNA from Pre-Clovis Human Coprolites in Oregon, North America.'" *Science* 325 (5937): 148. http://dx.doi.org/10.1126/science.1167672.

Rasmussen, Morten, Xiaosen Guo, Yong Wang, Kirk E. Lohmueller, Simon Rasmussen, Anders Albrechtsen, Line Skotte, Stinus Lindgreen, Mait Metspalu, Thibaut Jombart, Toomas Kivisild, Weiwei Zhai, Anders Eriksson, Andrea Manica,

Ludovic Orlando, Francisco M. De La Vega, Silvana Tridico, Ene Metspalu, Kasper Nielsen, María C. Ávila-Arcos, J. Víctor Moreno-Mayar, Craig Muller, Joe Dortch, M. Thomas P. Gilbert, Ole Lund, Agata Wesolowska, Monika Karmin, Lucy A. Weinert, Bo Wang, Jun Li, Shuaishuai Tai, Fei Xiao, Tsunehiko Hanihara, George van Driem, Aashish R. Jha, François-Xavier Ricaut, Peter de Knijff, Andrea B Migliano, Irene Gallego Romero, Karsten Kristiansen, David M. Lambert, Søren Brunak, Peter Forster, Bernd Brinkmann, Olaf Nehlich, Michael Bunce, Michael Richards, Ramneek Gupta, Carlos D. Bustamante, Anders Krogh, Robert A. Foley, Marta M. Lahr, Francois Balloux, Thomas Sicheritz-Pontén, Richard Villems, Rasmus Nielsen, Jun Wang, and Eske Willerslev. 2011. "An Aboriginal Australian Genome Reveals Separate Human Dispersals into Asia." *Science* 334 (6052): 94–98. http://dx.doi.org/10.1126/science.1211177.

Rasmussen, Morten, Yingrui Li, Stinus Lindgreen, Jakob Skou Pedersen, Anders Albrechtsen, Ida Moltke, Mait Metspalu, Ene Metspalu, Toomas Kivisild, Ramneek Gupta, Marcelo Bertalan, Kasper Nielsen, M. Thomas P. Gilbert, Yong Wang, Maanasa Raghavan, Paula F. Campos, Hanne Munkholm Kamp, Andrew S. Wilson, Andrew Gledhill, Silvana Tridico, Michael Bunce, Eline D. Lorenzen, Jonas Binladen, Xiaosen Guo, Jing Zhao, Xiuqing Zhang, Hao Zhang, Zhuo Li, Minfeng Chen, Ludovic Orlando, Karsten Kristiansen, Mads Bak, Niels Tommerup, Christian Bendixen, Tracey L. Pierre, Bjarne Grønnow, Morten Meldgaard, Claus Andreasen, Sardana A. Fedorova, Ludmila P. Osipova, Thomas F. G. Higham, Christopher Bronk Ramsey, Thomas v. O. Hansen, Finn C. Nielsen, Michael H. Crawford, Søren Brunak, Thomas Sicheritz-Pontén, Richard Villems, Rasmus Nielsen, Anders Krogh, Jun Wang, and Eske Willerslev. 2010. "Ancient Human Genome Sequence of an Extinct Palaeo-Eskimo." *Nature* 463 (7282): 757–62.

Raviele, Maria E. 2010. "Assessing Carbonized Archaeological Cooking Residues: Evaluation of Maize Phytolith Taphonomy and Density through Experimental Residue Analysis." PhD diss., Anthropology, Michigan State University, Lansing.

Raviele, Maria E. 2011. "Experimental Assessment of Maize Phytolith and Starch Taphonomy in Carbonized Cooking Residues." *Journal of Archaeological Science* 38 (10): 2708–13. http://dx.doi.org/10.1016/j.jas.2011.06.008.

Reddy, Seetha N. 1994. "Plant Usage and Subsistence Modeling: An Ethnoarchaeological Approach to the Late Harappan of Northwest India." PhD diss., Department of Anthropology, University of Wisconsin, Madison.

Reddy, Seetha N. 1997. "If the Threshing Floor Could Talk: Integration of Agriculture and Pastoralism During the Late Harappan in Gujarat, India." *Journal of Anthropological Archaeology* 16 (2): 162–87. http://dx.doi.org/10.1006/jaar.1997.0308.

Reddy, Seetha N. 1998. "Fueling the Hearths in India: The Role of Dung in Paleoeth-nobotanical Interpretation." *Paléorient* 24 (2): 61–69. http://dx.doi.org/10.3406 /paleo.1998.4677.

Reddy, Seetha N. 2003. *Discerning Palates of the Past: An Ethnoarchaeological Study of Crop Cultivation and Plant Usage in India.* Ann Arbor, MI: International Mono-graphs in Prehistory.

Redman, Charles L. 1992. "The Impact of Food Production: Short Term Strategies and Long-Term Consequences." In *Human Impact on the Environment: Ancient Roots, Current Challenges*, edited by Judith E. Jacobson and John Firor, 35–49. Boulder: Westview Press.

Redman, Charles L. 1999. *Human Impact on Ancient Environments.* Tucson: The University of Arizona Press.

Redman, Charles L., Steven R. James, Paul R. Fish, and J. Daniel Rogers, eds. 2004. *The Archaeology of Global Change: The Impact of Humans on Their Environment.* Washington, DC: Smithsonian Books.

Reed, David M. 1999. "Cuisine from Hun-Nal-Ye." In *Reconstructing Ancient Maya Diet*, edited by Christine D. White, 183–96. Salt Lake City: University of Utah Press.

Reich, David, Richard E. Green, Martin Kircher, Johannes Krause, Nick Patterson, Eric Y. Durand, Bence Viola, Adrian W. Briggs, Udo Stenzel, Philip L. F. Johnson, Tomislav Maricic, Jeffrey M. Good, Tomas Marques-Bonet, Can Alkan, Qiaomei Fu, Swapan Mallick, Heng Li, Matthias Meyer, Evan E. Eichler, Mark Stonek-ing, Michael Richards, Sahra Talamo, Michael V. Shunkov, Anatoli P. Derevianko, Jean-Jacques Hublin, Janet Kelso, Montgomery Slatkin and Svante Pääbo. 2010. "Genetic History of an Archaic Hominin Group from Denisova Cave in Siberia." *Nature* 468 (7327): 1053–60. http://dx.doi.org/10.1038/nature09710.

Reichert, Edward Tyson. 1913. *The Differentiation and Specificity of Starches in Relation to Genera, Species, Etc.* Washington, DC: The Carnegie Institution of Washington.

Reidhead, Vann A. 1976. "Optimization and Food Procurement at the Prehistoric Leonard Haag Site, Southeast Indiana: A Linear Programming Analysis." Unpub-lished PhD diss., Indiana University, Bloomington.

Reidhead, Vann A. 1980. "The Economics of Subsistence Change: Test of an Optimi-zation Model." In *Modeling Change in Prehistoric Subsistence Economies*, edited by Timothy K. Earle and Andrew L. Christenson, 141–86. New York: Academic Press.

Reinhard, Karl J., Phil R. Geib, Martha M. Callahan, and Richard H. Hevly. 1992. "Discovery of Colon Contents in a Skeletonized Burial: Soil Sampling for Dietary Remains." *Journal of Archaeological Science* 19 (6): 697–705. http://dx.doi.org /10.1016/0305-4403(92)90039-6.

Reinhard, Karl J., Donny L. Hamilton, and Richard H. Hevly. 1991. "Use of Pollen Concentration in Paleopharmacology: Coprolite Evidence of Medicinal Plants." *Journal of Ethnobiology* 11 (1): 117–32.

Reitz, Elizabeth J., and Elizabeth S. Wing. 2008. *Zooarchaeology*. 2nd ed. Cambridge University Press, Cambridge.

Reitz, Elizabeth J., Lee A. Newsom, and Sylvia J. Scudder, eds. 1996. *Case Studies in Environmental Archaeology*. London: Plenum Press.

Reitz, Elizabeth J., C. Margaret Scarry, and Sylvia J. Scudder, eds. 2008. *Case Studies in Environmental Archaeology*. 2nd ed. Springer, New York.

Renfrew, Colin, and Paul Bahn. 2008. *Archaeology: Theories, Methods, and Practice*. 5th ed. London: Thames and Hudson.

Renfrew, Jane M. 1973. *Palaeoethnobotany: The Prehistoric Food Plants of the Near East and Europe*. New York: Columbia University Press.

Rennie, D. A., E. A. Paul, and L. E. Johns. 1976. "Natural Nitrogen–15 Abundance of Soil and Plant Samples." *Canadian Journal of Soil Science* 56 (1): 43–50. http://dx.doi.org/10.4141/cjss76-006.

Reynolds, Amanda C., Julio L. Betancourt, Jay Quade, P. Jonathan Patchett, Jeffrey S. Dean, and John Stein. 2005. "$^{87}Sr/^{86}Sr$ Sourcing of Ponderosa Pine Used in Anasazi Great House Construction at Chaco Canyon, New Mexico." *Journal of Archaeological Science* 32 (7): 1061–75. http://dx.doi.org/10.1016/j.jas.2005.01.016.

Rhode, David. 1990. "On Transportation Costs of Great Basin Resources: An Assessment of the Jones-Madsen Model." *Current Anthropology* 31 (4): 413–19. http://dx.doi.org/10.1086/203863.

Richards, Michael P., and Richard E. M. Hedges. 1999. "Stable Isotope Evidence for Similarities in the Types of Marine Foods Used by Late Mesolithic Humans at Sites Along the Atlantic Coast of Europe." *Journal of Archaeological Science* 26 (6): 717–22. http://dx.doi.org/10.1006/jasc.1998.0387.

Richards, Michael P., T. Douglas Price, and Eva Koch. 2003. "The Mesolithic and Neolithic Transition in Denmark: New Stable Isotope Data." *Current Anthropology* 44 (2): 288–95. http://dx.doi.org/10.1086/367971.

Richards, Michael P., and Ralf W. Schmitz. 2008. "Isotope Evidence for the Diet of the Neanderthal Type Specimen." *Antiquity* 82 (317): 553–59.

Richards, Michael P., and Erik Trinkaus. 2009. "Isotopic Evidence for the Diets of European Neanderthals and Early Modern Humans." *Proceedings of the National Academy of Sciences of the United States of America* 106 (38): 16034–39. http://dx.doi.org/10.1073/pnas.0903821106.

Richerson, Peter J., and Robert Boyd. 1992. "Cultural Inheritance and Evolutionary Ecology." In *Evolutionary Ecology and Human Behavior*, edited by Eric Alden Smith and Bruce Winterhalder, 61–92. New York: Aldine de Gruyter.

Richerson, Peter J., and Robert Boyd. 2005. *Not by Genes Alone: How Culture Transformed Human Evolution*. Chicago: University of Chicago Press.

Rick, Torben C., and Jon M. Erlandson, eds. 2008. *Human Impacts on Ancient Marine Ecosystems: A Global Perspective*. Berkeley: University of California Press.

Riehl, Simone. 1999. *Bronze Age Environment and Economy in the Troad: The Archaeobotany of Kumtepe and Troy*. Tübingen: Mo Vince Verlag.

Riehl, Simone. 2009. "Archaeobotanical Evidence for the Interrelationship of Agricultural Decision-Making and Climate Change in the Ancient Near East." *Quaternary International* 197 (1–2): 93–114. http://dx.doi.org/10.1016/j.quaint.2007.08.005.

Riehl, Simone, and Katleen Deckers. 2008. "Vorbericht zu Einigen Eisenzeitlichen und Mittelalterlichen Pflanzenresten vom Tell Halaf." In *Tell Halaf*, edited by W. Orthmann, M. Novak, and L. Martin, 105–18. Wiesbaden: Harrassowitz.

Rindos, David. 1984. *The Origins of Agriculture: An Evolutionary Perspective*. Orlando: Academic Press.

Ristaino, Jean B., Carol T. Groves, and Gregory R. Parra. 2001. "PCR Amplification of the Irish Potato Famine Pathogen from Historic Specimens." *Nature* 411 (6838): 695–97. http://dx.doi.org/10.1038/35079606.

Ritchie, William A. 1969. *The Archaeology of Martha's Vineyard: A Framework for the Prehistory of Southern New England: A Study in Coastal Ecology and Adaptation*. New York: The American Museum of Natural History Press.

Rizzi, Ermanno, Martina Lari, Elena Gigli, Gianluca De Bellis, and David Caramelli. 2012. "Ancient DNA Studies: New Perspectives on Old Samples." *Genetics, Selection, Evolution.* 44 (1): 1–19. http://dx.doi.org/10.1186/1297-9686-44-21.

Robinson, David. 2001. "$\delta^{15}N$ as an Integrator of the Nitrogen Cycle." *Trends in Ecology & Evolution* 16 (3): 153–62. http://dx.doi.org/10.1016/S0169-5347(00)02098-X.

Robinson, Mark A., and Vanessa Straker. 1991. "Silica Skeletons of Macroscopic Plant Remains from Ash." In *New Light on Early Farming: Recent Developments in Palaeoethnobotany*, edited by Jane M. Renfrew, 3–13. Edinburgh: Edinburgh University Press.

Robyt, John F. 2009. "Enzymes and Their Action on Starch." In *Starch: Chemistry and Technology*, edited by James N. BeMiller, and Roy L. Whistler, 237–92. San Diego, CA: Academic Press.

Rolfsen, P. 1980. "Disturbance of Archaeological Layers by Processes in the Soil." *Norwegian Archaeological Review* 13 (2): 110–18. http://dx.doi.org/10.1080/00293652.1980.9965336.

Rollo, Franco. 1985. "Characterisation by Molecular Hybridization of RNA Fragments Isolated from Ancient (1400 B.C.) Seeds." *Theoretical and Applied Genetics* 71:330–33.

Rollo, Franco, Augusto Amici, Roberto Salvi, and Annrosa Garbuglia. 1988. "Short but Faithful Pieces of Ancient DNA." *Nature* 335 (6193): 774. http://dx.doi.org /10.1038/335774a0.

Rollo, Franco, A. La Marca, and A. Amici. 1987. "Nucleic Acids in Mummified Plant Seeds: Screening of Twelve Specimens by Gel-Electrophoresis, Molecular Hybridization and DNA Cloning." *Theoretical and Applied Genetics* 73 (4): 501–5. http://dx.doi.org/10.1007/BF00289186.

Römpler, Holger, Nadin Rohland, Carles Lalueza Fox, Eske Willerslev, Tatyana Kuznetsova, Gernot Rabeder, Jaume Bertranpetit, Torsten Schöneberg, and Michael Hofreiter. 2006. "Nuclear Gene Indicates Coat-Color Polymorphism in Mammoths." *Science* 313 (5783): 62. http://dx.doi.org/10.1126/science.1128994.

Röpke, Astrid, Astrid Stobbe, Klaus Oeggl, Arie J. Kalis, and Willy Tinner. 2011. "Late-Holocene Land-Use History and Environmental Changes at High Altitudes of St. Antonien (Switzerland, Northern Alps): Combined Evidence from Pollen, Soil and Tree-Ring Analyses." *The Holocene* 21 (3): 485–98. http://dx.doi .org/10.1177/0959683610385727.

Rösch, Manfred. 2005. "Pollen Analysis of the Contents of Excavated Vessels— Direct Archaeobotanical Evidence of Beverages." *Vegetation History and Archaeobotany* 14 (3): 179–88. http://dx.doi.org/10.1007/s00334-005-0015-9.

Rose, Fionnuala. 2008. "Intra-Community Variation in Diet During the Adoption of a New Staple Crop in the Eastern Woodlands." *American Antiquity* 73 (3): 413–39.

Rosen, Arlene Miller. 1987. "Phytolith Studies at Shiqmim." In *Shiqmim I: Studies Concerning Chalcolithic Societies in the Northern Negev Desert, Israel (1982–84)*, edited by T. E. Levy, 243–249, 547–548. BAR International Series 356. Oxford: British Archaeological Reports.

Rosen, Arlene Miller. 2007. *Civilizing Climate: Social Responses to Climate Change in the Ancient Near East*. Lanham: Altamira Press.

Rosen, Arlene Miller, and Steven Weiner. 1994. "Identifying Ancient Irrigation: A New Method Using Opaline Phytoliths from Emmer Wheat." *Journal of Archaeological Science* 21 (1): 125–32. http://dx.doi.org/10.1006/jasc.1994.1013.

Rossen, Jack. 1999. "The Flote-Tech Flotation Machine: Messiah or Mixed Blessing?" *American Antiquity* 64 (2): 370–72. http://dx.doi.org/10.2307/2694286.

Rossen, Jack, and James Olson. 1985. "The Controlled Carbonization and Archaeological Analysis of U.S. Wood Charcoals." *Journal of Field Archaeology* 12:445–56.

Rovner, Irwin. 1983. "Plant Opal Phytolith Analysis: Major Advances in Archaeobotanical Research." In *Advances in Archaeological Method and Theory*, edited by Michael B. Schiffer, 225–60. New York: Academic Press.

Rowley-Conwy, Peter. 1994. "Dung, Dirt and Deposits: Site Formation under Conditions of near-Perfect Preservation at Qasr Ibrim, Egyptian Nubia." In *Whither*

Environmental Archaeology, edited by Rosemary-Margaret Luff and Peter Rowley-Conwy, 131–38. Oxford: Oxbow Books.

Royal Botanic Gardens, Kew. 1985. "Plant Micromorphology Bibliography." Accessed January 27, 2012. http://kbd.kew.org/.

Rubiales, Juan M., Laura Hernández, Fernando Romero, and Carlos Sanz. 2011. "The Use of Forest Resources in Central Iberia During the Late Iron Age: Insights from the Wood Charcoal Analysis of Pintia, a Vaccaean Oppidum." *Journal of Archaeological Science* 38 (1): 1–10. http://dx.doi.org/10.1016/j.jas.2010.07.004.

Ruddiman, William F. 2003. "The Anthropogenic Greenhouse Era Began Thousands of Years Ago." *Climatic Change* 61 (3): 261–93. http://dx.doi.org/10.1023 /B:CLIM.0000004577.17928.fa.

Ruddiman, William F., and Erle C. Ellis. 2009. "Effect of Per-Capita Land Use Changes on Holocene Forest Clearance and CO_2 Emissions." *Quaternary Science Reviews* 28 (27–28): 3011–15. http://dx.doi.org/10.1016/j.quascirev.2009.05.022.

Ruddiman, William F., Zhengtang Guo, Xin Zhou, Hanbin Wu, and Yanyan Yu. 2008. "Early Rice Farming and Anomalous Methane Trends." *Quaternary Science Reviews* 27 (13–14): 1291–95. http://dx.doi.org/10.1016/j.quascirev.2008.03.007.

Ruffner, Charles M., and Marc D. Abrams. 2002. "Dendrochronological Investigations of Disturbance History for a Native American Site in Northwestern Pennsylvania." *Journal of the Torrey Botanical Society* 129 (3): 251–60. http://dx.doi.org /10.2307/3088775.

Runge, Freya. 2000. *Opal-Phytolithe in Den Tropen Afrikas*. Paderborn: Books on Demand GmbH.

Runge, Jürgen. 2002. "Holocene Landscape History and Palaeohydrology Evidenced by Stable Carbon Isotope (Delta C–13) Analysis of Alluvial Sediments in the Mbari Valley (5 Degrees N/23 Degrees E), Central African Republic." *Catena* 48 (1–2): 67–87. http://dx.doi.org/10.1016/S0341-8162(02)00010-3.

Russell, Emily W. B. 1983. "Indian-Set Fires in the Forests of the Northeastern United States." *Ecology* 64 (1): 78–88. http://dx.doi.org/10.2307/1937331.

Sadori, Laura, and Francesca Susanna. 2005. "Hints of Economic Change During the Late Roman Empire Period in Central Italy: A Study of Charred Plant Remains from 'La Fontanaccia,' near Rome." *Vegetation History and Archaeobotany* 14 (4): 386–93. http://dx.doi.org/10.1007/s00334-005-0010-1.

Sage, Rowan F. 2004. "The Evolution of C4 Photosynthesis." *New Phytologist* 161 (2): 341–70. http://dx.doi.org/10.1111/j.1469-8137.2004.00974.x.

Sahlins, Marshall D. 1976. *Culture and Practical Reason*. Chicago: University of Chicago Press.

Salamon, Michal, A. Coppa, M. McCormick, M. Rubini, R. Vargiu, and N. Tuross. 2008. "The Consilience of Historical and Isotopic Approaches in Reconstructing the Medieval Mediterranean Diet." *Journal of Archaeological Science* 35 (6): 1667–72. http://dx.doi.org/10.1016/j.jas.2007.11.015.

Sallon, Sarah, Elaine Solowey, Yuval Cohen, Raia Korchinsky, Markus Egli, Ivan Woodhatch, Orit Simchoni, and Mordechai Kislev. 2008. "Germination, Genetics, and Growth of an Ancient Date Seed." *Science* 320 (5882): 1464. http://dx.doi.org/10.1126/science.1153600.

Samuel, Delwen. 1996. "Investigation of Ancient Egyptian Baking and Brewing Methods by Correlative Microscopy." *Science* 273 (5274): 488–90. http://dx.doi.org/10.1126/science.273.5274.488.

Samuel, Delwen. 1999. "Brewing and Baking in Ancient Egyptian Art." In *Food in the Arts: Proceedings of the Oxford Symposium on Food and Cookery 1998*, edited by Harlan Walker, 173–81. Totnes, Devon, UK: Prospect Books.

Samuel, Delwen. 2000. "Brewing and Baking." In *Ancient Egyptian Materials and Technology*, edited by Paul T. Nicholson and Ian Shaw, 537–76. Cambridge: Cambridge University Press.

Samuels, Stephan R., ed. 1991. *Ozette Archaeological Project Research Reports, Volume I: House Structure and Floor Midden*. Report of Investigations 63. Pullman: Department of Anthropology, Washington State University and Pacific Northwest Regional Office, National Park Service.

Sands, Rob. 2013. "Portable Wooden Objects from Wetlands." In *The Oxford Handbook of Wetland Archaeology*, edited by Francesco Menotti and Aidan O'Sullivan, 306–22. Oxford: Oxford University Press.

Sauer, Jonathan D. 1993. *Historical Geography of Crop Plants: A Select Roster*. Boca Raton, FL: CRC Press.

Scarry, C. Margaret. 1993a. "Agricultural Risk and the Development of the Moundville Chiefdom." In *Foraging and Farming in the Eastern Woodlands*, edited by C. Margaret Scarry, 157–81. Gainesville, FL: University Press of Florida.

Scarry, C. Margaret. 1993b. *Foraging and Farming in the Eastern Woodlands*. Gainesville, FL: University Press of Florida.

Scarry, C. Margaret. 2003. "The Use of Plants and Mound-Related Activities at Bottle Creek and Moundville." In *Bottle Creek: A Pensacola Culture Site in South Alabama*, edited by Ian W. Brown, 114–29. Tuscaloosa: University of Alabama Press.

Scarry, C. Margaret, and John F. Scarry. 2005. "Native American 'Garden Agriculture' in Southeastern North America." *World Archaeology* 37 (2): 259–74. http://dx.doi.org/10.1080/00438240500095199.

Scarry, C. Margaret, and Vincas P. Steponaitis. 1997. "Between Farmstead and Center: The Natural and Social Landscape of Moundville." In *People, Plants, and Landscapes: Studies in Paleoethnobotany*, edited by Kristin J. Gremillion, 107–22. Tuscaloosa: University of Alabama Press.

Schiffer, Michael B. 1987. *Formation Processes of the Archaeobotanical Record*. Albuquerque: University of New Mexico.

Schlanger, Nathan. 1994. "Mindful Technology: Unleashing the Chaîne Opératoire for an Archeology of Mind." In *The Ancient Mind: Elements of Cognitive Archaeology*, edited by Colin Renfrew and Ezra B.W. Zubrow, 143–51. Cambridge: Cambridge University Press. http://dx.doi.org/10.1017/CBO9780511598388.015.

Schlumbaum, Angela, and Ceiridwen J. Edwards. 2013. "Ancient DNA Research on Wetland Archaeological Evidence." In *The Oxford Handbook of Wetland Archaeology*, edited by Francesco Menotti, and Aidan O'Sullivan, 569–583. Oxford: Oxford University Press. http://dx.doi.org/10.1093/oxfordhb/9780199573493.013.0034.

Schlumbaum, Angela, Jean-Marc Neuhaus, and Stefanie Jacomet. 1998. "Coexistence of Tetraploid and Hexaploid Naked Wheat in a Neolithic Lake Dwelling of Central Europe: Evidence from Morphology and Ancient DNA." *Journal of Archaeological Science* 25 (11): 1111–18. http://dx.doi.org/10.1006/jasc.1998.0338.

Schlumbaum, Angela, Marrie Tensen, and Viviane Jaenicke-Després. 2008. "Ancient Plant DNA in Archaeobotany." *Vegetation History and Archaeobotany* 17 (2): 233–44. http://dx.doi.org/10.1007/s00334-007-0125-7.

Schlumbaum, Angela, Sabine van Glabeke, and Isabel Roldan-Ruiz. 2012. "Towards the Onset of Fruit Tree Growing North of the Alps: Ancient DNA from Waterlogged Apple (*Malus* sp.) Seed Fragments." *Annals of Anatomy-Anatomischer Anzeiger* 194 (1): 157–62. http://dx.doi.org/10.1016/j.aanat.2011.03.004.

Schmidt, Peter R. 2009. "Variability in Eritrea and the Archaeology of the Northern Horn During the First Millennium BC: Subsistence, Ritual, and Gold Production." *African Archaeological Review* 26 (4): 305–25. http://dx.doi.org/10.1007/s10437-009-9061-5.

Schoch, Werner H., Barbara Pawlik, and Fritz H. Schweingruber. 1988. *Botanische Makroreste: Ein Atlas zur Bestimmung Häufig Gefundener und Ökologisch Wichtiger Pflanzensamen*. Bern: Paul Haupt.

Schoen, J. F. 1983. "Identification of Seed-Like Structures: A Taxonomic Review of Sclerotial-Forming Fungi." *Seed Science and Technology* 11:639–50.

Schoeninger, Margaret J. 2009. "Stable Isotope Evidence for the Adoption of Maize Agriculture." *Current Anthropology* 50 (5): 633–40. http://dx.doi.org/10.1086/605111.

Schoeninger, Margaret J., and Michael J. DeNiro. 1984. "Nitrogen and Carbon Isotopic Composition of Bone Collagen from Marine and Terrestrial Animals."

Geochimica et Cosmochimica Acta 48 (4): 625–39. http://dx.doi.org/10.1016/0016
-7037(84)90091-7.

Schoeninger, Margaret J., Michael J. DeNiro, and Henrik Tauber. 1983. "Stable Nitrogen Isotope Ratios of Bone Collagen Reflect Marine and Terrestrial Components of Prehistoric Human Diet." *Science* 220 (4604): 1381–83.

Schuenemann, Verena J., Kirsten Bos, Sharon DeWitte, Sarah Schmedes, Joslyn Jamieson, Alissa Mittnik, Stephen Forrest, Brian K. Coombes, James W. Wood, David J. D. Earn, William White, Johannes Krause, and Hendrik N. Poinar. 2011. "Targeted Enrichment of Ancient Pathogens Yielding the pPCP1 Plasmid of *Yersinia pestis* from Victims of the Black Death." *Proceedings of the National Academy of Sciences of the United States of America* 108 (38): E746–52. http://dx.doi.org/10.1073/pnas.1105107108.

Schuldenrein, Joseph. 2003. "Landscape Change, Human Occupation, and Archaeological Site Preservation at the Glacial Margin: Geoarchaeological Perspectives from the Sandts Eddy Site (36NM12), Middle Delaware River Valley, Pennsylvania." In *Geoarchaeology of Landscapes in the Glaciated Northeast: Proceedings of a Symposium Held at the New York Natural History Conference VI*, edited by John P. Hart and David L. Cremeens, 181–210. Albany, NY: The New York State Education Department.

Schulze, E.-D., R. Ellis, W. Schulze, P. Trimborn, and H. Ziegler. 1996. "Diversity, Metabolic Types and Delta C–13 Carbon Isotope Ratios in the Grass Flora of Namibia in Relation to Growth Form, Precipitation and Habitat Conditions." *Oecologia* 106 (3): 352–69. http://dx.doi.org/10.1007/BF00334563.

Schwarcz, Henry P. 1991. "Some Theoretical Aspects of Isotope Paleodiet Studies." *Journal of Archaeological Science* 18 (3): 261–75. http://dx.doi.org/10.1016/0305-4403(91)90065-W.

Schwarcz, Henry P. 2000. "Some Biochemical Aspects of Carbon Isotopic Paleodiet Studies." In *Biogeochemical Approaches to Paleodietary Analysis*, edited by Stanley Ambrose and M. Katzenberg, 189–209. New York: Kluwer Academic.

Schwarcz, Henry P., Jerry Melbye, M. Anne Katzenberg, and Martin Knyf. 1985. "Stable Isotopes in Human Skeletons of Southern Ontario: Reconstructing Paleodiet." *Journal of Archaeological Science* 12 (3): 187–206. http://dx.doi.org/10.1016/0305-4403(85)90020-2. Accessed 2011.

Schwartz, Deborah, and Roy L. Whistler. 2009. "History and Future of Starch." In *Starch: Chemistry and Technology*, edited by James N. BeMiller, and Roy L. Whistler, 1–10. Amsterdam: Academic Press.

Schwartz, Glenn M., Hans H. Curvers, Fokke A. Gerritsen, Jennifer A. MacCormack, Naomi F. Miller, and Jill A. Weber. 2000. "Excavation and Survey in the

Jabbul Plain, Western Syria: The Umm El-Marra Project, 1996–1997." *American Journal of Archaeology* 104 (3): 419–62. http://dx.doi.org/10.2307/507225.

Science. 2011. "Submission Requirements and Conditions of Acceptance." Accessed November 26. http://www.sciencemag.org/site/feature/contribinfo/prep/gen_info.xhtml.

Scully, Richard W., and Richard W. Arnold. 1981. "Holocene Alluvial Stratigraphy in the Upper Susquehanna River Basin, New York." *Quaternary Research* 15 (3): 327–44. http://dx.doi.org/10.1016/0033-5894(81)90034-X.

Sealy, Judith C., and Nikolaas J. van der Merwe. 1985. "Isotope Assessment of Holocene Human Diets in the Southwestern Cape, South Africa." *Nature* 315 (6015): 138–40. http://dx.doi.org/10.1038/315138a0.

Sealy, Judith C., and Nikolaas J. van der Merwe. 1986. "Isotopic Assessment and the Seasonal Mobility Hypothesis in the Southwestern Cape of South Africa." *Current Anthropology* 27 (2): 135–50. http://dx.doi.org/10.1086/203404.

Sealy, Judith C., and Nikolaas J. van der Merwe. 1988. "Social, Spatial and Chronological Patterning in Marine Food Use as Determined by ^{13}C Measurements of Holocene Human Skeletons from the Southwestern Cape, South Africa." *World Archaeology* 20 (1): 87–102. http://dx.doi.org/10.1080/00438243.1988.9980058.

Sealy, Judith C., Nikolaas J. van der Merwe, Julia A. Lee-Thorp, and John L. Lanham. 1987. "Nitrogen Isotopic Ecology in Southern Africa: Implications for Environmental and Dietary Tracing." *Geochimica et Cosmochimica Acta* 51 (10): 2707–17. http://dx.doi.org/10.1016/0016-7037(87)90151-7.

Sedov, Sergey, Elizabeth Solleiro-Rebolledo, Pedro Morales-Puente, Angélica Arias-Herreia, Ernestina Vallejo-Gomez, and Carolina Jasso-Castaneda. 2003. "Mineral and Organic Components of the Buried Paleosols of the Nevado de Toluca, Central Mexico as Indicators of Paleoenvironments and Soil Evolution." *Quaternary International* 106–7:169–84. http://dx.doi.org/10.1016/S1040-6182(02)00171-4.

Segalen, Martine. 1986. *Historical Anthropology of the Family.* Translated by J. C. Whitehouse and Sarah Matthews. Cambridge: Cambridge University Press. http://dx.doi.org/10.1017/CBO9780511621864.

Seidemann, Johannes. 1966. *Stärke-Atlas.* Berlin: Paul Parey.

Sever, Thomas, and Daniel E. Irwin. 2003. "Landscape Archaeology: Remote-Sensing Investigation of the Ancient Maya in the Peten Rainforest of Northern Guatemala." *Ancient Mesoamerica* 14 (1): 113–22. http://dx.doi.org/10.1017/S0956536103141041.

Shack, Dorothy N. 1969. "Nutritional Processes and Personality Development among the Gurage of Ethiopia." *Ethnology* 8 (3): 292–300. http://dx.doi.org/10.2307/3772758.

Shahack-Gross, Ruth. 2011. "Herbivorous Livestock Dung: Formation, Taphonomy, Methods for Identification and Archaeological Significance." *Journal of Archaeological Science* 38 (2): 205–18. http://dx.doi.org/10.1016/j.jas.2010.09.019.

Shahack-Gross, Ruth, Rosa-Maria Albert, Ayelet Gilboa, Orna Nagar-Hilman, Ilan Sharon, and Steve Weiner. 2005. "Geoarchaeology in an Urban Context: The Uses of Space in a Phoenician Monumental Buliding at Tel Dor (Israel)." *Journal of Archaeological Science* 32 (9): 1417–31. http://dx.doi.org/10.1016/j.jas.2005.04.001.

Shahack-Gross, Ruth, Mor Gafri, and Israel Finkelstein. 2009. "Identifying Threshing Floors in the Archaeological Record: A Test Case at Iron Age Tel Megiddo, Israel." *Journal of Field Archaeology* 34 (2): 171–84. http://dx.doi.org/10.1179/00934 6909791070943.

Shahack-Gross, Ruth, Fiona Marshall, Kathleen Ryan, and Steve Weiner. 2004. "Reconstruction of Spatial Organization in Abandoned Maasai Settlements: Implications for Site Structure in the Pastoral Neolithic of East Africa." *Journal of Archaeological Science* 31 (10): 1395–411. http://dx.doi.org/10.1016/j.jas.2004.03.003.

Shahack-Gross, Ruth, Fiona Marshall, and Steve Weiner. 2003. "Geo-Ethnoarchaeology of Pastoral Sites: The Identification of Livestock Enclosures in Abandoned Maasai Settlements." *Journal of Archaeological Science* 30 (4): 439–59. http://dx.doi.org/10.1006/jasc.2002.0853.

Shanks, Michael, and Ian Hodder. 1995. "Processual, Postprocessual and Interpretive Archaeologies." In *Interpreting Archaeology: Finding Meaning in the Past*, edited by Ian Hodder, Michael Shanks, Alexandra Alexandri, Victor Buchli, John Carman, Jonathan Last, and Gavin Lucas, 3–29. London: Routledge.

Shannon, Claude E., and Warren Weaver. 1949. *The Mathematical Theory of Communication*. Urbana: University of Illinois Press.

Shannon, Jack C., Douglas L. Garwood, and Charles D. Boyer. 2009. "Genetics and Physiology of Starch Development." In *Starch: Chemistry and Technology*, edited by James N. BeMiller, and Roy L. Whistler, 23–82. San Diego, CA: Academic Press.

Shearer, Georgia, and D. H. Kohl. 1988. "Natural ^{15}N Abundance as a Method of Estimating the Contribution of Biologically Fixed Nitrogen to N_2-Fixing Systems: Potential for Non-Legumes." *Plant and Soil* 110 (2): 317–27. http://dx.doi.org/10.1007/BF02226812.

Shearer, Georgia, D. H. Kohl, and B. Commoner. 1974. "The Precision of Determinations of the Natural Abundance of Nitrogen–15 in Soils, Fertilizers and Shelf Chemicals." *Soil Science* 118 (5): 308–16. http://dx.doi.org/10.1097/00010694 -197411000-00005.

Sheets, Payson D. 1982. "Prehistoric Agricultural Systems in El Salvador." In *Maya Subsistence: Studies in Memory of Dennis E. Puleston*, edited by K. V. Flannery, 99–118. New York, NY: Academic Press.

Sheets, Payson D. 2002. *Before the Volcano Erupted: The Ancient Cerèn Village in Central America*. Austin: University of Texas Press.

Shelton, China P. 2009. "Food, Economy, and Identity in the Sangro River Valley, Abruzzo, Italy, 650 B.C.-A.D. 150." PhD diss., Department of Archaeology, Boston University.

Shelton, China P., and Chantel E. White. 2010. "The Hand-Pump Flotation System: A New Method for Archaeobotanical Recovery." *Journal of Field Archaeology* 35 (3): 316–26. http://dx.doi.org/10.1179/009346910X12707321358838.

Shennan, Stephen. 1997. *Quantifying Archaeology*. 2nd ed. Iowa City: University of Iowa Press.

Sherard, Jeffrey L. 2009. "Analysis of Daub from Mound V, Moundville: Its Role as an Architectural Indicator." *Bulletin of the Alabama Museum of Natural History* 27:29–42.

Sherratt, Andrew. 1987. "Cups That Cheered: The Introduction of Alcohol to Prehistoric Europe." In *Economy and Society in Prehistoric Europe: Changing Perspectives*, edited by Andrew Sherratt, 81–114. Princeton, NJ: Princeton University Press.

Sherratt, Andrew. 1991. "Palaeoethnobotany: From Crops to Cuisine." In *Paleoecologia e Arqueologia II: Trabalhos Dedicados a A. R. Pinto Da Silva*, edited by F. Queiroga and A. P. Dinis, 221–36. Portugal: Centro de Estudos Arqueológicos Famalicenses.

Sheuyange, Asser, Gufu Obaa, and Robert B. Weladji. 2005. "Effects of Anthropogenic Fire History on Savanna Vegetation in Northeastern Namibia." *Journal of Environmental Management* 75 (3): 189–98. http://dx.doi.org/10.1016/j.jenvman.2004.11.004.

Shewry, P. R., M. A. Kirkman, S. R. Burgess, G. N. Festenstein, and B. J. Miflin. 1982. "A Comparison of the Protein and Amino Acid Composition of Old and Recent Barley Grain." *New Phytologist* 90 (3): 455–66. http://dx.doi.org/10.1111/j.1469-8137.1982.tb04478.x.

Shillito, Lisa-Marie. 2011. "Simultaneous Thin Section and Phytolith Observations of Finely Stratified Deposits from Neolithic Çatalhöyük, Turkey: Implications for Paleoeconomy and Early Holocene Paleoenvironment." *Journal of Quaternary Science* 26 (6): 576–88. http://dx.doi.org/10.1002/jqs.1470.

Shillito, Lisa-Marie, and Matthew J. Almond. 2010. "Comment On: Fruit and Seed Biomineralization and Its Effect on Preservation by E. Messager et al.; In: Archaeological and Anthropological Sciences (2010) 2:25–34. Doi 10.1007/S12520-010-0024-1." *Archaeological and Anthropological Sciences* 2 (3): 225–29.

Shishlina, Natalya I., Eugeny I. Gak, and Alexander V. Borisov. 2008. "Nomadic Sites of the South Yergueni Hills on the Eurasian Steppe: Models of Seasonal Occupation and Production." In *The Archaeology of Mobility: Old World and New*

World Nomadism, edited by Hans Barnard and Willeke Wendrich, 230–49. Los Angeles: Cotsen Institute of Archaeology, University of California Los Angeles.

Siemens, Alfred H., and Dennis E. Puleston. 1972. "Ridged Fields and Associated Features in Southern Campeche: New Perspectives on the Lowland Maya." *American Antiquity* 37 (2): 228–39. http://dx.doi.org/10.2307/278209.

Sievers, Christine, and Lyn Wadley. 2008. "Going Underground: Experimental Carbonization of Fruiting Structures under Hearths." *Journal of Archaeological Science* 35 (11): 2909–17. http://dx.doi.org/10.1016/j.jas.2008.06.008.

Sillen, Andrew, Judith C. Sealy, and Nikolaas J. van der Merwe. 1989. "Chemistry and Paleodietary Research: No More Easy Answers." *American Antiquity* 54 (3): 504–12. http://dx.doi.org/10.2307/280778.

Simpson, Edward H. 1949. "Measurement of Diversity." *Nature* 163 (4148): 688. http://dx.doi.org/10.1038/163688a0.

Smalley, John, and Michael Blake. 2003. "Sweet Beginnings: Stalk Sugar and the Domestication of Maize." *Current Anthropology* 44 (5): 675–703. http://dx.doi.org/10.1086/377664.

Smart, Tristine Lee, and Ellen S. Hoffman. 1988. "Environmental Interpretation of Archaeological Charcoal." In *Current Paleoethnobotany: Analytical Methods and Cultural Interpretations of Archaeological Plant Remains*, edited by Christine A. Hastorf and Virginia S. Popper, 167–205. Chicago: University of Chicago Press.

Šmilauer, Petr, and Jan Lepš. 2014. *Multivariate Analysis of Ecological Data using Canoco 5*. Cambridge: Cambridge University Press.

Smith, Alexia. 2005. "Agriculture, Culture, and Climate: Examining Change in the Bronze and Iron Age Near East." PhD diss., Department of Archaeology, Boston University. Ann Arbor, MI: University Microfilms, Boston, MA.

Smith, Alexia, and Naomi F. Miller. 2009. "Integrating Plant and Animal Data: Delving Deeper into Subsistence: Introduction to the Special Section." *Current Anthropology* 50 (6): 883–84. http://dx.doi.org/10.1086/605867.

Smith, Alexia, and Natalie D. Munro. 2009. "A Holistic Approach to Examining Ancient Agriculture: A Case Study from the Bronze and Iron Age Near East." *Current Anthropology* 50 (6): 925–36. http://dx.doi.org/10.1086/648316.

Smith, Beverley A., and Kathryn C. Egan. 1990. "Middle and Late Archaic Faunal and Floral Exploitation at the Weber I Site (20SA581), Michigan." *Ontario Archaeology* 50:39–54.

Smith, Bruce D. 1978. *Prehistoric Patterns of Human Behavior: A Case Study of the Mississippi Valley*. New York: Academic Press.

Smith, Bruce D. 1984. "*Chenopodium* as a Prehistoric Domesticate in Eastern North America: Evidence from Russell Cave, Alabama." *Science* 226 (4671): 165–67. http://dx.doi.org/10.1126/science.226.4671.165.

Smith, Bruce D. 1985. "*Chenopodium berlandieri* ssp. *jonesianum*: Evidence for a Hopewellian Domesticate from Ash Cave, Ohio." *Southeastern Archaeology* 4 (2): 107–33.

Smith, Bruce D. 1986. "Preceramic Plant Remains from Guilá Naquitz." In *Guilá Naquitz: Archaic Foraging and Early Agriculture in Oaxaca, Mexico*, edited by Kent Flannery, 265–74. Orlando: Academic Press.

Smith, Bruce D. 1989. "Origins of Agriculture in Eastern North America." *Science* 246 (4937): 1566–71. http://dx.doi.org/10.1126/science.246.4937.1566.

Smith, Bruce D. 1998. *The Emergence of Agriculture.* New York: Scientific American Library.

Smith, Bruce D. 2001a. "Documenting Plant Domestication: The Consilience of Biological and Archaeological Approaches." *Proceedings of the National Academy of Sciences of the United States of America* 98 (4): 1324–26. http://dx.doi.org/10.1073/pnas.98.4.1324.

Smith, Bruce D. 2001b. "Low-Level Food Production." *Journal of Archaeological Research* 9 (1): 1–43. http://dx.doi.org/10.1023/A:1009436110049.

Smith, Bruce D. 2005. "Reassessing Coxcatlan Cave and the Early History of Domesticated Plants in Mesoamerica." *Proceedings of the National Academy of Sciences of the United States of America* 102 (27): 9438–45. http://dx.doi.org/10.1073/pnas.0502847102.

Smith, Bruce D. 2006. *Rivers of Change.* Tuscaloosa: University of Alabama Press.

Smith, Bruce D. 2007a. "Niche Construction and the Behavioral Context of Plant and Animal Domestication." *Evolutionary Anthropology* 16 (5): 188–99. http://dx.doi.org/10.1002/evan.20135.

Smith, Bruce D. 2007b. "The Ultimate Ecosystem Engineers." *Science* 315 (5820): 1797–98. http://dx.doi.org/10.1126/science.1137740.

Smith, Bruce D. 2009a. "Core Conceptual Flaws in Human Behavioral Ecology." *Communicative & Integrative Biology* 6 (6): 533–34. http://dx.doi.org/10.4161/cib.2.6.9613.

Smith, Bruce D. 2009b. "Resource Resilience, Human Niche Construction, and the Long-Term Sustainability of Pre-Columbian Subsistence Economies in the Mississippi River Valley Corridor." *Journal of Ethnobiology* 29 (2): 167–83. http://dx.doi.org/10.2993/0278-0771-29.2.167.

Smith, Bruce D. 2011a. "A Cultural Niche Construction Theory of Initial Domestication." *Biological Theory* 2 (6): 260–71. http://dx.doi.org/10.1007/s13752-012-0028-4.

Smith, Bruce D. 2011b. "General Patterns of Niche Construction and the Management of 'Wild' Plant and Animal Resources by Small-Scale Pre-Industrial

Societies." *Philosophical Transactions of the Royal Society of London. Series B, Biological Sciences* 366 (1566): 836–48. http://dx.doi.org/10.1098/rstb.2010.0253.

Smith, Bruce D. 2011c. *Subsistence Economies of Indigenous North American Societies.* Lanham, MD: Rowman and Littlefield.

Smith, Bruce D. 2014. "The Domestication of *Helianthus annuus* L. (Sunflower)." *Vegetation History and Archaeobotany* 23:57–74. http://dx.doi.org/10.1007/s00334 -013-0393-3.

Smith, Bruce D. 2013. "Modifying Landscapes and Mass Kills: Human Niche Construction and Communal Ungulate Harvests." *Quaternary International* 297: 8–12. http://dx.doi.org/10.1016/j.quaint.2012.12.006.

Smith, Bruce D., and C. Wesley Cowan. 1987. "Domesticated *Chenopodium* in Prehistoric Eastern North America: New Accelerator Dates from Eastern Kentucky." *American Antiquity* 52 (2): 355–57. http://dx.doi.org/10.2307/281788.

Smith, Bruce D., and Melinda A. Zeder. 2013. "The Onset of the Anthropocene." *Anthropocene* 4:8–13. http://dx.doi.org/10.1016/j.ancene.2013.05.001.

Smith, Bruce N., and Samuel Epstein. 1971. "Two Categories of $^{13}C/^{12}C$ Ratios for Higher Plants." *Plant Physiology* 47 (3): 380–84. http://dx.doi.org/10.1104/pp.47.3.380.

Smith, C. Earle. 1967. "Plant Remains." In *The Prehistory of the Tehuacan Valley*, vol. 1, edited by Douglas S. Byers, 220–55. Austin: University of Texas Press.

Smith, David G., and Gary W. Crawford. 2002. "Recent Developments on the Archaeology of the Princess Point Complex in Southern Ontario." In *Northeast Subsistence-Settlement Change A.D. 700–1300*, edited by John P. Hart, and C. Reith, 97–116. Bulletin 496. Albany: New York State Museum.

Smith, Eric Alden, and Bruce Winterhalder. 1992. "Natural Selection and Decision Making: Some Fundamental Principles." In *Evolutionary Ecology and Human Behavior*, edited by Eric Alden Smith and Bruce Winterhalder, 25–60. New York: Aldine de Gruyter.

Smith, Helen, and Glynis E. M. Jones. 1990. "Experiments on the Effects of Charring on Cultivated Grape Seeds." *Journal of Archaeological Science* 17 (3): 317–27. http://dx.doi.org/10.1016/0305-4403(90)90026-2.

Smith, W. 2003. *Archaeobotanical Investigations of Agriculture at Late Antique Kom El-Nana (Tell El-Amarna). Excavation Memoirs 70.* London: Egypt Exploration Society.

Sobolik, Kristin D. 1988. "The Importance of Pollen Concentration Values from Coprolites: An Analysis of Southwest Texas Samples." *Palynology* 12 (1): 201–14. http://dx.doi.org/10.1080/01916122.1988.9989344.

Soffer, O., J. M. Adovasio, J. S. Illingworth, H. A. Amirkhanov, N. D. Praslov, and M. Street. 2000. "Palaeolithic Perishables Made Permanent." *Antiquity* 74:812–21.

Solazzo, Caroline, William W. Fitzhugh, Christian Rolando, and Caroline Tokarski. 2008. "Identification of Protein Remains in Archaeological Potsherds by Proteomics." *Analytical Chemistry* 80 (12): 4590–97. http://dx.doi.org/10.1021/ac800515v.

Soler, Jean. 1997. "The Semiotics of Food in the Bible." In *Food and Culture: A Reader*, 1st ed., edited by Carole Counihan and Penny Van Esterik, 55–66. New York: Routledge.

Soltis, P. S., D. E. Soltis, and C. J. Smiley. 1992. "An *rbcL* Sequence from a Miocene *Taxodium* (Bald Cypress)." *Proceedings of the National Academy of Sciences of the United States of America* 89 (1): 449–51. http://dx.doi.org/10.1073/pnas.89.1.449.

Søreide, Fredrik. 2011. *Ships from the Depths: Deepwater Archaeology*. College Station: Texas A&M University Press.

Speich, Hans. 1942. "Ueber die Optik der Kartoffelstärkekörner." *Berichte der schweizerischen botanischen Gesellschaft* 52:175–214.

Speir, T. W., and D. J. Ross. 1981. "A Comparison of the Effects of Air-Drying and Acetone Dehydration on Soil Enzyme Activities." *Soil Biology & Biochemistry* 13 (3): 225–29. http://dx.doi.org/10.1016/0038-0717(81)90025-0.

Sponheimer, Matthew., T. Robinson, L. Ayliffe, B. Roeder, J. Hammer, B. Passey, A. West, T. Cerling, D. Dearing, and J. Ehleringer. 2003. "Nitrogen Isotopes in Mammalian Herbivores: Hair δ^{15}N Values from a Controlled Feeding Study." *International Journal of Osteoarchaeology* 13:80–87.

Springer, Gregory S., D. M. White, H. D. Rowe, B. Hardt, L. Nivanthi Mihimdukulasooriya, Hai Cheng, and R. L. Edwards. 2010. "Multiproxy Evidence from Caves of Native Americans Altering the Overlying Landscape During the Late Holocene of East-Central North America." *The Holocene* 20 (2): 275–83. http://dx.doi.org/10.1177/0959683609350395.

Stacey, Maurice, and Sydney A. Barker. 1960. *Polysaccharides of Micro-Organisms*. Oxford: Oxford University Press.

Stahl, Ann Brower. 2002. "Colonial Entanglements and the Practices of Taste: An Alternative to Logocentric Approaches." *American Anthropologist* 104 (3): 827–45. http://dx.doi.org/10.1525/aa.2002.104.3.827.

Staland, Hanna, Jonas Salmonsson, and Greger Hörnberg. 2010. "A Thousand Years of Human Impact in the Northern Scandinavian Mountain Range: Long-Lasting Effects on Forest Lines and Vegetation." *The Holocene* 21 (3): 379–91. http://dx.doi.org/10.1177/0959683610378882.

Steele, K. W., and R. M. Daniel. 1978. "Fractionation of Nitrogen Isotopes by Animals: A Further Complication to the Use of Variations in the Natural Abundance of ^{15}N for Tracer Studies." *Journal of Agricultural Science* 90 (01): 7–9. http://dx.doi.org/10.1017/S002185960004853X.

Steffen, Will, Paul J. Crutzen, and John R. McNeill. 2007. "The Anthropocene: Are Humans Now Overwhelming the Great Forces of Nature?" *Ambio* 36 (8): 614–21. http://dx.doi.org/10.1579/0044-7447(2007)36[614:TAAHNO]2.0.CO;2.

Stein, Julie K. 1983. "Earthworm Activity: A Source of Potential Disturbance of Archaeological Sediments." *American Antiquity* 48 (2): 277–89. http://dx.doi.org/10.2307/280451.

Stephens, David W., and John R. Krebs. 1986. *Foraging Theory*. Princeton: Princeton University Press.

Stephens, Scott L., Robert E. Martin, and Nicholas E. Clinton. 2007. "Prehistoric Fire Area and Emissions from California's Forests, Woodlands, Shrublands, and Grasslands." *Forest Ecology and Management* 251 (3): 205–16. http://dx.doi.org/10.1016/j.foreco.2007.06.005.

Sterling, C. 1987. "The Light Microscope in Food Analysis." In *Food Analysis: Principles and Techniques*, edited by D. W. Gruenwedel and J. R. Whitaker, 175–201. CRC.

Stevens, Chris J. 1996. "Iron Age and Roman Agriculture in the Upper Thames Valley: Archaeobotanical and Social Perspectives." Unpublished PhD Thesis, Department of Archaeology, University of Cambridge, Cambridge.

Stevens, Chris J. 2003a. "The Arable Economy, in Prehistoric and Anglo-Saxon Settlements to the Rear of Sherborne House, Lechlade: Excavations in 1997, Edited by C. Bateman, D. Enright, and N. Oakey." *Transactions of the Bristol and Gloucestershire Archaeological Society* 121:23–96 (76–81).

Stevens, Chris J. 2003b. "An Investigation of Agricultural Consumption and Production Models for Prehistoric and Roman Britain." *Environmental Archaeology* 8 (1): 61–76. http://dx.doi.org/10.1179/env.2003.8.1.61.

Stevens, Chris J. 2007. "Charred Plant Remains, in a Middle Iron Age Settlement at Weston Down Cottages, Hampshire, Edited by Catriona Gibbson and Stephane Knight." *Proceedings of Hampshire Field Club* 62:5–36.

Stevens, Chris J. 2011. "Crop Husbandry as Seen from the Charred Botanical Samples from Yarnton." In *Yarnton: Iron Age and Romano-British Settlement and Landscape: Results of Excavations 1990–98*, edited by Gill Hey, Paul Booth, and Jane Timby, 534–68. Thames Valley Landscapes Monograph No. 35. Oxford: University School of Archaeology and Oxford Archaeology.

Steward, Julian H. 1933. "Ethnography of the Owens Valley Paiute." *University of California Publications in American Archaeology and Ethnology* 33:233–350.

Steward, Julian H. 1955. *Theory of Culture Change*. Urbana: University of Illinois Press.

Steward, Julian H. 1959. "The Concept and Method of Cultural Ecology." *Readings in Anthropology* 2:81–95.

Stewart, G. R., M. H. Turnbull, S. Schmidt, and P. D. Erskine. 1995. "C–13 Natural-Abundance in Plant-Communities Along a Rainfall Gradient—a Biological

Integrator of Water Availability." *Australian Journal of Plant Physiology* 22 (1): 51–55. http://dx.doi.org/10.1071/PP9950051.

Stewart, R. Michael. 1994. *Prehistoric Farmers of the Susquehanna Valley: Clemson Island Culture and the St. Anthony Site*. Occasional Publications in Northeastern Anthropology 13. Bethlehem, CT: Archaeological Services.

Stewart, R. Michael, Jay F. Custer, and Donald Kline. 1991. "A Deeply Stratified Archaeological and Sedimentary Sequence in the Delaware River Valley of the Midde Atlantic Region, United States." *Geoarchaeology: An International Journal* 6 (2): 169–82. http://dx.doi.org/10.1002/gea.3340060204.

Stewart, Wilson N., and Gar W. Rothwell. 2010. *Paleobotany and the Evolution of Plants*. 2nd ed. Cambridge: Cambridge University Press.

Steyn, Pieter L., and Constant C. Delwiche. 1970. "Nitrogen Fixation by Nonsymbiotic Microorganisms in Some California Soils." *Environmental Science & Technology* 4 (12): 1122–28. http://dx.doi.org/10.1021/es60047a007.

Stinchcomb, Gary E., Timothy C. Messner, Steven G. Driese, Lee C. Nordt, and R. Michael Stewart. 2011. "Pre-Colonial (A.D. 1,100–1,600) Sedimentation Related to Prehistoric Maize Agriculture and Climate Change in Eastern North America." *Geology* 39 (4): 363–66. http://dx.doi.org/10.1130/G31596.1.

Stinchcomb, Gary E., Timothy C. Messner, Forrest C. Williamson, Steven G. Driese, and Lee C. Nordt. 2013. "Climatic and Human Controls on Holocene Floodplain Vegetation Changes in Eastern Pennsylvania Based on the Isotopic Composition of Soil Organic Matter." *Quaternary Research* 79 (3): 377–90. http://dx.doi.org/10.1016/j.yqres.2013.02.004.

Stiner, Mary C., Natalie D. Munro, and Todd A. Surovell. 2000. "The Tortoise and the Hare: Small-Game Use, the Broad-Spectrum Revolution, and Paleolithic Demography." *Current Anthropology* 41 (1): 39–79. http://dx.doi.org/10.1086/300102.

Stoker, Anke. 2010. "Hidden and Disappeared Mediterranean Archaeo-Landscapes Revealed in Historic Aerial Photographs." In *Landscapes through the Lens: Aerial Photographs and Historic Environment*, edited by David Cowley, Robin A. Standring, and Matthew J. Abicht, 33–42. Oxford: Oxbow Books.

Stone, Glenn Davis. 1996. *Settlement Ecology: The Social and Spatial Organization of Kofyar Agriculture*. Arizona Studies in Human Ecology. Tucson: University of Arizona Press.

Stone, Glenn Davis, Robert McC. Netting, and M. Priscilla Stone. 1990. "Seasonally, Labor Scheduling, and Agricultural Intensification in the Nigerian Savanna." *American Anthropologist* 92 (1): 7–23. http://dx.doi.org/10.1525/aa.1990.92.1.02a00010.

Struever, Stuart. 1968. "Flotation Techniques for Recovery of Small-Scale Archaeological Remains." *American Antiquity* 33 (3): 353–62. http://dx.doi.org/10.2307/278703.

Stuiver, Minze, Paul D. Quay, and H. G. Ostlund. 1983. "Abyssal Water Carbon–14 Distribution and the Age of the World Oceans." *Science* 219 (4586): 849–51. http://dx.doi.org/10.1126/science.219.4586.849.

Suess, Hans. 1955. "Radiocarbon Concentration in Modern Wood." *Science* 122 (3166): 415–17. http://dx.doi.org/10.1126/science.122.3166.415-a.

Sugita, Shinya. 1994. "Pollen Representation of Vegetation in Quaternary Sediments: Theory and Method in Patchy Vegetation." *Journal of Ecology* 82:881–97.

Sullivan, Alan P. 1996. "Risk, Anthropogenic Environments, and Western Anasazi Subsistence." In *Evolving Complexity and Environmental Risk in the Prehistoric Southwest*, edited by Joseph A. Tainter and Bonnie Bagley Tainter, 145–67. New York: Addison-Wesley.

Surovell, Todd A., J. Byrd Finley, Geoffrey M. Smith, P. Jeffrey Brantingham, and Robert Kelly. 2009. "Correcting Temporal Frequency Distributions for Taphonomic Bias." *Journal of Archaeological Science* 36: 1715–24.

Sutton, David E. 2001. *Remembrance of Repasts: An Anthropology of Food and Memory*. Oxford: Berg.

Svensson, Peter. 2004. "CDs and DVDs Not So Immortal after All." *USA Today* May 5, 2004.

Swift, M. J., O. W. Heal, and J. M. Anderson. 1979. *Decomposition in Terrestrial Ecosystems*. Berkeley: University of California Press.

Swinkles, J. J. M. 1985. "Sources of Starch, Its Chemistry and Physics." In *Starch Conversion Technology*, edited by G. M. A. van Beynum and J. A. Roels, 15–45. New York: Marcel Dekker, Inc.

Szpak, Paul, Christine D. White, Fred J. Longstaffe, Jean-François Millaire, and Víctor F. Vásquez Sánchez. 2013. "Carbon and Nitrogen Isotopic Survey of Northern Peruvian Plants: Baselines for Paleodietary and Paleoecological Studies." *PLoS ONE* 8 (1): e53763. http://dx.doi.org/10.1371/journal.pone.0053763.

Taberlet, Pierre, Eric Coissac, F. Pompanon, Ludovic Gielly, Christian Miquel, Alice Valentini, Thierry Vermat, G. Corthier, Christian Brochmann, and Eske Willerslev. 2007. "Power and Limitations of the Chloroplast *trn*L (UAA) Intron for Plant DNA Barcoding." *Nucleic Acids Research* 35 (3): e14. http://dx.doi.org/10.1093/nar/gkl938.

Tanaka, Katsunori, Takeshi Honda, and Ryuji Ishikawa. 2010. "Rice Archaeological Remains and the Possibility of DNA Archaeology: Examples from Yayoi and Heian Periods of Northern Japan." *Archaeological and Anthropological Sciences* 2 (2): 69–78. http://dx.doi.org/10.1007/s12520-010-0036-x.

Tanno, Ken-ichi, and George Willcox. 2006. "How Fast Was Wild Wheat Domesticated?" *Science* 311 (5769): 1886.

Tanno, Ken-ichi, and George Willcox. 2012. "Distinguishing Wild and Domestic Wheat and Barley Spikelets from Early Holocene Sites in the Near East." *Vegetation History and Archaeobotany* 21:107–15.

Tarighat, Somayeh S., David L. Lentz, Stephen F. Matter, and Robert Bye. 2011. "Morphometric Analysis of Sunflower (*Helianthus annuus* L.) Achenes from Mexico and Eastern North America." *Economic Botany* 65 (3): 260–70. http://dx.doi.org/10.1007/s12231-011-9165-0.

Tauber, Henrik. 1981. "^{13}C Evidence for Dietary Habits of Prehistoric Man in Denmark." *Nature* 292 (5821): 332–33. http://dx.doi.org/10.1038/292332a0.

Taylor, J. P., B. Wilson, M. S. Mills, and R. G. Burns. 2002. "Comparison of Microbial Numbers and Enzymatic Activities in Surface Soils and Subsoils Using Various Techniques." *Soil Biology & Biochemistry* 34 (3): 387–401. http://dx.doi.org/10.1016/S0038-0717(01)00199-7.

Taylor, Mike. 2012. "It's Not Academic: How Publishers Are Squelching Science Communication." Accessed September 28, 2013. http://blogs.discovermagazine.com/crux/2012/02/21/its-not-academic-how-publishers-are-squelching-science-communication/#.UbJlauBFpm2.

ter Braak, Cajo J. F. 1985. "Correspondence Analysis of Incidence and Abundance Data: Properties in Terms of a Unimodal Response Model." *Biometrics* 41 (4): 859–73. http://dx.doi.org/10.2307/2530959.

ter Braak, Cajo J. F. 1986. "Canonical Correspondence Analysis: A New Eigenvector Technique for Multivariate Direct Gradient Analysis." *Ecology* 67 (5): 1167–79. http://dx.doi.org/10.2307/1938672.

ter Braak, Cajo J. F. 1987. "The Analysis of Vegetation-Environment Relationships by Canonical Correspondence Analysis." *Vegetatio* 69 (1–3): 69–77. http://dx.doi.org/10.1007/BF00038688.

ter Braak, Cajo J. F. 1988. "Partial Canonical Correspondence Analysis." In *Classification and Related Methods of Data Analysis*, edited by H. H. Bock, 551–58. Amsterdam: North-Holland.

ter Braak, Cajo J. F. 1994. "Canonical Community Ordination. Part I: Basic Theory and Linear Methods." *Ecoscience* 1 (2): 127–40.

ter Braak, Cajo J. F. 1995. "Ordination." In *Data Analysis in Community and Landscape Ecology*, edited by R. H. G. Jongman, C. J. F. ter Braak, and O. F. R. van Tongeren, 91–173. Cambridge: Cambridge University Press. http://dx.doi.org/10.1017/CBO9780511525575.007.

ter Braak, Cajo J. F. 1996. *Unimodal Models to Relate Species to Environment*. Wageningen: DLO-Agricultural Mathematics Group.

ter Braak, Cajo J. F., and Petr Šmilauer. 2002. *Canoco Reference Manual and Cano-draw for Windows User's Guide: Software for Canonical Community Ordination (Version 4.5)*. Ithaca, NY: Microcomputer Power.

ter Braak, Cajo J. F., and Piet F. M. Verdonschot. 1995. "Canonical Correspondence Analysis and Related Multivariate Methods in Aquatic Ecology." *Aquatic Sciences* 57 (3): 255–89. http://dx.doi.org/10.1007/BF00877430.

Terral, Jean-Frederic. 1997. ""Beginnings of Olive Domestication (*Olea europaea* L.) in North-Western Mediterranean Areas Shown by Morphometric Analyses Applied on Archaeological Charcoal." *Comptes Rendus de l'Academie des Sciences. Serie II A." Sciences de la Terre et des Plantes* 324 (5): 417–25.

Terral, Jean-Frédéric, and Aline Durand. 2006. "Bio-Archaeological Evidence of Olive Tree (*Olea europaea* L.) Irrigation During the Middle Ages in Southern France and North Eastern Spain." *Journal of Archaeological Science* 33 (5): 718–24. http://dx.doi.org/10.1016/j.jas.2005.10.004.

Terral, Jean-Frédéric, Claire Newton, Sarah Ivorra, Muriel Gros-Balthazard, Claire Tito de Morais, Sandrine Picq, Margareta Tengberg, and Jean-Christophe Pintaud. 2012. "Insights into the Historical Biogeography of the Date Palm (*Phoenix dactylifera* L.) Using Geometric Morphometry of Modern and Ancient Seeds." *Journal of Biogeography* 39 (5): 929–41. http://dx.doi.org/10.1111/j.1365-2699.2011.02649.x.

Terral, Jean-Frederic, Elidie Tabard, Laurent Bouby, Sarah Ivorra, Thierry Pastor, Isabel Figueiral, Sandrine Picq, Jean-Baptiste Chevance, Cecile Jung, Laurent Fabre, Christophe Tardy, Michel Compan, Roberto Bacilieri, Thierry Lacombe, and Patrice This. 2010. "Evolution and History of Grapevine (*Vitis vinifera*) under Domestication: New Morphometric Perspectives to Understand Seed Domestication Syndrome and Reveal Origins of Ancient European Cultivars." *Annals of Botany* 105 (3): 443–55. http://dx.doi.org/10.1093/aob/mcp298.

Terrell, John Edward, John P. Hart, Sibel Barut, Nicoletta Cellinese, Antonio Curet, Tim Denham, Chapurukha M. Kusimba, Kyle Latinis, Rahul Oka, Joel Palka, Mary E. D. Pohl, Kevin O. Pope, Patrick Ryan Williams, Helen Haines, and John E. Staller. 2003. "Domesticated Landscapes: The Subsistence Ecology of Plant and Animal Domestication." *Journal of Archaeological Method and Theory* 10 (4): 323–68. http://dx.doi.org/10.1023/B:JARM.0000005510.54214.57.

Tester, Richard F. 1997a. "Starch: The Polysaccharide Fractions." In *Starch: Structure and Functionality*, edited by P. J. Frazier, P. Richmond, and A. M. Donald, 163–71. Special Publications, no. 205. London: Royal Society of Chemistry.

Tester, Richard F. 1997b. "Properties of Damaged Starch Granules: Composition and Swelling Properties of Maize, Rice, Pea and Potato Starch Fractions in Water at

Various Temperatures." *Food Hydrocolloids* 11 (3): 293–301. http://dx.doi.org/10.1016/S0268-005X(97)80059-8.

Tester, Richard F., John Karkalas, and Xin Qi. 2004. "Starch—Composition, Fine Structure and Architecture." *Journal of Cereal Science* 39 (2): 151–65. http://dx.doi.org/10.1016/j.jcs.2003.12.001.

Therin, Michael. 1998. "The Movement of Starch Grains in Sediment." In *A Closer Look: Australian Studies of Stone Tools*, edited by Richard Fullagar, 61–72. Sydney: University of Sydney Archaeological Computing Laboratory.

Therin, Michael. 2006. "Starch Movement in Sediment." In *Ancient Starch Research*, edited by R. Torrence and H. Barton, 91–93. Walnut Creek, California: Left Coast Press.

Therin, Michael, Richard Fullagar, and Robin Torrence. 1999. "Starch in Sediments: A New Approach to the Study of Subsistence and Land Use in Papua New Guinea." In *The Prehistory of Food: Appetites for Change*, edited by Chris Gosden and Jon Hather, 438–62. London: Routledge.

Théry-Parisot, Isabelle. 2001. *Économie des Combustibles au Paléolithique: Expérimentation, Taphonomie, Anthracologie. Dossier de Documentation Archéologique 20*. Paris: C.N.R.S.

Théry-Parisot, Isabelle, Lucie Chabal, and Julia Chrzavzez. 2010. "Anthracology and Taphonomy, from Wood Gathering to Charcoal Analysis: A Review of the Taphonomic Processes Modifying Charcoal Assemblages, in Archaeological Contexts." *Palaeogeography, Palaeoclimatology, Palaeoecology* 291 (1–2): 142–53. http://dx.doi.org/10.1016/j.palaeo.2009.09.016.

Théry-Parisot, Isabelle, and Auréade Henry. 2012. "Seasoned or Green? Radial Cracks Analysis as a Method for Identifying the Use of Green Wood as Fuel in Archaeological Charcoal." *Journal of Archaeological Science* 39 (2): 381–88. http://dx.doi.org/10.1016/j.jas.2011.09.024.

Thiébault, Stéphanie. 2006. "Wood-Anatomical Evidence of Pollarding in Ring-Porous Species: A Study to Develop?" In *Charcoal Analysis: New Analytical Tools and Methods for Archaeology: Papers from the Table-Ronde Held in Basel 2004*, edited by Alexa Dufraisse, 95–102. Oxford: Archaeopress.

Thieme, Donald M. 2001. "Historic and Possible Prehistoric Impacts on Floodplain Sedimentation, North Branch of the Susquehanna River Valley, Pennsylvania, U.S.A." In *River Basin Sediment Systems: Archives of Environmental Change*, edited by Darrel Maddy, Mark G. Macklin, and Jamie C. Woodward, 375–403. Rotterdam: Balkema. http://dx.doi.org/10.1201/9781439824672.ch13.

Thomas, David Hurst. 1978. "The Awful Truth About Statistics in Archaeology." *American Antiquity* 43 (2): 231–44. http://dx.doi.org/10.2307/279247.

Thomas, David Hurst. 1980. "The Gruesome Truth About Statistics in Archaeology." *American Antiquity* 45 (2): 344–45. http://dx.doi.org/10.2307/279296.

Thompson, G. B. 1996. *The Excavation of Khok Phanom Di: A Prehistoric Site in Central Thailand, Volume IV: Subsistence and Environment: The Botanical Evidence (the Biological Remains, Part II). Reports of the Research Committee of the Society of Antiquaries of London, No. 53.* London: The Society of Antiquaries of London.

Thompson, Robert G., John Hart, Hetty Jo Brumbach, and Robert Lustech. 2004. "Phytolith Evidence for Twentieth-Century B.P. Maize in Northern Iroquoia." *Northeast Anthropology* 68:25–40.

Tieszen, Larry L., and Tim Fagre. 1993a. "Effect of Diet Quality and Composition on the Isotopic Composition of Respiratory CO_2, Bone Collagen, Bioapatite, and Soft Tissues." In *Prehistoric Human Bone-Archaeology at the Molecular Level*, edited by Joseph B. Lambert and Gisela Grupe, 121–55. Berlin: Springer-Verlag. http://dx.doi.org/10.1007/978-3-662-02894-0_5.

Tieszen, Larry L., and Tim Fagre. 1993b. "Carbon Isotopic Variability in Modern and Archaeological Maize." *Journal of Archaeological Science* 20 (1): 25–40. http://dx.doi.org/10.1006/jasc.1993.1002.

Tipples, K. H. 1969. "The Relation of Starch Damage to the Baking Performance of Flour." *Bakers Digest* 43:28–32.

Tolar, T., S. Jacomet, A. Veluscek, and K. Cufar. 2010. "Recovery Techniques for Waterlogged Archaeological Sediments: A Comparison of Different Treatment Methods for Samples from Neolithic Lake Shore Settlements." *Vegetation History and Archaeobotany* 19 (1): 53–67. http://dx.doi.org/10.1007/s00334-009-0221-y.

Toll, Mollie S. 1988. "Flotation Sampling: Problems and Some Solutions, with Examples from the American Southwest." In *Current Paleoethnobotany: Analytical Methods and Cultural Interpretations of Archaeological Plant Remains*, edited by Christine A. Hastorf and Virginia S. Popper, 36–52. Chicago: University of Chicago Press.

Torrence, Robin. 2006. "Description, Classification, and Identification." In *Ancient Starch Research*, edited by Robin Torrence and Huw Barton, 115–43. Walnut Creek, CA: Left Coast Press.

Torrence, Robin, and Huw Barton, eds. 2006. *Ancient Starch Research*. Walnut Creek, CA: Left Coast Press.

Torrence, Robin, Richard Wright, and Rebecca Conway. 2004. "Identification of Starch Granules Using Image Analysis and Multivariate Techniques." *Journal of Archaeological Science* 31 (5): 519–32. http://dx.doi.org/10.1016/j.jas.2003.09.014.

Treydte, Kerstin, Gerhard H. Schleser, Fritz H. Schweingruber, and Matthias Winiger. 2001. "The Climatic Significance of $\delta^{13}C$ in Subalpine Spruce (Lötschental,

Swiss Alps): A Case Study with Respect to Altitude, Exposure and Soil Moisture." *Tellus, Series B* 53:593–611. http://dx.doi.org/10.1034/j.1600-0889.2001.530505.x.

Trigger, Bruce. 1968. "Settlement as a Reflection of Social Structure." In *Settlement Archaeology*, edited by K. C. Chang, 117–33. Palo Alto: National Press.

Trigger, Bruce G. 2006. *A History of Archaeological Thought*. 2nd ed. Cambridge: Cambridge University Press. http://dx.doi.org/10.1017/CBO9780511813016.

Trimble, Stanley W. 1974. *Man-Induced Soil Erosion on the Southern Piedmont, 1700–1970*. Ankeny, Iowa: Soil and Water Conservation Society.

Tryon, Christian A. 2006. "The Destructive Potential of Earthworms on the Archaeobotanical Record." *Journal of Field Archaeology* 31 (2): 199–202. http://dx.doi.org/10.1179/009346906791072007.

Tsartsidou, Georgia, Simcha Lev-Yadun, Nikos Efstratiou, and Steve Weiner. 2008. "Ethnoarchaeological Study of Phytolith Assemblages from an Agro-Pastoral Village in Northern Greece (Sarakini): Development and Application of a Phytolith Difference Index." *Journal of Archaeological Science* 35 (3): 600–613. http://dx.doi.org/10.1016/j.jas.2007.05.008.

Tsartsidou, Georgia, Simcha Lev-Yadun, Nikos Efstratiou, and Steve Weiner. 2009. "Use of Space in a Neolithic Village in Greece (Makri): Phytolith Analysis and Comparison of Phytolith Assemblages from an Ethnographic Setting in the Same Area." *Journal of Archaeological Science* 36 (10): 2342–52. http://dx.doi.org/10.1016/j.jas.2009.06.017.

Tucker, Compton J., Jorge E. Pinzon, Molly E. Brown, Daniel A. Slayback, Edwin W. Pak, Robert Mahoney, Eric F. Vermote, and Nazmi El Saleous. 2005. "An Extended AVHRR 8-km NDVI Dataset Compatible with MODIS and SPOT Vegetation NDVI Data." *International Journal of Remote Sensing* 26 (20): 4485–98. http://dx.doi.org/10.1080/01431160500168686.

Tukey, John W. 1977. *Exploratory Data Analysis*. Reading, MA: Addison-Wesley.

Turner, Nancy. 1999. "Time to Burn." In *Indians, Fire and the Land in the Pacific Northwest*, edited by Robert Boyd, 185–218. Corvallis: Oregon University Press.

Turner, Nancy, Yilmaz Ari, Fikret Berkes, Iain Davidson-Hunt, Z. Fusun Ertuğ, and Andrew Miller. 2009. "Cultural Management of Living Trees: An International Perspective." *Journal of Ethnobiology* 29 (2): 237–70. http://dx.doi.org/10.2993/0278-0771-29.2.237.

Tweddle, John C., Kevin J. Edwards, and Nick R. J. Fieller. 2005. "Multivariate Statistical and Other Approaches for the Separation of Cereal from Wild Poaceae Pollen Using a Large Holocene Dataset." *Vegetation History and Archaeobotany* 14 (1): 15–30. http://dx.doi.org/10.1007/s00334-005-0064-0.

Twiddle, C. L., and M. Jane Bunting. 2010. "Experimental Investigations into the Preservation of Pollen Grains: A Pilot Study of Four Pollen Types." *Review of Palaeobotany and Palynology* 162 (4): 621–30. http://dx.doi.org/10.1016/j.revpalbo .2010.08.003.

Twiss, Page C. 1992. "Predicted World Distribution of C3 and C4 Grass Phytoliths." In *Phytolith Systematics: Emerging Issues*, edited by George Rapp, Jr., and Susan C. Mulholland, 113–28. New York: Plenum Press. http://dx.doi.org/10.1007/978-1 -4899-1155-1_6.

Twiss, P. C., Erwin Suess, and R. M. Smith. 1969. "Morphological Classification of Grass Phytoliths." *Soil Science Society of America Proceedings* 33:109–15.

Ur, Jason. 2003. "CORONA Satellite Photography and Ancient Road Networks: A Northern Mesopotamian Case Study." *Antiquity* 77 (295): 102–15.

Valamoti, Soultana M., and Glynis Jones. 2003. "Plant Diversity and Storage at Mandalo, Macedonia, Greece: Archaeobotanical Evidence from the Final Neolithic and Early Bronze Age." *Annual of the British School at Athens* 98:1–35. http://dx.doi .org/10.1017/S0068245400016816.

Valamoti, Soultana M., Delwen Samuel, Mustafa Bayram, and Elena Marinova. 2008. "Prehistoric Cereal Foods from Greece and Bulgaria: Investigation of Starch Microstructure in Experimental and Archaeological Charred Remains." *Vegetation History and Archaeobotany* 17 (S1): 265–76. http://dx.doi.org/10.1007/s00334-008 -0190-6.

Vale, Thomas R., ed. 2002. *Fire, Native Peoples, and the Natural Landscape.* Washington, D.C.: Island Press.

Van Bergen, P. F., H. A. Bland, M. C. Horton, and R. P. Evershed. 1997. "Chemical and Morphological Changes in Archaeological Seeds and Fruits During Preservation by Desiccation." *Geochimica et Cosmochimica Acta* 61 (9): 1919–30. http://dx.doi .org/10.1016/S0016-7037(97)00051-3.

van der Leeuw, Sander, and Charles L. Redman. 2002. "Placing Archaeology at the Center of Socio-Natural Studies." *American Antiquity* 67 (4): 597–605. http:// dx.doi.org/10.2307/1593793.

van der Merwe, Nikolaas J. 1989. "Natural Variation in ^{13}C Concentration and Its Effect on Environmental Reconstruction Using ^{13}C/^{12}C Ratios in Animal Bones." In *Chemistry of Prehistoric Human Bone*, edited by T. Douglas Price, 105–25. Cambridge: Cambridge University Press.

van der Merwe, Nikolaas J, and Ernesto Medina. 1991. "The Canopy Effect, Carbon Isotope Ratios and Foodwebs in Amazonia." *Journal of Archaeological Science* 18 (3): 249–59. http://dx.doi.org/10.1016/0305-4403(91)90064-V.

van der Merwe, Nikolaas J., and J. C. Vogel. 1978. "¹³C Content of Human Collagen as a Measure of Prehistoric Diet in Woodland North-America." *Nature* 276 (5690): 815–16. http://dx.doi.org/10.1038/276815a0.

VanDerwarker, Amber M. 2005. "Field Cultivation and Tree Management in Tropical Agriculture: A View from Gulf Coastal Mexico." *World Archaeology* 37 (2): 275–89. http://dx.doi.org/10.1080/00438240500095298.

VanDerwarker, Amber M. 2006. *Farming, Hunting, and Fishing in the Olmec World.* Austin: University of Texas Press.

VanDerwarker, Amber M. 2010a. "Correspondence Analysis and Principal Components Analysis as Methods for Integrating Archaeological Plant and Animal Remains." In *Integrating Zooarchaeology and Paleoethnobotany: A Consideration of Issues, Methods, and Cases,* edited by Amber M. VanDerwarker and Tanya M. Peres, 75–95. Berlin: Springer. http://dx.doi.org/10.1007/978-1-4419-0935-0_5.

VanDerwarker, Amber M. 2010b. "Simple Measures for Integrating Plant and Animal Remains." In *Integrating Zooarchaeology and Paleoethnobotany: A Consideration of Issues, Methods, and Cases,* edited by Amber M. VanDerwarker and Tanya M. Peres, 65–74. Berlin: Springer. http://dx.doi.org/10.1007/978-1-4419-0935-0_4.

VanDerwarker, Amber M., and Kandace R. Detwiler. 2002. "Gendered Practice in Cherokee Foodways: A Spatial Analysis of Plant Remains from the Coweeta Creek Site." *Southeastern Archaeology* 21 (1): 21–28.

VanDerwarker, Amber M., and Bruce Idol. 2008. "Rotten Food and Ritual Behavior: Late Woodland Plant Foodways and Special Purpose Features at Buzzard Rock II, Virginia (44RN2/70)." *Southeastern Archaeology* 27:61–77.

VanDerwarker, Amber M., and Robert P. Kruger. 2012. "Regional Variation in the Importance and Uses of Maize in the Early and Middle Formative Olmec Heartland: New Archaeobotanical Data from the San Carlos Homestead, Southern Veracruz." *Latin American Antiquity* 23 (4): 509–32. http://dx.doi.org/10.7183/1045-6635.23.4.509.

VanDerwarker, Amber M., Jon B. Marcoux, and Kandace D. Hollenbach. 2013. "Farming and Foraging at the Crossroads: The Consequences of Cherokee and European Interaction through the Late Eighteenth Century." *American Antiquity* 78 (1): 68–88. http://dx.doi.org/10.7183/0002-7316.78.1.68.

VanDerwarker, Amber M., and Tanya M. Peres, eds. 2010. *Integrating Zooarchaeology and Paleoethnobotany: A Consideration of Issues, Methods, and Cases.* Berlin: Springer. http://dx.doi.org/10.1007/978-1-4419-0935-0.

VanDerwarker, Amber M., C. Margaret Scarry, and Jane M. Eastman. 2007. "Menus for Families and Feasts: Household and Community Consumption of Plants at Upper Saratown, North Carolina." In *The Archaeology of Food and Identity,* edited by Katheryn C. Twiss, 16–49. Carbondale, IL: Center for Archaeological Investigations, Southern Illinois University.

VanDerwarker, Amber M., and Bill Stanyard. 2009. "Bearsfoot and Deer Legs: Archaeobotanical and Zooarchaeological Evidence of a Special-Purpose Encampment at the Sandy Site, Roanoke, Virginia." *Journal of Ethnobiology* 29 (1): 129–48. http://dx.doi.org/10.2993/0278-0771-29.1.129.

van der Veen, Marijke. 1987. "The Plant Remains." In *The Excavation of an Iron Age Settlement at Thorpe Thewles, Cleveland, 1980–1982. CBA Research Report 65*, edited by D. H. Heslop, 93–99. London: Cleveland County Archaeology.

van der Veen, Marijke. 1989. "Charred Grain Assemblages from Roman-Period Corn Driers in Britain." *The Archaeological Journal* 146:302–19.

van der Veen, Marijke. 1990. "Agriculture in North East England." *Archaeometry* 32:224–25.

van der Veen, Marijke. 1991. "Consumption or Production? Agriculture in the Cambridgeshire Fens." In *New Light on Early Farming: Recent Developments in Palaeoethnobotany*, edited by Jane M. Renfrew, 349–61. Edinburgh: Edinburgh University Press.

van der Veen, Marijke. 1992a. *Crop Husbandry Regimes: An Archaeobotanical Study of Farming in Northern England, 1000 BC–AD 500. Sheffield Archaeological Monographs 3*. Sheffield: Department of Archaeology and Prehistory, University of Sheffield.

van der Veen, Marijke. 1992b. "Garamantian Agriculture: The Plant Remains from Zinchecra." *Libyan Studies* 23:7–39.

van der Veen, Marijke. 1996. "The Plant Remains from Mons Claudianus, a Roman Quarry Settlement in the Eastern Desert of Egypt—an Interim Report." *Vegetation History and Archaeobotany* 5 (1–2): 137–41. http://dx.doi.org/10.1007/BF00189444.

van der Veen, Marijke. 1998. "A Life of Luxury in the Desert? The Food and Fodder Supply to Mons Claudianus." *Journal of Roman Archaeology* 11:101–16.

van der Veen, Marijke. 1999a. "The Economic Value of Chaff and Straw in Arid and Temperate Zones." *Vegetation History and Archaeobotany* 8 (3): 211–24. http://dx.doi.org/10.1007/BF02342721.

van der Veen, Marijke, ed. 1999b. *The Exploitation of Plant Resources in Ancient Africa*. New York: Kluwer Academic/Plenum Publishers. http://dx.doi.org/10.1007/978-1-4757-6730-8.

van der Veen, Marijke. 2004. "The Merchants' Diet: Food Remains from Roman and Medieval Quseir Al-Qadim, Egypt." In *Trade and Travel in the Red Sea Region: Proceedings of Red Sea Project I Held in the British Museum, October 2002*, edited by

Paul Lunde, and Alexandra Porter, 123–30. BAR international Series 1269. Oxford: Archaeopress.

van der Veen, Marijke. 2007a. "Formation Processes of Desiccated and Carbonized Plant Remains—the Identification of Routine Practice." *Journal of Archaeological Science* 34 (6): 968–90. http://dx.doi.org/10.1016/j.jas.2006.09.007.

van der Veen, Marijke. 2007b. "Luxury Food as an Instrument of Social Change: Feasting in Iron Age and Early Roman Britain." In *The Archaeology of Food and Identity*, edited by Katheryn C. Twiss, 112–29. Center for Archaeological Investigations Occasional Paper No. 34. Carbondale, IL: Southern Illinois University.

van der Veen, Marijke. 2011. *Consumption, Trade and Innovation: Exploring the Botanical Remains from the Roman and Islamic Ports at Quseir Al-Qadim, Egypt.* Frankfurt: Africa Magna Verlag.

van der Veen, Marijke, and Nick Fieller. 1982. "Sampling Seeds." *Journal of Archaeological Science* 9 (3): 287–98. http://dx.doi.org/10.1016/0305-4403(82)90024-3.

van der Veen, Marijke, and Glynis E. M. Jones. 2006. "A Re-Analysis of Agricultural Production and Consumption: Implications for Understanding the British Iron Age." *Vegetation History and Archaeobotany* 15 (3): 217–28. http://dx.doi.org/10.1007/s00334-006-0040-3.

Vandorpe, Patricia, and Stefanie Jacomet. 2007. "Comparing Different Pre-treament Methods for Strongly Compacted Organic Sediments Prior to Wet-Sieving: A Case Study on Roman Waterlogged Deposits." *Environmental Archaeology* 12 (2): 207–14.

van Heerwaarden, Joost, John Doebley, William H. Briggs, Jeffrey C. Glaubitz, Major M. Goodman, Jose de Jesus Sanchez Gonzalez, and Jeffrey Ross-Ibarra. 2011. "Genetic Signals of Origin, Spread, and Introgression in a Large Sample of Maize Landraces." *Proceedings of the National Academy of Sciences of the United States of America* 108 (3): 1088–92. http://dx.doi.org/10.1073/pnas.1013011108.

Van Liere, W. J., and J. Lauffray. 1954. "Nouvelle Prospection Archeologique dans la Haute Jazireh Syrienne." *Les Annales Archéologique Arabes Syriennes* 4/5:129–48.

van Tongeren, O. F. R. 1995. "Cluster Analysis." In *Data Analysis in Community and Landscape Ecology*, edited by R. H. G. Jongman, C. J. F. ter Braak, and O. F. R. van Tongeren, 174–212. Cambridge: Cambridge University Press. http://dx.doi.org/10.1017/CBO9780511525575.008.

van Zeist, Willem, and Johanna A. H. Bakker-Heeres. 1982. "Archaeobotanical Studies in the Levant 1. Neolithic Sites in the Damascus Basin: Aswad, Ghoraifé, Ramad." *Palaeohistoria* 24:165–256.

van Zeist, Willem, and Johanna A. H. Bakker-Heeres. 1984a. "Archaeobotanical Studies in the Levant 2. Neolithic and Halaf Levels at Ras Shamra." *Palaeohistoria* 26:151–70.

van Zeist, Willem, and Johanna A. H. Bakker-Heeres. 1984b. "Archaeobotanical Studies in the Levant 3. Late-Palaeolithic Mureybit." *Palaeohistoria* 26:171–99.

van Zeist, Willem, and Johanna A. H. Bakker-Heeres. 1985. "Archaeobotanical Studies in the Levant 4. Bronze Age Sites on the North Syrian Euphrates." *Palaeohistoria* 27:247–316.

van Zeist, Willem, and W. A. Casparie, eds. 1984. *Plants and Ancient Man: Studies in Palaeoethnobotany.* Rotterdam: A.A. Balkema.

van Zeist, Willem, and Rita M. Palfenier-Vegter. 1981. "Seeds and Fruits from the Swifterbant S3 Site." *Palaeohistoria* 23:105–68.

van Zeist, Willem, Krystyna Wasylikowa, and Karl-Ernst Behre, eds. 1991. *Progress in Old World Palaeoethnobotany.* Rotterdam: A.A. Balkema.

Vento, F. J., H. B. Rollins, M. Stewart, P. Raber, and W. Johnson. 1989. "Genetic Stratigraphy, Paleosol Development and the Burial of Archaeological Sites in the Susquehanna, Delaware, and Upper Ohio Drainage Basins, Pennsylvania." Unpublished manuscript, Pennsylvania Bureau for Historic Preservation, Harrisburg.

Verhoevan, Arno. 2010. "Posthole Archaeology." *Medieval and Modern Matters* 1:269–76.

Viau, André E., Konrad Gajewski, Phillippe Fines, David E. Atkinson, and Michael C. Sawada. 2002. "Widespread Evidence of 1500yr Climate Variability in North America During the Past 14000yr." *Geology* 30 (5): 455–58. http://dx.doi.org/10.1130 /0091-7613(2002)030<0455:WEOYCV>2.0.CO;2.

Virginia, Ross A., and Constant C. Delwiche. 1982. "Natural [15]N Abundance of Presumed N_2-Fixing and Non-N_2-Fixing Plants from Selected Ecosystems." *Oecologia* 54 (3): 317–25. http://dx.doi.org/10.1007/BF00380000.

Vogel, J. C., A. Fuls, and R. Ellis. 1978. "Geographical Distribution of Kranz Grasses in South-Africa." *South African Journal of Science* 74 (6): 209–15.

Vogel, J. C., and Nikolaas J. van der Merwe. 1977. "Isotopic Evidence for Early Maize Cultivation in New York State." *American Antiquity* 42 (2): 238–42. http://dx.doi .org/10.2307/278984.

Voorhies, Barbara. 1976. *The Cantuto People: An Archaic Period Society of the Chiapas Littoral, Mexico.* Papers of the New World Archaeological Foundation 41. Provo, UT: Brigham Young University, New World Archaeological Foundation.

Wada, Eitaro, Toshiki Kadonaga, and Sadao Matsuo. 1975. "[15]N Abundance in Nitrogen of Naturally Occurring Substances and Global Assessment of Denitrification from Isotopic Viewpoint." *Geochemical Journal* 9 (3): 139–48. http://dx.doi.org/10 .2343/geochemj.9.139.

Wadley, Lyn, Marlize Lombard, and Bonny Williamson. 2004. "The First Residue Analysis Blind Test: Results and Lessons Learnt." *Journal of Archaeological Science* 31 (11): 1491–501. http://dx.doi.org/10.1016/j.jas.2004.03.010.

Wagner, Gail E. 1976. "IDOT Flotation Procedure Manual." Unpublished manuscript, Illinois Department of Transportation, District 8.

Wagner, Gail E. 1982. "Testing Flotation Recovery Rates." *American Antiquity* 47 (1): 127–32. http://dx.doi.org/10.2307/280058.

Wagner, Gail E. 1988. "Comparability among Recovery Techniques." In *Current Paleoethnobotany: Analytical Methods and Cultural Interpretations of Archaeological Plant Remains*, edited by Christine A. Hastorf and Virginia S. Popper, 17–35. Chicago: University of Chicago Press.

Wales, Nathan, J. Alberto Romero-Navarro, Enrico Cappellini, and M. Thomas P. Gilbert. 2012. "Choosing the Best Plant for the Job: A Cost-Effective Assay to Prescreen Ancient Plant Remains Destined for Shotgun Sequencing." *PLoS ONE* 7 (9): e45644. http://dx.doi.org/10.1371/journal.pone.0045644.

Walker, Phillip L., and Michael J. DeNiro. 1986. "Stable Nitrogen and Carbon Isotope Ratios in Bone Collagen as Indices of Prehistoric Dietary Dependence on Marine and Terrestrial Resources in Southern California." *American Journal of Physical Anthropology* 71 (1): 51–61. http://dx.doi.org/10.1002/ajpa.1330710107.

Walters, Robert C., and Dorothy J. Merritts. 2008. "Natural Streams and the Legacy of Water-Powered Mills." *Science* 319 (5861): 299–304. http://dx.doi.org/10.1126/science.1151716.

Wanner, Heinz, Jürg Beer, Jonathan Bütlkofer, Thomas J. Crowley, Ulrich Cubasch, Jacqueline Flücklger, Hugues Goosse, Martin Grosjean, Fortunat Joos, Jed O. Kaplan, Marcel Küttel, Simon A. Müller, I. Colin Prentice, Olga Solomina, Thomas F. Stocker, Pavel Tarasov, Mayke Wagner, and Martin Widmann. 2008. "Mid- to Late Holocene Climate Change: An Overview." *Quaternary Science Reviews* 27 (19–20): 1791–828. http://dx.doi.org/10.1016/j.quascirev.2008.06.013.

Ward, Joe H., Jr. 1963. "Hierarchical Grouping to Optimize an Objective Function." *Journal of the American Statistical Association* 58 (301): 236–44. http://dx.doi.org/10.1080/01621459.1963.10500845.

Warinner, Christina. 2010. "Life and Death at Teposcolula Yucundaa." Unpublished PhD diss., Department of Anthropology, Harvard University, Cambridge.

Warinner, Christina, Nelly Robles García, and Noreen Tuross. 2013. "Maize, Beans and the Floral Isotopic Diversity of Highland Oaxaca, Mexico." *Journal of Archaeological Science* 40 (2): 868–73. http://dx.doi.org/10.1016/j.jas.2012.07.003.

Warinner, Christina, Jade d'Alpoim Guedes, and David Goode. 2011. "Paleobot.org: Establishing Open-Access Online Reference Collections for Archaeobotanical Research." *Vegetation History and Archaeobotany* 20 (3): 241–44. http://dx.doi.org/10.1007/s00334-011-0282-6.

Warinner, Christina, Joäo F. Matias Rodrigues, Rounak Vyas, Christian Trach-
sel, Natalia Shved, Jonas Grossmann, Anita Radini, Y. Hancock, Raul Y. Tito,
Sarah Fiddyment, Camilla Speller, Jessica Hendy, Sophy Charlton, Hans Ulrich
Luder, Domingo C. Salazar-García, Elisabeth Eppler, Roger Seiler, Lars H.
Hansen, José Alfredo Samaniego Castruita, Simon Barkow-Oesterreicher, Kai
Yik Teoh, Christian D. Kelstrup, Jesper V. Olsen, Paolo Nanni, Toshihisa Kawai,
Eske Willerslev, Christian von Mering, Cecil M. Lewis, Jr., Matthew J. Collins,
M. Thomas P. Gilbert, Frank Rühli, Enrico Cappellini. 2014. "Pathogens and
host immunity in the ancient human oral cavity." Nature Genetics 46 (4):336–44.
doi:10.1038/ng.2906.

Warinner, Christina, and Noreen Tuross. 2009. "Alkaline Cooking and Stable Isotope
Tissue-Diet Spacing in Swine: Archaeological Implications." Journal of Archaeological Science 36 (8): 1690–97. http://dx.doi.org/10.1016/j.jas.2009.03.034.

Warinner, Christina, and Noreen Tuross. 2010. "Tissue Isotopic Enrichment Associated with Growth Depression in a Pig: Implications for Archaeology and Ecology."
American Journal of Physical Anthropology 141:486–93.

Wasylikowa, Krystyna, and Jeff Dahlberg. 1999. "Sorghum in the Economy of the
Early Neolithic Nomadic Tribes at Nabta Playa, Southern Egypt." In The Exploi-
tation of Plant Resources in Ancient Africa, edited by Marijke van der Veen, 11–31.
New York: Kluwer Academic. http://dx.doi.org/10.1007/978-1-4757-6730-8_2.

Wasylikowa, Krystyna, Jóazef Mitka, Fred Wendorf, and Romuald Schild. 1997.
"Exploitation of Wild Plants by the Early Neolithic Hunter-Gatherers of the
Western Desert, Egypt: Nabta Playa as a Case-Study." Antiquity 71 (274): 932–41.

Watson, Patty Jo. 1976. "In Pursuit of Prehistoric Subsistence: A Comparative
Account of Some Contemporary Flotation Systems." Midcontinental Journal of
Archaeology 1:77–100.

Watson, Patty Jo. 1991. "A Parochial Primer: The New Dissonance as Seen from the
Midcontinental United States." In Processual and Postprocessual Archaeologies: Mul-
tiple Ways of Knowing the Past, edited by Robert W. Preucel, 265–74. Carbondale,
IL: Southern Illinois University Press.

Watson, Patty Jo. 1997. "The Shaping of Modern Paleoethnobotany." In People, Plants,
and Landscapes: Studies in Paleoethnobotany, edited by Kristin J. Gremillion, 13–22.
Tuscaloosa: University of Alabama Press.

Watson, Patty Jo. 2009. "Archaeology and Anthropology: A Personal Overview of
the Past Half-Century." Annual Review of Anthropology 38 (1): 1–15. http://dx.doi
.org/10.1146/annurev-anthro-091908-164458.

Watson, Patty Jo, Steven A. LeBlanc, and Charles L. Redman. 1971. Explanation in
Archeology: An Explicitly Scientific Approach. New York: Columbia University Press.

Watts, W. A. 1978. "Plant Macrofossils and Quaternary Paleoecology." In *Biology and Quaternary Environments*, edited by D. Walker and J. C. Guppy, 53–67. Canberra: Australian Academy of Science.

Webb, Elizabeth A., Henry P. Schwarcz, and Paul F. Healy. 2004. "Detection of Ancient Maize in Lowland Maya Soils Using Stable Carbon Isotopes: Evidence from Caracol, Belize." *Journal of Archaeological Science* 31 (8): 1039–52. http://dx.doi.org/10.1016/j.jas.2004.01.001.

Webster, David, David Rue, and Alfred Traverse. 2005. "Early *Zea* Cultivation in Honduras: Implications for the Ilitis Hypothesis." *Economic Botany* 59 (2): 101–11. http://dx.doi.org/10.1663/0013-0001(2005)059[0101:EZCIHI]2.0.CO;2.

Weier, John, and David Herring. 2000. "Measuring Vegetation (NDVI & EVI)." Accessed July 15, 2013. http://earthobservatory.nasa.gov/Features/MeasuringVegetation/measuring_vegetation_1.php.

Weiner, Annette B. 1995. "Culture and Our Discontents." *American Anthropologist* 97 (1): 14–21. http://dx.doi.org/10.1525/aa.1995.97.1.02a00040.

Weiser, Andrea, and Dana Lepofsky. 2009. "Ancient Land Use and Management of Ebey's Prairie, Whidbey Island, Washington." *Journal of Ethnobiology* 29 (2): 184–212. http://dx.doi.org/10.2993/0278-0771-29.2.184.

Weismantel, Mary J. 1988. *Food, Gender, and Poverty in the Ecuadorian Andes*. Philadelphia: University of Pennsylvania Press.

Weiss, Ehud, and Mordechai E. Kislev. 2004. "Plant Remains as Indicators for Economic Activity: A Case Study from Iron Age Ashkelon." *Journal of Archaeological Science* 31 (1): 1–13. http://dx.doi.org/10.1016/S0305-4403(03)00072-4.

Weiss, Ehud, Mordechai E. Kislev, Orit Simchoni, Dani Nadel, and Hartmut Tschauner. 2008. "Plant-Food Preparation Area on an Upper Paleolithic Brush Hut Floor at Ohalo II, Israel." *Journal of Archaeological Science* 35 (8): 2400–2414. http://dx.doi.org/10.1016/j.jas.2008.03.012.

Welch, Paul D., and C. Margaret Scarry. 1995. "Status-Related Variation in Foodways in the Moundville Chiefdom." *American Antiquity* 60 (3): 397–419. http://dx.doi.org/10.2307/282257.

Wendland, Wayne M., and Reid A. Bryson. 1974. "Dating Climatic Episodes of the Holocene." *Quaternary Research* 4 (1): 9–24. http://dx.doi.org/10.1016/0033-5894(74)90060-X.

Wesolowski, Veronica, Sheila Maria Ferraz Mendonça de Souza, Karl J. Reinhard, and Gregorio Ceccantini. 2010. "Evaluating Microfossil Content of Dental Calculus from Brazilian Sambaquis." *Journal of Archaeological Science* 37 (6): 1326–38. http://dx.doi.org/10.1016/j.jas.2009.12.037.

Wetterstrom, Wilma. 1978. "Cognitive Systems, Food Patterns, and Paleoethnobotany." In *The Nature and Status of Ethnobotany*, edited by R. Ford, 81–95. Ann Arbor: University of Michigan Museum of Anthropology.

Wheeler, Elisabeth A. 2011. "InsideWood—a Web Resource for Hardwood Anatomy." *IAWA Journal* 32 (2): 199–211.

Wheeler, Ryan J., James J. Miller, Ray M. McGee, Donna Ruhl, Brenda Swann, and Melissa Memory. 2003. "Archaic Period Canoes from Newnans Lake, Florida." *American Antiquity* 68 (3): 533–51. http://dx.doi.org/10.2307/3557107.

Whelchel, David L., ed. 2005. *Ozette Archaeological Project Research Reports, Volume III: Ethobotany and Wood Technology*. Report of Investigations 68. Pullman: Department of Anthropology, Washington State University and Pacific Northwest Regional Office, National Park Service.

White, Christine D., Mary Pohl, Henry P. Schwarcz, and Fred Longstaffe. 2004. "Feast, Field, and Forest: Deer and Dog Diets at Lagartero, Tikal, and Copan." In *Maya Zooarchaeology*, edited by Kitty Emery, 141–58. Los Angeles: University of California, Cotsen Institute of Archaeology 51.

White, Chantel E. 2011. "The Hand-Pump Flotation Tank." Accessed October 30. http://www.microcommons.org/items/show/29.

Whiting, Alfred F. 1944. "The Origin of Corn: An Evaluation of Fact and Theory." *American Anthropologist* 46 (4): 500–515. http://dx.doi.org/10.1525/aa.1944.46.4 .02a00060.

Wilk, Richard R., and Robert McC. Netting. 1984. "Households: Changing Forms and Functions." In *Households: Comparative and Historical Studies of the Domestic Group*, edited by Robert McC. Netting, Richard R. Wilk, and Eric J. Arnould, 1–28. Berkeley: University of California Press.

Wilkinson, Keith, and Chris J. Stevens. 2003. *Environmental Archaeology: Approaches, Techniques and Applications*. Stroud, Gloucestershire, UK: Tempus.

Wilkinson, Leland, MaryAnn Jill, Stacey Miceli, Gregory Birkenbeuel, and Erin Vang. 1992. *SYSTAT Graphics*. Evanston, IL: Systat Inc.

Wilkinson, Tony J. 1993. "Linear Hollows in the Jazira, Upper Mesopotamia." *Antiquity* 67 (256): 548–62.

Wilkinson, Tony J., J. H. Christiansen, J. Ur, M. Widell, and M. Altaweel. 2007. "Urbanization within a Dynamic Environment: Modeling Bronze Age Communities in Upper Mesopotamia." *American Anthropologist* 109 (1): 52–68. http://dx.doi .org/10.1525/aa.2007.109.1.52.

Wilkinson, Tony J., Charles French, Jason A. Ur, and Miranda Semple. 2010. "The Geoarchaeology of Route Systems in Northern Syria." *Geoarchaeology: An International Journal* 25 (6): 745–71. http://dx.doi.org/10.1002/gea.20331.

Willcox, George. 1974. "A History of Deforestation as Indicated by Charcoal Analysis of Four Sites in Eastern Anatolia." *Anatolian Studies* 24:117–33. http://dx.doi .org/10.2307/3642603.

Willcox, George. 2004. "Measuring Grain Size and Identifying Near Eastern Cereal Domestication: Evidence from the Euphrates Valley." *Journal of Archaeological Science* 31 (2): 145–50. http://dx.doi.org/10.1016/j.jas.2003.07.003.

Willerslev, Eske, Enrico Cappellini, Wouter Boomsma, Rasmus Nielsen, Martin B. Hebsgaard, Tina B. Brand, Michael Hofreiter, Michael Bunce, Hendrik N. Poinar, Dorthe Dahl-Jensen, Sigfus Johnsen, Jørgen Peder Steffensen, Ole Bennike, Jean-Luc Schwenninger, Roger Nathan, Simon Armitage, Cees-Jan de Hoog, Vasily Alfimov, Marcus Christl, Juerg Beer, Raimund Muscheler, Joel Barker, Martin Sharp, Kirsty E. H. Penkman, James Haile, Pierre Taberlet, M. Thomas P. Gilbert, Antonella Casoli, Elisa Campani ,and Matthew J. Collins. 2007. "Ancient Biomolecules from Deep Ice Cores Reveal a Forested Southern Greenland." *Science* 317 (5834): 111–14. http://dx.doi.org/10.1126/science.1141758.

Willerslev, Eske, and Alan Cooper. 2005. "Review Paper: Ancient DNA." *Proceedings of the Royal Society B: Biological Sciences* 272 (1558): 3–16. http://dx.doi.org/10.1098 /rspb.2004.2813.

Willerslev, Eske, Anders J. Hansen, Jonas Binladen, Tina B. Brand, M. Thomas P. Gilbert, Beth Shapiro, Michael Bunce, Carsten Wiuf, David A. Gilichinsky, and Alan Cooper. 2003. "Diverse Plant and Animal Genetic Records from Holocene and Pleistocene Sediments." *Science* 300 (5620): 791–95. http://dx.doi.org/10.1126 /science.1084114.

Williams, David. 1973. "Flotation at Siraf." *Antiquity* 47 (188): 288–92.

Williams, Gerald W. 2002. "Aboriginal Use of Fire: Are There Any 'Natural' Plant Communities?" In *Wilderness and Political Ecology: Aboriginal Influences and the Original State of Nature*, edited by Charles E. Kay and Randy T. Simmons, 179–214. Salt Lake City: University of Utah Press.

Willis, K. J., and K. D. Bennett. 1994. "The Neolithic Transition—Fact or Fiction? Palaeoecological Evidence from the Balkans." *The Holocene* 4 (3): 326–30. http:// dx.doi.org/10.1177/095968369400400313.

Wilson, D. G. 1984. "The Carbonisation of Weed Seeds and Their Representation in Macrofossil Assemblages." In *Plants and Ancient Man: Studies in Palaeoethnobotany*, edited by Willem van Zeist and W. A. Casparie, 199–206. Rotterdam: A. A. Balkema.

Wilson, David Raoul. 1982. *Air Photo Interpretation for Archaeologists*. New York: St. Martin's Press.

Wilson, S. M. 1985. "Phytolith Analysis at Kuk, an Early Agricultural Site in Papua, New Guinea." *Archaeology in Oceania* 20:90–97.

Winter, Klaus, and Joseph A. M. Holtum. 2002. "How Closely Do the d¹³C Values of Crassulacean Acid Metabolism Plants Reflect the Proportion of CO_2 Fixed During Day and Night?" *Plant Physiology* 129 (4): 1843–51. http://dx.doi.org/10.1104/pp.002915.

Winterhalder, Bruce. 2002. "Models." In *Darwin and Archaeology: A Handbook of Key Concepts*, edited by John P. Hart and John Edward Terrell, 201–24. Westport, Connecticut: Bergin and Garvey.

Winterhalder, Bruce, and Carol Goland. 1993. "On Population, Foraging Efficiency, and Plant Domestication." *Current Anthropology* 34 (5): 710–15. http://dx.doi.org/10.1086/204214.

Winterhalder, Bruce, and Carol Goland. 1997. "An Evolutionary Ecology Perspective on Diet Choice, Risk, and Plant Domestication." In *People, Plants, and Landscapes: Studies in Paleoethnobotany*, edited by Kristin J. Gremillion, 123–60. Tuscaloosa: University of Alabama Press.

Winterhalder, Bruce, and Douglas Kennett. 2006. "Behavioral Ecology and the Transition from Hunting and Gathering to Agriculture." In *Behavioral Ecology and the Transition to Agriculture*, edited by Douglas J. Kennett, and Bruce Winterhalder, 1–21. Berkeley: University of California Press.

Winterhalder, Bruce, Douglas J. Kennett, Mark N. Grote, and Jacob Bartruff. 2010. "Ideal Free Settlement of California's Northern Channel Islands." *Journal of Anthropological Archaeology* 29 (4): 469–90. http://dx.doi.org/10.1016/j.jaa.2010.07.001.

Winterhalder, Bruce, and Eric Alden Smith. 2000. "Analyzing Adaptive Strategies: Human Behavioral Ecology at Twenty-Five." *Evolutionary Anthropology* 9 (2): 51–72. http://dx.doi.org/10.1002/(SICI)1520-6505(2000)9:2<51::AID-EVAN1>3.0.CO;2-7.

Wollstonecroft, Michèle M., Zdenka Hroudová, Gordon C. Hillman, and Dorian Q Fuller. 2011. "*Bolboschoenus glaucus* (Lam.) S. G. Smith, a New Species in the Flora of the Ancient Near East." *Vegetation History and Archaeobotany* 20 (5): 459–70. http://dx.doi.org/10.1007/s00334-011-0305-3.

Wood, W. R., and D. L. Johnson. 1978. "A Survey of Disturbance Processes in Archaeological Site Formation." In *Advances in Archaeological Method and Theory*, edited by Michael B. Schiffer, 315–81. New York: Academic Press.

Woodson, Alex. 2007. "Wikipedia Remains Go-to Site for News." *Reuters* July 8, 2007. http://www.reuters.com/article/2007/07/08/us-media-wikipedia-idUSN0819429120070708.

Wootton, M., and P. Ho. 1989. "Alkali Gelatinization of Wheat Starch." *Stärke* 41 (7): 261–65. http://dx.doi.org/10.1002/star.19890410706.

Wright, David R., Richard E. Terry, and Markus Eberl. 2009. "Soil Properties and Stable Carbon Isotope Analysis of Landscape Features in the Petexbatun Region of Guatemala." *Geoarchaeology: An International Journal* 24 (4): 466–91. http://dx.doi.org/10.1002/gea.20275.

Wright, Lori E. 1994. *The Sacrifice of the Earth: Diet, Health, and Inequality in the Pasión Maya Lowlands*. Chicago: Anthropology Department, University of Chicago.

Wright, Lori E. 1997. "Ecology or Society? Paleodiet and the Collapse of the Pasion Maya Lowlands." In *Bones of the Maya: Studies of Ancient Skeletons*, edited by Stephen Whittington and David Reed, 181–95. Washington, DC: Smithsonian Institution Press.

Wright, Lori E. 2006. *Diet, Health, and Status among the Pasion Maya: A Reappraisal of the Collapse*. Nashville: Vanderbilt University Press.

Wright, Patti J. 2003. "Preservation or Destruction of Plant Remains by Carbonization?" *Journal of Archaeological Science* 30 (5): 577–83. http://dx.doi.org/10.1016/S0305-4403(02)00203-0.

Wright, Patti J. 2005. "Flotation Samples and Some Paleoethnobotanical Implications." *Journal of Archaeological Science* 32 (1): 19–26. http://dx.doi.org/10.1016/j.jas.2004.06.003.

Wright, Patti J. 2008. "Understanding the Carbonization and Preservation of Sunflower and Sumpweed Remains." *Midcontinental Journal of Archaeology* 33 (2): 139–53. http://dx.doi.org/10.1179/mca.2008.009.

Wright, Patti J. 2010. "Methodological Issues in Paleoethnobotany: A Consideration of Issues, Methods, and Cases." In *Integrating Zooarchaeology and Paleoethnobotany: A Consideration of Issues, Methods, and Cases*, edited by Amber M. VanDerwarker and Tanya M. Peres, 37–64. Berlin: Springer. http://dx.doi.org/10.1007/978-1-4419-0935-0_3.

Wright, Rita P., David L. Lentz, Harriet F. Beaubien, and Christine K. Kimbrough. 2012. "New Evidence for Jute (*Corchorus capsularis* L.) in the Indus Civilization." *Archaeological and Anthropological Sciences* 4 (2): 137–43. http://dx.doi.org/10.1007/s12520-012-0088-1.

Wykoff, Milton W. 1988. "Iroquoian Prehistory and Climate Change: Notes for Empirical Studies of the Eastern Woodlands." Unpublished PhD diss., Department of Anthropology, Cornell University, Ithaca.

Wykoff, Milton W. 1991. "Black Walnut on Iroquoian Landscapes." *Northeast Indian Quarterly* 4:4–17.

Wymer, Dee Anne. 1993. "Cultural Change and Subsistence: The Middle and Late Woodland Transition in the Mid-Ohio Valley." In *Foraging and Farming in the*

Eastern Woodlands, edited by C. Margaret Scarry, 138–56. Gainesville: University Press of Florida.

Wynn, Jonathan G., and Michael I. Bird. 2008. "Environmental Controls on the Stable Carbon Isotopic Composition of Soil Organic Carbon: Implications for Modelling the Distribution of C_3 and C_4 Plants, Australia." *Tellus. Series B, Chemical and Physical Meteorology* 60 (4): 604–21. http://dx.doi.org/10.1111/j.1600-0889.2008.00361.x.

Yang, XiaoYan, JinCheng Yu, HouYuan Lü, TianXing Cui, JingNing Guo, and Quan-Sheng Ge. 2009. "Starch Grain Analysis Reveals Function of Grinding Stone Tools at Shangzhai Site, Beijing." *Science in China Series D: Earth Sciences* 52 (8): 1164–71.

Yarnell, Richard A. 1964. *Aboriginal Relationships between Culture and Plant Life in the Upper Great Lakes Region*. Anthropological Papers 23. Ann Arbor: University of Michigan Museum of Anthropology.

Yarnell, Richard A. 1972. "*Iva annua* var. *macrocarpa*: Extinct American Cultigen?" *American Anthropologist* 74 (3): 335–41. http://dx.dci.org/10.1525/aa.1972.74.3.02a00060.

Yarnell, Richard A. 1978. "Domestication of Sunflower and Sumpweed in Eastern North America." In *The Nature and Status of Ethnobotany*, edited by R. I. Ford, 289–99. Anthropological Papers 67. Ann Arbor: University of Michigan Museum of Anthropology.

Yarnell, Richard A. 1982. "Problems of Interpretation of Archaeological Plant Remains of the Eastern Woodlands." *Southeastern Archaeology* 1:1–7.

Yashina, Svetlana, Stanislav Gubin, Stanislav Maksimovich, Alexandra Yashina, Edith Gakhova, and David Gilichinsky. 2012. "Regeneration of Whole Fertile Plants from 30,000-y-Old Fruit Tissue Buried in Siberian Permafrost." *Proceedings of the National Academy of Sciences of the United States of America* 109 (10): 4008–13. http://dx.doi.org/10.1073/pnas.1118386109.

Yoffee, Norman, and Andrew Sherratt. 1993. "Introduction: The Sources of Archaeological Theory." In *Archaeological Theory: Who Sets the Agenda*, edited by Norman Yoffee, 1–10. Cambridge: Cambridge University Press. http://dx.doi.org/10.1017/CBO9780511720277.001.

Young, Michael W. 1971. *Fighting with Food: Leadership, Values and Social Control in a Massim Society*. Cambridge: Cambridge University Press.

Yuan, Yue, Tong-Jian Shen, Priyamvada Gupta, Nancy T. Ho, Virgil Simplaceanu, Tsuey Chyi S. Tam, Michael Hofreiter, Alan Cooper, Kevin L. Campbell, and Chien Ho. 2011. "A Biochemical-Biophysical Study of Hemoglobins from Woolly Mammoth, Asian Elephant, and Humans." *Biochemistry* 50 (34): 7350–60. http://dx.doi.org/10.1021/bi200777j.

Zalasiewicz, Jan, Mark Williams, Richard Fortey, Alan Smith, Tiffany L. Barry, Angela L. Coe, Paul R. Bown, Peter F. Rawson, Andrew Gale, Philip Gibbard, F. John Gregory, Mark W. Hounslow, Andrew C. Kerr, Paul Pearson, Robert Knox, John Powell, Colin Waters, John Marshall, Michael Oates, and Philip Stone. 2011. "Stratigraphy of the Anthropocene." *Philosophical Transactions of the Royal Society* 369 (1938): 1036–55. http://dx.doi.org/10.1098/rsta.2010.0315.

Zarrillo, Sonia, and Brian Kooyman. 2006. "Evidence for Berry and Maize Processing on the Canadian Plains from Starch Grain Analysis." *American Antiquity* 71 (3): 473–99. http://dx.doi.org/10.2307/40035361.

Zarrillo, Sonia, Deborah M. Pearsall, Scott J. Raymond, Mary Ann Tisdale, and J. Dugane Quon. 2008. "Directly Dated Starch Residues Document Early Formative Maize (*Zea mays* L.) in Tropical Ecuador." *Proceedings of the National Academy of Sciences of the United States of America* 105 (13): 5006–11. http://dx.doi.org/10.1073/pnas.0800894105.

Zeanah, David W. 2004. "Sexual Division of Labor and Central Place Foraging: A Model for the Carson Desert of Western Nevada." *Journal of Anthropological Archaeology* 23 (1): 1–32. http://dx.doi.org/10.1016/S0278-4165(03)00061-8.

Zeder, Melinda A. 2009. "The Neolithic Macro-(R)evolution: Macroevolutionary Theory and the Study of Culture Change." *Journal of Archaeological Research* 17 (1): 1–63. http://dx.doi.org/10.1007/s10814-008-9025-3.

Zeder, Melinda A. 2012. "The Broad Spectrum Revolution at 40: Resource Diversity, Intensification, and an Alternative to Optimal Foraging Explanations." *Journal of Anthropological Archaeology* 31 (3): 241–64. http://dx.doi.org/10.1016/j.jaa.2012.03.003.

Zeder, Melinda A., Daniel G. Bradley, Eve Emshwiller, and Bruce D. Smith, eds. 2006. *Documenting Domestication: New Genetic and Archeological Paradigms*. Berkeley: University of California Press.

Zeder, Melinda A., Eve Emshwiller, Bruce D. Smith, and Daniel G. Bradley. 2006. "Documenting Domestication: The Intersection of Genetics and Archaeology." *Trends in Genetics* 22 (3): 139–55. http://dx.doi.org/10.1016/j.tig.2006.01.007.

Zeder, Melinda A., and Bruce D. Smith. 2009. "A Conversation on Agricultural Origins: Talking Past Each Other in a Crowded Room." *Current Anthropology* 50 (5): 681–91. http://dx.doi.org/10.1086/605553.

Zhang, Hai, Andrew Bevan, Dorian Fuller, and Yanming Fang. 2010. "Archaeobotanical and GIS-Based Approaches to Prehistoric Agriculture in the Upper Ying Valley, Henan, China." *Journal of Archaeological Science* 37 (7): 1480–89. http://dx.doi.org/10.1016/j.jas.2010.01.008.

Zhao, Zhijun. 2007. "Flotation Techniques and Their Application in Chinese Archaeology." In *From Concepts of the Past to Practical Strategies: The Teaching of*

Archaeological Field Techniques, edited by Peter Ucko, Qin Ling, and Jane Hubert, 207–12. London: Saffron Books.

Zhao, Zhijun. 2010. *Zhiwu Kaogu: Lilun, Fangfa He Shixian* 植物考古学：理论，方法和实现 *(Paleoethnobotany: Theory, Methods, Practice).* Beijing: Science Press.

Zhao, Zhijun, Deborah Pearsall, Robert Benfer, and Dolores Piperno. 1998. "Distinguishing Rice (*Oryza sativa* Poaceae) from Wild *Oryza* Species through Phytolith Analysis, II: Finalized Method." *Economic Botany* 52 (2): 134–45. http://dx.doi.org/10.1007/BF02861201.

Zhao, Zhijun, and Deborah M. Pearsall. 1998. "Experiments for Improving Phytolith Extraction from Soils." *Journal of Archaeological Science* 25 (6): 587–98. http://dx.doi.org/10.1006/jasc.1997.0262.

Zheng, Yunfei, Guoping Sun, Ling Qin, Chunhai Li, Xiaohong Wu, and Xugao Chen. 2009. "Rice Fields and Modes of Rice Cultivation between 5000 and 2500 BC in East China." *Journal of Archaeological Science* 36 (12): 2609–16. http://dx.doi.org/10.1016/j.jas.2009.09.026.

Zohary, Daniel, and Maria Hopf. 2000. *Domestication of Plants in the Old World. The Origin and Spread of Cultivated Plants in West Asia, Europe and the Nile Valley.* Oxford: Oxford University Press.

Zong, Y., Z. Chen, J. B. Innes, C. Chen, Z. Wang, and H. Wang. 2007. "Fire and Flood Management of Coastal Swamp Enabled First Rice Paddy Cultivation in East China." *Nature* 449 (7161): 459–62. http://dx.doi.org/10.1038/nature06135.

Zurro, Débora, Marco Madella, Ivan Briz, and Assumpció Vila. 2009. "Variability of the Phytolith Record in Fisher-Hunter-Gatherer Sites: An Example from the Yamana Society (Beagle Channel, Tierra Del Fuego, Argentina)." *Quaternary International* 193 (1–2): 184–91. http://dx.doi.org/10.1016/j.quaint.2007.11.007.

JENNIFER V. ALVARADO is a Laboratory Assistant in the Department of Anthropology, University of California, Santa Barbara, USA, and an Associate Biologist at Rincon Consultants, Inc.

KENNETH ANDERSEN received his Ph.D. from the Centre for GeoGenetics, Natural History Museum of Denmark, University of Copenhagen, Denmark.

ENRICO CAPPELLINI is an Assistant Professor at the Centre for GeoGenetics, Natural History Museum of Denmark, University of Copenhagen, Denmark.

JESSE CASANA is an Associate Professor in the Department of Anthropology, University of Arkansas, USA.

JADE D'ALPOIM GUEDES is an Assistant Professor in the Department of Anthropology, Washington State University, USA.

GAYLE FRITZ is a Professor in the Department of Anthropology, Washington University in St. Louis, USA.

DAPHNE E. GALLAGHER is a Lecturer in the Department of Anthropology, University of Oregon, USA.

KRISTEN J. GREMILLION is a Professor in the Department of Anthropology, The Ohio State University, USA.

AMANDA G. HENRY is the Head of the Research Group on Plant Foods in Hominin Dietary Ecology at the Max Planck Institute for Evolutionary Anthropology, Leipzig, Germany.

JOHN M. MARSTON is an Assistant Professor in the Departments of Archaeology and Anthropology, Boston University, USA.

TIMOTHY C. MESSNER is an Assistant Professor of Anthropology in the Department of Anthropology, State University of New York, Potsdam, USA.

SHANTI MORELL-HART is an Assistant Professor in the Department of Anthropology, McMaster University, Canada.

MARK NESBITT is Curator of the Economic Botany Collection at the Royal Botanic Gardens, Kew, UK.

DEBORAH M. PEARSALL is a Professor Emerita in the Department of Anthropology, University of Missouri, Columbia, USA.

CHINA P. SHELTON is a Lecturer in the Department of Sociology, Framingham State University, USA.

ALEXIA SMITH is an Assistant Professor in the Department of Anthropology, University of Connecticut, USA.

BRUCE D. SMITH is a Senior Research Scientist and Curator of North American Archaeology in the Department of Anthropology, Smithsonian National Museum of Natural History, USA.

ROBERT SPENGLER is a Postdoctoral Fellow at the German Archaeological Institute, Berlin, Germany.

CHRIS J. STEVENS is an ERC Research Associate in the Institute of Archaeology, University College, London, UK.

GARY E. STINCHCOMB is an Assistant Professor in the Watershed Studies Institute and Department of Geosciences, Murray State University, USA.

AMBER M. VANDERWARKER is an Associate Professor in the Department of Anthropology, University of California, Santa Barbara, USA.

NATHAN WALES is a Postdoctoral Fellow at the Centre for GeoGenetics, Natural History Museum of Denmark, University of Copenhagen, Denmark.

CHRISTINA WARINNER is an Assistant Professor in the Department of Anthropology, University of Oklahoma, USA, and a Research Affiliate of the Molecular

Research Group at the Institute of Evolutionary Medicine, University of Zürich, Switzerland.

PAUL WEBB is is Cultural Resource Program Leader for TRC Environmental Consultants, Inc.

CHANTEL E. WHITE is a Postdoctoral Research Associate in the Department of Anthropology, University of Notre Dame, USA.

apatite, 279, 283, 288. *See also* enamel apatite

archaeobotany. *See* paleoethnobotany

Archaic period, 72, 209, 213, 285–86, 346

Arizona, 125, 306, 312, 361

artifact: within botanical sediment samples, 96, 104, 109–10; as element of foodways, 382–86; preservation of DNA on, 299; preservation of pollen on, 52, 54, 63, 66–67; preservation of phytoliths on, 68–69; preservation of starch on, 42, 47–49; sampling of microremains from, 91–92

Asia: continent, 14, 335; East, 6, 13, 83; South, 6, 13; Southeast, 83; Southwest, 4, 13–14, 116, 118–19, 124, 128, 131, 134–35, 171, 176, 189, 196, 199, 201, 236. *See also* China; India; Iran; Iraq; Israel; Japan; Jordan; Mesopotamia; Syria; Turkey; Yemen

ASTER. *See* Advanced Spaceborne Thermal Emission and Reflection Radiometer

atmospheric carbon. *See* carbon dioxide

Australia, 47, 301. *See also* Oceania

Avena sativa (oat), 30

AVHRR. *See* Advanced Very High Resolution Radiometer

baking. *See* cooking, wet

banana. See *Musa*

baobab. See *Adansonia digitata*

barcoding, 308–9

barley. See *Hordeum vulgare*

bean. See *Phaseolus*

behavioral ecology, 8, 173, 339–40, 353, 354

behavioral modeling, 65, 173, 178, 261, 339–54, 373–74. *See also* crop, processing; ethnoarchaeology

Belize, 97, 111, 325

B horizon, 59–60

biomineralization, 21, 26

biomolecule, ancient. *See* ancient DNA; proteomics; RNA

bioturbation, 33, 59–60, 79, 86, 88

biplot, 187–92, 195–96

birefringence pattern, 39, 41, 45. *See also* starch

blackberry. See *Rubus*

bog: anaerobic conditions, 24; coring of, 87

Bolboschoenus, 131

Bolivia, 326

bone collagen, 279, 283, 285, 286–87, 289

bottle gourd. See *Lagenaria siceraria*

box plot, 165–66, 170, 205, 208, 210, 211–12, 216, 222–27, 229–32

bract, 117, 130, 139, 200

Britain: England, 172, 184, 193, 196, 201, 237, 238, 245, 253, 320, 366; Scotland, 200, 241, 252; Wales, 188, 195. *See also* Stonehenge; Upper Thames

British Columbia, 25, 70, 364. *See also* Kwädáy Dän Ts'ínchí; SGang Gway Midden site

Bronze Age, 97, 176–77, 194, 195, 197, 199, 200, 209, 237, 243, 321, 324

broomcorn millet. See *Panicum miliaceum*

burning. *See* fire

C_3. *See* photosynthesis, C_3

C_4. *See* photosynthesis, C_4

CA. *See* correspondence analysis

Cahokia, 121, 172, 207

calculus, dental. *See* dental calculus

CAM (Crassulacean acid metabolism). *See* photosynthesis, CAM

CANOCO, 187, 202, 204

canonical correspondence analysis (CCA), 181–82, 192–93, 197, 199, 203. *See also* correspondence analysis

canopy effect, 269, 282

carbon cycle, 263–65, 276–79, 282

carbon dioxide (CO_2), 264, 277, 279, 282–83

carbon fixation, 264, 282. *See also* photosynthesis

carbonization (charring), 21, 25–27, 30, 55, 68, 117, 121, 123, 132, 133, 136, 140, 241–44, 250, 253, 254, 304. *See also* preservation

Carya (hickory), 208, 217, 221–23, 225, 227–29, 346–47, 350

caryopsis, 133

CCA. *See* canonical correspondence analysis

Central America. *See* Belize; Guatemala; Honduras; Mesoamerica; Mexico; Neotropics; Panama

central place foraging model, 340, 342, 345, 350–51

centuriated fields, Roman, 321–23

ceramics, 28, 54, 91, 95, 101, 261, 266, 311, 383–85

cereal: agriculture, 195–96, 235–36, 253, 289, 322, 324, 330; DNA from, 306–7, 311; identification of, 128, 133–34; preservation, 243; processing remains, 30, 116, 184, 190, 195–96,

decontamination, 300. *See also* contamination
décrue sowing, 367–68
dehusking, 239, 241, 245, 249–50, 253–54
Delaware River valley, 265, 270
DEM. *See* digital elevation model
dendrochronology, 262, 359
density (statistical measure), 66, 80, 84, 112,
    164, 166–67, 170–71, 184, 205, 208–12, 214, 216,
    223–32
dental calculus, 45, 47–48, 91–92
depositional process: impact on DNA pres-
    ervation, 297, 300; of phytoliths, 55, 58–60,
    63–65, 72; of pollen, 52–54, 61, 66–67, 70; of
    seeds, 209; understanding of, 4–5, 14, 117, 167,
    189; variation in, 7. *See also* formation pro-
    cess; post-depositional process; preservation
desiccation: of botanical remains, 1, 3, 21–23,
    84, 92, 94, 96, 118, 136; impact on nucleic
    acid preservation, 298, 311
detrended correspondence analysis (DCA),
    189, 192. *See also* correspondence analysis
dewberry. See *Rubus*
diagenesis. *See* taphonomy
diet breadth model (DBM), 341–42, 344–49,
    352, 354
digital elevation model (DEM), 328–29
digital imagery, 7, 12, 129, 144–45, 148–52, 157–59.
    See also remote sensing; satellite imagery
digital photography. *See* photography, digital
Diospyros virginiana (persimmon), 217–18, 221,
    224, 227–28, 363
discriminant analysis (DA), 181–82, 185–86,
    193, 195–98, 200, 201, 202–3
dispersal: loss of mechanism in domesticates,
    133–34; of phytoliths, 58–59; of pollen, 52,
    63; of seeds, 32, 367; by wind, 32, 52
disturbance indicators, 71, 169, 197, 262,
    269–70, 273
diversity index, 164, 168–69, 172–74
DNA: data archiving of, 156; preservation of,
    25, 27, 145, 296–301; types of, 293–94, 297.
    See also ancient DNA
DNA sequencing: high-throughput/next-
    generation, 297, 304–6; shotgun, 305; third-
    generation, 312. *See also* ancient DNA;
    polymerase chain reaction
domestication: botanical markers of, 27, 118,
    129, 132–35, 139–44, 201, 236, 346; origins of,
    8, 285–88, 295–96, 307–11, 372–73

domestication syndrome, 133, 312
doxa, 377–78, 389
dry screening. *See* screening, dry
dung: as fuel, 31, 58, 64, 90, 176, 195; in sedi-
    ments, 58, 64, 90, 195. *See also* manure

Eastern Woodlands (of North America), 363
e-book, 157
ecofact, 92, 380
ecological engineering. *See* niche construction
Ecuador, 55, 64, 68–69. *See also* Jama River
    valley
Egypt, 22, 44, 97, 116–17, 122, 197, 295, 309–10.
    See also Nile River valley
eigenanalysis, 188
einkorn. See *Triticum, monococcum*
elite. *See* social status
El Niño-Southern Oscillation, 258
email, 121, 144, 151–52, 154
emmer. See *Triticum, dicoccum*
enamel apatite, 283
England. *See* Britain
environmental archaeology, 5, 8–9, 11
enzyme: in carbon fixation, 264, 277; DNA
    polymerase, 302, 304; DNase, 302; starch
    digestion, 37, 39–42, 44–48
equifinality, 283
Eragrostis tef (teff), 133
erosion, 24, 33, 70, 322, 333
ethnoarchaeology, 58, 69, 73
ethnobotany, 145, 310, 315, 354, 373–75, 377–78,
    382
Euphrates River, 176–77, 330
Europe: Central, 135, 198, 335; continent, 4, 22,
    28, 116, 118, 138, 175, 236, 270, 321–22, 376; dis-
    tinct methods employed in, 119–21, 145, 178,
    181, 193–94, 202; Northern, 117, 236, 270, 320;
    tradition of paleoethnobotany in, xx, 1, 3,
    13, 87, 193; Southeastern, 199, 272; Southern,
    273. *See also* Britain; France; Greece;
    Mediterranean; Roman period
exine, 52–53

factor analysis, 194
fallowing, 65, 197, 266, 268, 363, 364–65, 388
feature (archaeological): bias, 79: detection
    of, 319–21, 324–25, 327–31, 335; sampling
    of, 64, 78–84, 87, 89, 91, 93, 96, 112, 138, 166,
    208–11, 213

feces. *See* coprolite

fiber, 19, 27, 29, 281, 385. *See also* Textile

fiber-optic lighting, 123

Ficus carica (fig), 364

file transfer protocol (FTP), 151

fire: in landscape management, 258, 266–67, 269, 368–69; as mechanism for seed preservation, 27, 32, 117; scars, 262; as waste-disposal mechanism, 242. *See also* carbonization

fig. See *Ficus carica*

flintknapping, 209

floodplain, 198, 238–40, 265–66, 268–70, 359, 367

flotation: contamination during, 138–39, 301; device-assisted, 102–5, 108, 110–13; efficiency, 97, 106, 112–13, 119; historical development of, 4–7, 14, 134, 236, 284; limitations of, 99, 110–13, 117, 245; manual, 100–102; sampling for, 80, 82, 84, 92–94, 166, 214, 216; screen size for, 112; training in, 78, 108–9; versus screening, 97, 107, 111. *See also* fraction; sampling; screening

fodder, 29, 31, 176, 178, 238, 242, 253, 289

food chain. *See* food web

food processing, 30, 44–45, 66, 68, 116, 170, 183, 209–10, 214, 228, 231–32, 347, 350–51, 359, 362. *See also* crop, processing

food value estimate, 164, 165

food web, 278–81, 283, 290, 356

foodways, 205–8, 374–83, 387–89

forager, 8, 236, 248, 284–87, 345–48, 350–52, 356

formation process: archaeological, 5, 60–61, 78, 80, 110, 241, 374; of macrobotanical remains, 28–32; of phytoliths, 55–56, 59, 63–65, 68–69, 72; of pollen, 51–52, 61–63, 66–68, 69–72; of starch grains, 37–42. *See also* depositional process; post-depositional process; preservation

formative period (of Mesoamerica), 199, 206, 285

foxtail millet. See *Setaria italica*

fraction: heavy, 101–5, 109–10, 112–13, 119, 122, 214; light, 101–5, 109, 111, 113, 119, 122, 138, 214

France, 24, 100, 325–26

fruit: biomineralization of, 21; coat, 141–42; cultivation of, 322, 362–65, 369; in diet, 207; DNA from, 297; identification of, 132–33, 139; macrobotanical finds of, 19, 22, 30,

57, 97, 116, 118, 136, 218, 221, 223–24, 227–28, 231–32; phytoliths from, 51; starch from, 37

FTP. *See* file transfer protocol

garden: archaeology, 90; botanical, 130; cultivation, 198, 201, 322, 330, 360, 364, 388; rockwork, 360–62; root, 359–61; weeds, 125

gelatinization, 35, 41, 44–45, 47, 49. *See also* starch

GenBank, 12, 155–56, 158–59

gender, 7, 206–7, 209–10, 354, 367, 376

genome: chloroplast, 307–8; location within cell, 294; nuclear, 307; mitochondrial, 307–8; and plant evolution, 295, 309–10; reconstruction from ancient DNA, 296, 301, 306. *See also* Ancient DNA; DNA; DNA sequencing

geoarchaeology, 257

Geographic Information System (GIS), 197, 209, 212, 216, 226–31, 232, 237, 318

geomorphology, 259, 261, 265–66, 269–70, 330–31

GIS. *See* Geographic Information System

glacier, 258, 299

glume: base, 175, 238, 239–45; chaff, 250, 253; charred, 244; glume-rich assemblage, 240, 243–44, 253; phytolith, 160, 245; processing of, 238–246; survival of, 244–45; tissue, 66, 68, 238, 241, 245–46, 250–53, 296. *See also* bract; crop, processing; ratio, cereal-grain-to-glume-base; ratio, glume-to-grain

Google: Books, 2, 9, 152–53; Earth, 318, 321, 327; image search, 151; Ngram, 2, 9; other products, 152; Scholar, 153

Gossypium (cotton), 57, 310

grain. *See* cereal; crop, processing; pollen; seed; starch granule

grape. See *Vitis*

grass: and carbon isotopes, 268–69, 277, 282, 286; cultivation of, 367; ecology, 72, 177, 266–67, 361; grassland, 59, 173, 177, 369; phytoliths, 64, 200, 262, 268, 384; pollen, 62, 66; seed identification, 127, 132

gray literature, 12

Great Basin (North America), 21, 347, 350, 352, 356, 359, 361, 365, 368

Great Plains (North America), 59, 125

Greece, 30, 103, 184, 186, 193, 198, 299

grid, use of in sampling, 79, 122

ground stone: artifacts, 48, 54, 66, 68–69, 91, 201, 209, 236; experimental tools, 47; technology 349. *See also* stone
groundwater, 54–55, 278, 368
Guatemala, 70, 72, 330
Gulf Coast (Mexico), 175, 199, 207
gut contents, 25, 45–46, 62. *See also* coprolite; latrine

habitus, 8, 377, 388–89
hand picked samples, 96, 214
hand-pump flotation device, 6, 102–3, 106, 108, 112–13. *See also* flotation, device
Harappa, 28
HBE. *See* human behavioral ecology
herbarium, 130, 150, 298, 310
herbivory, 290–91
hickory. See *Carya*
hillfort, 238–41, 245, 251–54
hilum, 37–38, 40, 45, 138. *See also* starch
hollow ways, 324–25
Holocene, 201, 257, 259, 260, 265–72, 274, 315, 322, 330, 347, 365–66, 369
Honduras, 372, 382, 388
Hordeum vulgare (barley): agriculture, 237, 309–10; crop processing, 30, 239, 247; markers of domestication in, 134; phytoliths, 58; starch, 39–40. *See also* cereal; crop, processing
household: activities, 65, 209–10, 232, 252–54; area, 171, 207; sediments, 64; size, 213, 253; social unit, 213, 236–37, 250, 252–54, 261, 376, 380
human behavioral ecology (HBE), 8, 173, 339–54
human-environmental interaction, 3, 8–9, 13–14, 19, 70–73, 257–59, 272–74, 343, 355–58, 367–69, 373
humic acid, 304
hunter-gatherer. *See* forager
hypothesis: generation, 339, 341–43, 383; null, 193, 203; testing, 7, 163–64, 169, 173–78, 187, 246, 253, 310, 339–42, 347, 349
hypsithermal, 265

Iceman. *See* Ötzi
identification: of activity areas, 65, 89, 170, 175, 197, 210–11, 216, 222–23, 231–32, 373; advances in, 6, 129, 145, 158; of agricultural strategies, 170, 176–78, 285; of diet, 285–86, 374; of domestication, 27, 133–36; of dung fuel use, 31, 58, 176; of environmental change, 71, 88, 171–73, 265, 268, 357–58; equipment for, 119–23, 145; of genetic markers, 305–9, 313; history of, 1; of macroremains, 19–20, 22, 95–97, 109–10, 116–17, 132–36, 245; of outliers, 182–83, 185, 203, 208, 211, 222–23; paleoethnobotanical procedures for, 115–16, 118–21, 123–24, 131–38, 145, 198; of phytoliths, 55, 137–38, 200; of plant impressions, 21, 28; of pollen, 52–53, 67, 87, 137–38, 201; reference material for, 124–31, 154, 158, 214; of starch, 35, 39, 44–45, 137–38, 201; of tubers, 27, 136–37; of waterlogged material, 116–17, 137; of wood, 137
IKONOS, 318, 327, 331
illuviation, 59–60
impression: cordage, 28; plant, 21, 28; seeds, 28; textile, 28
India, 64, 67, 134, 213, 272–73, 363. *See also* Indus River valley
Indus River valley, 335. *See also* Harappa
inheritance-and-dispersal model, 59
initial sorting, 109–10, 118–22
Inka, 206, 209, 237
International Association of Wood Anatomists, 137
International Work Group for Palaeoethnobotany (IWGP), xx, 136
Internet: growth of, 36, 151–52; use by paleoethnobotanists, 129, 157. *See also* computing; data, database; data, online repository; data, sharing; email; World Wide Web
interobserver bias, 147
intersite: analysis, 93, 111, 163, 165, 169, 198, 236; approaches, 236; variation, 7, 58, 78, 82–86, 165, 170, 235–54
intrasite: analysis, 89, 170, 205–13; variation, 7, 78–82, 167, 170, 174, 205–33
involucre, 21
Inter-Tropical Convergence Zone, 258
Iran, 83, 178, 236, 327–28
Iraq, 105, 332. *See also* Mesopotamia
Iron Age, 26, 111, 199–200, 237, 241, 243–44, 246–47, 252, 254
irrigation: agriculture, 197, 312, 315, 330; effect on phytoliths, 58, 60, 374; features on landscape, 320, 327–29; and plant growth, 332, 334; in wild plant cultivation, 359

isotope: carbon, 73, 237, 263–64, 277–79, 281–88, 290; nitrogen, 279–83, 287, 289–91; oxygen, 388
isotope analysis, stable. *See* stable isotope analysis
isotope geochemistry, 261, 263–66, 268
isotopic: depletion, 279; enrichment, 264, 268–70, 279–81, 287, 289; fractionation, 264–65, 277–81
Israel, 113, 114, 184, 196, 209, 325
Iva annua (marshelder, sumpweed), 22, 131, 135, 219, 346, 367
IWGP. *See* International Work Group for Palaeoethnobotany

Jama River valley, 55, 57
Japan, 104, 138, 364–65
Jordan, 97–98, 102, 108, 112, 176, 364
Juglans (walnut), 121, 217, 221–25, 227–29, 346

Kentucky, 22, 176, 346. *See also* Cumberland Plateau
key (identification), 129, 132
Kwäday Dän Ts'inchí, 25

Lagenaria siceraria (bottle gourd), 57, 217, 221, 223–32, 367
lake-dwelling sites, 1, 24
lake sediment: formation processes of, 58, 69–71, 72–73; pollen recovered from, 51, 52, 69–71; phytoliths recovered from, 51, 58, 69, 72; wood recovered from, 24. *See also* bog; waterlogged
Lake Titicaca, 326–27
lamella, 38–39. *See also* starch
landrace, 133, 135, 295
Landsat, 316–19, 330–31. *See also* multispectral satellite imagery
landscape: human impact on, 71–72, 273, 322, 329, 354; management of, 356–64, 373; phenology, 331–35; reconstruction, 54, 315–16, 330–31; stability, 265
land use: botanical identification of, 110, 173, 201; environmental impact of, 258, 262, 265–70, 273, 315; modeling of, 316; impact of modern, 327, 329; remote sensing of, 315–16, 319–20, 322, 332–33; sustainability of, 14. *See also* agriculture; human-environmental interaction; landscape

latrine, 25, 51, 62. *See also* coprolite; gut contents
LBK. *See* linear pottery culture
leaf, 46, 56, 264, 307, 362
legume: domestication of, 133; isotopic analysis of, 279–80, 282, 289; pods, 133; processing, 184, 195–96; seeds, 97, 125, 132; starch, 38, 40; wild, 219, 221. *See also* crop, processing
Levant. *See* Israel; Jordan; Syria
Libya, 21, 97, 329
LiDAR. *See* Light Detection and Ranging
life assemblage, 29, 42. *See also* redeposited assemblage
Light Detection and Ranging (LiDAR), 318–19, 325–26, 331, 335
lighting for microscopy, 123
linear discriminant function analysis. *See* discriminant analysis
linear pottery culture (LBK), 289. *See also* Neolithic
linear programming, 343, 347, 350
listserv, 12, 151, 154
Little Ice Age (LIA), 257, 261, 267–73
logarithmic transformation, 166, 170, 242
longue durée, 388, 390

magnification, 95, 97, 120–23, 138, 167
maize. See *Zea mays*
Mali, 28
mammoth, 290, 301, 313
Manihot esculenta (manioc), 40, 57, 384–85
manure, 279, 289, 374. *See also* dung
marginal value theorem, 340, 342, 349
marshelder. See *Iva annua*
mass spectrometry (MS), 100, 275, 284, 311
mast, 344, 346–47, 365–66
matK, 308
matrix: conceptual, 378; mathematical, 216; molecular, 37; sediment, 20, 54, 79–80, 84, 91–92, 95, 107, 117
Maya: agriculture, 315, 325, 331; isotopic markers of diet, 289–91; region, 97, 111, 330
maypop. See *Passiflora incarnata*
Medieval Warming Period (MWP), 257, 261, 267–68, 270, 272
Mediterranean, 12–13, 135, 171, 321–22, 325, 332,
Mesoamerica, 97, 144, 206, 285–88, 380–81, 383–84. *See also* Belize; Central America; Guatemala; Honduras; Maya; Mexico; Neotropics

Mesopotamia, 315, 324, 328, 330, 332. *See also*
  Euphrates River; Iraq; Syria; Turkey; Uruk
  period
metadata, 148, 154, 317
Mexico, 175, 199, 206–7, 286–87, 295, 329. *See
  also* Gulf Coast; Soconusco; Tehuacan
  Valley; Teotihuacan; Yucatan Peninsula
microarray, 156
microfossil, 47, 51, 65–66, 73, 136, 153, 261, 298
microorganism, 20, 24, 46–47, 306, 310
microscopy: equipment for, 121; imaging, 149,
  151, 156; light, 27, 37, 39, 44, 136; scanning
  electron (SEM), 37, 39, 124, 136, 138, 141, 143,
  145; transmission electron (TEM), 38. *See
  also* photography
millet. See *Panicum miliaceum* (broomcorn
  millet); *Pennisetum glaucum* (pearl millet);
  Setaria italica (foxtail millet)
Mimbres culture, 349
mineralization. *See* biomineralization
Mississippian culture, 172, 284. *See also*
  Cahokia
mitochondrion. *See* organelle, mitochondrion
Moderate Resolution Imaging Spectroradiometer (MODIS), 318–19, 331–33. *See
  also* multispectral satellite imagery
MODIS. *See* Moderate Resolution Imaging
  Spectroradiometer
monsoon, 258–59
Monte Carlo permutation testing, 193, 203.
  See also multivariate statistics
Mound Builders, 284
Moundville, 170, 172
moving wall, 152
mRNA. *See* RNA, messenger
MS. *See* mass spectrometry
multidimensional statistics. *See* multivariate
  statistics
multiproxy analysis, 89, 93, 165
multispectral satellite imagery, 7, 316–19, 325,
  330–31. *See also* Advanced Spaceborne
  Thermal Emission and Reflection
  Radiometer (ASTER); Advanced Very
  High Resolution Radiometer (AVHRR);
  Landsat; Moderate Resolution Imaging
  Spectroradiometer (MODIS); Satellite
  Pour l'Observation de la Terre (SPOT)
multivariate statistics, 6–7, 163, 173, 178, 181–203
Musa (banana, plantain), 100, 116–17, 200, 362

National Science Foundation (NSF) (United
  States), 10–11, 15, 154, 156
Native American, 261, 309, 364. *See also*
  Cherokee; Mimbres culture; Mississippian
  culture; Mound Builders; Paiute;
  Woodland, culture
Natufian, 196
NDVI. *See* Normalized Differential
  Vegetation Index
Neanderthal, 64, 289, 291, 301
Near East. *See* Asia, Southwest
Neolithic: Aceramic/Pre-Pottery, 134, 199;
  Early, 102, 196, 197, 236; Final, 194; general,
  28, 99, 198, 210, 237; Late, 24, 197; transi-
  tion, 272. *See also* linear pottery culture
  (LBK)
neotropics, 273, 347. *See also* Mesoamerica;
  tropics
New Archaeology. *See* processual theory
New Guinea, 91, 200, 201, 349, 362, 376
New York, 200
New World, 116, 125, 134, 139, 170, 174–75,
  206–9, 325–26. *See also* Mesoamerica; neotropics; North America; South America
next-generation sequencing. *See* DNA
  sequencing
niche: association of taxa with, 196; resource
  depression, 349; width, 168–69, 172–73
niche construction theory, 8, 196, 258, 349, 354,
  355–63, 367–70
Nicotiana tabacum (tobacco), 19, 46, 307
Nile River valley, 116
NISP. *See* number of identified specimens
nitrogen cycle, 276, 279–81, 282
nitrogen fixation, 279–81
non-plant inclusions, 138–39
nonelite. *See* social status
Normalized Differential Vegetation Index
  (NDVI), 331–34
North America: Eastern, 135, 139, 141, 143,
  262, 265–69, 284–86, 335, 346, 362–66;
  New England, 260, 266; Northeast, 257;
  Northwest coast: 24, 356–61; tradition of
  paleoethnobotany in, 1, 3–4, 13; Western,
  356. *See also* Arizona; British Columbia;
  Great Basin; Kentucky; New York;
  Ontario; Oregon; Pennsylvania; United
  States; Woodland
North Atlantic Oscillation, 258–59

NSF. *See* National Science Foundation
number of identified specimens (NISP), 112
nutshell, 27, 119, 137, 170, 228–31

oak. See *Quercus*
oat. See *Avena sativa*
Oceania, 13. *See also* Australia; New Guinea
off-site sampling. *See* sampling, off-site
Ohio River valley, 172–73
old field ecosystems, 266, 268
Old World, 116, 124, 126–28, 133, 170, 181, 206–7,
    209, 329. *See also* Africa; Asia; Europe;
    Oceania
online data repository. *See* data, online
    repository
Ontario, 260
open access: database, 155–56, 158; journal, 157.
    See also data, database
open-air sites, 22, 87, 216, 231
OpenContext, 12, 156
oppidum, 252
optimal diet, 342, 344–46, 348, 350, 352
optimal foraging theory, 341–43, 345
ordination, 186–87, 189, 192–93
Oregon, 24
organelle: amyloplast, 36–37, 40; chloroplast,
    36–37, 293–94, 299, 305, 307–8; mitochon-
    drion, 293–94, 307–8; plastid, 36–37, 297
Oryza sativa (rice): agriculture, 64–65, 116,
    362; ancient DNA, 298; phytolith, 64–65,
    200, 298; processing, 64, 116, 134; starch,
    37, 40; waste, 64, 116. *See also* cereal; crop,
    processing
Ötzi (Iceman), 25, 62, 117
outlier (statistical): depiction of, 211–12,
    222–27; identification of, 182–83, 202–3, 208,
    211–12, 216, 222–27, 229, 231
overrepresentation, 54, 94, 111

Paiute, 359–60
Paleobot.org, 12, 127, 152, 158
paleoclimatology, 257–59, 263–64, 267–68,
    270–73, 335
paleodietary reconstruction, 275–276, 279,
    281, 283–84, 288–89. *See also* stable isotope
    analysis
paleoenvironment: proxies for 69–71, 87–88,
    263, 266, 273; reconstruction of, 4, 87, 110,
    258, 273–74

paleoethnobotany: alternate terms for, xix, 1–2,
    9; definition, xix; future of, xx–xxi, 3, 11–14,
    65–66, 69, 72–73, 159, 164, 178, 290, 298, 312,
    335, 387; historical development of, xix–xxi,
    1–4, 95, 115, 124, 147, 178
Paleolithic, 28, 209
palynology: climatic studies, 259; use in
    paleoethnobotanical research, 86–87, 137,
    262, 266–67
Panama, 58–59, 71, 287
Panicum miliaceum (broomcorn millet), 40
panicoid grasses: *Andropogon*, 266; *Panicum*,
    367
paradigmatic axis, 378–79
parching, 45, 253. *See also* cooking, dry
parenchyma, 117–18, 136–37
partial canonical correspondence analysis
    (pCCA), 193. *See also* canonical correspon-
    dence analysis (CCA); correspondence
    analysis (CA)
Passiflora incarnata (maypop), 224, 227
pastoralism, 31, 239, 284, 290–91, 330
PCA. *See* principal components analysis
pCCA. *See* partial canonical correspondence
    analysis
PCR. *See* polymerase chain reaction
Pearson's *r*, 211, 216
peat bog, 24, 54, 72, 87. *See also* preservation;
    waterlogged
peduncle, 30
Pennisetum glaucum (pearl millet), 28, 134
Pennsylvania, 260, 270
PEPC. *See* phosphoenolpyruvate
    carboxylase
pericarp, 21, 139, 141
persimmon. See *Diospyros virginiana*
Peru: Andean, 64, 80, 194, 206, 326; coastal,
    22; maize from, 295. *See also* Chimú; Inka;
    Lake Titicaca; Sausa; Tiwanaku period;
    Wanka II period
pH, 24, 46–48, 56, 72
Phaseolus (bean), 207, 223, 229–31, 279, 327, 367
phosphoenolpyruvate carboxylase (PEPC),
    277
photography: aerial, 316, 320, 322, 324–25, 327;
    conventional, 110, 124, 132, 148; digital, 124,
    129, 148–51; digital scanning, 324–25
photosynthesis: C_3, 73, 237, 262–64, 268,
    276–78, 282, 285–87, 289, 291; C_4, 237,

sedimentation: floodplain, 265–66, 268, 270; load, 261, 265, 269–70, 329

seed: coat, 133, 138–43 (*see also* fruit, coat); dispersal mechanisms, 32, 133–34, 367; identification methods, 124, 130–31, 137; imagery, 12, 124–29, 148–51; manuals, 124–28, 214; rain, 32; transport, 31–32, 352

SEM. *See* microscopy, scanning electron

semi-crystalline structure, 35

semiarid climate, 332, 356

semiquantitative analysis, 283

Setaria italica (foxtail millet), 40

SGang Gway Midden site, 364

Shannon-Weaver index, 168

shea. See *Vitellaria paradoxa*

sherd, 96, 110, 200, 383

shotgun DNA sequencing. *See* DNA sequencing, shotgun

shotgun proteomics. *See* proteomics

Shuttle Radar Topography Mission (SRTM), 319, 328. *See also* digital elevation model

sieving. *See* screening

silica, 55–56, 63, 68, 87, 245, 262, 304

Simpson's diversity index, 168–69

single nucleotide polymorphism (SNP), 307

site formation processes, 59, 78, 80

slackwater effect, 265

slash-and-burn. *See* agriculture, slash-and-burn

SMAP-style flotation system, 102, 104, 107, 112. *See also* flotation, devices

SNP. *See* single nucleotide polymorphism

social networking, 152, 156–57

social status, 170, 205–8, 210, 213

Society for American Archaeology (SAA), 9, 152–54

socioecological system, 236, 257

socioeconomic system, 236, 259

Soconusco, 287

soil organic matter (SOM), 263–65, 268–69, 278, 280

Solanum tuberosum (potato), 40, 310, 327

SOM. *See* soil organic matter

sonication, 69, 92, 383

Sorghum, 40, 135, 197, 277

sorting, 70, 109–10, 113, 118–23, 137, 246

South America, 144, 206, 236–37, 273, 287, 327. *See also* Amazon Basin; Bolivia; Ecuador; Lake Titicaca; Peru

Southwest Asia. *See* Asia, Southwest

speleothem, 269–70

spelt. See *Triticum, spelta*

spikelet, 64, 134, 241–54

sporopollenin, 52–53

SPOT. *See* Satellite Pour l'Observation de la Terre

squash. See *Cucurbita*

SRTM. *See* Shuttle Radar Topography Mission

stable isotope analysis: history of, 278–81; theoretical basis of, 276–81; use in archaeology, 276, 283–88. *See also* isotope; isotope geochemistry; paleodietary reconstruction

stain (iodine), 40

standard score. *See* Z-score

standardization: flotation, 112; mesh size, 112; sample size, 112, 165–66

starch: amylose, 36–40, 42; amylopectin, 36–40, 42; reserve, 37; transitory, 37, 46. *See also* starch granule

starch granule: deposition, 46–48; formation, 35–40; hilum, 37–38, 40, 44–45; lamella, 38–39; life history, 42–44; morphology, 36–40; preservation, 46–47, 91; taphonomy, 42–50. *See also* birefringence pattern; starch

statistics: descriptive, 166, 178; multivariate, 6–7, 163–64, 169, 173–74, 178, 181–82, 193–94, 197–203, 205, 210, 232; relative, 62, 80, 112, 164, 167–69, 170–74, 228–30; simple, 163–64, 169, 171, 173–74, 178; standardized, 164–68, 170–71, 173, 178, 182, 211, 216

steppe, 89, 173, 176–77, 332–33. *See also* grass, grassland

stepwise pattern, 281

stone: clearance, 320–23, 325; flagstone, 63; limestone, 278; natural, 47, 96; tools, 47–48, 68, 91, 101, 201; walls, 321–23, 329. *See also* ground stone

Stonehenge, 321

storage: activity, 73, 170, 214, 231–32, 235, 239–41, 246, 247–48, 250–53, 346, 363, 388; of data, 150–51, 156, 158, 306; deposit, 89, 184, 195, 208, 210, 228, 231–32, 359; function of artifacts, 68, 73, 231; pit, 144, 240–41, 243–45, 247–48; within plant tissues, 37, 46, 311, 385; of samples, 48, 84, 106–8, 109, 121–22; structure, 170, 236; underground storage organ, 37, 116, 40, 358, 369

waterlogged: identification of remains, 136–37; macrobotanical remains, 1, 3, 83, 95, 113, 117; pollen, 54, 63, 69; preservation, 23–25, 100; processing of remains, 94–100, 107; sampling of remains, 79, 84. *See also* DNA, preservation of

wattle-and-daub architecture, 28

website. *See* Internet; World Wide Web

weed: annual, 237; assemblage, 31, 196–97, 203, 246, 252–53; ecology, 197; seed, 175, 184, 237–39, 245–46, 252–54; transport into site, 31–32; weeding, 361, 388; weedy, 71, 118, 139, 141, 194, 362. *See also* dung, as fuel; ratio, weed-to-grain; ratio, wild-seed-to-cereal

wet screening. *See* screening, wet

wheat. See *Triticum*

whisker (in box plot), 166, 211

Wikipedia, 158–59

witness tree, 262, 364

wood: analysis, 123, 137; charcoal, 26–27, 30, 96, 111, 117, 171; construction, 360; fuel, 31, 178, 207–8, 236, 364–65; identification, 137, 152; preservation, 20, 22–25; phytoliths, 384; sorting, 119, 121

Woodland: culture, 175, 268–69, 284, 346; Late, 172, 175, 335; Middle 172; region, 363. *See also* Mississippian culture; Mound Builders; Moundville; Ohio River valley

World Wide Web (WWW), 151, 159

Xinjiang, 22

X-ray crystallography, 38

Yangtze River: delta, 71, 362; valley, 335

Yellow River, 335

Yemen, 329

Yucatan Peninsula, 315

Zea mays (maize, corn): agriculture, 172–73, 207, 261, 266–68, 270–72, 347–49, 361, 367, 388; carbon isotopes of, 227, 282, 284–88, 289; cob, 217, 297, 306, 388; cupule, 167, 174–75, 217, 229; dishes, 381–82, 389; domestication, 133, 310; genetics, 295, 310, 312; identification, 135–36; kernel, 119, 167, 174–75, 208–9, 217, 229, 306; phytolith, 57, 68, 70, 224, 384; pollen, 66; processing, 170–71, 174–75, 207, 231–32; starch, 36, 40, 68. *See also* ratio, kernel-to-cupule

zooarchaeology: integration with paleoethnobotany, 199, 274, 275–76, 290, 380; methods for DNA analysis in, 299; popularity versus paleoethnobotany, 8–9; use of behavioral ecology in, 344, 349; use of statistics in, 168, 199

zoophilous taxa, 62–63. *See also* pollination, by animal

Z-score, 164, 167, 352–53

www.ingramcontent.com/pod-product-compliance
Lightning Source LLC
Chambersburg PA
CBHW022126020426
42334CB00015B/784